ESSAYS OF A LIFETIME

SUNY series in Hindu Studies

WENDY DONIGER, EDITOR

SUMIT SARKAR

Essays of a Lifetime
Reformers • Nationalists • Subalterns

Essays of a Lifetime: Reformers, Nationalists, Subalterns by Sumit Sarkar was first published by Permanent Black D-28 Oxford Apts, 11 IP Extension, Delhi 110092 INDIA, for the territory of SOUTH ASIA.

Not for sale in South Asia

Cover design by Anuradha Roy

Published by State University of New York Press, Albany

© 2019 Sumit Sarkar

All rights reserved

No part of this book may be used or reproduced in any manner whatsoever without written permission. No part of this book may be stored in a retrieval system or transmitted in any form or by any means including electronic, electrostatic, magnetic tape, mechanical, photocopying, recording, or otherwise without the prior permission in writing of the publisher.

For information, contact State University of New York Press, Albany, NY
www.sunypress.edu

Library of Congress Cataloging-in-Publication Data

Names: Sarkar, Sumit- author.
Title: Essays of a lifetime : reformers - nationalists - subalterns / Sumit Sarkar.
Other titles: Selections.
Description: Albany, NY : State University of New York Press, [2019] | Series: SUNY series in Hindu studies | Includes bibliographical references and index.
Identifiers: LCCN 2018027697 | ISBN 9781438474311 (hardcover : alk. paper) | ISBN 9781438474328 (pbk : alk. paper) | ISBN 9781438474335 (e-book)
Subjects: LCSH: India--History--British occupation, 1765-1947. | Nationalism--India. | Social change--India. | Bengal (India)--History--British occupation, 1765-1947.
Classification: LCC DS463 .S2722 2019 | DDC 954.03/5--dc23
LC record available at https://lccn.loc.gov/2018027697

10 9 8 7 6 5 4 3 2 1

Contents

Preface and Acknowledgements   vii

I. BHAKTI AND SAMAJ: SOCIAL REFORM AND RELIGIOUS MODERNITY

1. Rammohun Roy and the Break with the Past — 1
2. The Complexities of "Young Bengal" — 25
3. The Pattern and Structure of Early Nationalist Activity in Bengal — 53
4. The Radicalism of Intellectuals: A Case Study of Nineteenth-Century Bengal — 86
5. One or Many Histories? Identity Formations in Late-Colonial Bengal — 105
6. Kaliyuga, Chakri, and Bhakti: Ramakrishna and His Times — 151
7. Vidyasagar and Brahmanical Society — 237
8. The Kalki-Avatar of Bikrampur: A Village Scandal in Early-Twentieth-Century Bengal — 312

II. NATIONALISTS AND SUBALTERNS

9. Nationalism: Ideology and Mobilisation — 369
10. The Conditions and Nature of Subaltern Militancy: Bengal from Swadeshi to Non-Cooperation, c. 1905–1922 — 416
11. Primitive Rebellion and Modern Nationalism: Forest Satyagraha in the Non-Cooperation and Civil Disobedience Movements — 474

12.	The Logic of Gandhian Nationalism: Civil Disobedience and the Gandhi–Irwin Pact 1930–1931	489
13.	Popular Movements and National Leadership 1945–1947	536
14.	The Return of Labour to South Asian History	576

III. TRIBUTES

15.	Thinking about P.C. Joshi	614
16.	Edward Thompson	621
17.	In Memory of Eric Hobsbawm	626

Preface and Acknowledgements

These essays were written over a period of more than four decades. Some have been included in books that I wrote: *A Critique of Colonial India* and *Writing Social History*. Some appeared as articles in other books: *Subaltern Studies*, for instance. Others were published in journals like *Annales*, *Historical Materialism*, and *Economic and Political Weekly*. In the present collection they have been arranged thematically, not chronologically. As a result there may, within the same section, be striking differences in emphasis, concerns, and even language. All, however, are connected by a common set of preoccupations that I have come back to, time and again, in new ways: social and religious values – old and modern – nationalism, subaltern activism.

A very legitimate question may be asked: Why do I need to bring together essays that have been published earlier? What is perhaps worse is that they are here published unaltered, even though I do not agree any more with many of the points I raised then. In fact, some of them positively embarrass me now, and I can see all could do with considerable revision – which is now beyond my capacity. The most obvious explanation is, of course, that they raised discussions and debates when they first appeared, and most are no longer easily available. Friends have often asked me to make them accessible and my ever-kind publisher has obliged – as always.

But there is, perhaps, a more serious explanation. The essays were written over a long time span, when a lot kept changing in the world of Indian history-writing. This collection, though based on the work of a single historian, may provide a clue to the broad nature of those changes. For that reason, too, it was important to leave them in the form in which they were first written. Let me identify some of the changes. In the early 1970s, some of us Bengali historians were struggling against the weight of a cultural and political inheritance: that of the Bengal Renaissance on the one hand, and of the nationalist movements on the other. Both had enjoyed a long period of unchallenged ascendancy in popular estimation and in Indian historiography – except in very reactionary circles.

Born in a family with generations of modern, liberal socio-religious reformism behind it, and overlaid by a new Leftist content that my father had added, I felt, in a spurt of youthful rebelliousness, that Leftist values and Brahmo liberalism did not sit well together. So, a lot of the essays on social reform probed the limits of the so-called Renaissance heritage quite severely. I now find it interesting that even then I did criticise Rammohun Roy for not doing more about caste – a point that I developed more forcefully in another essay, "The 'Women's Question' in Nineteenth-Century Bengal". Of course, given the prevailing indifference to issues of social justice of those times, my references were all too brief. "The Women's Question" was a part of *A Critique of Colonial India* but has not been included in the present collection. It took issue with renaissance emancipatory claims about gender at a time when gender was not yet central to mainstream history-writing, feminist historians having barely begun their journey.

Along with those of Asok Sen and Barun De, my writings provoked deep shock among Bengali Left liberals who felt – maybe with some justification – that this was iconoclasm of a totally unacceptable kind. A senior C.P.I. activist even blamed me for betraying my father's views on the Renaissance. Interestingly, without telling me, my father – Susobhan Chandra Sarkar, a towering teacher of history who had written much on the Renaissance himself – published a strong rejoinder rebuking the activist, justifying alternative readings of history, and saying that socialism should be a broad enough road on which many different people may travel together with ease.

This was also a time when "Cambridge School" historians had begun to question and problematise Indian nationalism. With hindsight, I feel that they had a lot to offer, though I still believe that their blindness to popular anti-colonial struggles was a major and strange limitation. But they were practically the first historians to work with archival records and private papers, and they looked closely at local social contexts like caste. At the time, however, we found their cavalier attitude to Indian nationalism highly offensive. Since their writings emanated from a Western – worse, British – academic context, we all too easily slipped into branding them "neo-imperialist".

Bipan Chandra (professor of history at J.N.U.) and many others reacted against the Cambridge School by looking closely and respectfully at, and identifying profoundly with, the work of great nationalist leaders. I could not make myself go that way, and my article on Gandhian nationalism should make it evident. As the shining promise at the dawn of Independence began to dim by the late 1960s and early '70s, and as a new wave of popular struggles began in various forms against the post-colonial ruling classes, I felt it was more important to explore the historical limits of mainstream nationalism, especially the class perspective of its leadership. The ongoing Vietnam War, and the residual excitement of May 1968, made quite a lot of us think for some time, independently and in isolation from one another, that the struggles of peasants and workers were more significant for national and social liberation than the leadership provided by the elites.

Already, Ranajit Guha had gathered around him a group of young scholars in England who were thinking on similar lines about how to re-vision Indian history. That was the nucleus of the Subaltern Studies collective, with which I, too, became associated for a while. When I visited Oxford for a year in 1976–7, I met the group, and I still remember the very exciting and stimulating discussions I had with Professor Guha at his Sussex home, where the two of us, once or twice, stayed up all night and I listened to him on the Indian peasantry, practically spellbound.

I was very fortunate to meet and strike up a friendship with E.P. Thompson and Dorothy Thompson that lasted till their death. I remember with enormous gratitude their great warmth and wonderful hospitality whenever my wife and I visited them thereafter. His magnum opus, *The Making of the English Working Classes*, had reached us, very belatedly, just before I went to Oxford and met him. That, and his later work, and the many discussions, political and historical, with him over the years inspired me as nothing else had ever done before or has since. The articles on subaltern militancy and Adivasi struggles came out of those encounters.

As a teacher of history at Delhi University for thirty years, between 1974 and 2004, I thoroughly redesigned the course on social history. It used to be focused on social reforms alone, but I brought in caste, Adivasis, and other subaltern lives as well. With hindsight, I realise that this – especially the caste dimension – was really quite unprecedented for postgraduate history courses anywhere at the time. This was a great experience. My students and I explored these themes together through detailed ethnographic studies, Phule's and Ambedkar's writings, those of Periyar that had been translated, and whatever caste histories were then available. We also read a lot of social fiction together. I learnt much from my students, who came from diverse backgrounds and who often made my classes far richer by bringing in their own experiences and perspectives on social history and on the suggested readings. This was the blessed time before the semester system was arbitrarily imposed on the university and made such easy, prolonged, yet thoughtful classroom discussions over days and weeks impossible: something that had made us all grow intellectually. Perhaps the whole point of introducing the semester system was precisely to block that path.

Since the post-Mandal stormy agitations hit Delhi University most severely in the early 1990s, these discussions sometimes turned into extremely acrimonious debates among students and colleagues alike. But the classroom certainly gained in immediate relevance. My later writings on caste came out of that churning.

In another course on early modern Europe that I taught, I discussed some of the *Annales* writings. I was never completely convinced by their project of writing total history, but found the concept of *histoire integrale*, which imbues a very specific local community with a larger sense of historical depth, far more exciting. We also studied early-modern German histories – especially by David Sabean and Hans Medick, among others – which explored the details of the everyday lives of ordinary people over a long duration.

The *alltagsgeschichte* tradition did not focus on individual lives but on broad patterns and habits of work and leisure. Carlo Ginzburg's work, on the other hand, introduced us to the enormous excitement of *microhistoria*: a detailed study of an ordinary sixteenth-century Italian miller who, in a small way, preached doctrines that brought the wrath of the Inquisition upon him – a happy occasion for historians, as Inquisition officials recorded his life and beliefs in his own words and in the supplementary words of his fellow villagers, all ordinary men like himself.

In the early 1990s I read Peter Linebaugh and Marcus Rediker with great interest as they identified working-class lives, work, and resistance in unexpected places: on board ship – which now appeared as a global site of capitalist production – in piracy, and in sailors' resistance to ship authorities. These confused the boundaries between social crime and insurrection and made us rethink both on new lines.

Sometime in the mid 1990s I went on the first and last academic leave of my life (though I continued to take my university classes). I joined the Nehru Memorial Museum and Library as a Senior Research Fellow, going back to my university after a year. But, in that year, reflections on many of my readings began to crystallise. Strangely, I returned to some of my older interests, but now in a different key: no longer so much to critique liberal reformism for its dependence on empire, but to see Vidyasagar against the context of contemporary orthodoxy, and reconfigure his agenda on education and gender in that light. I did not go back to the Brahmo movement which, after all, had been a familiar world to me. But I approached a Hindu saint, Ramakrishna, who seemed remote and alien to my socialist, secular worldview. I found in the *Kathamrita*, a diary kept by his disciple (who recorded his conversations for years), a rare text and a window to a guru's actual religious musings. Equally interesting was his following: not just the great nineteenth-century luminaries of Bengal, but also poor, lower-middle-class, little-educated clerks in modern government and mercantile offices, all from a world that had so far been ignored by historians. I pondered over what their guru – insulated from their work experiences and gruelling family responsibilities as he was – brought to their lives. And I thought about what highly sophisticated intellectuals found in his simple, rustic language and homely parables that so moved them. I especially probed the intermingling of different classes and intellectual-devotional orders around the figure of a single religious leader to reflect on the broader issues of a time of transition when the older hopes in liberal social and religious change had declined but the new energies of nationalism had not yet appeared. The intermingling of different lives became a point of strong interest – historians often study them in mutual isolation.

Microhistories alert us to unexpected undercurrents that work beneath the surface of events of conventional historical importance. Much had already been written by Indian historians by this time on subaltern resistance, especially to the colonial state. I was becoming more interested in ordinary lives which sometimes flare into extraordinary deeds – not necessarily admirable – which cannot be classified as open resistance to power. In Ginzburg's study, Inquisition records revealed this world. But in the absence of a huge bureaucratic apparatus that would be capable of keeping track of ordinary people, criminality alone provides us with similar stories which contemporaries sometimes recorded in some detail because of their sensation value. Accidentally, in the course of my readings on nineteenth-century religious and social movements in contemporary vernacular sources, I came across a newspaper report on a village scandal at Doyhata in East Bengal. It brought out a form of unorganised subterranean deviance which never led to any sect or movement, but to murder and mayhem for just one night in just one village. There were unexpected crossings of caste boundaries as a low-caste, uneducated, and poor guru inspired a high-caste, highly educated disciple to kill another and expose his own family women to the gaze of a stranger in a particularly gross manner. This was an improvised ritual and belief structure which would have left no traces at all in historical records, had it not involved violent crime.

I felt attracted to such small happenings that stuck out from the main historical plot structures and went against the grain of all expectations, or which came out of the realm of ordinary people and did not take on national or major religious dimensions. All this made me write about the Doyhata episode, which remains something of a personal favourite even now. I remember an article in the *Economic and Political Weekly*, shortly after it was published, which expressed surprise and dismay at what a Leftist and secular historian was coming to. But all historians are entitled to try and understand their Others.

Of late, labour histories have emerged as a most dynamic new trend in modern Indian historiography. As I read the works of Chitra Joshi, Rajnarayan Chandavarkar, Prabhu Mohapatra, Rana Behal, Ravi Ahuja, and many others with great interest, I recalled that my first book, on the Swadeshi Movement in Bengal, did have a chapter on the early-twentieth-century labour upsurge – well before systematic labour-history writings began in our country. I also recalled the animated discussions in the early 1970s with my younger friend Dipesh Chakrabarty, who had then just begun his research on jute workers. I wrote an overview of some of the recent works on Indian labour to see what had changed in labour history since then.

The pieces in the third section are very short tributes to historians and to a political leader who meant a lot to me.

So far, we Indian historians have written the histories that we wanted to write, following no agenda but our own. That seems to be a fast-vanishing luxury. I wish with all my heart all success to the present generation, and to the generations that will come after them, who struggle to write history as it should be written.

Some of the articles in the first section of this book, written between 1972 and 1981, were earlier published in *A Critique of Colonial India* (Calcutta: Papyrus, 1985). "Rammohun Roy and the Breach with the Past" was presented at a Nehru Memorial Museum and Library seminar in 1972 and published in V.C. Joshi, ed., *Rammohun Roy and the Process of Modernization in India* (New Delhi, 1975). "The Complexities of Young Bengal", presented at Calcutta's Centre for Studies in Social Sciences in 1973, came out in *Nineteenth Century Studies* (October 1973). "The Radicalism of Intellectuals" was reprinted from the *Calcutta Historical Review* (vol. 11, July–December 1977). "Primitive Rebellion and Modern Nationalism" was presented to the Bhubaneswar session of the Indian National Congress in 1977 and published in K.N. Panikkar, ed., *National and Left Movements in*

India (Delhi: Vikas, 1980). "The Logic of Gandhian Nationalism" and "Popular Movements and National Leadership 1945–1947" were presented at seminars in the Nehru Memorial Museum and Library in 1976 and 1980. They were reprinted from the *Indian Historical Review* (vol. III, July 1976) and the *Economic and Political Weekly* (Annual Number, 1982). "The Pattern and Structure of Early Nationalist Activity in Bengal" was prepared for the International Congress of Historians held at San Francisco in August 1975; it could not be presented because the Government of India, in the wake of the Emergency, excluded some of us from the official delegation, an honour which I was happy to share with Irfan Habib. "A Note on Forest Satyagraha" was unpublished and appeared for the first time in *A Critique of Colonial India*. I would like to thank Swapan Majumdar of Jadavpur University and Arijit Kumar of Papyrus for prodding me into publication, and Subimal Lahiri for going through the proofs of the 1985 edition of *A Critique of Colonial India*, published by Papyrus, Calcutta.

"One or Many Histories: Identity Formations in Late-Colonial Bengal" was written for *Annales*, but in the event I provided them a shorter version and the longer incarnation herein is published for the first time. "Kaliyuga, Chakri and Bhakti: Ramakrishna and His Times" first appeared in my collection titled *Writing Social History* (Delhi: Oxford University Press, 1998). "The Conditions and Nature of Subaltern Militancy" appeared in *Subaltern Studies III* (Delhi: Oxford University Press, 1984); "The Kalki-Avatar of Bikrampur: A Village Scandal in Early-Nineteenth-Century Bengal" was first published in *Subaltern Studies VI* (Delhi: Oxford University Press, 1989). "The Return of Labour to Indian History" first appeared in *Historical Materialism*, vol. 12 (2004).

In the "Tributes" section, "Thinking About P.C. Joshi" was first published in Gargi Chakravartty, ed., *'People's Warrior': Words and Worlds of P.C. Joshi* (New Delhi: Tulika, 2004). "Edward Thompson" and "In Memory of Eric Hobsbawm" both appeared as *EPW* obituaries soon after the deaths of the two inspiring historians.

1

Rammohun Roy and the Break with the Past

On the bicentenary of his birth, the title of "Father of Modern India" bestowed on Rammohun by many might appear utterly sacrosanct; an exploration of the assumptions lying behind such a statement still seems not unrewarding. If this ascription of parentage is to mean anything more than a rather pompous and woolly way of showing respect, the implication surely is that something like a decisive breakthrough towards modernity took place in Rammohun's times and in large part through his thought and activities. I propose to investigate, in the first place, the precise extent and nature of this "break with the past". Second, the unanimity with which a very wide and varied spectrum of our intelligentsia – ranging from avowed admirers of British rule through liberal nationalists to convinced Marxists – has sought a kind of father figure in Rammohun and a sense of identification with the "renaissance" inaugurated by him remains a historical fact of considerable importance. Subsequently I will try to analyse some of the implications of this well-established historiographical tradition based on the concept of a break in a progressive direction in Bengal's development at the beginning of the nineteenth century.

For the sake of clarity it would be convenient to begin by stating in a very schematic and somewhat provocative manner the propositions I intend to try and establish.

1. Rammohun's writings and activities do signify a kind of a break with the traditions inherited by his generation.

2. This break, however, was of a limited and deeply contradictory kind. It was achieved mainly on the intellectual plane and not at the level of basic social transformation; and the "renaissance" culture which Rammohun inaugurated inevitably remained confined within a Hindu-elitist and colonial (one might almost add comprador) framework.
3. What may be loosely described as the negative aspects of the break became increasingly prominent as the nineteenth century advanced. The Bengal Renaissance from one point of view may be presented not as a "torch-race", as Nirad C. Chaudhuri once described it, but as a story of retreat and decline. And perhaps a certain process of degeneration can be traced even in some of Rammohun's later writings.
4. The limitations and contradictions of Rammohun can be traced back ultimately to the basic nature of the British impact on Indian society. The conceptual framework required for the proper analysis of this impact is not the tradition-modernisation dichotomy so much in vogue today in Western historical circles, but the study of colonialism as a distinct historical stage.[1]
5. With few exceptions, history-writing on Rammohun and on the entire Bengal Renaissance has remained prisoner to a kind of "false consciousness" bred by colonialism which needs to be analysed and overcome in the interests of both historical truth and contemporary progress.

I

It is generally agreed that Rammohun's true originality and greatness lay in his attempt to synthesise Hindu,[2] Islamic, and Western cultural traditions; the precise character of this "synthesis", however,

---

[1] For a brilliant analysis of this important theoretical problem, see Bipan Chandra, "Colonialism and Modernization", Presidential Address, Modern India Section of the Indian History Congress, Jabalpur Session, 1970.

[2] Thus Brajendranath Seal and Susobhan Chandra Sarkar are in perfect agreement on this point, despite their otherwise quite different attitudes – Seal,

has often been obscured by a flood of laudatory rhetoric. Synthesis has often meant either eclectic and indiscriminate combination, or a kind of mutual toleration of orthodoxies. H.H. Wilson in 1840 quoted the Brahman compilers of a code of Hindu laws under Warren Hastings as affirming "the equal merit of every form of religious worship; . . . God appointed to every tribe its own faith, and to every sect its own religion, that man might glorify him in diverse modes . . ."[3] Ramakrishna Paramahansa was saying very similar things a hundred years later, and both Mughal tolerance and early British non-interference were grounded upon a politic acceptance of the need for a coexistence of orthodoxies. Such attitudes seem very attractive when compared to early-modern European religious wars, but they also have certain fairly obvious conservative implications.[4] It needs to be emphasised that "synthesis" with Rammohun, at least in the bulk of his writings, meant something very different; it implied discrimination and systematic choice, directed by the two standards of "reason" and "social comfort" which recur so often in his works. This is the true Baconian note struck, for instance, in the famous letter to Lord Amherst in 1823. Here, as elsewhere, panegyrists and debunkers alike have tended to miss the real point. The entire debate on the foundation of the Hindu College seems more than a little irrelevant as the "conservatives" were also quite intensely interested in learning the language of the rulers on purely pragmatic grounds, and there is surely nothing "progressive" in English education per se. What remains remarkable is Rammohun's stress on "Mathematics, Natural

---

Rammohun the Universal Man (Calcutta, n.d.), pp. 2–3; Sarkar, *On the Bengal Renaissance* (Calcutta, 1979), pp. 14–15.

[3] Cited in K.K. Datta, *Survey of India's Social Life and Economic Condition in the 18th Century* (Calcutta, 1961), p. 2.

[4] Barun De has dealt with this ossifying role of both Mughal and early-British "toleration" in two very stimulating articles—"A Preliminary Note on the Writing of the History of Modern India" in *Quarterly Review of Historical Studies*, vol. III, no. 1, 2 (Calcutta, 1963–4); and "Some Implications of Political Tendencies and Social Factors in (Early) Eighteenth Century India", in *Studies in the Social History of India (Modern)*, ed. O.P. Bhatnagar (Allahabad, 1964).

Philosophy, Chemistry, Anatomy and other useful Sciences",[5] a bias totally and significantly lost in the ultimate Macaulay-style literary education introduced in 1835 mainly under the pressure of financial needs![6]

It would be quite unhistorical, however, to attribute Rammohun's rationalism entirely to a knowledge of progressive Western culture. His earliest extant work, *Tuhfat-ul Muwahhidin* (c. 1803–4), was written at a time when, on Digby's testimony, Rammohun's command over English was still imperfect;[7] yet this "Gift to Deists" was marked by a radicalism trenchant enough to embarrass many later admirers.[8] Here the criteria of reason and social comfort are used with devastating effect to establish the startling proposition that "falsehood is common to all religions without distinction."[9] Only three basic

---

[5] "Letter to Lord Amherst, 11 December 1823", *English Works of Rammohun Roy* (henceforth *EW*), vol. IV (Calcutta, 1947), pp. 105–8.

[6] "I am sure you will do all you can to educate the natives for office and to encourage them by the possession of it . . . We cannot govern India financially without this change of system." Ellenborough, President of the Board of Control, to Bentinck, 23 September 1830, quoted in A.F. Salahuddin Ahmed, *Social Ideas and Social Change in Bengal, 1818–1835* (Leiden, 1965), pp. 151–2. Financial economy demanded more employment of Indians on small salaries, but Orientalist educational policy could not produce this kind of cadre.

[7] In an introduction to an 1817 London reprint of two tracts of Rammohun, Digby stated that the "Brahmin . . . when I became acquainted with him, could merely speak it [English] well enough to be understood upon the most common topics of discourse, but could not write it with any degree of correctness." Rammohun seems to have perfected his knowledge of English only after entering the service of Digby. They met each other first in 1801, but Rammohun became his *munshi* only in 1805. S.D. Collet, *Life and Letters of Raja Rammohun Roy*, ed. D.K. Biswas and P.C. Ganguli (Calcutta, 1962), pp. 23–4, 37–8.

[8] Collet dismissed it as "immature" (op. cit., p. 19). Rajnarain Bose in his preface to the 1884 English translation of the *Tuhfat* rather condescendingly referred to it as an "index to a certain stage in the history of his [Rammohun's] mind. It marks the period when he had just emerged from the idolatry of his age but had not yet risen to . . . sublime Theism and Theistic Worship . . ." Reprinted in Rammohun Roy, *Tuhfat-ul Muwahhidin* (Calcutta, 1949).

[9] Roy, *Tuhfat-ul Muwahhidin*, op. cit., Introduction.

tenets – common to all faiths and hence "natural" – are retained: belief in a single Creator (proved by the argument from design), in the existence of the soul, and faith in an afterworld where rewards and punishments will be duly awarded – and even the two latter beliefs are found acceptable only on utilitarian grounds.[10] Everything else – belief in particular divinities or "in a God qualified with human attributes as anger, mercy, hatred and love",[11] the faith in divinely inspired prophets and miracles, salvation through "bathing in a river and worshipping a tree or being a monk and purchasing forgiveness of their crime from the high priests",[12] and the "hundreds of useless hardships and privations regarding eating and drinking, purity and impurity, auspiciousness and inauspiciousness"[13] – is blown up with relentless logic and shown to be invented by the self-interest of priests feeding on mass ignorance and slavishness to habit. Such beliefs and practices are condemned as both irrational and "detrimental to social life and sources of trouble and bewilderment to the people."[14] We have come perilously close, in fact, to the vanishing point of religion, and the logic seems to have frightened even the later Rammohun himself. Prolific translator of his own works, he never brought out English or Bengali editions of the *Tuhfat*.

In Rammohun's later writings, too, the concepts of reason and social comfort or utility tend to crop up at crucial points in the argument. The illogicalities of the orthodox Christian doctrines of the Trinity and atonement through Christ are brilliantly exposed. The prefaces to the Upanishad translations and the *Brahma-Pauttalik Sambad*[15] ruthlessly analyse the irrationalities of contemporary Hindu image-

[10] ". . . they (mankind) are to be excused in admitting and teaching the doctrine of existence of soul and the next world although the real existence of soul and the next world is hidden and mysterious for the sake of the welfare of the people (society) as they simply, for the fear of punishment in the next world . . . refrain from commission of illegal deeds." Ibid., p. 5.

[11] Ibid., p. 8. This is an assumption fairly common, incidentally, in later Brahmo *upasana*.

[12] Ibid., p. 8.

[13] Ibid., p. 5.

[14] Loc. cit.

[15] Almost certainly by Rammohun, according to Stephen Hay.

worship, and religious reform is urged time and again for the sake of "political advantage and social comfort".[16] From 1815 onwards, Rammohun tried to anchor his monotheism on the Upanishads as interpreted by Sankara, yet there is never really any question of a simple return to the Vedanta tradition. Vedantic philosophy had been essentially elitist, preaching Mayabad and monism for the ascetic and intellectual while leaving religious practices and social customs utterly undisturbed at the level of everyday life. Rammohun's originality lay firstly in his deft avoidance of extreme monism. Mayabad in his hands gets reduced to the conventional idealist doctrines of dependence of matter on spirit and the creation of the world by God,[17] and the Vedantic revival is thus reconciled with a basically utilitarian and this-worldly approach to religion. Even more striking is Rammohun's scathing attack on the double-standard approach so very common in our religious and philosophical tradition – this is bluntly attributed to the self-interest of the Brahmans:

> Many learned Brahmans are perfectly aware of the absurdity of idolatry, and are well informed of the nature of the purer mode of divine worship. But as in the rites, ceremonies, and festivals of idolatry, they find the source of their comforts and fortune, they . . . advance and encourage it to the utmost of their power, by keeping the knowledge of their scriptures concealed from the rest of the people.[18]

The "purer mode of divine worship" should be open to householder and ascetic alike.[19] The practical relevance of all this for social reform

---

[16] Rammohun to Digby, 18 January 1828, *EW* IV, p. 96.

[17] "The term Maya implies, primarily, the power of creation, and secondarily its effect, which is the Universe. The Vedanta, by comparing the world with the misconceived notion of a snake, when a rope really exists, means that the world, like the supposed snake, has no independent existence, that it receives its existence from the Supreme Being. In like manner the Vedanta compares the world with a dream: as all the objects seen in a dream depend upon the motion of the mind, as the existence of the world is dependent upon the being of God . . ." *The Brahmanical Magazine*, no. 1, Calcutta 1821, *EW* II, p. 146.

[18] Preface to the *Translation of the Ishopanishad*, Calcutta, 1816, *EW* II, p. 44.

[19] Ibid., p. 43.

becomes clear through a reading of Rammohun's tracts on sati, where concremation with its shastric promises of heavenly bliss is proved inferior to ascetic widowhood which may lead to "eternal beatitude" and "absorption in Brahma".[20] Mrityunjay Vidyalankar had anticipated this argument in 1817,[21] but the author of the *Vedanta Chandrika* obviously could not relate his humanitarian stand on a particularly gruesome abuse to a general philosophy. And surely only Rammohun in his generation could have written the deeply moving closing section of the *Second Conference* with its passionate repudiation of the unequal treatment of women "thus dependent and exposed to every misery, you feel for them no compassion, that might exempt them from being tied down and burnt to death!"[22]

In sheer intellectual power, Rammohun stands far above his contemporaries, and a comparison with Ramram Basu, for instance,[23] is utterly ludicrous. Yet certain limits and qualifications need to be emphasised.

In the first place, the uniqueness of Rammohun's rationalism cannot be taken as finally settled till much more is known about the intellectual history of eighteenth-century India, and particularly perhaps about its Islamic components. Brajendranath Seal found in the *Tuhfat* clear evidence of the influence of early Muslim rationalism (the Mutazalis of the eighth century and the Muwahhidin of the twelfth);[24] what remains unexplored is the precise way in which

[20] *First and Second Conferences between An Advocate For, and An Opponent Of, The Practice of Burning Widows Alive* (Calcutta, 1818, 1820), *EW* III, pp. 91, 111.

[21] *Friend of India*, October 1819, summarised Mrityunjay's arguments, quoted in Brajendranath Bandyopadhyay, *Mrityunjay Vidyalankar* (Sahitya-Sadhak-Charitmala), vol. I, pp. 29–34.

[22] *EW* III, p. 127.

[23] Such a comparison has been made by Brajendranath Bandyopadhyay in *Sahitya-Sadhak-Charitmala*, vol. I; and more recently by David Kopf in *British Orientalism and the Bengal Renaissance* (Berkeley, 1969), chapter XII, apparently on the strength of an invocation to Brahma at the beginning of Ramram Basu's *Lipi-mala* (1802).

[24] Brajendranath Seal, *Rammohun the Universal Man* (Calcutta, n.d.), p. 4. The detailed discussion of the same question in Nagendranath Chattopadhyay,

this tradition was transmitted to the young Rammohun studying Persian and Arabic at Patna. A comparison of the *Tuhfat* with the *Dabistan-i Mazahib* of the mid seventeenth century – of which there does not exist as yet any adequate English translation – might prove quite illuminating. The "remarkably secular" character of much later Mughal historical writing may be another significant pointer in this context.[25] The Hindu intelligentsia of nineteenth-century Bengal (and maybe Rammohun, too, to some extent, after he had mastered English) turned their backs entirely on such traces of secularism, rationalism, and non-conformity in pre-British Muslim-ruled India – and their historians have by and large faithfully echoed the assumption of a completely new beginning with the coming of English education. An uncritical use of the renaissance concept is seldom a helpful analytical tool.

As has been implied already, a certain retreat from the fairly consistent and militant rationalism of the *Tuhfat* is evident in Rammohun's later religious and social tracts.[26] The slide back took place at both the levels of social practice and intellectual argument and can be explained partly, though not perhaps entirely, by Rammohun's reform-from-within technique. In 1819, private meetings of the Atmiya Sabha had freely discussed and criticised "the absurdity of the prevailing rules respecting the intercourse of the several castes with each other . . . the restrictions on diet . . . (and) the necessity of an infant widow passing her life in a state of celibacy."[27] But Rammohun in his published writings and public life paraded his outward

---

Mahatma Raja Rammohun Rayer Jivan-Charita (3rd edition, Calcutta, 1897), chapter 17, is acknowledged by the author to have been entirely based on Brajendranath's ideas.

[25] Barun De, "A Preliminary Note on the Writing of the History of Modern India", op. cit.

[26] For an analysis of the difference between the *Tuhfat* and the post-1815 religious writings, see Susobhan Sarkar, "Religious Thought of Rammohun Roy", idem, *On the Bengal Renaissance*, op. cit.

[27] *India Gazette*, quoted in *Asiatic Journal*, 18 May 1819; J.K. Majumdar, ed., *Raja Rammohun Roy and Progressive Movements in India* (Calcutta, 1941), p. 18.

conformity to most caste rules (even to the extent of taking a Brahman cook with him to England!), wore the sacred thread to the end of his days, limited his direct attack on caste to a single *Vajra-suchi* translation, and, concentrating all his social-reform energies on the single-sari issue, possibly even added to a slight extent to Vidyasagar's difficulties by hunting up all the texts glorifying ascetic widowhood. Such deviousness was perhaps not even tactically very wise, since the contradiction between theory and practice soon became the commonest orthodox charge against Rammohun, and one to which the reformer could only make the not entirely satisfactory rejoinder that his critics were equally inconsistent.[28] On the conceptual level, the claims of reason are now balanced and increasingly limited by Upanishadic authority as well as by a conservative use of the social comfort criterion. Even in the *Tuhfat*, belief in the soul and in an afterlife were accepted as socially advantageous although doubtfully rational. In the Introduction to *Kenopanishad* (1823), we get the following key passage:

> When we look to the traditions of ancient nations, we often find them at variance with each other; and when . . . we appeal to reason as a surer guide, we soon find how incompetent it is, alone, to conduct us to the object of our pursuit . . . instead of facilitating our endeavours or clearing up our perplexities, it only serves to generate a universal doubt, incompatible with principles on which our comfort and happiness mainly depend. The best method perhaps is, neither to give ourselves up exclusively to the guidance of the one or the other; but by a proper use of the lights, furnished by both, endeavour to improve our intellectual and moral faculties, relying on the goodness of the Almighty Power . . .[29]

Collet's biography quotes Sandford Arnot stating that

---

[28] See, for example, *Chari Prasna* (1822) and *Pashanda-Peeran* (1823) and Rammohun's replies, *Chari Prasner Uttar* (May 1822) and *Pathya-Pradan* (1823), published together in *Rammohun Granthabali* (Calcutta, n.d.), vol. VI. The *Brahma-Pouttalik Sangbad* (1820) defends the observance of caste, diet, and other social rules by the believer in Brahma as a matter of expediency even while emphasising their relative unimportance, pp. 138, 158, 164.

[29] *EW* II, p. 15.

> As he [Rammohun] advanced in age, he became more strongly impressed with the importance of religion to the welfare of society, and the pernicious effects of scepticism ... He often deplored the existence of the party which had sprung up in Calcutta ... partly composed of East Indians, partly of the Hindu youth, who, from education had learnt to reject their own faith without substituting any other. These he thought more debased than the most bigoted Hindu ... .[30]

In sharp contrast to the sense of rational discrimination which had been the keynote of the *Tuhfat*, the later Rammohun also reveals a certain eclecticism, a desire to be all things to all people, so much so that in England both Unitarian and Evangelical Christians tried to claim him as their own. James Sutherland described him in 1830 "on questions of religious faith" as "in general too pliant, perhaps from his excessive fear of giving offence or wounding the feelings of anybody", a contrast indeed with the young man who had written the *Tuhfat*.[31]

While the *Tuhfat* was soon almost forgotten, the religious writings and activities of the later Rammohun did leave a permanent legacy in the shape of the Brahmo Samaj. Yet it can be questioned whether Brahmoism was ever anything more than a rather unsatisfactory halfway house. It leaves an impression of incompleteness even when considered in purely intellectual terms as a modernist critique of orthodox Hinduism. While fire was concentrated from the beginning on image-worship, caste was not attacked with anything like the same zeal till the 1860s, and the fundamental belief in karma – perhaps an even more formidable barrier to radical social change – seems to have escaped serious criticism.[32] More important is the fact that

---

[30] Collet, op. cit., p. 371.

[31] Ibid., p. 370.

[32] In the *Kavitakarer Sahit Vichar* of 1820 (summarised in Nagendranath Chattopadhyay, op. cit., pp. 124–7) and the *Brahmanical Magazine*, no. 11, 1821 (*EW* II, p. 156), Rammohun came very near to an acceptance of the Karma doctrine – "The Supreme Ruler bestows the consequences of ... sins and holiness ... by giving them other bodies either animate or inanimate" (*EW* II, p. 156). To the true Vedantist, of course, Karmaphal belongs to the subsidiary world of illusion, but then Rammohun never accepted the full monist logic.

Brahmoism – in spite of the retreat from unadulterated rationalism begun by the later Rammohun and continued on a greatly enhanced scale by Debendranath and Keshabchandra – still remained far too intellectual and dry a creed to be ever successful as a popular religion. It failed to make any attempt to link up with the popular lower-caste monotheistic cults which seem to have been fairly numerous in eighteenth-century Bengal, particularly in the Nadia-Murshidabad region.[33] Rammohun did include a favourable reference to earlier monotheistic movements in his *Humble Suggestions* (1823),[34] but neither he nor his followers followed up the hint. Here as in so many other things English education placed an impenetrable barrier between the nineteenth century and the immediate pre-British past, which perhaps had contained certain healthy non-conformist elements along with much that was undoubtedly utterly ossified. In a conversation with Alexander Duff, Rammohun once made an interesting comparison between contemporary India and Reformation Europe;[35] we have only to pursue this optimistic analogy a little to see how it breaks down at practically every point. The Protestant Reformation had united the intellectual polemics of men like Erasmus with the less sophisticated but much more virile tradition of late-medieval popular heresy. The Catholic hierarchy in sixteenth-century Europe represented a highly organised and very often partly foreign system of exploitation, a kind of nodal point around which all the tensions of contemporary society had accumulated. Brahman oppression of lower castes, while far less systematic, was and is a reality; but it was hardly the most crucial problem for an Indian then being rapidly exposed to the full blast of colonial exploitation. Above all, the Reformation

---

[33] Kalikinkar Dutta mentions in particular the Karta Bhaja, the Spashta-dayaka, and the Balarami sect: op. cit., p. 8.

[34] *EW* II, p. 200.

[35] "As a youth," he (Rammohun) said to Mr Duff, "I acquired some knowledge of the English language. Having read about the rise and progress of Christianity in apostolic times, and its corruption in succeeding ages, and then of the Christian Reformation which shook off these corruptions and restored it to its primitive purity, I began to think about something similar might have taken place in India, and similar results might follow here from a reformation of the popular idolatry." Collet, op. cit., p. 280.

had succeeded not because its theology was intrinsically superior, but due to its linkage with a host of other factors – incipient nationalism directed against the papacy, the princely drive to establish territorial sovereignty, the greed for church lands, the bourgeois quest for hegemony over civil society – all conspicuously and inevitably absent in colonial Bengal. To expect a European-style Reformation in such a context reveals a rather pathetic kind of false consciousness.

The negative, alienating aspects of the English education which Rammohun and his generation so ardently welcomed are of course fairly obvious today. In fairness to Rammohun, certain qualifications should be made here. The traditional Sanskrit- or Persian-educated literati were also utterly alienated from the masses; the 1823 letter pleaded for Western scientific values, and not necessarily for English as the medium of instruction; and there were elements of a kind of mass approach in Rammohun's pioneering translations of the shastras into the vernacular, his promotion of Bengali journalism, and the efforts by Atmiya Sabha members and Hindu College students to bring out Bengali versions of English scientific and literary texts.[36] The seventh issue of the *Sambad Kaumudi* contained "An Address to the Hindoo Community, demonstrating the necessity of having their children instructed in the principles of the Grammar of their own language, previous to imposing upon the Study of Foreign Languages",[37] and in 1833 the students of Rammohun's Anglo-Hindu school started the Sarbatattva-deepika Sabha, pledged to the use of Bengali alone.[38] Yet the general attitude of our intelligentsia towards Western culture and particularly the English language contrasts

---

[36] Rammohun is said to have written a geography textbook (Nagendranath Chattopadhyay, op. cit., pp. 325–6). The Atmiya Sabha member Brajamohan Majumdar was working on a translation of Fergusson's *Astronomy* on the eve of his death: S. Hay, ed., *A Tract Against Idolatry* (Calcutta, 1963), Introduction. Salahuddin Ahmed (op. cit., chapter I) cites a 1832 reference in the Bentinck Papers to translations by Hindu College students.

[37] Summary in *Calcutta Journal*, 31 January 1882; J.K. Majumdar, op. cit., p. 288.

[38] *Sambad Kaumudi*, quoted in *Samachar Darpan*, 19 January 1833, ibid., pp. 273–5.

oddly with that displayed, for instance, by Sultan Mahmud II of the Ottoman Empire in an address to medical students in 1838: "You will study scientific medicine in French ... my purpose in having you taught French is not to educate you in the French language; it is to teach you scientific medicine and little by little to take it into our language ..."[39] In intellect and general culture Rammohun and other stalwarts of our renaissance were certainly far superior to this not particularly enlightened Sultan; but colonial subjection often puts blinkers on and distorts the greatest of minds.

If the culture of the Bengal Renaissance was highly elitist in character, it soon became also overwhelmingly and increasingly alienated from the Islamic heritage. Rammohun himself had been deeply rooted at first in the composite upper-class Persian culture of the eighteenth century, as both the *Tuhfat* and the *Mirat-ul-Ukhbar* bear witness. Explaining Rammohun's exclusion from the committee which founded the Hindu College, Hyde East stated that the Orthodox Hindus "particularly disliked (and this I believe is at the bottom of the resentment) his associating himself so much as he does with Mussulmans ... being continually surrounded by them, and suspected to partake meals with them."[40] In 1826 Adam reports him as about to commence on a life of Muhammad,[41] an interesting project which never materialised. A long historical footnote to the *Ancient Rights of Females* (1822) blamed Rajput "tyranny and oppression" almost as much as Muslim misrule for the degeneration of India from a supposed golden age in which Brahmans and Kshatriyas had balanced each other.[42] Yet already in Rammohun there are also strong traces of that concept of Muslim tyranny – and of British rule as a deliverance from it, hence fundamentally acceptable – which soon became a central assumption of virtually every section of the intelligentsia, conservative, reformist, and radical alike. In the Appeal to the King in Council against the 1823 Press Regulation, it is stated that "under

[39] Bernard Lewis, *The Emergence of Modern Turkey* (Oxford, 1968), p. 85.
[40] Letter of Hyde East to the Earl of Buckinghamshire (Fulham Papers), cited in Salahuddin Ahmed, op. cit., p. 36.
[41] Collet, op. cit., p. 201.
[42] *EW* I, p. 1.

their former Muhammadan Rulers, the natives of this country enjoyed every political privilege in common with Mussulmans, being eligible to the highest offices in the state". But "their property was, often plundered, their religion insulted, and their blood wantonly shed", till "Divine Providence at last, in its abundant mercy, stirred up the English nation to break the yoke of those tyrants and to receive the oppressed Natives of Bengal under its protection."[43] The basic theme, without Rammohun's qualifications, crops up throughout the nineteenth century at the most unexpected of places: in the Derozian Maheshchandra Deb condemning the seclusion of women in Hindu society before the Society for Acquisition of General Knowledge,[44] and in the rationalist Akshaykumar Dutt adversely comparing Muslim with British rule,[45] just as much as in Bankimchandra. An analysis of the ramifications of this concept, which research today is incidentally rapidly demolishing as in any way a just appraisal of the late Mughal India, surely would be the most interesting and most neglected of themes. British historiography certainly played a crucial role here,[46] and with the rapid disappearance of knowledge of Persian, the region's westernised intelligentsia became entirely dependent on it for knowledge of their immediate past. This is perhaps one contribution of British Orientalism to the Bengal Renaissance which merits more attention than it has received in the past.

Consideration of Rammohun's attitude to British rule leads, naturally, to a discussion of his political and economic ideas. Two rather tentative suggestions may be made in this connection. In the first place, it is just possible that the pattern of retreat fairly evident in Rammohun's religious and social thought has its counterpart also in his political ideas. The *Autobiographical Letter* contains a tantaliz-

[43] Collet, op. cit., Appendix I B, pp. 431, 449.
[44] Mahesh Chundra Deb, "A Sketch of the Condition of the Hindoo Women (1839)", in Gautam Chattopadhyay, ed., *Awakening in Bengal* (Calcutta, 1965), pp. 94–5.
[45] *Sangbad Prabhakar* 21.8.1247/1840; Benoy Ghosh, ed., *Samayikpatre Banglar Samajchitra* (Calcutta, 1962), vol. I, pp. 160–1.
[46] For this, see J.S. Grewal, *Muslim Rule in India—The Assessments of British Historians* (New Delhi, 1970).

ingly brief reference to Rammohun's early travels being animated by "a feeling of great aversion to the establishment of the British power in India",[47] and a Bangladeshi historian has recently speculated on the possibility of some connections with anti-British zamindar and even peasant groups in Rangpur.[48] The evidence here is admittedly still very scanty; certainly the Rammohun who is so much more familiar to us all somehow managed to combine an impressive interest in and sympathy for liberal and nationalist movements in England, France, Naples, Spain, Ireland, and even Latin America with a fundamental acceptance of foreign political and economic domination over his own country. Within this basic framework, Rammohun did blaze the trail, of course, for several generations of moderate constitutionalist agitation, focusing on demands like Indianisation of services, trial by jury, separation of powers, freedom of the press, and consultations with Indian landlords, merchants, and officials on legislative matters. His critique of the zamindari system and plea for an absolute ban on "any further increase of rent on any pretence whatsoever" strike a sympathetic chord in progressive hearts even today.[49] Yet here too perhaps a tendency towards growing moderation and a kind of centrism may be traced. The *Bengal Herald*, of which Rammohun was a principal proprietor, on 9 May 1829 announced as its objective an opposition "equally to anarchy, as to despotism",[50] and by 1832 Rammohun was paying the price for this centrism in the shape of

---

[47] The authenticity of this letter, published by Sandford Arnot after Rammohun's death, has been often challenged; but it is difficult to imagine what motive Arnot could have had in completely inventing the passage I am using. (Collet, op. cit., Appendix VIII, p. 497.) See also Victor Jacquemont's testimony (1829): "Formerly when he (Rammohun) was young, he told me this in Europe, the ruler of his country, was odious to him. The blind patriotism of youth made him detest the English and all who came with them." J.K. Majumdar, ed., *Indian Speeches and Documents on British Rule* (Calcutta, 1937), p. 41.

[48] Mufakharul Islam, "Rammohun Royer Ajnatabas", *Itihas* (Dacca), Bhadra-Agrahayan, 1376.

[49] "Questions and Answers on the Revenue System of India" (1832), *EW* III, p. 45.

[50] Cited in J.K. Majumdar, op. cit., p. 328.

an attack from two fronts. His evidence before the Commons Select Committee was denounced as unduly harsh on zamindars by the Dharma Sabha organ *Samachar Chandrika*;[51] much more surprising, and little known, is the whole series of articles in the *Bengal Hurkaru*,[52] violently attacking the reformer for being too soft in his critique of Company maladministration and far too tactful on the question of zamindari oppression of the peasants. "How could Rammohun Roy in these replies", it asks, "*forget* the Seventh Regulation of 1799 . . . the very plague-spot of our administration? Rammohun went to England as a 'voice from India' to tell the wrongs, and the sufferings, and to assert the rights of her children, we find . . . in these papers a mere Zamindar."[53]

The *Bengal Hurkaru* also attacked Rammohun for not being unqualified enough in his support for English colonisation in India, and the newspaper was edited by James Sutherland, an ex-associate of James Silk Buckingham of *Calcutta Journal* fame. This brings us to the second point: the need to analyse, in greater depth than has been usual so far,[54] the close links between British free-traders – the carriers, very often, of Utilitarian ideas – and men like Rammohun or Dwarkanath who combined zamindari with money-lending and business enterprise.[55] With both groups, enthusiastic acceptance of the basic British connection was combined with a more or less sharp

---

[51] *Samachar Chandrika*, quoted in *Samachar Darpan*, 7 July 1832; ibid., pp. 490–3.

[52] *Bengal Hurkaru*, 20 and 22 June, 22 November 1832; ibid., pp. 483–8, 496–501.

[53] Ibid., pp. 484, 488.

[54] See, however, Salahuddin Ahmed, op. cit., chapters I and V, for some discussion on this point.

[55] Dwarkanath's multifarious business activities need no elaboration; Rammohun built up his fortune initially through money-lending and dealings in Company papers, from the proceeds of which he started purchasing land from 1799. (Collet, op. cit., p. 14.) He later developed close connections with agency houses and in a letter to the Court of Directors (23 July 1833) asking for a loan after the collapse of Mackintosh and Co., stated that the latter had been "My Agents as well in general pecuniary transactions as in receiving my rents and managing my landed property." (*EW* IV, p. 129.)

critique of many aspects of Company administration and economic policy. Rammohun and Dwarkanath took a very prominent part in the Town Hall meeting organised by free-traders in December 1829 which petitioned parliament "to throw open the China and India trade, and to remove the restrictions against the settlement of Europeans in India": they improved the occasion by a full-throated defence of indigo planters.[56] The *India Gazette* of 2 July 1829, incidentally, had published a letter from an indigo planter attacking zamindari oppression of peasants and demanding rent reductions, to which a zamindar had replied four days later with a catalogue of misdeeds associated with indigo.[57] In a speech in 1836, Dwarkanath declared that twenty years ago the Company had treated all natives as servants, but things had changed vastly for the inhabitants of Calcutta thanks to the British free-traders; he proceeded to repay that debt by joining in the protest against a "black act" which had sought to curtail the right of European settlers in the *mofussil* to appeal to the Supreme Court against the decisions of district tribunals.[58]

In a very interesting article on the "Prospect of Bengal" published by the *Bengal Herald* of 13 June 1829, an English writer tried to teach his "Native friends" a few lessons in comparative social history. The growth of a "middling class" had brought about the English Revolution of the seventeenth century, while Spain and Poland still remained backward and miserable due to the absence of such a development. In Bengal after 1813, "the lesser restrictions on commerce and greater introduction of Europeans" had vastly enhanced the value of land, and "by means of this territorial value, a class of society has sprung into existence, that were [*sic*] before unknown; these are placed between the aristocracy and the poor, and are daily forming a most influential class." The inflow of English manufactures from "Liverpool, Glasgow, etc." was extremely welcome, since sooner or later "a reciprocity of trade must take place . . . if England expects that India will prove a

---

[56] Collet, op. cit., p. 270; J.K. Majumdar, op. cit., pp. 438–9.

[57] Quoted in Salahuddin Ahmed, op. cit., p. 102.

[58] Kishorichand Mitra, *Dwarkanath Tagore*, Bengali translation, ed. Kalyan Kumar Dasgupta (Calcutta, 1962), pp. 60–1.

large mart for her produce, she must remove the restrictive, almost prohibitory duties on Asiatic produce . . ."[59] The Rammohun–Dwarkanath section of our intelligentsia seems to have swallowed in toto this free-trader logic and visualised a kind of dependent but still real bourgeois development in Bengal in close collaboration with British merchants and entrepreneurs. The utter absurdity of this illusion is very obvious today. A single Dwarkanath did not herald a bourgeois spring and the years from 1813 to 1833 – coinciding almost exactly with the most active period of Rammohun's public life – saw the number of houses paying *chaukidari* tax in Dacca go down from 21,361 to 10,708.[60] The catastrophic decline in cotton handricrafts threw at least a million out of jobs in Bengal,[61] in "a revolution . . . hardly to be paralleled in the history of cornmerce."[62] The founding father of our Renaissance remained utterly silent about such developments.

Within the next generation, the Bengali "middle class" was rapidly squeezed out of even comparador-type business activities and left dependent on the professions, services, and land – almost entirely divorced, in other words, from productive functions since, thanks to the Permanent Settlement, rent receipts flowed in with a minimum of entrepreneurial effort. Bourgeois-liberal values remained bereft of material content. In Rabindranath's *Gora* – the best literary summation perhaps of the cultural world of "renaissance" Bengal – none of the characters seem to have to work for a living; the contrast, say, with Dickens, where "work plays an essential part in the characters" approach to life, is illuminating.[63]

II

Rammohun's achievements as a moderniser were thus both limited and extremely ambivalent. What is involved in this estimate is not really his personal stature, which was certainly quite outstanding;

---

[59] J.K. Majumdar, op. cit., pp. 434–7.
[60] N.K. Sinha, *Economic History of Bengal*, vol. III (Calcutta, 1970), p. 4.
[61] Ibid., pp. 7–8.
[62] Proceedings of the Board of Trade, July 1828, cited in ibid., p. 8.
[63] Humphry House, *The Dickens World* (London, 1961), p. 55.

the limitations were basically those of his times – which marked the beginning of a transition, indeed, from pre-capitalist society, yet in the direction, not of full-blooded bourgeois modernity, but of a weak and distorted caricature of the same which was all that colonial subjection permitted.

This is emphatically not the conventionally accepted view of Rammohun or of the renaissance he inaugurated. It must be obvious that this interpretation is entirely based on published and fairly well-known material and has not involved original research. That being so, a brief analysis of the assumptions underlying the established historiographical tradition seems called for.

From the Dharma Sabha down to R.C. Majumdar and David Kopf, Rammohun of course has had numerous critics and debunkers, but, instead of exposing his real contradictions and limits, criticism has in the main either picked on utterly irrelevant and trivial issues like the alleged Muslim mistress or the illegitimate Rajaram, or concentrated on trying to disprove Rammohun's claim to priority in such things as English education, campaign against sati, or monotheism – accepting by implication therefore their presumably revolutionary nature. The early attacks were clearly motivated solely by the desire to preserve the social and religious status quo. Attempts have been made occasionally to find proto-nationalists among the Dharma Sabha men,[64] but even at the height of the anti-sati agitation, the *Samachar Chandrika* declared: "None of our countrymen feel a pleasure in hearing anything to the disadvantage of the Honourable Company; they always pray for the welfare of the Government... We have been subject to no distress under the government of the Company; it is only the abolition of Suttees which has given us disquietude..."[65]

If Rammohun was closely allied with British free-trader liberals, no less intimate were the links between *Samachar Chandrika* and *John Bull*, the Tory defender of Company interests founded by the Reverend James Bryce.[66]

---

[64] By David Kopf, for example, op. cit., pp. 266–72.

[65] *Samachar Chandrika* quoted in *John Bull*, 9 March 1830, in J.K. Majumdar, op. cit., p. 330.

[66] The strange but very significant alliance between the Hindu orthodoxy

Around the turn of the century, Hindu revivalism did strike a rather temporary alliance with extremist nationalism, and this led sometimes to an interesting revaluation of Rammohun. While still clinging to the father image, the highly revisionist Brahmo Bipin Chandra Pal argued that English education had little or nothing to do with Rammohun's achievements; he went on to present the latter as almost the first of the Hindu revivalists who rightly rejected Western rationalism and instead tried to balance reason with shastric authority.[67]

The fact that denigration or revaluation of Rammohun from the Hindu orthodox or revivalist angle has been motivated by a desire to validate a defence of the social status quo is fairly obvious; what require closer analysis perhaps are the premises of the "progressive" hero-worship tradition particularly, though not exclusively, associated in Bengal with Brahmoism. Several strands can be distinguished here. Full-throated admiration for Rammohun and the entire Bengal Renaissance had been connected occasionally with avowedly pro-British views. Jadunath Sarkar provided a classic instance of this, with his well-known purple passage at the end of the Dacca University *History of Bengal* (1948) on Plassey as "the beginning ... of a glorious dawn, the like of which the history of the world has not seen elsewhere ... truly a Renaissance, wider, deeper, and more revolutionary than that of Europe after the fall of Constantinople ..."

J.K. Majumdar, who edited three invaluable volumes of documents on Rammohun, also published in 1937 a collection of *Speeches and Documents on British Rule, 1821–1918* marked by a quite remarkably sycophantic principle of selection: Gandhi figures in it for example only as the recruiting sergeant of 1918. Such attitudes, of course, had become relatively rare after the development of nationalism, but liberal patriots remained warm admirers of Rammohun as the pioneer of social reform and constitutionalist agitation.

The Marxist approach has been somewhat more ambivalent. From Rabindra Gupta (Bhowani Sen) in the Ranadive period to

---

and the *John Bull* is vividly reflected in a large number of extracts published by J.K. Majumdar: cf. for example, nos. 34, 36, 39, 184, and 185.

[67] Bipin Chandra Pal, "Yuga-Prabartak Rammohun", in *Nabayuger Bangla* (Calcutta, 1955); a reprint of Pal's article in *Banga-bani* 1328–31 (1921–4).

recent Naxalite iconoclasm, it has certainly included the occasional violent attack on the renaissance of the intellectuals, coupled with glorification of instances of popular or peasant resistance to British rule. By and large, however, writings of this type have been mainly on the agitational or journalistic level and have confined themselves to liberally distributing labels like "bourgeois" or "feudal" without going into the trouble of detailed critical analysis. More serious Marxist history-writing, with some justice, has tended to dismiss such attempts as too immature and sectarian, but its own selective emphasis on certain "progressive" aspects (thus, in the case of Rammohun, instances of rationalism, internationalism, and sympathy for the peasantry are highlighted while the pro-British stance is mentioned only in an undertone) perhaps could do with closer scrutiny. In certain periods in the history of the Left in India, this bid to link up with worthwhile elements of the nineteenth century cultural heritage surely had considerable immediate justification. The very influential *Notes on the Bengal Renaissance* (1946), for instance, was written at a time when the Communists were just breaking out of the isolation from the nationalist mainstream produced by the events of 1942, and when, in the words of its introduction, "disintegration threaten(ed) every aspect of our life" – the aftermath of famine and the shadow of the coming Partition of Bengal.[68] The *Notes* explicitly denied to itself the status of a full Marxist analysis; the same historian later offered a much more critical estimate of the Bengal Renaissance in a review of Nirad C. Chaudhuri's *Autobiography* (1952) and by implication in an article on the Mutiny (1957), as well as a more rigorous analytical scheme in an article on Rabindranath (1961) interpreting Bengal Renaissance culture in terms of a conflict between two trends, "Westernist" or "modernist", and "traditionalist".[69]

The Marxist historian's preference for the Westernist trend is understandable,[70] but the sense of discrimination shown in the article just

---

[68] S.C. Sarkar, *On the Bengal Renaissance*, op. cit., p. 3.

[69] Sarkar, op. cit., articles 5, 7, 8.

[70] "In today's battle over the shape of India's future, it is surely westernism rather than traditionalism which beckons us towards a better, happier life." Susobhan Sarkar, "Rabindranath Tagore and the Renaissance in Bengal", in idem, *On the Bengal Renaissance*, op. cit., p. 159.

referred to should be carried a step further. An unqualified equation of the "westernisers" – among whom Rammohun must surely rank as the first and perhaps the greatest – with modernism or progress almost inevitably leads on to a more positive assessment of British rule and English education, and the nineteenth-century panegyric of both then is either warranted by the facts or is in conformity with the general Marxist assessment of colonialism. Marx did refer in an 1853 article to the "regenerating" role of British rule in India, but he immediately went on to emphasise that "the Indians will not reap the fruits of the new elements of society scattered among them by the British bourgeoisie" till the workers seize power in Britain or "till the Hindus themselves shall have grown strong enough to throw off the English yoke altogether",[71] and his few stray remarks on the benefits of the free press or Western education should be compared with the tremendous enthusiasm and even exultation with which he followed the events of 1857.

The key concept needing more precise definition in this context is "modernisation". Western historians of underdeveloped countries have become terribly fond nowadays of the "tradition–modernisation" polarity, under cover of which the grosser facts of imperialist political and economic exploitation are very often quietly tucked away in a corner. In the post-1917 world, modernisation clearly involves a choice between the capitalist and the socialist paths of development; what is not so obvious is that even in the nineteenth century, when the bourgeois West seemingly offered the one model for progress, the precise pattern of "learning from the West" had varied considerably, and a principal determinant here had been the degree of political independence an underdeveloped country had been able to retain. In countries which escaped political conquest either completely or for a fairly long period – Japan, of course, but also to a much more limited extent Ottoman Turkey and Egypt under Muhammad Ali – the pattern of modernist change was significantly different from that witnessed in British India. The interests of political survival in

---

[71] Karl Marx, *The Future Results of the British Rule in India* (1853), reprinted in *On Colonialism* (Moscow, n.d.), pp. 84, 88.

a Western-dominated world compelled indigenous rulers to try to imitate Europe first of all in the fields of army and administration, then of economic life – the whole approach was far more pragmatic. The intellectuals learnt less of Shakespeare and Mill and very much more of modern technology and science, and from the very beginning attempts were made to assimilate the latter into the language of the country. Such a pattern, it is tempting to speculate, might have emerged in our country too, if, say, Tipu Sultan had somehow survived or the 1857 revolt been successful; there is no real reason to think that this would have been an unmitigated disaster.

A second kind of pattern can be traced in nineteenth-century Russian history, where westernising reform from the top starting with Peter ultimately produced an intelligentsia of quite a remarkable kind. Attempts have been made to draw an analogy between the Westerner–Slavophil debate and the conflict of trends in nineteenth-century Bengal: the differences are really far more significant.[72] What was absent in India was, first, the intellectual's agonised sense of alienation from the masses, culminating in the "going to the people" movement; and second, the remarkable jump to one or other form of socialist ideology, bypassing conventional bourgeois liberalism. The "advantages of backwardness" which Trotsky discerned in Russian history manifested themselves also in China, where, after the dismal failure of the Japanese-style "self-strengthening" movement, national renovation came under the leadership of a man who seems to have made the leap straight from Classical Confucian learning to Marxism. And perhaps the most telling object lesson of all comes, in this as in so many other things today, from embattled Vietnam, which passed under full colonial control only in the 1880s, and where only thirty years – and no break at all in the tradition of resistance – separated the 1885 Scholars' Revolt from Ho Chi Minh's embracing of Marxism in Paris.

In India, full-scale colonial rule lasted the longest, and there was ample time for the growth of dependent vested interests, the elaboration of hegemonic infrastructure producing "voluntary" consent

---

[72] Sarkar, op. cit., p. 152.

side by side with more direct politico-military domination. The English-educated intelligentsia in its origins was very much a part of this system, nowhere more so than in Bengal; that it later turned to nationalist and even sometimes Marxian ways did not automatically imply that the old presuppositions had been entirely and consciously overcome. A critical re-examination of the Bengal Renaissance, of its limits and contradictions and hidden assumptions, has therefore an importance far transcending the purely academic.

2

The Complexities of "Young Bengal"

No group in the history of our "renaissance" aroused more controversy in its own time than Young Bengal, and opinions about the pupils of Derozio have remained polarised ever since the *Oriental Magazine* made snide remarks about their habit of "cutting their way through ham and beef, and wading to liberalism through tumblers of beer",[1] and Kishorichand Mitra compared his elder brother's generation to the summit of Kanchenjunga, the first to catch the dawn.[2] As often happens in such debates, however, the discussion has crystallised into stereotypes which, for all their opposition, share some features in common. We all tend to assume that the Derozians were a more or less unified group – of anarchical and alienated iconoclasts or heroic radicals, according to personal, social, and political taste – sharply distinct from their contemporaries, and not changing very much over time. Though references are occasionally made to some of them becoming more moderate with the years, this has never been fully worked out, and the impression persists of a "generation without fathers and

---

[1] *Oriental Magazine*, vol. 1, no. 10, October 1843, reprinted in E.W. Madge, *Henry Derozio: The Eurasian Poet and Reformer*, ed. Subir Raychoudhuri (Calcutta, 1967), p. 42.

[2] Kishorichand Mitra, "Hare Memorial Lecture on Hindu College" (June 1861), in Pearychand Mitra, *Biographical Sketch of David Hare*, Bengali trans. Sushil Kumar Gupta (Calcutta, 1964), Appendix II.

children",[3] worthy of remembrance only because of a single flash of youthful rebellion in the 1830s.

Unlike the Decembrists of Russia, however, the Derozians did not perish in Siberian exile, but lived, most of them, to an active and highly respectable old age; and in other respects, too, it is my contention that the current assumptions are somewhat oversimplified. I think this can be shown even on the basis of existing published data, but it is good to remember the wide but not necessarily inevitable gaps that still exist in our knowledge of Young Bengal. Apart from the Society for Acquisition of General Knowledge (SAGK) *Proceedings* and the *Bengal Spectator* files made easily available recently by Gautam Chattopadhyay and Benoy Ghosh, the really first-hand materials about the Derozians (as distinct from later biographies) exist today only in the stray extracts from the *Enquirer* and other notices in the *India Gazette*, *Bengal Hurkaru*, and a few other journals, and the *Samachar Darpan* quotations from the *Jnananvesana* collected by Brajendranath Bandyopadhyay. Diligent research may yet unearth the files of these and other Derozian journals, and one hopes that the primary sources used, usually with tantalising brevity, by Sibnath Sastri in his *Ramtanu Lahiri o tatkalin Bangasamaj* are not lost for all time.[4]

Considerations of incomplete data apart, both the "conservative" and the "progressive" interpretations of Young Bengal, and, perhaps of the entire Bengal "renaissance", suffer from the habit of attempting over-facile straight-line connections and identifications between the past and the present. Inevitable to some extent and even worthwhile at times, such identifications become dangerous if they lead us to ignore the concrete context in which ideas superficially similar

---

[3] This implicit comparison with the Decembrists has been made by Amit Sen [pseud. S.C. Sarkar] in *Notes on the Bengal Renaissance*, reprinted in S.C. Sarkar, *On the Bengal Renaissance* (Calcutta, 1979), p. 27.

[4] These include the diaries of Ramgopal Ghosh and Radhanath Sikdar and an unpublished autobiography of Sibchandra Deb. One might add also Haramohan Chatterji's manuscript history of the Hindu College used by Kishorichand Mitra and Thomas Edwards, and Kishorichand's diary used in Manmathanath Ghosh's biography.

to our own or attractive to us today had to operate in the past. That the Derozians thrilled to the ideals of European radicalism is no doubt exciting and interesting news; the more important historical problem surely is the limited and inevitably distorted applicability of such ideas by an intelligentsia reared in a colonial environment and as yet largely identified with it. Perhaps we have all been somewhat guilty of a Whig interpretation of our nineteenth-century heritage.

I seek here to test the validity of the current assumptions about the Derozians in the context, first, of the intellectual and material environment of Young Bengal, and second, of the available data concerning Derozian thought.

II

The unity of Young Bengal as a distinct group has been derived usually from the unique influence of Derozio. Perhaps some oversimplification may be suspected even at this preliminary level, for the Derozians in course of their fairly long lives came under many other – and not always homogeneous –influences. David Hare with his free-thinker reputation has been occasionally bracketed with Derozio,[5] but it is important to remember that Hare's relations with Radhakanta Deb remained extremely friendly throughout and that this well-established patron of Young Bengal did little to prevent the dismissal of Derozio from the Hindu College and of Krishnamohan Banerji and Rasikkrishna Mullick from his own Pataldanga School.[6] The conversion to Christianity of Maheshchandra Ghosh and Krishnamohan through the efforts of Alexander Duff indicates the working of another, and this time quite sharply opposed, kind of influence. Derozio, it seems, some later stories of a deathbed recantation not-

---

[5] S.C. Sarkar, "Derozio and Young Bengal", in Atul Gupta, ed., *Studies in the Bengal Renaissance* (Jadavpur, 1958).

[6] J.C. Bagal, *Unabingsa satabdir bangla* (2nd ed. Calcutta, 1963), p. 87. For an illuminating and extremely provocative view of David Hare, see Barun De, "The Role of David Hare in Colonial 'Acculturation' during the Bengal Renaissance": unpublished paper presented to the Asiatic Society on 29 September 1972.

withstanding, had "died as he had lived, searching for truth",[7] and Duff according to his own testimony had concentrated all his efforts on persuading Krishnamohan and his friends to accept the Reformation as their model in place of "the terrible issue of French illumination and reform in the last century"[8] – to abandon, in other words, at least part of the legacy of the man contemptuously described by Duff's biographer as "a Eurasian of some ability and much conceit."[9] Then again, while some Derozians are known to have been quite critical of Brahmoism in the 1830s and '40s,[10] Tarachand Chakrabarti, their acknowledged leader in the days of the "Chuckervarty Faction", had been close to Rammohun in the 1820s and became the first secretary of the Brahmo Sabha, and of course Ramtanu Lahiri and Sibchandra Deb became prominent members of the Sadharan Brahmo Samaj in their declining years. The Brahmos had changed greatly over time, but so perhaps had the pupils of Derozio, to the point of becoming, in a few cases, ardent believers in spiritualism and theosophy.[11]

The evidence regarding the specific content of Derozio's own teachings is also not entirely free from ambiguity, and for this we

---

[7] Thomas Edwards, *Henry Derozio: The Eurasian Poet, Teacher and Journalist* (Calcutta, 1884), p. 126. Edwards cites the testimony of Maheschandra Ghosh, who was present when the Rev. Hill visited Derozio in a last effort to reclaim the lost sheep. Maheschandra, he argues, had every incentive to present Derozio as a Christian after his own conversion, but he always denied the story of a deathbed recantation spread by Hill (and repeated later by E.W. Madge, op. cit., pp. 16, 49).

[8] Alexander Duff, *India and India Missions* (Edinburgh, 1839), p. 629.

[9] George Smith, quoted in Edwards, op. cit., p. 90. A considerable part of Edwards' biography is in fact taken up by a refutation of Duff and Smith.

[10] Cf. Ramtanu Lahiri's famous comment discontinuing his subscription to the *Tattvabodhini Patrika* on 24 July 1846: "The followers of Vedanta temporise". See Sibnath Sastri, *Ramtanu Lahiri o tatkalin Bangasamaj* (Calcutta, 1903, 1909), pp. 164–5.

[11] Pearychand Mitra and Sibchandra Deb became interested in spiritualism from the 1860s, and Pearychand was prominent also in the Bengal branch of the Theosophical Society established by Blavatsky and Olcott in 1882. See Sibnath Sastri, op. cit., pp. 125, 132; Brajendranath Bandyopadhyay, "Pearychand Mitra", *Sahitya-sadhak charitmala*, no. 21 (Calcutta, 1955), p. 189.

have to thank the Derozians themselves. None of them, not even the prolific Pearychand Mitra who could find the time to write a fairly sympathetic life of Ramkamal Sen, ever attempted a full-scale biography of their dead teacher. Such reticence, along with the establishment of David Hare as a father figure through the annual Hare Memorial Lectures, perhaps indicates a search for respectability on the part of the Derozians from the 1840s onwards.[12] The standard biography by Edwards (written, incidentally, soon after the Ilbert Bill furore) concerns itself mainly with Derozio's role as a Eurasian (Anglo-Indian) reader, revealing a bias interesting in its own way but somewhat irrelevant for our present purpose. The oft-quoted passage in Pearychand's *Biographical Sketch of David Hare* remains on the whole at the level of somewhat vague generalities: "He used to impress upon his pupils the sacred duty of thinking for themselves . . . to live and die for truth – to cultivate and practice all the virtues . . . He often read examples from ancient history of the love of justice, patriotism, philanthropy and self-abnegation . . . Some were impressed with the excellence of justice, some with the paramount importance of truth, some with patriotism, some with philanthropy."[13] Relatively little of Derozio's prose writings have survived, but the lost essay on Kant had been warmly praised by the Principal of Bishop's College,[14] and the posthumously published translation from Maupertuis reveals a remarkable interest about a mid-eighteenth-century philosopher whose reputation, ruined by Voltaire in his own lifetime, has been rehabilitated only in our present century.[15] From the famous April 1831 letter to Wilson, we learn that Derozio had introduced his students to the Philo-Cleanthes dialogue of Hume blowing up the argument by design, but had balanced it by the allegedly more convincing refutations of scepticism by Reid

---

[12] This has been suggested by Barun De, op. cit.
[13] Pearychand Mitra, *Biographical Sketch of David Hare* (Calcutta, 1877), p. 27.
[14] Edwards, op. cit., p. 40.
[15] Ibid., p. 186. The translation was published in the *Calcutta Quarterly Magazine*, 1833. For Voltaire and Maupertuis, see Norman Hampson, *The Enlightenment* (London, 1968), pp. 225, 228–31.

and Dugald Stewart. One hopes that here Derozio was being a bit diplomatic, for otherwise this preference would leave us with a rather poor impression of his philosophical insight.[16] As regards political ideas and activities, Edwards tells us that Derozio at first opposed the Anglo-Indian agitation of 1829–30 because many "descendants of European foreigners" were being kept away from it: here we have a hint of Derozio's own relatively unprivileged position within the Eurasian community due to his Portuguese origin.[17] He later became very active in that movement, however, and his wider political interests were revealed by the inclusion in a speech at a Eurasian meeting of favourable references to the Reform Bill as "but a preliminary step to the introduction of more important reforms."[18] Finally, the last article by Derozio (*East Indian*, 17 December 1831) made a memorable plea for Hindu–East Indian unity eloquently buttressed by a quotation from Burns.[19]

Two points seem to emerge from this rather chaotic and incomplete data as central to Derozio's teachings: an impulse towards freethinking which among his pupils inevitably became directed against Hindu religious and social orthodoxy, and an emphasis upon integrity in thought and conduct. Perhaps Haramohan Chatterji's testimony may be taken as the fairest summary: "the 'College boy' was a synonym for truth . . . The principles and practices of the Hindu religion were openly ridiculed and condemned . . . the sentiments of Hume had been widely diffused and warmly patronised . . . the question at a very

---

[16] The letters to Wilson are reproduced in Edwards, op. cit., pp. 77–89. For a summary of Hume's *Dialogues* concerning natural religion, as well as of Reid's rather inept refutation of it, see Leslie Stephen, *History of English Thought in the Eighteenth Century*, vol. I (London, 1876), chapters 1 and 6.

[17] Edwards, op. cit., p. 112.

[18] *India Gazette*, 3 August 1831.

[19] "The East Indians complain of suffering from proscription – is it for them to proscribe? . . . It is their best interest to unite and cooperate with the other native inhabitants of India . . . Man to man the world over/Shall brothers be for a' that." Edwards, op. cit., pp. 162–3. Here we find an echo of that same identification with India, almost unique for an Anglo-Indian, which found such eloquent manifestation in some of Derozio's poetry.

large meeting was carried unanimously that Hindu women should be taught . . ."[20]

The Hindu tradition had always combined a very considerable degree of abstract intellectual freedom with insistence upon rigid social conformity, and Rammohun and the early Brahmos on the whole maintained this dichotomy.[21] The really alarming thing about the Derozians of the early 1830s was therefore their open rejection of rituals and defiance of caste and religious taboos in the name of a new conception of integrity. Krishnamohan's *The Persecuted* (November 1831), written soon after he had been forced to leave his home following the beef-eating incident on the night of 23 August 1831, brings out this point very well. Mohadeb would have been quite satisfied with a purely formal penance by his son caught eating forbidden food: "I care not for the most dissolute life you may lead. But do preserve our caste."[22] But Banylal after some inner conflict refuses to sacrifice "the Truth" even for his aged father, and has to leave his house because of the campaign organised by the orthodox editor Lallchand, who himself then promptly takes brandy in secret with the remark: "Now Banylal! do with perfect freedom what has cost you so dear."[23] Another very interesting figure is Debnath the rich Hindu patron of Lallchand who at the same time urges his son to go to an English school: "Why do you shrink at the idea of dressing fashionably and being like a gentleman? . . . How happy would these young men have been if they had not learnt their absurdities about truth, if they had just refrained from publicly declaring themselves hostile to our religion . . ."[24]

---

[20] Cited in Edwards, op. cit., p. 68.

[21] Rammohun paraded his outward conformity to most caste rules, and his son Radhaprasad observed the orthodox Hindu funeral ceremonies for his father – as the *Samachar Chandrika* noted with glee. Quoted in *Samachar Darpan*, 12 April 1834. See Brajendranath Bandyopadhyay, ed., *Sambadpatre sekaler katha*, vol. II (henceforth *SSK* II; Calcutta, 1941), p. 192. Close associates of Rammohun like Prasannakumar Tagore never abandoned pujas.

[22] Krishnamohan Banerji, *The Persecuted*, Act II, scene 2, pp. 10–12.

[23] Ibid., Act III, scene 1, p. 21.

[24] Ibid., Act IV, scene 2, p. 28.

With all its immaturities and exaggerations, Banylal's revolt has an element of grandeur about it, but it is interesting, and tragic, to see how quickly this image changes virtually into its opposite even in the writings of fairly sympathetic observers. In Michael Madhusudan's *Ekei ki bole sabhyata?* (1860), written by a man himself a bit of a Derozian in outlook and temperament if not in strict chronology, Nabakumar follows up a speech on women's emancipation with the call: "Gentlemen, in the name of freedom, let us enjoy ourselves."[25] The young men of the Jnanatarangini Sabha meet in their "Liberty Hall" of a brothel, while their wives and sisters have to spend their time playing cards at home. The old dichotomy has come back perhaps in some ways at a grosser level. Even more revealing is Dinabandbu Mitra's *Sadhabar ekadasi* (1866) with its magnificent portrait gallery of youths for whom westernisation has come to mean a smattering of English plus a maximum of wine, hypocritical advocates of temperance, a lawyer, a Vikrampur rustic trying to enter Calcutta society, a Brahmo deputy magistrate appropriately named Kenaram, and, most memorable of all Nimchand Dutt, the one person in the farce who is not a hypocrite or a fool but highly intelligent and steeped in the culture both of Europe and of his own country (no wonder many suspected a connection with Madhusudan), but whose erudition has led only to complete cynicism and dissipation.

The transition from Banylal to Nabakumar and Nimchand, one is tempted to suggest, epitomises the tragedy of Young Bengal, and the crucial problem for the historian surely is to analyse and explain this process of degeneration and withering away of the original radical impulse. *The Persecuted* gives us certain clues in this direction, with its preface fulsomely acknowledging "the great encouragement [the author] has received from the English community" and an appendix of "Notes and Illustrations" revealing that the play was largely aimed at a white audience. Another interesting scene is that between Banylal and his servant; the latter tries to give him some advice, but is promptly abused by the hero as a "fool . . . you would not have been a servile

---

[25] Madhusudan Dutta, *Ekei ki bale sabhyata*, Act II, scene I; *Madhusudan rachanabali* (Calcutta, 1965), pp. 250–1.

servant otherwise."[26] Dependence on foreign rulers and alienation from the masses were to remain for long the two cardinal limitations of our entire "renaissance" intelligentsia.

For the young men taught by Derozio to look upon Western education in terms other than narrowly utilitarian and as a gateway to new values, the inevitable conflict of generations must have produced initially a deep sense of isolation, a feeling, in Nabakumar's words, that the whole country was for them an immense prison-house.[27] Prior to the switch-over from Persian in the law courts and the virtual confinement of service jobs to the English-educated which came about in the late 1830s and 1840s, opportunities for advancement were not too frequent, particularly for youths with an atheistic or anarchical reputation. Both the *Samachar Chandrika* and the *Sambad Purnachandroday* commented gleefully on the woes of the "atheists" trying to eke out a livelihood as schoolteachers or clerks at Rs 16 per month, in sharp contrast to the highly successful men of the previous generation like Radhakanta Deb or Ramkamal Sen who had not allowed knowledge of English to shake their religious faith.[28] With the exception of Dakshinaranjan Mukherji, none among the prominent Derozians came from particularly well-established or rich families,[29] and a connection between their initial difficulties and their early radicalism is probably not too far-fetched.

The colonial structure, however, soon began providing several ladders of social and economic ascent for the Hindu College products,

---

[26] *The Persecuted*, Act I, scene 1, p. 4.

[27] *Ekei ki bale sabhyata*, Act II, scene 1, p. 250.

[28] *Samachar Chandrika*, 2 May 1831, *Sambad Purnachandroday*, 7 September 1835, in *SSK* II, pp. 676–7, 694–5.

[29] Thus Tarachand Chakrabarti, Krishnamohan Banerji, Ramgopal Ghosh, and Ramtanu Lahiri could study in Hindu College thanks only to the free studentships provided through Hare. The college fee of Rs 5 per month was quite high for its time, and Kisorichand draws an interesting contrast between the gilded youth who could pay fees and the far more serious group, mainly from relatively poor families, sent up every year from Hare's school. Sibnath Sastri, op. cit., chapters 4, 6; Kisorichand Mitra, "Hare Memorial Lecture", pp. 205–6.

as well as ways of ending their sense of isolation. The missionaries constituted one such refuge and the testimony of Krishnamohan cited by Duff is illuminating in this context: "I considered upon my lonely condition – cut off from men to whom I was bound by natural ties and thought that nothing but a determination on the subject of religion could give me peace and comfort."[30] On a more materialistic plane too, the poor Kulin boy could live his last days on a very comfortable missionary pension and marry three of his daughters to Englishmen.[31] The price for all this, however, had been the embracing of a faith surely at least as irrational as the one he had abandoned, and one that his teacher had refused to accept even on his deathbed.

A second, and much more commonly used ladder was government service. The Bentinck Papers show Rasikkrishna Mullick describing his economic distress and social persecution, and Hare and Ryan urging the governor general to give "honourable or appropriate employment" to English-educated Hindu youths.[32] Harachandra Ghosh was made Sadar Amin in Bankura in 1832, Rasikkrishna Mullick and Gobindachandra Basak became deputy collectors around 1837–8, Chandrasekhar Deb, Sibchandra Deb, and Kishorichand Mitra were appointed deputy magistrates between 1843 and 1846,[33] and Radhanath Sikdar was earning Rs 600 per month at the surveyor general's office by 1856.[34] The *Friend of India* of 13 February 1845

---

[30] Alexander Duff, op. cit., p. 627.

[31] H. Das, "The Rev. Krishnamohan Banerji – Brahmin-Christian, Scholar and Patriot (1813–1885)", *Bengal Past and Present*, vol. 38, June–December 1929.

[32] Cited in A.F. Salahuddin Ahmed, *Social Ideas and Social Change in Bengal 1818–835* (Leiden, 1965), p. 45.

[33] Bimanbehari Majumdar, *History of Indian Social and Political Ideas from Rammohun to Dayananda* (Calcutta, 1967), chapter 3; Jogeschandra Bagal, op. cit., pp. 188–9; S.R. Mehrotra, *The Emergence of the Indian National Congress* (Delhi, 1971), p. 31.

[34] Benoy Ghosh, *Banglar samajik Itihaser dhara* (Calcutta, 1968), pp. 178–87. The author cited the New Calcutta Directory of 1856. The bulk of the Bengali Hindu salaries listed in the Directory range from Rs 25 to Rs 60 per month.

made the point brutally clear with its comment that the "exaggerated statements and inflammatory addresses" of the Chuckervarty Faction had already "died into an echo" and "a few Deputy-Magistracies, judiciously bestowed will doubtless prevent their revival."[35]

Derozian journals like the *Jnananvesana* repeatedly urged their readers to take to the path of independent trade, as distinct from acting as *mutsuddies* to British businessmen, investing in Company papers, or taking up service or clerical jobs.[36] Pearychand Mitra and Ramgopal Ghosh did become fairly successful businessmen, and Tarachand Chakrabarti was also connected with trade for a brief while, but it is important to consider how "independent" or conducive to integrity this third ladder of advancement really could be in mid-nineteenth-century Bengal. Kalachand Seth and Company of 1839 (with which Pearychand and Tarachand had been associated) and Pearychand Mitra & Sons of 1855 were both engaged essentially in the export–import business, and R.C. Ghosh & Company traded in Arakan rice;[37] their activities obviously fell far short of the Dwarkanath Tagore level, and Bengali entrepreneurship of even this comprador type was being rapidly eliminated after the 1847 crash.

Certain tentative hypotheses about Derozian ideology suggest themselves from this brief survey of its intellectual and material setting. One would expect to find within it, first, a greater variety at any given moment of time than has been usually asumed to be present; second, a process of toning down of political and perhaps also of social radicalism under the twin constraints of age and ascent to social respectability; and third, a progressive blurring of distinctions between the Derozians and other sections of the intelligentsia. I intend below to try and test these hypotheses in the light of what is known about the specific content of Derozian thought.

[35] Mehrotra, op. cit., p. 31.
[36] *Jnananvesana* extracts in *Samachar Darpan*, 21 April 1838, 26 January 1839, in *SSK* II, pp. 331–2, 467–8.
[37] Brajendranath Bandyopadhyay, *Pearychand Mitra*, op. cit., pp. 179–80; Arabinda Poddar, *Renaissance in Bengal: Quests and Confrontations, 1800–1860* (Simla, 1970), pp. 128–31.

III

Information about early Derozian attitudes towards religion is extremely scanty and comes mainly from hostile sources, but we do get the impression of an interesting though short-lived atheistic phase all but unique in our nineteenth-century intellectual history. The *Samachar Chandrika* referred to atheists and admirers of Charvak among Hindu College boys,[38] and repeatedly called for governmental intervention: non-interference in religious and social matters by the foreign rulers was evidently desirable only so long as it helped in defence of the status quo.[39] Duff recalled in 1839 the alarm he had felt on first meeting the Hindu College boys: "Many had become, or were rapidly becoming, sceptics; and others direct atheists."[40] A visitor to the Hindu College, who asked students to write an essay on the highly respectable Anglican theologian Paley's system of ethics, got more than he had bargained for when "one went directly to refute Paley, and establish the mortality of the soul and the futility of any hopes as to futurity."[41] The popularity of Tom Paine's *Age of Reason* in Calcutta in the early 1830s has often been noted,[42] though the publication of a partial translation of it in the then strongly conservative *Sambad Prabhakar* indicates that it was being used also by orthodox Hindus in their polemics with Christian missionaries.[43] Krishnamohan, we

---

[38] The *Samachar Darpan* of 6 November 1830 reprinted from the *Chandrika*, a letter from an irate parent of a Hindu College boy making this interesting reference to the ancient Indian materialist philosopher. See *SSK* II, pp. 231–2.

[39] *Samachar Chandrika*, 5 May and 9 May 1831, in *SSK* II, pp. 235–7. One notices in this context how far-fetched is David Kopf's discovery of "proto-nationalism" in the Dharma Sabha campaign against the ban on sati. See Kopf, *British Orientalism and the Bengal Renaissance* (California, 1969), pp. 266–72.

[40] Duff, op. cit., p. 608.

[41] George Smith, *The Life of Alexander Duff*, vol. I (London, 1879), pp. 169–70.

[42] Edwards, op. cit., pp. 34–5; *Bengal Hurkaru*, 23 January 1832, quoted in Bhabatosh Dutta, ed., *Bankimchandrer Iswarchandra Gupter jibancharit o kabitva* (Calcutta, 1968), p. 206.

[43] Bhabatosh Dutta, op. cit., pp. 107–8.

are told, "became a professional atheist" after seeing the austerities imposed on his mother following his father's death,[44] and he went through a brief anti-Christian phase also, during which he and his friends went about the streets of Calcutta parodying missionary Bengali.[45] The *Jnanasindhu Tarango*, a philosophical journal brought out during 1832 by Rasikkrishna Mullick, has unfortunately disappeared;[46] if its files are ever rediscovered, more authentic and detailed information about this first phase of Derozianism might become available at last.

Nowhere was the Derozian retreat from their own early radicalism more evident, however, than on the level of religion and philosophy. Duff noted that "avowed atheism" was on the decline already by 1832,[47] and Krishnamohan in an essay on Hindu caste published in 1851 mentioned "Deism" and "Vedantism" as the only rival to Christianity in the anti-orthodox camp;[48] evidently Philo's arguments against natural religion had been forgotten fairly quickly. Who the "deists" might have been is not very clear; perhaps Krishnamohan is referring here to Derozians like Rasikkrishna Mullick and possibly many others who remained monotheists without becoming either Christians or Brahmos.[49] Derozians of this type became rather coy about their religious ideas after they had got over their youthful exuberance of the early 1830s, as can be seen from the strict exclusion of "religious discussions of all kinds" from the purview of the Society for the Acquisition of General Knowledge (1838).[50] Dakshinaranjan

[44] H. Das, op. cit., in *Bengal Past and Present*, vol. 37, January–June 1929, p. 138.

[45] *India Review*, October 1842, quoted in Jogeschandra Bagal, "Kishnamohan Bandyopadhyay", *Sahitya-sadhak-charitmala*, no. 72 (Calcutta, 1955), pp. 36–7.

[46] Jogeschandra Bagal, *Unabingsa satabdir bangla*, p. 180.

[47] Duff, op. cit., p. 667.

[48] *Hindu Caste*, p. 40. Bound with a number of missionary tracts and available in the National Library.

[49] Jogeschandra Bagal, op. cit., pp. 182–3, 191. Only a handful of the Derozians formally became Christians or Brahmos.

[50] "Prospectus and Rule of the SAGK", rpnt in Gautam Chattopadhyay, ed., *Awakening in Bengal in Early Nineteenth Century* (Calcutta, 1965), p. lix.

Mukherji, once the wildest of the Derozians and as such virtually ignored in Sibnath Sastri's *Ramtanu Lahiri*, was reported by Rajnarain Basu to have settled down in Oudh like a good Hindu by the 1860s, and to have got his son married to an Ajodhya Brahmin's daughter.[51] With Pearychand Mitra the retreat turns into a rout, for in his biography of Ramkamal Sen (the man who along with Radhakanta was mainly responsible for securing the dismissal of Derozio) written in 1880 he even stated that Ramkamal's kind of religion was far preferable to the irreligion of Young Bengal and the theories imbibed from Huxley, Spencer, Mill, or Bradlaugh.[52]

The Derozians thus left little distinctive or permanent impression on the plane of religion and philosophy (even Deism was preached much more boldly by that highly unorthodox Brahmo Akshaykumar Dutt); it is time to consider now their ideas and activities in the field of social reform. Apart from a few broadsides on the question of caste,[53] the central issue here was the emancipation of women in all its facets: the need for education, the evils of child-marriage and Kulin polygamy, parental arrangement of marriages, the seclusion of women, and the ban on widow-remarriage. As Maheshchandra Deb reminded his SAGK audience in January 1839, all these were things that passed "under their eyes every day and hour of their existence within the precincts of their own respective domiciles. Most of the Derozians must have been married in their teens at parental command and their new-fangled notions and habits no doubt often caused acute adjustment problems."[54] The *Jnananvesana* pleaded eloquently for women's education and emancipation,[55] drew up lists of Kulin

---

[51] Manmathanath Ghosh, *Raja Dakshinaranjan Mukhopadhyay* (Calcutta, 1917), pp. 205–8.

[52] Pearychand Mitra, *Ramkamal Sen*, Bengali translation ed. Jogeschandra Bagal (Calcutta, 1964), p. 60.

[53] Mostly by Krishnamohan Banerji; cf. his SAGK paper, "Reform Civil and Social", in Gautam Chattopadhyay, op. cit., p. 192. See the 1851 essay on caste, op. cit.

[54] Maheschandra Deb, "A Sketch of the Condition of Hindoo Woman", in Gautam Chattopadhyay, op. cit., p. 90.

[55] Quoted in *Samachar Darpan*, 5 January 1833, 29 April 1837; see *SSK* II, pp. 95–7, 98–9.

polygamists quite in the style of Vidyasagar,[56] and in October 1837 spoke of an abortive plan "some 3–4 years back" of organising a society for widow-remarriage.[57] The very first number of the *Bengal Spectator* (April 1842) carried a letter again anticipating Vidyasagar in its justification of widow-remarriage as both rational and in accordance with a proper interpretation of the shastras.[58] Derozians like Radhanath Sikdar actively supported Vidyasagar's great campaign, and they even went a step further by supporting registration of such marriages – the need for which to prevent abuses Vidyasagar realised only later on.[59]

Young Bengal's contributions to social reform are thus undoubted, yet several qualifications need to be made even here. There is first the very obvious fact that the Derozians were never able to organise anything like a real campaign on any social-reform issue; for that Bengal had to wait for Vidyasagar. Second, the Derozians were by no means alone in this field even in the 1830s. Women's education within limits was advocated even by Radhakanta Deb, the 1837 *Jnananvesana* letter on widow-remarriage expected support from several English- and at least one Indian-edited journal (Prasannakumar Tagore's *Reformer*), and the missionary daily *Samachar Darpan* actively campaigned for the emancipation of women.[60] Unexpected support came even from a traditional pandit like Gourishankar Vidyabagish, who was closely associated with the *Jnananvesana* and later edited the *Sambad Bhaskar*. Social radicalism was no monopoly of the Hindu College student, as Vidyasagar was to prove within a few years.

[56] *Samachar Darpan*, 23 April 1836. Ramchandra Chattopadhyay of Moyapara headed the list with sixty-two wives; see *SSK* II, pp. 252–3.

[57] *Samachar Darpan*, 21 October 1837, see *SSK* II, pp. 263–4.

[58] Benoy Ghosh, *Samayikpatre Banglar Samajchitra*, vol. III (Calcutta, 1964), pp. 44–9 (henceforth SBS III).

[59] Jogeschandra Bagal, *Unabingsa satabdir bangla*, pp. 216–17. Benoy Ghosh, *Banglar samajik itihaser dhara*, pp. 288–9.

[60] The most interesting example is the letter, allegedly written by some Chinsura women, demanding not only education, widow remarriage, and a ban on polygamy, but also the rights of choosing husbands voluntarily and moving freely in society. *Samachar Darpan*, 21 March 1835, in *SSK* II, pp. 257–8.

In the third place, closer analysis reveals the Derozian stance on social reform to be less uniform than appears at first sight, and not entirely free from occasional traces of backsliding. In a paper presented to the SAGK in January 1842, Pearychand Mitra sharply criticised Krishnamohan Banerji for the latter's tendency to blame the Hindu shastras for all the current social ills of the country, and argued that the position of women had not been all that atrocious in ancient India.[61] Pearychand's series of lectures on The State of Hindoostan under the Hindoos (September 1839–August 1841) struck at times a positively revivalist note in its evocation of the "grandeur and magnificence" of ancient India with its republics and benevolent rajas limited by the influence of Brahmins, its idyllic unchanging village communities, its fairly prosperous agriculture and flourishing external commerce.[62] A certain toning down in the demand for social reform followed almost inevitably, and we see Pearychand embarking on a cautious defence of early marriages as justified by the climate of our country.[63] In an 1853 pamphlet written for the British Indian Association, Pearychand excluded widow-remarriage, child-marriage, and interdining from the scope of the legislature.[64] The Bengal Spectator of July 1842, while strongly advocating widow-remarriage, expressed its distaste of the idea of appealing to the government for a law on the subject.[65]

The revivalist theme can certainly find considerable justification in terms of an incipient sense of national pride; what is depressing is that its edge was for a very long time directed mainly against the Muslims, not the British, and the Derozians prove no exception here. Maheshchandra Deb's Sketch of the Condition of Hindoo Women (January 1839) balanced its criticism of the Hindu shastras with the

---

[61] Pearychand Mitra, "A few desultory remarks on the 'cursory review of the institutions of Hindooism affecting the interest of the female sex', contained in the Rev. K.M. Banerjea's Prize Essay on Native Female Education". See Gautam Chattopadhyay, op. cit., pp. 272–97.

[62] Ibid., pp. 131, 166–81, 261–2, 335–51.

[63] Ibid., pp. 280–1.

[64] "Notes on the evidence on Indian affairs (1853)", quoted in Bimanbehari Majumdar, op. cit., chapter IV.

[65] SBS III, pp. 91–2.

argument that "the cause of that state of seclusion and imprisonment in which the females of this land are preserved may be traced to the tyranny of the Mehomedan Emperors."[66] Pearychand in 1840 expressed the hope that "the ancient Hindu spirit of enterprise, which the storm of Moslem oppression has entirely extinguished . . . will now be kindled and burnt in the bosoms of the rising generation, who will . . . open sources of employment in the extensive field of commerce . . ."[67] His optimism here was as ill-founded as his history, as occasional reports in contemporary newspapers about facts like the decline of Dacca,[68] or the rising curve of British cotton twist and cloth exports, should have warned him.[69]

The virtually ubiquitous presence of the concept of Muslim tyranny (and of British rule as a deliverance from it) is surely one of the most striking features of nineteenth-century "renaissance" thought, and the Derozian acceptance of these assumptions is a reminder that in certain crucial respects our "radicals" were not all that different from the "moderates" or even the "conservatives". Adam's *Report* notwithstanding, the *Jnananvesana* of 17 November 1838 asserted that primary education had been virtually non-existent as long as "the wretched oppressive Yavanas" had ruled the country.[70] Even the language here is reminiscent of the *Samachar Chandrika*, denouncing the "haughtiness of these Yavanas" and expressing the hope that "Moosoolmans will be driven out" of public jobs once Persian is deprived of its court language status.[71] Udaychandra Addhya's SAGK paper pleading for the vernacular as medium of instruction has rightly earned much modern praise. The essay begins, however, with the statement that Bengali had become greatly debased during the centuries of Yavana rule, and cites as proof the contemporary

[66] Gautam Chattopadhyay, op. cit., p. 94.
[67] Ibid., p. 350.
[68] *Samachar Darpan*, 7 May and 20 August 1831 (the second one is in extract from the *Samachar Chandrika*): see *SSK* II, pp. 336–7.
[69] *India Gazette*, 5 July 1831.
[70] *SSK* II, p. 76.
[71] Quoted in *India Gazette*, 26 December 1831, and cited by A.F. Salahuddin Ahmed, op. cit., p. 149.

neglect of the works of Kabikankan, Kashiram Das, Krittibas, and Bharatchandra[72] – conveniently forgetting the fact that each of these poets had lived and worked under "Muslim tyranny". But most interesting of all – because directly political – is the way this theme suddenly cropped up in the famous clash between Dakshinaranjan and Principal Richardson at the SAGK meeting of 8 February 1843. Richardson tried to prevent the conversion of the Sanskrit College Hall into what he feared would be "a den of treason" by reminding "the meeting of the security the natives now enjoyed, in comparison with the condition of their ancestors, under the Mahomedan Government." That the young speaker stood his ground, ably supported by the president of the meeting (Tarachand Chakrabarti) has often been recalled by us with pride; what is not always remembered is that Dakshinaranjan in his resumed speech promptly "admitted the superiority, with all its faults, of the Company's over the Mahomedan rule."[73]

Recent admirers of Young Bengal like Gautam Chattopadhyay have with considerable justice rejected as slanderous the fairly common description of the Derozians as a group of denationalised Anglicists. They have cited in this context facts like Udaychandra's plea for the mother tongue, Rasikkrishna, Dakshinaranjan, and Pearychand's critiques of the 1833 Charter Act and of the Company's police, judicial, and revenue administration, as well as a few more extreme manifestations of anti-British temper – of which the most striking perhaps is Kailashchandra Dutt's imaginary account of an armed rebellion against "Lord Fell Butcher" in 1945.[74] As has happened elsewhere, however, admirers and critics alike seem to have played down the variety within Derozian thought and exaggerated its uniqueness.

Many Derozians were certainly not indifferent to their mother tongue, and of course Pearychand Mitra and Radhanath Sikdar made a major contribution to its development through the *Alaler*

---

[72] Gautam Chattopadhyay, op. cit., Appendix I, pp. i–ii.

[73] Ibid., pp. 392, 394, 398, giving the *Bengal Hurkaru* report of the meeting (13 February 1843).

[74] Ibid., Introduction, pp. xvii–xviii.

gharer dulal and the *Mashik Patrika*. But the more dubious honour of starting effective public oratory in English also belongs to the Derozians (Rasikkrishna Mullick and Ramgopal Ghosh the "Indian Demosthenes"). Only six out of the twenty-four papers of the SAGK that have been preserved were in Bengali and the *Bengal Hurkaru* reports show that while speeches in Bengali were the rule at Landholders' Society meetings, the British India Society worked entirely in English.[75] Despite Udaychandra Addhya and maybe a few others,[76] in the Orientalist-Anglicst debate of the mid-1830s the "third force" advocating the vernacular medium was represented much more by the Serampore missionaries and William Adam than by the Derozians as a group.[77] In March 1833 the *Jnananvesana* asserted that "nothing can be more desirable than the formation of a society for publishing scientific books in Bengalee";[78] a similar plea, however, had been made two years before by the *Reformer*.[79]

With few exceptions, Derozian political radicalism remained within the bounds set by Rammohun. Fairly sharp criticism of the Company's monopoly rights and administrative practices was combined with a basic loyalty to the British connection and close links could thus be preserved for a long time with non-official Anglo-Indian public opinion increasingly dominated by the free-trader–Utilitarian nexus.[80]

[75] Cf., for example, *Bengal Hurkaru*, 3 March and 21 March 1838; 29 June and 11 September 1844.

[76] The Sarbatattvadipika Sabha of 1833 pledged to the use of Bengali alone included some Derozians like Nabinmadhab De, but none of the more well-known figures of that group. Gautam Chattopadhyay has quoted from a very powerful plea for the vernacular medium made by an unnamed Bengali and reprinted in the Alexander's *East India and Colonial Magazine* of January–June 1837. See Chattopadhyay, op. cit., Introduction, pp. xix–xx; but where is the evidence that the author was a Derozian?

[77] Kopf, op. cit., chapters 10 and 14; *Samachar Darpan*, 5 February 1834; see *SSK* II, pp. 215–17; William Adam, *Third Report on the State of Education in Bengal* (1838), ed. Anathnath Basu (Calcutta, 1941), section XII, p. 308.

[78] Quoted in *India Gazette*, 29 March 1833.

[79] Ibid., 10 August 1831.

[80] For the role of the non-official Britons in moulding the Bengali intelligentsia from the 1820s down to the early 1840s, see A.F. Salahuddin Ahmed, op. cit., pp. 6–10; and S.R. Mehrotra, op. cit., pp. 2–4.

Rasikkrishna's 1833 critique of the judicial and revenue administration attributed the evils to the fact that "a body of merchants has been placed over us as our sovereigns;" he evidently wanted more British magistrates in the districts, and not less, and after mildly criticising the Permanent Settlement, asserted "that the only way now to improve the condition of ryuts, is to effect a reformation in the organisation of Mofussil Courts . . ."[81] The SAGK papers generally steered clear of concrete political subjects, while on a more abstract plane Krishnamohan criticised absolute monarchy but still felt that "the ignorance and irregularity of the vulgar would call for the establishment of a nobility with certain peculiar rights."[82]

Instances of a bolder anti-colonial stance are not entirely lacking, though (as on the vernacular issue) the examples cited by Gautam Chattopadhyay are not always of indisputably Derozian origin.[83] It was after all the *Reformer* that was suspected of sedition by the *Calcutta Courier* in 1834, not the *Jnananvesana*.[84] But the *Hindu Pioneer* of Kailashchandra Dutt did publish a striking article in 1835 entitled "India under foreigners", for once praising Muslim rule as having "patronised merit wherever it was to be found" and boldly asserting that "the violent means by which foreign supremacy has been established, and the entire alienation of the people of the soil from any share in the government, nay, even from all offices of trust and power, are circumstances which no commercial, no political benefits can authorise or justify."[85] At the inaugural meeting of the short-lived Deshahitaishini Sabha (October 1841), the Derozian Saradaprasad

---

[81] *Jnananvesara* articles: "Government of the Company and Revenue System of India", reprinted in *India Gazette*, 8 April and 10 May 1833.

[82] Krishnamohan Banerji, "On the Nature and Importance of Historical Studies" (May 1838); see Gautam Chattopadhyay, op. cit., pp. 21–2.

[83] Cf. the letter by "A Friend to Improvement" published in the *Reformer* and reprinted in the *Calcutta Monthly Journal*, April 1831, which cited the American example to prove the capabilities of an independent India. Ibid., Introduction, pp. xiii–xiv.

[84] *Samachar Darpan*, 5 November 1834, in SSK II, pp. 191–3.

[85] Quoted by Bimanbehari Majumdar, op. cit., pp. 53–4, from the *Asiatic Journal*, May–August 1838.

Ghosh bluntly declared that "our deprivation of the enjoyment of political liberty is the cause of our misery and degradation." He urged journalists "to write continually on political subjects, pointing out the evils of the Government", talked in terms of petitioning parliament and ended on the following interesting note: "You do not, like the brave and noble minded American, aspire as high as to free yourself from the yoke of British sway . . . you only desire to be freed from the tyranny and oppression of the local government of this country."[86]

Discretion was fast proving the better part of valour, however, by the time the Bengal British India Society was being formed in April 1843 in the wake of George Thompson's weekly lectures and the furore aroused by the *Friend of India* and the *Englishman* over the Richardson incident. At the first meeting of the new society, Ramgopal Ghosh moved a resolution emphasising "pure loyalty" and stated that "he desired nothing more sincerely than the perpetuity of the British sway in this country."[87] Another resolution, moved by Pearychand and Ramgopal, excluded students from membership,[88] and in December 1844 a society memorial to Hardinge urged principals to maintain strict moral discipline in their institutions[89] – a far cry indeed, all this, from the atmosphere of the early 1830s! It seems not at all unlikely that George Thompson was at least partly responsible for this evident toning down. He had reminded his audience in his weekly lectures that "England is the fountainhead from which your benefits must flow",[90] and his speeches sometimes read almost like refutations of Saradaprasad Ghosh: "For the work of agitation and petitioning as carried on in England, you are not yet prepared . . . Sit down and draw out a statement of . . . evils. Let them be intelligently exhibited and convincingly illustrated . . . We then, who have access to the people and Parliament of England, thus assisted by you will be able in your own language to make known

---

[86] *Bengal Hurkaru*, 6 October 1841, quoted in Mehrotra, op. cit., pp. 27–8.
[87] *SBS* III, p. 605.
[88] *Bengal Spectator*, 25 April 1843, in *SBS* III, p. 149.
[89] *Bengal Hurkaru*, 9 December 1844.
[90] Ibid., 8 February 1843.

your wishes and your wants."[91] Perhaps the role of nineteenth-century Indophile Britishers of the type of Thompson needs some revaluation as a restraining quite as much as an inspiring influence on the local intelligentsia.

With its sober monthly meetings (usually chaired by Englishmen: Thompson, followed by Theobald) and occasional respectful petitions the British India Society hardly marked any advance in political technique over the Landholders' Society. Both the *Bengal Spectator* and the British India Society repeatedly pleaded for more administrative jobs for Indians, and the latter prepared a pamphlet comparing the number of offices held by Hindus under Muslim and British rule[92] – but Indianisation of services was an intelligentsia demand as old as Rammohun. Ramgopal's famous speeches defending the Black Acts do mark a kind of a break (Dwarkanath and Prasannakumar had supported the Anglo-Indian campaign in 1836 against an earlier attempt to restrict white judicial privileges),[93] but once again the Derozian cannot make much claim to uniqueness. The whole attitude of the local intelligentsia was shifting to a certain extent, and the alliance with non-official whites was fast breaking down (perhaps as an aftermath to the 1847 commercial crisis, plus the unpopularity provoked by missionary zeal, emphasised by Mehrotra). The changed situation was symbolised by the British Indian Association of 1851 which united the orthodox and the Derozians, the big landlords with the relatively parvenu intelligentsia, but kept the Anglo-Indians out. The limits of this change were revealed soon enough by the outburst of Mutiny loyalism, in which the Derozians fully shared, with Dakshinaranjan obtaining the dubious distinction of a confiscated Oudh *taluk* (given by Canning at Duff's advice, interestingly enough) and spending his last days doing much "to remove the racial antipathies between the English and the Indians."[94]

[91] Quoted in Mehrotra, op. cit., p. 30.
[92] "Evidences relative to the efficiency of native agency in the administration of this country" (1844); see Mehrotra, op. cit., pp. 30–1.
[93] Ibid., pp. 6–7.
[94] Sir Roper Lethbridge's testimonial, quoted in Manmathanath Ghosh, *Raja Dakshinaranjan Mukhopadhyay* (Calcutta, 1917), p. 155.

Where the British India Society can claim a certain uniqueness as compared to its zamindar predecessor is in its definite pro-peasant stance. As exposure material, the letters describing the woes of Miyazan in the *Bengal Spectator*,[95] were soon to be surpassed by Akshaykumar Dutt's series in the *Tattvabodhini Patrika*,[96] and the suggestion of a permanent settlement in rent rates, made by Pearychand in his 1846 *Calcutta Review* article,[97] did not go beyond the Rammohun tradition. But the secretary of the British India Society was writing on the basis of a very interesting and detailed questionnaire on land relations circulated by his organisation in July 1843, the replies to which (preserved in the pages of the *Bengal Hurkaru*) surely form important source materials for agrarian history. In the case of the *Calcutta Review* article, however, a gap is noticeable between premises and conclusion which illustrates the limits of Derozian reformism. The answers to the questionnaire, though provided usually by individual local landholders or zamindari *naibs*, had still repeatedly stated that the zamindars were doing absolutely nothing either to improve cultivation methods or to promote education.[98] Pearychand in sharp contrast placed his main bet on the zamindar made benevolent by English education.[99] His views on the class nature of education are indeed engagingly frank: "The education of the Ryot and of the Zemindar ought to go hand in hand. The Vernacular schools are intended for the former, and English ones and Colleges are for the latter."[100] Equally revealing is the reference to peasant resistance: the

---

[95] *Bengal Spectator*, 1 November and 15 December 1842. In *SBS* III.

[96] *Tattvabodhini Patrika*, nos. 81, 84, 88, Baisakh-Agrahayan 1772 S.E. (1850), in *SBS* II (Calcutta, 1963), pp. 108–32. There is here a sharp criticism also of indigo planters – something absent in Rammohun and not very prominent in Derozian writings.

[97] Pearychand Mitra, "The Zamindar and the Ryot", *Calcutta Review*, vol. VI, July–December 1846.

[98] Replies of Ramloll Dutt (a landed proprietor of Rajpore, 24 Parganas) and Gopee Kissen Mitter (from Birbhum, on the basis of information supplied by a local naib). See *Bengal Hurkaru*, 12 October and 12 November 1844, reporting monthly meetings of the British India Society.

[99] *Calcutta Review*, vol. VI, p. 350.

[100] Ibid.

ryots near the city, he says, "appear to have acquired many vices – they forge Kobojes, break their agreements with Indigo planters, evade payment of Khajana, and make *Dharma Ghut* or combine *en masse* not to pay rent to the Zernindar."[101] Pearychand ends with an appeal to the zamindar: "When the ryots are well protected, they find it easier to pay your claims . . . your happiness and the happiness of your ryots, are identified with each other."[102]

The uncritical acceptance of the liberal assumption of natural identity of interests proved even more of an inhibiting force in the understanding of the basic economic relationship between Britain and India. The Derozians swallowed, hook, line, and sinker, the free-trader logic. They eagerly modelled themselves on George Thompson's London British India Society, which at its inaugural meeting (6 July 1839) had referred to India as "a country of vast extent and great fertility; whose inhabitants are docile, intelligent and industrious . . . a country capable of supplying many of our demands for tropical produce, and the desire and capacity of whose population to receive the manufactures, and thus stimulate the commerce of Great Britain, would under a just and enlightened rule, be incalculably developed."[103] The decline of Indian handicrafts passed unnoticed by the Derozians, just as with Rammohun. The biography of Ramkamal Sen quoted copiously from Wilson's letters denouncing the industrial devastation being caused by his countrymen in India,[104] but there is no evidence that Pearychand (or Ramkamal, for that matter) allowed such things to cloud his optimism about the British connection. The article on raw cotton written by Pearychand for the Agri-Horticultural Society looked upon that commodity purely in terms of its export possibilities – at a time when Indian mills had already started springing up in Bombay.[105] No doubt the author's own comprador activities were partly responsible for such blindness.

[101] Ibid., p. 344.
[102] Ibid., pp. 351–2.
[103] Mehrotra, op. cit., p. 17.
[104] Pearychand Mitra, *Ramkamal Sen*, pp. 21–2.
[105] Pearychand Mitra, *Krishi-path* (Calcutta, 1861), rpnt in *Pearychand rachanabali*, ed. Asitkumar Bandyopadhyay, Calcutta, 1971, pp. 288–90.

The Complexities of "Young Bengal"

A sympathetic account of Young Bengal published in the *Calcutta Monthly Journal* of May 1837 described the Derozians as ardent free-traders and young men among whom "the very word Tory was a sort of ignominy."[106] The basic tragedy of the Derozians lay precisely here, in their pathetic eagerness to affiliate themselves with the latest in bourgeois liberalism. In the continent of its birth, bourgeois liberalism in the nineteenth century was, within limits, a progressive and even revolutionary force, but its finest ideals and categories had a tendency to turn into their opposites whenever attempts to apply them in the colonial context were made by foreign administrators (even when subjectively honest or benevolent) or indigenous intellectuals.[107] This was a process of inversion which was ultimately rooted in the basic fact that the very same historical forces that were bringing breathtaking development to the West were producing underdevelopment in the colonial and semi-colonial world, till by 1900, in the words of a brilliant recent work on economic history, "India, the brightest jewel in the British Crown was one of the poorest nations in the world."[108] The trouble lay not so much in imitation of the West as in the kind of West that was being imitated – socialism, too, was after all just as much alien and "Western" in nineteenth-century Russia.

It may be argued, of course, and with considerable justice, that the Derozians had little choice in the matter. As a colonial intelligentsia, the British liberal model was virtually imposed upon them. They had far less opportunity or freedom to choose between alternative ideologies than their counterparts in Russia, and the English medium automatically tended to seal them off from the masses. Yet it is worth remembering that the England of the 1830s and '40s was as yet far from mid-Victorian stability; it was still the country of intense class struggle, the land, not just of the Benthamites, free-traders, Brougham and Thompson, but also of Owen and the Chartists and brilliant

---

[106] Quoted in Bhabatosh Dutta, op. cit., pp. 88–9.

[107] For a brilliant analysis of this process of inversion, see Asok Sen, "The Bengal Economy and Rammohun Roy", paper presented at a seminar on Rammohun at the Nehru Museum, New Delhi, October 1972.

[108] Amiya Bagchi, *Private Investment in India, 1900–1939* (Cambridge, 1972), p. 3.

literary exposures like *Hard Times*. Echoes of something of this other England did occasionally reach Calcutta through the Anglo-Indian press. The *India Gazette* of 5 July 1831 (with Derozio then on its editorial staff, and his pupils presumably among its avid readers) published a very remarkable letter violently attacking a pamphlet issued by the Society for the Diffusion of Useful Knowledge entitled *The Results of Machinery Exhibited: An Address to the Working-men of the United Kingdom*. "The odious plague-spot of Whig perfidy is broad on the book", stated the correspondent, since the author was obviously "an advocate for the people's submission to misery." The letter quoted approvingly from More's *Utopia*, and incidentally also denounced the Reform Bill as yet another proof of Whig selfishness and treachery. The *Bengal Hurkaru* occasionally published Chartist news, distorted via the *Times*.[109]

If the Derozians ignored such warnings and went on with their pale imitation of the Society for Diffusion of Useful Knowledge (deferentially substituting "acquisition" for "diffusion" in the title of their SAGK) they remained indifferent also to the world of popular anti-British struggles, momentarily unveiled for example in the letters on a Chuar campaign published in the *India Gazette* of January 1833. A British army officer is here complaining that "the folks in Calcutta believe we have but child's play, but they are sadly mistaken; . . . the regular troops are quite unfit for this irregular warfare", and though "so many villages have been burnt, Ganganarayan is still holding out."[110] The only reference to such things in the SAGK *Proceedings* was made by Harachandra Ghosh. His description of the district of Bankura, of which he had been the Sadar Amin, ended on the following note: "unless most active exertions are made by Government to elevate their character by establishing educational institutions, these people will ever remain in ignorance and would commit great mischief by their seditious disturbances which are constantly occurring."[111]

---

[109] *Bengal Hurkaru*, 18 February 1843.

[110] *India Gazette*, 21 and 25 January 1833.

[111] "A Topographical and Statistical Sketch of Bankoorah", July 1838; see Gautam Chattopadhyay, op. cit., p. 67.

The contrast with the Russian revolutionary intelligentsia, with its leap to socialism as early as the 1840s and passionate striving for peasant revolution, is painfully evident. The valid Russian parallel to Young Bengal is in fact not Decembrism and certainly not Narodnism, but perhaps at best the "small deeds" liberalism of the Zematvo gentry after the 1860s.[112] In concrete terms, Young Bengal produced (if temperamental affinity is taken to be more important than strict chronology) one supreme literary genius in Madhusudan; a number of honest and conscientious officials, providing some public benefits for their places of birth or residence (Sibchandra Deb who did a lot for Konnagar, Harachandra Ghosh, Rasikkrishna Mullick), but excluded from the levers of real power by the racialist colonial structure; an able librarian and prolific writer (Pearychand Mitra); a fine surveyor who discovered the highest peak in the world, only to find his priority questioned and the honour appropriated by his white boss Sir George Everest; some sincere and devoted teachers, like Ramtanu Lahiri; a couple of fairly successful second-ranking comprador businessmen; and the prototype of the later moderate politician in Ramgopal Ghosh. Its impact on Bengali society as a whole, as distinct from its intelligentsia crust, was very nearly nil. A sad falling off, surely, from the excitement and generous visions of the days of the Academic Association and the *Enquirer*, when the world had seemed to lie at the feet of these young pupils of Derozio, who had then fondly believed that "the rays that have emanated from the Hindu College . . . must eventually dissipate the mists of ignorance and superstition."[113]

In the absence of private papers, it is impossible to reconstruct today what the Derozians themselves felt about all this, to know whether they were ever haunted by regrets and a sense of unfulfilled hopes. But perhaps it will not be too far-fetched to look upon the epidemic of drinking which blighted so many of their lives as not just a bad habit picked up from the West, but an indication sometimes

---

[112] George Fischer, *Russian Liberalism from Gentry to Intelligentsia* (Harvard, 1958), chapter I.
[113] *Enquirer*, quoted in *India Gazette*, 6 September 1831.

of an inner agony of spirit. Maybe the best symbol of the tragedy of a generation has been provided for us by Dinabandhu Mitra, whose Nimchand greets the policeman's lantern with Milton's "Hail, Holy light."[114]

[114] *Sadhabar ekadasi*, Act II, scene 3, in *Dinabandhu rachanabali*, Calcutta (1967), p. 146.

3

The Pattern and Structure of Early Nationalist Activity in Bengal

I. Introduction

Considered in general terms, the history of the Indian national movement reveals interesting crests followed by troughs. Very obvious in the Gandhian era (e.g. the heightened tempo of 1919–22, 1930–4, 1942, and 1943–6, as contrasted to the years in between), the same pattern can be seen, though at progressively lower planes, if we glance back at the pre-First World War decades. Terrorism with its romantic appeal has occasionally somewhat concealed the post-Swadeshi slump, yet Aurobindo at least had no doubts in June 1909 that there had been a major retreat.[1] Again, though Extremist enthusiasts during the Swadeshi upsurge may have often condemned the political activities of all their predecessors as unadulterated "mendicancy", there is surely a difference, at least in Bengal, over the years *c.* 1867–85, and the undoubtedly dull two decades immediately preceding the Partition of 1905.

Explanations of this advance–retreat pattern have so far tended to be of two kinds. Repression has often been taken to be the decisive

---

[1] "When I went to jail the whole country, was alive with the cry of Bande Mataram, alive with the hope of a nation . . . When I came out of jail I listened for that cry, but there was instead a . . . silence. A hush had fallen on the country, and men seemed bewildered . . ." Aurobindo Ghose, *Uttarpara Speech*, 4th edition (Calcutta, 1943), p. 2.

factor, and certainly its importance cannot be denied in the early 1930s and '40s, as well as for the terrorist and left-leaning movements virtually throughout. But despite much talk of Swadeshi "martyrs", it is very difficult to explain the collapse of the Bengal movement in 1908–9 by police terror alone,[2] while in the 1870s and '80s repression amounted to little more than the short-lived Vernacular Press Act, Surendranath's two-month imprisonment in 1883, and sporadic official attempts to discourage participation in the Congress.[3]

Bipan Chandra has argued that the Indian nationalist leadership, whether Moderate, Extremist, or Gandhian, throughout followed "the basic strategy of pressure–compromise–pressure leading to political advance that would be brought about through the actions of the duly constituted authorities." The perspective was always one of step-by-step advance, and not direct seizure of power: concessions were wrested from the British through "negotiations backed by controlled mass action", the great advantage of this method being that "the political activity of the masses, was rigidly controlled from the top" and bourgeois hegemony safely maintained.[4] The periodic ebb tides thus appear by implication a matter of conscious choice by a nationalist leadership which is on the point of attaining some formal or tacit concessions and which is afraid of mass action getting out of hand. Some may see in this a sophisticated version of R.P. Dutt's well-known betrayal thesis grounded upon the Bardoli

---

[2] Prosecutions were actually instituted against Swadeshi agitators in only 10 cases in Bengal and 105 cases in Eastern Bengal and Assam during 1905–9; only about half of these were successful, with the accused getting terms ranging from two weeks to a year. The only two cases of firing recorded for the entire 1903–8 period involved Jamalpur railwaymen on strike and Sherpur Muslim rioters, not Swadeshi crowds. For a more detailed discussion, see Sumit Sarkar, *Swadeshi Movement in Bengal 1903–1908* (New Delhi, 1973), pp. 76–8, 502.

[3] Most notably by Sir Auckland Colvin on the eve of the 1888 Allahabad Congress. See Bipinchandra Pal, *Memories of My Life and Times*, vol. II (Calcutta, 1952; 2nd edition, 1973), chapter VI; and Briton Martin, *New India, 1885* (California, 1969), Epilogue.

[4] Bipan Chandra, "Elements of Continuity and Change in the Early Nationalist Activity", *Proceedings of the Indian History Congress, Muzaffarpur Session* (n.p., 1972), pp. 8–9.

decision of 1922 and the argument seems not unconvincing as an interpretation of the Gandhian era. I am not so sure, however, about the application to earlier decades of the three assumptions involved in Bipan Chandra's theory – conscious and effective control over the tempo of the movement, the attainment of real, though partial, concessions at the end of each round, and fear of popular extremism. The Morley–Minto reforms in their final shape hardly satisfied even the most Moderate of the Bengal politicians, the scuttling of Hume's mass contact drive of 1887–8 was not connected with any substantial concessions, and, prior to the Rowlatt satyagraha explosion of 1919, the recurrent problem for the nationalist leadership seems to have been not excess of mass enthusiasm but its relative absence.

Above all, repression can succeed, and a leadership can throttle the energies of its mass following, only if the movement as a whole suffers from certain structural inadequacies. My attempt here is to investigate, through two case studies of Bengal in 1867–85 and 1903–8, the possible causal connections between the zig-zag pattern of nationalist activity and what I am calling the "structure" of nationalism. I use the term "structure" in a very broad sense to cover not just the interplay of interest groups so absorbing to Namierite historians, but the entire complex of objectives, techniques, socio-cultural ideals, and values, organisational forms, communication media, and social composition which together make up the texture of a movement. The Swadeshi period will be discussed first, partly because it is easier from the midstream to trace the course of the rivulets making up the torrent, but also because it happens to have been my field of special study; and a secondary purpose of this essay is to test the relevance of some of my general conclusions for an earlier period of nationalist history.

II. 1903–1908

It is generally agreed that the years from the announcement of the Partition Plan in 1903 to the Alipore Bomb Case in 1908 saw a significant attempt by Bengal's nationalism to break out of what has been variously described as its "elitist", "*bhadralok*", "Western-educated", or "upper middle-class" confines and to attain the stature of a mass movement. That this attempt did not succeed is also evident enough, since what remained after 1908 were the two opposite but related poles of old-style "mendicancy" and a "revolutionary" movement betraying its elitist character, both by its style of activity (individual terror, or at best ambitious schemes for military coups, never guerrilla bases in the countryside or urban insurrections) and by its upper-caste social composition.[5]

In trying to explain this sequence of significant effort and ultimate failure, I attempted a fourfold classification of trends within the Swadeshi movement in terms of political objectives and methods.[6] I distinguished between (i) the "Moderate" tradition, with piecemeal reform culminating at best in colonial self-government as its aim, "agitation" to win over British public opinion through logically faultless exposures of the "un-British" ways of the Anglo-Indian bureaucracy as its method, and demanding little in the way of sustained mass work; (ii) "Constructive Swadeshi", urging the necessity of autonomous self-help efforts (Swadeshi enterprise, national schools, village organisation) to end the alienation of the English-educated elite, often somewhat indifferent to active politics but aiming at slow but real national self-regeneration – the classic epitome of all this being Rabindranath's "Atmasakti" concept; (iii) "Political Extremism", with complete swaraj or political independence as its theoretical ideal (though in practice Extremist leaders would often be satisfied with "half a loaf", as Tilak once put it),[7] "extended boycott", or "passive resistance", anticipating much of Gandhism as its basic technique, necessarily demanding for its success a high level of mass participation; and (iv) "Terrorism", seeking immediate independence through methods of individual violence and military conspiracy,

---

[5] A total of 165 out of the 186 persons convicted of revolutionary crime, or killed in committing them in the period 1907–17, came from the three upper castes of Brahmin, Kayastha, and Baidya. *Sedition Committee (Rowlatt) Report* (Calcutta, 1918), annexure II.

[6] This and the succeeding paragraph represents a highly condensed version of the thesis developed in my *Swadeshi Movement in Bengal 1903–1908*, op. cit., chapter II.

[7] *Tenets of the New Party* (Calcutta, 2 January 1907) in Tilak, *Writings and Speeches* (n.p., n.d.), p. xxiv.

ardently revolutionary in subjective intent, highly elitist and hence not very effective in practice. Cutting across these trends were certain ideological debates concerning socio-cultural values, which I tried to subsume under what I now consider to be the somewhat oversimplified and inadequate categories of "modernism" on the one hand, and "traditionalism" or "revivalism" on the other.[8]

From the point of view of the development of nationalism into a mass movement, the potentially most fruitful path was the combination of (ii) and (iii), of village-level constructive work with passive resistance. As the recent grassroots studies of Hitesranjan Sanyal have revealed, this was more or less the way in which the Gandhian movement was able to mobilise the countryside in the 1920s and 1930s in pockets like Tamluk and Contai subdivisions in Midnapur (under Birendranath Sasmal), Arambagh in Hooghly, and parts of Bankura and Purulia.[9] In the Swadeshi period, too, there was the very interesting development of the "samiti" movement, with its cadres of full-time volunteers numbering some 8500 by mid 1907, particularly formidable in the districts of Backergunj, Faridpur, Dacca, and Mymensingh, and engaging in a wide variety of mass activity (and not merely or even predominantly elitist conspiracy) down to the summer or autumn of 1908.[10] Among other positive aspects might be mentioned a notable revival of village handicrafts,[11] efforts to organise national schools in East Bengal villages which badly frightened the authorities,[12] a labour movement under nationalist inspiration and guidance which set up short-lived trade unions among printers, railwaymen, and jute workers,[13] the development of popular

---

[8] The virtual equation which I then made between westernism, modernism, and a progressive stance in general ignored the specific and the inevitable distortions of a "modernisation" proceeding under colonial hegemony. I have tried to develop this point in "Rammohun Roy and the Break with the Past", above.

[9] Cf. the articles of Hitesranjan Sanyal.

[10] For details, see Sarkar, *Swadeshi Movement in Bengal, 1903–1908*, op. cit., chapter VII.

[11] Ibid., chapter III.

[12] Ibid., chapter IV.

[13] Ibid., chapter V.

vernacular journalism, and the exploration of numerous imaginative techniques of mass contact ("rakhi-bandhan" and "arandhan", Swadeshi songs, plays, *jatras*, and festivals, etc.).[14]

Yet the limits are equally obvious. Muslim participation in the samitis was non-existent, except to some extent in the Anti-Circular Society with its Brahmo and determinedly non-communal leadership. Despite the earnest efforts of a group of Swadeshi Muslim leaders, Muslim separatism gained ground steadily and there were communal riots in several East Bengal districts during 1906–7, with Muslim peasants ranged against Hindu landlords and moneylenders.[15] From the very beginning, zamindari officials and Muslim vendors faced each other as accused and plaintiff in an ominously big proportion of Swadeshi cases.[16] Even in Aswinkumar Dutt's Barisal the Dumartala village samiti of which some detailed information has been preserved had a priest as president, two *tahsildars*, four unlicensed medical practitioners, the son of a zamindari official, a Bansal Settlement office clerk, and some non-resident Calcutta students as members – not a single peasant.[17] In Amritalal Bose's *Sabash Bangali*, a contemporary play giving a vivid description of the Swadeshi days, no peasant appears on stage, and the movement in Pashdanga village remains clearly a matter of schoolboys led by their patriotic headmaster.[18] The volunteers in Mukunda Das' *jatra Palli-Seva* do not have to worry overmuch over their "rice and dal", as all have some land, and by implication men to till it for them.[19]

[14] Ibid., chapter VI.

[15] Ibid., chapter VIII.

[16] As for instance in the Narsingdi Salt Case (December 1905), the Rajbari Salt Case (January 1906), the Uluberia Salt Case (January 1906), and the Narayangunj Case (June 1907). Reports on the first three cases are to be found in the contemporary pamphlet *Swadeshi Cases* (Calcutta, 1906); for the fourth, see *Bande Mataram*, 21 June 1907.

[17] Samitis in the Backergunj District, in Government of India, Home Political Progs Deposit, April 1909, n. 2, pp. 63–4, National Archives of India, New Delhi.

[18] Amritalal Bose, *Sabash Bangali* (Calcutta, December 1905).

[19] Mukunda Das, *Pulli-Seva* (n.d.), scene II, p. 7, included in *Mukunda Daser Granthabali* (Calcutta, 1951).

If the Hindu peasantry remained passive and their Muslim counterparts turned occasionally hostile, the responsibility at least in part lay no doubt with the Swadeshi leadership, which seems to have made little or no effort to develop an agrarian programme that could have integrated nationalist demands with the concrete socio-economic grievances and aspirations of the rural masses. The Indian Association had championed the *raiyats* in the debates leading to the 1885 Act, but its only reaction to the tenancy amendment bill of 1907 was to deplore unnecessary government intervention in landlord–tenant relations.[20] Asutosh Chaudhuri, who had created a sensation in 1904 by calling for self-help as opposed to mendicancy at the Burdwan Provincial Conference, denounced on the floor of the Bengal Legislative Council the provision for executive intervention in cases of illegal rent enhancement, arguing that "the tenant can surely get relief from a munshiff's court."[21] Even Rabindranath, whose post-1907 essays reveal a deep and agonising awareness of the alienation between the educated elite and the masses, could in practice attempt or recommend little more than benevolent village reconstruction efforts by zamindars.[22] Surendranath's *Bangalee* welcomed rent remissions at Tagore's Shelaidaha estate,[23] but it also supported rejection by the Muktagacha zamindars of a Muslim *raiyat* petition against an alleged 50 per cent *abwab*, and saw in the whole affair an instance as to how Lieutenant Governor Fuller "has demoralised the Mussalman ryots of Mymensingh."[24]

As surrogates for a peasant programme, the Swadeshi intelligentsia descended upon patriotic rhetoric, a mingling of politics with Hindu religiosity and revivalism, and the use of zamindari and upper-caste pressure, enforcing the boycott via the closure of village marts to foreign goods and the social ostracism of recalcitrants.[25]

---

[20] *Bangalee*, 15 February 1907.
[21] Ibid., 16 November 1906.
[22] For the evolution of Rabindranath's attitudes, see Sarkar, *Swadeshi Movement in Bengal, 1903–1908*, pp. 52–5, 62–3, 82–5, 90–1.
[23] *Bangalee*, 13 May 1906.
[24] Ibid., 27 May 1906.
[25] *Swadeshi Movement in Bengal 1903–1908*, chapter VI.4.

The counter-productive nature of most of these methods is fairly obvious. Apart from Muslim alienation, there is some evidence also indicating the aloofness and even hostility of subordinate rural Hindu castes. A Namasudra conference in March 1908 demanded "freedom of trade",[26] and the Mahishyas of Midnapur entered the national movement on a large scale only with Sasmal's Union Board agitation of 1921.[27] An aspect of Gandhism which found no Swadeshi anticipation, incidentally, is Harijan (untouchable) uplift.

Both the lack of an agrarian programme and the nature of the substitutes developed in its place were evidently connected with the social composition of the Swadeshi movement. The groups attracted by Swadeshi comprised educated youths, lawyers, teachers, journalists, doctors, zamindari officials, some (though by no means all) big landlords, as well as sections of the clerical staff of government offices, firms, and a few industries.[28] Though a fairly heterogeneous lot in many ways, a connection with land in the form usually of intermediate tenures was an almost ubiquitous element within this so-called "middle-class" or "*bhadralok*" social stratum. In Sarupkhati (Backergunj district), to give only one example out of many, "nearly half the volunteers are said to be talukdars, that is to say persons with a tenure, holding interest in the land."[29] Rising prices and the overcrowding of the professions may have made such tenure-holders more conscious of the value of their (often quite small) rent incomes, thus inhibiting an agrarian programme even more than in the 1870s and '80s. To this must be added the alienation from productive functions, the contempt or at best condescension for manual labour, the Hindu gentry's superiority complex *vis-à-vis* their Muslim tenants or share-croppers – the whole complex of "*bhadralok*" attitudes, in fact, flowing in part from caste traditions,

---

[26] *Bengalee*, 20 March 1908.

[27] Hitesranjan Sanyal, op. cit.

[28] For more details see *Swadeshi Movement in Bengal 1903–1908*, pp. 355–9, 503–7.

[29] Government of India Home Political Press Deposit, October 1907, n. 19, para 7.

but tremendously encouraged throughout the nineteenth century by a colonial society grounded upon the Permanent Settlement, the destruction of productive opportunities in industry and trade, and a highly elitist English education. The current obsession of many Western historians with the *bhadralok* is not entirely misplaced; where they go seriously (and, one is sometimes tempted to add, deliberately) astray is in the attempt to interpret limitations as motive forces, reducing the whole of nationalism to a mere product of narrow elite grievances and injured vanity. The Namierite cynicism applied to the nationalists is never extended to the British rulers,[30] far too direct and crude an economic motivation is assumed for political actions and ideals,[31] and the whole underlying structure of colonial exploitation is quietly conjured away.[32]

Even if the Swadeshi intelligentsia had managed to evolve a more "populist" stance, however, the countryside might have remained unresponsive, as had happened with the Narodniks in Russia. As compared to the pre-1885 period, the peasant world of early-

---

[30] Thus J.H. Broomfield, the foremost and very consistent advocate of the *bhadralok* interpretation of Bengal nationalism, describes Lord Carmichael as "a man with a mission", hails Lord Lytton as "another man with a mission", and in his conclusion asserts that "the basic objective of British policies in Bengal throughout this half-century was to combat Hindu bhadralok exclusiveness", not the preservation of their own vested interests. J.H. Broomfield, *Elite Conflict in a Plural Society* (California, 1968), pp. 42, 187, 331.

[31] For a discussion of the extent of the linkages between educated unemployment, price rise, and nationalism, see *Swadeshi Movement in Bengal, 1903–1908*, pp. 510–12.

[32] Cf. for instance Anil Seal's engagingly coy statement: "the patterns of Indian trade were fitting conveniently into the international needs of the British economy." *The Emergence of Indian Nationalism: Competition and Collaboration in the Late Nineteenth Century* (Cambridge, 1968), p. 1. More recently, Judith Brown has argued that even the drain of wealth theories were entirely oriented to the interests of the educated elite, since "they recommended a drastic reduction in the number of foreigners in the administration – a remedy which dovetailed neatly with their own wish for more jobs in government service." *Gandhi's Rise to Power: Indian Politics 1915–1922* (Cambridge, 1972), p. 21. That men like Naoroji or R.C. Dutt "recommended" many other things is conveniently omitted.

twentieth-century Bengal seems significantly quiet, though detailed research on this so far rather neglected period in agrarian history might well modify this picture. The concessions obtained by the upper strata of the peasantry by the Tenancy Act of 1885, combined with the boom in jute cultivation, had possibly reduced tensions in the countryside to a certain extent. The price rise must have hurt the poorer sections of the peasants, but as the Mymensingh riots of 1906–7 revealed, the discontent usually turned against the immediate local oppressor (zamindar, *mahajan*, trader, even sometimes the Swadeshi agitator trying to oust cheaper foreign articles from the market) and the distant British overlord was not automatically affected.[33] The lack of integration between national and social discontent stands out in fact as the crucial structural limitation of the Swadeshi movement, and our second case study will try to indicate that this has relevance also for an earlier phase of our nationalist history.

III. 1867–1905

Viewed from the heights of the post-1903 national movement, nineteenth-century Bengal politics at first seems a rather dull plateau-land of unmitigated elite mendicancy without any very sharp discontinuities. Most of the issues raised by the early Congress resolutions had been anticipated by provincial associations like the British Indian in the 1830s,[34] and indeed by Rammohun, who had focused on demands like Indianisation of services, trial by jury, separation of powers, freedom of the press, and consultations with Indian landlords, merchants, and officials on legislative matters. The basic technique of occasional public meetings and respectful petitions to the authorities in Calcutta or London had also been pioneered in the 1820s by Rammohun as well as by his Dharma Sabha rivals, and the

---

[33] *Swadeshi Movement in Bengal, 1903–1908*, chapter VIII.3.

[34] As for instance in the 1852 petitions of the British Indian, Bombay, and Madras associations on the eve of the renewal of the East India Company Charter. B.B. Majumdar, *Indian Political Associations and Report of Legislature, 1818–1917* (Calcutta, 1965), appendix; S.R. Mehrotra, *The Emergence of the Indian National Congress* (Delhi, 1971), chapter II.

ubiquitous presence of a faith in the "providential" British connection appears obvious throughout.

Yet closer observation reveals certain interesting and important breaks. By the turn of the century, even the most Moderate of our politicians had become acutely aware of the link between India's poverty and British economic exploitation through drain of wealth, destruction of handicrafts, and excessive revenue burdens,[35] however much they might still rely on "mendicant" means for remedying such evils. But the "Father of Modern India" had remained utterly silent about deindustrialisation, even though the period of his maximum public activity coincided almost exactly with a decline in the number of houses paying *chaukidari* tax in Dacca from 21,361 to 10,708 between 1813 and 1833.[36] Rammohun had even welcomed the import of cheap and finer English salt on the grounds that those unemployed could be easily diverted to agriculture and other occupation as "gardeners, domestic servants and daily labourers."[37] Rammohun did show some concern about the "large sum of money" being "annually drawn from India by Europeans retiring from it with the fortunes realised there",[38] and even went to the trouble of trying to calculate its amount;[39] his solution, however, was a cautious support for colonisation, "a system which would encourage Europeans of capital to become permanent settlers with their families."[40] For Rammohun as well as for the Derozians, the remedy for current evils in the administration and the economy of the country was on the

---

[35] R.C. Dutt's three perennial themes: see Preface to *Economic History of India under Early British Rule* (London, 1901).

[36] N.K. Sinha, *Economic History of Bengal*, vol. III (Calcutta, 1970), p. 4.

[37] S.C. Sarkar, ed., *Rammohun Roy on Indian Economy* (Calcutta, 1970), p. 82, quoted in Asok Sen, "The Bengal Economy and Rammohun Roy", paper presented at a seminar organised by the Nehru Memorial Museum and Library, New Delhi, October 1972, forthcoming, p. 38.

[38] *Questions and Answers on the Revenue System of India*, Answer to Question 52 (London, 1831), rpnt in Nag & Burman, eds, *The English Works of Raja Rammohun Roy*, part III (Calcutta, 1947), p. 52.

[39] Ibid., pp. 73–7.

[40] Ibid., p. 52.

whole greater collaboration and not less, with free-trader groups, though not with the East India Company. Rasikkrishna Mullick in his 1833 critique of Company justice and revenue administration wanted more British magistrates in the districtes,[41] while Pearychand Mitra in 1840, with an optimism as unfounded as his history, expressed the hope that "the ancient Hindu spirit of enterprise, which the storm of Moslem oppression has entirely extinguished ... will now be kindled and burnt in the bosoms of the rising generation, who will ... open sources of employment in the extensive field of commerce."[42] Most striking of all perhaps is the assumption implicit in Kailashchandra Dutt's unusually militant patriotic outburst: "The violent means by which Foreign Supremacy has been established and the entire alienation of the people of the soil from any share in the government ... are circumstances which ... *no commercial, no political benefits* can ever authorise or justify."[43]

Indo-British commercial collaboration in Bengal suffered a major blow in 1847 with the collapse of the Union Bank, and already by 1851 the British Indian Association was including in its list of grievances the "lack of encouragement of the manufacturers and commerce of the country, which had been depressed in consequence of throwing open the trade with India."[44] The crucial turning point in Bengal at the level of theory came twenty years later with Bholanath Chandra's "A Voice for the Commerce and Manufacturers of India", serialised in *Mukherji's Magazine* between March 1873 and June 1876, though there had also been some Anglo-Indian anticipations: notably Robert Knight's *India: A Review of England's Relations Therewith* (1868) and the unusually sophisticated analysis of the drain by James Geddes, "Our Commercial Exploitation of

---

[41] *Jnananvesana* articles, *Government of the Company*, and *Revenue System of India*, reprinted in *India Gazette*, 8 April, 10 May 1833.

[42] Reprinted from the Society for Acquisition of General Knowledge Proceedings in Gautam Chattopadhyay, *Awakening in Bengal* (Calcutta, 1965), p. 351.

[43] "India under Foreigners", in the *Hindu Pioneer* of October 1835, rpntd in *Nineteenth Century Studies*, vol. I, no. 4, October 1973.

[44] Mehrotra, op. cit., p. 61.

the Indian Populations".⁴⁵ Bholanath, who had once worked with the Union Bank and had then started an independent trading concern – only to see it go bankrupt in 1863⁴⁶ – roundly asserted that "the English want to reduce us all to the condition of agriculturists."⁴⁷ He called for protective tariffs, or, if these were not forthcoming, the use of "the only but most effectual weapon – moral hostility . . . resolving to non-consume the goods of England", so as to "dethrone King-Cotton of Manchester, and once more re-establish there the Indian sway in the cotton world."⁴⁸ There is a pointed reference also to the "abstraction of capital from India since 1757, under which she is now left but an empty shell."⁴⁹ That Bholanath in 1873 was arguing a relatively novel case is indicated by the fact that his whole essay was a polemic against Krishnamohan Mullick, who in a three-volume *Brief History of Bengal Commerce* (1872) and a rejoinder published in *Mukherji's Magazine* of May 1873 had argued that the rise in export–import figures *ipso facto* indicated growing prosperity, the decline in handicrafts being both inevitable and beneficial for the poor (as Manchester cloth was so much cheaper).⁵⁰ Krishnamohan Mullick may have been an obscure and elderly Anglophile, but precisely similar arguments had been put forward in 1872 by no less a person than

---

⁴⁵ In *Calcutta Review*, 1872. The writings and motivations of men like Knight and Geddes deserve much more detailed study than they have received so far. Judging from an open letter criticising the railway guarantee system and demanding more public works written in 1866 to Secretary of State Cranborne, Knight looked upon himself as a spokesman of British capitalists settled in India as opposed to London financial groups: "We shall never find English capitalists on the London Stock Exchange very ready to embark (on public works investment) . . . without a state guarantee. On the other hand, the English capitalists on the spot—I mean the mercantile community in India itself . . . are the very men to project such works, *as the leaders of the Native wealthy community.*" *National Paper*, 9 January 1867.

⁴⁶ Manmathanath Ghosh, *Manishi Bholanath Chandra* (Calcutta, 1924, 1939), pp. 82, 160.

⁴⁷ Quoted in ibid., p. 154.

⁴⁸ Ibid., pp. 165, 155.

⁴⁹ Ibid., p. 170.

⁵⁰ Ibid., pp. 137, 153.

Bankimchandra, in a more or less forgotten passage of his otherwise deservedly famous "Bangadesher Krishak" (The Peasantry of Bengal).[51]

Analysis of the structure and social composition of nationalist associations reveals a second kind of discontinuity, and once again the critical years seem to be the 1860s and '70s. "The present territorial aristocracy of this province (Bengal) . . . in large measure our own creation . . . is a potent influence on our side", reported Curzon to Hamilton on 12 February 1903.[52] While 39 per cent of Congress delegates between 1892 and 1909 were lawyers,[53] and even bankers and merchants were fairly prominent in the N.W. Provinces and Oudh if not in Bengal,[54] big landlords generally kept away. There were only 6 zamindars among the 48 executive committee members of the Indian Association between 1876 and 1888 whose occupations have been recorded, as compared to 26 lawyers and 8 journalists.[55] Things had been quite different, however, down to the 1860s. On the basis of evidence like Bhabanicharan Bandyopadhyaya's *Kalikata Kamalalay* (Calcutta, 1823) and Dwijendranath Tagore's reminiscences recorded by Bipinbihari Gupta,[56] S.N. Mukherjee has argued that much of early- and mid-nineteenth-century Calcutta's politics, religious, and social reform is best understood in terms of the interplay of competing factions headed by leading aristocratic families of the

---

[51] Bankimchandra denounced protection as grievously wrong in theory, rejected the conception of drain (though later admitting in an 1892 footnote that this had been a major mistake), and argued that the unemployed weaver could easily take to other occupations. *Bankim Rachanabali*, vol. II, Sahitya Sansad Edition (Calcutta, 1954), pp. 309–13.

[52] Quoted in Anil Seal, op. cit., p. 226.

[53] Ibid., p. 280.

[54] Between 1885 and 1901, Congress delegates from the North-West Provinces and Oudh included 551 Brahmins, 294 Kayasthas and 404 Khattris, Agarwals, and other mercantile castes. Well over half of the latter group were classed as bankers or traders. C.A. Bayly, "Patrons and Politics in Northern India", in Gallagher, Johnson, and Seal, eds, *Locality, Province and Nation: Essays on Indian Politics 1870–1940* (Cambridge, 1973), p. 30.

[55] Anil Seal, op. cit., p. 215.

[56] Bipinbihari Gupta, *Puratan Prasanga* (Calcutta, 1913, 1923; combined edition, 1966).

city – the "*daladali*" of the "*abhijat bhadralok*".[57] Rammohun's Atmiya Sabha consisted of Calcutta and suburban zamindars,[58] the Brahmo movement for quite some time remained largely an extension of the Jorasanko Tagores as opposed to the Sobhabazar Deb-dominated Dharma Sabha, and the British Indian Association with its Rs 50 annual membership was an overwhelmingly landlord concern whose secretary, Krishtadas Pal, earned the following uncomplimentary reference from Bholanath Chandra: "A man of the people by birth, he disappointed his nation by spending his energies in Zamindari harness."[59] Even Vidyasagar found the patronage of the Paikpara Sinhas useful, if Krishnakamal Bhattacharyya's testimony is to be accepted.[60]

Krishnakamal has also asserted that Vidyasagar owed part of his great prestige to the contacts he had established with white society,[61] and indeed rebel groups like the Derozians in the 1830s and early '40s and Keshabchandra Sen's followers in the 1860s who lacked aristocratic backing seem to have tried to compensate for it by cultivating such connections.[62] But a more serious political challenge to zamindar predominance began developing from the 1860s, spearheaded successively by Girish Chunder Ghosh (with his *Bengalee*, started in 1862 in conscious rivalry with the *Hindoo Patriot*, which by then had become entirely a zamindar organ),[63] the *Amrita Bazar Patrika*

[57] S.N. Mukherjee, "Class, Caste and Politics in Calcutta, 1815–1838", in B. Leach and S.N. Mukherjee, eds, *Elites in South Asia* (Cambridge, 1970).

[58] Benoy Ghosh, *Banglar Samajik Itihaser Dhara* (Calcutta, 1968), p. 236.

[59] Manmathanath Ghosh, op. cit., p. 190, quoting from Bholanath's biography of Digambar Mitra (Calcutta, 1893).

[60] Bipinbihari Gupta, op. cit., p. 49.

[61] Ibid., pp. 49–50.

[62] A glance through the *Bengal Hurkaru* files would indicate that Europeans were on the whole more prominent at the meetings of the British India Society than they had been in the Landholders' Association; the proceedings of the latter were conducted mainly in Bengali, while the former worked entirely in English. *Bengal Hurkaru*, 3 March, 21 March 1838; 29 June, 11 September 1844. The Anglophilism and Christian contacts of Keshabchandra were notorious.

[63] Krishnakamal Bhattacharyya, as recorded in Bipinbihari Gupta,

and the short-lived Indian League of Sisirkumar Ghosh, and the far more successful Indian Association of 1876. Support came mainly from the non-zamindar professional intelligentsia, rapidly growing in number as English education expanded and penetrated deeper into the countryside. Sisirkumar had tried to rally the *mofussil bhadralok* through district associations before floating the Indian League,[64] while Anandamohan Bose and Surendranath Banerjea mobilised Calcutta students through the Students' Association of June 1875 and public lectures on Garibaldi, Mazzini, Chaitanya, and Sikh power.[65] Both the Indian League and the Indian Association fixed a low annual membership fee of Rs 5 with, hopefully, a reduced rate of Re 1 for "Artisans, Munduls and other heads of villages and bonafide tillers of the soil."[66] The Indian Association Town Hall protest meeting against the Vernacular Press Act on 17 April 1878 was held in the teeth of opposition from the zamindars of the British Indian Association and even many Bar leaders, and the *Brahmo Public Opinion* hailed it editorially on 25 April 1878 as marking "an epoch in the social and political history of Bengal."[67]

Contemporaries often interpreted this rift in terms of a conflict between the old aristocracy and an emergent "middle class". Thus Sibnath Shastri in his autobiography recalled how the Indian Association had been started to meet the need for a political organisation of Bengal's "*Madhyabitta sreni*" (middle class).[68] Like other European

---

op. cit., p. 329. See also Manmathanath Ghosh's statement: "The politics of the *Bengalee* often clashed with those of the *Hindoo Patriot* the avowed organ of the landed aristocracy." *Life of Chandra Ghosh* (Calcutta, 1911), p. 5.

[64] Such associations were set up (mainly through district tours by Sisirkumar and his brother Hemanta Kumar) at Dacca in March 1872 and at Burdwan, Murshidabad, Santipur, and Ranaghat soon afterwards. B.B. Majumdar, op. cit., p. 139.

[65] J.C. Bagal, *History of the Indian Association 1876–1951* (Calcutta, 1953), pp. 5–7; Bipinchandra Pal, *Memories of My Life and Times*, vol. I (Calcutta, 1932, 1973), chapter XI.

[66] B.B. Majumdar, op. cit., p. 140; J.C. Bagal, op. cit., p. 16.

[67] J.C. Bagal, op. cit., pp. 34–7.

[68] Sibnath Shastri, *Atmacharit* (1952 edition, Calcutta), p. 133.

analogies drawn optimistically by our nineteenth-century intelligentsia, the parallel is not entirely exact. The "aristocracy" here was not particularly old, and consisted mainly of the nouveaux riche who had made their pile in the late eighteenth century as hangers-on of early Company administrators and through comprador trade, and had turned to investments in zamindari and Calcutta real estate after 1793. The "middle class", on the other hand, far from being based on industry or commerce, was always only too eager to buy itself a niche in the Permanent Settlement hierarchy through intermediate tenures after having climbed the ladder of success via English education and the liberal professions. The *Amrita Bazar Patrika* in fact repeatedly equated the "Middle Class" with the tenure-holding "gentry", and asserted that "amongst all civilised countries the gentry or middle class carries the greatest influence in all matters, and so it is in Bengal . . . but unfortunately the existence of such a class is not even so much as acknowledged by the Government."[69]

The conflict therefore was hardly a fundamental or irreconcilable one, but as Kalyankumar Sengupta has argued, "the salaried and the professional people who had little or no rentier income championed tenant rights", utilising the struggle of the peasantry in the 1860s, '70s, and early '80s in defence of occupancy rights and against rent enhancements "to win a political battle against the absentee landlords and their supporters, the conservative intelligentsia."[70] Girish Chunder Ghosh, states his biographer, started the *Bengalee* as a "weekly on behalf of the Ryot, who then had no special organ or advocate to voice his grievances", and the prospectus of the new

---

[69] The same article attacked the zamindars as "sunk in sensuality and sloth . . . and indifferent to the interest of those dependent on them", while "the masses compose the Ryotary class, but [are] plunged in deep ignorance . . ." *Amrita Bazar Patrika*, 11 September 1873, quoted in B.B. Majumdar, *History of Indian Social and Political Ideas from Rammohun to Dayananda* (Calcutta, 1967), pp. 133–4. See also a similar passage in the *Amrita Bazar Patrika* of 9 December 1869, quoted in Benoy Ghosh, op. cit., pp. 172–3.

[70] Kalyankumar Sengupta, "The Politics of Bengal Rent: Ideology and Interests of the Intelligentsia, 1875–1885", paper presented at the 29th International Congress of Orientalists, Paris, July 1973, pp. 4, 6.

journal declared its intention to "faithfully and fearlessly represent the Ryot to the Ruler and the Ruler to the Ryot."[71] Dwarkanath Vidyabhushan's *Somprakash* called in 1862 for an alliance between the middle and the lower orders to fight zamindari oppression,[72] and along with the early *Bengalee* it repeatedly urged a permanent settlement of rents.[73] The Indian Association went a step further in the early 1880s, organising peasant meetings and trying to start "Rent Unions" on the eve of the Tenancy Act of 1885.[74] What the British Indian Association zamindars felt about such developments was well expressed in the following angry analysis of the new brand of politicians made by J.M. Tagore in June 1833:

> They have neither status nor stake in society, and to attain the one or the other or both, they resort to various kind of agitations social, religious, reformatory, and so on . . . They are for the most part, East Bengal men, joined in by some England-returned natives, who also hail from that part of the country. Many of them have seen something and read still more of the doings of the Irish agitators . . . they would fair try their chance in the socialistic line . . . When they convene public meetings, they fill them with schoolboys, and then exclaim that they have the public with them. They go to the ryots, pretend to be their friends, sow seeds of dissension between them and the zamindars, and thus set class against class.[75]

[71] Manmathanath Ghosh, *Life of Grish*, op. cit., p. 109.

[72] *Somprakash*, 20 Sravana 1269/1862, in Benoy Ghosh, ed., *Samayil patre Banglar Samajchitra*, vol. IV (Calcutta 1966), pp. 66–7.

[73] Cf., for instance, *Somprakash*, 1 Asar 1271/1864, to Sravana 1272/1865, 9 Magh 1278/1872, in Benoy Ghosh, *Samayil*, op. cit., pp. 85, 100, 109. For the similar views of Girish Chunder Ghosh, see Manmathanath Ghosh, op. cit., pp. 5, 160, and Girish Chunder, "The Permanent Settlement", *Bengalee*, 25 July 1866, rpnt in *Nineteenth Century Studies*, vol. 13, July 1973.

[74] The Indian Association Memorandum to the Government of Bengal on the proposed Rent Bill (27 June 1881) claimed that "public meetings of the ryots . . . have been held in different parts of the country – at Kissengunge, Foradaha, Gooshpara, and Gopalpur, in the Nuddea district, at Lagusai in Bearbhoom, at Rahita in the Twenty-Four Parganas, at Boidyabatti in Hooghly, at Burdwan, and in the town of Calcutta itself . . ." J.C. Bagal, op. cit., appendix A, para 2.

[75] J.M. Tagore to S.C. Bayley, Member of Viceroy's Council, 1 June 1883, quoted from the Ripon Papers by S.R. Mehrotra, op. cit., p. 363.

Pattern and Structure 71

The frightened conservative zamindar was no doubt exaggerating things a bit, but it seems clear enough that the Bengal politics of *c*.1867–85 was marked not merely by an internal split somewhat akin to the "shetia"–intelligentsia conflict traced by Christine Dobbin in Bombay city,[76] but also by development of a range of new political techniques which repeatedly seem to foreshadow the Swadeshi days. There were first the annual Hindu Melas for about ten years from 1897 onwards, the prototype of Swadeshi festivals like the Shivaji Utsava, inspired by Rajnarain Bose's proposals "for the Promotion of National Feeling among the Educated Natives of Bengal" (1856) and organised by Nabagopal Mitra with the patronage of the Tagores (particularly Ganendranath and Dwijendranath).[77] The Mela tried to promote the spirit of self-reliance through exhibitions of indigenous crafts, patriotic songs, and physical culture;[78] associated with it were a "National Society" which organised periodic lectures, a "National School" founded in 1872 "for the cultivation of Arts, Music, and for Physical Training", and the weekly *National Paper* – all run by the indefatigable "National" Nabagopal Mitra.[79] The 1871 exhibition included a new type of charkha invented by Sitanath Ghosh of Jessore,[80] the Sanjibani Sabha recalled by Rabindranath in his autobiography tried to set up a match-workshop and a weaving concern,[81] while a more serious Swadeshi venture was Jyotirindranath Tagore's Inland River Steam Navigation Service of 1881 which won enthusiastic support from Barisal and Khulna passengers but

[76] Christine Dobbin, "Competing Elites in Bombay City Politics in the Mid-19th Century (1852–1883)", in Leach and Mukherjee, op. cit.

[77] J.C. Bagal, *Hindu Melar Itibritta* (n.p., 1945, 1968), pp. 91–101, gives the full fext of Rajnarain's prospectus, with its call for a "Nationality Promotion Society", to encourage physical culture, "Hindu music", "Hindu Medicine", and the strict use of the vernacular in conversation, correspondence, and public gatherings, etc.

[78] A point emphasised, for instance, in the playwright Monomohan Bose's speech at the second session of the Mela in 1868, in J.C. Bagal, op. cit., pp. 10–11.

[79] Ibid., *passim*, esp. pp. 61–8, 83–5.

[80] Ibid., p. 24.

[81] Rabindranath Tagore, *Jibansmriti*, pp. 110–16.

was eventually ruined by British competition.[82] The 1860s and '70s also saw a spurt of patriotic poems and songs, as well as of plays like Dinabandhu Mitra's *Nil-Darpan* (1860), Monomohan Basu's *Harischandra* (1875), Jyotirindranath Tagore's "historical" dramas, and the violently anti-British *Sarat-Sarojini* (1874) and *Surendra-Binodini* (1875) of Upendranath Das, which served as the immediate provocation for the Dramatic Performances Act in 1876. A major landmark here had been the foundation of the National Theatre in 1872 hailed by Sisirkumar Ghosh as a "democratic stage", no longer dependent like its predecessors on the whims of aristocratic patrons.[83]

If all this seems to foreshadow the temper of "Constructive Swadeshi", the first rumblings of "Political Extremism" can also be heard in this same period. The obvious name here is Bankimchandra,[84] though it is difficult and dangerous to generalise about such a great and complex figure. The Indian Association later became the most Moderate of political bodies, but its early activities had included, not just the all-India tours of Surendranath and Lalmohan Ghosh's visit to England on the highly elitist Civil Service issue, but the foundation of night schools in Calcutta,[85] and fairly successful efforts to start district and even village branches in many parts of Bengal,[86] as well

[82] *Somprakash* of 28 Magh 1291/1885 reported how passengers at Bagerhat waited in the rain for hours for Jyotirindranath's *Lord Ripon*, and refused to board the British Flotilla Company's steamer: Benoy Ghosh, *Samayikpatre Banglar Samajchitra*, vol. IV, pp. 179–80.

[83] Amritalal Bose's memories, in Bipinbihari Gupta, op. cit., p. 226.

[84] One might mention here the brilliant satires of mendicant elite politics in *Babu* and *Hanuman-babu-sangbad*, in *Loka Rahashya* (1874, 1888), *Amar Durgotsava* in *Kamalakanter Daptar* (1875), as well as of course the Bande Mataram hymn written in 1875 and in *Anandamath* (1881–2).

[85] Ten such night schools were reported to be functioning by the *Brahmo Public Opinion* of 7 August 1879, quoted in J.C. Bagal, *History of the Indian Association*, op. cit., p. 46.

[86] In 1895, the association claimed 121 branches, all but 4 of them within the Bengal Presidency. Among Bengal's districts, Midnapur, and Pabna headed the list with 29 branches each, followed by Nadia and Faridpur (8); Hooghly (7); 24 Parganas (6); Howrah, Jessore and Khulna (4 each); Burdwan and Mymensingh (3 each); Bogra and Sylhet (2 each); and Darbhanga, Bankura,

as the pro-ryot activities already mentioned. The Decennial Report of the Indian Association stated in 1883: "It is too often brought forward as a matter of reproach that our political agitation is confined to a few educated Babus. The Association is resolved to wipe off this reproach."[87] Though nationalist attempts to promote trade unions still lay in the future, the association attempted a major agitation on the Assam tea labour issue, with Dwarkanath Ganguli undertaking a dangerous trip to the plantation region to collect exposure material for his serial in *Bengalee*, "Slavery in the British Dominion".[88] Dwarkanath had been preceded by a fellow-Brahmo, Ramkumar Vidyaratna, while another Brahmo stalwart, Sasipada Banerji, worked all his life among Baranagore labourers, starting night schools and a working men's club for them and bringing out from 1873 the first labour journal in India, the monthly *Bharat Sramajivi*.[89] Recalling Sasipada's activities in the 1870s on the eve of the Swadeshi upsurge, Sitanath Tattvabhushan pointed to them as an object lesson and a critique of "the current method of agitation, both social and political, the method that consists in writing, speaking, memorialising, and holding conferences . . ."[90] Again, though the full-blown theory of passive resistance was a Swadeshi creation, Bholanath Chandra's call for "non-consumption" of foreign goods was followed by a boycott pledge taken by some Dacca youths in 1876.[91] One might argue also that passive resistance of a very effective kind had been worked out already by the peasants of Bengal, in the great indigo struggle

---

Birbhum, Murshidabad, Rajshahi, Rangpur, Backergunj and Nowgong (1 each). Of these, 17 in Pabna, 14 in Midnapur, and 1 each in 24 Parganas and Nowgong are described as "Village Unions" or "Ryots' Associations". J.C. Bagal, op. cit., appendix F.

[87] Ibid., p. 90.

[88] 25 September 1886–9 April 1887. Recently reprinted as *Slavery in British Dominion*, compiled by K.L. Chattopadhyay (Calcutta, 1972).

[89] For Sasipada Banerji, see Sitanath Tattvabhushan, *Social Reform in Bengal – A Side-Sketch* (Calcutta, 1904).

[90] Ibid., p. 22.

[91] *Sadharani*, 7 Chaitra 1282/1876, quoted in Soumendra Gangopadhyay, *Swadeshi Andolan o Bangla Sahitya* (Calcutta, 1367/1960), p. 11.

of 1859–60 as well as the Pabna rent strike of 1873; middle-class nationalism in fact lagged behind fifty years, being able to take up the cue effectively only under Gandhi at Champaran and Kaira. Finally, passing mention has to be made of the (admittedly not very serious) secret society game apparently being played by many Calcutta students in the late '70s and early '80s, along with the young Tagores under Rajnarain Bose.[92]

Yet the sum total of all this obviously remained well below the Swadeshi aggregate, and in any case the anticipations of a less elitist and more militant kind of politics were fading away rapidly after about 1885. The Hindu Mela had died out by the late '70s and even at its height, the exhibitions of indigenous products had an overwhelmingly upper-class character, as indicated by the prizes awarded in 1869 and the *Amrita Bazar Patrika*'s comment next year comparing it to the fancy fair of English country ladies.[93] The 1880s saw a significant change in dramatic fashions, patriotic themes being ousted by Girish Chunder Ghosh's domestic and often strongly revivalist plays. By the mid 1880s, the Indian Association was fast toning down its early anti-zamindar slant. It expressed its "disappointment" over the final draft of the Bengal Tenancy Bill but did nothing further about it in the way of petitions, let alone peasant meetings.[94] The 1886–7 report of the association argued that "the old enmity between Zamindars and Raiyats is fast disappearing", and emphasised the need for "that harmony between the two communities upon which the welfare of the country so largely depends." Indian Association activities in the countryside were now confined to the socially and politically much less explosive temperance issue.[95] The concomitant of this was the fact that the British Indian Association, which had boycotted the National Conference of December 1883, fully participated in the second conference of 1885, which had as its sessional presidents

---

[92] Bipinchandra Pal, *Memories of My Life and Times*, vol. I (Calcutta, 1932, 1973), pp. 199–200.

[93] J.C. Bagal, *Hindu Melar Itibritta*, pp. 13–14, 21.

[94] J.C. Bagal, *History of the Indian Association*, p. 72, quoting from the 1884 Annual Report of the Association.

[95] Ibid., pp. 109, 101–2.

zamindars like Jaykrishna Mukherji and Narendrakrishna Deb. In the same year, Raja Rajendranarayan Deb replaced the old Derozian Krishnamohan Banerji as president of the Indian Association.[96] The 1882 Association Report was already complaining that work in the districts was much hampered by the "want of a band of self-less workers."[97] In the absence of a full-time political cadre of the type developed by the Swadeshi samitis, the terrorist secret societies, and later by Gandhi, the district and village branches probably remained largely paper organisations. Even Surendranath in 1905 depended mainly on new student societies for mass contact, and not on his old Indian Association network,[98] and there is a significant lack of correlation between the 1895 list of branches and the later Swadeshi storm centres.[99]

Repression and/or fear of mass extremism are hardly acceptable as explanations for this mid '80s decline, much less so even then for the Swadeshi collapse. Once again, therefore, we have to turn to a study of internal limitations.

I would like to argue, in the first place, that the cultural milieu of the intelligentsia of mid-nineteenth century so-called "renaissance" Bengal, inhibited the development of nationalist politics in several distinct ways. With the exception of Surendranath, most politically active men of the 1860s, '70s, and '80s, looked upon this side of their work as a definitely secondary occupation, far less important than educational, social, religious, or literary endeavours. This is clearly brought out by the autobiographical literature of the age: thus Debendranath Tagore's *Atmajivani* (Calcutta, 1898) contained no reference at all to the British Indian Association, of which he had

---

[96] Ibid., pp. 65–6, 83–6. The executive committee elected in 1870, in sharp contrast, had excluded all titled names, while the sessional presidents at the 1883 National Conference had been the Derozian schoolteacher Ramtanu Lahiri, the *vakil* Kalimohan Das (uncle of C.R. Das), and Annada Chandra Khastagir (maternal grandfather of J.M. Sengupta): ibid., pp. 14, 65–5.

[97] Ibid., p. 57.

[98] See Sarkar, *Swadeshi Movement*, op. cit., p. 338, for the relative unimportance of the Indian Association in Swadeshi days.

[99] Thus Backergunj had only one branch in 1895, ibid., appendix F.

been the first secretary, while Sibnath Shastri is almost equally taciturn about his political activities in the late 1870s.[100] The current fashion of virtually ignoring ideologies as mere rationalisations of material interests and of reducing politics to the "political arithmetic" of competing pressure groups seems particularly inadequate for periods like the one under discussion.

The simple "traditionalist–modernist" model I used for the Swadeshi age is very difficult to apply to the rich and complex cultural world of the 1860s and '70s. Such a dichotomy operated only at moments of acute tension over concrete social-reform issues (e.g. suttee, widow-remarriage, the Age of Consent debate); usually the situation was far more complicated. As a first and highly simplified approximation, we may perhaps identify four groups: secular reform of the Vidyasagar brand, more or less indifferent towards religious enthusiasm whether of the old or new variety and concentrating on a kind of piecemeal social engineering;[101] Brahmoism, at the height of its influence in the 1860s and '70s, declining rapidly thereafter; the positivist circles somewhat neglected by historians, but studied in some detail recently by Sabyasachi Bhattacharya;[102] and the rising tide of Hindu revival. One has only to draw up such a list to become

---

[100] There is less than a page about the Indian Association in Sibnath Shastri's otherwise detailed and fascinating *Atmacharit*, op. cit., pp. 133–4.

[101] Vidyasagar was certainly an agnostic and possibly an atheist; some of his off-the-cuff remarks about religion have been recorded in Bipinbihari Gupta, op. cit., pp. 131–2, 179–80, 293. He was not attracted either by the then fashionable surrogate of positivism; indeed, his refusal to generalise or to accept any ideological system is perhaps the best index to his unique greatness (I owe this point to Professor Asok Sen of the Centre for Studies in Social Sciences, Calcutta). Dwarakanath Vidyabhushan's *Somprakash* developed a somewhat similar attitude; see for example its very interesting critiques of the Keshab Sen group for excessive religiosity, 10 Jyaistha 1277/1870, 9 Falgun 1277/1871, in Benoy Ghosh, *Samajikpatre Banglar Samajchitra*, vol. IV (Calcutta, 1966), pp. 218, 222.

[102] Sabyasachi Bhattacharya, "Positivism in Nineteenth Century Bengal: Diffusion of European Intellectual Influences in India", in R.S. Sharma, ed., *Indian Society: Historical Probings in Memory of D.D. Kosambi* (New Delhi, 1974).

aware of further complexities and subdivisions: the bitter internecine quarrels among the Brahmos, for example, or the obvious differences between the revivalism of the Bankim–Akshay Sarkar as contrasted to the Sasadhar Tarkachudamani–Krishnaprasanna Sen groups.[103]

Sectarian quarrels occasionally did provide an indirect stimulus to nationalist activity. Thus the sudden enthusiasm for "national" ways displayed by the Jorasanko Tagore—Rajnarain Bose—Nabagopal Mitra group in the mid 1860s probably had something to do with its losing struggle with Keshabchandra Sen to retain the allegiance of the younger Brahmos.[104] A decade later, the revolt against Keshabchandra which led to the foundation of the Sadharan Brahmo Samaj was accompanied for a few years by intense political activity on the part of men like Sibnath Shastri, Anandamohan Bose, Dwarkanath Ganguli, and Krishnakumar Mitra, and this group of radical young Brahmos seem to have been the real backbone of the Indian Association in its early days. But on the whole the negative or inhibiting aspects were much more important in the long run. First and most obvious was the element of distraction, the swamping of early political ardour by enthusiasm for social reform or religion. A good example here would be Sibnath Shastri, who in 1876 inspired a group of like-minded young Brahmos (including the later Extremist leader Bipinchandra Pal) to take a vow to keep away from government service on the ground that "self-government is the only form of political government ordained by God",[105] but who from the 1880s became increasingly engrossed with the organisational and missionary routine of the Sadharan Brahmo sect. Mention may be made also of Sisirkumar Ghosh, the founder of the *Amrita Bazar Patrika* and the India League, who abandoned nationalist politics for Vaishnavism,

---

[103] For a good discussion by a contemporary, see Bipinchandra Pal, op. cit., chapter XXII.

[104] Thus the *National Paper* of 2 January 1867 violently attacked the "spurious Brahmoism" of Keshabchandra's "young band" for its denationalised semi-Christian ways. The most detailed account of this split is in Ajitkumar Chakrabarti, *Maharshi Debendranath Tagore* (Allahabad, 1916; Calcutta, 1971), pp. 269–345.

[105] Bipinchandra Pal, op. cit., pp. 252–61.

and Akshaykumar Sarkar, editor of the radical political weekly *Sadharani* in the 1870s and of the purely revivalist organ *Navajivan* in the 1880s. What may be called the Aurobindo Ghosh model has been perhaps a little too common in the history of our nationalism.[106]

A second negative aspect was the strong Hindu note pervading the entire cultural atmosphere of our "renaissance", which could not but have an alienating effect, not only immediately but perhaps even more in the twentieth century, as an educated Muslim counter-elite began developing in Bengal. "National" Nabagopal Mitra with his "Hindu" Mela and his "National" Association is a striking instance, and the *National Paper* brushed aside criticism of this equation with the argument that "the Hindus . . . certainly form a nation by themselves and as such a society established by them can very properly be called a National Society."[107] The Hindu Mela, it must be remembered, was organised not by revivalist or orthodox Hindus but mainly by Adi Samaj Brahmos. The Positivists present another curious case: they often boasted of their atheism,[108] yet their attitude towards Hindu social customs ranged from cautious reform to outright hostility to change,[109] and indeed one of their chief

---

[106] The extremist and revolutionary leader who became the seer of Pondicherry.

[107] *National Paper*, 4 December 1872, quoted in J.C. Bagal, *Hindu Melar Itibritta*, p. 64. Jogendranath Vidyabhushan, who later became Assistant Secretary of the Indian Association, did suggest changing the name to Bharat Mela, but his plea was ignored. Brajendranath Bandyopadhyay, *Sahitya-Sadhak-Charitmala*, vol. III, no. 31 (Calcutta, 1943), p. 24.

[108] Thus Krishnakamal Bhattacharya in later life recalled with evident pride a comment made about himself by Dwijendranath Tagore: "He knows how to write and how to fight and how to slight all things divine." Bipinbihari Gupta, op. cit., pp. 17–18.

[109] Krishnakamal supported widow remarriage, but his sympathies were with Comte in the Comte–Mill controversy over representative government and votes for women, and he expressed his horror at the idea of divorce among Hindus. Ibid., pp. 6–7, 17–18, 72. Another convert, Girish Chunder Ghosh, argued in an article on the conditions of Indan women that the "evils are considerably exaggerated", and talked about the "lofty sense of female honour"

European mentors, Principal Lobb of Hooghly College, had urged the acceptance of Comte precisely because his was "a system which can be grafted upon Hinduism, which Hindus can make their own and which by espousing they will not be obliged to sacrifice . . . their national customs and traditions . . ."[110]

Respect or reverence for Hindu traditions was perhaps not unnatural: far more ominous was the virtually all-pervading assumption that British rule had been preceded by centuries of "Muslim tyranny" and therefore had to be welcomed as a deliverance from an age of darkness. One comes up against this syndrome time after time throughout nineteenth-century Bengal: in Rammohun and Derozians as much as among their Dharma Sabha critics, in the entire patriotic literature of the period (and not just in a few stray passages of Bankimchandra),[111] in the *National Paper*, in the speeches of Keshabchandra Sen, and (most surprising of all perhaps) even in Sibnath Shastri.[112] The conventional distinction between conservatives

---

maintained by the celibacy of widows. *Hindoo Patriot*, 10 August 1854, rpntd in Manmathanath Ghosh, ed., *Selections from the Writings of Grish Chunder Ghosh*, op. cit., pp. 182–4. The basically conservative stance of Positivism has been emphasised both by Sabyasachi Bhattacharya and by Pradip Sinha, *Nineteenth Century Bengal: Aspects of Social History* (Calcutta, 1965), chapter 6.

[110] Letter to Girish Chunder Ghosh, 24 September 1867, rpntd in Manmathanath Ghosh, ed., op. cit., p. 230.

[111] For a slightly biased but valuable study, see Md. Maniruzzaman, *Adhunik Bangla Kavye Hindu–Musalman Samparka 1857–1920* (Dacca, 1970).

[112] For a general discussion of this theme, along with illustrative quotations from Rammohun, the Derozians, Keshabchandra, and Bankimchandra, see Tanika Sarkar, "The Concept of Muslim Tyranny: An Unbroken Tradition", *Presidency College Magazine*, 1972; Derozian views are discussed in "The Complexities of Young Bengal", above. The *National Paper* of 6 February 1867 eloquently described India as "suffering for centuries under the yoke of Mahomedan despotism, when nothing could be done without the permission of the Ruling Power, when private affairs, such as marriage ceremonies, etc., required the sanction of the authorities [*sic*] . . . [and] the very idea of freedom . . . was driven out . . ." Sibnath Shastri in his *Ramtanu Lahiri O Tatkalin Bangasamaj* (Calcutta, 1903, 1955) referred to the Krishnanagar rajas as "bearing upon their shoulders the storms of Yavana (Muslim) rule";

and progressives breaks down on this crucial issue as well as on the related question of the basic attitude towards foreign rule.

Apart from this link via the Muslim tyranny concept, a more direct connection between culture and loyalty was encouraged through the contacts with Englishmen assiduously cultivated by virtually all the groups and sub-groups of the mid-nineteenth-century Bengali intelligentsia, as well as sometimes by the very logic of their activities. The Anglophilism of even Vidyasagar, a man of unimpeachable integrity and independence in his personal relations with whites, stemmed perhaps from a not unfounded conviction that the kind of piecemeal modernisation upon which he had set his heart was impossible in the given context without co-operation with the rulers. Autonomous social forces for such changes simply did not exist in a colonial society. Among the Brahmos, Keshabchandra's loyalism was of a particularly gross kind, but his Adi Samaj critics were not fundamentally different: thus the *National Paper* categorically stated that it "would be an unfortunate day for the country when the English would pack up their belongings and embark for England."[113] Nabagopal Mitra, his patron Dwijendranath Tagore later recalled, was an adept in the art of running after British officials, and asked once to arrange some indigenous paintings for the Hindu Mela where he had commissioned an artist to draw a picture of Indians kneeling before Britannia.[114] "National" is evidently a term with connotations that vary with the times. The Sadharan Brahmos were on the whole much more independent, and several among them later played a leading part in the Swadeshi movement,[115] but they too developed connections

---

he added in the very next sentence that "in the Yavana Period native rajas were quite independent in many matters", and seemed utterly unaware of the contradiction.

[113] 20 March 1867.

[114] Bipinbihari Gupta, op. cit., p. 298.

[115] Thus Krishnakumar Mitra and Monoranjan Guha Thakurta were among the deportees of 1908; Premotosh Bose and Prabhatkusum Roychaudhuri were pioneering labour organisers. Extremist leaders included Sundarimohan Das as well as of course Bipinchandra Pal (though his Brahmoism was by then highly revisionistic); and there were quite a number of Brahmos also

Pattern and Structure

with British Unitarians, the possible political implications of which have not been studied so far.

As in social matters, the Positivist stance on politics was somewhat ambiguous. Richard Congreve, with whom the Jogendrachandra Ghosh circle maintained a voluminous correspondence, was a consistent critic of imperialism even during the Mutiny uproar, and James Geddes was also a prominent Civilian Positivist. Yet Indian converts seldom advanced beyond a fairly tepid and conventional kind of nationalism,[116] and that some of their European mentors were giving quite a different kind of advice is indicated by the following passage in Lobb's correspondence with Girish Chunder Ghosh: "There is much danger in the present state of things that men here should be led away by visionary dreams of commercial activity and political aggrandisement. The problems of commerce and politics must I think be worked out by the West, but Bengal can accomplish a revolution most important to the interests of humanity if she concentrates her attention upon man's spiritual future . . ."[117]

The concentration upon "man's spiritual future" soon abandoned Positivist for Hindu revivalist forms, but, as the above letter indicates by implication, there is no intrinsic connection between revivalism and radical nationalist politics – despite the temporary and not entirely fortunate alliance between the two in the Swadeshi period. Bipinchandra Pal in fact categorically stated in March 1903 that after the Ilbert Bill days "Politics have been neglected in the interest of abstract religion. And in consequence, religious songs have supplanted the old national songs."[118] It should also be remembered that

---

among the early terrorists. The Nababidhan Samaj in sharp contrast retained its reputation for Anglicism and loyalty. Bipinchandra Pal, *Memories of My Life and Times*, vol. II (Calcutta, 1951, 1973), p. 444.

[116] Sabyasachi Bhattacharya's article is mainly based on the Congreve Papers, and includes a brief discussion of Positivist political activity. Strangely enough, however, there is no mention of Girish Chunder Ghosh.

[117] Lobb to Girish Chunder Ghosh, 19 February 1868, in *Life of Grish*, op. cit., p. 236.

[118] *New India*, 19 March 1903; rpntd in Bipinchandra Pal, *Swadeshi and Swaraj* (Calcutta, 1954), p. 94.

orthodoxy or revivalism, too, had its white patrons, almost as much as reform, from *John Bull*'s support for the *Samachar Chundrika* in the early 1830s down to Blavatsky and Olcott's Theosophy racket in the 1880s.

The net result of all this was a kind of political journalism and activitity which was frankly and neatly described by Akshaychandra Sarkar's *Sadharani* when it stated that "there was no politics except weeping".[119] Rammohun and the Derozians had not felt the need for tears as they had been pretty sure that collaboration would deliver the goods in the shape of a subordinate but still real modernisation. Optimism was waning with the spread of the conviction that British rule was basically exploitative and racialist but the self-confidence and strength needed for launching anything like a really radical movement still lay in the Swadeshi future, when the Japanese victory over Russia would come as a major shot in the arm to Asian pride. Among the other factors usually cited as explanations for the Swadeshi outburst, educated unemployment and rising prices already figured fairly often in journalistic complaints of the 1860s and '70s,[120] but we do still get the impression of a kind of mid-Victorian middle-class economic and social stability which was to break down in the next century. Racial discrimination as revealed above all in the Ilbert Bill uproar was probably a far more potent source of tension: the crux of the Civil Service agitation lay precisely here and not in the relatively insignificant number of extra jobs that a raised age limit and simultaneous examinations could have been expected to provide.[121] The cumulative effect of these things, plus the growing

---

[119] Brajendranath Bandyopadhyay, *Sahitya-Sadhak-Charitmala*, vol. III, no. 39 (Calcutta, 1956), p. 10.

[120] Thus the *Somprakash* of 21 Baisakh 1288/1881 complained that 10,000 were applying for jobs with salaries of Rs 10–Rs 15. Benoy Ghosh, *Samayik patre Banglar Samajchitra*, vol. IV (Calcutta, 1966), p. 143. The *Tattvabodhini Patrika* was referring to rising prices already by Sravana 1778/1856, ibid., vol. II, Calcutta 1963, p. 184.

[121] Yet this racial factor is deliberately played down in much recent British writing on Indian nationalism. "The argument that the rule of strangers in India goaded their subjects into organising against it is not our concern": Anil

sense of frustration as "weeping" or mendicancy failed to bring about even slight changes, led ultimately to the sharp turn towards radical nationalism in 1905; time was evidently needed for such factors to mature.

We have seen in the Swadeshi model that the crucial structural limitation of our nationalism probably lay in the field of elite mass communications. Things appear more promising in this respect at first sight in the 1867–85 period. Far from rural tensions being dormant, as was to happen in the Swadeshi age, the peasant world of Bengal was then extremely restive. The "Blue Mutiny" was followed by the sustained struggle of Pabna *raiyats* in defence of occupancy rights and against rent enhancements, and soon afterwards came the turmoil preceding the Tenancy Act of 1885.[122] Intelligentsia reactions were equally significant: virtually unanimous support, plus some organisational help, for the indigo rebels; less unequivocal, but still considerable, literary sympathy for Pabna; peasant rallies organised by the Indian Association on the eve of the 1885 Act.

Yet certain crucial limitations of this apparent elite–peasant rapprochement need to be emphasised. Intelligentsia support for peasants was reformist, never revolutionary. Indigo after all was a single and glaring abuse, condemned by many Europeans and by the lieutenant governor himself; the preface to the *Nil-Darpan* of Dinabandhu Mitra ended with fulsome praise for Canning and Grant.[123] The Pabna upsurge frightened to a certain extent even a generally pro-peasant weekly like *Somprakash*, and the author of "Bangadesher Krishak" in the wake of the rising advised Mir Musharaf Husain to withdraw his *Zamindar Darpan* play: "We have been pained and disgusted by the Pabna ryots. It is unnecessary to add fuel to the

---

Seal, "Imperialism and Nationalism in India", in Gallagher, *et al.*, *Locality, Province and Nation*, op. cit., pp. 5–6.

[122] For a detailed recent analysis, see Benoy Bhushan Chaudhuri, "Peasant Movements in Bengal, 1850–1900", *Nineteenth Century Studies*, vol. I, no. 3, July 1973.

[123] *Dinabandhu Rachanabali*, Sahitya Sansad Edition (Calcutta, 1968), p. 1.

fire."[124] The oft-repeated intelligentsia plea for a permanent fixity of rents would have benefited only the topmost layer of the peasantry, and there is no evidence of concern about non-occupancy ryots, let alone share-croppers or agricultural labourers. Above all, sympathy for the peasantry certainly did not always synchronise with a clear-cut nationalist stance; quite a reverse kind of relationship seems to have operated in many cases. The young Civilian Rameshchunder Dutt, author of *An Apology for the Pabna Rioters* (1873), found in such disturbances "some evidence that the moral of a civilised mode of administration has not been entirely lost on the millions of Bengal."[125] The later nationalist, R.C. Dutt of drain of wealth fame, ardently defended the system of permanent zamindari. A similar comment has to be made about the early friends of labour in Bengal. District magistrates subscribed readily to the *Bharat Sramajivi*, and the limits of Sasipada Banerji's work among labour are vividly revealed by the comments innocently made by his admirer Sitanath Tattvabhushan.[126]

It is tempting, particularly for left-inclined historians of today, to draw a sharp distinction between such manifold instances of bhadralok moderation, timidity, or "comprador" behaviour and the supposedly pure stream of popular militant anti-imperialism as manifested in the peasant struggles.[127] Unfortunately, however, research is increasingly revealing that these movements had their own, and not entirely dissimilar limitations. Kalyankumar Sengupta and Benoy Bhushan Chaudhuri have their differences about the interpretation of the Pabna rising but they both agree that it was a movement of the relatively better-off or at most of the "middle" peasant, not really of the lowest state in the countryside. Sengupta talks about the "legalistic-passive" character of the whole struggle.[128] Chaudhuri

[124] *Somprakash*, 7 June 1873; *Bangadarshan*, Bhadra 1280/1873, cited in Kalyankumar Sengupta, op. cit.

[125] *Bengal Magazine*, September 1873, rpntd in *Nineteenth Century Studies*, vol. I, no. 3, July 1973, p. 312.

[126] Sitanath Tattvabhushan, op. cit., pp. 8–9.

[127] A good example of such an interpretation is Suprakash Roy, *Bharater Krishak-Bidroha O Ganatantrik Sangram*, vol. I (Calcutta, 1966).

[128] Kalyankumar Sengupta, "Peasant Struggle in Pabna, 1873, its Legalistic Character", *Nineteenth Century Studies*, op. cit., p. 328.

emphasises that loyalty to British authority was never questioned: "It is surprising how the peasant's vision of a new order was associated with the Queen." Even at its most radical point the Pabna movement demanded that the peasants "are to be the ryots of Her Majesty the Queen, and Her only."[129] Such a pathetic faith in a distant superior, as contrasted to the immediate oppressor, is not perhaps particularly surprising: an obvious parallel would be the Russian peasants' long-continued reverence and love for their "Little Father", the Tsar.

The conclusion that emerges is that in nationalism, as in other movements, very little happens automatically, as a spontaneous reflection of material conditions. There is need for conscious effort, for an ideology, if a social group or class, to use Gramscian language, is to rise from the "economic-corporative" to the "hegemonic" level of political action.[130] The great contribution of our nineteenth-century intelligentsia was their gradual development of such an ideology, in the shape of the drain of wealth theory. That its formulation and acceptance may or may not have had something to do with narrow elite grievances, as present-day Western scholars like to argue, is about as relevant to the understanding of the historical significance of this development as would a Freudian analysis of possibly even less savoury unconscious motives of nationalist or other political leaders. The failure, to a very great extent conditioned by colonialism itself, lay in the long continued and never entirely overcome absence of effective instruments of hegemony, of techniques and programmes for bridging the elite–mass gap.

---

[129] Benoy Bhushan Chaudhuri, "The Story of a Peasant Revolt in a Bengal District", *Bengal Past and Present*, vol. XCII, pt II, no. 174, July–December 1973, pp. 253–4.

[130] Antonio Gramsci, *Selections From Prison Notebooks* (New York, 1971), *passim*, esp. pp. 3–4, 52–5.

4

The Radicalism of Intellectuals
A Case Study of Nineteenth-Century Bengal

HISTORICAL EVALUATIONS OF the intelligentsia bred through English education under colonial rule in nineteenth-century Bengal have tended to incline towards one of two opposed stereotypes. The dominant interpretation remains heavily eulogistic and centres around the concept of a "reniassance". Its proponents have included extremely diverse groups: men affiliated to the actual movements of religious or social reform, British liberals eager to emphasise the benefits of English education and often finding in it a balm for their own feelings of guilt, Indian nationalists cherishing "liberal" or "modernistic" values, and a considerable number of Marxist intellectuals.[1]

Less apparent on the whole at the level of formal research, yet not uninfluential at times, has been the opposite tendency towards iconoclastic denigration of the "renaissance" heroes for their alienation of the masses and their illusions concerning foreign rule. Occasionally present in the writings of some twentieth-century nationalists who had extended their hostility towards foreign rule to include education

[1] For a discussion of the ideological and social roots of the "renaissance" model, see Barun De, "A Critique, of the Historiography, of the Trend Entitled 'Renaissance' in 19th Century India", paper presented to the Indo-Soviet Symposium on Economic and Social Development of India and Russia from the Seventeenth to the Nineteenth Century, Moscow, May 1973.

in a foreign medium,² this trend has normally been pronouncedly left in its political colour and as such has replaced the intellectual hero with the peasant rebel. An uneasy oscillation between high praise for "renaissance" intellectuals and admiration for popular outbreaks like that of 1857 (roundly denounced by the former) has thus characterised much of Indian Marxist writing on nineteenth-century history. Such ambivalence has obvious links with the debates about the progressive potentialities or otherwise of the "national bourgeoisie", endemic within our left movement from the Roy–Lenin controversy of 1920 right down to the present day.³ The two attitudes are not unrelated also to more general assumptions concerning the nature of colonialism particularly in its earlier, free-trader "liberal" phase. One might compare, for instance, R.P. Dutt's assertion regarding an "objectively progressive" phase of British rule in India, grounded upon Marx's somewhat isolated comment on its "regenerative" role,⁴ with the more recent Gunder Frank model of metropolitan domination leading to "development of under-development" in the colonial world throughout the history of world capitalism.⁵

In the context of Bengal, however, the two approaches, for all their apparent mutual opposition, share a tendency to seek for affinities, father figures, and sustenance in the past through an assumption of straight-line connections amounting almost to a kind of

---

² One might recall Gandhi's description of Rammohun as a "pigmy", which provoked an angry rejoinder from Tagore.

³ Thus the ultra-left "Ranadive Period" (1948–50) in the history of the Communist movement saw attacks on "renaissance" heroes by Rabindra Gupta (Bhowani Sen), and more recently, the CPI (ML) has tended to be even more iconoclastic. Intellectuals affiliated to the present CPI have on the whole been much more attracted by the "renaissance" model; cf., for example, S.C. Sarkar, *On the Bengal Renaissance* (Calcutta, 1979), or Gautam Chattopadhyay, *Awakening in Bengal in the Early 19th Century* (Calcutta, 1965), Introduction.

⁴ R.P. Dutt, *India Today*, 2nd edition (Bombay, 1947), p. 82, referred to an "objectively progressive or regenerating role, corresponding to the period of free trade capitalism", of British rule in India.

⁵ A. Gunder Frank, *Capitalism and Under-development in Latin America* (Pelican, 1971).

"Whig" interpretation of history. The enthusiastic response of one school to Rammohun, Young Bengal, or Brahmoism is matched by the romantic glorification of all nineteenth-century peasant outbreaks as revolutionary in the modern sense, headed by leaders assumed to have been "fish in water".[6] The models of heroic radical thinkers or peasant rebels have had a natural appeal for present-day intellectuals, living in a Bengal which in course of the last fifty years, lost its pre-eminence on the national plane, went through famine followed by Partition, and witnessed the repeated failure of apparently quite promising and powerful left movements. Such models nevertheless tend to somewhat distort the past through eulogy and denigration alike.

In recent years there have been the beginnings of a third kind of interpretation, seeking to understand and evaluate the work of the nineteenth-century intellectuals in terms of their own specific context without assuming over-simple connections or continuities between the past and the present. Insofar as that context was moulded fundamentally by colonialism, this approach at times superficially resembles "ultra left" denunciations of the "renaissance" myth. What distinguishes it from the latter is the stress on objective constraints, permitting considerable sympathy and understanding for men like Rammohun or Vidyasagar even while probing their limitations, and the absence of excessive romanticism concerning all "anti-British" or "popular" outbreaks. The basic framework of this interpretation was outlined by Barun De.[7] It has been put forward also in a number of articles included in a recently published volume on Rammohun,[8] and, in perhaps its most well-rounded form, by Asok Sen.[9]

---

[6] Ranajit Guha, "The Image of a Peasant Revolt in a Liberal Mirror", *Journal of Peasant Studies*, October 1974, p. 42.

[7] Barun De, op. cit.

[8] V.C. Joshi, ed., *Rammohun Roy and the Process of Modernisation in India* (Delhi, 1975): see the articles by Asok Sen, Barun De, Pradyumna Bhattacharya, and Sumit Sarkar.

[9] Asok Sen, "Iswarchandra Vidyasagar and His Elusive Milestones", Occasional Paper No. 1, Centre for Studies in Social Sciences, Calcutta, August 1975.

The Radicalism of Intellectuals

My intention is to explore the possibilities of this third kind of approach with reference to the nature and limits of individuals or groups in nineteenth-century Bengali intellectual life generally accepted in "renaissance" historiography as radical or "progressive".

II

It seems useful to begin with a definition of "radicalism"; or rather, of what can be and has been legitimately expected of nineteenth-century "radical" figures by their present-day admirers. On the model of the famous Russian Westerner-Slavophile dichotomy, S.C. Sarkar in an influential and important paper made a sharp distinction between two trends within our "renaissance", "westernism" (or "liberalism") as contrasted to "traditionalism" (or "revivalism"). "Westernism", explicitly proclaimed by him to be more progressive, was further defined by him to include the components of social reform, rationalism, and secular humanism.[10]

Broadening this definition somewhat, we might list the logical implications of such a model of nineteenth-century "radicalism" to include: (i) propagation not so much of English education (which was no reformist monopoly),[11] as of its possible scientific aspects and values, and campaigns for specific reforms in society (e.g. ban on sati, education of women, widow-remarriage, polygamy, child marriage, occasional attacks on caste, etc.); (ii) the development of a certain amount of freethinking and rationalism in religious matters; and (iii) a consequent secularism which could, it was hoped, transcend the barriers between Hindus and Muslims; (iv) a sympathetic concern for peasants; and (v) germs of something like protonationalism – though these admittedly were not peculiar to radical trends alone. The nineteenth-century intellectuals were impelled by their situation to re-model their own social and ethical norms of behaviour, as

---

[10] S.C. Sarkar, "Rabindranath Tagore and the Renaissance in Bengal", (1961) in S.C. Sarkar, op. cit., pp. 152–9.

[11] Conservatives like Radhakanta Deb were equally enthusiastic and had far more to do with the foundation and early management of the Hindu College.

well as to define their attitudes towards the peasant masses and the foreign rulers. The issues posed by this model are thus certainly not irrelevant or a mere creation of the present, and it is interesting that the first number of the Derozian journal *Bengal Spectator* (April 1842) defined its objectives in broadly similar terms.[12] What requires further investigation is, first, how distinct the "radicals" really were in their ideas and actions from the "conservatives" or "traditionalists"; second, the internal consistency and efficacy of their programmes; and third and most important, the specific ways in which the colonial situation warped, hindered, or frustrated the most "progressive" or "modern" of aspirations.

At the most concrete level of all, advocacy of or opposition to specific changes in education and social life, there was certainly a significant distinction between reformers and conservatives, a contrast which occasionally touched explosion point over issues like sati or widow-remarriage. Rammohun's plea for "Mathematics, Natural Philosophy, Chemistry, Anatomy, with other useful Sciences" certainly struck a new, modernistic note,[13] and a recent detailed study indicates that his Bengali prose-style marks a significant advance over that of his conservative critics like Mrityunjay Vidyalankar.[14] Vidyasagar in both respects was his logical, and perhaps greater, successor (though even the allegedly over-anglicised Derozians showed considerable concern for developing the vernacular[15]) with his repudiation of anti-scientific philosophies, creation of a recognisably modern Bengali, drive

---

[12] The aims of the journal were defined editorially as "improvement in customs and manners", "encouragement of education, agriculture and commerce", and "reform of rules of government" (my translation). Benoy Ghosh, *Samayikpatre Banglar Samajchitra*, vol. III (Calcutta, 1964), p. 75.

[13] Letter to Lord Amherst, 11 December 1823, in Nag and Burman, eds, *English Works of Rammohun Roy*, part IV (Calcutta, 1947), p. 108.

[14] Pradyumna Bhattacharya, "Rammohun Roy and Bengali Prose", in V.C. Joshi, op. cit., pp. 199–212.

[15] Udaychandra Addhya pleaded for the vernacular medium at a session of the Derozian Society for Acquisition of General Knowledge (Gautam Chattopadhyay, op. cit., appendix I, pp. i–ii). Pearychand Mitra made a notable contribution towards the development of a colloquial Bengali prose style.

for mass (including women's) education through vernacular textbooks and as inspector of primary schools.[16] The campaigns against sati and for widow-remarriage remain memorable achievements, brought about through a combination of skilful shastric exegesis, passionate humanistic pleas on behalf of women which strike a chord even today, and, in the case of Vidyasagar, a lifetime of truly heroic and selfless endeavour.[17] The Derozians had anticipated Vidyasagar in advocating widow-remarriage and attacking Kulin polygamy in the 1830s and '40s,[18] and the young Brahmos of the 1860s and '70s went along with and sometimes beyond him in a militant campaign for equal rights for women and the throwing down of caste barriers conducted first under and then against the leadership of Keshabchandra Sen. Some of them, most notably Sasipada Banerji, started philanthropic work among industrial labourers, through night-schools, cheap journals, and campaigns against drink.

Yet the shadows of colonial society repeatedly fell between desire and fulfilment. The Macaulay-style purely literary education introduced in 1835 was far removed from Rammohun's dreams, and Vidyasagar resigned in disgust from his post of Assistant Inspector of Schools within three years of his appointment. The financial needs of the colonial administration played a determining role in both cases.[19] The *sadhu bhasha* or chaste prose style developed by the

[16] By far the best account is in Asok Sen, op. cit.

[17] One might cite, for instance, Rammohun's comment: "What! lament is that, seeing the women thus dependent and exposed to every misery, you feel for them no compassion, that might exempt them from being tied down and burnt to death." *A Second Conference between All Advocates for, and An Opponent of the Practice of Burning Widows Alive*, Calcutta, 1820, *EW*, III, p. 127. Vidyasagar ended his second tract in favour of widow-remarriage with the question: "For what sins of theirs are women born in India?" (My translation.) *Vidyasagar Rachana Samgraha*, vol. II (Calcutta, 1972), p. 165.

[18] For some details, see "The Complexities of Young Bengal", above.

[19] "We cannot govern India financially without this change of system", wrote Ellenborough to Bentinck on 23 September 1830, advising him "to educate the natives for office and to encourage them by the possession of it". A.F. Salahuddin Ahmed, *Social Ideas and Social Change in Bengal,*

nineteenth-century literati was a new and major achievement, but it was far removed from the language of the toilers, unlike Luther's German or the "language of artisans, countrymen and merchants" preferred by the Royal Society after the Puritan Revolution.[20] In social reform, the pioneers often failed to live upto the ideals of their youth. One might cite in this context Rammohun's parading of outward conformity to caste rules and concentration on the single issue of sati (his Atmiya Sabha at private meetings had gone much further in 1819).[21] The Derozians upon entering middle age increasingly sought social respectability through conformism,[22] and Keshabchandra Sen performed a remarkable volte-face in the Cooch Behar marriage affair.[23] Reform in practice in any case affected only a very small minority. Widow-remarriage, for instance, in itself an upper-caste issue, is even now highly disapproved and fairly rare in respectable society, and the Brahmo struggles in the 1860s and '70s against caste and the seclusion of women were fought out mainly within the confines of their own community.[24] Lower-caste movements of

---

1818–1835 (Leiden, 1965), pp. 151–2. For the constraints on education in Vidyasagar's period, see Asok Sen, op. cit., pp. 18–28.

[20] Pradyumna Bhattacharya, op. cit.

[21] *India Gazette*, quoted in *Asiatic Journal*, 18 May 1819, in J.K. Majumdar, ed., *Raja Rammohun Roy and Progressive Movements in India* (Calcutta, 1941, p. 18. The report referred to Atmiya Sabha meetings criticising caste restrictions on marriage and diet and the ban on widow remarriage.

[22] Sumit Sarkar, op. cit., pp. 515–16.

[23] After being largely instrumental in persuading the government to pass a modernistic marriage act for those willing to abjure loyalty to the principal religions, Keshabchandra married his own under-age daughter into the Cooch Behar royal family, breaking its provisions.

[24] Keshabchandra's group broke away in the mid 1860s from Debendranath mainly on the demand for exclusion of those still wearing the sacred Brahminical thread from Brahmo pulpits. In the 1870s, women's liberation took the form of ladies being permitted to sit with their menfolk at prayer meetings of the Samaj. Sibnath Shastri, *Ramtanu Lahiri o Tatkalin Bangasamaj* (Calcutta, 1903, 1955), chapters 10–13. Ajitkumar Chakrabarti, *Maharshi Debendranath Tagore* (Allahabad, 1916; Calcutta, 1971), vol. II, chapters I, 3–4, 8.

a "sanskritising" type often worked at cross-purposes with the aims of social reformers.²⁵

One might add that even at the theoretical level reform ideals often seem more than a little incomplete. Rammohun fought against sati by hunting up all the texts he could find hailing ascetic widowhood, thus possibly somewhat adding to Vidyasagar's difficulties. Vidyasagar's whole campaign left untouched the fate of the adult widow who, perchance, might not want or be able to marry again, but who on humanistic grounds surely had the right to a normal life free of barbarous austerities. The Brahmo drive against the seclusion of women was often accompanied by an insistence upon puritanical norms of behaviour, so much so that the very term "Brahmo" has become in colloquial Bengali almost a synonym for prudishness. One is reminded of the scathing comment of a modern Women's Liberation leader about "the Victorian feeling that the female must relinquish sexuality if she is to be in any sense autonomous, a variant on the bondage of 'virtue' which demands sexual inhibition in a woman if she is to maintain her social and therefore her economic position."²⁶ As for Sasipada Banerji's work among Baranagore labour, a biographer admiringly notes that "the merchants themselves bore testimony to its tangible moral effects, declaring that those of their hands who attended Sasi Babu's school were the very people that were found to be most careful and painstaking in their work."²⁷ Further light on the nature of Sasipada's activities has been thrown by the recent discovery of some issues of his journal *Bharat Sramajivi*. The recurrent advice it gave to labourers and peasants was to work hard in their callings, and to try to rise above it on an individual basis through education, small savings, plus a bit of usury.²⁸ The Baranagore jute mills

---

²⁵ "For one convert that Mr Malabari may make, at the cost of much social obloquy, among the highly educated classes Hinduism sweeps whole tribes into its net." H.H. Risley's Note of 22 March 1886, quoted in C. Heimsath, *Indian Nationalism and Hindu Social Reform* (Princeton, 1964), p. 156.

²⁶ Kate Millett, *Sexual Politics* (London, 1971), pp. 77–8.

²⁷ Sitanath Tattvabhushan, *Social Reform in Bengal: A Side-Sketch* (Calcutta, 1904), pp. 8–9.

²⁸ Extracts from twelve issues of the *Bharat Sramajeebi* (Baisakh-Chaitra

were owned, incidentally, by whites. False consciousness here had gone so far that a "progressive" reformer, occasionally hailed even as a pioneer labour leader, was busy inculcating virtues that obviously served capitalist interests out of sheer altruism, all in the cause of foreign capital.

With women and labour alike, even the very limited Victorian models could not be attained in the conditions of Bengal. Women's rights remained an affair of male philanthropy, not of any autonomous feminist movement as in the West, and there was no labour aristocracy to provide a social basis for Sasipada Banerji.[29]

The pattern of early radical outbursts, retreat with growing age, and general incompleteness in theory and ineffectiveness in practice recurs in the history of nineteenth-century strivings for rationalistic changes in religion. Prolific translator of his own works, Rammohun never produced English or Bengali versions of his early and extremely remarkable *Tuhfat-ul-Muwahhidin*, and his later and far more influential writings balanced appeals to reason by a conservative use of his favourite "social comfort" criterion along with an increasing dependence on Upanishadic authority.[30] The Derozian impulse towards scepticism and atheism which had frightened orthodox Hindus and Christian missionaries alike ebbed away within a few years.[31] Akshaykumar Dutt, who is said to have once horrified Debendranath Tagore with his proof of the uselessness of prayer through simple arithmetic, remained a lone Deist in the Brahmo movement.[32]

1286/1879–80) discovered and edited by Kanailal Chattopadhyay, in *Ekshan* (Calcutta), XI 5–6, Puja 1975. In particular nos. 8–9 of the journal.

[29] Acknowledgements are due here to Dipesh Chakrabarty's paper on Sasipada Banerji which he has kindly permitted me to use. See *Indian Historical Review*, January 1976.

[30] For studies of the evolution of Rammohun's religious thought, see S.C. Sarkar, "Religious Thought of Rammohun Roy", in idem, *On the Bengal Renaissance*, op. cit.; and Sumit Sarkar, "Rammohun Roy and the Break with the Past", above.

[31] "Complexities of Young Bengal", above.

[32] Work plus prayer equals harvest. Akshaykumar is said to have argued: but work = harvest, therefore prayer = O. Ajitkumar Chakrabarti, op. cit., p. 193.

Vidyasagar probably had similar ideas, but wisely kept them to himself to prevent *odium theologicum* disrupting his efforts at piecemeal social engineering. Positivists like Krishnakamal Bhattacharya, in sharp contrast, boasted of their atheism but tended to be much more cautious and even conservative on isssues of practical reform.[33]

As distinct from such individuals or groups, Brahmoism did attain the level of a real and continuous, though much divided, movement. Spreading out beyond its early confines of a handful of big Calcutta zamindar families, it came to embrace or at least influence a considerable section of the educated community in the districts, often of fairly humble (though probably never peasant) social origin. It still leaves the impression, however, of being no more than a rather unsatisfactory halfway house. While fire was concentrated from the beginning on image-worship (perhaps largely because missionaries were attacking the whole of Hinduism for its "idolatry"), more important things like caste were not seriously attacked till the 1860s, nor was the fundamental karma assumption really challenged. Few attempts were made to link up with traditions of popular lower-caste monotheism. Brahmoism in fact remained essentially concerned, as Asok Sen puts it, "to take care of the soul of newly settled gentlemen."[34] Above all, Brahmin oppression, while not exactly a non-issue, was surely not the most crucial problem for India under colonial rule. It was not, as the Catholic hierarchy had become in sixteenth-century Europe, the nodal point around which a host of social contradictions had accumulated. The parallel with the Protestant Reformation, so much in vogue among Brahmos and their admirers from Rammohun onwards,[35] breaks down in fact at

---

[33] Krishnakamal supported widow-remarriage, but sympathised with Comte in the Comte–Mill debate on representative government and votes for women, and was horrified by the idea of divorce. Bipinbihari Gupta, *Puratan Prasanga* (Calcutta, 1966), pp. 6–7, 17–18, 72. Another Positivist, Girish Chunder Ghosh, felt that as regards the conditions of Indian women, "the evils are considerably exaggerated". *Hindoo Patriot*, 10 August 1854.

[34] Asok Sen, op. cit., p. 59.

[35] Cf. Rammohun's conversation with Alexander Duff, recorded in S.D. Collet, *Life and Letters of Raja Rammohun Roy* (Calcutta, 1962), p. 280.

every point and reveals itself to have been yet another example of the false consciousness of a colonial intelligentsia.

Colonial rule also gravely hindered the formation of a genuinely secular or non-communal outlook (particularly relevant in a multi-religious society like Bengal) even among the critics of Hindu orthodoxy. Such people, with very rare exceptions, tended to share with conservatives or outright revivalists the assumption that British rule had rescued Bengal from centuries of "Muslim tyranny".[36] Various reasons might be forwarded for this strange, not very well known, but virtually ubiquitous and ultimately disastrous phenomenon. The English-educated found very few Muslims among their peers due to factors not yet fully explored but certainly not unconnected with the socio-economic patterns of post-Permanent Settlement Bengal. A break had taken place with pre-nineteenth-century Indo-Islamic culture through the displacement of Persian by English, and more generally by the myth of the "renaissance" itself, for awakening has to presuppose a dark age. Anglo-Indian historiography played a crucial part, through Tod on Elliot and Dowson, for example.[37] Above all, perhaps, the Muslim tyranny syndrome provided a convenient justification for the intelligentsia's fairly abject acceptance of foreign rule. And when patriotic sentiments did start developing, as from the 1860s, the Muslims could still serve as useful whipping boys.[38]

Left-leaning admirers of nineteenth-century radicals have often emphasised the existence among them of considerable pro-peasant sympathies. Despite his zamindar status, Rammohun advocated the extension of the Permanent Settlement principle to the *raiyats'* rents, and pro-peasant pleas were made by numerous later reformist journals like the Derozian *Bengal Spectator*,[39] the Brahmo *Tattvabodhini*

---

[36] Tanika Sarkar, "The Concept of "Muslim Tyranny – An Unbroken Tradition", *Presidency College Magazine*, Calcutta, 1973.

[37] In Muhammad Habib's brilliant critique of Elliot in *Politics and Society during the Early Medieval Period* (New Delhi, 1974), pp. 3–32.

[38] Bankimchandra would be the obvious example.

[39] *Bengal Spectator*, 1 November, 15 November, 15 December 1942. Benoy Ghosh, *Samayik Patre Banglar Samajchitra*, vol. III.

Patrika,[40] the *Somprakash* of Dwarkanath Vidyabhushan,[41] and the *Bengalee* of Girish Chunder Ghosh.[42] Intellectuals sympathised with, and in some cases gave organisational support to, the indigo rebellion of 1859–60. Twenty years later, the Indian Association was fighting for pro-*raiyat* changes in the Rent Bill through peasant meetings and rent unions, and its challenge to the zamindar-dominated British Indian Association was often seen by contemporaries in Europeans terms, as a struggle between an old aristocracy and an emergent "middle class".[43]

Actually the conflict was never very fundamental and was patched up quickly enough after the passage of the 1885 Tenancy Act.[44] The "middle class" in colonial Bengal was not based on properly bourgeois forms of industry, trade, or even land management. Its members were only too eager to buy themselves positions in the vast and growing Permanent Settlement hierarchy, through intermediate tenures or superior "*raiyat*" rights, once they had climbed the ladder of success via English education and the liberal professions. As a recent detailed study has shown, the Indian Association campaign on the Rent Bill revealed an interesting concern for making occupancy rights saleable, not necessarily residential and free of all restrictions on

[40] *Tattvabodhini Patrika*, Baisakh, Sravana and Agrahayana 1772 S.E. 1850; Benoy Ghosh, op. cit., II.

[41] *Somprakash*, 20 Sravana 1269/1862, Asar, 1271/1864, 14 Bhadra and 4 Aswin 1271/1864, 9 Magh 1278/1872, 6 Aswin 1271/1874; Benoy Ghosh, op. cit., IV.

[42] Girish Chunder Ghosh, "The Permanent Settlement", *Bengalee*, 25 July 1866, rpntd in *Nineteenth Century Studies*, July 1973.

[43] The *Somprakash* of 20 Sravana 1269/1862 called for an alliance between the middle and lower orders to fight zamindari oppression: Benoy Ghosh, op. cit., IV, pp. 66–7. Sibnath Shastri related the Indian Association to the political needs of a "*madhyabitta sreni*" (middle class), *Atmacharit* (Calcutta, 1952), p. 133.

[44] The 1886–7 Report of the Indian Association argued that "the old enmity between zamindars and raiyats is fast disappearing," and emphasised the need for "that harmony between the two communities upon which the welfare of the country so largely depends." J.C. Bagal, *History of the Indian Association* (Calcutta, 1953), pp. 101–2, 109.

sub-letting – all of which "would obviously be of great help to 'ryots' settled in Calcutta or other urban centres and enjoying occupancy rights over agricultural lands."[45]

Attempts have been made also to discover elements of nationalism from the very beginnings of the "renaissance". Rammohun (and to a possibly greater extent some of the Derozians) did occasionally criticise Company administration, and they formulated demands which remarried basics to the later national movement right down to at least 1905: Indianisation of services, and a measure of representative government. They also pioneered the classic "Moderate" techniques of press campaigns, public meetings, and petitions. Unlike the post-1870s generation of nationalist intellectuals,[46] however, what was conspicuously absent was any awareness of the basic fact of British economic exploitation through drain of wealth or decline of handicrafts. Rammohun remained utterly silent about the process of deindustrialisation, though the population of towns like Dacca was declining catastrophically in his lifetime.[47] He did once refer to what a later generation would call the drain, but only to suggest European colonisation as a solution, "a system which would encourage Europeans of capital to become permanent settlers with their families."[48] "Progressive" intellectuals down to the 1850s eagerly sought links with British "liberal" free trader groups, the very force that was ruining Bengal's production economy. The Derozians, for example, modelled their 1843 political society on George Thompson's London British India Society of 1839, which at its inaugural meeting had referred to India as "a country capable of supplying many of our demands for tropical produce, and the desire and capacity of

---

[45] Asok Sen, op. cit., p. 67.

[46] The turning point probably came with Bholanath Chandra's "A Voice for the Commerce and Manufactures of India", *Mukherji's Magazine*, Calcutta, March 1873–June 1876.

[47] The number of houses paying *chaukidari* tax in Dacca was 21,361 in 1813 and 10,708 in 1833; N.K. Sinha, *Economic History of Bengal*, vol. III (Calcutta, 1970), p. 4.

[48] *Questions and Answers on the Revenue System of India* (August 1831), answer to Question No. 52, *EW* III, p. 52.

The Radicalism of Intellectuals

whose population to receive the manufactures, and thus stimulate the commerce of Great Britain, would under a just and enlightened rule, be incalculably developed."[49]

The breakthrough towards a recognisably nationalist ideology in the 1860s and '70s via patriotic literature, institutions like the Hindu Mela, and economic analysis often went hand in hand with the virtual swamping of socio-religious reform movements by Hindu revivalism. Reformers had indeed relied heavily on the support of the foreign government no doubt mainly because of an awareness of the lack of sufficiently strong internal social forces for modernistic change.[50] The loyalism of some (though by no means all) Brahmos, most notably Keshabchandra Sen, was quite notorious. Yet the comfortable assumption often made that revivalism, however harmful in its social or intellectual effects, did contribute directly and greatly to anti-colonial political radicalism does not seem particularly well founded. To take first an example from the earlier period, if Rammohun or the Derozians were not proto-nationalists, neither were their conservative critics. The *Samachar Chandrika* even at the height of its campaign against the sati ban paraded its general loyalism.[51] A year later, it was urging governmental intervention against Hindu College boys allegedly turning atheist.[52] Non-interference in social matters by the foreign rulers was evidently desirable only so long as it helped to defend the status quo. The level of nationalistic politics seems to have actually declined in the Bengal of the late 1880s and '90s, the years particularly characterised by revivalism. Bipin Chandra Pal stated in March 1903 that after the Ilbert Bill days, "Politics have

---

[49] Quoted in S.R. Mehrotra, *The Emergence of the Indian National Congress* (Delhi, 1971), p. 17.

[50] Such surely is the explanation for the Anglophilism of even a man like Vidyasagar.

[51] "We have been subject to no distress under the government of the Company; it is only the abolition of Suttees which has given disquietude": *Samachar Chandrika*, quoted in *John Bull*, 9 March 1830, rpntd in J.K. Majumdar, op. cit., p. 330.

[52] *Samachar Chandrika*, 5 and 9 May 1831, Bropendranath Bandyopadhyay, *Sambad Patre Sehaler Katha*, vol. II (Calcutta, 1941) pp. 235–7.

been neglected in the interest of abstract religion. And in consequence religious songs have supplanted the old national songs."[53]

Things changed radically for a few years with the Swadeshi upsurge of 1905–8, though even here any complete identification of extremism with Hindu revivalism would be over-simple.[54] What is more important, revivalism despite some short-term advantages, proved politically extremely harmful. Not only did it contribute to Muslim alienation, the easy surrogate it seemed to provide for the far more difficult work of linking up the swaraj ideal with the concrete socio-economic demands of the masses probably hindered the conversion of Extremism into a genuinely broad-based movement. Despite the very striking anticipations of Gandhian satyagraha in the passive resistance creed of Aurobindo and Pal, and of much of Gandhian constructive village work in Rabindranath's pleas for self-help, the ultimate legacy of the Swadeshi movement was the heroic but basically sterile path of individual terror.[55]

III

The history of the nineteenth-century Bengali intelligentsia thus emerges as fundamentally a story of repeated failure, and by way of conclusion it is tempting to speculate on the possible causes of this tragedy.

The parallel occasionally attempted by admirers of the Bengal "renaissance" with nineteenth-century Russian intellectual history seems fruitful only in terms of the difference it reveals. Missing here is the intellectuals' agonised sense of alienation from the masses, so much deeper than occasional humanitarian sympathies and culminating in the "going to the people" movement. Nor is there any counterpart of that consistent opposition to autocracy, even at the

---

[53] *New India*, 19 March 1903.

[54] One might cite the example of the Anti-Circular Society, extremist in politics but bitterly opposed to revivalism. A dissident, secular, even anti-religious trend was present even among the early terrorists. Sumit Sarkar, *Swadeshi Movement in Bengal, 1903–1908* (New Delhi, 1973), pp. 58–61, 365–6, 486–7.

[55] Ibid., chapters II, IX, and XI.

cost of emigration or Siberian exile, or of that remarkable jump to one or other form of socialist ideology, bypassing conventional bourgeois liberalism. Narodnism, too, is missing, the distorted but not entirely irrelevant mirror of the peasants' objective strivings for the "first road" of capitalist development through the emancipation of the small producer. Above all, the achievement under Lenin of an organic linkage between a significant section of the socialist intelligentsia and the working class, enabling the breakthrough from spontaneity to consciousness and realising at least in part his What is To Be Done programme – all that is obviously absent in our past, and to a considerable extent in our present, too.

The "advantages of backwardness", long stagnation followed by sudden leaps forward, are noticeable in Russian history, as well as in China or Vietnam, countries where colonial rule was either never fully established, or did not last very long. Not any advantage of backwardness, but a relentless process of inversion, seems characteristic of modern India. Institutions and ideals which did contribute to undoubted progress in the metropolitan country, though often at great human cost – e.g. free-trader liberalism or full-scale private property in land, turned into their opposites here – reflecting the basic fact that the very same forces that brought breathtaking progress in the West produced underdevelopment in the colonial world.

The full logic of colonialism worked itself out in British India, and particularly in Bengal, where it lasted the longest. There was ample time for the growth of dependent vested interests and for the elaboration, in Gramscian language, of a hegemonic infrastructure producing voluntary consent side by side with direct politico-military domination. The latter in normal times could be kept relatively veiled, thus contributing, unlike in Tsarist Russia, to a plethora of deep-seated liberal illusions. Such illusions took three main forms: a long-continued faith in basic British good intentions, persisting well into the nationalist period; a belief in English education as the sovereign panacea;[56] and eager acceptance of liberal socio-political ideals. The Derozians, for example, a contemporary sympathetic account tells us,

---

[56] After mentioning many instances of zamindari exploitation of peasants, Pearychand Mitra suggested that education – Western for the landlord,

were ardent free-traders among whom "the very word Tory was a sort of ignominy."[57] The tragedy lay precisely here, in this pathetic eagerness to affiliate themselves with the latest in bourgeois liberalism.

Our nineteenth-century intellectuals certainly had less freedom to choose between alternative ideologies than their Russian counterparts, while their English education automatically tended to seal them off far more from the peasantry. Yet absence of opportunities is not the whole explanation. Echoes of another England, still in the 1830s and '40s a land of bitter class struggle and working-class politics, did occasionally reach Calcutta through journals which the Derozians were almost certainly reading, but without their leaving any impression on them.[58] Again, while Utilitarianism in general was greatly admired and imitated, Ricardian anti-landlord rent theory found no takers.

More fundamentally, therefore, the limitations of our intellectuals, "radical" and "conservative" alike, were connected with the socio-economic structure moulded by colonialism. In Bengal, this meant firstly the progressive tightening of British control over industry and commerce, after a very short-lived "bourgeois" spring in the age of Dwarkanath Tagore. Swadeshi industrial endeavours in the early twentieth century soon petered away,[59] while the more successful Marwari challenge had little influence on Bengali social and cultural life due to the isolation and unpopularity of that immigrant

---

vernacular for the ryot – would solve everything: "The Zamindar and the Ryot", *Calcutta Review*, December 1846. Cf. also, Ranajit Guha, op. cit., for the intellectual response to the indigo movement, and the Bharat Sramajeebi's faith in education for solving labour problems.

[57] *Calcutta Monthly Journal*, May 1837, quoted in Bhabatosh Dutta, ed., *Bankimchandrer Iswarchandra Gupter Jibancharit o Kabitva* (Calcutta, 1968), pp. 88–9.

[58] The *India Gazette* of 5 July 1831 (Derozio was then on its staff) published a remarkable letter attacking the Society for the Diffusion of Useful Knowledge in English for its "Whig perfidy" in praising the results of machinery, and even quoted from More's *Utopia*. The *Bengal Hurkaru* occasionally published news about the Chartists (e.g. issue of 18 February 1843).

[59] Sumit Sarkar, *Swadeshi Movement*, op. cit., chapter III, p. 12.

community. Equally important was the elaboration of the vast Permanent Settlement hierarchy of rentiers, big and small, sucking in virtually everyone with pretensions to respectability, and unproductive at every level since rent receipts flowed in without much entrepreneurial effort or innovation. A zamindar like Joykrishna Mukherji of Uttarpara gained the reputation of being an unusually enterprising landlord on the strength of the improvements he tried to encourage among his peasants. After each of these he promptly tried to hike up the rents.[60] He did not go in for real capitalist farming, obviously because the traditional mode of exploitation, consolidated and systematised by British rule, brought in profits so much more easily.

The bourgeois values imbibed by the intelligentsia through their Western education and contacts thus remained bereft of material content or links with production. The intellectuals were attracted easily enough towards liberal social reform, nationalist politics, and (from the 1920s) even socialist ideology; the concrete impact of all this, however, on Bengali society as a whole was, and still remains, severely limited.

It is tempting to seek solace in the history of the peasantry, to bathe in the supposedly pure stream of popular militant anti-imperialism as manifested in peasant uprisings. Unfortunately, however, detailed research seems to indicate that these movements had their own and not entirely dissimilar, limitations. Directed against immediate local oppressors, such movements seldom questioned the ultimate but distant British authority. In the Pabna rent strike of 1873, for instance, the most radical demand raised was that peasants were "the ryots of Her Majesty the Queen, and of Her only". A modern historian comments: "It is surprising how the peasants' vision of a new order was associated with the Queen."[61] Not so very surprising or unique perhaps: one is reminded of the pathetic faith of generations of Russian peasants in their "Little Father", the Tsar.

---

[60] Such facts become obvious from Nilmoni Mukherjee's somewhat eulogistic but extremely detailed and valuable *A Bengal Zamindar: The Life and Times of Joy Krishna Mukherji* (Calcutta, 1975).

[61] B.B. Chaudhuri, "The Story of a Peasant Revolt in a Bengal District", *Bengal Past and Present*, July–December 1973, pp. 253–4.

During the Swadeshi movement, the discontent of Muslim peasants against predominantly Hindu zamindars or *mahajans* could be given a communal and positively anti-patriotic twist with the greatest of ease.[62] What was lacking here was an ideology, either nationalist or social-revolutionary. That came, and even then only sporadically and in scattered areas, only in the 1920s and '30s, with Gandhian village work and Communist Kisan Sabha activities. In the labour movement, too, the grip of economism has never been really broken yet in our country.

The breakthrough in a sustained way from what Gramsci called the "economic-corporative" to the "hegemonic" level of political action yet remains to be achieved in India.[63] In such a situation, an overenthusiastic search for father figures or precursors seems neither historical nor particularly useful. One is reminded of Marx's warning given in the context of a country which had gone through a mighty revolution, that "the social revolution . . . can only create its poetry from the future, not from the past."[64]

---

[62] Sumit Sarkar, *Swadeshi Movement*, chapter VIII.3.

[63] Antonio Gramsci, *Selections from the Prison Notebooks* (New York, 1971), *passim*, esp. pp. 3–4, 52–5.

[64] Karl Marx, *The Eighteenth Brumaire of Louis Bonaparte – Surveys from Exile* (Penguin, 1973), p. 149.

5

One or Many Histories? Identity Formations in Late-Colonial Bengal

THE POST-MODERNIST WAVE appears to be receding a little, and histories going beyond the narrowly "culturalist" or "discursive" are no longer considered necessarily outdated. For those, like myself, who have remained critical of the dominant moods of the late 1980s and '90s, this might be the moment for a stock-taking that would not be primarily polemical, and is able to take fuller account of some significant gains for historical understanding brought about through the recent wholesale questioning of earlier assumptions, alongside the many deeply problematic features. Foremost among the potential advances, I suggest, in terms of its relevance for South Asian historiography, is the critique of unilinear modes of thinking, and the simultaneous foregrounding and problematisation of questions of identity. I intend here to explore the possibilities (as well as sometimes the problems) of a quest for a more differentiated vision of the past, with particular reference to caste identities in late-colonial Bengal.

Caste was till very recently a neglected theme in histories of "modern" India, which have focused so far on colonial rather than post-colonial times. Such history-writing has remained stuck for a long time within a single basic, colonial / anti-colonial binary, within which it was difficult not to evaluate caste identities primarily in terms of their "divisive" impact on what should have been a great and united struggle for freedom from foreign subjection. Left-nationalist, Leftist, and, most notably, early Subaltern Studies scholarship did complicate this model in helpful ways, emphasising the autonomous initiatives of peasants, tribals, and workers and the tensions between such impulses and "mainstream" nationalism. But the implicit criteria for evaluation of such movements still remained their "contribution", or otherwise, to anti-colonialism. Even the recent "postcolonial" and "culturalist" turn, beginning in South Asian scholarship with the critique of "Orientalist" colonial discourses initiated by Edward Said and taken up in a big way both within and beyond late Subaltern Studies, failed to really break with that paradigm. The resultant colonial discourse / indigenous authenticity binary seems often in danger of remaining a variant of the earlier dichotomy, with alien, "Western", cultural hegemony substituted for political and economic exploitation, and political nationalism merely giving place to cultural.[1]

The problem can be refigured in terms of today's influential language of identity. A central theme in what follows will be the ways in which the late-colonial era of Indian history became exceptionally abundant in its range of identity projects. But one consequence of unilinearity has been that, among them, some came to be assumed as "natural" (e.g. "national", "communal",[2] "class" – all frequently conceptualised in homogenised ways), while others were marginalised or ignored (notably, "gender", "caste", "regional" solidarities).

---

[1] For a fuller discussion, see my "Postmodernism and the Writing of History", in Sumit Sarkar, *Beyond Nationalist Frames* (New Delhi: Permanent Black, 2002), as well as the Introduction to that volume. See also idem, "The Decline of the Subaltern in Subaltern Studies", in Sarkar, *Writing Social History* (Delhi: Oxford University Press, 1997), chapter 3.

[2] In its peculiar, Indian-English sense of aggressive religious identity-politics that have prioritised and sharpened conflicts between religious groups (primarily, Hindu and Muslim) in twentieth and early-twenty-first century South Asia. Here "real" freedom is identified as liberation, not from British, but from alleged Hindu or Muslim domination. Colonial /anti-colonial is displaced by Hindu / Muslim, but the binary mode of thinking continues, often in aggravated form. The Hindu chauvinist, "Hindutva" variant of communalism currently dominates the Indian government, and constitutes a very serious threat to the country's secular and democratic institutions.

For identities in the first group could be related, in fairly direct ways, with the central antinomy of colonial / anti-colonial: the second was difficult to accommodate within that linear narrative.

We need to be open to the possibilities of many histories and trajectories that demand evaluation in terms of multiple criteria: and here, one would think, postmodernist scepticism about homogenised, unilinear, teleological approaches should have been helpful. Should have, but hardly have, so far. Despite bows to Derrida, Spivak, or Bhabha, the focus on identity in South Asian postcolonial theory has rarely gone along with the exploration of the multiplicities and hybridity that constitute the real gains of the new ways of thinking. "Class" nowadays is often discarded as a discredited and harmful Marxist relic inextricably mired in economism. But what follows is often a simple substitution: the "identities" valorised in place of class (notably, in radical circles, women, along with subordinated castes and above all Dalits) get projected in ways every bit as essentialised.[3]

I am putting forward a case for a measure of disaggregation, the breaking up of single, linear narrative: but how far down this road is it helpful to proceed? There has been a tendency, in the wake of Lyotard, to reject all "grand narratives" as politically oppressive, and displace them through a valorisation of "fragments". But fragments are not necessarily immune from power relations, nor are they totally detachable from wider processes. Mine will be a plea for "many histories", but there remains a need to explore the multitude of interrelations and crosscurrents: threads across time, which intermingle and break apart, might seem lost, and yet may get recuperated and resumed.[4] The search for interconnections should not be

---

[3] "Dalit", literally "ground down", means acutely oppressed. It is the term favoured as self-description today by many located at the lowest level of caste society. Earlier terms for them had been "Untouchable", "Scheduled Castes" (still the official designation), and Gandhi's term "Harijan".

[4] Some possible readings of Foucault's difficult, yet deeply suggestive, concept of genealogy might be of help here. See, for instance, Jan Goldstein's description of one, among several, of its implications: "while the components of a genealogy are knit together in the manner of narrative, that narrative is resolutely non-teleological: events are eruptions, outcomes are local and

abandoned, but has to be made much more complicated, freed from all forms of reductionism and assumptions of necessary and unchanging priority or determination, whether by class, caste, religion, economy, or culture. A reduction of the discipline to the contemplation of arbitrarily isolated fragments can impoverish history-writing as much as operating with homogenised totalities.

A general statement about the need to keep in mind interconnections is of course easy enough to make. The real challenge lies in its embodiment within a concrete research project, avoiding the pitfalls of homogenisation and total disaggregation alike.

In what follows I start by raising some questions of method concerning the study of caste, and then focus on a particular period in the history of late-colonial Bengal. Higher and lower caste formations will be looked at, not in the isolated manner that has been usual, but through an emphasis on interactions and mutual conditionings, and some research-based material will be presented concerning the three major caste ideologies-cum-movements of Namasudras, Mahishyas, and Rajbansis. A brief concluding section will seek to tease out some more general implications.[5]

II

My study of identity formations, and more specifically caste, locates itself in late-nineteenth- and early-twentieth-century Bengal. The choice requires some explication.

Late-colonial India was marked by the emergence of a plethora of organisations claiming to represent a wide range of projected identities:

---

radically contingent . . ." Jan Goldstein, ed., *Foucault and the Writing of History* (Cambridge, Mass., and Oxford: Basil Blackwell, 1994).

[5] The Mahishyas (*c.* 2.5 million by the 1901 Census), Rajbansis (*c.* 2 million), and Namasudras (1.86 million) were located in the south-western, northern, and south-central parts of the Bengali-speaking part of the British-ruled Bengal Presidency. After the Partition of 1947, most of the Namasudra- and Rajbansi-inhabited areas became part of East Pakistan (subsequently Bangladesh), though over the years substantial numbers have migrated to India's West Bengal.

Indian, regional, religious or communal, caste, labour, peasant, tribal, women. The context was the revolution in communications (railways, postal services, improved roads, the spread of the printing press which in India came as an innovation of the colonial era), combined with the multifarious pressures of foreign rule and the opportunities it also offered in selective and shifting ways to particular categories of Indians. Particular attention has been paid in recent years to the ways in which colonial discourses and institutions helped to stimulate such processes, often in conflictual ways. Here, there has been much discussion of the role of the census (which was started in 1871). The logic of enumeration sharpened dividing lines between communities which earlier had much more fluid or ill-defined boundaries, and stimulated bitter competition for jobs or political opportunities between Hindu and Muslim elites, higher and lower castes, different regional or ethnic groups. Even the categories of caste and religion, for long conceptualised in Orientalising modes of thinking as all but timeless, now are widely seen as, in significant part, constructs of the era of colonial modernity. In addition, recent work on environmental history has highlighted the ways in which processes of "sedentarisation" (the spread of settled peasant agriculture into drier parts of the subcontinent) were stimulated by the colonial drive to enhance export of agricultural commodities. Such changes probably helped to extend and consolidate hierarchies of "official" religions, caste, and patriarchy.

That a crucial hardening of identities was happening during these decades is evident: what has been less often noticed is the logic of simultaneous development of many identity projects, which must have meant frequent interpenetrations, overlaps, and mutual undercutting. Thus the rise of regional, communal, or caste loyalties could weaken calls for "national" unity against foreign rule, and vice versa. To take a second instance, the consolidation of Brahmanical disciplines provoked counter-affirmations by subordinated caste formations. Simultaneous, multiple development, in other words, contributed to both a hardening and a potential fragility, of identities. One possible, indeed frequent, response, then became the projection of enemy "Others", through which differences being construed as "internal" to the group or community could be subordinated or suppressed.[6]

Bengal is the part of the subcontinent with which I am most familiar, and has been the field of much of my research. The choice of caste in conjunction with Bengal, however, might seem more puzzling, for the dominant language of politics today in the Indian state of West Bengal gives little space to it, in sharp contrast, for instance, to neighbouring Bihar.[7] Historical studies of caste correspondingly began rather late for colonial Bengal, but then there has come a spurt of valuable work in recent years, above all the research of Sekhar Bandopadhyay.[8]

My own interest in the history of caste in late-colonial Bengal has been quite belated. It had remained marginal, for instance, in the doctoral work I did on the Swadeshi phase of anti-colonial politics (1903–8) that I had basically built around multiple forms of emergent anti-colonial nationalism as complicated by questions of class.[9] The movement against Curzon's decision to partition Bengal in 1905 had

---

[6] Such processes have been most evident in relation to the development of nationalisms – both anti-colonial and religious or communal. For an important explication of this argument, see Pradip Kumar Datta, *Carving Blocs* (Delhi: Oxford University Press, 1999), chapter 1, and *passim*. See also Sumit Sarkar, "Identity and Difference: Caste in the Formation of the Ideologies of Nationalism and Hindutva", in idem, *Writing Social History*, chapter 9.

[7] Post-1947 Hindu minority migration has reduced the saliency of caste-based politics even more in Muslim-majority Bangladesh, the other part of the geographical area in focus here. Many of the movements I will touch upon were actually located for the most part in what is today Bangladesh.

[8] *Caste, Politics and the Raj: Bengal, 1872–1937* (Calcutta: K.P. Bagchi, 1990), and *Caste, Protest and Identity in Colonial India: The Namasudras of Bengal, 1872–1947* (Surrey: Curzon Press, 1997). See also the earlier work of Hitesranjan Sanyal, *Social Mobility in Bengal* (Calcutta: Papyrus, 1981); and Swaraj Basu, *Dynamics of a Caste Movement: The Rajbansis of North Bengal, 1910–1947* (Delhi: Manohar, 2003).

[9] "Swadeshi", meaning one's own country, is the term commonly used to describe the boycott of British imports and promotion of indigenous enterprise which became the key features of the middle-class protest against the Partition of Bengal.

evolved many new techniques that in some ways briefly anticipated the methods of Gandhian mass passive resistance of the 1920s and '30s. But it remained confined to a literati that was predominantly Hindu and rent-receiving, while in many regions (notably, the East Bengal countryside) the peasants whom they were exploiting happened to be Muslims. Mass participation, the prerequisite for effective passive resistance, consequently remained fairly limited, and the middle-class leadership never incorporated non-payment of taxes within its strategy of passive resistance. (It could have led to peasants in their turn refusing to pay rents to them.) The Swadeshi middle class added to its problems through shifting to an aggressively Hindu idiom (a characteristic of this "Extremist" phase of nationalism) and using coercive methods to make peasants give up imported cloth and salt, though these were cheaper than their indigenous substitutes. Meanwhile the emergent Muslim counter-elite in the new province of East Bengal and Assam was being attracted by the prospect of more jobs and state favours, in a classic pattern of divide-and-rule strategies playing effectively upon internal tensions. Hindu–Muslim clashes broke out in some East Bengal Hindu landlord estates in 1906–7. With mass support, always limited, ebbing away in face of some British repression, the more determined of the nationalists either went back to Moderate techniques or shifted to methods of conspiracy and individual violence: perspectives of mass passive resistance gave way to elitist revolutionary terrorism.[10]

I had been aware, of course, that the Hinduism of my middle-class protagonists had been overwhelmingly high caste in social composition and values,[11] and my narrative made passing references to

---

[10] The above is a very brief, and necessarily somewhat simplified, summary of the core argument of my *Swadeshi Movement in Bengal, 1903–1908* (New Delhi: People's Publishing House, 1973).

[11] The term commonly used to describe this literati, "*bhadralok*", signifies an amalgam of high-caste status (Brahmin, Vaidya, Kayastha)), rentier interests in land, and a "gentlemanly" style of living untainted by manual labour. The word "caste" has two indigenous referents: (i) "*varna*", the largely theoretical fourfold classification of Hindus into hierarchically situated Brahmans, Kshatriyas, Vaishyas, and Sudras, plus the lowest category of "Untouchables",

some lower-caste groups (notably, the Namasudras) that had shared the reservations of many Muslims. But I had felt little impulse then to try to construct autonomous narratives of caste formations and movements in something like their own terms, maybe perhaps in part because caste then had implicitly appeared little more than a distorted expression of class. More specifically, a considerable literature of tracts and pamphlets produced by lower-caste activists and organisations had then passed me by, even though I had used much more of regional language, non-official source material for my thesis than had been at all common at that time.

Going back to the research area of thirty years back has thus proved an experience both salutary and exciting. In particular – and this may help to explain the conjoining of Bengal and caste – my current research seems to be unearthing an interesting, and analytically helpful, pattern of ups and downs in the saliency of questions of caste within the public spheres constituted in the late-colonial era above all through the spread of vernacular print. I had referred a little while back to the apparent unimportance of caste in the recent politics of Bengal. It was surprising, therefore, to come across a census commissioner in 1901 stating that claims to higher status and disputes over questions of caste precedence were most numerous in "Bengal Proper" (i.e. the Bengali-speaking region), and not in the Bihar part of what then was the single province of Bengal Presidency.[12] The classified catalogue of printed Bengali texts in the India Office Library, London, lists only twenty-four entries under the "Castes and Tribes" category for the entire period up to 1905, but 140 titles are mentioned for 1905 and

---

"Scheduled Castes", or "Dalits"; (ii) each *varna* has many subdivisions, usually termed "*jatis*", between whom the barriers regarding intermarriage, interdining, etc., operate. *Jati* then is much the more common meaning of "caste" today, but claims to higher status often take the form of demands for recognition as being of a higher *varna*.

[12] "It is a curious circumstance that, with scarcely an exception, these claims to higher caste, or to new and more pretentious names, are confined to Bengal Proper." E.A. Gait, *Bengal Census Report, 1901* (Calcutta: Bengal Secretariat, 1903), p. 384.

1920, a big majority of them written by people of lower-caste origin, or in support of the claims of subordinated *jatis*. The corpus seems to have diminished again from around the mid 1920s.

The present essay forms part of still-unfinished research on the rise and decline of a "language" of caste in early-twentieth-century Bengal. Unlike the bulk of existing social-anthropological or historical work on caste, which understandably, in the interests of intensive study of a manageable corpus of data, has tended to concentrate on narratives of particular castes and caste movements (or interactions within a village or locality chosen for fieldwork), I am trying to develop a perspective that can fruitfully juxtapose higher- and lower-caste movements and texts, and foreground their interpenetrations and mutual conditionings.

Certain methodological corollaries are associated with this choice. Such an approach may help us go beyond a series of unhelpful polarities common in the current anthropological and historical literature on caste. One such opposition has been that between the Dumontian emphasis on structural harmony and consensus through effective and continuous Brahmanical ideological hegemony, and, as its polar opposite, a power / resistance binary model. Historians working within the Subaltern Studies paradigm have been particularly fond of the latter approach, which posits a total disjunction between the "domains" of high-caste power and subordinate autonomy.[13] My data, in contrast, indicates more complex patterns of selective appropriations and inversions, difficult to fit into either a model of successful integration or consensus, or of a totally distinct subaltern world.

A second, not unrelated, dualism has been that between essentialist and extreme "constructivist" approaches to caste. The initial Indological focus on "classical" ancient Sanskrit texts had tended to interpret caste in terms of a basically unchanging *varna* hierarchy, uniform

---

[13] The first effort to extend the "subalternist" approach to the study of caste began, significantly, with a critique of Dumont. Partha Chatterjee, "Caste and Subaltern Consciousness", in Ranajit Guha, ed., *Subaltern Studies VI* (Delhi: Oxford University Press, 1989).

across subcontinental space and time. Mid-twentieth-century structural-functionalist social anthropology, basing itself on fieldwork and participant observation, visualised a more mobile model, with *jatis* capable of moving up or down a fixed, hierarchical caste ladder through initiatives which M.N. Srinivas termed "sanskritising", imitating upper-caste rituals and social mores. In both approaches, however, the entities being studied, *varna* or *jati*, were assumed to be more or less given. In significant contrast, the recent counter-orthodoxy has emphasised the constructed or "imagined" nature of caste and other identities, their "invention" through colonial policies and / or discursive strategies – most notably, census classification and enumeration. The notions of construction deployed here have been somewhat simplistic and reductive. Engrossed in critiques of colonial discourse, recent scholarship has tended to underplay the significance of both indigenous agency, and conflicts more internal to colonised society not simply produced by colonialism.[14] But an emphasis on the fluidity of identities would remain central to my argument, too.

III

Caste was a minor theme in the discussions and debates within the vibrant public sphere that had been constituted in nineteenth-century Bengal through the coming of print. There were not many aggressive assertions of Brahmanical privilege, probably because there was still a virtual absence of subordinated-caste "voices" – in marked contrast with some other regions of British-ruled India, notably Maharashtra and Tamilnadu, where strong anti-Brahmanical movements had already emerged by the 1870s through the work of Jyotiba Phule and the beginnings of a "Dravidian" repudiation of "Aryan" Brahmans as outsiders.

---

[14] So much so that even drawing attention to such conflicts is occasionally being read as prima facie evidence of a pro-colonialist bias. For a recent, surprising, instance, see Nick Dirks' polemic against Chris Bayly and Cambridge South Asian scholarship in *Castes of Mind: Colonialism and the Making of Modern India* (New Delhi: Permanent Black, 2001), pp. 313–16.

The major reformist trend in Bengal, that associated with the Brahmo religious and social-reform movement founded by Rammohun Roy in the early nineteenth century, was critical of caste in principle but did little about it in practice. The intense intra-*bhadralok* debate that did develop between reformers and advocates of orthodoxy or revivalism focused rather upon the issues of polytheism and image-worship (violently denounced by Christian missionaries and Brahmos), and centrally on what by the mid nineteenth century had come to be termed *stri-swadhinata* (women's emancipation, or, more precisely, the "freeing" of women). This involved efforts, mainly initiated by men but gradually taken up also by women of similar social status who began entering the vernacular public sphere by the mid nineteenth century, to promote women's education, end sati, legalise widow-marriage, abolish polygamy, and restrict evils associated with child-marriage. Not much changed in actual social life: indeed, the practices being denounced by high-caste reformers were simultaneously often spreading downwards, being taken up by upwardly mobile caste groups eager to win respectability and higher status through "sanskritising" initiatives. But gender issues seem to have constituted the first site for the emergence of notions of individualised rights, with even the conservative defence of customs like sati combining textual arguments with a new insistence on the element of consent: the widow allegedly ascending the funeral pyre willingly, as against reformers who were accused of taking away the right to choose a heroic sacrificial death.[15] By the last quarter of the century, a backlash against reform in religious and social life, increasingly strengthened by emerging nationalist sentiments, counterposed against individual rights the superior claims of indigenous community solidarities. Reform was denounced as surrender to alien Western notions, while the community, predictably, was imagined along firmly hierarchised lines. This was also the era of maximum efficacy of what Partha Chatterjee in a much-quoted phrase called "the nationalist

---

[15] Tanika Sarkar, "A Pre-history of Rights? The Age of Consent Debates in Colonial Bengal", in idem, *Hindu Wife, Hindu Nation: Community, Religion and Cultural Nationalism* (Delhi: Permanent Black, 2001).

resolution of the womens' question".¹⁶ Reform through legislation by an alien state was opposed as involving the loss of what remained of indigenous cultural and religious autonomy, and debates in public about *stri-swadhinata* became rarer for a time.

The central conservative argument, at once conservative and communitarian, crystallised around the term *adhikaribheda:* differentiated claims to powers and privileges, making up a hierarchised yet harmonious entity in which each strata of religious belief and practice, caste and gender, would know its proper place and respect the duties and claims appropriate to its station in life. *Adhikaribheda* was pitted initially against Brahmo religious reform efforts and as refutation of claims to equal rights of women.¹⁷ Soon it would be refurbished to beat back lower-caste demands for higher status or denunciation of Brahmanical privilege. Meanwhile Orientalist scholarship – European, from William Jones onwards, and then also high-caste Indian – had helped to constitute a second line of argument that centred around the Aryan civilisational myth. The supposedly higher "Aryan" values, it came to be widely assumed, had gradually spread from the Indo-Gangetic valley southwards, conquering, or assimilating through peaceful cultural means, less civilised peoples and integrating them in appropriate places in a vast but unified hierarchy apexed by the "twice-born" higher castes. Caste hierarchy thus acquired a new and prestigious "historical" dimension. Lower-caste spokesmen in Maharashtra and Tamilnadu were quick to appropriate this myth in inverted form, asserting on its basis that the Brahmanical groups were alien invaders who had subjugated autochthonous original peoples. No

---

¹⁶ Partha Chatterjee, "The Nationalist Resolution of the Women's Question", in Kumkum Sangari and Sudesh Vaid, eds, *Recasting Women: Essays in Colonial History* (Delhi: Kali for Women, 1989); see also Partha Chatterjee, *The Nation and Its Fragments: Colonial and Postcolonial Histories* (Delhi: Oxford University Press, 1994), chapters 6, 7.

¹⁷ In an interesting debate in the pages of a Bengali monthly in 1884, a plea that women should have equal rights with men was refuted by the argument that every being did have a claim to specific powers (*adhikar*), but these were necessarily differentiated. Otherwise a horse would have the right to sit at the table, and a gentleman would not be able to ride on the shoulders of his palanquin-bearer. *Nabyabharat*, May–June / June–July 1884.

such inversion is noticeable, however, in Bengal lower-caste writings.

A "language" of caste suddenly became prominent from the early 1900s, with a proliferation of lower-caste pamphlets and memorials and simultaneous affirmations of high-caste privilege. This at first sight seems to confirm the kind of colonial impact / indigenous response model I questioned a while back. In 1901, Census Commissioner Risley ordered "*jatis*" to be hierarchically arranged in the census returns according to notions of social precedence prevalent in each locality, provoking a flood of claims and counter-claims, and providing a major stimulus to caste organisation. In 1910 his successor, Gait, attempted through a very controversial circular to define the category "Hindu" more precisely, seeking to exclude from it untouchable groups not allowed to enter temples or get served by respectable Brahman priests. The move aroused great resentment and fear in high-caste circles, much discussion about the proper definition of a Hindu, and, as we shall see, some efforts at ameliorative reforms from the top to maintain Hindu unity. It needs to be noted, though, that both these moves were short-lived. The 1911 census reverted to a simple alphabetical order, and the Gait circular was quickly withdrawn in face of *bhadralok* criticism. Efforts at upward mobility and claims to higher status certainly did not end, and indeed continued on a growing scale – even after independence, when from 1951 questions regarding caste stopped being asked in census enumeration.[18] Nor was census intervention entirely external to the society officialdom was trying to govern, define, and mould. Given the vast disproportion in numbers, the British could only rule through shifting structures of alliances with indigenous groups – most of the time of high-caste or elite-Muslim status, and these often provided significant inputs into "colonial knowledge". Thus Risley in 1901 had ordered caste classification in census returns "by social precedence as recognised by native public opinion" – to which Gait, then in charge of the Bengal census, added the practical gloss that "the decision must rest with enlightened public opinion, and not with public opinion generally".

[18] Except for the "Scheduled Castes" or Dalits, for whom the Indian constitution of 1950 established a system of reservations as a form of affirmative action.

The highly skewed nature of education and literacy ensured that the "enlightened" operationally meant the upper-caste literati alone.[19]

The new discursive prominence of caste was connected to a number of interrelated developments at both higher- and lower-caste levels, among which the census was only one determinant among several. Identities and traditions could also be invented from "below", autonomously. The beginnings of a Namasudra upthrust in parts of south-central Bengal, for instance, go back to the early 1870s, well before the decennial census, which began only in 1871, could have had any significant impact. Census status was seldom the sole or even major theme in the large number of lower-caste tracts published during the first decade of the new century, when the 1901 classificatory system was in operation.[20] More important than official policies, perhaps, was the spread of vernacular print culture downwards from its earlier *bhadralok* Hindu confines. The lower-caste tracts that started coming out in significant numbers from the early 1900s were often written by people living in villages, and printed in obscure small towns.[21] There was a parallel leap in the same period in

---

[19] *Census (India), 1901*, vol. I.1, p. 538; *Census (Bengal), 1901*, vol. VI.I, pp. 354, 378–84. A few sample figures regarding caste-differentiated literacy: in 1911 the three major high castes in Bengal, namely, Brahmans, Vaidyas, and Kayasthas, had vernacular literacy rates of 39.9 per cent, 53.2 per cent, and 30.9 per cent. The corresponding figure for Namasudras was 4.9 per cent. Sekhar Bandopadhyay, *Caste, Politics and the Raj*, op. cit., p. 109. Indigenous inputs into colonial knowledge have been attracting a lot of scholarly attention in recent years: see, for instance, Kapil Raj, "Circulation and the Emergence of Modern Mapping: Great Britain and Early Colonial India, 1764–1820", in Claude Markovits, *et al.*, eds, *Society and Circulation* (New Delhi: Permanent Black, 2003); Phillip B. Wagoner, "Precolonial Intellectuals and the Production of Colonial Knowledge", *Comparative Studies in Society and History*, 45.iv, October 2003.

[20] Five out of a sample of seven Namasudra tracts published between 1909 and 1943 that I have studied in detail did not mention the census at all: see "Identities and Histories: Some Lower-Caste Tracts from Early Twentieth-century Bengal", in Sumit Sarkar, *Beyond Nationalist Frames*, chapter II.

[21] There was a parallel leap in the same period of Muslim pamphlets written by equally obscure rural or small-town authors.

the number of Muslim pamphlets written by equally obscure village or small-town authors. This spread was related to a gradual expansion of literacy: even the 4.9 per cent Namasudra vernacular literates of 1911 represented a considerable advance over the 3.3 per cent reported in 1901.[22] And both processes were underwritten by a long-term boom in the prices of jute exports, from *c.* 1907 till the mid 1920s, which provided a brief "new frontier of opportunity" for those sections of peasants who had sufficient resources to benefit from the processes of export-led commercialisation of the late-colonial era. The major jute-growing areas of Bengal were located in the eastern, south-central, and northern parts of the province, where the bulk of the rural population was either Muslim, or lower-caste Hindu (notably, the Namasudras in the south, and the Rajbansis in the northern districts). The "frontier" was operative also for some of the Mahishyas of south-west Bengal, who in addition were located in relative proximity to Calcutta and some of whom were moving into small business and professions.[23] There does seem to be a significant coincidence of dates here with the period of maximum proliferation of both lower-caste and Muslim vernacular pamphlets. For the frontier of opportunity proved short-lived: a secular decline in world agricultural prices set in from *c.* 1925–6, presaging the devastating Depression years of the 1930s, and affecting most of all the upper stratum of peasants who had gone in for export-driven commercialised agriculture.

The high-caste bhadralok responded in two major ways to what by the early 1900s was perceived as a threat from social levels about which they had been quite unconcerned earlier. There was a much more aggressive assertion of Brahmanical hegemony and hierarchy. In 1900, for instance, Jogendrachandra Ghosh, prominent zamindar and lawyer, published a treatise interestingly entitled *Brahmanism and the Sudra, or the Indian Labour Problem*. Ghosh was a great admirer of the more socially conservative aspects of the Positivism of Comte, and headed the Calcutta Positivist Society. He argued in this text

---

[22] Sekhar Bandopadhyay, *Caste, Protest and Identity*, op. cit.

[23] Sugata Bose, *Agrarian Bengal: Economy, Social Structure and Politics, 1919–1947* (Cambridge: Cambridge University Press, 1986), pp. 46, 63–4.

for an alliance between Western-educated Positivist intellectuals like himself, and traditional Brahman "pandits", who together would develop a kind of "Hindu self-government" in social and religious matters, while remaining strictly loyal to the British political authority. This was needed, he argued, particularly because there was already a possibility of a "dangerous upheaval from the lower depths of Hindu society... The discipline effected by the Rishis [ancient sages] and Brahmans in the heart and mind of the women and the masses was threatened by dangerous ideas coming from the West... things like Trade Unions and Socialism... strikes, pickets, etc." Cultural nationalism thus became the site for a refurbishing of hegemonies of caste and patriarchy, a note that became prominent during the peak of the Swadeshi upsurge, when it became common form to operate with a state / society dichotomy somewhat reminiscent of Slavophile ideas, with the latter exalted as the domain of a freedom which was however strictly hierarchised. The *Dawn,* an influential periodical of the Swadeshi years, stated bluntly in August 1903 that "in all ages and by virtue of a law of nature, there shall be inequalities between man and man", while Jogendrachandra Ghosh in 1900 concluded his treatise with a plea for "freedom at least in the regions of social and historical theory", blissfully unaware that he had just illuminated the ambiguities of that "freedom". In 1911, one of Bengal's biggest landlords, Brojendrakishore Raychaudhuri of Gauripur, inaugurated a Brahman Sabha in Calcutta with a speech deploring the prevalent "social anarchy" and defending Brahmanical privilege in unambiguous and aggressive terms. His arguments found an echo in less sophisticated language from a tract written by a totally obscure village schoolteacher the same year.[24] Aggressive conservatism

---

[24] Brojendrakishore Roychaudhuri, *Brahman Sabhay Bakrita* (Calcutta, 1911); Chintaharan Chattopadhyay, *Brahman* (Faridpur, 1911). Brojendrakishore, it may be added, had been a major patron of the Swadeshi movement – so much so that at one stage the government had considered taking action against him. "Conduct of zamindars of Gauripur in connection with the political agitation in Mymensingh district. Proposed attachment of their estates under Regulation III of 1818", Government of India Home Political A, February 1908, n. 102–3.

of this kind, it may be added, had often a close connection with open defence of landlord interests. We meet the Brahman Sabha again in 1940, vociferously opposing even the slightest reduction in the authority of zamindars over tenants. Concessions to sharecroppers who by then had become the actual cultivators of the soil in many areas also aroused great resentment.[25]

More significant ultimately, however, was a second strand where privilege was sought to be maintained in modified forms through a judicious measure of reform from top downwards, combined with the projection of an external Other, usually the Muslim. The key statement here was made by U.N. Mukherji, a well-connected Calcutta gentleman who in June 1909 wrote a series of articles in the pages of the leading Moderate-nationalist newspaper *Bengalee* under the very evocative title of "Hindus: A Dying Race". Mukherji began with some census data and projections from 1891 onwards that seemed to indicate a relative decline in the proportion of Hindus to Muslims in Bengal, attributed this to the wretched conditions of the lower castes as contrasted to the supposedly more virile, energetic, and prosperous Muslim peasants, and urged paternalistic upliftment at Brahmanical initiative as the means to Hindu survival, unity, and rejuvenation.[26] The importance of these articles, quickly reprinted as a pamphlet, lay in their multiple possible implications and appropriations. The title and general tenor of Mukherji's articles were clearly directed towards building Hindu unity under a refurbished high-caste leadership to counter the Muslim threat. Social reform was given a new caste upliftment emphasis largely absent earlier, but was simultaneously appropriated to a vision of inevitable biological rivalry between Hindus and Muslims, and consequent need for Hindu unity under reformed, but still high-caste, leadership. Mukherji here struck

---

[25] Bangiya Brahman Sabha's reply to a questionnaire circulated by the Bengal Land Revenue (Floud) Commission, *Report of the Land Revenue Commission, Bengal* (Alipur, 1940), vol. VI, pp. 409–33.

[26] The seminal importance of Mukherji was grasped first by Pradip Kumar Datta: see his "'Dying Hindu': Production of Hindu Communal Commonsense in Early 20th Century Bengal", *Economic and Political Weekly*, 19 June 1993, and idem, *Carving Blocs*, op. cit., chapter 1.

a note that has remained central to Hindu chauvinist and communal tendencies right down to the present. Yet he had also been sharply critical of high-caste neglect of subordinated castes, and highlighted the plight of the latter. What was for him no more than the means to a different end could become the primary purpose in other discursive strands. An undeservedly forgotten Brahman reformer, Digindranarayan Bhattacharya, spent the first three decades of the new century speaking and writing voluminously against Brahmanical domination and caste hierarchy, and addressing numerous lower-caste gatherings. His *Jatibheda* (Caste Distinctions, 1912) included quotations from Mukherji's analysis of census data, but went on to directly attack the basic principle of *adhikaribheda* in the name of an assertion of equal rights.[27] And there was also a possibility of actual lower-caste appropriations, as when Manindranath Mandal, a Pod,[28] wrote a biography of Digindranarayan hailing him as comparable to the Buddha, Chaitanya, and Muhammad.[29] Mandal in 1922 tried to set up a kind of united front of a whole range of lower-caste organisations. His own account of what proved to be a short-lived initiative mentioned that U.N. Mukherji had tried to dissuade him from such an experiment, but the move had been welcomed by Digindranarayan.[30] Yet it should be noted that the intersections between the strands of reform and lower-caste assertion as well as Hindu (or

---

[27] "God", Digindranarayan argued, has given "the same powers to all human beings, just as he has made the same sun for Brahmans and Chandals." *Jatibheda* (Faridpur, 1912), pp. 4–5.

[28] A lower-caste group spread over several districts of south-west and south Bengal.

[29] Manindranath Mandal, *Bange Digindranarayan* (Calcutta, 1927). Chaitanya, the medieval devotional saint, had the reputation of being sympathetic towards lower castes, and Buddhism of course rejected caste in principle. More surprising is the reference to Muhammad, particularly because the biography was published soon after bitter Hindu–Muslim riots during 1926 in Calcutta and many other parts of Bengal.

[30] Manindranath Mandal, *Bangiya Jana Sangha / Bengal People's Association* (Calcutta, 1923). A pamphlet giving details about this effort to float an umbrella organisation of Bengal's low-caste groups, it was dedicated to Digindranarayan.

anti-colonial nationalist) hegemonising moves could run both ways. Digindranarayan for some time in the late 1920s and early '30s was active also in the Hindu Mahasabha, an organisation with a marked anti-Muslim slant.

For the high-caste Hindu bhadralok, then, the hopes aroused by the Swadeshi years were quickly followed by a sense of insecurity, with the simultaneous rise of Muslim political groups and unprecedented lower-caste activism, both encouraged to some extent by the British. There was also an important class dimension. There is an exact coincidence of dates between Mukherji's serialised essays in *Bengalee* and an article by a district lawyer from East Bengal in another pro-nationalist journal, the *Modern Review*. Entitled "What Can be Done for the Namasudras", this urged the upper castes to go in for a series of ameliorative efforts similar to Mukherji's suggestions, but also went on to explain the urgency for such reform specifically in terms of an agrarian, anti-landlord agitation by Namasudras. "Egged on by their half-educated brethren", the latter had started a "misguided and suicidal agitation", cutting off connections with high castes and even ceasing to cultivate "the lands of the higher class Hindu landlords as *barga* [sharecropper] tenants".[31]

A broad correspondence between religious-cum-caste and class differences has been one of the more obvious features of early twentieth-century Bengal history. Rabindranath Tagore, to cite one notable contemporary instance, drew pointed attention in a number of his post-Swadeshi writings to the vast gap between the upper-caste Hindu landed gentry and Muslim or lower-caste rural masses.[32] But

[31] Binod Lal Ghosh, "What Can be Done for the Namasudras", *Modern Review*, June 1909.

[32] Tagore had enthusiastically espoused the Swadeshi agitation for some years, but then, from around 1907, turned sharply against it in the twin contexts of communal riots and revolutionary terrorist violence. The criticism was expressed through a number of essays and two famous novels, *Gora* (1907–9) and *Ghare Baire* (Home and the World), and developed into a most perceptive critique of nationalism itself. For more details, see Sarkar, *Swadeshi Movement in Bengal*, chapter 2, and "Nationalism and Stri-Swadhinata: The Contexts and Meanings of Rabindranath's *Ghare Baire*", in idem, *Beyond Nationalist Frames*, chapter 5.

the divide has been usually presented as a kind of historical constant, which does not really explain the evident sharpening of agrarian, caste, and communal conflict at particular times and places, as in the Swadeshi and post-Swadeshi years. Here some recent economic-historical research into shifts in Bengal agrarian relations is quite illuminating. The work of Nariaki Nakazato has revealed that the early years of the twentieth century had been marked by a major drive on the part of land-owning groups to shift from extraction of cash rents from tenants to produce-rent paying, sharecropping forms of surplus appropriation from the actual cultivators.[33] Peasant resistance against zamindars in course of the nineteenth century had led to a measure of tenancy protection (the rent acts of 1859 and 1885), by which landlord powers of rent enhancement and eviction had been somewhat curtailed as far as cash rents were concerned. But sharecropping was not subject to such legal restrictions, and in addition agrarian prices were rising in the early twentieth century due to the export boom. The gentry, some of them also traders in agricultural produce, consequently stood to gain from a shift from cash to produce rents. Both the old kind of landlords and tenure-holders, most of them high-caste *bhadralok* and upwardly mobile sections of peasants (usually Muslims, or some among the better-off lower-caste Hindus) who had won some protection through tenancy laws and were now often leasing out some of their lands, participated in this *barga* drive. Matters tended to come to a head particularly during settlement operations, when the British tried to gather precise information about and so regulate rural relationships. Settlement officers were empowered by Section 40 of the 1885 act to allow the commutation of produce into money rents, and, in an era of rising prices, it was in the obvious interest of the actual cultivators to pay rents in money rather than in kind.

The old kind of zamindar–peasant conflict was thus getting complicated through the new line of division between diverse kinds of landholding groups (zamindars, *bhadralok* tenure-holders, sec-

---

[33] Nariaki Nakazato, *Agrarian System in Eastern Bengal, c.1870–1910* (Calcutta, 1994).

tions of richer peasants usually of lower-caste status) and sharecroppers (*bargadars* or *bhagchasis*, to use the Bengali terms). There were conjunctures now when landlords and the tenant upper stratum (often generically called *jotedars* in Bengal) could combine against sharecroppers or agricultural labourers. The caste movements of Namasudras, Mahishyas, and Rajbansis, as they unfolded during these decades, bore the marks of these intersecting lines of conflict. Caste, we shall see, was both strengthened by class, and disrupted by it at times.

IV

The trajectories of Namasudras, Mahishyas, and Rajbansis provide interesting material for a measure of comparative history, for the three were located in significantly contrasting ecological and socio-economic contexts, and their movements developed varied and shifting relationships with alternative strands of anti-colonial and religious nationalist politics, class tensions, and gender-related problems.

IV.1

Among the three, the Namasudras were the most subordinated and the poorest. Their superiors and officials called them "Chandals", a term indicating very low, untouchable status, till their own efforts won them the more respectable designation. Living in the deltaic region of southern and south-central Bengal, many of them in course of the nineteenth century had achieved a measure of upward mobility, transiting from fishermen and boatmen towards settled agriculture by reclaiming potentially very fertile land along the expanding frontier of the active Ganga delta, clearing forests and swamps through their own arduous efforts. The Gopalganj subdivision of Faridpur district, where a fifth of all the Namasudras of Bengal lived, had been transformed by 1921 from a vast swamp into a region with a population density of 858 per sq. mile.[34] Gopalganj, which became the

[34] A British account dated 1852 had described the "Chandals" as "fish-sellers, ploughmen, coolies and slaves", but the 1901 census found 77.94 per cent of them engaged in agricultural occupations. These were further

centre of Namasudra religious and political upthrust, was located on an important riverine trade route linking East Bengal jute and rice-exporting regions with Calcutta. Upward mobility must have added to internal variations – indeed "Chandal" probably indicated not an unified distinct caste but people of diverse occupations and incomes called by this derogatory epithet by their social superiors, since they shared a roughly similar, despised social position. The first recorded movement among them, in 1872–3, had been provoked by Kayasthas and other high castes spurning an invitation to a funeral feast extended to them by a rich Chandal villager. Some Chandals then went on to withdraw agricultural services from their higher-caste superiors.[35] A generation later, Namasudra pamphlets were still complaining repeatedly about the habit among many "Brahmans, Vaidyas, and Kayasthas" of abusing them, calling them "Chandals".

The census for Namasudra and other lower-caste publicists was a resource rather than the primary impulse, of some help in the assertion of an identity which would be both unitary and more respectable. Such affirmation was bound up with the imagining of a history grounded in pure lineage: in the Namasudra case, the alleged descent from the union of a Brahman sage with a Sudra mother.[36]

---

subdivided into 1.15 per cent rent receivers, 95.71 per cent tenant farmers, and 3.56 per cent field labourers. Sekhar Bandopadhyay, *Caste, Protest, and Identity*, op. cit., pp. 20–1.

[35] Report of W.L. Owen, District Superintendent of Police, to District Magistrate, Faridpur, No. 66, Camp Bhanga, 18 March 1873: Government of Bengal, Judicial Proceedings, March 1873, n. 173. The Chandals also protested about the official practice of delegating the work of cleaning latrines in prisons to them alone. This, they claimed, went against the government promise "to treat all castes on terms of equality". It is interesting to see the conflict between an incipient notion of equal rights and *adhikaribheda* emerge at such an early date at a level very different from that of *bhadralok* society.

[36] Brahmanical codes accepted this as a more respectable kind of marriage than the case of a high-caste woman having relations with a lower-caste man: interesting evidence of double standards, as well as the interrelationships of caste and patriarchal order. "Chandals" had been defined as offsprings of the illicit union of a Brahmin woman with a Shudra man by the authoritative ancient Brahmanical text *Manusamhita*.

"Histories" of this kind constituted a major part of the Namasudra texts that began to be published from the early 1900s. The winning of more respectable status required also what the sociologist M.N. Srinivas called "sanskritising" social change: the imitation of higher-caste norms, in particular the takeover of Brahmanical customs like abstention from meat or liquor, the seclusion of women, early marriage, and a taboo on widow-remarriage. Many of these norms related to the tighter disciplining of women. The 1872–3 movement had as one of its several strands an effort to stop Chandal women from going to village markets as petty traders, which their menfolk now considered degrading. More was involved perhaps in such moves than "imitation". By an easy association of ideas, the insistence on pure descent spilled over into such patriarchal projects, among the Namasudras as well as a host of similar lower-caste movements right down to current times. Genealogical purity seemed to demand tighter control over the potentially liminal domain of feminine sexuality.[37]

But there was more to the Namasudra assertion than these conventional aspects, and these help us to understand the relative stability and persistent autonomy of their movement – in partial contrast, we will see, to those of the Mahishyas and the Rajbansis. Unlike the others, it was associated with a dissident religious sect, that of the Matuas, which developed also around the 1870s. This was led successively by two Namasudras, Harichand and then his son Guruchand "Thakur", inhabitants of Orakandi, a river port in Gopalganj. We are in the privileged position here of having access to two "internal" documents, in the form of a couple of long metrical hagiographies, along with a number of Matua songs.[38] The hagiographies are particularly

---

[37] I owe this point to Pradip Kumar Datta, *Carving Blocs*, p. 161.
[38] Tarakchandra Sarkar, *Sri Sri Harileelamrita* (Faridpur, 1916; Khulna, 1924), and Mahananda Haldar, *Guruchand Carit* (Khulna, 1943). Sekhar Bandopadhyay pioneered the historical study of the Matuas: see his "Popular Religion and Social Mobility in Colonial Bengal: The Matua Sect and the Namasudras", in Rajat Kanta Ray, ed., *Mind, Body and Society: Life and Mentality in Colonial Bengal* (Calcutta: Oxford University Press, 1995), and *Caste, Protest and Identity*, op.cit. I have attempted a more detailed discussion of these and some other lower-caste writings in my "Identities and Histories:

interesting because they indicate a number of significant shifts over time, as well as certain internal tensions. *Harileelamrita* appears more like a conventional devotional (bhakti) religious narrative, replete with stories of miracles and emphasising a piety which sometimes seems to transcend caste and even religious boundaries through ecstatic song and moments of communitas. Members of the Matua community were instructed to ignore caste rules: conversely, many passages particularly in the earlier hagiography describe even upper-caste people joining Harichand's movement. Namasudra identity politics, about which *Harileelamrita* is virtually silent, comes to the fore in the second text, which is also much more matter-of-fact and makes no claims that its hero performed miracles. The Matua message rather, has now become a combination of piety and work almost reminiscent of a puritan ethic.[39] This goes along with an oft-repeated insistence on education and enterprise. Very appropriate for a long-subordinated group now striving for a degree of upward mobility, the combination figures prominently in many other lower-caste as well as rural Muslim writings of the same era. An entrepreneurial streak had been mentioned in passing even in the metrical biography of Harichand, who is said to have miraculously grown double crops on his land, started an oil shop, and advised his followers to turn to trade. *Guruchand Carit* is much more detailed, with a whole section devoted to its hero's business activities. Guruchand had very successfully entered the riverine trade of Orakandi in rice, jute, and mustard seeds, and also gave loans to poorer peasants: not exploiting them unlike other moneylenders, we are assured, for he was kind enough to cancel the debts of those who surrendered their lands to him![40]

It is in the account of educational efforts, however, that the class sub-text often hinted at in these Matua writings comes to the

---

Some Lower-caste Narratives from Early Twentieth-century Bengal", in *Beyond Nationalist Frames*, chapter 2.

[39] The oft-repeated formula is *"hate kam mukhe nam"*, work and recite the holy name. There were anticipations of this in some passages of the earlier text, but the additional phrase used then, *"bhakti-ee prabal"* (devotion is mightiest), is now absent.

[40] *Harileelamrita*, pp. 49–51; *Guruchand Carit*, p. 100, and *passim*.

surface, in a foregrounding of exploitation – quickly followed by its tacit appropriation into the counter-elite project of a Namasudra upper stratum. Guruchand's efforts to start a high school at Orakandi around 1907 is justified in terms of the advantage that landlords and moneylenders were taking of Namasudra illiteracy, tricking them in everyday matters of rent or debt-payment receipts. Guruchand's plan for a school was bitterly opposed by the local Kayastha bhadralok, for the latter, we are told, were afraid that their sharecroppers and servants would no longer work for them, once educated. The bhadralok are reported to be saying that Namasudra education would disrupt the age-old principle of *adhikaribheda*, as enshrined notably in the ancient epic Ramayana. In the end a school was set up through help given by a Christian missionary, the Australian Baptist Mead, who also had good contacts with British officials. The text emphasised that this was an entirely tactical move: very few Matuas converted to Christianity. Around the same time, Guruchand is described as using a class-based argument to dissuade some Namasudras who, it seems, had been on the point of joining the Swadeshi movement. The rich educated men, he reminded them, can never be friends of the poor: "If a poor man accompanies a rich person, it is the first who carries the luggage..."[41] Yet this detailed exposure of class oppression culminates in a section, entitled "Namasudra Awakening, 1907", where all that happens is some relatives of Guruchand, along with a few others, manage to get minor administrative jobs through Mead's intercession with British officials. Upward mobility continued at an accelerating pace for the leading core. Guruchand's grandson, P.R. Thakur, obtained a barrister's degree in Britain and eventually became a member of the Constituent Assembly of independent India. *Harileelamrita* had been composed by a village poet who was able to get it published only through carefully listed small donations from fellow members of the Matua community. The author of *Guruchand Carit*, in sharp contrast, was an urban lawyer, and its copyright was held by P.R. Thakur. The bulk of the Namasudras, of course, remained as poor and subordinated as before.

Even more significant are certain silences. The hagiographies (the

[41] *Guruchand Carit,* pp. 140–6, 173–4.

second of which does refer to many historical events unconnected with devotional matters), as well as the other Namasudra tracts I have seen, contain no reference either to the 1872–3 withdrawal of services to high-caste landholders, or the 1907–9 movement of sharecroppers for commutation of produce into money-rent. For these we have to turn to official documents, which happen to be exceptionally rich for the latter period. Matters had then come to a head in the Gaurnadi police station area of Bakarganj, a district adjoining Faridpur, and located close to the Namasudra heartland. Many of the Gaurnadi peasants and sharecroppers were Namasudras, while the region also had an unusually heavy bhadralok small-landlord concentration, and a particularly oppressive form of produce-rent. Gaurnadi, further, was a stronghold of the Swadeshi movement, being the ancestral home of one of its most respected leaders, the schoolteacher-cum-petty landlord Aswinikumar Datta. Settlement operations were going on in this area from 1903–4, and the local British official, J.C. Jack, seems to have developed a degree of empathy with the plight of the sharecroppers. It reminded him, he stated in one report, of Arthur Young's account of the Metayer system in pre-Revolutionary France. Jack felt it was his duty to inform the Gaurnadi peasants and sharecroppers of the provision for commutation during the settlement operations, and this led to a flood of applications: 1164 of these came between June and August 1908, and the special officer Jack had appointed for that purpose granted commutation into money-rent to all but thirty of them. The alarm of the bhadralok gentry quickly expressed itself through petitions by "pleaders and Brahmin priests" to Jack's official superiors, as well as through a newspaper campaign by the local nationalist weekly, *Barisal Hitaishi*. In an interesting instance of class affinity proving stronger even than race, Jack was pulled up by his official superiors and commutations were discouraged. The sharecropper movement continued for some months, but then died away.[42]

[42] The main source is J.C. Jack, *Bakarganj Settlement Report, 1900–08* (Calcutta, 1915), Appendix G. This contains the entire correspondence between Jack and his superior officers concerning the commutation issue over which he had been pulled up by his superiors, and seems to have been his

The total silence of the extant Namasudra printed literature about this episode is not surprising. Its writers, and targeted readers, would obviously belong to the literate upper stratum of the community, and not the poorer Namasudra peasants or sharecroppers. Even tenancy reform issues, bearing on landlord–peasant and not peasant–sharecropper relationships, evoked little interest. The All Bengal Namasudra Association did not even bother to reply to the questionnaire circulated by the Floud Commission of 1938–40.[43] In 1909, in the 1920s, and then on a much bigger scale in the Communist-led Tebhaga movement of 1946–7, sharecropper movements developed in many parts of Bengal, often with some Namasudra participation, around the recurrent demands for two-thirds share of the produce (for which the Bengali term is *tebhaga*). There was no response from the leaders or activists of caste-identity politics. And the growing conservatisation of dominant groups in the Namasudra movement – what Sekhar Bandopadhyay has termed the displacement of initial protest by tendencies towards "accommodation" – expressed itself also in matters of Matua religious practices and family and gender norms. The closing sections of *Guruchand Carit* reveal the Matuas as increasingly adopting high-Hindu gods and rituals, contrary to the earlier thrust towards rejection of conventional religious-cum-caste practices. The *Harileelamrita* had occasionally referred to women participating actively and as equals in Matua congregational occasions. Collections of Matua songs published in the late twentieth century, in

---

way of making a quiet appeal to posterity. (Such correspondence is seldom included in other administrative reports of this kind.) See also *Barisal Hitaishi*, 3 August, 17 August, 7 September 1908: translated excerpts in Report of Native Papers (Eastern Bengal and Assam), for the relevant weeks. For a more detailed account of this episode, see my "Intimations of Hindutva: Ideologies, Caste and Class in Post-Swadeshi Bengal", in Sarkar, *Beyond Nationalist Frames*, chapter 3.

[43] *Report of Land Revenue Commission,* op. cit., vol. II, pp. 17–18. Other organisations which failed to respond included the All Bengal Scheduled Caste Federation and the Muslim League, though all of them had been classified by the commission among "Associations concerned with tenants".

sharp contrast, insist on the subordination of wives to their husbands and other conventional family norms.[44]

Despite such fissures, Namasudra caste politics was able to retain a solidarity and independence rather unusual for Bengal, maybe because internal differentiation, while growing, was less than among Mahishyas and Rajbansis, and the Matua cult could still provide a common rallying point. Persistent hostility towards the bhadralok gentry, in a situation where very few Namasudras were able to rise into the landlord class (which was overwhelmingly upper-caste Hindu in this part of Bengal), kept most of them away from both anti-colonial and Hindu-identity forms of nationalism. There was even an occasional tilt towards Muslim formations on the part of some Namasudra politicians. Here significant contrasts emerge with the trajectories of the other two major Bengal movements of subordinated castes, of Mahishyas and Rajbansis.

IV.2

Like "Namasudra", "Mahishya" was a new, more prestigious designation, sought and won through petitioning the census authorities by people claiming to speak on behalf of a community earlier known as Chasi Kaibarta. Their main concentration is in the south-western Bengal district of Midnapur (with spillovers across the Bhagirathi into the western part of the delta region and a growing influx also into the environs of Calcutta). Like the Namasudras, again, there is a history here of transition from fishing towards agricultural occupations. But with the Mahishyas this had begun at a much earlier date and had produced, by the nineteenth century or perhaps even before, a growing social distinction between "Jele" (the fishermen), and the "Hele" (cultivators, from "hal", plough) or "Chasi" Kaibartas, with the latter determined to demarcate themselves from their less successful

---

[44] For more details, see Sekhar Bandopadhyay, "Popular Religion and Social Mobility in Colonial Bengal: The Matua Sect and the Namasudras", in Rajat Kanta Ray, ed., *Mind, Body and Society: Life and Mentality in Colonial Bengal* (Calcutta: Oxford University Press, 1995), and idem, *Caste, Protest and Identity,* op. cit., chapter 2, and *passim*.

former caste brethren in a manner that one does not see with the Namasudras.[45] And while only 1.15 per cent of the Namasudras had been entered as rent receivers in the 1911 census (as against 95.7 per cent tenant-farmers and 3.56 per cent field labourers), the *Midnapur District Gazetteer* of the same year described a very different situation, with Mahishyas showing a substantial presence among "all interests in land ranging from the proprietor to the cultivator." The bhadralok, again, were rather thin on the ground in south-west Bengal: their proportion to the total Hindu population according to the 1931 census was 184 per 1000 in Faridpur, but only 71 in Midnapur.[46] There was less coincidence, therefore, between class and caste distinctions in Midnapur, while the relatively thin local presence of the three higher castes could also have reduced the intensity of caste conflict. A counterbalancing factor, however, was that many clerical and professional jobs in the small towns of the Mahishya belt had come to be held by educated bhadralok trained in nearby Calcutta, leading to resentments among the rapidly developing Mahishya counter-elite. Mahishya vernacular literacy, it needs to be added, while low, was still considerably higher than among Namasudras: 10.9 per cent as compared to 4.9 per cent by the 1911 census.

Such structural dimensions help to explain three key features of the Mahishya movement: an early beginning (and one mainly through the medium of print, quite unlike the initial Chandal withdrawal of agricultural services); a relatively moderate style and stance, virtually throughout; and an accommodation into "mainstream" bhadralok-led currents that was easier, quicker, and more nearly complete than with the Namasudras. This was helped by their somewhat higher

---

[45] The Namasudras had resented being called Chandals, but they did not go through an internal bifurcation whereby a poorer section was left branded by that pejorative term.

[46] L.S.S. O'Malley, *Midnapur District Gazetteer* (Calcutta, 1911), p. 58; *Census, 1911, 1931*. The exact figures should be taken with some reservation, keeping in mind not only possible errors in enumeration but also the way in which categories in pre-industrial rural society tend to overlap. A small tenant, for instance, quite commonly had to work also as sharecropper or labourer on someone else's land for survival.

ritual position as compared to the Namasudras: unlike them, they were *jalacharanya,* from whom high castes would accept water (the basic line of caste distinction in Bengal). An additional, so far little-noticed factor, could also have contributed to the moderate, strictly "sanskritising", form of the Mahishya upthrust. This is the prominence in it of the "Varna", "Patit", or "degraded Brahmans": ritual experts serving the Mahishyas, and therefore looked down upon and considered ritually impure by high castes. Poor Brahmans were often tempted to offer such services covertly to noveaux riche families from other lower castes too, as can be seen from contemporary tracts and literary representations – but the phenomenon seems to have been more common in relation to the Mahishyas.[47] Social-cum-ritual ascent of the community they were serving was necessary if such degraded Brahmins themselves were to acquire respectability and recognition from high-caste society, and a high proportion of the Mahishya tracts were written by them, or emphasised their grievances and demands.[48] Such groups are likely to have acted as carriers of Brahmanical norms and practices, and so enhanced moderate, assimilationist or sanskritising tendencies.

Mahishya tracts appear to have been considerably more numerous than Namasudra ones in the early twentieth century. There were also a number of journals specifically devoted to the Mahishya cause, like the *Mahishya Sevika*. Most of them have a fairly formal style and are replete with quotations from ancient texts. Verse, prominent in the Namasudra literature and obviously geared to a partly or wholly non-literate audience, is also quite rare. Namasudra pamphlets, even while putting forward quite moderate claims for recognition of higher status, sometimes tend to slip into more aggressive rhetorical flourishes attacking *bhadralok* behaviour: such extreme language is largely absent in the Mahishya literature. There is, in its place, the

---

[47] Those who have seen Satyajit Ray's *Pather Panchali* might recall the desperately poor Brahman villager Harihar, trying to survive through giving some lower-caste men the sacred thread which is the principal marker of "twice-born", high-caste status.

[48] Seven out of the fifteen Mahishya tracts that I have personally seen fall into this category.

frequent complaint that mainstream high Bengali literature has been unfair to the Mahishyas, mixing them up wrongly with the lowly Jele Kaibarta and often slandering them. This is a theme missing in Namasudra writing: its readers and authors would have had little acquaintance with such exalted *bhadralok* worlds. Another key theme in Mahishya tracts was the need to impose tighter patriarchal norms and restrictions on women, with a journal specifically targeted for a feminine audience and edited by a woman, coming out from 1911. This urged Mahishya women to help the cause through devotion to wifely and maternal duties, and particularly through imparting proper training to their children. They were advised to follow strictly the commands of their husbands and parents-in-law in all matters.[49]

Mahishya tract writers, otherwise so determined to align themselves with high-caste *bhadralok* values, departed from that script in one major way. Like in many other lower-caste and rural Muslim writings, claims to higher status (in the case of the Mahishyas, usually that of Kshatriya) are combined with much praise of the virtues of agricultural enterprise and labour: precisely the things which traditional upper-caste society has despised, so much so that there is a widespread ritual taboo on the Brahman touching the plough. "Men of peasant class form the real basis of Hindu society", proclaims a typical Mahishya text.

But terms like "peasant" or "labour" are seldom free of ambiguity in the corpus I am reviewing. It is often unclear whether the labour of sub-tenants, sharecroppers, or agricultural labourers is not being quietly annexed to the figure of the landholding, reasonably prosperous, and upwardly mobile peasant which is central to the Mahishya movement and its self-image. The Mahishya tracts were not immune from the class tensions stimulated by the early-twentieth-century spread of sharecropping, notably in the Contai and Tamluk subdivisions of south-east Midnapur. Here coastal land once used for salt manufacture had been leased by the British in large blocks to *chakdars* using sharecroppers. In a move reminiscent of what was happen-

---

[49] Krishnabhabini Biswas, ed., *Mahishya-Mahila*, pt I (Calcutta, July, 1911), pp. 6–8.

ing in Gaurnadi around the same time, local British settlement officers tried to initiate some moves to provide security of tenure to such *bhagchasis*.[50] The Namasudra texts, we have seen, had kept silent about such conflicts: the Mahishya response was more vocal and aggressive in its defence of the privileges of the *chakdars*, and of landholders against sharecroppers and subordinate tenants in general. For months on end during 1909, *Nihar*, the local Contai weekly which was edited by a Mahishya, published a long series of essays attacking every move by settlement officials to improve sharecropper conditions. It vehemently opposed recourse to Section 40 of the 1885 Act to commute produce into money-rent, as well as the grant to sharecroppers of documents (*parchas*) that could formalise their status and conditions. All such moves were denounced as part of a gigantic effort to "convert mere cultivators into tenants."[51]

Where Midnapur came to differ most obviously from the Namasudra regions of south-central Bengal was the way anti-colonial nationalism here was able to effect a junction with, and largely absorb, the movement for caste-based upward mobility. Swadeshi in Midnapur, as elsewhere, had remained an affair of the educated bhadralok of the district headquarters and some other towns, turning early into revolutionary terrorism and leaving the Mahishya countryside unaffected. A significant change came about, however, through the Gandhian Non-Cooperation Movement of 1921–2, led very effectively in Midnapur by Birendranath Sasmal, prosperous Mahishya landholder from the Contai region who became the first barrister to get a London degree in his community. The Midnapur Congress

---

[50] A.K. Jameson, *Final Report on the Survey and Settlement Operations in the District of Midnapur, 1911 to 1917* (Calcutta, 1918), pp. 51–6, 113, and passim.

[51] *Nihar*, 19 January, 6 April, 20 April 1909, and many other issues: the series continued for more than six months, till July 1909. *Government of Bengal, Report on Native Newspapers*, relevant weeks. It may be interesting to add here that grant of such documents to sharecroppers was the central item in the successful reforms, termed Operation Barga, carried out by the Communist-led Left Front government of West Bengal in the late 1970s and '80s.

under his initiative was able to build a powerful and permanent base in the countryside, and particularly among the Mahishyas, through the characteristically Gandhian combination of occasional strictly peaceful mass disobedience of laws that adversely affected large sections of Indian society in cross-class ways, and sustained constructive work in villages. Sasmal inaugurated the Congress breakthrough into the Midnapur countryside through a successful boycott of the new Union Boards in 1921 that were enhancing taxes for villagers, while the subsequent all-India salt satyagraha of 1930 proved highly effective in a region once renowned for manufacturing salt from sea water. The junction with wider nationalism was not free from tensions. Birendranath Sasmal was deprived of a chance to become the top leader of the Bengal Congress in the mid 1920s by a cabal of Calcutta-based high-caste Congress party bosses who felt aggrieved by the rise of this lower-caste figure from the countryside. But Mahishya-dominated east and south Midnapur remained, through the nationalist era, the strongest base in Bengal of organised Gandhian mass struggle, while Mahishya identity politics, at its peak in the first two decades of the new century, clearly went into long-term decline.

Recent historical research has amply documented the ambivalences of Gandhian nationalism about internal divisions within Indian society, its frequent tilt in favour of indigenous property structures and hesitation about any total break with Brahmanical hierarchy.[52] Such moderation may well have helped in the mobilisation of a community like the Mahishyas that included landlords and peasants alike with an investment in Brahmanical forms of respectability. But certain spillover effects of Gandhian nationalism remain striking, providing some contrast with most forms of caste-based identity politics. In the early days of Gandhian nationalism, and particularly in areas not penetrated much by its cadres, all manner of rumours circulated about the Mahatma, imagining him in semi-millenarian ways, occasionally stimulating very diverse movements with goals and methods vastly

---

[52] The historical literature here is quite vast, and includes notably much of the work of Subaltern Studies in its early phase. For an overview stressing these limits, see Sumit Sarkar, *Modern India, 1885–1947* (New Delhi: Macmillan, 1983).

different from those actually envisaged by Gandhi and his disciples. Organised Gandhian movements could also find their styles and methods of agitation being taken over in whole or in part by plebeian groups with other kinds of objectives. For these did convey object lessons in the possibility of unarmed people acquiring the courage and inner strength to withstand brutal repression, without violence but also without fear. The message could be applied to other conflict situations, against landlords or other indigenous oppressors as much as against the foreign rulers. Extension of the first kind was witnessed among tribal groups in the western part of Midnapur district in early 1922, who went around looting village markets and destroying liquor shops amidst slogans hailing Gandhi. The second form was manifest in the way both the 1921 anti-Union Board no-tax campaign and the 1930 salt satyagraha was immediately followed by sharecroppers of the Contai-Tamluk coastal belt agitating peacefully against the *chakdars* and withholding payments to them. In significant contrast to the Mahishya leaders of 1909, the local Congress now tried to mediate between landholders and their *bhagchasis* through village-level joint meetings, and by the 1930s some of the sharecropper demands had been met. The *Nihar*, now a nationalist organ, also reported these matters much more sympathetically. The logic of Gandhian mass nationalism, depending for its efficacy on the active participation of large numbers, did demand a measure of accommodation, alongside restraints: a moderate caste movement engaged in upward mobility through petitions and lobbying of officials had no such compulsions.[53] One needs to add also that, in Midnapur as in several other regions marked by sustained Gandhian rural work, substantial numbers of nationalist activists disillusioned by Gandhian constraints eventually turned towards more radical, Socialist, or Communist ideologies.

[53] Sumit Sarkar, "The Conditions and Nature of Subaltern Militancy: Bengal from Swadeshi to Non-Cooperation, *c.* 1905–22", in Ranajit Guha, ed., *Subaltern Studies III* (Delhi: Oxford University Press, 1984); Hitesranjan Sanyal, "The Quit India Movement in Medinipur District", in Gyanendra Pandey, ed., *The Indian Nation in 1942* (Calcutta: K.P. Bagchi, 1988); ibid., *Swarajer Pathe* (Calcutta: Papyrus, 1994). The untimely death of Sanyal left unfinished his pioneering research on rural Gandhians in Midnapur and some other West Bengal districts, based on years of village-level interviews.

Midnapur by mid century had become one of the principal bases of the Bengal Communists, though the Congress, too, retained a significant presence.

IV.3

With the Rajbansis of the North Bengal districts of Rangpur, Dinajpur, Jalpaiguri, and Coochbehar we encounter yet another kind of pattern. Large parts of this plains region had been for long a frontier zone, with a relatively scanty population and poor communications before the coming of railways in the late nineteenth century. The bulk of the area was technically divided up into big zamindaris, almost all of them held by high-caste Hindus. But operationally more significant, from the point of view of agrarian relations, was the figure of the *jotedar*, the substantial farmer who had leased in land from zamindars, acquired firm tenant status by the late nineteenth century, and got his lands cultivated by sharecroppers (here termed *adhiars*). Share-cropping in parts of North Bengal has a long history, with the East India Company surveyor Buchanan noting its presence already in the early years of the nineteenth century. But it probably intensified with the spread of commercialised agriculture, notably the rapid growth of jute cultivation in districts like Rangpur.

High-caste Hindus were relatively thin on the ground here, big landlords apart.[54] While much of the region had a Muslim majority, Rajbansis were the most numerous group among the Hindus, comprising two-thirds of the latter in Rangpur. As with the Mahishyas, this meant that the Rajbansis straddled several social levels, constituting a big part of the *jotedars* and the *adhiyars* alike. But the agrarian structure ensured here a sharper class division within the same community than in Midnapur, which was in significant part a small-peasant economy. A Rajbansi tract of 1908 even acknowledged, with unusual prescience and frankness, that "differences in conditions of life had made the same *jati* have two *sreni*".[55]

[54] Brahmans, Kayasthas, and Vaidyas per mille numbered only 51 in Rangpur, 28 in Dinajpur, and 27 in Jalpaiguri, according to the 1931 census. The proportion was considerably lower than even in Midnapur.

[55] Harakishore Adhikari, *Rajbansi Kulapradip* (Calcutta, 1908).

While the *bhadralok* were relatively few in number, they had come to control the bulk of white-collar jobs and professions in North Bengal towns, stimulating tensions with the emergent Rajbansi (as well as Muslim) educated counter-elites. Rajbansis, however, faced a special problem in their bid for social ascent: the stigma of real or alleged ethnic and cultural distinction and inferiority. Many British officials, as well as some *bhadralok* commentators, classed the Rajbansis with a tribal group in the same region, the Koches. Rajbansis spoke a particular variant of Bengali and had many religious, social, and particularly marriage and sexual behaviour patterns distinct from high-Hindu norms. Rajbansi upper-crust affirmations therefore took the forms of a demand for census recognition as Kshatriyas, totally different from the Koch, and determined efforts to purge their customs of "non-Aryan" modes and construct a more prestigious "history" of the community. The Rajbansis, it was argued, were really descended from ancient Kshatriya warriors who had been forced to take refuge in a non-Aryan uncivilised frontier region (and so had forgotten upper-caste ways of life) in order to escape the wrath of Parashuram, the ancient slayer of Kshatriyas in an epic legend. Significantly, unlike the Namasudras and even the Mahishyas, there was a close synchrony of Rajbansi memorials with the decennial census, with 1891, 1901, and 1911 being the early peak points. Panchanan Barma, the first lawyer from this community (as Birendranath Sasmal had been the first barrister from the Mahishyas), organised a Kshatriya Samiti in 1910, and in January 1913 several thousand Rajbansis adopted the sacred thread in a collective ceremony.[56]

Anti-colonial nationalist organisations were relatively weak in this region, and mainly confined to the *bhadralok* in the towns. Insofar as it sought wider linkages, the Rajbansi leadership, in a pattern different from both Namasudras and Mahishyas, tended to seek an alignment with Hindu orthodox groups and eventually with Hindu identity politics with an anti-Muslim slant. Even at its beginnings

---

[56] Swaraj Basu, *Dynamics of A Caste Movement: The Rajbansis of North Bengal, 1910–1947* (Delhi: Manohar, 2003), the most detailed account so far. See also Ranajit Dasgupta, *Economy, Society, and Politics in Bengal: Jalpaiguri, 1869–1947* (Delhi: Oxford University Press, 1992), pp. 87–92, and *passim*.

during the 1891 census, its initiators had contacted the orthodox Rangpur Dharma Sabha and sought its sanction for Rajbansi Kshatriya status. This alignment became more pronounced from the mid 1920s as chauvinist Hindu trends, along with their Muslim counterparts, gathered strength after the breakdown of the Hindu–Muslim unity which Gandhian nationalism had briefly achieved during the Non-Cooperation and Khilafat upsurge of 1919–22. The Kshatriya Samiti during the mid 1920s was actively involved in a virulently anti-Muslim campaign on the issue of alleged abductions of Hindu girls by Muslim men – indeed, it initiated this campaign in the Rangpur region, though then the leadership quickly passed to Calcutta-based high-caste organisations. Yet the *Rangpur District Gazetteer* of 1911 had made a special point of mentioning that "Hindus and Muslims of the cultivating classes regard each other with the most complete toleration."[57] Perhaps it was precisely this fluidity of boundaries that made the construction of rigid distinctions more urgent for an elite identity project that aimed at gaining respectability in terms of high-Hindu norms. Rajbansi women had been accustomed to go freely to local markets, and traditionally the community had somewhat relaxed patterns of marital arrangement and sexual behaviour. The panic whipped up about Muslim abductors by the male leaders of the Kshatriya Samiti thus helped to enforce tighter patriarchal norms on "their" women.[58]

The high level of internal division within the putative caste community eventually became a major problem for the Rajbansi caste movement. The Kshatriya Samiti was able to maintain for a generation a strong electoral presence within what was (till 1951) a limited, property-related franchise. Panchanan Barma and other Kshatriya members of the Bengal legislative council pursued there a policy of

---

[57] *Rangpur District Gazetteer*, p. 48.
[58] Pradip Kumar Datta, "'Abductions' and the Constellation of a Hindu Communal Bloc in Bengal of the 1920s", *Studies in History*, XIV.i, January–June 1998; ibid., *Carving Blocs*, chapter 4. As with the demographic panic about Muslims allegedly breeding faster than Hindus inaugurated by U.N. Mukherji in 1909, the image of the Muslim male lusting for and raping Hindu girls became, and remains, a recurrent chauvinist Hindu stereotype.

firm alliance with the British against Congress nationalism. During debates on tenancy matters, Barma supported some restrictions on landlord power in the interests of the *jotedars*, but, predictably, consistently opposed any moves to safeguard the interests of the *adhiars*.[59] But the lower levels of Rajbansi society did not always share such social and political conformism. During 1919–22, rumours about Gandhi sparked off no-rent movements among some Rangpur peasants, and there were numerous protests in the same region against levies on local market transactions imposed by both zamindars and big *jotedars* which were a major burden for the petty commodity production of poorer peasants and sharecroppers.[60] Some twenty years later, the Communist-led Kisan Sabha made its first entry into Jalpaiguri, Dinajpur, and Rangpur through an effective campaign against such market impositions in 1939–40, and speedily undercut the influence of the Rajbansi caste association among the poorer members of that community. In the winter of 1946–7, Rajbansi peasants and sharecroppers of large parts of Jalpaiguri, Dinajpur, and Rangpur, along with tribals and some Muslims, came together in the famous Tebhaga struggle, with *adhiars* demanding a two-thirds share of the produce as against the existing half or less, in what was possibly the biggest agrarian movement in Bengal's history. Both conventional nationalism and caste identity momentarily found themselves utterly displaced by the militant politics of class.[61]

V

Let me now draw together the threads of my argument and try to move from empirical details towards some tentative, more general formulations.

There is first the question of context and content, the relationship of the present to the past in historical writing. The surge in research

---

[59] Dasgupta, op. cit., pp. 126–8; Datta, *Carving Blocs*, p. 158.

[60] Dasgupta, op. cit., chapter 6; Sarkar, "Conditions and Nature", op. cit.

[61] Dasgupta, op. cit., chapters 9–10; Sunil Sen, *Agrarian Struggle in Bengal, 1946–47* (New Delhi: People's Publishing House, 1972); Abani Lahiri, *Postwar Revolt of the Rural Poor in Bengal: Memoirs of a Communist Activist* (Calcutta: Seagull, 2001).

about religious and caste identities in scholarship concerning India since the late 1980s has been related, very obviously, to contemporary events. These years have seen the spectacular rise of an aggressive, right-wing Hindu nationalist or "Hindutva" formation, previously considered marginal, which today controls the central Indian government. As a movement associated with predominantly high-caste interests and values, Hindutva has simultaneously provoked numerous lower-caste and Dalit forms of identity politics, and many have sought to find in these a counterpoint to the onslaught on the secular and democratic bases of the Indian polity. It has been natural in such a conjuncture for secular-minded historians to explore antecedents, in efforts to understand the threat and suggest possible counterpoints. And no doubt there has been a bit of both in this essay, with its conjoint exploration of a post-Swadeshi high-caste ideology that at times appears to foreshadow today's Hindutva, and lower-caste part-alternatives. But presentism has its dangers, too, and maybe there is a problematic element even in Benjamin's beautiful and moving aphorism of history as "a memory . . . [that] flashes up at a moment of danger" – if it is taken as an immediate guide to historical practice.[62] For then we are tempted to carry over into the past not only current concerns in ways that can degenerate into sheer instrumentalism, but our present-day ordering of relative significance of events and tendencies. Radical hopes of imminent agrarian revolution during the 1960s and '70s had been an essential backdrop to intensive study and valorisation of autonomous peasant or subaltern militancy. Conversely, the post-1980s moods of worldwide disillusionment concerning possibilities of transformative projects have contributed to the major shift in historical attention from questions of class and socio-economic relationships towards identity politics often conceived

---

[62] Walter Benjamin, "Theses on the Philosophy of History", in idem, *Illuminations*, ed. Hannah Arendt (New York: Schocken Books), 1968, p. 255. Benjamin was not trying to provide a recipe for academic history-writing, but engaged in profound philosophical meditation shot through with calls for revolutionary action, at a moment of supreme crisis. "Theses" was written in spring 1940, a few months before his tragic suicide as one of Fascism's most illustrious victims.

in culturalist ways. The past, in other words, is made in both instances into an excessively familiar country. Along with the likely imbalances in historical analysis, this can also contribute to an unwitting acceptance of the present, too, as given, inevitable, and closed. An alternative assumption, that times past could have been marked instead often by a radical alterity, might in contrast open up past and present alike through encouraging processes of defamiliarisation.[63] Or perhaps history-writing should seek to maintain a creative tension between the Otherness of the past and an unavoidable element of linkages with the present. For an assumption of total difference would logically block comprehension. It can also encourage an exotic cultural relativism: the study of the past as utterly different, only in "its own terms", gazed at "in wonderment" as Lyotard had suggested one needs to do with regard to pre-modern narratives.[64]

A concomitant of presentist modes have been assumptions of unilinearity, of straight-line, uninterrupted linkages.[65] And that, again, tends to be associated with essentialisations of categories and values: colonialism and nationalism conceptualised in a homogenised, Manichaean manner; classes or castes as given, proletarians, peasants or subalterns

---

[63] I am drawing here on the insights of an important recent essay: Pradip Kumar Datta's "Hindutva and Its 'Myhistory'", *Seminar*, 522, February 2003.

[64] "All that we can do is gaze in wonderment at the diversity of discursive species, just as we do at the diversity of plant or animal species." J.F. Lyotard, *The Postmodern Condition: A Report on Knowledge* (1984; rpnt. Manchester University Press, 1992), p. 26. For critics like Seyla Benhabib, this is unacceptable, for it reduces other cultures and/or past times to exhibits in an ethnological museum, and assumes an absence of internal tensions and potentials for change. "Feminism and the Question of Postmodernism", in idem, *Situating the Self: Gender, Community and Postmodernism in Contemporary Ethics* (Cambridge: Polity Press, 1992). For another powerful critique, see Michele Moody-Adams, *Fieldwork in Familiar Places: Morality, Culture and Philosophy* (Harvard, 1997), "Introduction", and "The Use and Abuse of History".

[65] Nothing, of course, could have been more alien to the predominant tenor of Benjamin's thinking, with its sharp repudiation of unilinearity. "Theses", it would be recalled, suggested that "nothing has corrupted the German working class so much as the notion that it was moving with the current", and emphasised the need to "blast open the continuum of history".

as always potentially autonomous, progressive, worthy of valorisation. Plebeian autonomy and militancy cannot be uniformly valorised, made into an essence: their manifestations have also taken the form of internecine violence, pogroms, oppression of those less fortunate than themselves, effective appropriation by superior classes/castes. I have come to feel increasingly that there is much of value in Foucault's call for a historical vision that is "capable of liberating divergence and marginal elements" and is able to respond to even "haphazard conflicts" and "the singular randomness of events".[66] In my presentation of data from Bengal, it would have been noticed, I have tried to emphasise the many interruptions, shifting, multiple appropriations across "levels", identity formations that never really get fully stabilised but remain in danger of disruption through intersections with each other.[67]

Solidarities of nation, religious community, caste, class, gender – none of these can be taken as given or inevitable constants, nor can they be arranged, a priori, in any unchanging, determinate hierarchy of relative importance or attraction. It is more helpful to consider them as constructed, contingent projects playing on one of the many tensions or potential conflicts in a given situation or social group. I find very helpful here Gramsci's remarks about "contradictory consciousness", the ways in which one tends to belong "simultaneously to a multiplicity of mass human groups", with a "disjointed and episodic conception of the world".[68]

[66] Michel Foucault, "Nietzsche, Genealogy, History", in Paul Rabinow, ed., *The Foucault Reader* (Penguin, 1984), pp. 87–8.

[67] Two further instances. Caste was displaced by class solidarity as the counter-elite Rajbansi Kshatriya Sabha collapsed in face of the Tebhaga movement in the mid 1940s, and yet in recent years there has been a certain revival of the former through a "Kamtapur" movement for regional, autonomy. Gender-related reformism was marginalised by nationalism in its Extremist phase, but I have argued that there was a considerable revival, indeed extension, of such concerns following the decline of Swadeshi: see Sumit Sarkar, "Nationalism and Stri-Swadhinata . . .", op. cit.

[68] Antonio Gramsci, *Selections from the Prison Notebooks*, ed. Q. Hoare and G. Nowell-Smith (New York: International Publishers, 1971), p. 323, and *passim*.

Here, once again, it might be advisable to try to maintain a tension between two methodological and ethical approaches that tend to fly apart into polar opposition. Many today would be suspicious of a residue of "Leninist" condescension in Gramsci's language, and be attracted by the notion of multiple identities or hybridity, rather than their transcendence through what they fear would become another monolithic project, potentially "totalitarian" in its universalism. But there are problems also with eclectic approaches that merely observe the oscillations in relative importance of identity projects and remain satisfied with a model of fleeting solidarities all more or less on the same plane of significance and value. For then two questions remain, not only unanswered but even unasked. Is it entirely impermissible to suggest tentative linkages between particular conjunctures and variations in relative potency of alternative solidarities? And is it really possible to avoid some evaluation in terms of consequences and potential implications?

The Bengal material I have presented suggests that the oscillations across time of a more or less similarly located set of people between divergent kinds of solidarity – between caste and class mobilisations, for instance – were related less to material conditions and more to what might be termed the subjective horizon of expectation at particular moments. Signs of rift between the British authorities and nationalism-inclined high-caste Hindu landlords during the Swadeshi years probably stimulated hopes of some modifications in matters of tenancy, rent, and share of crops among the largely Muslim or lower-caste peasants and sharecroppers. This was evident in Gaurnadi, with a sympathetic British settlement official, but not in the adjoining district of Faridpur where agrarian conditions were similar. After the rebuke administered to Jack, officials there were careful not to inform produce-rent payers of the option of converting to money-rent.[69] Discussions of tenancy reform in the Bengal Legislative Council in

---

[69] J.C. Jack, the official whose commutation initiative had been aborted by his superiors at Gaurnadi, explicitly makes this point when describing his settlement work in the neighbouring district. J.C. Jack, ed., *Faridpur Settlement Report* (Calcutta, 1916).

the mid 1920s stimulated a further round of agrarian unrest,[70] while *tebhaga* was very directly related to the hope of transformative change stimulated by the effective agitational and organisational work of the Communist-led Kisan Sabha. Such issues had little relevance for the better-off strata among lower castes or Muslims, for whom the shifts in horizons would be related more to census status, and job and political opportunities through the official grant of reservations. At the same time, it would be dangerous to assume that the narrower vision of identity politics was confined only, or always, to emergent counter-elites. There have been long years when for the underprivileged hopes of radical change have appeared quite impossible, and so it has seemed more sensible to adhere to other kinds of identity. This might be religious solidarity, in the context of upper-caste overtures of limited sanskritisation combined perhaps with the projection of another religious group as the ever-threatening Other – we might recall U.N. Mukherji – or the pinning of all hopes on caste-reserved jobs or seats. Such moves would directly benefit only a minority, but others might hope to gain a little through kinship or clientage connections – or at least a bit of vicarious pride at the ascent of a few of their caste brethren.

Given today's political and academic moods, I find it important to highlight limits of two kinds concerning caste-centred identity politics that seem to emerge from the Bengal data. One was the failure to evolve effective techniques of mass praxis, in significant contrast, as I have tried to indicate in passing, to both Gandhian nationalism and left-wing social radicalism. The other problem, particularly marked in Bengal and a possible explanation for the waning of lower-caste challenges in the province from the mid 1920s, was the tendency of putative lower-caste formations towards repeated fragmentation into mutually hostile narrow identities. In certain other regions – particularly in the late-colonial era, the Maharashtra of Phule and Ambedkar, and Tamilnadu through the movement inspired by Periyar – more generalised critiques of caste domination

---

[70] Tanika Sarkar, *Bengal 1928–1934: The Politics of Protest* (Delhi: Oxford University Press, 1987), pp. 40–1.

came to be elaborated through inversion of the theory of Aryan cultural assimilation and, occasionally, through a radical rejection of social inequality and injustice. These had the potential of overriding distinctions and conflicts between different lower-caste groups, and uniting them, if only intermittently, on a common anti-Brahmanical platform. We have already seen that occasional rhetoric apart, such counter-hegemonic possibilities remained absent in Bengal caste movements. And there was also the other great failure, that of the Marxian Left, which refused till fairly recently to see in caste anything more than an epiphenomenon of class. The two strands, of class- and caste-related radicalism, never really came together in late-colonial Indian politics. Indian Marxists operated on a shifting combination of two registers: promoting the specific, class-related economic demands of workers or peasants, and involvement in the anti-colonial struggle. Caste leaders in Bengal, as we have seen, were generally uninterested or even hostile to both.

Here our data points towards a final, general theme: the recurrent tension between what adopting Charles Taylor's terminology might be called the politics of universal rights and entitlements (in both its liberal and socialist forms), and the politics of difference, which demands the recognition of identities of distinct groups, and often suspects in universal schemas a desire to impose an oppressive, homogenised uniformity.[71] There is a widespread understanding today that a major shift has taken place in recent years from the first to the second – more precisely, from class and class struggle towards diverse forms of identity politics built around the fault lines of ethnicity, religion, caste, gender, or sexual preference. This is also a change which many welcome in a fairly unqualified manner. Why identity politics is so often thought to exclude themes of class might seem somewhat intriguing, for the latter in strict logic is surely also a kind of identity, particularly when class is looked at primarily from the point of view of consciousness, felt solidarities, and commonalities. (That, typified

---

[71] Charles Taylor, "The Politics of Identity", along with the comments on this paper in Amy Gutman, ed., *Multiculturalism: Examining the Politics of Identity* (Princeton, 1994).

for instance in the Thompsonian approach, has been on the whole the most fruitful strand within Marxian history-writing.) The shift might then appear merely additive, drawing belated and welcome attention to sites of power and solidarities of resistance neglected much too long within conventional Marxism.

I think the change is both deeper and more problematic. This becomes clear once one recalls the transformative vision embedded in the classic Marxian conception of class. The proletariat, for Marx, has the potential, unique among all other classes, for abolishing itself ultimately through revolution, instead of becoming a new putatively permanent ruling class the way the bourgeoisie had replaced feudal lords. The Marxian project, then, had envisaged transformation through self-transformation of an "identity" of a very special kind.

Not many today would share many features of this vision: the unique potential attributed to the "proletariat" (itself not too clear a category), the ascription to it (or often in practice to its self-appointed spokesmen) of a leading role that has repeatedly turned despotic, the disregard for tensions of other kinds and of identities emerging from out of them. But if the vision had been no more than utopian, sometimes dangerous, it did at its best try to condition the practice of Marxian movements in one particular way that I think is relevant for my present argument. This was the effort to simultaneously affirm, yet go beyond, the merely sectional demands of the working class in order to build alliances of all the toilers and the wretched of the earth. That, I would like to emphasise, had been one of the key meanings of the protean word "hegemony" – a meaning which, strangely, has been almost lost in recent times.[72]

[72] It might be helpful to recall for a moment some nearly forgotten figures and texts. Lenin's *What is to be Done?* had counterposed "hegemony" to "economism", "socialist" to "trade-union consciousness", and called on social democrats to become "tribunes of the people". Gramsci refined that distinction through his language of "economico-corporative" and "hegemonic" moments. Discussions of hegemony in recent years, in contrast, have tended to concentrate on the question of power operating not just through sheer coercion but through the effective production of internalised consent, interpellation: Gramsci seen through the prisms of Althusser and Foucault. To

Postmodernist moods, emerging from the ruins of the radical aspirations of the 1960s and '70s, have tended in contrast to reject transformative projects in principle as guilty of the sins of universalism and teleology, valorised resistance – the more dispersed the better – against total change, and insisted on the absolute separation of the particular or fragmentary from any more general perspectives. In many contexts, this might seem to make considerable sense: in defence of the cultural autonomy and dignity of immigrant minorities, for instance, through discourses of multiculturalism. Yet, even in such situations where counter-hegemonic transformations are difficult to imagine, stress on the distinctiveness of totally isolable "authentic" cultures raises both practical and theoretical problems. We are back, really, with the pitfalls of extreme cultural relativism, which tends to homogenise differences and can take little account of power relations and capacities for internal change within cultures and communities. It is prone also to assume an unwarranted determinism by origin.[73]

Suddenly, today, things might just be changing again. Tens of millions across the globe have been out on the streets in common protest against war and capitalist globalisation. What is new and remarkable about this "movement of movements" is that it is at once worldwide yet decentralised, coming together not through submerging but often on the basis of a multitude of diverse identities and affirmations. Perhaps another world may not be impossible, after all.

---

take one instance: the first meaning of hegemony is almost entirely omitted from Jeremy Hawthorn's generally helpful *Glossary of Contemporary Literary Theory* (London, 1992).

[73] I have found very helpful Michele Moody-Adams' analysis of three assumptions of cultural relativism that she finds untenable: cultures as "fundamentally self-contained and isolable"; as " internally integrated wholes"; and "cultural influence on belief and action . . . understood deterministically". Moody-Adams, op. cit., p. 21 and *passim*.

6

Kaliyuga, Chakri, and Bhakti
Ramakrishna and His Times

[Head]-master: "Tell me, does he read a lot of books?"
Brinde [servant girl]: "Why should he need books/ Its all in his Words."

The master had just come from his books. He was amazed to discover that Thakur Sri Ramakrishna never read books.

> — *from the description of Mahendranath Gupta's first visit to Ramakrishna, February 1882, in "M", Ramakrishna Kathamrita, I, p. 17* [1]

THE SUDDEN ENTRY OF print of culture and Western education, along with the creative indigenous response to them through vernacular prose, valorised book learning to an unprecedented extent among the colonial middle class of nineteenth-century Bengal. Sacred Hindu texts became widely available in

---

Reprinted with minor changes, from *Economic and Political Weekly*, 18 July 1992. Another version has been published as "Occasional Paper I: An Exploration of the Ramakrishna-Vivekananda Tradition", in the series Socio-Religious Movements and Cultural Networks in Indian Civilisation, Indian Institute of Advanced Study, Shimla, 1993. Earlier drafts of parts of this essay have appeared as "The Kathamrita as Text: Towards an Understanding of Ramakrishna Paramahansa", Occasional Paper No. 22, Nehru Memorial Museum and Library, New Delhi, 1985, and "Ramakrishna and the Calcutta of His Times" ("The Calcutta Psyche"), *India International Centre Quarterly*, Winter 1990–1. Also published in my *Writing Social History* (Delhi: Oxford University Press, 1997). The present text owes much to the searching criticisms and corrections of Tanika Sarkar and to comments by Hitesranjan Sanyal and Dipesh Chakrabarty.

[1] I am using the 1980–2 reprints of "M" (Mahendranath Gupta)'s five-

written form for the first time, and printed matter became far more accessible than manuscripts could ever have been. Higher education, now being made indispensable for respectable jobs and professions, was imparted through a foreign language, far removed from everyday speech, which could be learnt only through books. Contact with a culture which claimed superior status by virtue of its rationality and science stimulated efforts to use self-consciously "rational" arguments to modify or defend institutions and ideas now felt to be "traditional". Time acquired new meaning and disciplinary authority through an equally abrupt entry of clocks and watches, and there was among some a sense of moving forward in consonance with its linear progress. Foreign rule, however humiliating, had brought the gift of "modern" culture for the new English-educated literati, and maybe its evils could be reduced or eliminated through gradual reform. A premium, consequently, was placed on varied forms of social activism: education, religious and social reform, revivalism, philanthropy, patriotic endeavour.

And yet, at the very heart of it all, there was that strange, sudden trek of the Calcutta *bhadralok* in the late 1870s and early 1880s to a man who seemed to represent the very opposite of all such valorisations and initiatives. Ramakrishna Paramahansa (1836–86), hitherto obscure Dakshineswar temple priest of humble village-Brahman origin, had virtually no English and not even much formal vernacular (or Sanskrit) schooling. He thought little of rationalistic argument, considered organised efforts to improve social conditions futile, preached an apparently timeless message of bhakti in rustic language, and claimed to have seen, many times, the Goddess Kali face to face. The cult that developed around Ramakrishna remained an essentially *bhadralok* affair in Bengal, with some extensions later, again invariably among educated people, in other provinces and abroad through the efforts of Vivekananda and the Ramakrishna Mission. Some fifty years after Ramakrishna's death, a short story imagined two devout elderly

---

volume *Sri-Sri Ramakrishna-Kathamrita* (Calcutta, 1902, 1904, 1908, 1910, 1932: henceforth KM). The translations are mine.

women meeting at Benaras: the city lady was full of Ramakrishna, the village woman had never heard of him.[2]

Today, an average middle- or lower-middle-class Hindu household in Bengal can be expected to have a portrait of Ramakrishna somewhere, along with, quite possibly, a well-thumbed copy of the *Kathamrita*.

It was the *Kathamrita* which first aroused my interest, as a historian, in Ramakrishna, with its claim to be a diary-based record of the conversation of the Dakshineswar saint between February 1882 and August 1886. Not just scattered saintly *obiter dicta*, in other words, but actual conversation: here, it was tempting to assume, we have something close to G.M. Young's definition of the ideal social history document through which we can eavesdrop on the people of the past talking among themselves. More significantly, the *Kathamrita* was a product of something like a luminal moment, a two-way crossing of social frontiers – the rustic Brahman becoming the guru of the city *bhadralok*, the latter falling under the spell of an idiom, values, and personality very different from their own. Both trajectories needed to be problematised and explored, for perhaps they could add something to our understanding of village culture and religion on the one hand, and the contradictions of *bhadralok* life on the other.

The passage in the *Kathamrita* which describes Mahendranath Gupta's first visit to Ramakrishna introduces us to this intersection of apparently very distinct worlds. The diarist-author had stood third in the B.A. examinations in 1874, and in 1882 he was headmaster of a North Calcutta school controlled by Ishwarchandra Vidyasagar, the "ocean of learning", famous social reformer and philanthropist.[3] It was natural for a man like Mahendranath to assume that wisdom and reading books were all but synonymous: the five-volume compendium he prepared from his diary, however, would eventually celebrate the surrender of men like him to a near-illiterate villager who never read books. Brinde, the sevant girl, almost certainly illiterate, had no

---

[2] Bibhutibhushan Bandopadhyay, *Drobomoyeer Kashibas*, in idem, *Galpasamagra* (Calcutta, 1975).
[3] Biographical sketch of Mahendranath Gupta, appended to KM I.

problem in accepting that true wisdom and holiness had nothing to do with written culture. But Ramakrishna was not interested in having devotees like her, and he is said to have disliked the crowds of villagers that came to see him when he occasionally visited Kamarpukur, where he had been born.[4] The *Kathamrita*, as well as biographical accounts of Ramakrishna, in contrast, repeatedly describe how the saint often went out of his way to win over *bhadralok* devotees.[5] This might appear to be a "natural" process of upward mobility. It was conditioned, however, by a colonial situation which had obliged many members of traditional village or small-town-based upper-caste literati to move to the metropolis, try to take to English education, or – like Ramakrishna – become a rather new kind of guru for middle-class *bhadralok*. The ascent into urban *bhadralok* society also left traces in Ramakrishna's discourse in a changing pattern of stresses and silences which can tell us something about varied appropriations of apparently common religious traditions at different social levels.

For men like Mahendranath there was clearly an initial hesitation, but also a passionate eagerness to cross this threshold. The attraction for opposites here reveals a deep disquiet among sections of the *bhadralok*, at least in some moods, about assumptions and styles of activity which on the surface ruled their lives. There were reasons, we shall see, why such a sense of aridity and dissatisfaction manifested itself precisely in the 1870s and 1880s. A certain differentiation within *bhadralok* social space also needs to be taken into account. English education brought reasonable success in professions and services for some, though even there the highest rungs would be occupied by Englishmen. For many more, it came to connote only humble clerical jobs (*chakri*) in government or mercantile offices, once again usually British controlled. Ramakrishna's message developed a particular resonance in this second, often half-forgotten, world

---

[4] *Life of Sri Ramakrishna Compiled from Various Authentic Sources* (Mayavati 1924, rpnt. Calcutta, 1964), pp. 290–1. Henceforth *Life*.

[5] The major canonical biography is Swami Saradananda, *Sri Sri Ramakrishna-Lilaprasanga* (Calcutta, 1911–19, rpnt. 1979). Henceforth "L". All intimate disciples of Ramakrishna were of educated *bhadralok* origin, with the solitary exception of Latu, the Bihari servant of Ramchandra Datta.

of the unsuccessful *bhadralok*. *Chakri*, I intend to argue, is crucial for understanding Ramakrishna and situating him within the overall context of colonial domination. It helps also to highlight a sense of internal difference, inadequate awareness of which, I feel, has made the recent studies of the *Kathamrita* by Partha Chatterjee somewhat monochromatic.[6] The Ramakrishna tradition, at least arguably, may have become in our own times an undifferentiated "religion of urban domesticity". Reading that back into the beginnings of that cult, in terms of a homogenised colonial middle class confronting Western cultural domination appears to me to be more than a little teleological.

If Ramakrishna attracted *bhadralok* through his "Otherness", this was to a considerable extent an Other constructed by the *bhadralok* themselves. There is no direct written testimony left by the saint: we know about him only from *bhadralok* disciples and admirers, and the texts they composed simultaneously illuminate – and transform. This is not necessarily a disadvantage, for the logic of *bhadralok* appropriations constitutes our major field of interest. The *Kathamrita* occasionally beckons beyond it towards a less assimilated Ramakrishna, by virtue of its effort to preserve direct conversation and its relatively non-canonised character.[7] But on the whole it is not a perhaps unapproachable "original" Ramakrishna-by-himself, but

---

[6] Partha Chatterjee, "A Religion of Urban Domesticity: Sri Ramakrishna and the Calcutta Middle Class", in Partha Chatterjee and Gyanendra Pandey (eds), *Subaltern Studies VII* (Delhi, 1992); see also Partha Chatterjee, *The Nation and Its Fragments* (Delhi, 1994), chapter III.

[7] Thus the Ramakrishna described in the KM (its author, incidentally, never formally joined the Ramakrishna Mission) did not wear saffron, used polished slippers or shoes, slept on a bed under a mosquito net: visitors were often surprised by his appearance and dress (KM III, p. 1). Later iconic representations of Ramakrishna invariably present him in the garb of a conventional *sannyasi*. The one contemporary photograph that exists is hardly ever used in the canonical literature. I have seen only one reproduction of it, in Brojen Banerji and Sajanikanta Das, *Sri Ramakrishna Samasamayik Drishtite* (Calcutta, 1952). This shows Ramakrishna in a dance of ecstasy with Brahmos at Keshabchandra Sen's house in September 1879: he is not markedly different in dress from the other *bhadralok*, apart from a rather shabby rusticity.

Ramakrishna as constituted in the gaze of the late-nineteenth-century *bhadralok*, who are of central importance in any exploration of the Ramakrishna-Vivekananda tradition.

The *Kathamrita* was published from fifteen to fifty years after the sessions with Ramakrishna and covers a total of only 186 days spread over the last four and a half years of the saint's life. The full text of the original diary has never been made publicly available. Considered as a constructed "text" rather than simply a more or less authentic "source", the *Kathamrita* reveals the presence of certain fairly self-conscious authorial strategies. There is in particular a deployment of paradox which simultaneously points towards an overarching harmony. The high degree of "truth-effect" undeniably conveyed by the *Kathamrita* to twentieth-century readers is related to its display of testimonies to authenticity, careful listing of "types of evidence",[8] and meticulous references to exact dates and times. We are reminded that the nineteenth century had brought a new vogue for precise biographies and histories. But the man whose conversation was being presented had been attractive to the *bhadralok* partly because he had been bored by formal logic, preferred parables and analogies to precise argumentation, and often expressed a deep aversion for the discipline of time.[9]

There is, then, a deliberate foregrounding, throughout, of the learned literate knowledge/unlearned oral wisdom polarity. We never meet Brinde again: her one appearance was clearly to set the scene for this contrast. Quotations from high-Hindu sacred texts (*shastras*) and references to abstract religious philosophical doctrines embellish the *Kathamrita* as chapter headings and footnotes – in obvious stylistic contrast to Ramakrishna's own colloquial idiom. The point being made, however, is precisely that there is no fundamental conflict. The paradoxes which abound in the *Kathamrita* raise

---

[8] Each volume of the KM begins with an analysis of "Three Kinds of Evidence" – "direct and recorded on the same day", "direct but unrecorded", and "hearsay and unrecorded" – and the text claims to be based on the first type. Vivekananda's praise of the author for having kept himself "entirely hidden", unlike Plato with Socrates, is quoted, along with testimonies from Ramakrishna's wife and some other prominent disciples.

[9] KM I, p. 30 (5 March 1882).

doubts about *bhadralok* assumptions (like the inherent superiority of textual learning which underlay Mahendranath's initial query to Brinde) but eventually reinforce accepted categories.[10] A wonderful affinity is shown to prevail between Ramakrishna's unlearned wisdom and the shastras, mutually confirming the avatar status of the saint and the eternal validity of the holy texts. As the *Lilaprasanga*, the canonical biography brought out by the Ramakrishna Mission, stated in 1911: "The coming of the *thakur* this time as an illiterate was to prove the truth of all the *shastras*."[11] We need to ponder over the implications of a textual strategy – and movement – that felt the need to simultaneously display and reconcile learned/illiterate, city-educated/rustic differences.

Ramakrishna, then, was an appropriate and partially *bhadralok*-constructed Other with whom an urban group plagued with a sense of alienation from roots could relate without undue discomfort. Late-nineteenth-century Bengal had its rural rebels, its troublesome tribal, low-caste, or Muslim illiterates; the 1870s and 1880s in particular were marked by acute agrarian tension over rents and tenant rights. *Bhadralok* society, even the clerical underdogs of which could at times have a bit of rental income through petty intermediate tenure-holding in the Permanent Settlement hierarchy,[12] naturally preferred empathy with the countryside through a figure like Ramakrishna. Despite the apparent vehemence of his rejection of book-learning and activism, acceptance of Ramakrishna, we shall see, did not usually involve any sharp or total break with normal forms of *bhadralok* life and activity. These could still be carried on, but in a new way, enriched by a spirituality and inner life suited to the times, which helped to mitigate a deepening sense of anomie.

There was little obviously new in Ramakrishna's teachings. That may have been one of his strengths, for through Ramakrishna the city *bhadralok* could imagine themselves to be reaching back to

[10] For an argument stressing this dual nature of paradox, particularly in religious discourse, see Megan McLaughlin, "Gender Paradox and the Otherness of God", *Gender and History*, III.2, Summer 1991.

[11] L I, pp. 264–5.

[12] See Asok Sen, "Agrarian Structure and Tenancy Laws in Bengal, 1850–1900", in Sen, *et al.*, *Perspectives in Social Sciences 2* (Calcutta, 1982).

lost traditional moorings in the countryside, in simple faith conveyed through rustic language. The central message was one of bhakti, valorising, as bhakti has often done, quiet inner devotion over textual exegesis, time-consuming ritual, and external action. The catholicity of "many views, many paths" (*yata mat, tato path*), which became one of Ramakrishna's principle titles to fame, also has many earlier – and nineteenth-century – counterparts. What is significant, and valuable for historical analysis, is the way Ramakrishna contextualised such themes through parables and similes drawn from contemporary everyday rural and *bhadralok* life. Thus the critique of the printed word takes the form of a comment about English-educated people who refuse to believe that a house is collapsing before their eyes till it is confirmed by that characterstic nineteenth-century innovation, the newspaper.[13] And very specific forms of *bhadralok* social activism are listed in a story Ramakrishna seems to have particularly liked to relate, for it is repeated no less than six times in the *Kathamrita*:

> Sambhu Mallik wanted to talk about hospitals, dispensaries, schools, roads, and tanks . . . Giving just alms at Kalighat, not seeing Kali herself! (Laughter) . . . So I told Sambhu, if you meet *Iswara*, will you ask him to build some hospitals and dispensaries? (Laughter). The *bhakta* will never say that. He will rather say, Thakur, let me stay near your lotus-feet, keep me always near you, give me pure bhakti.[14]

His audience was clearly appreciative, in the early 1880s. We will have to consider why, and for how long – since Vivekananda would subsequently make systematic philanthropy the central thrust of the mission he founded in Ramakrishna's name.

Images drawn from quotidian life have been common in Indian religious discourses, and particularly in bhakti. But the precise situating of such images, in juxtaposition with other kinds of historical evidence, is much easier with a firmly datable nineteenth-century figure

---

[13] KM I, p. 219 (22 October 1885).

[14] KM I, p. 51 (27 October 1882). The passage is repeated with minor variations in KM I, pp. 127–8 (15 June 1884); KM II, p. 166 (11 October 1884); KM III, p. 215 (18 October 1885); KM IV, p. 50 (January 1884); and KM V, p. 206 (6 December 1884).

like Ramakrishna than it would be, say, with Kabir or Mirabai. Thus, Ramakrishna's conception of evil repeatedly linked together *kamini*, *kanchan*, and the *dasatya* of *chakri*: lust, as embodied invariably in women, gold, and the bondage of the office job. Wives with their luxurious ways instil into their husbands a thirst for money, and this in turn forces men into office work. The temptations of *kamini* and *kanchan* are age-old themes, but their association with *chakri* is new. We meet this triad again in a multitude of late-nineteenth-century vernacular plays, farces, and tracts as the correlated evils of Kaliyuga, the last and worst of the fourfold succession of eras in the traditional Hindu conception of cyclical time. A 2000-year-old motif took on new specific contours under colonial rule, which had abruptly introduced the discipline of clock time, and imposed it so far mainly in government offices and mercantile firms.

Language is vital here: we can get close to Ramakrishna – who left behind no systematic exposition – only through images. The parables through which Ramakrishna expounded his conception of bhakti held out the image of a traditional, paternalistic, caring overlord to whom the devotee could come close through faithful service – the polar opposite of the impersonal, alien sahib of the nineteenth-century office. The alternative, and on the whole preferred, model was an escape from all effort and tension, even of loving service, through an unquestioning, childlike surrender to the Mother Goddess, Kali. The first kind of devotion represented a well-known Vaishnava *bhava* (mood), the second embodied the alternative Shakta tradition as modified in the eighteenth century by Ramakrishna's favourite poet. But bhakti in both forms, I intend to argue, had been modulated by felt evils of a specific, historically conditioned kind. It had at first a mainly clerical lower-middle-class ambience, but could attract the more successful *bhadralok*, too, in their more inward-turning moods.

For Ramakrishna, the woman to whom one could not relate as to a mother, invariably represents the threat of *kamini*, lust incarnate. Not least among the many paradoxes of the Ramakrishna movement is the way a saint with such apparent misogynist traits came to have many enthusiastic women devotees: middle-aged or elderly *bhadralok* housewives and widows, even actresses of prostitute origin. This was happening after a generation of male *bhadralok* initiatives concentrated on women's questions and seeking what by the 1860s was being called "*stri-swadhinata*", the "freeing" of women through education and reform from the more obvious of patriarchal disabilities and prejudices (sati, the ban on widow remarriage, polygamy). Ramakrishna cared nothing about such efforts, and yet one of the principal leaders of social reform, the Brahmo Keshabchandra Sen – who had persuaded the government to pass a very modern marriage law for his sect in 1872 – became in the late 1870s the first really prominent *bhadralok* admirers of the Dakshineswar saint. Once again, the interrelations between Ramakrishna and the *bhadralok* offer an entry point into crucial tensions and contradictions, this time related to gender. There were interesting shifts within the Ramakrishna movement, too. Sarada Devi, Ramakrishana's wife, was kept very much in the background in the saint's lifetime, living in a tiny room, cooking and looking after her husband, and talking to women devotees alone. Ramakrishna rigorously abstained from sexual relations with Sarada, and worshipped her as an embodiment of the Divine Mother one night as the culminating point of his years of passionate spiritual quest (*sadhana*).[15] After Ramakrishna's death Sarada Devi became a major cult figure of the movement in her own right, revered as Sri Ma or Holy Mother. Shifting constructions and images of womanhood in fact will be quite central to our analysis: gender has to be not an afterthought, but at the very core of any understanding of Ramakrishna and Vivekananda.

My principal focus is on the initial interaction between Ramakrishna and the Calcutta *bhadralok* in the late 1870s and early 1880s as embedded above all in the *Kathamrita*. This provides, I argue, an exceptionally privileged but little-explored ground for understanding some of the ways in which Hindu religious traditions came to be modified to meet the new pressures and demands of colonial middle-class life. What we call Hinduism today is, in its crystallised form, to a considerable extent a relatively new, late-nineteenth-century

---

[15] *Life*, p. 250.

construction, and the Ramakrishna movement played a significant role in its emergence.[16] This happened particularly through the varied appropriations of Ramakrishna that continued across time and seemed to abruptly change their nature a decade or so after Ramakrishna's death through the efforts of his best-known disciple. Vivekananda achieved a tour de force which apparently inverted much of his master's teaching. He gave crucial importance to organised philanthropy, serving the "*daridranarayan*" (God embodied in poor folk): the conversation with Sambhu Mallik consequently had to be excised totally from the canonical biography.[17] Emphasis was shifted from bhakti towards the other two *margas* (ways) of high-Hindu spiritual quest, Vedantic *jnana* (knowledge), and karma (redefined now as social service rather than ritual), and Ramakrishna's catholicity was made into an argument for the essential superiority of an aggressive and muscular Hinduism. Vivekananda's tours abroad and across India raised the social status of the Ramakrishna movement in Bengal, and the humble world of clerical *chakri* lost some of its centrality.

Vivekananda, however, must not be reduced to a mere series of inversions of Ramakrishna, for the shifts were related to the opening up of dimensions virtually unknown to his master. Schematically, these can be represented as the problematisations of Western domination, of "Bharatvarsha" seen through the prism of an ideally unified Hindu world, and of the village, low castes, and poor people generally as standing in need of wholesale upliftment. Vivekananda, again, like Ramakrishna before him, quickly became open to multiple appropriations, though in his case the existence of authenticated writings and correspondence make the question of a "real" or "original" Swamiji less chimerical. There is Vivekananda the "patriot-prophet", patron saint for a whole generation of Swadeshi enthusiasts, revolutionary terrorists, and nationalists in general. More

---

[16] I am borrowing the term "crystallisation" from W. Cantwell Smith, "The Crystallisation of Religious Communities in Mughal India", in idem, *On Understanding Islam: Selected Studies* (The Hague, 1981), chapter 9.

[17] L I, pp. 370-3, gives a longish account of Ramakrishna's contacts with Sambhu Mallik, but completely omits the conversation quoted six times in KM.

relevant today, and ominously so, is the image of the Swami as one of the founders of twentieth-century "Hindutva", of a unified and chauvinistic Hinduism.

I can only hope to lightly touch on some of these many dimensions here. A comprehensive discussion obviously demands a separate paper, which would also have to explore in detail the new social compulsion and aspiration of the 1890s which must have conditioned Vivekananda's initiatives. But it is equally impossible to leave Vivekananda out of a study of Ramakrishna. His influence has indelibly marked nearly all the texts we have about Ramakrishna – though the *Kathamrita* less so than most – and there was never any conscious or complete rupture.[18] We cannot ignore the question as to how that continuity remained possible. Vivekananda was recognised by most people as Ramakrishna's authentic heir, and his reputation, in fact, helped to establish, extend, and perpetuate Ramakrishna's own image as apostle of an apparently very different kind of devotion. A quietistic, inward-looking bhakti, which in certain circumstances can develop into its apparent opposite: there are implications here of deep contemporary interest and concern.

II

Ramakrishna's interaction with the Calcutta *bhadralok* has given us an initial impression of a series of opposites which attract each other, a bridging of different "worlds" or "levels" of frontiers that were "difficult" and yet "had to be crossed".[19] It is time to attempt greater precision about what worlds we are talking about, and when and why they were sought to be bridged.

Binaries like elite/popular, city/country, or *bhadralok*/peasant are of limited help in exploring the tensions that structure the *Kathamrita*. Ramakrishna, for a start, was not a peasant, but a poor Brahman from

---

[18] The contrasts between KM and L are particularly relevant here – see Walter G. Neevel (Jr), "The Transformation of Ramakrishna", in Bardwell L. Smith, *Hinduism: New Essays on History of Religion* (London, 1976).

[19] "A difficult borderland and . . . frontiers that had to be crossed" – terms used by Raymond Williams while discussing writers like George Eliot, Thomas Hardy, and D.H. Lawrence in an analysis of a somewhat similar problematic, in *The Country and the City* (London, 1973), p. 316.

Kamarpukur village in Hooghly district. The family plot was tiny; it was, nevertheless, cultivated by agricultural labourers.[20] Gadadhar Chattopadhyay (born in 1836) as a boy played with children of low-caste artisans. His high-caste status helped him to become a friend, however, of the local zamindar's son, and the scanty formal schooling he received was at a *pathshala* run in that landlord's house. Around 1850 he was brought to Calcutta by his elder brother Ramakumar. The paddy grown on the family plot was not sufficient to balance the rising cost of cloth and other necessities, and Ramakumar's own income as *smriti* expert from rulings on ritual disputes was also drying up.[21]

Kamarpukur, once noted for weaving and other crafts, had started to decline. It was afflicted by "Burdwan fever" (malaria), and hit, like so many parts of the western Bengal moribund delta, by a combination of ecological change, disruption of drainage due to railways, and decline of crafts before imported manufactures. The traditional high-caste literati, experts in Sanskrit learning alone, were facing a crisis as English education increasingly became the prerequisite for entry into the respectable professions.

Ramakrishna's own family, however, was saved from ruin by the patronage of the upstart Kaivarta zamindars of Janbazar in Calcutta. Rani Rashmoni had just completed the Dakshineswar temple but was finding *pujaris* (priests) difficult to get because of her low-caste origin. Ramakrishna and Ramakumar eventually obliged.[22] Ramakrishna's passionate and wayward *sadhana* soon made him abandon formal priestly duties and many at that time thought he had gone mad. Rashmoni and then her son-in-law Mathur, however, continued looking after his simple needs. A deed of endowment stabilised Ramakrishna's position in 1858, though on a rather minimal basis.[23] Other patrons and devotees started coming in after Mathur's death in 1871: the philanthropist Sambhu Mallik, who had a garden house adjoining Dakshineswar temple; a high official of the Nepal durbar

[20] L I, Purbakatha o Balyaajivan, p. 41; *Life*, p. 5.
[21] L I, pp. 122–4.
[22] *Life*, pp. 45–57.
[23] The cash payment amounted to Rs 5 per month, together with stipulated quantities of food and cloth: KM II, p. ix (for text of deed of endowment); L II, Dibyabhave o Narendra, p. 350.

posted in Calcutta named Biswanath Upadhyaya; and, from 1875, after Ramakrishna had sought out and impressed the Keshab Sen circle, a growing number of English-educated professional men, clerks, and students.[24]

Details like these, placed against a background of crisis of the traditional literati, help us to understand some of the complexities in Ramakrishna's attitude towards well-off learned folk, the masters of the written or printed word. They add a deeper social meaning to the orality/literacy contrast with which we began and which in different forms will accompany us throughout our essay. *Baramanush* or *baralok* (rich, literally big people) patrons were essential for survival, even if they occasionally happened to be of low-caste origin or embodied cultural values in many ways alien to Ramakrishna. They had, in fact, to be sought for – and yet were resented at the same time.

Ramakrishna loved to recall that his father, despite poverty, had never accepted gifts from Shudras.[25] That to him was the role model of the unbending old-world Brahman, asserting ritual purity at all costs over wealth and power: admirable, but unrealistic, for Ramakrishna himself was spending his adult as a dependent of a Kaivarta zamindar. From this, perhaps, followed a self-mocking description. Ramakrishna once confessed that from boyhood on he had been a "*sukher paira* [pigeon that seeks comfort]. I frequented well-off households, but ran away from houses where I saw suffering."[26] Ramakrishna admits to a weakness, mildly ridicules himself, and at the same time confesses that he had been unable to rid himself of an unfortunate trait. Implicit here is the danger of an opposite, degenerate model of the Brahman turned self-seeker, currying favour from rich but low-caste patrons – the very type, one could add, of the decadent Brahman of many texts denouncing Kaliyuga. The "mad" sadhana through which Ramakrishna eventually gained recognition as holy man and preceptor typified a third, subtler form of negotiation with the *baramanush* of the world, through which patronage could be won without loss of self-respect. In the days of his "madness", when

---

[24] *Life*, pp. 250–8, 269–70, 297–303, 307–10, 370–5, 430–50, 470–1.
[25] *Life*, p. 7; L I, p. 40.
[26] KM V, p. 45 (10 June 1883).

recognition was still to come, Ramakrishna had prayed: "Mother, if the zamindars of my *desh* [village home] show me respect, I will believe that all this [his visions] is true. Then even they came to talk to me on their own." Acknowledgement by the *baramanush* remains indispensable, but the zamindars now come "on their own" to the hitherto humble, unknown temple *pujari*. Holy madness also gives a licence to mock authority. Ramakrishna recalled with considerable satisfaction that his "madness" had permitted him then to say "things bluntly and straight out to people. I showed no deference for anyone, had no fear of *baralok*."[27] He had even slapped Rani Rashmoni once, for being inattentive during a devotional song.[28] The years of tempestuous sadhana were over, and Ramakrishna was now a respectable guru of the *bhadralok*; he still looked back on those mad years with pride.

The ambiguity persisted throughout. Thus Ramakrishna, by then quite a well-established figure, took special care to button himself up while going to visit Vidyasagar. In course of their conversation, however, he informed Vidyasagar that the celebrated reformer was like a ship, he himself a tiny boat. But ships may run aground in small streams, boats sail freely on rivers big or small.[29] Subservience and resentment, we shall see, would jostle at the heart of Ramakrishna's central conception of bhakti, with divinity at times patterned by him on the model of the *baramanush* patron in a relationship that was acceptable but not tension-free. For a man like Ramakrishna, resentment would always fall far short of overt critique. The occasional mockery of the powerful would be inextricably mingled with deference. Ramakrishna's attitudes recall perhaps that "sideward glance" of "muffled challenge" with which the St Petersburg clerk looks at his superiors in Dostoyevski's *Poor Folk*.[30] Such ambiguity towards power would be shared by many in Ramakrishna's *bhadralok* audience, and, more particularly, by its clerical component.

---

[27] KM II, p. 49 (4 June 1883).

[28] KM II, pp. 2–3 (16 October 1882).

[29] KM III, p. 16 (5 August 1882).

[30] Mikhail Bakhtin, *Problems of Dostoyevski's Poetics* (Leningrad, 1929, Moscow, 1963; trans. Manchester, 1984), p. 210.

If Ramakrishna was ambivalent towards the superior ones of his world, the *baralok*, a second kind of ambiguity surfaces in the parables drawn from nature and rural life which are so abundant in his discourse. Virtual absence of formal learning kept Ramakrishna's original world not too distant from the oral culture of peasants, artisans, and village women. But birth in a high-caste family with some reputation for ritual expertise already meant a certain distancing, and Ramakrishna himself moved away from the village towards the new world of city *bhadralok*. The *Kathamrita* conversations provide rich evidence about the tensions of a never-quite-completed movement: they help us to appreciate, too, the ways through which Ramakrishna's language itself became an additional attraction for his urban devotees. Late-nineteenth-century *baralok* writing had changed recently in the direction of greater chastity and decorum, with the prose of Vidyasagar and Bankimchandra rejecting as vulgar the style associated with earlier literary figures like Iswar Gupta. Such self-imposed restraints perhaps at times became slightly oppressive, as creating an uncomfortable distance from everyday speech. The *Kathamrita* insisted on keeping Ramakrishna's colloquialisms, and presented to its readers a language that seemed attractively earthy and unsophisticated, and yet perfectly understandable. The remarkable thing about Ramakrishna's nature imagery is the unselfconscious ease with which he passes from similes conventionally beautiful to others that would seldom be mentioned in chaste late-nineteenth-century *bhadralok* writing. The blue from a distance, but colourless close by, indicates the equal validity of *sarkar* and *nirakar* types of devotion – conceiving divinity as with or without form.[31] Steadfastness in yogic devotion is conveyed by the image of a bird sitting with total concentration on its egg.[32] But villagers defecating around a Kamarpukur pond can serve Ramakrishna's purpose as well, and as often as sea or birds,[33] and there are also caustic comments about the Brahmo habit of dwelling constantly on the beauty of God's creation. They admire the garden,

[31] KM I, p. 59 (28 October 1882).
[32] KM III, pp. 19–20 (24 August 1882).
[33] KM I, p. 74 (December 1882).

said Ramakrishna, and forget to look for its owner or *bahu*.³⁴ There is no "dissociation if sensibility" in Ramakrishna,³⁵ no marking out of a distinct realm of subject or diction as proper or poetic. Nature in his conversation is different from the way it is represented in the occasional formal set descriptions Mahendranath Gupta gives of the surroundings of Dakshineswar, in imagery derived through Bankimchandra's prose and ultimately from canons of Sanskrit aesthetics. It differs also from the style of the "romantic" poetry of nature being developed, precisely around the 1880s, by Biharilal Chakrabarti and Rabindranath.

Nature to Ramakrishna was not yet a spectacle of sheer beauty, to be admired through a distinct and self-conscious aesthetic sensibility. It was also something impregnated with human labour. It is remarkable how often the everyday toil of peasants, artisans, and women is made to convey messages with a positive content – unlike, we shall see, most of Ramakrishna's images drawn from city life. The peasant, sticking to his ancestral land even if crops have failed in a year of drought, working carefully and hard to bring just the right amount of water to his field from a distance, is often made to epitomise the perseverance needed for true bhakti.³⁶ The housewife who prepares fish in various ways to suit the distinct palates of her many children becomes the symbol of the multiplicity of paths to the divine.³⁷ The *bhakta* can remain in the world but not be lost in its temptations, like village women minding their babies, talking to customers while they work at the *dheki* (husking machine), careful

---

³⁴ KM II, p. 75 (28 November 1883); KM V, p. 62 (18 August 1883); KM I, p. 150 (19 October 1884).

³⁵ The phrase used by T.S. Eliot to emphasise the contrast between the literature of the times of Shakespeare and Donne, and that of Milton and his successors. See also Raymond Williams, *The Country and the City*, op. cit., for a similar disjunction in the evolution of the pastoral.

³⁶ KM I, p. 71 (14 December 1882); KM II, p. 33 (8 April 1883); KM IV, p. 84 (23 March 1884); KM V, p. 104 (2 January 1884), p. 135 (22 February 1885).

³⁷ KM I, p. 21 (February 1882).

that their hands do not get injured.[38] Evident in such parables is a love and delight in the sensuous details of rural workaday life, where individual labour can be seen to produce immediate, palpable results: land yielding crops, women turning fish into many dishes, grain being husked into rice. City life – and more particularly the life of the intellectual and the clerk – must have appeared singularly bereft of this feel of sensuous productivity, to Ramakrishna as well as to his audience.

The valorisation of rural labour, again, is often associated with the questioning of the dry abstract arrogance of formal written culture, the *jnana* of pandits or of the English-educated. Seeing is better than hearing, and hearing is better than reading, Ramakrishna liked to say.[39] True religious awareness is like the practical knowledge about varieties of yarn picked up by the apprentice, never from books, but through serving a master-weaver.[40] Such passages indicate not a general "withdrawal" from *jnana* and karma, as has been recently argued,[41] but a valorisation of village labour and oral practical wisdom over city life and the written culture of the literati, old or new.

Ramakrishna's fables are often imbued with a strong note of peasant wisdom and practicality. The pandit crossing the Ganga boasts of his *shastric* knowledge. But then a storm begins and he does not know how to swim. His companion says: "I may not know *sankhya* and *patanjali*, but I can swim."[42] Of the three friends who meet a tiger in the forest, the true *bhakta* is the one who climbs up a tree, not the man who resigns himself to death, or even the third who calls on Iswara for succour. The *bhakta* loves God so much that he says: "Why bother Iswara with this?" His of course is also the most practical choice.[43]

---

[38] KM III, p. 59 (27 December 1883); KM IV, p. 146 (14 September 1884).
[39] KM II, p. 216 (22 October 1885); KM III, p. 75 (30 June 1884).
[40] KM II, p. 39 (15 April 1883).
[41] Partha Chatterjee, "A Religion of Urban Domesticity", op. cit.
[42] KM IV, pp. 74–5 (24 February 1884).
[43] KM II, p. 46 (2 June 1883).

Perhaps a note of "plebeian" practicality can be inferred also from Ramakrishna's passionate desire to see Kali face to face during the days of his intense sadhana.[44] Later on, too, he insisted that he was literally seeing and talking with the goddess during his frequent trances – and this was the sole claim to superior religious power Ramakrishna ever made. Once again, *seeing* was held to be superior to hearing, say, a text read out by a pandit. Interesting in this context is Ramakrishna's denigration of reading, though that too uses the eyes: evidently he was not particularly used to silent reading, that central practice of developed literate culture. "Seeing" would be the only way through which plebeians with little or no education could claim devotional equality with, or primacy over, the *baralok* masters of textual learning. As with the work of peasants, artisans, or women, devotion here yields direct, sensuous results.

Direct perception had been privileged as the only valid form of knowledge in the *pratakshyabad* of the ancient Indian materialist tradition of Lokayata, which has been denigrated down the ages as a philosophy of the vulgar people.[45] Perhaps we have in Ramakrishna traces of a "religious materialism" not utterly dissimilar to what Carlo Ginzburg has diagnosed for his sixteenth-century North Italian miller – minus, of course, that social radicalism which makes Menocchio so remarkable.[46] But Ramakrishna, as usual, perhaps like Hindu traditions in general, straddles different levels or worlds. The primacy of visual perception is assumed also in a wide variety of Hindu religious and philosophical traditions, though this is *manspratyaksha* – spiritual or mystic seeing – rather than anything comparable to everyday visual experience. One recalls the justly famous ancient hymn which claims to have seen the Absolute Purusha, resplendent like the sun, dispelling all darkness. *Sannyasis* claiming yogic powers, along with preachers of bhakti, have often counterposed

[44] L I, Sadhakbhava, pp. 111–14; *Life*, p. 68.
[45] Surendranath Dasgupta, *History of Indian Philosophy*, vol. III (Cambridge, 1961); Debiprasad Chattopadhyay, *Lokayata* (New Delhi, 1959, 1975), chapter I.
[46] Carlo Ginzburg, *The Cheese and the Worms* (Harmondsworth: Penguin Books, 1982).

their superhuman powers of seeing the divine against the Brahman claim to textual knowledge,[47] and Ramakrishna clearly fits in with such traditions.

Such affinities are not surprising, for continued familiarity with the rural world of nature, labour, and oral culture is accompanied in Ramakrishna by a certain distancing. The labour of artisans, peasants, and women has become a parable of perseverance and devotion: little remains of the sweat and pain of toil. This is a rural Brahman sensibility, perhaps, which does not aestheticise village life – unlike romantic literature – but seeks to reduce it to lessons in religion and morality.

A similar process can be seen at work in the selection Ramakrishna made, in the *Kathamrita* conversations with *bhadralok* devotees, of some forty-odd songs from his favourite composer, Ramprasad Sen. The songs of this eighteenth-century Kali-*bhakta* can still be heard in village lanes and on the lips of beggars. They often present a faith heroically preserved in and through enormous suffering, poverty, inequality, and exploitation:

> Who calls you, Tara, compassionate to the poor!
> To some you give wealth, elephants, and chariots.
> While others are fated to work for wages, without enough rice
> And *sag* . . .
> You have brought me to this world, and beaten me as iron is beaten.
> I will still call to you, Kali, see how much courage I have.[48]

Little remains of this anguish, suppressed anger, and sublimation, of what is recognised to be injustice, in the songs sung by Ramakrishna to city audiences of middle-aged householders and educated young men. His choice highlighted the more obviously doctrinal pieces, along with the ones where the mood of triumphant union with Kali marginalises or eliminates sufferings. To borrow for a moment

---

[47] Madeleine Biardeau, *Hinduism: The Anthropology of a Civilisation* (Delhi, 1989), pp. 73–5.

[48] Sibaprasad Bhattacharji, *Bharatchandra o Ramprasad* (Calcutta, 1967), p. 218; Sashibhushan Dasgupta, *Bharater Shakti-Sadhana o Shakta-Sahitya* (Calcutta, 1960), p. 230.

Kaliyuga, Chakri and Bhakti

from Weber, a movement is taking place from a "theodicy of suffering" towards a "theodicy of good fortune".[49]

Ramakrishna's parables of village life do occasionally mention instances of zamindari oppression – but always as things which have to be accepted, facts of life no different from droughts or other natural calamities.[50] Rural hierarchy is accepted and even idealised at times in the figure of the benevolent *baramanush* patron. This contrasts significantly, we shall see, with Ramakrishna's views on certain forms of power in city-life.

Ramakrishna spent thirty-five years of his life in a suburb of Calcutta, but it was only during the last ten years or so that he suddenly gained acceptance and renown among the Calcutta *bhadralok*. The timing coincided, significantly, with a kind of hiatus in *bhadralok* history. By the 1870s and 1880s, the "renaissance" dream of improvement and reform under British tutelage was turning sour. The Brahmos had split up, Vidyasagar was increasingly frustrated and lonely, and racial tensions were mounting under Lytton and through the Ilbert Bill furore. The alternative, patriotic vision of solving the country's ills by drastically modifying or overthrowing foreign rule did not, however, appear really viable till around 1905. Organisations like the Indian Association or the early Congress still had a very limited appeal, even among the *bhadralok*.

The hiatus bred, in the first place, a disquiet about the multifarious schemes and endeavours of the *bhadralok*, so many of which seemed to end in a whimper. Ramakrishna's rejection of social activism, embodied for instance in his scornful comments about Sambhu Mallik's philanthropy, thus won an appreciative audience – even though its own foundations were rather different. Subordination of external action to inner piety came naturally for someone affiliated to traditions of bhakti and there was, perhaps, also an element of plebeian cynicism. Philanthropy merely boosted the ego of the

---

[49] Max Weber, "The Socoal Psychology of World Religion", in H.H. Garth and C. Wright Mills, *Max Weber, Essays in Sociology* (London, 1948, 1977), pp. 271–5.

[50] See, for example, KM II, pp. 271–7 (2 June 1883); KM II, p. 61 (15 June 1883).

do-gooding *baramanush*: it was sheer arrogance for anyone to think that he had the power to really improve the world.[51]

For the *bhadralok*, the hiatus between the myths of renaissance improvement and nationalist deliverance encouraged moods of introspection and nostalgia. There was a partial turning away from forward-looking male activism towards a series of logically distinct but often intermingled "Others": past as contrasted to present, country *vs* city, a deliberate feminisation as opposed to active masculinity, the attractive playfulness and irresponsibility of the child and the *pagal* as against the goal-oriented instrumental rationality of the adult male.[52] One can now begin to understand the scope and power of Ramakrishna's appeal, which fitted in with, and helped to stimulate, such broader trends. His earthy parables seemed to bring back a rural world from which the city *bhadralok* now sometimes felt they had unwisely uprooted themselves. Ramakrishna's lifelong love for women's roles – acting feminine parts in boyhood, dressing up as a woman for a time in Mathur's house, even allegedly having periods – was chronicled with respect and admiration by Mahendranath Gupta and other biographers.[53] Feminisation in any case had a respectable pedigree in certain forms of Vaishnava devotion.[54] Even more attractive was Ramakrishna's childlike surrender to the Shakta divine mother: "Attaining Iswara makes you into a five-year-old boy"[55] – a womb reversion, almost, allowing uninhibited scope to what in other contexts would be termed irresponsible, unmanly, irrational behaviour.

What was happening, however, was not a rupture or neat separation into activist and inward-turning groups, but a commingling of moods. In Bankimchandra's *Anandamath*, for instance – published

---

[51] See, for instance, KM II, p. 157 (11 October 1884), where Ramakrishna recalls a conversation with Kristodas Pal, or his meeting with Vidyasagar, KM III, p. 15 (5 August 1882).

[52] See note 63 for reference to the culturally specific meanings of *pagal* (usually translated as "mad") in Bengal.

[53] *Life*, p. 176.

[54] See, for instance, Ramakanta Chakrabarti, *Vaisnavism in Bengal* (Calcutta, 1985), chapter XI, and *passim*.

[55] KM I, p. 214 (22 October 1885).

incidentally in 1882, the year in which Mahendranath began his trips to Dakshineswar – the *sannyasis* are engaged in a hard masculine project of overthrowing British-backed Muslim rule, and they explicitly distinguish their Vaishnavism from the non-violent bhakti of Chaitanya. Yet their "Bande Mataram" hymn is addressed to a nurturing bounteous motherland, and the novel contains a dream sequence where Kalyani sees Vishnu cradled and enveloped by an indistinct all-embracing mother figure.[56] In Bengali poetry the "epic" style of Michael Madhusudan Datta in the 1850s and 1860s had glorified heroic action in defiance of overwhelming odds. Precisely around the 1880s, this began to be partially displaced by the more introspective Romantic lyricism of Biharilal Chakrabarti and Rabindranath, where nature was given a new centrality. A rural retrospect became prominent also in autobiographies, which were now being composed in unprecedented number thanks to the simultaneous entry of print culture and vernacular prose. They were coming to acquire a "developmental" format, in which a man's life became "a study of his progress towards and absorption into his historical role"[57] – and yet it was reformist authors using this format who seemed to linger most over idealised memories of childhood spent in traditional rural families.[58] Introspection and intimate detail, marginalised in the central narrative of adult public activity, could be given freer rein in memories of childhood, and these consequently became channels for "expressing difficulty and ambivalence".[59]

Probably under Ramakrishna's influence, the Brahmos associated with Keshabchandra Sen began conceptualising and addressing

---

[56] Bankimchandra Chattopadhyay, *Anandamath* (1882), in *Bankim Rachanabali*, vol. I (Calcutta, 1360/1953).

[57] Benedict Anderson, "A Time of Darkness and A Time of Light", in A. Reid and O. Mann, *Perceptions of the Past in South East Asia* (Heinemann, 1979, 1982), p. 226.

[58] For a more detailed discussion, see Sumit Sarkar, "Renaissance, Kaliyuga and Kalki: Construction of Time and History in Colonial Bengal", paper presented at International Round-table of Historians and Anthropologists, Bellagio, August 1989 (a revised version is in the present book).

[59] Carolyn Steedman (ed.), *The Radical Soldier's Tale* (London, 1988), pt I, p. 103.

divinity in maternal terms. Ramakrishna's spell helped to turn another once-militant Brahmo, Bejoykrishna Goswami, into a Vaishnava mystic who wanted to "become like a child, just like what he had been in infancy".[60] The childlike behaviour valorised by Ramakrishna or Bejoykrishna, it must be added, was modelled on a construction of childhood, possibly specific to upper-caste Hindu society, which was different from both Puritanical discipline and romantic glorification of pure natural growth. The Hindu child "is closely integrated into family life without having any of its responsibilities. He has no personal timetable . . . no rules of hygiene or cleanliness imposed from outside . . . He seems to live by pure whim . . ."[61] Biographers of Ramakrishna love to describe what they term his *balak-bhava* (the mood of relating to divinity as a child), including lack of inhibitions about nudity or soiling himself in public.[62] The child model thus slides into that of the *pagal*, and, partly again under Ramakrishna's influence, the runaway irresponsible male and the *pagal* as embodiment of holy folly became long-lasting stereotypes in Bengali literature.[63]

Direct references to colonial domination are extremely rare in Ramakrishna's discourse, but surely it is not far-fetched to see in the series of "Others" fostered by his example traces of an implicit rejection of values imposed by the nineteenth-century West. Colonialism counterposed to European active virile masculinity the stereotype of the conquered native as effeminate, irritatingly childish, or at best pleasantly childlike.[64] The educated Bengali did not surrender, without qualification, to this "colonial discourse", as uncritical admiration of Edward Said has led some to assume. Excluded anyway from the

---

[60] Mahatma Bijoykrishna Goswami in *Jivan-Vrittanta* (Calcutta, n.d.), p. 387.

[61] Biardeau, *Hinduism*, op. cit., pp. 33–4.

[62] See, for instance, the section entitled "Balakbhava" in Satyacharan Mitra, *Sri Sri Ramakrishna Paramahansa: Jibani o Upadesh* (Calcutta, 1897), pp. 150–2.

[63] For a study of the *pagal* in religious life, see June McDaniel, *The Madness of the Saints: Ecstatic Religion* in *Bengal* (Chicago, 1989).

[64] Ashis Nandy, *The Intimate Enemy: Loss and Recovery of Self under Colonialism* (Delhi, 1983), pp. 7–8, 11–16, 52–3.

privileged male occupations of military and political command and successful independent entrepreneurship, and relegated to dull and lowly clerical jobs, such people were perhaps expressing a muffled defiance through a preference for feminisation, childlike behaviour, and the irresponsible unreason of the *pagal*. These provided a wider scope to certain human possibilities than the rigid code of Victorian responsible male behaviour sought to be imposed as the *bhadralok*'s role model. Ramakrishna and his devotees freely expressed their emotions, plunged into ecstatic dances, wept in public: the *Kathamrita* describes the master uninhibitedly fondling and "playing" with his teenager disciples.[65] Ramakrishna in effect subverted the distinctions between adult and child, male and female, work and play, which the "civilising" mission of the West was making more rigid in colonial Bengal. Such subversion was particularly attractive during the hiatus between the renaissance and the nationalist myths, but its appeal extended beyond the 1870s and 1880s and a specific social dimension. It stood in marked contrast particularly to the imposed world of formal routinised education and time-bound *chakri*.

Not all sections of the Calcutta *bhadralok* were equally open to Ramakrishna's influence in the late 1870s and early 1880s. Rani Rashmoni and Mathur of the Janbazar family apart, the really big zamindars of Calcutta showed little interest in Ramakrishna. A few well-off householders became devotees, he was occasionally invited to the garden houses of the rich, and there were some sessions with Marwari businessmen of Barabazar.[66] But on the whole the insistence of Ramakrishna's first biographer, Ramachandra Datta, that his master had been the guru not of the rich but of the *madhyabitta* (middle class) seems acceptable – with the further, vital, clarification that the higher or more successful stratum of the Calcutta professional middle class also remained more or less immune from the spell of Dakshineswar in the saint's own lifetime.[67] The disciples who became *sannyasis* under Vivekananda suffered from acute scarcity of funds till the

[65] *Life*, pp. 32, 323–5, 338, 345, and *passim*.
[66] KM I, chapter 21 (20 October 1884, pp. 178–86), is an account of a visit of Ramakrishna to the Marwaris of Barabazar.
[67] Ramachandra Datta, *Sri Sri Ramakrishna Paramahansa Dever Jivan-Vrittanta* (Calcutta, 1890), pp. 86–9.

late 1890s. Lawyers, journalists, teachers (except Mahendranath),[68] and writers seldom figure in the *Kathamrita*, and politicians like Surendranath Banerjea never bothered to pay Ramakrishna a visit. Among the major figures of what today is often called the Bengal Renaissance, only Keshabchandra Sen became close to him, and it was journals run by the Nababidhan Brahmo group that first made Ramakrishna known among the English-educated.[69] There were brief encounters – usually at Ramakrishna's initiative, and none of them too happy, with leaders of the other two Brahmo factions (Debendranath Tagore and Shibath Shastri), with the Hindu revivalist orator Sasadhar Tarkachudamoni, as well as with Vidyasagar, the poet Michael Madhusudan, and the novelist Bankimchandra.[70] But the one major literary figure who became a devotee, the actor-playwright Girish Chandra Ghosh, had failed in the school-leaving examination and had then spent years as a clerk. It is the world of *chakri*, of clerical jobs in mercantile and government offices, that really dominates Ramakrishna's Calcutta milieu. His devotees included a sprinkling of deputy magistrates and subjudges, along with a few who held relatively senior jobs in mercantile offices: the upper rungs in both kinds of service would have been British preserves. More often, the disciples were struggling clerks or young men who might soon have to start looking for clerical posts.[71]

The stresses and silences about Calcutta in Ramakrishna's discourses confirm and supplement the inferences derived from data about his city contacts. Despite long years in Dakshineswar (a northern suburb of the metropolis) and lengthy sojourns at the Janbazar mansion in

---

[68] Mahendranath's near-uniqueness is indicated by the nickname of "master" (teacher), which he came to be known by in Ramakrishna's circle. Evidently there were no other teachers around.

[69] For details about Ramakrishna's relations with Brahmos, see Brojen Banerji and Sajanikanta Das, op. cit., and Sankariprasad Basu, *Vivekananda o Samakalin Bharatvarsha* (Calcutta, 1979), chapter 13.

[70] KM, *passim*. Bankimchandra, for instance, horrified Ramakrishna by declaring with provocative cynicism that food, sleep, and sex were the principal goals of human life. Vidyasagar remained polite, but never followed up Ramakrishna's sole visit to him.

[71] For some details, see my "Kathamrita as Text", pp. 24–6.

Kaliyuga, Chakri and Bhakti 177

the heart of central Calcutta, Ramakrishna remained in many ways an outsider to the city. The poignant nostalgia of the *dasi* (servant woman) is a favourite image of his, serving her master's family with devotion, looking after his children, and yet thinking all the time of her distant village home.[72] It conveys, perhaps, something of his own mood. Ramakrishna could display, even in the 1880s, a rustic sense of wonder at times about city marvels.[73] But, in total contrast to rural labour, most urban work processes failed to arouse his interest – even though Dakshineswar was an area where jute mills were springing up. The city rich do not constitute a distinct category in his conversation, being conflated with the rural zamindar in the image of the *baramanush, baralok*, or babu. The limits of Ramakrishna's city contacts and appeal are indicated also by the silences about the middle-class professions of law, journalism, and teaching. The one specifically urban life situation which becomes really vivid in Ramakrishna's discourse is the life of the clerk (*kerani*): "What a mess! A salary of twenty rupees – three children – no money to feed them properly; the roof leaks, no money to repair it; impossible to buy new books for the son, to give him the sacred thread; have to beg eight annas from one, four annas from another!"[74] Other passages graphically describe the unemployed *kerani* desperately running around for another job, as well as the travails of time-bound office work.[75]

A poor Brahman like Ramakrishna had a natural empathy for clerks – poor, overwhelmingly upper caste, with bhadralok aspirations but without the resources, often, to fulfil them.[76] I have argued elsewhere that the anguish and frustrations of genteel poverty in this world

---

[72] KM I, p. 22 (February 1882); ibid., p. 131 (15 June 1884); ibid., p. 7 (2 April 1882).

[73] KM I, p. 52 (27 October 1882). This describes his "childlike" pleasure about the sights and sounds of the white part of the city: gas lights, well-lit houses, girls playing the piano.

[74] KM V, p. 109 (9 March 1884).

[75] KM V, p. 44 (2 June 1883), p. 4 (2 April 1882).

[76] For Ramakrishna, as we have just seen, the many burdens of the *kerani* include, notably, trying to educate his son and meeting the costs of the sacred thread investiture ceremony.

of the unsuccessful *bhadralok* – pandits losing patronage in the new era, obscure hack-writers, humble schoolteachers, clerks, unemployed educated youth, high school or college boys with highly uncertain job prospects – produced a late flowering of what may be called Kaliyuga literature in mid- and late-nineteenth-century Bengal.[77] Embodied in a mass of cheap vernacular tracts, plays, and finding a visual counterpart in many Kalighat paintings,[78] these constitute the most relevant context for understanding Ramakrishna and his appeal. This "low life of literature",[79] together with Ramakrishna's conversation (in which the Kalighat motif recurs with some frequency), provides an entry into a grossly neglected world. Historians of the "Bengal Renaissance" have concentrated on the well-known intellectuals, the older kind of work on nationalism focused on politics inspired or manipulated from the top, while Subaltern Studies concerned itself primarily with peasant movements and consciousness.[80] What for convenience may be termed lower-middle-class groups have entered historical narratives, if at all, mainly under economistic rubrics as victims of educated unemployment or price rise. Yet their importance in a variety of late-nineteenth-century and twentieth-century movements is obvious enough – and so is, in cultural terms, their vital intermediate role. Theirs has been a predominantly high-caste, yet depressed world, entry into which has been the first step in upward mobility for neo-literates from lower down

---

[77] See Sumit Sarkar, "Kalki-avatar of Bikrampur: A Village Scandal in Early Twentieth Century Bengal", in Ranajit Guha (ed.), *Subaltern Studies VI* (Delhi, 1989; reproduced in the present volume); idem, "Calcutta in the Bengal Renaissance", in Sukanta Chaudhuri (ed.), *Calcutta: The Living City*, vol. I (Delhi, 1990); idem, "Kali-yuger Kalpana o Aupanibeshik Samaj", in G. Chattopadhyay (ed.), *Itihas Anusandhan 4* (Calcutta, 1989).

[78] W.G. Archer, *Bazar Paintings of Calcutta* (London, 1953); Mildred Archer, *Indian Popular Painting in the Indian Office Library* (London, 1977).

[79] I am borrowing this term from Robert Darnton, "The High Enlightenment and the Low-Life of Literature in Pre-Revolutionary France", *Past and Present*, no. 51, May 1971.

[80] In its initial phase, that is to say; today some of its practitioners are more interested in the Saidian project of deconstructing a colonial discourse assumed to be all-pervasive.

the social hierarchy. And if the Kaliyuga myth has been relatively open to occasional appropriations from below,[81] it could also extend its appeal to the late-nineteenth-century high *bhadralok* in their more introspective and pessimistic moods. This was possible, I intend to argue, particularly because of the new and crucial centrality of *chakri* within the Kaliyuga literature of colonial Bengal.

For some two thousand years, from the Vana Parva of the Mahabharata onwards, Kaliyuga has been a recurrent and powerful dystopia, a format for voicing a variety of high-caste male anxieties. Its many evils – located in the present and the future, for Kaliyuga is supposed to have begun soon after the end of the Mahabharata war – traditionally include oppressive *mleccha* (alien and impure) kings, Brahmans corrupted by too much rational argument (the "science of disputation"), over-mighty Shudras expounding the scriptures and ceasing to serve the Brahmans, girls choosing their own partners, and disobedient and deceiving wives having intercourse with menials, slaves, and even animals.[82] The nineteenth century made a selection, with new stresses, from this impressive catalogue. Brahman corruption and rationalistic criticism of traditional verities were obviously relevant themes. Little was made (except in some later, early-twentieth-century texts) of the Shudra threat,[83] which never became much of an issue in nineteenth-century Bengal (as contrasted to Maharashtra). Women remain a key target, but no longer primarily for sexual immorality: pride of place now went to the "modern" wife, allegedly ill-treating her mother-in-law, enslaving the husband, and wasting money on luxuries for herself.[84] The crucial

---

[81] For an example, see my "Kalki-Avatar of Bikrampur", op. cit.

[82] These, along with natural calamities, are the principal features of Kaliyuga in "Vana Parva" ("Markandaya Samasya", 187–90) of the Mahabharata. I am using the English translation of Pratapchandra Roy (Calcutta, n.d.), vol. III, pp. 397–413, along with the standard nineteenth-century Bengali version of Kaliprasanna Sinha and Gopal Haldar (eds), *Mahabharata* (Calcutta, 1974), vol. II, pp. 194–200.

[83] Thus Pasupati Chattopadhyaya's *Kalir Bamun* (Calcutta, 1922) hits out at a lower-caste "sanskritising" movement.

[84] Jayanta Goswami, *Samajchitre Unabinghsha Satabdir Bangla Prahasan*

innovation in a multitude of late-nineteenth-century tracts and farces was the close interrelationship postulated between the disorderly wife, the "modern" craze for money, and the *chakri* the husband is forced to take up to get the one and please the other – precisely, in other words, Ramakrishna's triad of *kamini–kanchan–chakri*.

And so the gods, on a visit to colonial India in *Debganer Marta Agaman* (1889), keep meeting "clerks . . . dozing as they return home from office. Their faces are worn out after the whole day's work . . . The sahib's kicks and blows the whole day, and when they return . . . the nagging of wives . . ."[85] A play entitled *Kerani-carit* (1885) makes the discipline of time its central focus: "We lose the day's salaries if we reach office a minute late . . . half the salary goes on fines . . . there is not a single gap in our day's routine." The clerk's wife complains that she now sees little of her husband, but is quickly consoled by the thought that the salary will fetch her jewellery.[86] And while little is said directly about colonial domination as *mleccha* rule, Harischandra Bandopadhyay's *Kaler Bau* (1880) contains a powerful subtext. "Slaves to government officials, we have to spend our time in homes as slaves to the wives", complains a husband. The figure of the suffering mother, neglected by a son who has been entrapped by the wiles of the modern wife, becomes here a metaphor for the enslaved "mother"-land, the *Bangamata* who has become the "slave [dasi] of the London queen".[87]

Placed in this context, Ramakrishna's oft-repeated comments about *kamini* and *kanchan* cease to sound like a mere reiteration of age-old verities and acquire a specific late-nineteenth-century resonance. As in many contemporary farces and Kalighat paintings,

---

(Calcutta, n.d.), summarises the plots of a large number of plays and farces around these themes.

[85] Durgacharan Roy, *Debganer-Marta Agaman* (Calcutta, 1889).

[86] Prankrishna Gangopadhyay, *Kerani-carit* (Calcutta, 1885). See also Anon., *Kerani-darpan* (Calcutta, 1874), with its vivid account of time discipline and racist humiliation in office work. I owe this reference to Anamitra Das.

[87] Jayanta Goswami, op. cit., p. 1036.

kamini at times conveys a fear of loss of male authority within the household: "Men are made fools and worthless, by women . . . If the wife, says, 'Get up', he gets up – 'sit down', he sits down." A caustic remark about an ex-devotee, now busy running errands for his wife, drew appreciative laughter from Ramakrishna's audience. But the central link is between *kamini* and the *dasatya* of *chakri* (bondage of the office job), mediated by *kanchan* – and direct references to colonial domination, extremely rare otherwise in Ramakrishna's discourse, here put in an appearance. "Look how many educated people trained in English, with so many degrees, accept *chakri*, and receive kicks from their master's boots every day. *Kamini* is the sole reason for all this."[88] Ramakrishna once told a favourite disciple that he should jump in the Ganga rather than "become a slave of someone by taking a job".[89] He was also quite explicit about what is objectionable about office work: "your face seems to have a dark shadow upon it. That's because you are working in an office. In the office you have to handle money, keep accounts, do so much other work. You have to be alert all the time."[90]

The precise nature and implications of this aversion to *chakri*, running through late-nineteenth-century Kaliyuga literature and Ramakrishna's conversation, need some analysis. *Chakri* was generally ill paid and increasingly difficult to obtain: but the "salary of twenty rupees" mentioned by Ramakrishna was not really negligible by contemporary standards, and educated unemployment was not yet the explosive issue it would become later. What made *chakri* intolerable at this specific conjuncture was rather its connotation of impersonal cash nexus and authority, embodied above all in the new rigorous discipline of work regulated by clock time. Disciplinary time was a particularly abrupt and imposed innovation in colonial India. Europe had gone through a much slower phased transition, spanning some five hundred years: from the first thirteenth- and fourteenth-century mechanical clocks with hour-hands alone, through the later

[88] KM III, p. 143 (12 April 1885); KM I, p. 73 (14 December 1882).
[89] KM II, p. 201 (1 March 1885).
[90] KM I, p. 121 (15 June 1884).

innovations of watches counting off minutes and seconds, down to the developed eighteenth- and nineteenth-century apparatus of disciplinary time in modern armies, bureaucracies, hospitals, schools, prisons, and factories.[91] Colonial rule telescoped the entire process for India within one or two generations.

In Bengal, particularly, government and mercantile offices (along with the new type of schools and colleges) became the principal locus for the imported ideas of bourgeois time and discipline. Factories were still rare (and mainly, so far, involved white employers and migrant non-Bengali labourers), capitalist farming non-existent, and few Bengalis served in the army. Calcutta in the late nineteenth century, however, was the headquarters of the British Indian bureaucracy, mercantile enterprise, and education. Regular hours of work throughout the year in offices must have contrasted sharply with the seasonal variation in labour tempo normal to village life. Mughal bureaucracy had had its clerks, of course, but jobs in British-controlled offices under bosses seeking to impose Victorian standards of punctuality and discipline must have still meant a considerable departure. Time-bound office work, again, had to be performed in the unfamiliar enclosed space of the modern city building. In school and office alike, there was the additional problem of an often imperfectly understood foreign language of command.

Chakri thus became a "chronotope" of alienated time and space,[92] late-nineteenth-century Kaliyuga's heart of darkness, the principal

---

[91] E.P. Thompson, "Time Work-Discipline, and Industrial Capitalism", *Past and Present*, no. 38, December 1967; Michel Foucault, *Discipline and Punish* (London, 1979).

[92] Mikhail Bakhtin, *The Dialogic Imagination* (Texas, 1981), *passim*. The dual burden of disciplinary time and foreign language is neatly summed up in a "funny" story that can still be heard in Bengal about the clerk's life, perpetually rushing from home to shopping to office and back: "Running, running, office come – tobuo to Sir late hoy" [Sir, still I am late]. I owe this reference to Sukumari Bhattacharji. For some interesting evidence about a hostility to "*naukri*" based on aversion towards disciplinary time persisting among artisans till today, see Nita Kumar, *The Artisans of Banaras: Popular Culture and Identity, 1880–1986* (Princeton, 1988), chapters 2, 4, and *passim*.

format through which awareness of subjection spread among colonial middle-class males. Unable as yet to resist foreign bosses effectively, the clerk – or the writer empathising with him – often passed on the blame in part to women. Awakening political consciousness thus became intertwined with a strengthening of patriarchal prejudices.

In course of time this predominantly lower-middle- class discourse on *chakri* merged with broader critiques of colonial domination, formulated by more sophisticated intellectuals. The office was one obvious and highly visible site of racial discrimination, manifested in salary differentials and the everyday behaviour of white bosses. British rule, it came to be argued, was directly responsible for making Indians dependent on servile clerical jobs, for it had destroyed handicrafts, ruined agriculture through excessive taxes, and blocked independent business through "one-way" free trade. Remedies were now sought through autonomous efforts at technical and "national" education, Swadeshi enterprise, and, increasingly, political struggle. Within offices, too, the first signs of clerical organisation and protest would become manifest from around 1905.[93]

All that lay in the future: for the moment, Ramakrishna could evoke a profound response through his promise of escape into an inner world of bhakti, into which one could retreat even while carrying on the duties imposed by a heartless time- and rule-bound society. This was Ramakrishna's specific, original contribution to the general critique of *chakri*. Over this inner world presides, significantly enough, an Iswara who, in Ramakrishna's parables, gets repeatedly conflated with the idealised figure of the traditional *baramanush* or babu – someone utterly different from the impersonal, distant office boss (usually called *manib* in the *Kathamrita* conversations). The raja, zamindar, or old kind of city patron pleased with the *seba* (devoted voluntary service, as contrasted to bondage or *dasatya*) of his *khansama*

---

[93] For some details, see my *Swadeshi Movement in Bengal 1903–1908* (New Delhi, 1973), chapter V. Interestingly, the first strike that attracted widespread attention and sympathy was by the clerks of Burn Iron Works, Howrah, and it was around a question of time discipline. The clerks were protesting against a new mechanical system of recording attendance: ibid., pp. 200–2.

(servant),[94] might ask the latter one day to sit next to him.[95] A poor man's son in this paternalistic, personalised mode of authority could become rich overnight if the *baramanush* wed his daughter to him.[96] It is essential, however, to get to know the babu directly, even if his officials (*amlas*) try to block your way – after which even the *amlas* will respect you. Maybe there is a hint here of the age-old rural dream in many lands of the distant overlord, just king, "little father" of the poor. "Willed submission" was an acceptable way of relating to such figures, at least in retrospect: they can serve, therefore, as prototypes of the divine.[97]

Running through all such parables is an implicit "Other": the modern British-controlled office governed by impersonal rules and abstract time schedules where the *amlas* are as troublesome as ever, but the superior (sahib) is no longer approachable. A story frequently related from the mid nineteenth century onwards about Ramprasad seems relevant here. The composer is supposed to have been caught by an official scribbling verses about Kali all over the account book of his employer. The eighteenth-century Calcutta *baramanush*, far from dismissing him, was moved to tears, and gave Ramprasad a lifelong pension. The written version of this take seems to have originated with Iswar Gupta in 1853–4, in a pioneering biographical essay which, incidentally, identified that bygone age as a lost golden Satyayuga, in which patrons like Krishanchandra Roy of Nadia still knew how to treat with honour the traditional literati.

The essay simultaneously valorised unlearned wisdom over formal training in poetry and religion alike.[98] The anguish of a declining traditional high-caste literati, and the misery of clerical *chakri*, thus

---

[94] KM IV, p. 11 (25 February 1883); ibid., p. 68 (February 1884); KM V, p. 104 (26 December 1883).

[95] KM II, p. 63 (15 June 1883).

[96] KM III, p. 83 (30 June 1884), pp. 160–1 (9 May 1885).

[97] For the centrality of "willed submission" to bhakti, see Kumkum Sangari, "Mirabai and the Spritual Economy of Bhakti", *Economic and Political Weekly*, XXV, 27–8, 7–14 July 1990.

[98] Extracts from Ishwarchandra Gupta's essay are given in Jogendranath Gupta, *Sadhak Kavi Ramprasad* (Calcutta, 1954).

come together to constitute the core of late-nineteenth-century Kaliyuga sensibility.

Kaliyuga, however, is not necessarily a symbol of pessimism alone. The worst of ages, it paradoxically has also been seen as the best of times. In it, according to much bhakti literature, deliverance comes easily, for mere recitation of the name of Hari may suffice. The paradox extends further, for women and Shudras, two major sources of corruption in all pre-modern Kaliyuga texts, can attain good simply through performing their "duties" to husbands and twice-born men.[99] Subalternity is privileged, provided, of course, it remains properly subaltern. The humble constitute the ideal *bhaktas*. Bhakti and Tantra, the two forms of religious practice repeatedly declared to be appropriate for Kaliyuga, are both explicitly open to women and Shudras, unlike brahmanical learning and ritual. Extreme degeneration could also foreshadow a total reversal, with Vishnu coming as Kalki avatar to restore Satyayuga. Here, however, the Brahman takes over again, for the restored norm will be of ideal caste and gender hierarchy.[100]

A "gender paradox" thus underlay conceptions of Kaliyuga: the insubordinate, unchaste woman was the principal source of evil,[101] but bhakti too had a feminine face, being personified by the pure and dutiful wife or mother. This paradox took on new forms in the nineteenth century as certain modulations were made in the remedial dimensions of Kaliyuga. From the 1880s onwards, most notably in the plays of Girischandra Ghosh and those influenced by him, the ideal woman (usually a wife) emerged as active helper in the restoration of moral order. Going beyond the model of exemplary patient suffering typified by Sita, she intervenes in a manner which is deferential yet assertive: a mode that anticipates, perhaps, some aspects of Gandhian

---

[99] Vishnupurana, cited in Kumkum Sangari, op. cit. I am grateful to Kumkum Sangari for drawing my attention to this important paradox. See also W.C. Beane, *Myth, Cult and Symbols in Shakta Hinduism* (London, 1977), pp. 237–9, and Madeleine Biardieu, op. cit., p. 105.

[100] Here there is a significant contrast with the egalitarian dimensions of Christian apocalypse.

[101] See Megan McLaughlin, op. cit.

passive resistance or satyagraha.[102] The woman may be helped by an old-world servant, representing the good Shudra, and gradually a sub-theme extolling simple peasant virtues starts entering the literature.[103] Inspiration for remedial action comes from figures of holy madness, sometimes obviously modelled on Ramakrishna, and occasionally, the Kalki avatar himself enters to restore Satyayuga.[104]

Ramakrishna's own ways of confronting the evils of Kaliyuga had, however, certain significantly distinct nuances. Nineteenth-century Kaliyuga literature could pass easily from denunciation of the disorderly woman to exaltation of the pure Hindu wife, for the evils it pilloried amounted to little more than a shrewishness which could be tamed or reformed. The evil woman in Kaliyuga literature was insubordinate, quarrelsome, lazy, and luxury-loving, but seldom really dangerous or sexually frightening. The trope had flourished on the margins of a much broader bhadralok discourse which from the 1820s had insistently and obsessively probed Hindu conjugality as its central concern. By the late nineteenth century, a very wide spectrum of Hindu sensibilities had come to regard the pure Hindu wife as the last unconquered space in a universe increasingly dominated by alien Western values.[105]

Ramakrishna was emphatically not interested in probing or celebrating Hindu conjugality, for deep within him lay an acute physical revulsion for heterosexual intercourse. He frequently equated it with defecation, and expressed a fear and abhorrence of the female body which aroused male lust: "Blood, flesh, fat, entrails, stools, urine – how can one love such a body?" The "limbs and opening" of women's bodies appeared "enormous" to him.[106] Sex to him consequently was

---

[102] For some examples, see Sarkar, "Kalki-avatar of Bikrampur", op. cit.
[103] Ibid.
[104] Aghorchandra Kabyatirtha, *Kalir Abasan, be Kalki-avatar Geetabhinoy* (Calcutta, 1902).
[105] Tanika Sarkar, "The Hindu Wife and the Hindu Nation: Domesticity and Nationalism in Nineteenth-century Bengal", *Studies in History*, July–December 1992; rpntd. in idem, *Hindu Wife, Hindu Nation* (Delhi: Permanent Black, 2001).
[106] KM III, p. 19 (24 August 1882), and many similar passages; KM IV, p. 201 (5 October 1884).

not any less disgusting when pursued within marriage: rather, it could then become associated with *kanchan* and the need for salaried jobs, and therefore doubly dangerous.

The redemptive wife was thus no resolution for Kaliyuga anxieties to Ramakrishna. Women became tolerable only if somehow totally desexualised, which for Ramakrishna meant looking on them as mothers — bringing them in other words under the powerful taboo of incest. "After much effort", Ramakrishna says, he was able to tolerate women devotees, by identifying all women as "manifestations of Ma Anandamoyee".[107] A shift in discourse from conjugality to motherhood, we shall see, did become common towards the end of the century,[108] and by 1905 Durga-Kali had emerged as collective redeemer and patriotic icon, a powerful symbol of the "mother"-land.

Ramakrishna's mother goddess, however, offered only individual solace, not any overall deliverance from the afflictions of Kaliyuga. Nor did the apocalyptic solution of an imminent Kalki avatar appeal to him much. There does exist one startling passage in the *Kathamrita* where Ramakrishna can be seen toying with such dreams while recalling insults suffered from Dakshineswar temple officials: "The Kalki-avatar will come at the end of Kaliyuga. A Brahman's son — he knows nothing, suddenly a horse and sword will come . . ."[109] Kalki as a Brahman "who knows nothing", and is, presumably like Ramakrishna himself, poor, seems to be a late-nineteenth-century innovation. It turns up again in *Kalir Abasan* (1902), written by the "poor Brahman" head pandit of a Calcutta school. And, in December 1904, a wandering poor Brahman sadhu who had once been a village schoolteacher turned up at a rural *bhadralok* household in Dacca district, actually claiming to be Kalki-avatar.[110] More indications, perhaps, of the social ambience of the Kaliyuga motif in late-nineteenth and early-twentieth-century Bengal.

---

[107] KM IV, p. 201.
[108] See Tanika Sarkar, "Bankimchandra and the Impossibility of a Political Agenda", *Oxford Literary Review*, 16.I, ii, 1994.
[109] KM IV, p. 101 (20 June 1884).
[110] For details of this Doyhata incident, see Sarkar, "Kalki-avatar of Bikrampur", op. cit.

Ramakrishna's main response to Kaliyuga was, however, along the paths of devotional and not apocalyptic bhakti. This took two basic forms in his discourse: the evocation of the paternalistic *baramanush* model as counterpoint to the alien world of *chakri*, and the way, more emotionally satisfactory for him, of total surrender to the Shakta mother goddess, becoming again a five-year-old child. Both ways were structured in terms adapted from patterns of religious discourse available to Ramakrishna. It is time to turn to the more formal, specifically religious, structure of Ramakrishna's teachings.

III

The more technically "religious" aspects of Ramakrishna's discourse compel the problematisation of a whole range of assumptions and themes. Conventional orality/literacy distinctions, for a start, begin to appear rather different as we listen to a holy man, quite often called illiterate by his disciples, using with considerable expertise abstruse doctrinal and philosophical concepts normally assigned to the realms of high or textual culture alone. Following a pattern common in much hagiography, the *Kathamrita* and other accounts by devotees simultaneously stress Ramakrishna's uniqueness, and his manifold connections with a variety of religious practices and doctrines: village cults, obscure sects like the Kartabhaja, the world of Tantrism, mainstream Vaishnava and Shakta traditions, even fleetingly Christianity and Islam. A saint, in hagiography, has to have very distinctive features (in this case, particularly, unlearned wisdom and supreme catholicity) and yet fit into normal religious modes. The problem of recurrence and uniqueness, or linkages and distinctions, concerns historical analysis, too, and goes beyond the (by no means unimportant) issue of Ramakrishna's personal qualities. What it can reveal also are some of the ways through which religious traditions were being reshaped amidst the new pressures of colonial life. Thus, it is insufficient to merely acclaim Ramakrishna's justly famous catholicity as a "traditional" or an "age-old" feature of "Hinduism": its precise origins and features, the nature of its appeal, and changing implications require exploration. Again, Ramakrishna evolved into a rather new kind of guru, related to yet distinct from established types of religious preceptors. He was, perhaps, a guru suited particularly well to the demands of colonial urban *bhadralok* life and anticipates in some ways (not all) the "godmen" of today. The two models of bhakti which constituted the core of his teachings, and which we have already seen manifested through parables, also have doctrinal aspects, antecedents, and linkages, among which that between mother worship and deep aversion for sexuality demands particular attention. Ramakrishna's conversation and attitudes here offer important insights into shifting late-nineteenth-century images of gender, which in turn were bound up with the development of discourses of nationalism. Finally, the possible audience-specific features of Ramakrishna's discourse need to be kept in mind. His devotees included middle-aged householders, a circle consisting mainly of adolescents of college- or even schoolgoing age, respectable housewives and widows, actresses of prostitute origin, and a lone disciple of non-*bhadralok* status, his Bihari servant Latu. Ramakrishna's message could well have varied slightly with his audience – and here the *Kathamrita* begins to fail us, for it offers direct access only to the first group. Audience-specificity raises the question of varied appropriations, and so we are led into a brief study of what became the dominant reading, that of Vivekananda.

Ramakrishna's conversation often has surprisingly deep "textual" foundations, even where it seems to be most context-determined, or a product of homespun wisdom alone. Thus bhakti to him, as in much contemporary Kaliyuga literature, was the counterpoint to the new nineteenth-century world of *chakri* which reduced the quantum of free time and left little room for contemplation or ritual. But the association of Kaliyuga with lack of time is also a very old theme, with bhakti as the corresponding appropriate and "easy" response for men who have lost in physical stature, span of life, and moral worth alike.[111] A more startling example is Ramakrishna's

[111] *Haribhakti* (Calcutta, 1909–10), a Vaishnava tract in simple language, argued that in Kaliyuga repetition of Harinama alone had to be sufficient for salvation, for the path of contemplation ("Jnana") was blocked by "worries about rice, dal, oil and salt . . . others get nervous about being late for office, and can think only of the angry face of the boss . . ." The theme of a compensatory easy way due to diminution of time in Kaliyuga is already

preference for the bhakti of a kitten, clinging helplessly to its mother in total dependence, over that of the baby monkey, who holds on to its parent with a certain will and effort of its own. The two images actually come unaltered from a philosophical dispute, way back in the thirteenth century in far-off Srirangam (Tamilnadu), between the "Tenkalai" and the "Barkalai" sects of the Sri Vaishnavas, followers of Ramanuja, the founder of Visista-advaitabad.[112]

Ramakrishna was particularly knowledgeable about the doctrinal categories of Gaudiya Vaishnavabad – not surprisingly, as Vaishnava bhakti in Bengal since the days of Chaitanya has combined mass appeal with a uniquely rich theological literature, in the vernacular as well as in Sanskrit. He made, for instance, analysis of three types of devotees (*sattvik*, *rajasik*, and *tamasik bhaktas*) which goes back to the *Bhagavat Purana*, adding a brilliant gloss that identified these subdivisions with types drawn from contemporary *bhadralok* life.[113] Ramakrishna was also perfectly capable of making precisely defined doctrinal choices: of *raganuga* (emotional or ecstatic) bhakti, for instance, over the more ritualised *vaidhi*. A much more unusual – indeed, somewhat puzzling – choice was Ramakrishna's preference for Ramanuja's philosophy of Visista-advaita, as against the orthodox Gaudiya Vaishnava version of dualistic bhakti, *achintabhedabheda*, about which he remained completely silent.[114] For the rest, a discourse on the five standard *bhavas* (moods) of Gaudiya Vaishnavabad was a regular feature of his conversation: relating to divinity as subject to ruler (*shanta*), servant to master (*dasya*), parent

---

present in the Vishnupurana (c. AD 100–500): W.C. Beane, op. cit., p. 238; and Kumkum Sangari, op. cit.

[112] KM I, p. 23 (February 1882); KM II, p. 69 (26 September 1883); KM III, pp. 60–1 (27 December 1883). The third reference draws an analogy between the (inferior) devotion of the baby monkey and the more ritualised *vaidhi* form of bhakti: the kitten, in contrast, embodies *raganuga*. For the thirteenth-century origins, see Jitendranath Bandopadhyay, *Panchopasana* (Calcutta, 1960), p. 103: then too, Tenkalai was the less ritualised variant.

[113] KM I, p. 57; Jitendranath Bandopadhyay, op. cit., pp. 15–17.

[114] I remain grateful to the late Hitesranjan Sanyal for drawing my attention to this problem.

to child (*vatsalya*), friend to friend (*sakhya*), and lover to beloved (*madhur*). He had tried out all these during the days of his "mad" sadhana, he told his disciples, but had now settled down into *dasya*. The model of acceptable authority, *seba*, willingly offered to the traditional *baramanush* or *baralok* Ramakrishna's counterpoint, as we have already seen, to the *dasatya* of *chakri*, and thus also had a firm doctrinal foundation.

What can explain such long lineages, the apparently textual bases of the discourse of a man supposedly illiterate? Despite the testimony of the servant-girl Brinde, Ramakrishna perhaps did have a few books, and he is said to have given one of them, a medieval monistic (Advaita Vedantic) text, to his favourite disciple Narendranath (Vivekananda). This *Ashtavakramsamhita* uses the image of an ocean in its account of the highest stage of high-Hindu spiritual realisation, and resemblances have been found between such passages and Ramakrishna's descriptions of his frequent experiences of samadhi in terms of immersion into an endless ocean.[115]

But the bulk of Ramakrishna's doctrinal knowledge evidently could not have come from private reading of books. The *Kathamrita* forces upon us a keener awareness of the complex interpenetrations of literacy and orality. Historians in recent years have been moving away from sharp elite/popular, textual/oral disjunctions towards an understanding of ways in which elements of high textual culture could sink into and intermix with predominantly oral practices. Distinctions may persist, not through any rigid separation of traditions, beliefs, or artefacts, but in differential appropriation or use of a broadly common heritage.[116] Such interfaces are perhaps particularly marked in a culture like that of Hinduism, which has had a literate elite for over two thousand years, but which still tried till the late eighteenth

---

[115] J. Moussatef Masson, *The Oceanic Feeling: The Origins of Religious Sentiment in Ancient India* (Dordrecht, 1880), pp. 37–43. Masson thinks that Freud's use of the term "oceanic feeling" in his *Civilisation and Its Discontents* (1930) was derived from Romain Rolland's study of Ramakrishna.

[116] Roger Chartier, "Culture as Appropriation: Popular Cultural Uses in Early Modern France", in S. Kaplan (ed.), *Understanding Popular Culture* (Mouton, 1984); Chartier, *Cultural Uses of Print in Early Modern France* (Princeton, 1987), Introduction.

century to keep its most sacred texts in purely oral form. Orality here in fact became an instrument of high-caste domination. Ramakrishna could have relatively easy access to "high" knowledge, despite poverty and lack of formal education, as he happened to be of Brahman birth.

In contrast to the specialised textual learning of the pandit, the traditional renouncer – holy man or *sannyasi* – normally picked up his skills through apprenticeship to a master and/or contacts with other similar wandering sadhus. Transmission, in other words, was through predominantly non-textual means, from watching, hearing about, or participating in a variety of religious practices. Ramakrishna, for whom, as we have seen, seeing and hearing were always privileged over reading, clearly belonged to a world of this kind, which could be high and non-textual at the same time, and which was furthermore marked by great heterogeneity.

The striking feature of Ramakrishna's original village world, as revealed by his occasional reminiscences and later accounts of Kamarpukur by devotees, was certainly catholicity. Gadadhar encountered in boyhood a multiplicity of cults – Dharma, Gajan, Manasa (or Vishalakshmi), Shitala – with mainly plebeian devotees but occasional high-caste participation. Devotional practices easily crossed sectarian barriers and could vary within the same family. Thus Gadadhar's father Khudaram began as a devotee of Shitala, and later made Raghuvir (Ram) his chosen deity, while the prosperous Pyne family of merchants worshipped both Siva and Vishnu. Ramakrishna's elder brother Ramkumar became a worshipper of Shakti without this troubling his Vaishnava father. The boy Gadadhar could imbibe mainstream Hindu traditions through watching folk theatre performances of epic and puranic tales (there were three such *jatra* parties in Kamarpukur), and he soon started acting them out himself with friends. In addition, two pilgrim routes intersected at Kamarpukur, from Burdwan to Puri with its Vaishnava associations, and from Calcutta to the Saivite centre of Tarakeshwar. Gadadhar developed an early interest in the constant flow of pilgrims and sadhus through his native village.[117]

---

[117] L I, Purbakatha o Balya-jivana, pp. 27–9, 40, 48–9, 51, 116.

Kaliyuga, Chakri and Bhakti

Numerous "sadhu-*sants, sannyasis* and *bairagi* babajis" used to pass through Dakshineswar, too, Ramakrishna once recalled, taking the river route down to the great pilgrimage centre of Gangasagar. "They don't come here any longer, now that the railway has been constructed."[118] A whole series of mentors thus came Ramakrishna's way, as, fired by an intense desire to literally see Kali's face, he pursued a sadhana initially passionate and wild enough to be thought by many to indicate possession or madness.[119] They brought with them formal knowledge of diverse doctrines and rituals, and so helped to structure Ramakrishna's devotional practices into recognisable and established forms. The flow of *sannyasis* through Dakshineswar thus provided a substitute, in Ramakrishna's case, for the years of wandering which is a standard constituent in the life histories of many religious leaders — in the nineteenth century for men as different as Sahajananda Swami (the founder of the Swaminarayan sect), Dayananda, and Rammohun.

The mysterious and the beautiful Bhairabi Brahmani came first, around 1861, and instructed Ramakrishna in Tantric practices and concepts which have provided an "esoteric", often somewhat disreputable, substratum to much of mainstream Bengal Shakta and Vaishnava traditions. Bhairabi assured Ramakrishna that his unusual states indicated not possession or madness but *mahabhava*, akin to what had been manifested in Chaitanya. She was followed by Vaishnavacharan, a Vaishnava pandit who was also a member of the largely low-caste Kartabhaja sect. Initiation into orthodox Vaishnava traditions came from the Ramayat sadhu Jatadhari, while between 1864 and 1866 Totapuri, a sadhu from Punjab, guided him on the very different path of Vedantic contemplation of the Absolute. Ramakrishna also made brief forays into Islam and Christianity, though these never became major constituents of his thought.[120]

The striking feature of these years of mad sadhana was thus religious experimentation. Ramakrishna, flouting all conventional norms of

---

[118] L II, Gurubhava-Uttarardha, p. 44.
[119] L I, Sadhakbhava, p. 82
[120] *Life*, pp. 139–40, 176, 189–205; L I Sadhak bhava, pp. 206–74.

Brahman *pujari* behaviour,[121] took up, followed, and then discarded the practices of one tradition after another. The Ramakrishna we meet in the *Kathamrita* was significantly different. He remained on the whole now on a single preferred path of devotion, a combination of *dasya* with *santan-bhava*, bringing together elements from Vaishnava and Shakta traditions, though still supremely catholic in his acceptance of many paths to the divine. It was this more relaxed, self-confident Ramakrishna, firmly grounded once again in normal caste practices,[122] secure in his guru status, less of a seeker and more the dispenser of holy wisdom, who went on his own initiative to meet Keshabchandra Sen in March 1875 – beginning an interaction with Brahmos, and, more generally, with the English-educated: the people he once described as "Young Bengal".[123]

The conversations of this later Ramakrishna in the *Kathamrita*, as well as – to an enhanced extent – hagiographical accounts, bear on them the marks of this trajectory, for they indicate certain patterns of selectiveness in reference to the years of religious experimentation. The stresses and silences here are significant in several different ways. Conditioned by the transition from poor Brahman villager to guru of English-educated city *bhadralok*, they simultaneously point to broader shifts within religious practices themselves and help us to understand the precise (and changing) meanings and implications of Ramakrishna's famous catholicity.

The village cults of Dharma, Gajan, Manasa, or Shitala figure only in reminiscences about boyhood, and the tone remains purely descriptive, without either praise or blame. They never enter Ramakrishna's many listings of alternative valid paths, where only mainstream forms of high Hinduism are mentioned along with references to (undifferentiated) Islam and Christianity. Such cults, Ramakrishna evidently thought, were irrelevant, perhaps almost unknown or forgotten among his *bhadralok* devotees, or in metropolitan life in

---

[121] Thus his sacred thread had "flown off by itself, as if in a summer storm". KM II, p. 79 (16 October 1882). Discarding the sacred thread is right and proper for a *sannyasi* – but then Ramakrishna had never formally taken *sanyas*, either.

[122] KM II, p. 113 (21 September 1884).

[123] L II, p. 44.

general. Manasa, other local or plebeian forms of the mother goddess like Chandi, and Dharma had provided the standard themes in much of pre-colonial Bengali literature. Ramakrishna's relative silence is a possible indication, therefore, of a shift in the nineteenth-century *bhadralok* milieu towards more sanskritised high-Hindu forms of devotion, grounded in brahmanical texts made much more widely accessible through printing and translation.

Tantrism, along with the Kartabhajas, figure much more prominently in the *Kathamrita* conversations, and one of Ramakrishna's favourite songs came from another "obscure" sect, the entirely low-caste Sahibdhani.[124] Reference or exposition, however, is usually combined with warnings, and the ambiguous tone deepened, to verge on virtual silencing, in later hagiograhical literature composed under Vivekananda's shadow. Tantrism down the centuries has provided a crucially important underside to Hindu religious traditions in Bengal. It constituted the doctrinal core of Shakta practices, influenced many types of Vaishnavism, and formed a vital substratum in the rituals and doctrines of predominantly low-caste "esoteric" Sahajiya cults – among which the Kartabhaja and the Sahibdhani are late examples. Open, unlike much of brahmanical knowledge and ritual, to low castes and women, the Tantric perspective of attaining spiritual goals in and through the body involves the ritual transgression of conventional norms about meat, fish, wine, and sexual intercourse (symbolically or with a wife alone, in *dakshinachara*, but literally and with any member of the circle, in *vamachara*). *Coitus reservatus*, the key element in such ritualised sex, could be replaced, however, in more respectable forms of Tantrism by the union of Shakti and Siva within one's own body through rousing the *kundalini* or by the sublimation of sex into the childlike love for the mother goddess.[125] Disreputable, yet often deeply attractive, Tantric and Sahajiya traditions

---

[124] Sudhir Chakrabarti, *Sahebdhani Sampraday Tader Gan* (Calcutta, 1985).

[125] Sir John Woodruffe, *Sakti and Sakta* (Madras, 1918, 1965), chapter 27; Heinrich Zimmer, *Philosophies of India* (New York, 1951, 1956), pt III, chapter V; Chintaharan Chakrabarti, *Tantras: Studies on their Religion and Literature* (Calcutta, 1963); N.N. Bhattacharji, *History of the Tantric Religion* (Delhi, 1982). *Dakshinachara* and *vamachara* refer to the "right-hand" and "left-hand" varieties of Tantric ritual. Kundalini is the "serpent power" which

have had a powerful appeal for castes and women – while providing at the same time a kind of secret second life to many high-caste men (as autographical literature well into the twentieth century occasionally reveals).[126]

Ramakrishna's conversation reveals considerable knowledge about Kartabhaja and Tantric practices and technical terms.[127] The Kartabhaja, whose practices included ritual violation of caste – and possibly sexual taboos at the annual festival at Ghoshpara – figure in one catalogue of valid forms of devotion, on par with Vaishnava, Shakta, Vedantic, and Brahmo.[128] And another account of their teachings is immediately followed by the assertion that "only the low can become high . . . cultivation is difficult on uplands".[129] Yet disciples were repeatedly warned also that the Kartabhaja combined big words with licence. "Theirs is a very dirty sadhana, like entering the house through a latrine."[130]

A similar ambivalence characterises Ramakrishna's many references to Tantrism, which arguably was much more fundamental to his entire way of thinking than has been generally acknowledged.[131]

---

supposedly lies coiled on the lowest extremity of the spinal cord, and has to be aroused.

[126] See, for instance, Motilal Roy, *Jivan-Sangini* (Calcutta, 3rd ed., 1968), pp. 39–48, and *passim*.

[127] So much so that the *Kathamrita* was used by Zimmer to illustrate his presentation of Tantrism, while Ramakrishna's "lucid" exposition of Kartabhaja tenets is taken to be authoritative in Ramakanta Chakrabarti, *Vaisnavism in Bengal* (Calcutta, 1985), chapter XX.

[128] For the Kartabhaja, apart from Sudhir Chakrabarti and Ramakanta Chakrabarti, see Debendranath De, *Kartabhaja Dharmar Itibritta* (Calcutta, 1968, 1990). I owe the last reference to Ratnabali Chatterji.

[129] KM IV, p. 169 (19 September 1884); KM II, pp. 30–1 (8 April 1883).

[130] KM V, p. 181 (23 March 1884).

[131] Walter Neevel has argued that Ramakrishna's ideas can be understood "more adequately in the categories of Tantric thought and practice than in the concepts of Sankara's advaita which the biographers primarily employ." See "The Transformation of Ramakrishna", in Bardwell L. Smith, *Hinduism: New Essays in the History of Religion* (London, 1976), p. 76. Following Zimmer, Neevel emphasises the allegedly "world-affirmative" aspects of Tantra,

Tantrism as expressed particularly through the songs of Ramprasad probably helped Ramakrishna to blend together – as Ramprasad had done a century before – the two major traditions of Bengal Hinduism: Shakta and Vaishnava. The much-quoted equation of money with soil (*taka mati, mati taka*) has an obvious affinity with the Tantric affirmation of the identity of "cremation-ground and dwelling place, gold and grass".[132] Affinities are noticeable also between Ramakrishna and his near-contemporary Bamakshepa, the *pagal* Tantric sadhu of Tarapith cremation-ground in Birbhum – another poor Brahman without formal learning who likewise combined catholicity with intense devotion to Kali. Bamakshepa, who avoided Calcutta and deliberately flaunted a rough and bawdy style of speech, perhaps indicates what Ramakrishna could have been if he had remained fixated in his *pagal* phase, and not evolved into a guru preferring a purely urban *bhadralok* audience.[133]

The *Kathamrita* discourse, however, is replete also with warnings about Tantric sadhana with women – even though that precisely was what Bhairabi Brahmani had taught Ramakrishna, making him sit on the lap of a beautiful nude young woman as the culminating point of a long process of training.[134] The Tantrism Ramakrishna himself talked about followed the safer forms of arousing the *kundalini*, and pursuit of *santan-bhava*. Conversations using or expounding Tantric terms are prefaced with the remark that these were "secret matters" (*guhya katha*), and Mahendranath preferred to put the bulk of such passages in the later volume of the *Kathamrita*, a violent attack on *vamachari* Tantrism by Vivekananda.[135]

---

as opposed to Vedantic ascetic renunciation; this, he argues, links Ramakrishna with Vivekananda's social service. Zimmer, however, had pointed out that Tantric "dionysian" affirmation was of the world "just as it is" – this could as well rule out ameliorative action.

[132] Jitendranath Bandopadhyay, *Panchopasana* (Calcutta, 1960), p. 270.
[133] Jogindranath Chattopdhyay, *Bamakshepa* (Calcutta, 1918).
[134] L I, pp. 204–5. Ramakrishna, we are assured, went immediately into samadhi.
[135] KM V, p. 181. I would like to acknowledge my indebtedness on this point to the ongoing work of Jeff Kripal, Chicago University research

The vital yet difficult and embarrassing interface between Tantric-Sahajiya traditions and Ramakrishna is reminiscent of similar problems encountered four centuries back by Chaitanya and his followers.[136] It clearly points also towards a contemporary transition. Tantric traditions were being made more respectable through excisions, and at times sought to be suppressed altogether, in *bhadralok* circles as stricter ideas about gentility developed in the shadow of "Victorian" norms in the nineteenth century.[137]

The multiplicity of religious experiences and experiments, along with the transition we have noticed from the years of mad sadhana to the more domesticated guru of the *Kathamrita*, conditioned the best-known feature of Ramakrishna's teaching – a specific blend of enormous catholicity with clear expression of preference. Catholicity for Ramakrishna was inseparable from bhakti: all forms and paths were valid, provided they were followed with genuine devotion. The mother loves to prepare varied dishes for her children, to suit their different tastes.[138] The sheer breadth of Ramakrishna's tolerance for other faiths evokes wonder and admiration today: "There is a pond with three or four *ghats* – Hindus call what they drink *jal*, Muslims *pani*, the English water. He is called Allah by one, God by others, some say Brahma, others Kali, still others Ram, Hari, Jesus, or Durga."[139]

Ramakrishna's catholicity would soon come to be displayed as a timeless essence of Hinduism: its precise meanings and implications become clearer, however, if contextualised against a background of shifting lines of demarcation between religious traditions. By the 1880s a variety of pressures and influences were helping to generalise

---

scholar, and particularly his "Revealing/Concealing the Social: A Texual History of Mahendranath Gupta's Ramakrishna's Kathamrita", Bengal Studies Conference, 1990.

[136] Hitesranjan Sanyal, *Bangla Kirtaner Itihas* (Calcutta, 1989), *passim*.

[137] One illustration of this would be Woodruffe's *Sakti and Sakta*, with its playing down of *vamachara* and argument that Tantra presents Vedic truths in forms appropriate for Kaliyuga.

[138] KM I, p. 21 (February 1882).

[139] KM I, p. 42 (October 1882).

certain identities and conflicts, and a transition from "fuzzy" to "enumerated" communities was well under way.[140] The early 1890s would see, for the first time, Hindu–Muslim riots spread across a large part of the subcontinent on a single issue (cow protection), while Christian missionary propaganda also provoked acute tensions at times. To Ramakrishna, however, Jesus could still come between Hari and Durga in a listing of varieties of devotion, and there is no developed sense of a sharply distinct "Hindu" identity – let alone any political use of it.[141] The total lack in him of the modern sense of history that print culture and colonial textbooks had stimulated kept Ramakrishna immune also from the myth of "medieval Muslim tyranny" evident in *bhadralok* discourse from the 1820s onwards. Whether out of innocence or deliberate choice, Ramakrishna represented a kind of protest against the creation of sectarian walls. Yet in his own way he did bear witness to changing times. Ramakrishna's acquaintance with Islam (or Christianity) were fairly minimal,[142] and the religious or philosophical concepts he used came entirely from what today would be considered "Hindu" traditions – unlike much of pre-colonial bhakti, with its close interrelationships with Sufism, or, at a very different level, Rammohun.

A twofold transition was under way in the late nineteenth century: the sharpening of distinctions between a "Hindu" and other religious identities, and the blurring of differences now being perceived as internal to Hindu dharma (in the sense, actually rather new, of Hindu "religion" or "Hinduism"). Ramakrishna himself had no conception of hostile "Others" in Christianity or Islam: his catholicity, nonetheless, did not really involve any "syncretism" between Hindu and other religions. It related principally to divisions within the Hindu world. Doctrinal tensions within nineteenth-century middle-class Hindu

---

[140] I am borrowing these terms from Sudipta Kaviraj.

[141] Consider for instance the following passage: "You can reach Iswara through any dharma, pursued with sincerity. Vaishnavas, Shaktas, Vedantists, Brahmos will all attain Iswara, and so will Muslims and Christians." KM II, p. 19 (11 March 1883). What is missing is the sense of "Hindu" as a cohesive identity or dharma.

[142] *Life*, pp. 207–8, 253–5.

society had been sharpened by Christian polemics against idolatry and Brahmo efforts to replace image-worship by adoration of the formless (*nirakar*) Brahman, who was *nirguna* – not to be described in terms of humanly conceived qualities. There were debates also about the relative efficacy of contemplation, devotion, and ritual (*jnana*, bhakti, and karma). Ramakrishna provided a healing touch in such conflicts – particularly welcome, perhaps, for Brahmos tired of internecine strife who became the earliest among his *bhadralok* admirers. Doctrinal subtleties and textual debates were relevant, he assured his devotees, as *sakara-saguna* worship (of divinities with form and qualities, given representation in images) and *nirakar sadhana*, *jnana*, bhakti, and karma were all alternative paths of attaining the same goal. Ramakrishna's catholicity embraced, we have seen, Vedic-Pauranic texts and rituals, Tantrism, and obscure sects like the Kartabhaja and the Sahibdhani. Vaishnava and Shakta concepts, images, and songs intermingled in his sessions with devotees, and *kirtan* and Ramprasad alike could send him off into the ecstatic condition that his disciples liked to call samadhi.

For the Ramakrishna of the *Kathamrita* years, however, celebration of difference always went along with clear expression of preferences. An obvious primacy was given to bhakti, and as ecstatic devotee of Kali, Ramakrishna was bound to prefer *sakara* worship. One can get to a roof in many ways, Ramakrishna liked to say, by staircase, ladder, or rope – but the ways must not get mixed up: "You have to stick firmly to one way to get to *Iswar*."[143] To each his own, so to say – but each should normally also stick to his own. Stable choice, rather than any really open or fluid syncretism or experimentation, despite his own earlier history, was Ramakrishna's advice in the 1880s.

Here we encounter the crucially important concept of *adhikaribheda*: immense catholicity, going along with firmly conservative maintenance of rules appropriate for each level, *jati*, or *sampraday* (community), which are all conceived as having a place in a multiplicity of orthopraxis. *Adhikaribheda* had emerged as a formal doctrine in the seventeenth-eighteenth century as a high-brahmanical

---

[143] KM IV, p. 135 (7 September 1884); KM V, p. 14 (13 August 1882).

way of accommodating difference in philosophy, belief, and ritual. A particular application of it was the concept of *smarta panchopasana* – the equal validity and orthodoxy of devotion to Ganapati, Vishnu, Siva, Shakti, and Surya.[144] The roots, perhaps, go much further back, to the notion, basic to Hindu concepts of hierarchy and caste of each human group having its *svadharma* (one's own religious path).[145]

Adhikaribheda is open to somewhat different implications, depending on whether looked upon from "below" or from "above". *Adhikaribheda* catholicity has allowed the formation and survival of a multitude of practices and beliefs, and numerous *sampradays* with a fluidity and openness in their initial phases which make even classification as Hindu or Muslim not always easy.[146] Living spaces have thus opened up for subordinate groups – low caste and women – within the interstices of an order marked by great caste and gender inequality and oppression: moments during which caste could be disregarded, rituals and taboos of superiors mocked or turned on their heads.[147] Such living spaces, however, also help hierarchy and oppression to endure by making them appear less unendurable. A fine study of Mira and Kabir has indicated how this dialectic of protest and subordination manifested itself, above all, through bhakti.[148]

Catholicity, grounded in *adhikaribheda*, can also have an opposite thrust. In official, high-caste doctrine, *adhikaribheda* often becomes synonymous with, not fluidity or openness, but neat compartmentalisation, the drawing up of more definite boundaries, and the arrangements of the various philosophies, ritual, beliefs and *sampradayas* in a fixed hierarchy culminating in high-Brahman practices and Advaita Vedantist philosophy. Mid-nineteenth-century conservative

[144] Umeshchandra Bhattacharji, *Bharat-darshan-sara* (Calcutta, 1949), pp. 287–8; Jitendranath Bandopadhyay, *Panchopasana*, op. cit., chapter IV.

[145] Madeleine Biardieu, op. cit., p. 45.

[146] Two obvious examples would be the Bauls of Bengal and the legend about Hindus and Muslims quarrelling over Kabir's body.

[147] For some examples, see Sashibhushan Dasgupta, *Obscure Religious Cults* (Calcutta, 1946), and Sudhir Chakrabarti, op. cit.

[148] See Kumkum Sangari, op. cit.

Bengali Hindu texts like Loknath Basu's *Hindu-dharma-marma* and Nandakumar Kabiranta's *Sandeha-nirasana* have a conception of orthopraxy at first sight almost as broad as Ramakrishna's but this is used essentially as a polemical weapon in defending the status quo in orthopraxy against Christians, Brahmos, and "atheists and rationalists".[149] Reformers are condemned as intolerant – banning even voluntary sati, forcibly trying to modify age-old customs of marriage and widowhood, insulting the simple faith of the masses in image-worship. Caste was irrelevant at the highest levels of Vedantic *jnana* and *sannyas*: being unimportant, no effort was needed to attack it in everyday practice.

The *adhikaribheda* of Ramakrishna has to be situated within this continuum between the two logically opposed poles of extreme fluidity and precise definition of hierarchy. Thus caste, on the whole, was not particularly prominent in his discourse, and he often recalled how, in the days of mad sadhana, his own sacred thread "had flown off by itself".[150] But Ramakrishna, too, argued that caste becomes unimportant through a natural process of spiritual realisation alone, and once used an abusive epithet about those who tried to end it through conscious effort. A joke he made was resented as an instance of high-caste prejudice by a Teli devotee.[151] In more general terms, we have seen Ramakrishna move in personal life from extreme religious experimentation towards an insistence on each sticking to his own practices and beliefs in a world of fairly rigid divisions. But this was still some distance removed from a single, clear-cut hierarchisation exalting the supremacy of Vedantic monism based on the *jnana* of learned, high-brahmanical culture. Ramakrishna occasionally admitted this superiority in theory but loved to reiterate his own preference for dualistic bhakti through Ramprasad's words: "I do not

---

[149] Thus, "*varna-bhiveda* (caste distinctions) are essential *mukti sadhan* (quest for salvation) . . . since the supreme Lord has given different (powers) to different jatis . . . What is bad is to lose one's dharma. The possibility of salvation remains so long as any dharma is devoutly followed". Loknath Basu, *Hindu-dharma-marma* (Calcutta, 1856, rpnt. 1873), pp. 2, 67.

[150] KM II, p. 2 (16 October 1882).

[151] KM II, pp. 27–8 (8 April 1883).

want to become sugar, for I love its taste." Ambiguity persisted also in the relationship between Vedic-Pauranic and Tantric traditions. In Vivekananda, we shall see, the transition world be completed, with Vedantic *jnana* firmly placed at the apex of a single, well-defined hierarchy. This was accompanied by a much sharper definition of dividing lines between Hindu and other religious traditions. In Ramakrishna, in contrast, the term "Hindu" is not particularly common, and the Hindu/Muslim/Christian demarcation often does not seem qualitatively too different from the distinctions between Shakta, Vaishnava, and Brahmo. The post-*Kathamrita* canonical literature, however, tended to read back such firm hierarchisation and dividing lines into Ramakrishna, emphasising his affinities with Vedanta.[152] The sacred thread and conventional *sannyasi* attire, to take another example, came back in most standard iconographic representations of Ramakrishna, in significant contrast to *Kathamrita* descriptions and the seldom reproduced 1879 photograph.[153]

Along with Ramakrishna's catholicity, many facets of the *bhadralok* cult that developed around him as guru provide entry points into a religious world in process of being reshaped and crystallised into modern Hinduism. The guru in Indian traditions has taken on multifarious and changing forms. Guru cults have been indispensable for most lower-caste Hindu or *be-shara* Sufi heterodoxies, as necessary concomitant to their rejection of the textual expertise of Brahmans and mullahs.[154] *Diksha* (initiation) from a guru is indispensable also for Tantric sadhana and many forms of Vaishnava devotion, and orthodox high-caste families often have *kula* gurus providing initiation through a secret mantra. Fundamental usually to all these forms is an initiation rite, and a conception of *parampara* or lineage. Thus the relationship between *kula* gurus and families initiated by them

---

[152] Walter Neevel, op. cit.; L I, II, *passim*.

[153] The photograph was published in Gurudas Barman, *Sri Sri Ramakrishnacarit* (Calcutta, 1910), a never-reprinted biography which lies today in the Rare Book Section of the National Library (Calcutta). It has been reproduced, to the best of my knowledge, only once – in Brojen Banerji and Sajanikanta Das, op. cit.

[154] Madeleine Biardieu, op. cit., pp. 73–5.

would be inheritable on both sides in a pattern similar to the lineage in matters of puja and life-cycle rituals between the upper-caste *jajman* and the family *purohit*. The guru would normally expect complete deference and obedience, might sometimes acquire a reputation for miraculous powers, and even come to be regarded as true object of worship. The *kula* gurus of orthodox families had a guiding role in crucial family decisions, while the gurus of lower-caste sects or Tantric circles presided over distinctive and generally secret rituals, involving ecstatic song and dance and, at times, ritualised sex. The subterranean world of non-brahmanical heterodoxies developed as a corollary an enigmatic *sandhya-bhasha*, or language of twilight, rich in double meanings, full of images drawn from everyday life which seemed simple but had deeper meanings for the initiated.[155]

Ramakrishna's circle was distinctive here in many ways. The need to find and stay near a *sat* guru (true guru), presumably himself above all, was a constant refrain in Ramakrishna's conversation. But relations with disciples remained relaxed and informal. Ramakrishna never claimed special miraculous powers, often expressed contempt for such *siddhai*, and disappointed some devotees by consulting a doctor during his last fatal illness. There were usually no initiation rites or mantras,[156] no insistence on total obedience, and not even very much outward deference as the Thakur uninhibitedly "played" with his boys and went together with them to watch plays. Ramakrishna did not seek to displace the *diksha*-giving *kula* guru in the lives of his upper-caste disciples: his remained a purely emotional influence, more or less independent of specific life-cycle moments or situations, and perhaps all the more powerful because of this relative detachment from everyday life. An open-market fluidity, suited to a metropolitan, mobile society thus distinguished Ramakrishna from more traditional types of gurus, and the printed word played a crucial role in the spread of his reputation.[157] There were some tendencies,

---

[155] Sashibhushan Dasgupta, *Obscure Religious Cults*, op. cit., *passim*. See also Daniel Gold, *The Lord as Guru: Hindi Sants in the Northern Indian Tradition* (Oxford, 1987).

[156] KM IV, p. 191 (20 October 1885); KM V, p. 121 (24 May 1884).

[157] Particularly, in the late 1870s, the journals brought out by the Keshab Sen group. For details, see Brojen Banerji and Sajanikanta Das, op. cit., *passim*.

however, towards the end of Ramakrishna's life and particularly after his death, towards his reabsorption into more familiar patterns of religious leadership. The *Kathamrita* records debates among disciples about Ramakrishna's possible avatar status,[158] the *Lilaprasanga* mentions some miraculous incidents,[159] many devotees began worshipping him formally after his death, and Sarada and the swamijis of the Ramakrishna Mission started giving *diksha* to new recruits.[160]

The *Kathamrita* accounts of sessions with Ramakrishna repeatedly highlight the Thakur's frequent trances, and these obviously enhanced his appeal. Ramakrishna, from boyhood on, had periodically lost consciousness, become motionless as a statue, and then seemed to be talking on very familiar terms with figures (usually Kali) visible to him alone. The possible physical or psychotic explanations here are less important than the interpretations given by different cultures to trance states.[161] Considered in early days to be a form of illness bordering on lunacy, or instances of spirit possession (and as such apparently responsible for attracting large crowds during Ramakrishna's brief visits to Kamarpukur),[162] the trances came to be invariably interpreted by *bhadralok* devotees as samadhi: the mystical communion in high-Hindu sadhana in which the individual *jivatma* merges for a while with *paramatma* or Brahman, the ultimate in spiritual realisation. A monistic Vedantic stamp was thus put on a man who on the whole seems to have preferred the ways of dualistic devotion.

[158] Girishchandra Ghosh and Ramchandra Datta in particular upheld the avatar thesis, and KM records sharp depates around this with Mahendralal Sircar – in, particular, KM IV, pp. 258, 264, 266–7, 275–6 (23–24 October 1885).

[159] These amount to no more than supernatural visions seen by Ramakrishna and not external transformations.

[160] KM IV, pp. 258–76, *passim*.

[161] I.M. Lewis, *Ecstatic Religion: An Anthropological Study of Spirit Possession and Shamanism* (Harmondsworth, Penguin, 1971, 1975), p. 39.

[162] During his occasional visits to Kamarpukur, "the place where the Master was staying was thronged to its utmost capacity with men and women since his ecstacy, resulting in frequent Samadhi . . . attracted the people." *Life*, pp. 290–1.

The trances were often preceded or accompanied by ecstatic songs and dances joined in by devotees. These had been important features of the secret inner life of plebeian sects (the sole written text of the Kartabhaja, for instance, had been *Bhaver Geet*, a collection of songs).[163] There was nothing secret, however, about Ramakrishna's circle, and not a trace of the ritualised sex central to the hidden life of many Tantric-cum-Sahajiya "esoteric" cults. Women too had abjured esoteric practices while retaining the centrality of song, the singing and dancing in this purely *bhadralok* cult remaining an indoor affair. Chaitanya and his followers had made song (*kirtan*) the principal mode of mass proselytisation, and Keshab Sen tried to revive this mode for Brahmoism in the 1870s. We never hear, however, of Ramakrishna leading *sankirtan* processions in streets.

The absence of distinctive secret rituals left its mark on Ramakrishna's language. Closer, in its use of everyday images drawn from rural life and labour, to the language of lower-caste sects than to the formal *sutra-bhashya* format of high-brahmanical exegesis, its meaning always remained single and on the surface. *Sandhya-bhasha* had been marked by a richness and fluidity of metaphor: the boatmen, river, or caged bird of the Bauls can be understood in many different ways.[164] Metaphor, in contrast, is rare in Ramakrishna: its place is taken by clear-cut analogies or parables, with the intended message often carefully verbalised.[165] Drained of metaphorical excess and iconoclastic content, the rustic turn of phrase and quotidian analogy of the twentieth-century urban guru, god-man or god-woman, ends up in banalities. Ramakrishna perhaps represents an early phase of this transition towards an urban consumer-oriented Hinduism.

[163] Ramakanta Chakrabarti, op. cit.; Debendranath De, op. cit.

[164] Charles H. Capwell, "The Esoteric Beliefs of the Bauls of Bengal", *Journal of Asian Studies*, XXXII.2 February 1974; Asitkumar Bandopadhyay, *Bangla Sahityer Itibritta* III.2 (Calcutta, 1966, 1981).

[165] I have been helped greatly while formulating this contrast by Kumkum Sangari's distinction between Kabir's reliance on "the intellectual clarity and 'distance' of analogy or allegory" and Mira's "blurred and displacing realm of metaphor".

Ramakrishna, then, did not offer to his devotees any definitive set of rituals or doctrines, the satisfaction of total surrender to a *diksha* guru, or promise of miracles. To the middle-aged householders who constituted his principal audience in the *Kathamrita*, his was a broad message of what in bhakti traditions has often been called *grihastha sannyas*.[166] Despite the repeated condemnations of *kamini* and *kanchan*, renunciation was not called for. The devotee could remain in the world, while not allowing himself to get immersed totally within it, on the model of the *dasi* in her master's household. "You have money and wealth, and yet you call Iswara – that is very good." A Brahmo sub-judge once summed up what might well have been a characteristic audience response when he declared that he was "filled with peace and happiness on hearing that there . . . [was] no need to leave the world, that Iswara can be attained even while living as a householder."[167] Thus wealth could still be pursued, though in a non-attached (*nishkama*) manner, and the wife could remain, though sex should be given up after one or two children. The pursuit of bhakti within one's household even had its advantages and was like fighting from inside a fort, for one's minimum material needs would be taken care of.[168] Here, in other words, was a kind of "this-worldly mysticism" – living in the world, pursuing the normal *bhadralok* way of life, but inwardly distancing oneself from its travails and frustrations as typified, above all, in the chronotype of *chakri*.[169] Schematically,

[166] See, for instance, the well-known analysis of Louis Dumont, "World Renunciation in Indian Religions", *Contributions to Indian Sociology*, IV, 1960.

[167] KM IV, p. 31 (16 December 1883); KM I, pp. 151–3 (19 October 1884).

[168] KM I, p. 153 (19 October 1884).

[169] I am adapting the concept of "distancing" from the work of the German social historian Alf Ludtke, who has developed the category of *Eigensinn* to analyse a variety of everyday working-class attitudes. These involve a kind of withdrawal or distancing into partially autonomous spaces, and, despite the vast differences in contexts and forms, I find Ludtke helpful in suggesting a way out of the somewhat rigid subordination/resistance binary. Alf Ludtke, "The Historiography of Everyday Life: The Personal and the Political", in R. Samuel and G. Stedman-Jones (eds), *Culture, Ideology and Politics: Essays for Eric Hobsbawm* (London, 1982); G. Eley, "Labour History, Social History,

this can be regarded as the polar opposite of Weberian worldly asceticism. The one allowed householder devotees to pursue wealth in moderation, in obviously traditional, non-innovative ways, with no premium placed upon diligence and economic success – rather its opposite. The other, in its ultimate seventeenth-century Puritan manifestation, had inculcated a work ethic based on a new conception of time and discipline, where salvation was sought "primarily through immersion in one's worldly vocation".[170]

The doctrinal component of *grihastha-sannyas* came from a blending of selected Vaishnava and Shakta elements: once, through Ramakrishna, we can watch the processes of continuity-cum-change at work within religious traditions. Ramakrishna disliked the more ritualistic, *vaidhi* forms of Vaishnava devotion, while rejecting, by implication, also the alternative, more simple and plebeian, emphasis upon formal reiteration of Hari-nama alone.[171] Emotional, *raganuga* bhakti, conveyed primarily through songs (*kirtan*), figure prominently, however, in accounts of Ramakrishna's sessions with his devotees. He was fairly knowledgeable about, but not deeply interested in, the intricacies of Gaudiya Vaishnava scholasticism, with the significant exception of the doctrine of the five *bhavas*, which enters his conversation very frequently. A link may be suggested here with *grihastha-sannyas*, for, as Dineshchandra Sen perceptively remarked many years ago, the remarkable thing about the Gaudiya Vaishnava theory of *bhavas* was the relationship established through it between religious sensibility and the emotions of everyday householderly life: parental affection, friendship, love (adulterous as well as conjugal), the devotion of servant to master.[172] The *dasya-bhava* Ramakrishna had come to prefer was expounded by him through a series of homologous parables. Here king and *khansama* (servant), *baralok*

Alltagsgeschichte: Experience, Culture and the Politics of the Everyday – A New Direction for German Social History?", *Journal of Modern History*, 61.ii, June 1989.

[170] Max Weber, *Sociology of Religion* (Boston, 1969), pp. 167, 270.
[171] KM II, p. 18 (11 March 1883).
[172] Dinesh Chandra Sen, *Brihat-Banga*, vol. II (Calcutta, 1935), p. 690.

patron and would-be client, babu and *durwan* (gatekeeper) have implications which are doctrinal as well as (obviously) social, for they are being used to assert the claims of dualistic bhakti over Vedantic monism. The *samanya jiva* (humble being) should not assume an immediate identity with the Absolute, he needs a prior mediation through devoted service, bhakti expressed through *seba*:

> The king is sitting. If the *khansama* goes and occupies the king's seat, saying, "King, what you are, I am, too", people will think him mad. But the king himself, pleased by the *khansama*'s service (*seba*), might tell him one day, "Why don't you come and sit, next to me – what you are, I am, too." Then if he sits, that would be all right.[173]

Personalised *seba* is the opposite of rule- and time-bound *chakri* governed by the cash nexus, *dasya-bhava* contrasts with *dasatya* – and yet the etymological near-identity of *dasya* and *dasatya* may not be entirely irrelevant. The servant–master model was not tension-free and demanded constant effort: it remained some distance removed from Ramakrishna's favourite bhakti image of the kitten clinging to its mother in total surrender. *Dasya-bhava* in Ramakrishna ultimately takes second place to *santan-bhava*, relating to divinity as child to mother. This had no place in Gaudiya Vaishnava scholastics but came to Ramakrishna from Shakta traditions, as modulated above all through Ramprasad's songs. *Santan-bhava*, unlike *dasya*, could be perceived as unmediated, effortless intimacy, made tension-free by complete surrender – and so Ramakrishna ultimately privileged Shakta over Vaishnava, Kali over every other deity.

Shakta–Vaishnava relations had been quite conflict-ridden at times,[174] but a coming together became noticeable from the eighteenth century with Tantrism often providing the unifying substratum. The Tantric centre of Tarapith, for instance, became a favourite haunt for Vaishnava as well as Shakta sadhus.[175] Formal Shakta doctrine was, and remained, essentially Tantric, but the emergence

---

[173] KM II, p. 63 (15 June 1883).
[174] There was an evident contrast between the Vaishnava emphasis on love and non-violence and Shakta animal sacrifices and blood imagery.
[175] Jogendranath Chattopadhyay, *Bamakshepa*, op. cit., p. 39.

of a rich tradition of religious poetry and song (*shyamasangit*) from Ramprasad onwards added a vital emotional dimension, absent in the often purely mechanical Tantric practices.[176] Derived in part from Vaishnava imagery, and repeatedly emphasising the essential identity of Kali and Krishna (and quite often many other forms of devotion), the resultant mix became an extremely powerful compound, richer perhaps in the range of human experience it could incorporate than Gaudiya Vaishnavbad. The aestheticised love-play central to Vaishnava song (*padabali*) had little to say about death or suffering other than *viraha* (separation from the beloved). Shyamasangit (Shakta songs) deliberately embraced sharper polarities: Mother Kali emerged as grotesque, terrible, and beautiful – cruel, wayward, and yet somehow endlessly loving.[177] Acceptance of total divine control was combined with a recognition of infinite divine caprice,[178] and the devotee's own response could oscillate across many registers: expression of sheer terror and anguish, deep resentment about the inequities of life, jubilant embracing of contradictions, a sense of triumph over suffering achieved perhaps through Tantric sadhana, the peace of complete childlike surrender to the Divine Mother. Such complexities of control – the times, in different ways, of both Ramprasad and Ramakrishna. Kali, again, is related in many ways to conceptions of Kal (time) and Kaliyuga: the Kaliyuga moods we have analysed as crucial for Ramakrishna had perhaps a special affinity for Shakta forms of devotion.[179] It may not be coincidental that a significantly

---

[176] Compare, e.g., the "mechanistic, and even crass" Tantric-Sahajiya text translated by Edward G. Dimock, *The Place of the Hidden Moon* (Chicago, 1966), pp. 235–48, with the richly emotive songs of Ramprasad, or the Shyamasangits, incorporated in the audio-cassettes of the twentieth-century singer Pannalal Bhattacharji.

[177] Sashibhushan Dasgupta, *Bharater Shakti-sadhana o Shakta Sahitya* (Calcutta, 1960), chapter 8; Asitkumar Bandopadhyay, *Bangla Sahityer Itibritta*, III.2 (Calcutta, 1966, 1981), chapter 3.

[178] As for instance in Dewan Ramdulal Nandi of Tripura's 'sakali tomar iccha icchamayee Tara tumi'".

[179] W.C. Beane, *Myth, Cult and Symbols in Sakta Hinduism* (London, 1977), chapter 5.

large number of composers of Shyamasangit came from more old-fashioned, often declining, zamindars and zamindari officials of late-eighteenth- and early-nineteenth-century Bengal.[180] Mother goddess cults had flourished also in diverse forms among many plebeian groups. Even in the 1880s Mahendralal Sircar, the doctor treating Ramakrishna during his last illness, could dismiss Kali as "that Santal bitch".[181] A major contribution of Ramakrishna, perhaps, was to help make Shakti worship much more respectable and widespread among Western-educated middle-class groups.

Shakta worship in Bengal had developed around the two poles of secret Tantric *chakras* (circles) and public Kali or Durga Pujas, organised often amidst great ostentation by zamindari households or other rich patrons. Ramakrishna, like Ramprasad a hundred years before, shifted the emphasis away from these poles towards a more intimate, yet domesticated and respectable, form of devotion in which Shyamasangit (sung individually, unlike the congregational Vaishnava *sankirtan*) acquired a central role. Ramakrishna, however, as we have seen, toned down considerably the accents of anguish and resentment which had been very noticeable in Ramprasad. He projected a much less tension-ridden conception of the mother goddess. Ramprasad's Kali was often unjust, cruel, partial towards her rich sons: the poet's ego retained an independent identity and, as in all real-life families the mother–son relationship was not bereft of tensions and contradictions. Such maturity seems to have been deliberately abandoned by Ramakrishna in an act of total surrender of ego, imagining himself to be a child, or indeed perhaps an infant, in a kind of womb reversion, completely free of problems, because unquestioning.

Ramakrishna went beyond the Ramprasad model also in his insistence that *santan-bhava*, looking upon all women as emanations of the mother goddess – and so, without exception, as mothers – was the only way one could hope to conquer the lure of *kamini*. A very strong personal note is evident in Ramakrishna's many passages about

---

[180] Asitkumar Bandopadhyay, op. cit.
[181] KM I, p. 235 (26 October 1885).

the horrors of the feminine body, as well as in his obsessive equation of sex with defecation. Sarada Debi recalled later that dysentery, of which her husband had been a chronic victim, often made his body an object of disgust for Ramakrishna. There seems to have developed in him a deep fear of matter flowing out of one's body, and the orifices of women appeared enormous and frightening.[182] One might also speculate that the Tantric sexual exercises Bhairabi Brahmani had made Ramakrishna undertake had contributed to a distaste and revulsion for heterosexual intercourse. But once again the personal in Ramakrishna is related also to the social-cum-historical: a very similar theme of overcoming sexuality by conceiving of the temptress as mother is prominent in Nathpanthi legends about Gorakhnath which have circulated for centuries in Bengal's countryside.[183]

Ramakrishna's mother-worship has also a wider dimension going beyond the limits of purely Shakta practices, for it may be related to certain major shifts within *bhadralok* constructions of womanhood. For much of the nineteenth century, *bhadralok* discourses had persistently problematised conjugality, constructing the woman, usually the-wife-as-victim, in need of male reformist succour, epitome of surrender to alien values, or last repository of indigenous virtue in a world otherwise lost to foreign Western domination. The pure woman – again, in late-nineteenth-century plays as wife more often than mother – could also occasionally figure as active agent in a deferentially assertive mode. Ramakrishna, who radically devalued all forms of conjugal relationships and presented woman-as-mother as sole counterpoint to the horrors of *kamini*, was a part of, and contributed to, a decisive shift in the direction of identifying ideal womanhood with an iconic mother figure.

The new, enormously valorised mother–son relationship quickly took on patriotic overtones. Already in the early 1880s, in Bankimchandra's *Anandamath*, with its "Bande Mataram hymn", the wild and terrible Kali is the "Mother as she has become", oppressed and starving, while the resplendent ever-bountiful Durga symbolises the

---

[182] KM IV, p. 68 (2 February 1884), p. 201 (5 October 1884).
[183] Asitkumar Bandopadhyay, op. cit., II.I (Calcutta, 1966, 1988).

future liberated "mother" land. The duty of the sons is an active one – the liberation of the mother from alien bondage. Durga Puja correspondingly from around the turn of the century started emerging from the households of zamindars to become *sarbajanin* – community-organised – in towns, and Hindu nationalists during the Swadeshi era made many efforts to appropriate Puja rituals and the Shyama-sangit form for the patriotic cause.[184]

Ramakrishna himself – for whom Kali was beautiful and ever-loving in her very wildness, in need of no transformation, demanding no activity but only total childlike surrender – remained quite far removed from this Hindu nationalist discourse. And yet the gulf between childlike immersion and activist duty was not unbridgeable, as Vivekananda would soon indicate.

Our focus so far has been primarily on the *Kathamrita*, and it is easy from that to slip into an assumption that Ramakrishna's teachings in the early 1880s constitute a single bloc. But speech is inherently "dialogic", modulated by contexts and audiences,[185] and Ramakrishna's devotees included many apart from the middle-aged householders who tend to predominate in Mahendranath's text. The *Kathamrita* does not give an equivalent direct access to other groups: the very young men who later become *sannyasis* (they are often present, but not possibly in their more intimate conversations with the saint – for "M", householder himself, never quite became a member of that inner circle), the wives, the prostitutes-turned-actresses. Ramakrishna's message may well have varied somewhat to suit such distinct audiences, making the range of possible appropriations even wider.

For middle-aged householders, as we have seen, Ramakrishna offered bhakti – embodied in *grihastha sannyas* – as an "easy way", soothing many tensions, demanding no learned understanding of doctrine or mastery over ritual, requiring virtually no sacrifice of normal *bhadralok* careers and lifestyles. These needed only to be carried out

---

[184] For some details, see Sumit Sarkar, *Swadeshi Movement in Bengal 1903–1908*, op. cit., chapter VI.

[185] V.N. Voloshinov, *Marxism and the Philosophy of Language* (Leningrad, 1930; London, 1973).

in a *nishkama*, detached, manner. In addition, the condemnation of social activism could perhaps be read by such people – some of them reasonably well-off – as a denial of the need to spend savings on too much charity or philanthropy.

But it might still be unduly cynical to explain Ramakrishna's appeal, even among this milieu, entirely in terms of his providing a comfortable "theodicy of good fortune". The element of playfulness and rejection of some of the inhibitions of normal *bhadralok* behaviour (becoming emotional in public, dancing in ecstacy) could have been particularly attractive to middle-aged householders in contrast to the dingy formalities of respectable adult life. The lure of a kind of sanctified escape from responsibility, at a time when these tend to crowd upon a man with the onset of middle age, should not be underestimated. Again, middle-aged devotees, even when reasonably successful, must as minor government officials and senior clerks have been frequently subject to the pinpricks of a superior and foreign officialdom. The critique of *chakri* would not have appeared meaningless here. Through Ramakrishna the householder could perhaps find the solace and comfort of an inner space, distanced from an everyday world dominated increasingly by money and alien power.

The message for the young men and boys was presumably somewhat different, and far more challenging than that imparted to householders, for it inspired some of them to make a definitive break with *kamini* and *kanchan* in the forms of marriage and conventional jobs. Quite often they had to overcome considerable parental hostility even for visiting Ramakrishna, for frequent trips to Dakshineswar could mean neglecting the formal studies which had become the indispensable qualification for respectable professional or clerical careers. Ramakrishna often encouraged such truancy and once made a pun which equated passing examinations with bondage.[186] For these teenagers here was a middle-aged man, revered saint and perhaps avatar, who mixed and talked freely with them in a manner at once serious and yet utterly informal. Such a combination would have been

---

[186] Swami Gambhirananda (ed.), *Apostles of Shri Ramakrishna* (Calcutta, 1967), p. 124.

rare with elders in hierarchised homes or with teachers in schools or colleges – the second major site, so far as *bhadralok* were concerned, of the new discipline of time. This transcending of the barriers of age and youth, work and play, in Ramakrishna's company perhaps had a particular attraction for adolescents engaged in a difficult transition from boyhood to adult responsibility.

We have already explored some of the ways in which *chakri*, the petty clerical job which was all that most of these young men could have otherwise aspired for, had come to be perceived as quintessentially unattractive. It was also getting more difficult to obtain, as Narendranath, academically the brightest among Ramakrishna's disciples, discovered through bitter personal experience when his father's sudden death in 1884 made him hunt desperately for some time for an office job.[187] Conjugality, the other sacrifice demanded of a *sannyasi*, apparently had few attractions, too. The *Kathamrita* is full of hints that the young married men drawn to Ramakrishna were neglecting their wives – with considerable encouragement, at times, from the saint himself. Biographical accounts of devotees mention with some regularity a repugnance for married life, at times preceding the first encounter with Ramakrishna.[188] The prospect, usually, was of marriage by parental arrangement with much younger, uneducated girls, well below the age of puberty.[189] Western education and tastes, confined overwhelmingly so far to males, may have created a new cultural

---

[187] *Life of Swami Vivekananda by his Eastern and Western Disciples* (Almora, 1912, 1963), pp. 88–90.

[188] See, for instance, the accounts of Yogananda (Yogindranath Chaudhuri), Saradananda (Sarat Chakrabarti), Sivananda (Taraknath Ghosh), and Turiyananda (Harinath Chattopadhyay) in Gambhiranandra, op. cit., pp. 148, 171, 202, 305; as well as the biography of a lay devotee, Saratchandra Chakrabarti's *Saadhu Nag Mahasay* (Calcutta, 1912, 1934).

[189] The *garbhadan* ritual demanded intercourse immediately after the first menses, and there was a massive agitation, particularly in Bengal, against the reformist-cum-government proposal to raise the age of consent to twelve years in 1891. Amiya Sen, *Hindu Revivalism in Late Nineteenth Century Bengal* (Delhi, 1993); Tanika Sarkar, "Rhetoric Against the Age of Consent: Resisting Colonial Reason and the Death of a Child-Wife", *Economic and Political Weekly*, 4 September 1993.

distance within the *bhadralok* family. More important, however, was the close interconnection between marriage and the sharpened struggle for survival bound up with the travails of *chakri*. "Nowadays parents marry their boys too young. By the time they finish their education, they are already fathers of children and have to run hither and thither in search of a job to maintain the family" – Ramakrishna had told Sarat and Sashi Chakrabarti, cousins who later became prominent figures in the Ramakrishna Mission.[190] The life stories of many disciples indicate more or less independent perceptions of the same crucial association of *kamini* with a *kanchan* obtainable, in niggardly amounts, only through *chakri*.

The skewed family situation, considered from the woman's angle, may go some distance towards explaining what otherwise appears the most puzzling of Ramakrishna's many paradoxes. The man whose conversation was full of extremely negative comments about the lust-filled bodies and luxurious and selfish ways of women still won the devotion of many women.[191] We even have accounts of women casting off inhibitions and purdah to go to Dakshineswar in a spirit of almost joyous abandon.[192] Ramakrishna's abhorrence of sex, and his advice to keep off intercourse after one or two children, perhaps struck a chord in married women. Sex may have often seemed a terrible duty for young girls married off to totally unknown men at a tender age, in an era when absence of contraceptives made childbearing frequent, dangerous, and extremely burdensome.[193] Middle-aged or

[190] Gambhirananda, op. cit., p. 171.

[191] Thus KM II, pp. 161–2 (11 October 1882); KM III, pp. 161–2 (9 May 1888), related a story about a guru who convinces a disciple that family affection is illusory, by giving him a medicine that apparently kills him: his mother and wife, though apparently full of sorrow, refuse the guru's offer that he could return to life if they are prepared to die in his place. The story is not directly about the evils of *kamini* at all – but, significantly, no male relative is put to the same test.

[192] L I, Gurubhava-Purbardha, pp. 31–6.

[193] A somewhat similar phenomenon has been noticed among early Methodist women: Henry Abelove, "The Sexual Politics of Early Western Methodism", in Obelkevich, *et al.* (ed.), *Disciplines of Faith* (London, 1987).

elderly housewives or widows may have found a way of overcoming loneliness and the tedium of household chores by setting themselves up in a maternal role *vis-à-vis* Ramakrishna. They loved to cook and bring food for him, which the holy man eagerly accepted and often asked for.[194] And while little survives of Ramakrishna's conversation with feminine audiences, one must not exclude the possibility that he added an extremely rare, non-personal and (in a limited sense) intellectual content to lives otherwise largely bereft of such mental sustenance.

A startling element was added to the circle of women devotees of Ramakrishna after his visit to Girish Ghosh's play *Chaitanya-Lila* (1884). The holy man blessed Binodini for her performance as the young Chaitanya: the man who normally abhorred feminine contact allowed actresses, recruited from among prostitutes, to touch his feet. Sex in such degraded form was presumably an object of pity and grace, not a threat – and perhaps, for a man who found even sex in marriage intolerable, prostitution was not all that specially repugnant. Ramakrishna's unexpected blessing of theatre women gave a new respectability to a profession despised by many,[195] and assuaged feelings of guilt: he became, in fact, in course of time a kind of patron saint for the Calcutta public theatre.[196] A wider impact became noticeable also when, in the mid 1890s, prostitutes – and not merely actresses drawn from them – began turning up in large numbers at the annual Ramakrishna birthday festivals at Dakshineswar, much to the horror of many *bhadralok*.[197] Binodini herself, with some limited encouragement from Girishchandra Ghosh, was emboldened to publish a moving, if somewhat flamboyantly repentant, account of her life as prostitute and actress.[198]

[194] Ibid., p. 33; L, li, Gurubhava-Uttarardha, p. 238.
[195] More specifically by Brahmos and those influenced by them.
[196] Naliniranjan Chattopadhyay, *Shri Ramakrishna o Banga Rangamancha* (Calcutta, 1978).
[197] Vivekananda to Ramakrishnananda, 23 August 1896 – *Patrabali*, II (Calcutta, 1949, 1960), pp. 127–8.
[198] Asutosh Bhattacharji (ed.), *Nati Binodini Rachana-Sangraha* (Calcutta, 1987).

The paradox of the Ramakrishna cult opening up certain spaces for women, in and through highly sexist assumptions and practices, is epitomised in the career of Sarada Debi. The wife who in her husband's lifetime was relegated firmly to Ramakrishna, blossomed out after Ramakrishna's death into a cult figure in her own right, the "Holy Mother" and embodiment of motherhood for Vivekananda and other devotees. Her sayings, taken down and presented by reverential devotees as Ramakrishna's had been, vividly illuminated this paradox in their autobiographical sections. Life with her husband at Dakshineswar is repeatedly recalled as a tale of bliss (*ananda*) and yet, without any felt sense of contradiction, we encounter at times in her very next words memories of a tiny, dismal room in an obscure corner of the temple compound with a doorway so low that you often hit your head entering it. Life was an endless round of preparing food, for Ramakrishna as well as for devotees who kept dropping in at all hours, and of waiting for nightfall to relieve herself by the river, for no-one had thought of providing a latrine for women. She learnt to read only after overcoming much opposition, particularly from Hriday, the cousin of Ramakrishna who had managed the material side of the saint's life till the early 1880s. There were weeks during which Sarada hardly saw her husband and could only hear him, talking and singing with male devotees, through the chinks of a bamboo curtain. And yet life had been bliss, for Ramakrishna had never called her by the contemptuous *tui* and never beaten her.

The memories of the years after 1886 take on a very different, increasingly self-confident, if still engagingly naïve, manner. Ramakrishna, Sarada tells us, appeared in a dream to tell her to start giving *diksha*, and she also began going into samadhi. We now have passages where she claims to be *jagater ma*, mother of the universe. Her body, precisely because it has endured so much suffering, is *devsharir*, divine.[199]

Prostitutes apart, all Ramakrishna's devotees came from the *bhadralok*, with a solitary exception: Latu, the illiterate Bihari servant the

---

[199] Abhaya Dasgupta (ed.), *Sri Sri Sarada Devi: Atmakatha* (Calcutta, 1980), pp. 12, 15, 18, 30–1, 34, 39, 67–8, 73, 75, 77, 79, 93, 109.

saint had inherited from his early disciple, the well-established North-Calcutta doctor Ramachandra Datta. Latu was given, appropriately, the task of cleaning up by the *bhadralok* disciples when Ramakrishna during his last days could not go out to defecate. The memoirs of Latu, taken down and published, provide certain fascinating sidelights. Son of a Chapra district shepherd, Latu retained all his life a dignity, independence, even a certain aggressiveness which not everyone liked and which many associated with his passion for wrestling. Serving Ramakrishna became for him a liberation from the burden of *naukri* in Ramachandra's household. He was fond of retelling Ramakrishna's *dasi* parable, adding to it a note of plebeian poignancy derived from an immediacy of experience: "He told me this story so that I could learn how to survive in the house of the *manib* (master). How else could my sorrows have ended?" *Seba* to Latu was sharply distinct from flattery: the *baralok* expect flattery, but not God. But *seba*, even for Ramakrishna, could be arduous, too, and Latu recalled how he was often scolded, and once was made to walk six miles to bring some special food for Ramakrishna. Sarada could talk freely with him, even in her years of rigorous purdah, and Latu's memories about her strike a note utterly different from the standard deification into abstract mother-figure: "How hard a life she had led. She stayed in that tiny room, for so many years, unnoticed by everyone."

Revered as one of Ramakrishna's intimate disciples, renamed Adbhutananda, Latu steadfastly refused to stay or even spend a night at the Belur Math founded by Vivekananda. "We are sadhus – why should we have land, houses, gardens, wealth? I won't stay in such a place."[200]

IV

The Dakshineswar temple, where Ramakrishna had lived for thirty years, and Belur Math, founded by his most illustrious disciple, face

---

[200] Chandrasekhar Chattopadhyay, *Sri Sri Latu Maharaj Smriti-Katha* (Calcutta, n.d.), pp. 10, 33, 45, 93, 95, 119–21, 370.

each other today on opposite banks of the Bhagirathi, presenting in many ways a vivid study in contrasts, even oppositions. The temple, like any major Hindu sacred site, is thronged with crowds which cut across class divides, noisy, colourful, not oversensitive to dirt. The holiness of the place permits women to shed inhibitions and bathe in the river ghat alongside menfolk. The approaches are cluttered with shops selling a variety of mementoes, trinkets, and eatables, and the atmosphere resembles that of a bazaar or mela. Solemnity reigns to some extent only inside the central shrine of Bhavatarini Kali, and, more evidently, in the corner room where Ramakrishna used to stay: here devotees sit, ponder, or pray. Belur Math is much more of an upper-middle-class devotional-cum-tourist spot, almost aggressively hygienic, it is full of guards and notices warning visitors off from bathing in the river and spoiling the lawns. An image of Ramakrishna, fully clothed in spotless white, constitutes the central shrine. A glass curtain preserves it from physical proximity or the touch of devotees or visitors. Asked where Vivekananda and his associates had themselves stayed, a swami points vaguely in the distance. He is much more interested in telling us that the main building had been constructed by Martin Burn in the 1930s, and that Kamala Nehru and Indira Gandhi had been regular visitors.

And yet Dakshineswar and Belur remain tied together by indissoluble links, each shedding its lustre on the other, leaving us with the problems of extremely varied worlds which still for some reason require a stable centre in the figure of Ramakrishna. Diverse appropriations of a founding father are of course common and not at all exceptional. While still worth exploration in terms of implications and contexts, the theme most relevant for our present study is the persistence of a need for affiliation with Ramakrishna across decades of sweeping change.

The power and weight of the canonical traditional as established by Vivekananda has somewhat obscured the range of meanings that the image of Ramakrishna has had the capacity to take on or inspire. There has been, for instance, a Tantric Ramakrishna, in considerable discordance with Vivekananda's violent condemnation of *vamachari* ways. An acrimonious controversy developed in the 1930s around the precise importance of Bhairabi Brahmani.[201] Ramakrishna's householder devotees, again, had little sympathy initially with Narendranath's band of young *sannyasis*, and there was even an unseemly quarrel between the two groups over Ramakrishna's ashes.[202] Middle-aged householders, led by Ramachandra Datta, instituted a distinct cult centred at Kankurgachi in east Calcutta, emphasising a quietistic and highly ritualised devotion to Ramakrishna as an avatar, to the exclusion of social activism. This was, arguably, closer in some ways to the spirit of the Ramakrishna we meet in the *Kathamrita* than the Vivekananda adaptation.[203] The national and international fame of Vivekananda eventually eclipsed the Kankurgachi variant of Ramachandra Datta, but pure ritualised devotion has persisted as a subordinate yet vital strand even within the canonical Ramakrishna Mission tradition. Sarada Debi is a crucial figure here, with her claim that Ramakrishna had predicted that he would be "worshipped in every home" after death, and insistence on the importance of *diksha*, mantra, and other rituals.[204] Among the *sannyasis*, Ramakrishnananda (Sashibhushan Chakrabarti) in particular preferred the ways of ritualised bhakti and *puja*. The elaborate ceremonies he conducted at the Math were often summarily dismissed by Vivekananda in private letters as useless "bell-ringing".[205]

[201] Two early biographies emphasised Ramakrishna's Tantric connections: Satyacharan Mitra, *Sri Sri Ramakrishna Paramahansa: Jibani o Upadesh* (Calcutta, 1897), and Bhubanchandra Mukhopadhyay, *Ramakrishna Charitamrita* (Calcutta, 1901). Kalikrishnananda Giri, *Sri Ramakrishna Sri-guru Bhairabi Yogeswari* (Calcutta, 1936) refers to a controversy about the role of Bhairabi in the mid 1930s.

[202] *Life of Swami Vivekananda by his Eastern and Western Disciples*, op. cit., pp. 153–5.

[203] Swami Gambhirananda, *History of the Ramakrishna Math and Mission* (Calcutta, 1957), pp. 39–41; Ramachandra Datta, *Sri Sri Ramakrishna Parmahan sadever Jivan-Vrittanta* (Calcutta, 1890, rpnt. 1910); ibid., *Tattva Prakashik* (4th edn, Kankurgachi, 1912). The evils of *chakri* figure prominently in Ramachandra Dutta's play *Lilamrita* (Calcutta, 1900).

[204] *Sarada Devi: Atmakatha*, op. cit., pp. 67–8, 93, 106.

[205] "If you can give up bell-ringing, otherwise I will not be able to join you ... The only karma I understand is service to others, everything else is

From the mid 1880s Girish Ghosh and his epigone began projecting yet another, subtly distinct, Ramakrishna through the north Calcutta professional stage, reaching out to an audience considerably wider than the limited range of personal contact or even print. Girish personally was on excellent terms with householder and *sannyasi* devotees alike, and his representations served ultimately as a kind of bridge between quietistic, though no longer highly ritualised, bhakti and Vivekananda's new turn towards social service. In *Bilvamangal* (June 1886), *Nasiram* (May 1888), and *Kalapahar* (September 1896), Girish introduced the figure of the wandering *pagal* or "holy fool", mad to the conventional world but purveyor, really, of divine wisdom, often in words taken straight from Ramakrishna. Wisdom conveyed through wandering folly quickly established itself as a central figure in Rabindranath's *thakurda* (grandfather) figures.[206] The *pagal* of Girish Ghosh appears, at first sight, to embody pure irresponsibility or playfulness, justified on the ground that everything is determined by Hari: "predestination" here has produced implications diametrically opposed to the puritan work ethic. Only "Hari-nama" is needed, else one should behave like a five-year-old child.[207] But *pagal* figures like Nasiram, or Chintamani in *Kalapahar* do in fact preside over and inspire substantial moral change – though action itself is pushed along, significantly, by women: plebeian trickster figures, or deferentially assertive wives.[208] Inward-turning piety and activism, in other words, do not necessarily remain binaries in the Ramakrishna–

---

evil karma. Hence I bow to the Buddha. Do you understand? A big gap is emerging between your group and myself . . ." Vivekananda to Sashi (Ramakrishnananda), n.d., 1895, *Patrabali*, I (Calcutta, 1948, 1954), pp. 444, 446. The translation is mine: the official translation, in *Letters of Swami Vivekananda* (Mayavati, 1940; Calcutta, 1970), p. 249, tones down the language considerably.

[206] In plays like *Prayaschitta* and *Muktadhara*.

[207] "When you were a child, you, merrily sucked your mother's breasts, and the mother did all the worrying – now, if you, stop worrying Hari will do the worrying for you." Nasiram, in the play with that name – Ray and Bhattacharji (ed.), *Girish-Rachanbali*, IV (Calcutta, 1974).

[208] Like Batul in *Srivatsa-Cinta* (1884) or Bhajahari and Prafulla herself in *Prafulla* (1889), ibid.

Vivekananda tradition. The withdrawal into oneself that Ramakrishna had inspired undercut an activism thought to be based on arrogance, but could serve at times as a prelude, through inner purification, for a higher kind of outgoing action.

In Satischandra Chattopadhyay's *Annapurna* (1904), Gadadhar himself appears as a "mad" *pujari*, alongside a *thakurda* who distances himself from worldly concerns through dance and devotional song. A clerk sings about his office woes and recalls the happier experiences of Ramprasad with his employer. The heroine, Annapurna, eventually changes the heart of her drunkard husband through endurance and deferential assertion. But Gadadhar himself is now a figure deeply moved by scenes of poverty, and the play ends with a widowed Annapurna erecting a temple where the poor would be fed day and night. Satischandra is clearly writing in the shadow of Vivekananda who, as we shall see, had exalted the Hindu widow, considered ritually impure by tradition, into the ideal Hindu woman, retaining all the marks of austere widowhood but immersed in social service. Annapurna, which means bounteous provider of food, is, again, one of Durga's many names, and the Swadeshi movement would soon erect Durga-Annapurna into a central image of the motherland. A minor play thus epitomises a whole complex transition.

A visitor to Belur Math today is greeted by a signboard that highlights the current philanthropic work of the Ramakrishna Mission. The poor, however, are physically much more distant than at Dakshineswar, and no plebeian bazaar has been allowed to obstruct the spacious entrance to the Math. The contrast points towards a two-way transition. With Vivekananda, sophisticated son of a prominent Calcutta attorney who quickly acquired international and national fame after his Chicago address, the Ramakrishna cult moved from the clerical margins into the centre of high-*bhadralok* life. Rustic and homely parables, along with the *dasatya* of *chakri* theme, dropped out of Vivekananda's discourse, which took the form of lectures (Ramakrishna, incidentally, had detested oratory),[209] and essays in

---

[209] This in fact was a constant refrain in his conversation. See, for instance, his encounter with Sasadhar Tarkachudamani, the Hindu revivalist orator, in KM III, 72ff (30 June 1884).

English or chaste, sanskritised Bengali. The distancing produced by English education and urban middle-class life was often associated, however, with a deep awareness of the West as, simultaneously, stimulus and threat. Among the more sensitive of the nineteenth-century *bhadralok*, it had led also to repeated efforts to ameliorate the conditions of the underprivileged and oppressed: women, lower castes, the poor.

Vivekananda revived, at the heart of what had begun as inward-turning bhakti, the traditions of such *bhadralok* activism. First-hand experience of mass poverty, ignorance, and caste oppression, obtained through tours across the subcontinent in 1890–3, added to this revival a distinctive, sharper edge. Ramakrishna, poor himself, had considered poverty a part of natural or divine law, and had displayed a "peasant" cynicism about do-gooding efforts by rich and learned folk as instances of arrogance and futility: "You have read a couple of pages in English, and so consider yourself mightily learned ... [and] ... think you can do good for the world. Can you end droughts, famines, epidemics?"[210] Vivekananda cultivated contacts with precisely such people – princes, dewans, well-established men – as potential fund-givers throughout his tours of India, and fund-raising remained a major objective of his lectures in America and Europe. ("I give them spirituality, and they give me money."[211]) The money he hoped to use for far-reaching plans of elevating the *daridra-narayan*, God manifest in the poor. Organised philanthropy would be combined with popular education in true high Hinduism and modern science, via devices like magic lanterns.

Such, Vivekananda visualised, would be the primary tasks of his band of young educated *sannyasis*, and in practice training this elite came to be foregrounded over the more challenging objective of mass education.[212] What was entailed was a transformation within

---

[210] Gurudas Barmen, *Sri Sri Ramakrishna Charit* (Calcutta, 1910), quoting a conversation with Kristodas Pal, pp. 206–7.

[211] Letter to Sashi, 19 March 1894, *Letters of Swami Vivekananda*, p. 82.

[212] "I have given up at present my plan for the education of the masses. It will come by degree. What I now want is a band of fiery missionaries." Letter to Alasinga, 12 January 1895, ibid., p. 197.

his own group, which could be achieved only after intense debate. In the words of the official historian of the Ramakrishna Mission, "the conflicting aims of religion and social service seemed irreconcilable indeed". Vivekananda's "greatest triumph lay in re-orientating the outlook of his brother disciples from ideas of personal salvation to a sympathetic comprehension of the needs of the world".[213] He had to fight, in a way, against an entire Hindu tradition in which charity might at times be considered a part of the dharma of the king or householder, but where the *sannyasi*'s principal ideal was individual *moksha*, not improvement of the world.

Basic religious-philosophical concepts, consequently, had to be given new meanings. Karma became, for Vivekananda, not traditional caste-based rituals and obligations determined by previous birth, but non-traditional social service. The *jnana* of Vedantic monism was sought to be transformed, through a real *tour de force*, into a message of strength and strenuous efforts to help others. The monistic unity of all beings, Vivekananda argued, implied that "in loving anyone, I am loving myself."[214] Vedantic *jnana* was simultaneously exalted in unambiguous fashions over quietistic emotional bhakti, and the Tantric elements in Ramakrishna sought to be suppressed altogether in a firmly structured framework of *adhikaribheda* which now defined a clearly demarcated Hindu religion.[215] This was the kind of Hinduism which Vivekananda thought could be projected abroad as intellectually powerful enough to challenge and overcome the

---

[213] Swami Gambhirananda, *History of the Ramakrishna Math and Mission*, op. cit., pp. 123, 117–18.

[214] *Vedantism* in Complete Works of Swami Vivekananda (9th ed., 1964: henceforth CW), III, p. 130.

[215] Two examples, from many: "I thoroughly appreciate the power and potency of bhakti on men to suit the needs of different times. What we now want in our country, however, is not so much weeping, but a little strength. What a mine of strength is in this Impersonal God . . . That you get alone in the Vedanta – and there alone." Reply to Jaffna welcome address, 1897 – CW III, p. 130. "All of religion is contained in the Vedanta, that is, in the three stages of the Vedanta philosophy, the Dvaita, Visisthdvaita, and Advaita; one comes after the other." This he claimed to be "my Letter to Alasinga, 6 May 1895, *Letters*, p. 227.

arrogant claims of Christian missionaries – claims inseparable, often, from imperialist racism. Through its propagation, Vivekananda emerged as the first major exemplar of that familiar twentieth-century figure, the Indian guru who wins fame and disciples in the West. *Adhikaribheda* apexed by Vedanta seemed to have the potential, also, for unifying all Hindus through the incorporation of diversities within a single hierarchy. Nivedita would soon define Vivekananda's achievement at Chicago as the transformation of "the religious ideas of the Hindus" into "Hinduism", for through *adhikaribheda* "there could be no sect, no school, no sincere religious experience of the Indian people . . . that might rightly be excluded from the embrace of Hinduism."[216] The catholicity of Ramakrishna, modulated and transformed through this construction of a crystallised "Hindu" identity, thus became for Vivekananda the paradoxical ground for a claim to superior worth: "Our religion is truer than any other religion because it never conquered, because it never shed blood." Vivekananda in the same lecture went on to stress the need for "iron muscles and nerves of steel", and even visualised "the conquest of the whole world by the Hindu race . . . [a] conquest of religion and sprirituality."[217]

Vivekananda's rhetoric sounds powerful and self-confident, yet just beneath its surface fissures often lurk, manifesting themselves repeatedly through implicit or explicit contradictions. It is in terms of such tensions, which Vivekananda was too clear-sighted and honest to be able to brush aside, that we can best understand why an apparently wholesale inversion of the ideas of Ramakrishna, accompanied by the entry of themes quite unknown to the master, still remained in need of an ultimate anchorage in the quietistic bhakti of the Dakshineswar saint.

The tensions are clearest in Vivekananda's discourses about women and lower castes. His letters repeatedly associate degradation of women with caste oppression as the two central evils of Hindu society. The contrasts with Ramakrishna in both respects are obvious enough. Awareness of social degradation played no part in Ramakrishna's

---

[216] Nivedita, *Our Master and His Message*, Introduction to *CW* I, p. x.
[217] *From Colombo to Almora*, *CW* III, pp. 274–5.

twin images of women as epitome of danger through sexuality and emblem of maternal purity, and caste had figured rarely in his discourse. Vivekananda had nothing of Ramakrishna's obsessive terrors about the woman's body, and he was careful to substitute *kama* for *kamini*, avoiding the implication that lust was somehow peculiarly feminine.[218] Early letters from America enthusiastically acclaimed the free yet responsible and socially committed Western women he had met, several of whom had become his ardent disciples: "free as birds in air", whereas "look at our girls, becoming mothers below their teens . . . We are horrible sinners, and our degradation is due to our calling women 'despicable worms', 'gateways to hell' and so forth."[219] The disciple here came perilously close to a direct criticism of his master. But passages like these are generally confined to private correspondence. Public speeches concentrated fire on missionary slanders about Indian womanhood, and the futility and irrelevance of social-reform movements.[220] Missionary propaganda, arrogant and at times racist, had the habit of harping on themes like child marriage or the seclusion of women, and Vivekananda evidently found it demeaning to national-cum-religious pride to publicly repeat such criticism, however much he might privately detest many such practices.

The cult of Sarada Debi as "Divine Mother" which Vivekananda encouraged was perhaps one way of trying to resolve this tension: womanhood of one particular kind was being exalted, but through a markedly traditionalist idiom: the other attempted solution was ascetic widowhood channelled into social service. Vivekananda, Nivedita thought, had "looked, naurally enough, to widows as a class to provide the first generation of abbess-like educators" – he had a "horror" of the "unfaithful widow", and emphasised "trustful

---

[218] See, for instance, Vivekananda or Sashi, 24 June 1896, where he explicitly instructed the latter to substitute *kama* for *kamini* in the material he was preparing for Max Mueller: *Patrabali*, II, p. 100.

[219] Letters to Haripada Mitra, 28 December 1893; to Sashi, 19 March 1894, *Letters*, pp. 61, 81.

[220] See, for example, *From Colombo to Almora*, CW III, pp. 151–3, 198, 207ff.

and devoted companionship to the husband."²²¹ In India, though not among Western women disciples, several of whom were young, unmarried, and unconventional, feminine entry into public space presumably required careful regulation so as not to conflict with conjugal duty and decorum. The widow who still carried all the marks of traditional austerity provided the ideal material. The limits, even here, were revealed by Vivekananda's bitter public quarrel in the United States with Pandita Ramabai about the condition of Hindu widows – a quarrel which coincided in time with a gesture of financial support to Sasipada Banerji's home-cum-school for widows at Baranagar (April 1895).²²² Setting up widows' homes and educating their inmates was one thing: a militantly reformist widow who had turned Christian as a matter of mature voluntary choice represented a very different proposition.

Vivekananda's comments about caste reveal a similar pattern. His letters are full of an awareness and anger about caste oppression rare among the *bhadralok* intelligentsia of nineteenth-century Bengal, where even Brahmo rejection of caste had generally taken the form of token gestures within the bounds of the reformed community.²²³ Such awareness, he said, had been brought to him by the "experience I have had in the south, of the upper classes torturing the lower . . . Do you think our religion is worth the name? Ours is only 'Don't touchism'. Millions live on *mohua* plants, while *sadhus* and Brahmins 'suck the blood of these poor people'."²²⁴ But this new sensitivity towards caste oppression was also bound up with an ideal of a crystallised and unified Hindu society which, too, had been absent in Ramakrishna. Vivekananda's public lectures, in particular, normally situated the need to uplift lower castes in the context of the danger

---

[221] Nivedita, *The Master as I Saw Him* (Calcutta, 1910, 1963), pp. 142–3, 282–6.

[222] S.N. Dhar, *A Comprehensive Biography of Swami Vivekananda*, vol. I (Madras, 1975), chapter 9.

[223] As Brahmoism remained confined to the educated upper-caste *bhadralok*, intermarriage and interdining remained restricted to the Brahmans, Kayasthas, and Vaidyas who had become Brahmos.

[224] Letter to Sashi, 19 March 1894, *Letters*, p. 81.

of Christian and Muslim proselytisation: an argument that would come to acquire a central place in the discourses of twentieth-century "Hindutva".[225] There was also a simultaneous, violent condemnation of the emerging anti-Brahman movements in the South: "it is no use fighting among the castes . . . The solution is not by bringing down the higher, but by raising the lower up to the level of the higher . . . To the non-Brahman castes I say, be not in a hurry . . . you are suffering from your own fault. Who told you to neglect spirituality and Sanskrit learning?"[226] The hidden interlocutor, once again, must have been the missionary and colonial apologist for whom caste oppression, along with the subordination of women, proved the essential unworthiness and inferiority of Indians.

Bartaman Bharat (Modern India, March 1899),[227] Vivekananda's most famous work in Bengali, provides the supreme example of this radical logic that abruptly turns back on itself as it encounters the rock of patriotic-cum-Hindu faith. It elaborates an interesting conception of history where priestly (Brahman), royal (Kshatriya), and mercantile (Vaishya) power succeeded each other, not just in India but everywhere. All have their merits and deficiencies, but sharpest condemnation is reserved for the eras of priestly domination. Stereotypes of Hindu nationalist historiography are ruthlessly overturned as Vivekananda indicates a preference for the Buddhist and Islamic eras, when the decline in Brahman power had enabled the emergence of powerful empires: Rajput domination, in contrast, is represented as a virtual dark age. The global British empire obviously embodies the climax of Vaishya power, after which is predicted a "rising of the Shudra class, with their Shudrahood . . . when the Shudras of every country . . . remaining as Shudras – will gain absolute supremacy in every society . . . Socialism, Anarchism, Nihilism and suchlike sects are the vanguard of the social revolution that is to follow." ("I am a

---

[225] As in Shraddhanand's activities in the early 1920s, or earlier in Bengal, the "dying race" theme developed by U.N. Mukherji. Pradip Kumar Datta, "The "Dying Hindu": Production of Hindu Communal Common-sense in Early Twentieth-century Bengal", *Economic and Political Weekly*, 19 June 1993.

[226] *The Future of India*, *CW* III, pp. 294–8.

[227] I am using the official English translation in *CW* III.

socialist", Vivekananda had proclaimed to Mary Hale in the course of a letter outlining a similar argument in 1896.[228]) But then, very abruptly, comes an assertion that in British-ruled India "the whole population has virtually come down to the level of the Shudra." The only real Brahmans today are foreign professors, the Kshatriyas are British officials, the Vaishyas the British merchants. The whole tide of Vivekananda's argument now suddenly reverses itself. What is branded as blind imitativeness becomes the principal target, and a whole range of traditional practices and norms is implicitly re-valorised: the "Sita-Savitri-Damyanti" model, for instance, as opposed to the "unrestricted intermingling" of men and women. "Westerners hold caste distinctions to be obnoxious, therefore let all the distinct castes be jumbled into one." The rhetoric reaches its climax in the appeal: "forget not that the lower classes, the ignorant, the poor, the illiterate, the cobbler, the sweeper, are thy flesh and blood, thy brothers." This has often been cited as the pinnacle of Vivekananda's radicalism, but a retreat has really taken place, from the earlier vision of Shudra revolution to the submergence of caste or class differences, without basic internal transformation, into a nationalist brotherhood. The intended audience ("thy") is clearly the educated, while the people with "a rag round their loins" are expected only to proclaim at the top of their voice: "The Indian in my brother . . . India's gods and goddesses are mine." The concluding pages of *Bartaman Bharat* have become a standard college or high-school text; the earlier sections are much less familiar. The authorised *Life of Vivekananda* "by his Eastern and Western admirers" summarises much of Vivekananda's writings but omits all reference to *Bartaman Bharat*.

Bartaman Bharat ended with apparently self-confident rhetoric – but the letter to Mary Hale where Vivekananda called himself a socialist concluded on a suddenly world-weary tone: "The sum-total of good and evil in the world remains ever the same . . . Let every dog have his day in this miserable world" – till such time as "man gives up this vanity of a world and governments and all other botherations."[229] A profound pessimism in fact seems to repeatedly

---

[228] *Letters*, pp. 317–18.
[229] Ibid.

Kaliyuga, Chakri and Bhakti 231

undermine Vivekananda's utopian dreams. The argument that he used, for instance, to appropriate Vedanta for an ethic of social service is in a way deeply cynical, for it assumes that men will help others only if they realise that this is just another form of self-love. Asked by an American woman missionary in 1898 whether he foresaw any hope of eliminating child-marriage and cruelty to widows, Vivekananda sadly replied in the negative. Vivekananda, the missionary reports, seemed to have a "strange foreboding of ultimate failure" even "with the Hindu world at his feet" – "sitting there at twilight, in the large, half-lighted hall, it seemed like listening to a cry."[230]

Vivekananda's well-known oscillation between supremely self-confident activism and inward-turning world-weariness has been sought to be explained in terms of an inner psychological conflict going back to childhood days.[231] A more contextualised reading, however, is also possible, to supplement – and not necessarily supplant – the psychological analysis. The utopian image of a Bharatvarsha rooted in an ideal Hinduism that Vivekananda passionately tried to adhere to was contradicted repeatedly by the harsh facts of contemporary Hindu society that he was too clear-sighted and honest to be able to ignore. He found no way of resolving these contradictions. What needs to be recognised as tragedy may best be grasped in terms of a grid of alternative action parameters, none of which Vivekananda could adopt without ambiguity or self-doubt.

Vivekananda condemned caste and gender oppression, and found many Hindu practices – including revering the cow as Mother – utterly ridiculous.[232] Yet existing social-reform initiatives he considered superficial, with some justice, because confined to the educated elite – and demeaning to national pride. The public condemnation of many evils which he denounced in private was inhibited in him by the fear of strengthening Western slanders about a subject race.

Vivekananda, at the same time, could not share the facile nationalist faith that such internal problems were secondary and would sort

---

[230] Lucy E. Guiness, *Across India at the Dawn of the Twentieth Century* (London, 1898), p. 147. I owe this reference to Tanika Sarkar.
[231] See Ashis Nandy, *The Intimate Enemy* (Delhi, 1983).
[232] *Life of Swami Vivekananda*, p. 489.

themselves out after the winning of political freedom. His countrywide tours had given an unusual depth of meaning to a patriotism that embraced the entire subcontinent, and found memorable expression in the invocations to *"Bharat"* with which *Bartaman Bharat* ends. But Vivekananda had little faith or interest in existing forms of Moderate Congress political activity, repeatedly warned against attaching "political significance" to his ideas,[233] and seems to have looked upon the British empire, at times, as an opportunity to spread Hinduism abroad (on the analogy of Christianity under the Roman Empire).[234] Deep concern with poverty remained unrelated in Vivekananda to any awareness of colonial exploitations: there is a virtual silence about that already well-established staple of nationalist polemic, the drain of wealth theory.[235] Vivekananda, then, was not quite the "patriot-prophet" who would soon be reversed as patron saint by a whole generation of Swadeshi enthusiasts, revolutionary terrorists, and nationalists in general. Nivedita, who did more than anyone else, perhaps, to promote this image of Vivekananda, herself recognised its partially constructed character: "Just as Shri Ramakrishna, in fact, without knowing any books, had been a living epitome of the Vedanta, so was Vivekananda of the national life. But of the theory of this he was unconscious."[236]

Vivekananda, the apostle of anti-British nationalism today, belongs essentially to the past: what has become ominously relevant is the other, closely related image of the Swami as one of the founders of twentieth-century Hindutva, of a united, muscular, and aggressive Hinduism. He had no particular prejudice about Islam,[237] but there is little doubt that like very many Hindu nationalists of his times, or later, the Bharat of Vivekananda's dreams was essentially Hindu. The closing appeal for fraternal embrace in *Bartaman Bharat* somehow

[233] Letter to Alasinga, 27 September 1894, *Letters*, p. 148.

[234] *Problem of Modern India and Its Solution* (July 1899), *CW*, IV.

[235] With one notable exception – a violently anti-British letter to Mary Hale, 30 October 1899, referring to "blood-sucking" and a "reign of terror", *Letters*, pp. 394–6. But Vivekananda almost certainly did not consider drain of wealth to be the prime cause of mass poverty.

[236] Nivedita, *The Master as I Saw Him*, op. cit., p. 53.

[237] Nivedita recalls his warm admiration of Mughal achievements, ibid.

forgets to mention Muslims. Much more important is the crucial role of Vivekananda in crystallising a Hindu identity that is able to play simultaneously on the twin registers of catholicity and aggression: a pattern that has become standard in the discourses of today's RSS-VHP-BJP combine. And yet a gap remains, for Vivekananda could never reconcile himself totally to the harsh realities of caste and gender oppression, of mass poverty for which he refused to affix the responsibility solely on the Bristish, and of "hundreds of superstitions". The Triplicane Literary Society Address (1897) which claimed that Hinduism was "truer than any other religion" simultaneously demanded that such things be "weeded out".[238] It was quite impossible for Vivekananda to accept everything in Hindu society in a kind of aestheticised celebration of difference, as multicoloured flowers in a garland.[239]

Faced with such insurmountable tensions, Vivekananda came to perpetually oscillate between exuberant calls to action and moods of introspection, in a pattern that is particularly relevant because it helps us understand why an ultimate anchorage in Ramakrishna remained so indispensable. *Bartaman Bharat* had been preceded by months during which Vivekananda had immersed himself in the songs of Ramprasad, trying "to saturate his own mind with the conception of himself as a child". After a mystical experience at Kshir Bhawani in Kashmir, Vivekananda told Nivedita in October 1898: "It is all 'Mother' now! ... there is no more patriotism. I am only a little child."[240] This, evidently, was not the Mother of *Anandamath* or Swadeshi nationalism, a patriotic icon calling sons to the path of self-sacrificing action. It was Ramakrishna's Divine Mother, who wants nothing more than childlike surrender, an abjuration of the active responsible adulthood that Vivekananda himself had tried so hard to promote. In some ways, perhaps, it was Ramakrishna himself.

[238] *CW*, III, p. 278.
[239] That, roughly, is the dominant outlook of contemporary "Hindutva" as embodied above all in the Vishwa Hindu Parishad. See Tapan Basu, Pradip Dutta, Sumit Sarkar, Tanika Sarkar, Sambudha Sen, *Khaki Shorts and Saffron Flags: A Critique of the Hindu Right* (Delhi: Longman, 1993).
[240] *The Master as I Saw Him*, op. cit., pp. 124, 128.

The introspective mood came to dominate the last two years or so of Vivekananda's life, finding expression in words utterly moving and unforgettable:

> This is the world, hideous, beastly corpse. Who thinks of helping it is a fool . . . I am only the boy who used to listen with rapt wonderment to the wonderful words of Ramakrishna . . . That is my true nature; works and activities, doing good and so forth are only superimpositions. Now I again hear his voice, the same old voice thrilling my soul . . . I have long given up my place as a leader . . . Behind my work was ambition . . . behind my guidance the thirst for power. Now they are vanishing and I drift. I come! . . . I come, a spectator, no more an actor. Oh, it is so calm! . . .[241]

Quietistic, inward-turning bhakti, tolerant and non-proselytising, had thus been transformed, with conflicts but no major rupture, into a crystallised and assertive Hindu identity with activist programmes. But insurmountable contradictions – fundamentally perhaps the limits set to *bhadralok* idealism by hierarchies of caste, gender, and class within a colonial situation – blocked the realisation of such programmes, and both the expansion of outlook and the eventual return to origins helped to deepen the appeal of the initial message. Vivekananda's fame preserved and vastly extended the reach of the apparently very different image of Ramakrishna. It is noteworthy, for instance, that Mahendranath brought out four of the five volumes of his *Kathamrita* between 1902 (the year of Vivekananda's death) and 1910 – years precisely of Swadeshi nationalist militancy inspired to a consider extent by Vivekananda's posthumous image as patriot-prophet. A significant number of revolutionary terrorists, it may be added, beginning with two of the accused in the Alipur Bomb Case of 1908, sought shelter within the Ramakrishna Mission in the wake of political frustration or failure. Such recruits provoked occasional government suspicion, but the Mission kept itself determinedly aloof from nationalist politics.[242] It offered space for philanthropic and educational work, but also for quiet devotional piety. Vivekananda's

---

[241] Letter to Mary Hale, 17 June 1900; to Josephine MacLeod, 18 April 1900, *Letters*, pp. 422–3.
[242] Gambhirananda, *History of Ramakrishna Math and Mission*, op. cit., pp. 88–90, 202–4, 213.

return to Ramakrishna, it seems, had created something like a recurrent pattern.

The Ramakrishna heritage which flourishes today in Bengal incorporates, consequently, an enormous variety of appropriations around a central core of claimed affinity. At one extreme, fleets of cars draw up every evening outside the palatial Institute of Culture of the Ramakrishna Mission in south Calcutta, where learned religious-cum-philosophical discourses provide solace for the rich. The Mission itself carries on valuable educational and philanthropic work, and enough has survived within it of the original catholicity to keep it – so far – away from the contemporary politics of aggressive Hindutva typified by the VHP. But little remains of more grandiose dreams of uplifting the *daridra-narayan* on a countrywide scale, or of a "Shudra" revolution. Few even of Vivekananda's close associates, ever seem to have taken to heart his occasional passionate onslaughts against Brahmanical tyranny and gender oppression.

At another related but somewhat distinct level, crowds of varied social origin throng Dakshineswar, and portraits of Ramakrishna adorn countless middle- or lower-middle-class homes, an object of deep devotion for many humble men and, perhaps even more, women. The clerical ambience we noted as crucial for Ramakrishna's initial appeal never really disappeared, even though Vivekananda had moved into a higher social world. Of thirty-seven members, for instance, of a Ramakrishna Samiti functioning in Barisal town in 1910 – set up at the initiative of government clerical staff without any affiliation at first with Belur and combining a little philanthropy with collective readings of the *Kathamrita* – twenty-four came from clerical and related professions. At a later stage the clerks tried to "enlist certain respectable and sympathetic gentlemen of the town", and so a few pleaders and schoolteachers were included in the Executive Committee.[243]

The world of clerks in Bengal, of course, has changed vastly since Ramkrishna's times. Beginning with the Burn Company clerks' strike in October 1905, Bengal's office employees began developing trade

---

[243] Government of Bengal, Home Poll Confidential, 372/1910 (West Bengal State Archives).

union organisations of their own. From the 1950s the clerical world of Dalhousie Square has been one of the strongest bastions of the left and trade-union movement in West Bengal. Nor are offices today marked by any stringently enforced discipline of time: symbolically, perhaps, a portrait of Ramakrishna has become a common feature of many offices and banks. But Left political predominance has obviously not been accompanied by any equivalent cultural hegemony, and a depressing and dismal struggle for existence still characterises much of lower-middle-class life.

Agni-sanket (1984), by the bestselling novelist Sanjib Chattopadhyay, may provide us with an appropriate concluding note. The context is disillusionment with the Left Front government, the focus, once again, clerical life. *Kamini, kanchan,* and the miseries of lower-middle-class life have come together once more. Drudgery in office and home remains the lot of the less fortunate, while the successful few climb up by shattering kinship obligations. For both, women and sex are somehow to blame. "The whole world is turning around the woman's body. On all sides the manholes are open." Social conservatism has become utterly blatant. Watching girls being "teased" in crowded buses, the clerk-hero ruminates: "Where has that veil gone? Where that respect? No leader talks of moral ideals, or of our ancient traditions." The author presents no real, positive alternatives, neither Vivekananda's patriotic social service nor even Ramakrishna's quiet bhakti and *grihastha sannyas*. But a good woman changes the heart of the local rowdy, who leaves her as a dying gift a picture of Ramakrishna. The hero dreams about a "white-belt black-shirt" terrorist gang to punish evildoers, a taxi-driver blames Kaliyuga for soaring prices, and, in an apocalyptic fantasy ending, the burning body of the clerk goes around destroying symbols of corruption.[244] A deeply depressing, claustrophobic world, where failure and poverty only help to consolidate hierarchies of caste and gender – over which Ramakrishna presides, as an icon that gives perhaps a little comfort, but not hope.

[244] Sanjib Chattopadhyay, *Agni Sanket* (Calcutta, 1984), pp. 39, 57, 60, 104, and *passim*.

7

Vidyasagar and Brahmanical Society

Ramakrishna: "The work (*karma*) that you are doing is very good... But as your devotion (*bhakti*) and love for Him grows, your work will lessen... Man cannot improve the world, only He is doing it: He has made the sun and the moon, given affection to mothers and fathers, benevolence (*daya*) to the great, *bhakti* to the *sadhu bhakt*... Look, how wonderful the universe is. How many things: sun, moon, the stars; how many different kinds of living beings. Big and small, good and bad, some with more powers (*shakti*), some with less."

—**Vidyasagar:** "Has He given more *shakti* to some, less to others?" extract from "M" (Mahendranath Gupta), *Ramakrishna-Kathamrita*, vol. III (Calcutta, 1908; 15th edition, 1982), pp. 15 and 10, dtd 5 August 1882

THE *RAMAKRISHNA-KATHAMRITA* may seem an odd, perhaps positively eccentric, starting point for an essay on Vidyasagar. Ramakrishna's visit to Vidyasagar's house was never reciprocated, and in many ways the two clearly represented opposite poles. Mahendranath Gupta, the compiler of *Kathamrita*, who had arranged the visit at Ramakrishna's request, was in 1882 headmaster of a North Calcutta school started by Vidyasagar. He resigned his job soon afterwards, upon hearing that the latter had made an adverse comment about his neglect of his duties because of overfrequent visits to Dakshineswar.[1]

[1] Biographical note on "M" (Mahendranath Gupta), appended to *Ramakrishna-Kathamrita*, vol. I (Calcutta, 1901, 1980).

Mahendranath's account of Ramakrishna's conversations with Vidyasagar, based on his diary notings but published a quarter of a century later, seems to have been structured with exceptional care. It begins with praise of Vidyasagar by the diarist-compiler for great learning and unequalled compassion ("*dayar sagar*"): there is not a word about Vidyasagar the social reformer, no reference at all to widow remarriage. Then, step by step, Ramakrishna is presented as establishing the inferiority of "mere" learning and philanthropy to devotion. There is a brief moment of agreement, when Vidyasagar admires Ramakrishna's statement that no-one can know or describe what divinity is. But from there the paths diverge radically once more. For Vidyasagar, as described by Mahendranath, the unknowability of the supramundane makes it our supreme duty to try to do everything possible to improve this-worldly life.[2] For Ramakrishna, in total contrast, ignorance becomes the premise for faith and devotion, and it is folly and arrogance for men to think of improving the world. The universe inevitably consists of big and small, some with more power and others with less: it is beautiful because it is divinely structured in terms of hierarchical inequality. This reiteration of the principle of *adhikari-bheda*, much used in nineteenth-century Brahmanical discourses,[3] provoked Vidyasagar to make a retort implicitly asserting that inequality is not natural but social, and hence open to human remedial action. The retort clearly rankled with Ramakrishna, for the *Kathamrita* describes him recalling it on two later occasions as proof of the folly of Vidyasagar.[4]

Opposed mentalities, indeed world outlooks: but I think it is helpful to remember that Vidyasagar and Ramakrishna came from rather

---

[2] Vidyasagar once teased a Brahmo preacher who had lost his way while coming to his house: "Why do you think you know the road to heaven any better? You'd better give up this business fast." Chandicharan Bandopadhyay, *Vidyasagar* (Calcutta, 1895, 1969), p. 54.

[3] For a discussion of the centrality of this notion, see chapters 8 and 9 in Sumit Sarkar, *Writing Social History* (Delhi: Oxford University Press, 1997).

[4] "Vidyasagar is so learned, has such a reputation, yet he said such a silly thing, asking whether He could have given more powers to some, less to others – ". *Kathamrita*, vol. II, p. 64 (15 June 1883). See also ibid., vol. III, p. 205 (28 July 1885).

similar social worlds. Not primarily because Birsingha and Kamarpukur are villages close to each other, both then part of Jehanabad (Arambagh) subdivision of Hooghly district, but in terms of origins in rural, poor Brahman families in an area centred around Khanakul-Krishnanagar, noted for centuries for its Brahmanical learning. Families, moreover, which were or had become extremely poor: few among the other famous men of nineteenth-century Bengal rose from such conditions of extreme genteel poverty.[5] For both Vidyasagar and Ramakrishna, the move to Calcutta was crucial, but then their paths to influence and fame became utterly different. The social ascent of Vidyasagar, enjoying excellent relations with high British officials and leading zamindars particularly in the 1850s and 1860s, and with a monthly income at times of three to four thousand rupees from his textbook publishing business, was in external terms much more spectacular than that of the humble *pujari*-cum-mystic at Rani Rashmoni's Dakshineswar temple. Before coming to visit Vidyasagar, Ramakrishna took unusual care to see that his buttons were in place, and in course of their conversation said that Vidyasagar was like a big ship, while people like him were no more than fishing boats.[6] Yet by the early 1880s there was also a strong element of paradox in their respective positions. The "ocean of learning" was feeling more and more isolated among the Calcutta *bhadralok*, and had come to prefer the company of unlearned Santals at Katmatar, while it was precisely the English-educated who were flocking to Dakshineswar. When Ramakrishna died in August 1886, the liberal English newspaper *Statesman* was impressed by the manner in which his ashes had been

---

[5] Vidyasagar's father Thakurdas was earning Rs 10 a month when he brought his son to Calcutta in 1828, and though prices of most things then were extremely low, the Hindu College fee was Rs 5 per month. Rani Rashmoni's deed of endowment of February 1861 provided Rs 5 for Ramakrishna as *pujari* of her temple, plus stipulated amounts of cloth and food. *Vidyasagar Charit* (autobiographical fragment, published posthumously in 1891, reprinted in Tirthapati Datta, n.d., *Vidyasagar Rachanabali*, vol. I, Calcutta, 1994, p. 411); Sambhuchandra Vidyaratna, *Vidyasagar-Jivamarit* (Calcutta, 1891; rpntd. ed. Kumudkumar Bhattacharya, Calcutta, 1992), p. 13: *Ramakrishna-Kathamrita*, vol. II (Calcutta, 1904, 1982), p. iii.

[6] *Ramakrishna-Kathamrita*, vol. III, pp. 3, 16.

"reverentially carried" by his "followers – all graduates and undergraduates of the university."[7]

A juxtaposition of Vidyasagar with Ramakrishna can raise some interesting questions about different trajectories emerging from a little-explored world of poor high-caste literati: the underside, so to say, of the colonial "educated middle class" about which so much has been written in praise or condemnation. Nineteenth-century studies have oscillated between eulogies of "renaissance awakening" inspired by Western or English education, and critiques of colonial cultural subjugation brought about by the same institutions and ideas. The influence, or imposition, of the culture of the post-Enlightenment West figures as absolutely central in both interpretive models, while the "middle class", in a second assumption common to otherwise opposed poles, tends to get portrayed in excessively homogenised terms.[8]

It has never been easy to slot Vidyasagar into either of these alternative frames, for he combined indisputably "modernistic" ideas and reform initiatives with a rejection of all the external signs of "Westernism" and evident rootedness, by education and way of life, in "traditional" Brahman literati culture. At times such problems have heightened the quality of research. Benoy Ghosh's study, for instance, remains impressive through its grasp over detail and valuable insights, even though its "awakening" or "renaissance" mould would not be acceptable to many today.[9] And the early 1970s critique of the renaissance in terms of colonial constraints undoubtedly attained its point of maximum subtlety and depth in Asok Sen's *Iswarchandra Vidyasagar and His Elusive Milestones*.[10]

Sen's study had been a wide-ranging analysis of the constraints upon Vidyasagar, exploring the interrelations between education, social-reform endeavours, and the changing contours of colonial

---

[7] *Statesman*, 25 August 1886, rpntd in Ranabir Raychaudhuri, ed., *Calcutta a Hundred Years Ago* (Calcutta: Nachiketa Publications, 1988), p. 126.

[8] For a fuller elaboration of my problems with both these frameworks, see chapter 6 in Sarkar, *Writing Social History*.

[9] Benoy Ghosh, *Vidyasagar o Bangali Samaj*, vols I, II, III (Calcutta, 1957, 1958, 1959; combined volume, Calcutta: Orient Longman, 1973).

[10] Published Calcutta: Riddhi-India, 1977.

political economy. With the displacement of Marx by Saidian critiques of colonial discourse, emphasis has shifted from such specific explorations of the ways in which modernising initiatives had been frustrated in colonial conditions to supposedly more radical repudiations of post-Enlightenment modernity and radicalism. "Modernity", rather than the structures of capitalist colonialism, has become the principal polemical target, and the social is collapsed into the narrowly intellectual and discursive. The nineteenth-century literati now appear as more homogenised than ever, with their trajectories set by ideas inevitably tainted by their origin in the modern West. What, often with considerable vagueness, is called nationalism gets deconstructed into a series of disciplinary projects that are either derived from, or at best run parallel to, the patterns of colonial power-knowledge.[11]

Significantly, perhaps, few attempts have been made so far to incorporate Vidyasagar into this anti-modernist interpretive frame.[12] Some recent writings point, rather, in a different and to my mind more fruitful direction. Brian Hatcher and Sekhar Bandopadhyay have highlighted in distinct ways the relevance of Brahmanical ideas and contexts for understanding Vidyasagar. Hatcher's is an unusual, if narrow, focus upon Vidyasagar's educational plans and school textbooks: he finds in them not a simple acculturation by Victorian notions of improvement and discipline, but a coming together of "bourgeois and Brahmanical educational ideologies within a Bengali idiom of moral pedagogy."[13] In a brief but very original and important

---

[11] The most authoritative and influential expositions of this current orthodoxy have come of course from Partha Chatterjee, *Nationalist Thought and the Colonial World: A Derivative Discourse?* (Delhi: Oxford University Press, 1986), and *The Nation and Its Fragments* (Delhi: Oxford University Press, 1994); for the (slightly) revised version emphasising parallel disciplinary projects, see Partha Chatterjee, ed., *Texts of Power: Emerging Disciplines in Colonial Bengal* (Calcutta: Samya, 1996).

[12] With the partial exception, perhaps, of Shivaji Bandopadhyay, *Gopal-Rakhal Dvandvasamas: Upanibeshbad o Bangla Shishusahitya* (Calcutta, 1991), pp. 134–42, and *passim*.

[13] Brian A. Hatcher, *Idioms of Improvement: Vidyasagar and Cultural*

essay, Sekhar Bandopadhyay has argued that the relative failure of widow remarriage and other nineteenth-century social-reform initiatives cannot be explained solely by the "structural weaknesses of the reformist effort". One needs to take into account also "the power of tradition that refused to be reformed", as embodied in hierarchies of caste and gender that were necessarily interlocked, since caste purity depended in large part on strict regulation of marriage and female sexuality.[14] These were consolidated in some ways under British rule, but certainly did not originate from colonialism. Bandopadhyay rejects the tendency common nowadays to romanticise the precolonial "popular" as a realm of freedom. He argues that the Brahmanical "ideology of discipline" and "public control over private life" had penetrated deep into so-called "popular" Hinduism in Bengal well before the colonial presence. The taboo on widow remarriage, for instance, was far from being restricted to high castes alone, as has often been assumed. Turn-of-the-century census reports found it normative among the bulk of intermediate and even lower castes, with only very lowly placed groups still remarrying widows without inhibition.[15] Both resistance to, and (I shall argue) occasional support for, Vidyasagar's campaign was therefore not necessarily always confined to the upper-caste elite.

Hatcher's careful analysis remains in the end more textual than social, slipping at times into a bland language of disembodied

---

Encounter in Bengal (Calcutta: Oxford University Press, 1996), p. 117, and *passim*.

[14] H.H. Risley had declared in 1891 that "caste is mainly a matter of marriage". Five years later, Jogendranath Bhattacharya, leading Nadia pandit and expert in Hindu law, quoted Risley with appproval and reiterated: "The most important regulations by which the castes have been made exclusive are those which relate to marriage." H.H. Risley, *Tribes and Castes of Bengal*, vol. I, *Introductory Essay: Caste in Relation to Marriage* (Calcutta, 1891, 1981), pp. xlii; Jogendranath Bhattacharya, *Hindu Castes and Sects* (Calcutta, 1896, 1968), p. 9.

[15] Sekhar Bandopadhyay, "Caste, Widow-remarriage and the Reform of Popular Culture in Colonial Bengal", in Bharati Ray, ed., *From the Seams of History: Essays on Indian Women* (Delhi: Oxford University Press, 1995), pp. 9, 11, 14, and *passim*.

"cultural encounter". The Brahmanical focus in both Hatcher and Bandopadhyay, I feel, needs to be sharpened through a more layered, non-homogenised view of the high-caste literati world that would also give due regard to the many changes within it in the course of the nineteenth century. Vidyasagar's rise from poor-Brahman origins should be seen not just in terms of the heroic endeavour of an individual, but within a wider context of multiple pressures and opportunities playing upon the world of traditional pandits and ritual experts.

The unusually abundant biographical literature on Vidyasagar (itself a feature that needs to be problematised, I shall argue) permits many glimpses of a pandit world in movement.[16] Most of Vidyasagar's teachers in Sanskrit College, for instance, seem to have been first-generation migrants into Calcutta: Gangadhar Tarkabagish, grammarian, from Kumarhatta-Halisahar; Joygopal Tarkalankar, famous scholar of Sanskrit literature who had assisted Colebrooke and Carey and helped to edit the early Bengali newspaper *Samachar Darpan*, from Bajrapur village in Nadia; Premchandra Tarkabagish, master of Alankar (aesthetics), from Rayna (Burdwan district); Sambhuchandra Vacaspati, Vedanta expert, from Ujitpur village in Barisal; and Joynarayan Tarkapanchanan, who trained Vidyasagar in Nyaya, from the south-western environs of the city (Behala-Barisha, followed by Salkia).[17] Vacaspati apart, they had all come from villages or small towns within a fifty-mile or so radius of the new metropolis, for this also had been the heartland, from the fifteenth-sixteenth century onwards, of Vaidik and Rarhiya Brahman scholarship and training in Smriti and Nyaya. Most famous of all had been the Nadia belt from Nabadwip to Bhatpara, which had produced Raghunandan and

---

[16] No less than four full-length biographies of Vidyasagar were published within a decade of his death in 1891: by Sambhuchandra Vidyaratna (1891), Chandicharan Bandopadhyay (1895), Biharilal Sarkar (1895), and (in English) Subolchandra Mitra (1902). There has also been an abundance of anecdotes.

[17] Benoy Ghosh, op. cit., pp. 74–95, has carefully collated the information about Vidyasagar's teachers from biographical literature and the research of Brojendranath Banerji. Of the early biographies of Vidyasagar, Sambhuchandra is particularly informative about his Sanskrit College teachers: see pp. 16–32 of his book.

Raghunath Shiromani, masters of Nabya-Smriti and Nabya-Nyaya, and had enjoyed another late efflorescence in the eighteenth century through the patronage of Maharaj Krishnachandra of Nadia. The belt of old Brahman settlements and *tols-chatuspathi* extended southwards along the Bhagirathi from here through Halisahar, down to what are today the south-eastern outskirts of Calcutta – the Harinabhi-Rajpur-Changripota-Majilpur area – while across the river there was a parallel stretch from Ambica-Kalna and Guptipara through Tribeni down to Serampur and Uttarpara. And finally there was the region from which came Vidyasagar, Ramakrishna, and Rammohan: the Khanakul-Krishnanagar pandit *samaj*, with influence extending to Brahman settlements in the subdivisions of adjoining Arambagh and Ghatal. With a touch of local pride, Vidyasagar in an official report once described the village of Krishnanagar as "the chief centre of Hindu learning next to Nuddea".[18]

The pandits who had moved to Calcutta quite often lived in conditions of marked poverty,[19] but presumably prospects had become worse still in their original villages by the early nineteenth century, making city life preferable. Brahman scholars and ritual experts had been accustomed to live "not off the land but off patronage",[20] as *sabha-pandits* of maharajas and rajas, on bits of revenue or rent-free *brahmottar* or *devottar* lands donated by zamindars, and from gifts and fees from local notables and from householders with whom they had hereditary *jajmani* connections. They were therefore among the rural groups most vulnerable in times of trouble, and such times came in quick succession to south-western and central Bengal from the mid eighteenth century.

---

[18] Vidyasagar's Report on Progress of Normal and Village Schools, January 1857, included in General Report on Public Instruction, Lower Provinces, Bengal Presidency, 1856–7, Appendix A, and reprinted in Arabinda Guha, ed., *Unpublished Letters of Vidyasagar* (Calcutta: Ananda Publishers, 1971), p. 29.

[19] Benoy Ghosh has used the biography of a near-contemporary of Vidyasagar, Girishchandra Vidyaratna, to illustrate this poverty. Girishchandra's father had run *tols* in Rajpur and then North Calcutta, living virtually in a hovel. Harishchandra Bhattacharya, *Girishchandra Vidyasagar Jivani* (Calcutta, 1909), cited in Benoy Ghosh, op. cit., p. 78.

[20] Hatcher, op. cit., p. 36.

There had been the Maratha raids, affecting parts of the southwest and the west, followed twenty years later by the much more devastating famine of 1770, when Midnapur, Hooghly, Burdwan, and Nadia had figured among the worst-affected districts.[21] Vidyasagar's corner of Bengal was among the regions where the famine had been followed by decades of near-anarchy. His grandfather developed the habit of always travelling with an iron staff with which he once beat off and killed a bear just a few miles from Midnapur town.[22] Patronage flows must have been further restricted by the quick changes in superior land rights through Company revenue experiments culminating in the Permanent Settlement. The new rigorous regime of Sunset Laws would have made grants to Brahmans often appear an ill-affordable luxury. The British in the 1830s attempted large-scale resumption of revenue-free grants, while an enterprising zamindar like Joykrishna Mukherjee of Uttarpara, who had been part of the zamindari united front critical of this move, later became unpopular among many Hooghly Brahmans by resuming rent-free tenures on his own estates.[23] The decline of traditional crafts under the new regime of one-way free trade could also have deepened indirectly the crisis of rural literati families. It must have affected the old textile centre of Khirpai, for instance, close to Birsingha and the place where Vidyasagar's grandmother had probably sold the yarn she used to spin on her charkha as her only resource, in the years when Thakurdas had been too young to earn, and her husband had become a wanderer.[24] And finally, over the *longue durée*, there were the consequences of the

---

[21] N.K. Sinha, *Economic History of Bengal*, vol. II (Calcutta: Firma K.L. Mukhopadhyay, 1962), pp. 50–3.

[22] *Vidyasagar-Charit*, p. 409.

[23] The Calcutta *dals* headed by Radhakanta Deb and the Tagores came together on this issue to float the Bengal Landholders' Society in 1838. Nilmoni Mukherjee, *A Bengal Zamindar: Joykrishna Mukherjee of Uttarpara and His Times, 1808–1888* (Calcutta: Firma K.L. Mukhopadhyay, 1975), pp. 56–8. The later resumption of Brahman grants by Joykrishna led Vidyasagar to briefly oppose the zamindar whose name had figured at the head of the petition seeking legalisation of widow remarriage, in 1855. Mukherjee, op. cit., p. 274.

[24] *Vidyasagar-Charit*, p. 399.

shift in riverflows eastwards, making the old heartland of Brahmanical culture irreversibly part of a moribund delta – a process quickened after the mid nineteenth century by railway embankments blocking old drainage patterns and probably contributing to the devastating entry of malaria. An early biography of Vidyasagar bears witness to the panic inspired by malaria through an unexpected precision about places and dates: malaria first appeared, Chandicharan Bandopadhyay tells us, in Muhammadpur village in Jessore in 1825, spread over Nadia, Barasat and 24 Parganas, and then struck Burdwan and Hooghly in 1867–9.[25]

For a generation or two, in contrast, the expanding colonial metropolis of Calcutta appeared as a zone of new opportunities for a significant part of the traditional literati. "Native" life in Calcutta was initially dominated by noveau riche families, members of which amassed fabulous fortunes as *banians* and *dewans* through profitable collaboration with early British traders and administrators, experimented in independent entrepreneurship, and then settled down as urban real-estate owners and zamindars. Most of them came from non-Brahman, and indeed at times low-caste, groups. Such "compradore-rajas" were eager to patronise Brahman scholars and ritual experts in their *sabhas* ("courts") as part of their quest for respectability,[26] and it is significant that the citadel of nineteenth-century Calcutta orthodoxy was constituted by a Kayastha family, the Debs of Sobhabazar. Nabakrishna Deb, grandfather of Radhakanta, had built the family's fortunes through highly profitable collaboration with Clive and Warren Hastings. He is also reputed to have brought many learned Brahmans to Calcutta to adorn his court, among them scholars like Jagannath Tarkapanchanan and Baneswar Vidyalankar.[27]

---

[25] Chandicharan Bandopadhyay, *Vidyasagar* (Calcutta, 1895, 1969), p. 497.

[26] Pradip Sinha's term: see his *Calcutta in Urban History* (Calcutta, 1978), pp. 16–17.

[27] Loknath Ghosh, *The Native Aristocracy and Gentry of India* (Calcutta, 1881). I am using its Bengali translation, *Kalkatar Babu-Vrittanta*, Calcutta, 1983, pp. 74–5; Raja Binaya Krishna Deb, *The Early History and Growth of Calcutta* (Calcutta, 1905), pp. 60–1.

The various *dals* or factions of early-nineteenth-century Calcutta around rival notable families all had need of the services of Brahman pandits: even Young Bengal seems to have had one in tow, in Gourishankar Bhattacharyya, who helped Derozians bring out the *Jnananeswan* and later edited the reformist *Sambad Bhaskar*.

The continued prestige of pandits and ulema in colonial Calcutta till the 1830s was related even more, perhaps, to certain distinctive features of Company judicial administration. Hastings had laid down in 1780 that matters of "inheritance, marriage, caste and other religious usages or institutions were to be administered to Hindus according to the laws of the Shaster", and to Muslims by those of the Shariat.[28] "Judge-pandits" and experts in Islamic law therefore had to be appointed to assist Englishmen in the civil courts of the Company, and in the 1820s and 1830s they were appointed from Sanskrit College students who had mastered their Smriti texts and passed a subsequent Law Committee examination. In 1829, Vidyasagar's educational plans were decided after much family confabulation by the argument that joining Sanskrit College would open up for him considerable prospects of profitable employment.[29]

Till around the 1830s, then, Company administration needed the reproduction on a fairly extended scale of the Sanskrit (as well as Persian-knowing) literati, and the channelling of official patronage to the Calcutta Madrasa and the Sanskrit College made good administrative sense even apart from the classical tastes of emerging Orientalist scholarship. Sanskrit College (and even more Fort William College, where Company officials learned Indian classical

---

[28] J.D.M. Derrett, "The British as Patrons of the Sastra", in idem, *Religion, Law and the State in India* (London, 1968), p. 233.

[29] Thakurdas, Vidyasagar's father, however, who had had to give up hopes himself of following the family profession of teaching Sanskrit due to sheer financial need, and had become a bill collector for a shopkeeper instead, wanted his son to ultimately set up a *chatuspathi* in Birsingha. He made Vidyasagar turn down the offer of a Judge-Pandit's job in Tripura, after he had performed brilliantly in the Smriti and Law Committee examinations when only seventeen. *Vidyasagar-Charit*, p. 414; Chandicharan Bandopadhyay, op. cit., p. 53.

and vernacular languages) offered Indian scholars and experts salaries that were fairly high for the times. For the less fortunate or able, there was the possibility, given the continued high demand for Sanskrit, of starting *tols* in Calcutta. William Ward counted twenty-eight of them in 1820, possibly an underestimate. Vidyasagar's father Thakurdas had put up initially with a distant relative who was running such a *chatuspathi*, when a move to Calcutta had been forced on him by financial need. Some thirty years later, in the 1840s, Ramakrishna likewise came to Calcutta in the wake of his elder brother Ramkumar, who thought running a *tol* in the city offered better prospects than eking out a livelihood as Smriti expert-cum-astrologer in the obscure village of Kamarpukur.[30]

By the mid 1840s, however, Sanskrit College graduates were finding it increasingly difficult to get jobs, a problem that Vidyasagar tried to tackle by advising Hardinge in 1846 that teachers of the 101 vernacular schools the governor general had just decided to start should be recruited entirely from them. Vidyasagar's appointment as principal of Sanskrit College in January 1851 was directly connected with the crisis the college had come to face due to the employment crunch.[31] At a much less exalted level within the world of the traditional literati, Ramkumar by the early 1850s was finding survival as pandit of a Calcutta *tol* extremely difficult. He, along with his brother Gadadhar (Ramakrishna), had to become a *pujari* in 1855 at the new temple of Dakshineswar just built by Rani Rashmoni – initially with considerable heartburn, for temple priests were considered rather low in the pecking order of Brahmans, and the brothers, even worse, were accepting the patronage of a Kaibarta.[32]

[30] Swami Saradananda, *Sri Sri Ramaakrishna-Leelaprasanga, Volume I. Purvakatha o Balakbhabh* (Calcutta, 1911, 1982), pp. 122–3.

[31] Chandicharan Bandopadhyay, op. cit., pp. 82–3; Subolchandra Mitra, *Life of Pandit Iswar Chandra Vidyasagar* (Calcutta, 1902; rpntd, New Delhi: Ashish Publishing House, 1975), p. 113.

[32] Swami Saradananda, *Volume II: Sadhakbhava* (Calcutta, 1982), pp. 70–5. Kaibartas in the mid nineteenth century were mostly fishermen and agriculturists of intermediate-caste status in south-western Bengal, with a major concentration in Midnapur. Over the succeeding decades the culti-

Incidents like these were indicators of bigger changes. The window of opportunity that Calcutta had opened for the traditional literati was clearly closing, as a result of the triumph of Macaulay and the "Anglicists". The 1840s also marked the end of large-scale Bengali entrepreneurship, with the collapse of the Union Bank in 1847 being often taken as the benchmark. This further reduced potential patronage – even though the *sabhas* and pandits around leading families did not wither away immediately, and we shall see Vidyasagar trying to utilise them at times for his reformist projects. There was now less need of judge-pandits, too, for a formidable body of "Anglo-Hindu" jurisprudence had emerged which by 1864 could "assume" that sufficient expertise had accumulated to obviate the need for such appointments. The practice of having such judge-pandits for each district court started withering away from the 1840s.[33] Above all, English education was becoming virtually the sole channel for retaining or winning respectability and employment for a *madhyabitta* or middle class that could not live on zamindari or tenure-holding alone, and yet (unlike peasants, labourers, the bulk of lower castes, and Muslims) could afford, though often with great difficulty, to go to college.

But college fees were pretty high for the times (Presidency charged twelve rupees a month in the 1870s, and Vidyasagar started his Metropolitan Institution mainly to provide a cheaper education for the more indigent among the *bhadralok*),[34] and so only a limited number among the *madhyabitta* really had the chance of successful professional or service careers as lawyers, prominent writers, journalists, doctors, officials, or politicians. Below them a substratum proliferated that, over time, came to be associated – ideal-typically and for generations in Bengali literature whenever it sought to depict poverty – with the figures of the indigent traditional literati and the clerk in government

---

vators among them (the Hele, as distinct from the Jele, Kaibartas) were able to win for themselves the more prestigious name of Mahishya through a major caste movement.

[33] Sambhuchandra Vidyaratna, op. cit., p. 40.
[34] Chandicharan Bandopadhyay, op. cit., p. 369.

and mercantile offices caught in the toils of *chakri*.[35] Already in 1823, Bhabanicharan Bandopadhyay in his *Kalikata Kamalalay* had distinguished between *madhyabitta lok* and *daridra athaccha bhadra lok* (poor but respectable folk). He described the latter, however, as surviving through doing odd jobs for the big "*dewanjis*".[36] Patronage of the rich Indian was clearly more visible then than regular office work, entered into through some amount of formal education. Clerical jobs down to around the mid century seem to have been more the domain of the Eurasians. A smattering of English, picked up through personal contacts, had been sufficient for Thakurdas to get a bill collector's job with a businessman, and Vidyasagar in the 1840s and 1850s was able to get fairly important official posts for some friends and clients through contacts with prominent Englishmen.

With time, however, both education and employment became more bureaucratised, and the drudgery and humiliation of *chakri*, under foreign bosses and subordinated to a new discipline of clock time, became the crucial element in a late-nineteenth-century revival of the ancient trope of Kaliyuga.[37] By the 1880s, Ramakrishna would be describing in a vivid passage the plight of a college graduate, running from office to office, desperately begging for a job: for the professions and the services open to Indians were getting overcrowded, and newspapers were already full of complaints about educated unemployment. Changes in agrarian relations probably also contributed to the sense of a *madhyabitta* crisis. Thanks to the proliferation of intermediate tenures under the Permanent Settlement, a significant part of professional and even clerical groups also had

---

[35] Two obvious examples would be Haripada, *kerani* in Rabindranath's poem *Kinu Goalar Goli*, and Harihar, in Bibhutibhushan Bandopadhyay's *Pather Panchali*, now internationally known through Satyajit Ray's trilogy.

[36] Bhabanicharan Bandopadhyay, *Kalikata Kamalalay* (Calcutta, 1823; rpntd in Bandopadhyay, *Rasarachanasamagra*, Calcutta: Nabapatra Prakashana, 1987), p. 7.

[37] I have tried to explore this theme in a number of essays: see Chapters 5, 6, and 8, in Sarkar, *Writing Social History*, and "Colonial Times: Clocks and Kaliyuga in Nineteenth-Century Bengal", paper presented at Paris, Maison des Sciences de l'Hommes, June 1996.

some connections with land.³⁸ Fragmentation, however, tended to make such incomes from petty zamindari or tenure-holding insufficient, particularly after many easy ways of rent enhancement had been restricted by the tenancy laws of 1859 and 1885. The pattern of some years of hope and social ascent, followed by frustration, that we have traced through the traditional literati was reproducing itself after a gap of a few decades in the life of the "new", English-knowing intelligentsia.

Vidyasagar, I feel, needs to be placed within this broad context of a changing, multilayered *madhyabitta* society. Multilayered, though, not in the sense that there were rigid or insuperable partitions – both Vidyasagar and Ramakrishna in very different ways illustrate in fact just the opposite. The importance of keeping in mind the internal differentiation of the *bhadralok* world is precisely because the dividing lines were permeable. The most eminent of the *bhadralok* could have kinsmen eking out a living from clerical *chakri*, or among the ranks of the educated unemployed. He could recall, or imagine, lower-middle-class life as his past, or perhaps his future, and the racist humiliations which even the most successful of Indian officials or professional men would occasionally encounter could make vivid for them the indignity and degradation which was the constant lot of the clerk. The image of the *kerani* consequently had a power and reach much in excess of the actual, physical number of clerks, and a focus upon the *daridra athaccha bhadra* is analytically helpful for highlighting pressures and tensions in some ways common to the entire *madhyabitta*.

The manifestations of these pressures in everyday family life, marriage relationships, and widowhood are vital for my enquiry, for this obviously was the domain central to all Vidyasagar's reformist concerns. I argued, elsewhere and long back, that the fairly unusual concentration on the "women's question" in middle-class male circles through much of the nineteenth century needs to be problematised,

---

[38] A rough estimate made by the 1891 Bengal census found half the merchants, one-third of the shopkeepers, a tenth of schoolteachers, pleaders, and lawyers, one-fourth of the doctors, and one-sixth of the "clerical class" to have "some interest in land, generally as intermediate tenants." *Census 1891, Volume III (Bengal)*, ed. C.J. O'Donnell (Calcutta, 1893), p. 291.

for it cannot be explained entirely in terms of mimesis of the West. Young men, moving to the city in quest of education and jobs, married off in their teens by parents to brides much younger and generally illiterate, could have faced acute problems of conjugal adjustment, particularly if they happened to be first-generation reformers, Derozian or Brahmo, with nuclearity imposed on them through ostracism by their relatives. Issues like widow-burning, women's education, gender seclusion, arranged marriage, child marriage, polygamy, and the prohibition of widow marriage would be "under their eyes every day and hour of their existence within the precincts of their own respective domiciles."[39] These in addition were problems which the nineteenth-century intelligentsia would have thought to be within their reach, remediable – unlike, say, foreign rule, prior to the rise of effective, middle-class-led nationalism. Programmes emerged consequently of *stri-swadhinata*, in effect, a fairly limited and controlled emancipation of wives within a framework of more companionate conjugality, undertaken entirely at male initiative, and sometimes accompanied by a refurbished patriarchy as reformist husbands within nuclear units sought to impose new norms of religious and social conduct on not-too-enthusiastic wives.[40]

This, however, could only have been one kind of scenario among many. Our hypothetical young men doing reasonably well in Calcutta might soon have large numbers of relatives (or village-cum-*jati* affines) staying with and/or dependent on them. Out of a salary of fifty rupees a month as chief pandit of Fort William College in the mid 1840s, Vidyasagar was sending twenty home to his father in Birsingha as virtually sole support for the big joint family there, while maintaining in Calcutta with the remainder three brothers, five nephews, an old servant and a number of indigent boys whose education he was paying

---

[39] The quotation is from Maheshchandra Deb, *A Sketch of the Condition of Hindoo Women*, presented to the Derozian Society for Acquisition of General Knowledge in January 1839, and reprinted in Gautam Chattopadhyay, ed., *Awakening in Bengal in the Early Nineteenth Century* (Calcutta, 1965), p. 90.

[40] Sumit Sarkar, "The Women's Question in Nineteenth Century Bengal", in Sarkar, *A Critique of Colonial India* (Calcutta: Papyrus, 1985), pp. 71–6.

for.[41] The successful few might try to break away, fuelling charges of selfish, iconoclastic modernity: for the less fortunate or able, insistence on customary obligations could become an important strategy for survival. One response, therefore, to the pressures of changing colonial life, that probably deepened over time as they impinged upon one sector after another of the *madhyabitta*, was a renewed insistence upon the virtues of the "traditional" upper-caste Hindu undivided family. This was counterposed against the encroachment of market values and selfish, insubordinate individualism, and portrayed in ideological terms as a world characterised by mutuality of deference and benevolent paternalism, where kinship obligations had been sacred, and an endless hospitality had kept doors always open for everyone of equivalent status. That the burdens of such hospitality and openness would rest inevitably on the unpaid labour of wives and the toil of servants would of course be either elided, or prettified into a model of Annapurna, the mother or wife as bounteous provider of food, from whom services somehow flowed with tireless grace and beauty. Such norms constituted the implicit ideal Other of the many representations of Kaliyuga in a mass of mid- and late-nineteenth-century tracts, plays, and farces, produced by obscure authors among whom one notes a high proportion of Brahman surnames. In them the evils of contemporary life were regularly attributed to insubordinate, expensive, educated wives, neglecting domestic duties, making husbands disregard kinship obligations, nagging them for money and jewellery, and pushing menfolk into the humiliating dependence of clerical *chakri*.

Let us take one example, typical in everything except its surprising location: "The one priceless resource this enslaved and lifeless society of Bengal can have is the ideal Hindu household . . . [where] relatives are looked after, responsibility is taken for one's community and caste (*jatigoshthi*), poor and helpless sons and daughters of departed relations are brought up with care. . . ." All these, however, are becoming things of the past: "Today people are entirely dominated

---

[41] Sambhuchandra Vidyaratna, op. cit., p. 40; Chandicharan Bandopadhyay, op. cit., p. 78; Benoy Ghosh, op. cit., p. 159, and *passim*.

by calculations of selfish gain . . . Peace and happiness had reigned over Bengal's homes once, because women had been satisfied with little, and poor relations in trouble had been given shelter in well-off households."

The passage comes from Chandicharan Bandopadhyay's very sympathetic biography of Vidyasagar, which unlike several others supported women's education and widow remarriage.[42] But Chandicharan, we shall see, clearly did not agree with Vidyasagar's views about the undivided family, and a clue regarding his reasons is provided by repeated references to poor relations. He was a Brahmo from a Jessore–Khulna poor Brahman background, and owed his education and career to a relative who had been better off.

I have argued elsewhere that Ramakrishna, whose conversation was full of allusions to the evils of *kamini, kanchan,* and the *dasatya* of *chakri* (lust, money, the bondage of office work), needs to be placed in the setting of this late-nineteenth-century revival of Kaliyuga themes – but with a difference. We are told that many parents in the early 1880s disliked his influence over boys and young men, for they were afraid he was encouraging them to neglect studies and careers. For the bulk of his listeners, his was a message of *grihastha bhakti*, a move into a self-created inner, devotional space from where one could go on discharging one's domestic duties, but in a detached, non-worldly manner: neither any leech-like clinging to joint-family connections for material survival, therefore, nor activist efforts to transform domestic relations and reduce human suffering through human endeavour. For an intimate circle, he may have advised the path of *sannyas* or renunciation, which Vivekananda would later drastically modify in an activist direction, reviving Vidyasagar's philanthropy but not much of his transformative social programme.[43]

Chandicharan Bandopadhyay will be of help again, as we try now to move closer to Vidyasagar, approaching him through cross-sections of his writings and activities concerning Sanskrit College, primary

---

[42] Chandicharan Bandopadhyay, *Vidyasagar* (Calcutta, 1895, 1896, 1909, 1969), pp. 17–18.

[43] For a detailed analysis, see my "Kaliyuga, Bhakti, and Chakri: Ramakrishna and His Times", in *Writing Social History*.

and women's education, and gender – but first of all through a glance at representations of him in biography and anecdote. The passage I have quoted is a comment inserted into an account of Vidyasagar's ancestry, largely based, as all such accounts have been, on a posthumous autobiographical fragment. Its context is Vidyasagar's description of the household of Radhamohan Vidyabhushan, maternal uncle of his mother. This had been a joint family run in an ideal manner, without quarrels, and with a great reputation for generous hospitality. Bandopadhyay expressed surprise that despite seeing at first hand such an ideal Hindu household, Vidyasagar was "bitterly opposed to the undivided family. He used to say: 'Where husbands are run by their wives [a brief Kaliyuga motif even here!], where there is no affection between brother and brother, it is futile to try to maintain the joint family . . .'." A quick separation of brothers could reduce conflict. Also, "If a happy [and, implicitly, nuclear] family becomes prosperous, it is possible to help considerably one's brothers, their sons and daughters, other relations – but within a family torn by quarrels it is impossible to do any good even with a lakh of rupees."[44]

There was much bitter personal experience behind such a remark, we shall see: but the point can bear a wider generalisation. Vidyasagar sought, all his life, to transform his upper-caste surroundings in specific, concrete ways through tremendous, basically individual endeavours. Despite the total absence of inherited wealth or landed property (something quite unusual for such a prominent and materially successful man), he was able to achieve and maintain personal independence through skilful utilisation of the three basic determinants of nineteenth-century colonial middle-class life in Bengal: education, *chakri*, print culture. Vidyasagar learnt English late, from his English contacts and from friends who had studied in Hindu College, but mastered it sufficiently to translate or adapt numerous texts, even Shakespeare's *Comedy of Errors*. He rose high in a still somewhat informal structure of educational administration (Head Pandit of Fort William College, Assistant Secretary and then Principal of Sanskrit College, Assistant Inspector of Schools

---

[44] Chandicharan Bandopadhyay, op. cit., p. 18.

for Midnapur, Hooghly, Burdwan, and Nadia), but simultaneously was careful to establish financial independence through the Sanskrit Press Depository (1846–7), a printing press-cum-bookshop and publishing concern. That gave him enough private income to sustain an exceptional independence in official employment, and then the ability to quit when he realised by the late 1850s that his advice would no longer be acceptable to a more bureaucratised officialdom eager after 1857 to cut down expenses. His income from textbooks and the bookshop was very high for the times.[45] Nearly all of it he spent, however – at times running deep into debt – on widow remarriage and philanthropy.

For Vidyasagar's was never an individualism divested of collective concerns, and he refused to abandon his roots in Brahmanical, and specifically poor-Brahman, society, even while seeking to change its norms in specific ways: he soared, we might say, but refused to roam. Therein, up to a point, perhaps lay his strength, and certainly much of his human greatness – but also, I intend to argue, some of the roots of compromise, failure, and tragedy.

II

We look back on past happenings and figures as through a glass, darkly, through representations, never face to face. Discrepancies and fissures within and among representations, however, may help us at times to avoid getting entirely trapped in a hall of mirrors. "Sources" and their conditions of production, as well as our own perspectives, ueed to be constantly problematised, made part of the narratives we are trying to build about the past.

Later scholars have tended to take for granted the existence of an unusually large number of near-contemporary biographies of

---

[45] In the year ending 30 June 1870, for instance, the Sanskrit Press Depository published twenty-seven editions, with a total print run of 253,000 copies. Buckland estimated Vidyasagar's annual income from publishing at around Rs 3500–4000 a month. Swapan Basu, *Samakale Vidyasagar* (Calcutta, 1993), p. 179, citing C.E. Buckland, *Bengal under the Lieutenant-Governors*, vol. II (Calcutta, 1902), p. 1035.

Vidyasagar and Brahmanical Society 257

Vidyasagar, and the equally exceptional abundance of anecdotes; and then happily gone ahead to use them as quarries of valuable information. But why four biographies within eleven years of his death, when Rammohan, for instance (who, unlike Vidyasagar, left some kind of movement after him), had to wait nearly fifty years for the first?[46] And why so many anecdotes, unequalled numerically by those about any other nineteenth-century luminary? The puzzle deepens when we recall that the biographies were written in a decade dominated by social reaction and revivalism, not reform. For Vidyasagar's death in 1891 had coincided with a massive upsurge in Bengali middle- and lower-middle-class society against the official proposal to raise the age of consent from ten to twelve.[47]

Several of the biographers themselves present an even greater surprise. No doubt it was natural enough for Sambhuchandra Vidyaratna to write an appreciative life of his distinguished elder brother, even though he had once made Vidyasagar very angry by initially opposing the widow remarriage of the reformer's son, Narayanchandra.[48] And Chandicharan, as we have seen, was a Brahmo who supported women's education and widow remarriage, though he had reservations about Vidyasagar's dislike of the joint family. But Subol Mitra was unenthusiastic about widow remarriage, and the section about it

---

[46] The first full-length biography of Rammohan, by Nagendranath Chattopadhyay, came out only in 1881.

[47] For a detailed analysis, see Tanika Sarkar, "Rhetoric against Age of Consent: Resisting Colonial Reason and the Death of a Child-Wife", *Economic and Political Weekly*, vol. XXVIII, 36, 4 September 1993.

[48] This marriage, arranged by Narayanchandra on his own initiative, much to his father's delight and pride, occasioned the famous letter of Vidyasagar to Sambhuchandra (27 Sravana 1277/1870) rebuking him for the request he had evidently made to hold back, as Sambhuchandra's in-laws were threatening to sever social connections. The letter went on to declare: "The introduction of widow remarriage is the greatest deed of my life. I have spent my all in this cause, and if need be, remain prepared to give my life for it. . . . I am not a mere slave to Custom (*deshachar*) . . . what I think to be justified or necessary for the good of myself or my society, I will do: I will never be held back by fear of other people or relatives . . . It is my conviction that in such matters everyone must be free to decide on his own . . ." Benoy Ghosh, op. cit., p. 450.

in his English biography, though detailed and valuable, clearly is tilted on the side of Vidyasagar's critics.[49] The really interesting, indeed, paradoxical, case is Biharilal Sarkar, connected from 1883 till his death in 1921 with the *Bangabasi* newspaper group that spearheaded the virulent anti-reformist crusade against the Age of Consent bill, and who remained consistently conservative on every social issue. The edition I am using contains an autobiographical sketch that begins with an evocation of the principle of *adhikari bheda*, and refers to the way he had peddled from door to door Bengali translations of shastric texts brought out in cheap editions by the *Bangabasi* press.[50] We learn from the ensuing biography that one such text had been Panchanan Tarkaratna's edition of *Parasar Samhita*, which had sought to explicitly refute Vidyasagar's interpretation, upon which the reformer had grounded his scriptural justification for widow remarriage. The failure of widow remarriage, Biharilal states without equivocation, had been a "great good fortune for Hindu society". Another blessing was that no law had been passed banning polygamy despite Vidyasagar's efforts, and Biharilal has doubts even about the usually more acceptable issue of women's education. Education for Hindu women, he argues, has produced "poison". It should have been geared towards fostering "Annapurnas ... Not writing and reading [*lekhapara*], but learning the duties proper to Hindu wives – that is what education for them should mean."[51] And yet such a man had felt impelled in 1895 to write a long biography of Vidyasagar, which was in fact the most carefully compiled of all early accounts, and provided the basic matter for Subol Mitra's English *Life*.

No biography of Vidyasagar can avoid giving considerable space to his reform endeavours, A strategy of displacement is often at work, however, shifting emphasis and, particularly, praise to his *panditya* and *daya* (learning and compassionate philanthropy). Mahendranath Gupta's presentation is thus entirely typical. For Biharilal, to take

---

[49] Subolchandra Mitra, op. cit., chapter xvi, pp. 260–324.

[50] Biharilal Sarkar, *Vidyasagar*, ed. Asit Bandopadhyay (Calcutta, 1895, 1900, 1910, 1922, 1986), pp. 25, 30, 31.

[51] Ibid., pp. 181, 171, 310, 151.

the most obvious example, Vidyasagar's drive for widow remarriage flowed out of an unacceptable excess of compassion. His book ends with an appeal to "Hindus" to "energetically perform their proper, strictly shastra-determined duties with Vidyasagar's sincerity and determination."[52]

In biography and anecdote alike, Vidyasagar's learning and philanthropy invariably gained a special lustre from his poor-Brahman origins and conquest of adverse circumstances through sheer personal grit, determination, and self-discipline.[53] Instances of self-respect and independence of spirit while in government service are also lovingly narrated in virtually all writings and tales about him. Anecdotes, which need to be recognised as "among the principal products of a culture's representational technology",[54] are particularly revealing of the patterns of selectivity and emphasis at work in constituting memories about Vidyasagar. Written accounts and verbal narration of stories, of course, should not be segregated from each other in a case like Vidyasagar's, for the spate of early biographies clearly contributed to the preservation of tales by recording many of them in print. But stories spread very much further, in repeated cycles of orality and reading as they were reproduced in a variety of printed forms (school texts about the great man, for instance) and passed down in conversation. Unlike biographies, anecdotes have a built-in licence to be selective, for they are free of the need to appear comprehensive. It

---

[52] Biharilal Sarkar, op. cit., p. 369. Subolchandra Mitra also feels that Vidyasagar "materially injured the Hindu religion" through an excess of "kindness and self-reliance", which led him to try to remedy the "apparent distress of Hindu widows" and the "ostensible miseries of Kulin women" (pp. 673–4).

[53] For Subolchandra Mitra, to take a characteristic example, Vidyasagar provided an object lesson that "poverty is no bar to the attainment of success" (p. 85). He also emphasised that Vidyasagar, "nothing but a common man of the middle station of life", "in liberality . . . surpassed the richest millionaires" (p. 415). Hatcher has aptly commented that Vidyasagar's life became an exemplar of the moral pedagogy he had tried to inculcate through his textbooks (p. 185).

[54] Stephen Greenblatt, *Marvellous Possessions: The Wonder of the New World* (Oxford: Clarendon Press, 1991), p. 3.

is significant, therefore, that there seem to be few specific stories about what Vidyasagar himself had declared to be the greatest deed of his life – widow remarriage – at least as compared to the flood of tales illustrating Vidyasagar's compassion, conquest of adverse circumstances, and independence of spirit. The early biographies would be known today only to specialists, the more recent accounts only to a fairly limited number. But the average educated Bengali is quite likely to be familiar with tales of Vidyasagar as a student from a wretchedly poor family, reading under street lamps to save money on fuel, and cooking for his father in a tiny, filthy kitchen full of cockroaches.[55] Equally famous is his declared intention to live by selling potatoes, if need be, while chucking up his first Sanskrit College job. Anecdotes about dignity and independence in relation to white bosses are perhaps the most loved of all: Vidyasagar calmly putting up his feet on the desk to avenge a like insult from the English principal of Hindu College, and allegedly throwing a slipper at the actor playing the part of an indigo planter in a performance of Dinabandhu Mitra's *Nil-Darpan*. The proto-nationalistic ring in some of these tales is significant, though more perhaps as imagined retrospect than reality: the one about *Nil-Darpan* is probably a later emendation, for it was absent in the biographies of the 1890s.

That dominant representations of Vidyasagar have been selective appropriations is thus fairly obvious, and perhaps only to be expected. What still remains mysterious is why this sanitisation had to take the form of volubility and not silence: why conventional and even conservative men found it imperative to write and talk incessantly about a reformer whose efforts had largely failed. The emphasis in biographies and anecdotes upon poor-Brahman origins, ascent through self-help, and maintenance of dignity and independence before foreign employers might provide an important clue, for these were precisely the values that the *madhyabitta*, and particularly its poorer and less successful substratum, were likely to have admired,

---

[55] Asked by Hatcher to paint a portrait of Vidyasagar, a scroll painter in Midnapur came up with a picture of a youthful Iswarchandra reading under a street lamp. The same story figures in many modern texts for children. Hatcher cites as one example Rabidas Saharay's *Amader Vidyasagar* (Calcutta, 1985): Hatcher, op. cit., pp. 76–7.

aspired towards, but generally failed or lacked the courage to sustain in their own lives. And while the compassion of Vidyasagar is known to have extended to Santals and famine-stricken peasant women, it lay in the nature of things that its most regular recipients would be poor *bhadralok*. These were the people with whom he would have had everyday social contact, who could benefit from the low fees charged by the Metropolitan Institution, and for whom his excellent official contacts could sometimes provide jobs.

The available data about the three early biographers (other than his brother) appear quite relevant here, for all came from this milieu of poor *bhadralok*. Chandicharan Bandopadhyay (1858–1916) never had the resources to complete his education and depended on the patronage of a manager of the Narail zamindari estate. Biharilal Sarkar (1855–1921), too, did not get beyond the First Arts class; for the business ventures of his father, a former clerk at the surveyor general's office, had ended in financial ruin, and Biharilal had had to take up a job at a printing press. Subolchandra Mitra (1872–1913) likewise started as a humble press employee, though he later became the best known of the three through a fine dictionary-cum-encyclopaedia. None of the three could have had personal memories of the 1850s, when Vidyasagar's educational and reform campaigns had been at their height, but they could well have known many who had been recipients of his *daya* in the decades when philanthropy had perforce become his principal activity. "Who will be able to count", the otherwise often critical Biharilal asked rhetorically, "the number whose *chakri* had been arranged by Vidyasagar?" And Chandicharan lavished particular praise on the Hindu Family Annuity Fund Vidyasagar had initiated in 1872 to provide, on an insurance principle, an allowance of five rupees a month for widows and dependants of "Bengal's *madhyabitta daridra bhadra parihar* [poor, respectable middle-class families]."[56]

In a more speculative vein: the temporal location of all the early biographies of Vidyasagar in the decade immediately following the Age of Consent agitation may not have been entirely coincidental.

---

[56] Biharilal Sarkar, op. cit., p. 216; Chandicharan Bandopadhyay, op. cit., p. 503.

Triumphant revivalism was clearly not averse to an appropriation of a suitably sanitised Vidyasagar, in the hegemonising spirit of wasting no icon. (The ascendant Hindutva of recent years has similarly made many efforts to absorb even Ambedkar.) But maybe there was also a more complex and ambiguous connection. Hindu-revivalist nationalism had with apparent success inverted Vidyasagar's premises for reform in the most extreme conceivable manner. No compassion was wasted on Phulmonee, a child of ten or eleven raped to death by her husband in 1890. Rather, as the agitation attained its height in the early months of 1891, newspapers like *Bangabasi* and *Dainik-o-Samachar-Chandrika* defiantly admitted that Hindu shastras did impose a harsh discipline on women (in particular, child-wives and widows), did cause much suffering, even at times death: yet such suffering was necessary for the honour and glory of the Hindu community/nation, and alien interference could never be tolerated.[57] But such arguments, it should be noted, implicitly accepted what had been the starting point of Vidyasagar's reform drive: that some Hindu texts and customs imposed gross suffering on women.[58] The intense, taut, almost hysterical rhetoric could have sometimes concealed an inner tension, a half-formed self-doubt, maybe even an occasional pang of guilt that needed to be suppressed through excessive vehemence. By the mid 1890s the movement had subsided, and Vidyasagar himself was safely dead.[59] Incessant talk and writing about a suitably sanitised Vidyasagar could have provided a certain

---

[57] Tanika Sarkar, "Rhetoric against the Age of Consent". Of particular relevance for my argument is the quotation given in this essay from *Dainik-o-Samachar-Chandrika*, 11 January 1891: "Fasting [by widows] on *ekadashi* is a cruel custom and many weak-bodied widows very nearly die of observing it . . ."

[58] Such an admission was present also in the criticisms of widow remarriage made by Biharilal and Subolchandra: Vidyasagar had been motivated by an excess of compassion that subverted a necessary, though admittedly painful, discipline.

[59] He had also "redeemed" himself slightly in the eyes of conservatives, just before his death, by giving a somewhat ambiguous opinion about the Age of Consent Bill when officially asked for his views. See footnote 149 and corresponding text, below.

necessary release of tension, precisely in circles that had been, and remained, fundamentally conservative.

The sanitising process did have one outstanding contemporary critic, however – Rabindranath Tagore. In a speech at the annual Vidyasagar Memorial meeting in July 1895, Tagore declared that Vidyasagar's true greatness lay "not in compassion [*daya*], not in learning [*vidya*]", but in a determined, uncompromising humanism which had made him look at the life of women in a fundamentally distinctive way. Furthermore, "Vidyasagar had been alone in Bengal. It is as if he had no kith or kin in this land ... He was not happy here ... He had a deep contempt for this weak, petty, heartless, lazy, arrogant, argumentative people, for in every way he was then opposite ..."[60] Strange words, in a way, spoken amidst apparently universal praise for the departed reformer which had been joined in with enthusiasm even by conservatives. But they fit rather well with certain anomalies that occasionally burst through the placid surfaces of conventional narratives about Vidyasagar, and find further confirmation in the pattern of stresses and silences that characterise the autobiographical fragment published after his death.

The biographies repeatedly present Vidyasagar as an ever-dutiful and considerate son, elder brother, and father who maintained from Calcutta a big joint family in Birsingha. Vidyasagar's devotion to his mother in particular has become legendary. Yet despite the mass of personal detail, whether authentic or apocryphal, some things remain mysterious, and there are sudden explosions, never fully explained ruptures, in the accounts of his family relationships. Around 1867, to end "intermittent quarrels among the members of the large family", Vidyasagar arranged "separate boarding" for his brothers and only son, giving each of them a monthly allowance.[61] One brother brought a case against him a couple of years later about the ownership of the Sanskrit Press Depository.[62] And then there was that series

---

[60] Rabindranath Tagore, *Vidyasagarcharit*, 13 Sravana 1302/1895; rpntd, *Charitrapuja* (1907); *Rabindra-rachanabali*, vol. IV (Calcutta: Viswabharati, 1940, 1975), pp. 502, and *passim*.

[61] Subolchandra Mitra, op. cit., pp. 482–3.

[62] Chandicharan Bandopadhyay, p. 405; Subolchandra Mitra, op. cit.,

of mysterious letters, all dated 12 Agrahayan 1276/1869, through which Vidyasagar bade "lifelong farewell" to mother, wife, brothers, and Birsingha village (through the village *pradhan*). The letters at the same time stipulated in minute detail monthly allowances for each relative and money for the philanthropic institutions he had started in his village. He never visited Birsingha again.[63] And finally came the disinheritance of his son Narayanchandra, around 1872. Once again, the biographies reveal nothing of the reasons for this.

The autobiographical fragment is at first sight disappointing, for it is mostly about Vidyasagar's ancestry and ends with him at age nine, just joining Sanskrit College. It has been used in virtually all accounts of Vidyasagar, but so far as no more than a repository of information about his genealogy. Brian Hatcher is a partial exception, since he goes some distance towards treating it as a constructed text through which Vidyasagar tried to communicate "his own self-understanding".[64] But his analysis stops with the suggestion that the choice of stresses in the fragment indicates Vidyasagar's continued reverence for the Brahman as a man of learning, while also conveying a sense of crisis affecting rural Brahmans due to disorderly times and economic distress.[65] What I find much more revealing is an implicit,

---

p. 500. Mitra states that Vidyasagar had arranged a deputy-magistrateship for this brother, Dinabandhu, earlier, by speaking about him after much hesitation with the lieutenant governor: indication, simultaneously, of the still rather informal official appointments system, and the burden of ingratitude that seems to have been often Vidyasagar's lot.

[63] The ostensible reason for the break was a rather strange incident, in which Vidyasagar, for once, had promised not to encourage a particular widow remarriage, but his brother Sambhuchandra had gone ahead and arranged it. It can hardly explain such a dramatic rupture, affecting also his wife and mother who could not have anything to do with the affair. Chandicharan Bandopadhyay, op. cit., pp. 414–17. For the full text of these letters, see Benoy Ghosh, op. cit., pp. 454–7. The most complete account of the whole murky affair is in Asok Sen, op. cit., pp. 161–2.

[64] Hatcher, op. cit., p. 23, and chapter 1.

[65] The fragment emphasises the expertise of several ancestors in Sanskrit grammar, Smriti, and Nyaya, and mentions Thakurdas' lifelong regret that poverty had forced him to give up plans for a pandit's life and take up the

recurrent note critical of the high-caste joint family. Radhamohan Vidyabhushan of Patul village, along with his entire extended family, had given succour to his sister, Vidyasagar's maternal grandmother Ganga, after her husband had gone mad through Tantric excesses. For Chandicharan, this was convincing proof of the enduring value of the joint family. Vidyasagar did describe the Patul household in loving detail, but immediately added that such an ideal family was utterly atypical: "Affection among brothers usually does not last long in an undivided family."[66] The ancestor about whom Vidyasagar left by far the longest account, and whom he clearly admired most, was not a pandit running a *tol*, but his exceptionally independent-minded grandfather Ramjoy Tarkabhushan, who had broken with his joint family after quarrelling with elder brothers, left the original homestead of Banamalipur, and become a wanderer for many years. He retained a tremendous sense of dignity and self-respect even in his old age, rejected an offer of land from the local zamindar, and was openly contemptuous of the prominent men in Birsingha village.[67]

The second, recurrent stress in the fragment is about how, repeatedly, it is the women who have to bear the burden of family quarrels among men. What is more, Vidyasagar seems to be indicating, they often bear this undeserved suffering with a fortitude, dignity, and loving kindness rare among men. There is, in other words, not just compassion for women but respect, admiration, and a strong sense of male guilt – and the respect, it can be argued, was related to individual qualities and actions, not primarily to status as elders or even to motherhood as such.

Admiration for Ramjoy does not blind Vidyasagar to a realisation that much of the price of his independence had to be borne

---

job of bill collector for a Barabazar shop selling imported ironware. Hatcher, op. cit., chapter 1; *Vidyasagar-Charit (Swarachita)*, in Tirthapati Datta, ed., *Vidyasagar Rachanabali*, vol. I (Calcutta, 1994), pp. 400, 414.

[66] *Vidyasagar-Charit*, pp. 405–6.

[67] Vidyasagar recounts, with evident approval and delight, that Ramjoy called the village bigwigs cows, not men. Warned once about some human excreta on the path, he had replied: "I can see only cowdung." Ibid., p. 408.

by grandmother Durgadevi. She had had to bring up six sons and daughters by spinning yarn and selling it at Khirpai. Ill-treatment by in-laws had forced her out of Banamalipur: she returned to her home village of Birsingha, but there too faced much unkindness from her brother's family. (This, then, was the counter-example to Patul, and for Vidyasagar evidently far more characteristic of the extended family at work.) And then there is the story of an unnamed middle-aged widow running a roadside foodshop, who fed Thakurdas gratis regularly at a time when he was virtually starving on the streets of Calcutta – a generosity, Vidyasagar emphasises, "that would have been unthinkable if the shopkeeper had been a man." The other woman who figures prominently in Vidyasagar's narrative is Raimoni, another widow, sister of Jagatdurlabh Sinha, in whose house he initially put up in Calcutta. Her kindness and deep affection had given him solace when, as a boy who had left home for the first time, he was missing his grandmother. "I have never seen a woman to equal Raimoni", he declares, and mentions her as justification for what many have called his "partiality" towards women.[68] Surprisingly, if we recall the biographies and the many anecdotes, the autobiography says virtually nothing about Vidyasagar's mother. We should not build too much on an absence in what is an unfinished fragment, but here perhaps is another hint that the Vidyasagar of the biographies and anecdotes has been excessively sentimentalised.

The concluding chapters of Vidyasagar's biographies tend to become long catalogues of his philanthropic deeds. Interrupting this flow, however, particularly in Chandicharan, are occasional references to Vidyasagar's caustic remarks about his own social group, the high-caste *bhadralok* men: remarks so sharp that they make this "ocean of compassion" seem almost a misanthrope. "Why does he abuse me – I don't remember having ever tried to help him in any way?" Chandicharan reports Vidyasagar saying, in his last days, that the country could improve only if the present breed of men were totally uprooted, and human beings of a new kind planted on freshly tilled

---

[68] Ibid., pp. 401, 411. Both Biharilal and Subolchandra dilate on Raimoni's kindness, but avoid mentioning that she was a widow.

soil. "I much prefer my uncivilised Santals to your sort of respectably dressed men of Aryan descent."[69]

Biting, cynical sarcasm amidst a continued stream of philanthropic acts: the contradictions here are at the heart of Vidyasagar's lifelong endeavours and tragedy, as a man who valued his links with high-Hindu society, and yet had developed a very different set of values and sought to reform his milieu in specific but quite fundamental ways. The remaining sections of this essay will explore the unfolding of this dialectic of affinity and difference, first through Vidyasagar's educational initiatives, and then in terms of attempted reform of gender relations.

III

Vidyasagar never wrote a systematic treatise on education. The precise significance of his extremely innovative ideas and projects have to be reconstructed from scattered texts – official letters and notes,[70] school primers and textbooks written by him, and documents relating to Vidyasagar in the files of the government education department and archives of Sanskrit College.[71]

The changes Vidyasagar sought to make in Sanskrit College, as assistant secretary (1846–7) and later as principal (1850–8), were not just about reforms in a particular institution, for they can be seen to imply ultimately a distinctive educational-cum-social philosophy. Even the innovations that might appear trivial today, such as Vidyasagar's insistence on punctuality and regular attendance by students and teachers,[72] acquire greater meaning when one remembers

---

[69] Chandicharan Bandopadhyay, op. cit., pp. 518–20.

[70] The most important of these are Vidyasagar's proposals for reorganising Sanskrit College (16 December 1850), his Notes on the Sanskrit College, drawn up at the request of Lieutenant Governor Halliday (12 April 1852), and the controversy with J.R. Ballantyne, Principal, Benaras Sanskrit College, in 1853.

[71] These have been usefully collated and published in Arabinda Guha, ed., *Unpublished Letters of Vidyasagar*.

[72] Vidyasagar introduced a pass system for students wanting to go out

that clock time was no more than a generation or two old in India in the 1840s, having been a belated, colonial import. Its history has been surprisingly neglected in studies of colonial India. Bound up, as elsewhere, with new pressures for regularity and tighter work schedules, clocks and watches acquired somewhat distinct and varied implications through their links with structures of colonial power. The three principal early sites for time discipline in colonial Bengal were educational institutions, government and mercantile offices, and the railways.[73] Indigenous responses to it clearly had a differential character. Vidyasagar is a reminder that systematised, rule-bound education governed by clock time was widely perceived as indispensable for middle-class self-improvement under colonial conditions. Punctuality no doubt often remained a burden, but its normative role in schools and colleges was not questioned. Things were quite different in the alienated world of *chakri* or office work under foreign bosses, where disciplinary time entered into a distinctively late-nineteenth-century vision of Kaliyuga.[74]

Vidyasagar's plan of 16 December 1850 suggested a series of changes in the syllabus of Sanskrit College, all in a recognisably modern, rationalistic direction. It simultaneously sought to bring Sanskrit teaching into close contact with the development of both Bengali and English education. Thus, for Sanskrit grammar, which students so long had been forced to memorise through the very difficult *Mugdhabodha*, Vidyasagar suggested the learning of the basic rules "dressed in the easiest Bengali", followed by graduated Sanskrit readings. (He would himself soon supply the appropriate Sanskrit grammar in Bengali, the *Vyakarana-Kaumudi*.) Training in English, too, was necessary, but only in the higher classes, to avoid the danger of getting swamped by it at the expense of the vernacular.

---

during college hours, and tried to shame latecomers among teachers by standing at the gate every morning at 10.30. Chandicharan Bandopadhyay, op. cit., pp. 92, 104–5.

[73] Modern factories start getting important only in the later decades of the nineteenth century, and much of the workforce even then consisted of immigrants. Relatively few Bengali-speaking people were recruited into that other site of time-discipline – the modern colonial army.

[74] For a fuller discussion, see chapters 6 and 8.

Sanskrit College students, the plan emphasised, must "acquire great proficiency in Bengali" and "derive useful information" through it (for which he was already providing the wherewithal, through textbooks like *Jivancharit* and *Bodhodaya*), "and thereby have their views expanded before they commence their English studies". They could also learn Jyotish (mathematics and astronomy) much more profitably through Bengali translations of contemporary English texts, instead of Lilavati and Bhaskaracharya, which Vidyasagar thought "very meagre" by modern standards. Even more striking is the evident attempt to reduce the importance in the syllabus of the Smriti teachings of Raghunandan (whose texts constituted the principal barrier to reforms like widow remarriage or a higher age of consent throughout the nineteenth century) and the Navya-Nyaya of Raghunath Shiromani (whose logic Vidyasagar thought had been "similar to that of schoolmen"). Along with Navya-Nyaya, the philosophical portions of the pre-Vidyasagar syllabus had a strong tilt towards Vedanta, characteristic of high-Hindu metaphysics since medieval times. It included texts specifically refuting "the Bouddha or atheistical doctrine" and all other non-Vedantist schools. In their place, Vidyasagar wanted to introduce the *Sarvadarshanasangraha*, through which, he argued, the student would be able to see how "the different systems have attacked each other, and have pointed out each other's errors and fallacies. Thus he would be able to judge for himself" – particularly since some courses in European philosophy would also be introduced.[75] In 1858 Vidyasagar brought out a critical edition of this fourteenth-century text of Madhavacharya, which he said had become a very rare manuscript.[76] It may not be irrelevant to note that the *Sarvadarshanasangraha* remains the primary source for the little information we have about the suppressed ancient Indian materialist tradition of Lokayata, associated with Carvaka.[77]

---

[75] The full text of Vidyasagar's plan for the reorganisation of Sanskrit College, submitted to F.J. Mouat, Secretary, Council of Education, on 16 December 1850, is included in Debkumar Basu, ed., *Vidyasagar Rachanabali*, vol. I (Calcutta, 1974), pp. 376–92. The quotations in this paragraph are taken from this report.

[76] Ibid., pp. 364–5.

[77] S.N. Dasgupta, *A History of Indian Philosophy*, vol. I (Cambridge, 1922);

That the implications of Vidyasagar's reform plan went very much beyond mere syllabus revision becomes clear from his *Notes on the Sanskrit College* (12 April 1852), which summed up with admirable precision and logic the core of his educational perspectives. "The creation of an enlightened Bengali Literature", Vidyasagar now declared, "should be the first object of those who are entrusted with the superintendence of Education in Bengal." This required the "exertions of those . . . competent to collect the materials from European sources and . . . dress them in elegant, expressive and idiomatic Bengali." But for this, Vidyasagar felt, mastery of Sanskrit was also essential, as "mere English scholars are altogether incapable of expressing their ideas in elegant and idiomatic Bengali. They are so much anglicised that it seems at present almost impossible for them to do so even if they later learn Sanskrit." It is very clear then that "if students of the Sanskrit College be made familiar with English Literature, they will prove the best and ablest contributors to an enlightened Bengali Literature."[78]

In September 1853 Vidyasagar had to defend his syllabus against criticisms made of it by J.R. Ballantyne, principal of Benaras Government Sanskrit College. In course of that exercise he had to formulate his underlying assumptions with greater clarity and polemical sharpness. Ballantyne had suggested a greater emphasis on the "correspondences" between select aspects of European and Indian philosophical traditions as a way of reconciling the Brahmanical literati to the coming of Western ideas. This involved a very different pattern of choice between philosophical schools than Vidyasagar's. The Benaras principal wanted less of Mill's *Logic*, the inclusion of Bishop Berkeley's *Inquiry*, and the introduction of a commentary written by Ballantyne himself which had emphasised the alleged similarities between that classic text of European philosophical Idealism, and Vedanta and Sankhya. This was the specific context for Vidyasagar's blunt and

---

Debiprasad Chattopadhyay, *Lokayata: A Study in Ancient Indian Materialism* (New Delhi: People's Publishing House, 1959, 1978), chapter 1.

[78] The text of the *Notes* has been reprinted in many places: I am using Indramitra, *Karunasagar Vidyasagar* (Calcutta, 1969, 1992), pp. 652–4.

aggressive statement about Vedanta and Sankhya being "false systems of philosophy": a remark that has been often torn out of context to indicate either Vidyasagar's laudable westernised modernity, or (with some justice) his philosophical naivete and dogmatism. But Vidyasagar's position, it must be emphasised, was not an uncritical preference of Western to Indian thought, for Vidyasagar was equally dismissive of Berkeley. The really interesting thing about the reply to Ballantyne is the way it anticipated, and sought to refute, what by the late nineteenth century would become a central strategy of much Hindu revivalism, as well as of a brand of Orientalism from which it was often highly derivative.[79] "Lately a feeling is manifesting itself among the learned of this part of India, specially in Calcutta and its neighbourhood, that when they hear of a Scientific truth, the germs of which may be traced out in their Shastras, instead of shewing any regard for that truth, their triumph and the superstitious regard for their own Shastras is redoubled." Vidyasagar went on to make a most uncomplimentary characterisation of the "learned of India" as a "body of men whose longstanding prejudices are unshakeable" – referring presumably to the traditional Brahman literati, not the Sanskrit College students he was trying to train in a new way. He went on to reiterate and expand the alternative cultural perspective he had

---

[79] Ballantyne as principal of Benaras Sanskrit College, interestingly, contributed quite directly to the later development. of Hindu revivalism by insisting on the need to evolve a Sanskritised Hindi, distinct from Urdu. As early as 1847, he was advising his pupils that they should try to make the Hindi used by the pandits of the "holy city" of Benaras "the standard of all India". "It was the duty of himself and his brother Pundits not to leave the task of formulating the national language in the hands of the villagers, but to endeavour to get rid of the unprofitable diversity of provincial dialects –." This was in reply to a rather puzzled interjection of a student of his that it was difficult to understand "what you Europeans mean by the term Hindi, for there are hundreds of dialects . . . and what you call the Hindi will eventually merge in some future modification of the Oordoo, nor do we see any great cause of regret in this prospect." Christopher R. King, "Forging a New Linguistic Identity: The Hindi Movement in Banaras, 1868–1914", in Sandria B. Freitag, *Culture and Power in Banaras* (Delhi: Oxford University Press, 1990), pp. 184–5.

outlined in April 1852. Instead of trying "to reconcile the learned of the Country",

> what we require is to extend the benefit of education to the mass of the people. Let us establish a number of Vernacular *schools*, let us prepare a series of Vernacular class-books on useful and instructive subjects, let us raise up a band of men [who] should be perfect masters of their own language, possess a considerable amount of useful information and be free from the prejudices of their country. To raise up such a useful class of men is the object I have proposed to myself and to the accomplishment of which the whole energy of *our* Sanskrit College should be directed.[80]

Beginning, then, in 1844 with the suggestion for tackling the employment problem facing Sanskrit College graduates through giving them jobs in Hardinge's experimental village schools, Vidyasagar in course of a decade had progressed to an integrated plan for cultural renovation of the literati of Bengal. Considered in the perspective of conventional histories of education, Vidyasagar's scheme may be seen as a bringing together of Orientalist, Anglicist, and Vernacularist positions, achieved through significant changes within each of them. Translated more meaningfully into social terms, it needs to be understood as an attempt to bridge the growing gap between the traditional pandits and the westernised, English-educated intelligentsia: not through some kind of eclectic compromise, however, which roughly had been Ballantyne's advice, but by a determined effort to transform and get beyond both poles. Vidyasagar hoped to impart a fundamentally new vernacular-cum-rural turn to pandits and English-educated alike, and considerably broaden the social basis of the intelligentsia as a whole. That such a trend could unfold in mid-nineteenth-century Bengal, it needs to be added, should considerably complicate the westernist/traditionalist dichotomy in terms of which so much colonial middle-class history has been conceptualised.

Vidyasagar had had ample opportunities of watching this rupture

---

[80] Vidyasagar to F.I. Mouat, replying to Ballantyne's observations, 7 September 1853. Text in Benoy Ghosh, op. cit., pp. 525–30.

grow at first hand, for classes in Sanskrit College in his time took place in the same building as Hindu College, with the two institutions, however, carefully segregated from each other by walls. His class-friends would all be Brahmans (plus a few Vaidyas), mostly poor. Hindu College was catering to a more multi-caste clientele, including many sons of the relatively low-born Calcutta nouveaux riches; but it was at the same time considerably more exclusive in economic terms. Vidyasagar himself had managed to straddle both worlds, through mastering English and developing personal ties with a host of Hindu College products (including many of the Young Bengal variety), but he would have realised how insuperable the barriers might soon appear to many. And indeed the long-term consequences of the failure of Vidyasagar's dream have been very far-reaching. The logical implication of his educational strategy was a reunification of the literati on a basis oriented towards modernistic change, which would be at the same time geared towards mass vernacular education, and therefore at least potentially more democratic than pre-colonial Brahmanical culture. Instead, as the rift widened, the world of the old-fashioned pandits became increasingly narrow, immersed in futile grumbling about the many evils of Kaliyuga, often blindly conservative – while the "anglicised" have often swung between complete alienation and recurrent searches for "roots" in (largely invented or spurious) "traditions". In total contrast to Vidyasagar's vision, the occasional unificatory moments have tended to develop around revivalist-nationalistic programmes – right down to our own times, one is tempted to add, in Hindutva's twin base among Vishwa Hindu Parishad sadhus and a Non-Resident Indian-oriented elite that is highly westernised in a consumerist sense.

Two things were indispensable if Vidyasagar's plans were to succeed. There was the need for an "enlightened Bengali Literature", in particular a vernacular discursive prose capable of tackling in a creative and attractive manner a much wider range of themes than had been possible or necessary in pre-colonial times. The other, inter-related, prerequisite was the rapid spread of vernacular education. The two together could help to constitute a public space open to argumentation, and based on expanding literacy and print culture.

The first condition was largely met, for this was an autonomous area where the intelligentsia could operate on its own, and when the coming of print culture enabled wide dissemination and created some possibilities for financial independence. Western education on the whole was a stimulus rather than hindrance to the development of indigenous languages, in significant contrast to what happened in some other parts of the colonised world. Vidyasagar's own seminal and multiple contributions to the development of modern Bengali prose have of course been very widely recognised. They ranged from mundane but necessary things like the introduction of standardised punctuation and syntax,[81] the careful compilation of glossaries of new terms for modern concepts,[82] to the creation of a style that was chaste, dignified, yet free from the inaccessible and excessively sanskritised ornateness of the Bengali which many pandits still liked to use.[83] Rabindranath even felt this to have been Vidyasagar's greatest single achievement, and described it as an emancipation of the language simultaneously from "rustic barbarism" and "parochial scholasticism".[84] And for a man capable of the considerable literary qualities of a text like *Sitar Banobas*, it must have been a major sacrifice

---

[81] Vidyasagar's introduction of commas and semicolons made Bengali prose both more rigorous and more accessible, as a comparison with, say, Rammohan immediately reveals. On the importance of punctuation, see the perceptive comments of Carolyn Steedman, who reminds us that even for written English, rules for punctuation were still "in the process of being established" in the second half of the nineteenth century. *The Radical Soldier's Tale* (London: Routledge, 1988), p. 73, and *passim*.

[82] Vidyasagar's *Jivancharit* (1849) included a list of the Bengali terms he was coining for words like "colonial", "prejudice", "museum", "natural law", "theatre", "revolution", and "university". Debkumar Basu, op. cit., vol. I (Calcutta, 1966, 1969, 1974), pp. 234–6.

[83] Many among the old-fashioned literati disliked Vidyasagar's Bengali. Chandicharan Bandopadhyay, op. cit., p. 178, relates the story of Sanskrit scholars at a shastric debate in the palace of the zamindar of Krishnanagar ridiculing a pandit who had given a *vyavastha* (opinion on a point of religious law) in Bengali that seemed too close to Vidyasagar's: "What have you done? This can be too easily understood!"

[84] Rabindranath Tagore, *Vidyasagar-Carit*, p. 478.

to devote one's writing talents almost entirely to composing, as part of a deeply felt social commitment, school textbooks, adaptations, and reform tracts.[85]

The expansion-cum-improvement of vernacular schools in villages required, however, considerable financial inputs from the state and/or the rural gentry, as well as active support from the literati, old and new. For a brief period in the mid 1850s the conjuncture appeared favourable for Vidyasagar's dream. Colonial educational policy was not quite the monolith, determined solely by Macaulay's notorious Minute of 1835, that is sometimes assumed nowadays. Bengal officials in the early 1850s had been impressed by the apparent success of the "circle" experiment started in the North-Western Provinces under Thomason that had tried to set up a model school in each revenue district as a way of improving vernacular education. Wood's Education Despatch of 1854, though in the end contained within the "filtration" framework, had also visualised some expansion in vernacular education through the grant-in-aid system by which costs would be shared between the government and local patrons.

Around 1855–6 – the peak years also of his social reform drive – Vidyasagar was enjoying excellent relations with many high British officials in Bengal, from Lieutenant Governor Halliday downwards. This had helped him to develop links with a number of prominent zamindars, in particular some "improving" landlords like Joykrishna Mukhopadhyay of Uttarpara, who had recently acquired large estates in Hooghly district, and who around 1855 was combining efforts to promote new crops like potatoes and sugarcane with the establishment of both English and vernacular schools in the areas under his control.[86] Vidyasagar, finally, had become a major figure by the mid 1850s

---

[85] Bankimchandra's remark in 1871 that "beyond translating or primer-making Vidyasagar has done nothing" therefore appears peculiarly uncharitable. *Calcutta Review*, April 1871, quoted in Swapan Basu, *Samakale Vidyasagar* (Calcutta, 1993), p. 157.

[86] In June 1855, for instance, Joykrishna and his brother proposed the starting of fourteen village vernacular schools, and were able to obtain from the lieutenant governor a grant-in-aid of Rs 189 a month for each. Nilmoni Mukherjee, *A Bengal Zamindar*, pp. 102, 160.

among the literati, both traditional and new: active in the Brahmo-led Tattwabodhini Sabha and Patrika, friend of many with Young Bengal antecedents, and yet numbering among his closest associates pandits like Madanmohan Tarkalankar, who helped him start the Sanskrit Press Depository, and Taranath Tarkavacaspati, who combined running a *tol* at Ambica-Kalna with far-flung business interests. The peak of Vidyasagar's educational and reform campaign seems to have coincided in fact with a last flurry of enterprising landlordism and middle-class entrepreneurship in Bengal.[87] Vidyasagar's, in other words, was not quite a lone venture in the Bengal society of the 1850s. A British inspector of schools would note in April 1859 that "the learned Pundits of Sanskrit College have, as a body, been seized with a love of publishing books." They had become interested "in European Science and Literature" and "were writing in a language that ordinary people may read." Through their efforts, and particularly "under the able superintendence of Ishur Chunder Vidyasagar", the Bengali language was becoming "capable of being the elegant vehicle of scientific and other infornation".[88]

In May 1855, Halliday appointed Vidyasagar Assistant Inspector of Schools for the four districts of Hooghly, Burdwan, Midnapur, and Nadia, conjointly with his principalship of Sanskrit College, with a combined salary of Rs 500 a month. By the end of that year he had already established some twenty model schools, applying to Bengal Thomason's circle system, and also started a normal school to train village headmasters at Sanskrit College under the superintendence of his close friend, the rationalist Akshoykumar Dutta. In a parallel move Vidyasagar, who had already displayed his commitment to women's

---

[87] Thus the prominent Derozian Ramgopal Ghosh had prospered through rice trade with Burma, while Taranath Tarkavacaspati around 1850 was supplying imported yarn to 1200 weavers in Ambica-Kalna and Radhanagar, and exporting cloth to many places in North India. He was connected also with trade in timber and ghee. Such literati connections with successful business enterprise would become very rare after the 1850s. Benoy Ghosh, op. cit., pp. 161–2.

[88] H. Woodrow, Inspector of Schools, East Bengal, in General Report of Public Instruction, 1858–9, Appendix A, p. 30, cited in Arabinda Guha, ed., *Unpublished Letters of Vidyasagar*, p. 19.

education by enthusiastically backing Bethune's school for daughters of respectable families in Calcutta in 1849, utilised his new official position to start forty girls' schools in villages between November 1857 and June 1858.

Precision is needed about what exactly was new in these two initiatives of Vidyasagar, for it is possible both to exaggerate or unduly downplay their significance. The surveys made in 1835–8 by William Adam, Rammohan's Unitarian friend, had found a fairly widespread system of indigenous vernacular education in the villages, with some 100,000 *pathshalas* for the "indigent classes" in Bengal and Bihar, mostly under non-Brahman (often Kayastha) *gurumohasayas*. Adam discovered "the desire to give education to their male children" to be "deeply seated in the minds of parents even of the humblest classes", and thought that the *pathshalas*, of course quite radically modified and improved, could be "the institutions through which primarily, although not exclusively, we may hope to improve the morals and the intellect of the Native population."[89] Vidyasagar's plan of normal and model schools can be seen, therefore, as in a way a belated effort to implement Adam's suggestions.

The impressive number and apparent absence of direct Brahman control has led to an occasional romanticisation of these pre-colonial schools, which in some ways fitted better with rural conditions than the new system which colonial rule, actively helped by reformers like Vidyasagar, eventually established.[90] Poromesh Acharya has recently provided an important corrective here, emphasising both the

---

[89] William Adam, *First Report on the State of Education in Bengal, 1835*, ed. Anathnath Basu (Calcutta: Calcutta University, 1941), p. 7.

[90] Thus the *pathshalas* used to have classes from early morning to ten, and again from three to sundown, and were often closed during the harvesting season: certainly arrangements far better suited to rural conditions and a hot climate than the "modern" system. The changeover to a ten-to-four schedule was in the 1860s, after Vidyasagar had resigned his offrcial positions, but it came about through the influence of the Normal School for gurus which he had started. Kazi Shahidullah, "The Purpose and Impact of Government Policy on Pathshala Gurumohashoys in Nineteenth-Century Bengal", in Nigel Crook, ed., *The Transmission of Knowledge in South Asia* (Delhi: Oxford University Press, 1995), pp. 120, 122, 125.

extremely limited nature of the education supplied by these schools even at their best, as well as the split-up and hierarchised nature of the entire indigenous educational system which allowed little scope for social mobility. *Pathshala* education, of course entirely in Bengali, was basically confined to writing, arithmetic, and a bit of revenue and commercial accounting. (Reading was less important, since there were no printed textbooks and a necessarily limited number of manuscripts; this put a premium on memorising.[91]) The *pathshalas*, in other words, were geared to the everyday needs of would-be petty zamindari officials, traders, and better-off peasants: a source of strength, but also a limit. Adam's Reports were actually quite critical of the very limited content of indigenous elementary education.[92] The village school structure had little or nothing to do with the *tols, chatuspathis,* and *madrasas* – centres of Sanskrit and Arabic or Persian learning which were the preserve of Brahman males and other learned groups. The educational apparatus consisted of "separate classes of institutions without any link or relation of any kind, each catering to a distinct class or community."[93] The relative absence of high castes from village schools was thus a mark of inferiorisation and hierarchy (a crucial instance of *adhikaribheda*, in fact, the principle which Ramakrishna had extolled and Vidyasagar questioned in their only conversation), not autonomy. The *Chanakya-slokas*, for instance, which pupils were often made to memorise in the *pathshalas*, combined maxims of worldly wisdom with frequent reaffirmations of Brahmanical supremacy: the Brahman was the guru of all other castes, it declared, just as the husband was guru to his wife.[94]

The changes Vidyasagar and other mid-nineteenth-century colonial officials sought to introduce in the *pathshala* involved expansion

---

[91] One might recall in this context the terms which Vidyasagar's village teacher is said to have used when advising Thakurdas that his son should be taken to Calcutta and taught English: "His handwriting is very beautiful." Chandicharan Bandopadhyay, op. cit., p. 23.

[92] "[T]here is no text or schoolbook used containing any moral truths or liberal knowledge . . ." Adam, p. 9.

[93] Poromesh Acharya, "Indigenous Education and Brahmanical Hegemony in Bengal", in Crook, op. cit., p. 98.

[94] Poromesh Acharya, op. cit., pp. 105–11.

of its curriculum to include history, geography, ethics, and natural philosophy (i.e. elementary science), much greater use of textbooks, promotion through examinations, and in general an integration within the theoretically "complete and continuous" system that was being worked out for colonial education.[95] Hierarchies did not end, of course, particularly those based on economic or class differentials, and may even have been sharpened at times, both through the dichotomy in medium of instruction (English at higher levels) and by some of the changes brought about in the *pathshalas*.[96] At the same time, there was a new theoretical equality of opportunity independent of caste status, a chance for talented boys of families with some but not much resources to climb up an uniform educational ladder through personal grit, determination, and self-discipline.

There was a much more gradual and limited, but still strikingly new, opening for some girls, too, against formidable opposition. The widespread belief was that educated wives became widows, and while daughters in high-caste families could be occasionally taught a little within their parents' homes, the idea of sending them out to school was deeply shocking, and a very early marriage anyway obligatory. Conditions were no different in the villages: Adam's First Report made the categorical statement that "there are no indigenous girls' schools."[97] It is true that Radhakanta Deb, the great champion of sati against Rammohan and Bentinck and of ascetic widowhood against Vidyasagar, had been at the same time a promoter, of a kind,

---

[95] Hatcher, op. cit., p. 106; Poromesh Acharya, op. cit., p. 98.

[96] In 1863, a British official noticed a "marked difference" in the appearance of pupils of "improved" – as compared to unreformed – *pathshalas*. In the latter, cultivators' children were prominent, those of "the better class of villagers" relatively rare. Normal school pupils in contrast were largely "the Brahmin and writer-caste boys." Report of Inspector Medlicott, Government of Bengal Educational Proceedings, no. 51, January 1863, cited in Kazi Shahidullah, op. cit., p. 125. School fees in the new system were rigorously collected, and payable in cash only; school timings no longer made adjustments for agrarian rhythms; and the curriculum had become more abstract, detached from labour processes (e.g. the shift from zamindari and *mahajani* accounting to formal Western mathematics).

[97] Adam, op. cit., p. 7.

of the education of girls and is even said to have published a tract about it. This had specified, however, that only girls of poor parents could be sent out to school, while respectable families should have their daughters taught within the home – in both cases only till they were married off. A number of girls' schools were set up in Calcutta in the early 1820s, mostly at missionary initiative, but they were, significantly, located in the poorer parts of the city. The initiative then seems to have died out for a generation, and we may speculate whether the conservative consolidation against the ban on sati and Derozian iconoclasm may not have had something to do with this hiatus. What was striking about Bethune's endeavour in 1849 was that daughters of respectable families were now being encouraged to go out to a school, being transported there in a carriage that displayed a Sanskrit quotation said to have been hunted up by Vidyasagar.[98] In course of his drive for girls' schools in villages, too, Vidyasagar took special pride in those being attended by daughters of respectable, high-caste families, thus once again challenging directly conservative *bhadralok* prejudices.[99]

The characteristic features – and limits – of Vidyasagar's pedagogy are revealed most clearly through a glance at his primers and textbooks.[100] Three themes stand out. There is the motif of the poor boy

---

[98] The above paragraph is based on Chandicharan Bandopadhyay, op. cit., chapter VII, and Benoy Ghosh, op. cit., chapter IV.

[99] Vidyasagar's report to H. Woodrow (Officiating Director of Public Instruction, 10 December 1857) emphasised the importance of the girls' school he had managed to start at Koolingram, Burdwan district, as those sending their daughters there "are, for the most part, respectable men". A later report of his claimed that with consistent government support he could have started girls' schools "in almost every village in the districts under me, except perhaps the District of Nuddea." The qualification is revealing, for Nadia was the citadel of Brahmanical learning and orthodoxy. Arabinda Guha, op. cit., pp. 35, 36.

[100] The key texts here include *Jivancharit* (1849), *Bodhoday* (1851), *Nitibodh* (1851: published in the name of Vidyasagar's close friend Rajkrishna Bandopadhyay, but with the first seven sections written by himself), *Charitabali* (1856), and, of course, *Varnaparichay* in two parts (April, June 1855). *Varnaparichay* went through 152 editions totalling 3,500,000 copies in Vidyasagar's lifetime, and remained the standard Bengali primer right down

making good through diligence, devoted effort, and single-minded pursuit of learning. *Jivancharit* and *Charitabali* use material from William and Robert Chambers' *Exemplary and Instructive Biography* (Edinburgh, 1846) to present brief life-histories of leading Western scientists, along with those of Grotius, Valentine Duval (a shepherd boy who rose to become a historian), and Jenkins (son of an African prince who managed to get a British education). The concentration on scientists (Copernicus, Galileo, Newton, Herschell, Linnaeus) indicates Vidyasagar's rationalist preferences, and so perhaps is the insertion here of Grotius, founder of an international law which theoretically puts the same limits on the powers of all states, big or small, and prominent advocate of toleration in an age of religious bigotry. The life-histories are adaptations from English, yet a revealing displacement seems to be at work in many of the comments: diligence, which in the Western exemplars is by no means restricted to formal book-learning alone, tends inevitably, in the conditions of colonial, middle-class Bengal, to get focused solely on a single-minded pursuit of education. The biography of Duval ends with Vidyasagar remarking that *yatna* and *parisrama* (devoted effort and exertion) would have led the shepherd boy nowhere had he not harnessed that devotion to learning.[101] The *Varnaparichay* and, even more, *Bodhoday*, made the point sharper: "Those who are diligent about becoming educated will live happy lives because they will be able to earn money."[102]

The theme of improvement through education is inextricably bound up with a tremendous insistence on discipline, connoting both rigorous self-control and strict obedience to the commands of parents and teachers. The *Varnaparichay*, as Sibaji Bandopadhyay has emphasised

---

to contemporary times. Sibaji Bandopadhyay, *Gopal-Rakhal Dvandvasamas*, p. 135.

[101] I owe this point to Hatcher, op. cit., p. 181, who does not, however, make this distinction between Western exemplar and Indian adaptation explicit.

[102] *Bodhoday*, in Gopal Haldar, ed., *Vidyasagar Rachanasangraha* (Calcutta, 1972), vol. I, p. 182. The theme, of course, has become a Bengali proverb: "*Lekhapara kore je garighora chare se.*"

in an important study, is structured throughout by a binary contrast between disciplined diligence and errant disobedience, culminating at the end of Part I in the opposition of Gopal who will succeed in life, and Rakhal who will never learn to read.[103] This is a discipline, it should be added, that is presented in terms utterly stark and bleak, abstracted from human affect and paternalistic glosses. Children are actually told in one lesson that they should always try to please their parents, for if the latter had not been kind enough to feed and clothe them, their sufferings would have known no limit.[104] The Utilitarian, materialistic tone of Vidyasagar's textbooks in fact provoked some contemporary criticism from both orthodox Hindus and some Christian missionaries.[105] These are understandable enough, but the peculiar bleakness of the world of *Varnaparichay* remains a bit puzzling: it is almost as if Vidyasagar sometimes is fighting a part of himself, suppressing an inner Rakhal, projecting the path of discipline and obedience as something made necessary by a heartless world.[106] *Varnaparichay* ends with a really strange and cruel tale, quite out of place one would think in a children's primer. Bhuban, an orphan boy spoilt by his loving aunt, becomes a thief, is condemned to be hanged, and as a parting "gift" bites off his aunt's ear while saying goodbye.

Improvement, or social ascent, through stern discipline: but only up to a point, within limits set by existing property relations. *Bodhoday* affirms a highly status quoist version of a kind of labour theory of property: "The things we see around us must belong to one or other person. An object belongs to whoever has worked to produce

[103] Sibaji Bandopadhyay, op. cit., pp. 134–42, and *passim*.

[104] *Varnaparichay*, Part II, in T. Datta, ed., *Vidyasagar Rachanabali*, vol. I (Calcutta,1994), p. 1264.

[105] Biharilal Sarkar, op. cit., p. 153, was critical of the *Bodhoday*, which had declared that sense impressions constitute the only source of knowledge, and defined matter as objects that can be perceived. The missionary leader John Murdoch objected to the use of the "secularist" *Varnaparichay* in Christian schools. Swapan Basu, op. cit., p. 130.

[106] Vidyasagar's autobiographical fragment begins by recalling how disobedient he had been in his childhood and how often his father had had to scold or beat him: a relevant personal detail, but which does not, I feel, fully explain this tone.

it, or has inherited it from his forefathers. No one else has any right to it. Whoever owns an object should continue to own it." No respectable (*bhadra*) person should be a beggar, while having property is conducive to continuous effort. Vidyasagar's school texts are full of warnings about the immorality of theft: "One shouldn't lay one's hand on something belonging to another person, even if one's life is at stake."[107] There was, then, a clear class limit, and sometimes a caste frontier, too, though here it was more a question of expediency than believed-in principle. Vidyasagar had insisted in 1851 on opening Sanskrit College to Kayasthas, and in 1854 to other "respectable castes". But in 1855 he rejected as inexpedient a suggestion that a Subarnabanik student should also be admitted.[108] Though often very prosperous, he argued, "in the scale of castes the class stands very low", and he did not want to further "shock the prejudice of the orthodox Pundits of the Institution."[109] Despite a concern for primary education in the countryside very rare among members of his class, Vidyasagar, it needs to be added, was probably not the unqualified advocate for mass enlightenment that later admirers have at times made him out to be. Hatcher has cited a letter of his written in September 1859, which argues that educating "one boy in a proper style" was preferable to providing a smattering of learning to large numbers, for poor children would be taken out of school and put to work by their parents in any case.[110] Vidyasagar did set up a night school for "sons of the cultivating class" in Birsingha in 1853, but this seems to have been a special gesture made for his home village, and not part of his overall schemes.[111]

---

[107] *Bodhoday* (1851, 1886), in Debkumar Basu, ed., *Vidyasagar Rachanabali*, vol. I (Calcutta, 1966, 1974), pp. 282–3.

[108] Subarnabaniks were a prosperous trading community in Bengal who had a surprisingly low-caste status: supposedly because they had offended Ballal Sen, eponymous founder of the specific caste structure of Bengal.

[109] Letters dated 28 March 1851 and 21 November 1855, in Benoy Ghosh, op. cit., pp. 542–5.

[110] Letter to Rivers Thompson, 29 September 1859, cited in Hatcher, op. cit., p. 111.

[111] Vidyasagar also ran a free day-school and a girls' school at Birsingha,

Still it is possible to be over-harsh about Vidyasagar. Ranajit Guha has described his schoolbook morality as nothing but "hard-baked, bourgeois individualism",[112] and certainly there are not only similarities but obvious connections (through Chambers, for instance) with nineteenth-century middle-class British ideologies of improvement as moulded by amalgams of Evangelicalism and Utilitarianism.[113] Texts like *Varnaparichay* comprise the part of Vidyasagar's work that might appear readily assimilable to today's very influential emphasis on "disciplinary" projects, either derived from colonial discourses or running parallel with them.[114] Hatcher's book has effectively drawn attention, in significant contrast, to the possibility of the more indigenous roots of Vidyasagar's pedagogical values, in particular the traditions of *nitishastra*, embodied in texts like *Chanakya-slokas* and *Hitopadesha*, which also contained elements of an ethic of this-worldly improvement through strenuous learning.[115] But Hatcher, like the analysts of colonial discourse, remains within the parameters of a search for "influence" or origins. What tends to remain unasked is the question of the precise social contexts which made the emphasis on discipline appear unavoidable. (Not necessarily pleasant or attractive, the bleak world of *Varnaparichay*, its almost Machiavellian realism and ruthlessness, perhaps signifies a recognition of necessity rather than blithe imitation or enthusiastic

---

along with a charitable dispensary. His total expenses for these came to as much as Rs 500–600 a month. Subolchandra Mitra, op. cit., pp. 240–1.

[112] Ranajit Guha, *An Indian Historiography of India* (Calcutta: K.P. Bagchi, 1988), p. 61.

[113] For later generations, Samuel Smiles' *Self-Help* has come to epitomise this ideology: here, however, there can have been no direct influence, since that text was published only in 1859.

[114] See, for instance, Partha Chatterjee, ed., *Texts of Power: Emerging Disciplines in Colonial Bengal* (Calcutta: Samya, 1996). For a more nuanced version of a similar argument, see Sibaji Bandopadhyay, op. cit.

[115] A prize-winning Sanskrit poem by Vidyasagar in his student days, composed at a time (1838) when he had not mastered English, had already announced that "though a man be weak, poor, or of low birth, through learning he earns the respect worthy of a king." Hatcher, op. cit., pp. 165–7.

acceptance.) With the closing of opportunities for military careers and the decline of indigenous business enterprise, education in Bengal, by the mid nineteenth century, was becoming virtually the sole channel for respectable upward mobility: education, further, of a far more formal, examination-centred kind, for which the old kind of *pathshala*, however much in tune with earlier conditions, was quite unsuited. Recruitment into services and professions was becoming increasingly dependent on examinations and educational degrees. The informal patronage that Vidyasagar could still distribute through his personal relations with top British officials would soon become a thing of the past. And, once again, instead of a homogenised "middle class", a focus on its poorer elements seems helpful for situating Vidyasagar's initiatives. The strenuous moods of his school texts were not primarily meant for the gilded youth of Calcutta. They become meaningful only when placed in a context of genteel poverty, and here Vidyasagar's projects implied a striving for a real though limited expansion, an attempt, in the words of Asok Sen, to extend "opportunities of education for the poorer gentry in small towns and villages of Bengal."[116]

The attempt went some distance beyond them, perhaps, in terms of long-term appropriations by groups about whom Vidyasagar himself had shown little or no concern. Recent research has unearthed a mass of early-twentieth-century vernacular tracts composed by an emerging literati of Muslims and lower-caste authors located in obscure villages or small towns of rural Bengal.[117] They are imbued with an improvement ethic reminiscent often of Vidyasagar's combination of education with puritanical virtues and discipline, though there is also a greater focus on life outside the classroom, in particular on agricultural development. Given the continued, massive circulation of texts like *Varnaparichay*, one might even suspect a certain amount of direct, if unintended, influence.

[116] Asok Sen, op. cit., p. 42.

[117] I am indebted for this point to the very original research of Pradip Kumar Dutta: "Hindu–Muslim Relations in the Bengal of the 1920s" (unpublished thesis, Delhi University, 1996), chapter II, and *passim*.

Such developments lay much in the future in the 1850s. For Vidyasagar, the tragedy was that the favourable conjuncture that he had sought to utilise for major educational and other initiatives proved extremely short-lived. Educational administration was getting more bureaucratised under a brash young I.C.S. Director of Public Instruction, Gordon Young, who did not get on with Vidyasagar. Much more important was a new mood of financial stringency, fairly obviously connected with counterinsurgency expenses in the wake of 1857. Vidyasagar had gone ahead in the early summer of 1857 in starting girls' schools in his four districts, on the strength of a verbal assurance from Halliday that if "the inhabitants would provide suitable school houses, the expenses for maintaining the schools would be met by the Government." In the next year "the Supreme Government . . . refused their sanction to their establishment except under the Grants-in-aid Rules. My labours have thus become fruitless and the interesting little schools will have to be closed immediately."[118] Towards the end of 1858 Vidyasagar resigned in disgust from all his official posts.

Barriers of another kind, relating to the development of vernacular education for boys, become evident from an earlier report of Vidyasagar in January 1857. He had pointed out then that "the success of Vernacular Education will depend materially upon the encouragement given in the way of providing the Alumni of these institutions with offices under Government." Vidyasagar suggested that vernacular students should therefore be nominated "to lower posts in the Judicial or Revenue Departments", a proposal, needless to state, that was entirely ignored.

Colonial constraints – in the form of very material considerations and structures, not abstract ideas – are therefore entirely clear in the case of Vidyasagar's educational ventures. They had coalesced with the elite Brahmanical traditions of high castes, sometimes strengthening, but hardly creating them: for there is no evidence whatsoever of any major attempt at mass education (or organised efforts to improve the conditions of women, for that matter) by *bhadralok*

---

[118] Extract from General Report of Public Instruction, 1858–59, Appendix A, in Arabinda Guha, op. cit., p. 36.

men in pre-colonial times. The philanthropy of the more enterprising zamindars, on which too Vidyasagar had thought he could depend in the 1850s, was often a bit double-edged at its best,[119] and died away as enhancement of rent became more difficult with the tenancy acts of 1859 and 1885. And deepening employment problems clearly constricted middle-class attitudes over time. *Bhadralok* protests poured in when Lieutenant Governor Campbell suggested some diversion of funds from higher towards primary education in 1870.[120] Even anti-colonial nationalism did not change attitudes fundamentally. The "national education" of the Swadeshi era concentrated on trying to float an alternative university, and certain interesting experiments in districts like Barisal and Faridpur to start autonomous nationalist-oriented village schools among Namasudras and Muslims, which had worried the government considerably, soon died away.[121]

A report of an inspector of schools just a few months after Vidyasagar's resignation can serve as an appropriate, if depressing, epitaph for this section. At Jowgong village near Boinchee, Burdwan district, where a girls' school founded by Vidyasagar was still getting an official grant of Rs 32 per month, "not a girl, boy or pundit was in attendance" when it was visited on 25 January 1859. The inspector went from there to the neighbouring village of Koolingram, which, as we have seen, Vidyasagar had singled out for special mention in December 1857 as an instance of successful overcoming of the initial hostility of "respectable men".[122] A few girls could be seen there in January 1859, but "the poor Pundit of the Girls' School had . . . no friends". The headmaster of the boys' school was leading the opposition, and the girls' school had had to shift to another village a mile away.[123]

[119] There had been complaints in 1847 that Joykrishna Mukherjee was funding his Uttarpara English school by enhancing the rents of his tenants at Boinchee. Nilmoni Mukherjee, op. cit., p. 108.

[120] Asok Sen, op. cit., pp. 38–9.

[121] Sumit Sarkar, *Swadeshi Movement in Bengal, 1903–1908* (New Delhi, 1973), chapter IV.

[122] See fn. 90 above.

[123] Report of E. Lodge, Inspector of Schools, South Bengal, 10 March 1859, cited in Arabinda Guha, op. cit., pp. 50–1.

IV

Many stories have been current about the origins of Vidyasagar's passionate concern for the plight of women, in a society where child marriage was normative, widow remarriage prohibited, austere widowhood stringently enforced among high and most intermediate castes, and polygamy considered prestigious among Kulin Brahmans, Kayasthas, and Vaidyas. His mother first advised him to take up the cause of widows – according to one account. Others refer to first-hand experiences during visits to Birsingha in his college days: seeing a child-widow of his own age having to fast on *ekadosi*, and hearing about another forced into infanticide by parental command. He was particularly shocked when a favourite teacher of his at Sanskrit College, the elderly Vedanta scholar Sambhuchandra Vacaspati, married a child to run his household for him a few months before his death. (Vidyasagar is said to have wept on meeting the child-bride, doomed to early and lifelong widowhood, and walked out of his teacher's house, refusing to touch water there henceforth.[124]) Two widows are prominent, as we have seen, in his own autobiographical fragment, but as exemplars of warmth and compassion rather than suffering.

What is common to all these anecdotes is an emphasis on personal experience that can be read as a confirmation of the inference I had drawn from Maheshchandra Deb's essay.[125] There are no references at all to any stimulus provided by Western models of marital relations. And, contrary to an interpretive model which today is very influential, all biographies about Vidyasagar agree that the counterposing of shastra against *deshachar*, texts versus customs, eventually the core of his widow remarriage and anti-polygamy tracts, came as deliberate strategy, formulated after he had become convinced that certain practices were harmful and evil.[126] Vidyasagar's reform tracts hardly

---

[124] Chandicharan Bandopadhyay, op. cit., pp. 59–61, rejects as inauthentic the story about his mother, and relates the tales about infanticide and Vacaspati. Subolchandra Mitra, op. cit., p. 262, gives the story about *ekadosi*.

[125] See above, footnote 39 and corresponding text.

[126] Chandicharan Bandopadhyay, op. cit., pp. 237–8, vividly describes

bear out the assumption so often made nowadays that "the discursive struggle in which the social reformers were engaged was over tradition and culture; women were simply the site of this contestation."[127]

Vidyasagar's first essay on social reform, *Balyabibaher Dosh* (Evils of Child-Marriage, 1850), was marked in fact by a total absence of textual exegesis. Partly for that reason, it was also his most radical statement on gender relations, and it was able, within the space of a few brilliantly written pages, to unfold an integrated, comprehensive critique of child marriage, arranged marriages, marital oppression, taboos against educating women, and the horrors and evils of austere widowhood.[128]

The essay began with a trenchant denunciation of *both* text and custom, shastra and *laukik vyavahara*. The two in combination have produced, and sustain, all that Vidyasagar found objectionable in existing marital practices. Throughout the essay, he judged the existing institutions and practices against an ideal norm of companionate

---

sleepless nights spent by Vidyasagar hunting for shastric arguments to prove the case for widow remarriage, before he came across the Parasar passage he would make famous. The story may be overdramatised, as it seems unlikely that Vidyasagar would not have known about the passage earlier (see fn. 142, below), but the essential point regarding the primacy of personal experience over text is reiterated by Subolchandra Mitra, op. cit., p. 262, who adds that he "rightly" took no public step before discovering the shastric justification.

[127] Ratna Kapur and Brenda Cossman, *Subversive Sites: Feminist Engagements with Law in India* (New Delhi: Sage, 1996), p. 47, a pioneering feminist study of Indian legal discourse which unfortunately accepts at this point a little uncritically Lata Mani's thesis about the debate around sati. I have stated elsewhere my difficulties with Mani's argument, namely that nineteenth-century debates about the conditions of women were primarily a means to the end of establishing textualized versions of tradition, even when applied to Rammohan: see Sumit Sarkar "Orientalism Revisited: Saidian Frameworks in the Writing of Indian History", *Oxford Literary Review*, 16, 1994.

[128] *Saruasubhakari*, 1850; Gopal Haldar, ed., *Vidyasagar Rachanabali*, vol. II (Calcutta, 1972), pp. 3–9. This was an article in a short-lived monthly brought out by some Hindu College friends of Vidyasagar; it was published anonymously, but there is complete unanimity among biographers and critics that the author was Iswarchandra.

conjugality based on adult mutual love *(pronoy)*, and that, Vidyasagar says, can flow only from an "unity of minds".[129] This is impossible if girls are married off at eight, nine, or ten – which happens because *smriti-shastras* have promised some imagined otherworldly boons from such action, and people are also afraid of flouting long-continuing custom. All marriages, further, are arranged by parents as advised by often corrupt *ghataks* (professional go-betweens), and the couple do not even see each other before the ceremony – and so "in our country sincere marital love is rare: the husband is merely the breadwinner, the wife a domestic servant *(grihaparicharika)*." Child marriage, again, is directly connected with women being kept without education, for, even if they had been taught a little at their parental homes, after marriage will begin life in an "alien house *(paragriha)*", totally subjected to the authority of fathers and mothers-in-law, and filled with an endless round of "cleaning the house, preparing beds, cooking, serving food, and other duties which would have to be learned with perfection." The early marriage of girls also increases the number of widows, "and who has not witnessed first-hand the unbearable sufferings of widows? . . . All chance of pleasure must end as soon as their husbands die . . . they will not be allowed a drop of water, even if critically ill, on days of ritual fasting . . ." Never again would Vidyasagar condemn so uncompromisingly the rules of austere widowhood, identify patrilocal marriage for women as life in an "alien" home, or indeed critique child marriage directly. These did not become part of his action programmes, nor did he return to the interconnections he had worked out here between the need to raise the age of marriage, promotion of women's education, and improving the lot of widows.

The major plank of Vidyasagar's argument in this pamphlet is thus individual and conjugal happiness – but there is also a second register, of morality and social welfare that on the whole has figured more in social-reform literature but remains somewhat low-key here. The rigours of lifelong widowhood, imposed often on young girls, cause

---

[129] I intend to argue below that this implicit recognition of ideal conjugality as necessarily based on the union of adult minds and bodies is quite central to a proper assessment of Vidyasagar.

much immorality and lead to abortions and infanticide. Children born of a too-early marriage tend to be weak and unhealthy, nor can they get proper training from mothers who have been kept uneducated. Young men married off in their teens neglect their studies and are overburdened by the financial responsibilities of maintaining wife and children: earning money has to become the sole aim of life, leading, once again, to immoral ways. Vidyasagar, interestingly, comes close for a moment here to what became a standard late-nineteenth-century Kaliyuga theme, and figured often in Ramakrishna's conversation as the link between *kamini, kanchan,* and *chakri* – but then his argument moved in a very different direction, prioritising this-worldly happiness and welfare, not devotion or asceticism. Ramakrishna would certainly not have shared his enthusiasm for conjugal love.

Did the later, and very much better known, tracts advocating widow remarriage and criticising Kulin polygamy on largely textual grounds then mark a retreat for Vidyasagar, with gender injustice becoming no more than a site for arguments about valid and invalid tradition? Such a critique would be less than fair, for it fails to analyse the options that were open (or not open) to Vidyasagar when formulating a specific programme of reform and trying to organise a movement on its basis. The tract against child marriage could be daringly radical and reject shastric exegesis, precisely because it was more of a consciousness raising exercise than a specific proposal for an immediate, concrete reform. It raised no demand for a new law: did not need to, in strict logic, for of course there was no law prohibiting adult marriage – as widow remarriage was prohibited and its issue illegitimate till 1856. The basic point that has to be made is that under British Indian law personal and family matters were supposed to be regulated in accordance with the shastras for Hindus, and the shariat for Muslims.[130] Reform through external state legislation,

---

[130] Warren Hastings' Regulations had laid down, in 1772 and again in 1780, that "inheritance, marriage, caste and other religious usages or institutions were to be administered to Hindus according to the laws of 'shaster'." Numerous changes were made, of course, but in consultation with indigenous experts (hence the need for "judge-pandits" in courts) – till the "assumption", made in 1864, that judicial knowledge of Hindu law was complete. In practice,

and reform from within through scriptural exegesis and community debate, which today often get counterposed against each other (as in current controversies about Muslim personal law, for instance), were actually interdependent in Vidyasagar's time. He had to find shastric justifications for widow remarriage, if it was to become legal under "Anglo-Hindu" law: reason and humanity alone would not be sufficient. The intertwining of Brahmanical tradition and colonial law becomes clear when seen from the opposite side, too. The petition organised by Raja Radhakanta Deb against the Widow Marriage Bill in March 1856 combined alternative interpretations of the shastras and appeals to age-old custom with the argument that "the proposed law is also at variance with the several Statutes of the British Parliament and the Regulations of the East India Company."[131]

The author of *Balyabibaher Dosh* was not yet particularly important in official or elite Indian circles. The widow-remarriage tracts, in contrast, were published in 1855–6, at the peak of Vidyasagar's influence, and the plunge into shastric exegesis was obviously in significant part an attempt to convince leading pandits who, through their importance in the *sabhas* of big zamindars and at high-caste ritual occasions, could in turn help him get the support of the big men of Hindu society. Vidyasagar in other words was trying to utilise and manipulate, for reformist purposes, the traditions of the medieval raja-pandit nexus that had spilled over in modified forms into the Calcutta-based *dali* of the nineteenth century.[132] Soon after publishing

---

occasional consultations continued even afterwards. J.D.M. Derrett, *Religion, Law and the State in India*, op. cit., p. 233, and *passim*.

[131] The petition, which obtained 36,764 signatures, went on to cite regulations enacted in 1772, 1793, and 1831, and the unanimous opinion of the judges of the Sadr courts given to the Law Commission of 1837 that legalisation of widow remarriage would "at once dislocate the whole framework of Hindu jurisprudence". A similar combination is visible in the petition made by the "Professors of the Hindu law" of Nuddea, Tribeni, Bhartpara, Bansberia, Calcutta, and other places denouncing the efforts of a "*Modern* pandit, Vidyasagar", "in conjunction with a few young men of the rising class". For the texts of both these documents, see Subolchandra Mitra, op. cit., pp. 302–17.

[132] See the excellent discussion in Sekhar Bandopadhyay, op. cit., pp. 22–3.

Vidyasagar and Brahmanical Society 293

his first tract justifying widow remarriage, Vidyasagar even tried to win over the Sobhabazar Raj, approaching Radhakanta Deb through a nephew who had become an ally of his. That attempt failed,[133] but he was able to get a substantial section of leading zamindars, along with a number of pandits like Taranath Tarkavacaspati and some Sanskrit College teachers, to line up with Brahmos and Young Bengal intellectuals in the petitions that were organised from October 1855 onwards asking for the legalisation of widow remarriage.[134] Vidyasagar's subsequent campaign against Kulin polygamy in 1856–7 also got the support of many prominent zamindars: probably more easily, for in its extreme forms (Kulins with a hundred wives or more, many of whom never saw their husbands after marriage) this was an undeniable scandal, confined moreover to a limited circle of high-caste families claiming a peculiarly high status.[135] A law on the subject may well have been enacted but for the 1857 rebellion. In the late 1860s, when Vidyasagar revived the demand and published his two tracts against polygamy, support was forthcoming for a time even from the Sanatan Dharmarakshini Sabha that had lately been organised to defend Hindu orthodoxy.[136]

As Sekhar Bandopadhyay has emphasised, Vidyasagar's reform

---

[133] Radhakanta organised two shastric debates, but at the end of the second awarded the shawl that traditionally signified victory at such occasions to Brajanath Vidyaratna, leading Smriti expert of Nabadwip. Subolchandra Mitra, op. cit., pp. 268–9. Brajanath remained one of Vidyasagar's most bitter and formidable antagonists down to the 1880s.

[134] The signatories included the maharajas of Burdwan and Nadia, and the head of both branches of the Tagore family (Debendranath and Prasannakumar), and the first petition was headed by the unimpeachably respectable and orthodox Joykrishna Mukherjee of Uttarpara. Altogether some 25,000 signatures could be collected for reform: less than the number collected by its opponents, but still fairly impressive. Chandicharan Bandopadhyay, op. cit., pp. 255–6; Nilmoni Mukherjee, op. cit., pp. 142–3.

[135] Polygamy had become rampant because it often became the principal source of livelihood for Kulin young men, who would be paid handsome sums by the parents of daughters eager to move their families up in the hypergamous scale.

[136] A support that Vidyasagar cited as a particularly telling argument in his favour in the introduction to his first *Bahubibaha* tract (1870). This also

campaigns thus included an element of continuity with earlier ways of seeking change through *vyavasthas* (authoritative rulings on social matters) from prominent pandits.[137] There had been several attempts earlier to get individual widow marriages sanctioned in this way, notably one by Raja Rajballabh of Dacca in the mid eighteenth century, which had been blocked by the pandits of Maharaja Krishnachandra of Nadia. Shortly before Vidyasagar published his first tract on widow remarriage, Shyamacharan Das, a man of intermediate caste (Nabasakh) status living in North Calcutta, had managed to get a favourable *vyavastha* for the remarriage of his widowed child from a number of leading pandits. (The ruling used a passage from Manu but was careful to limit permission for remarriage to Shudra widows who had remained virgins.[138])

Vidyasagar's tracts, then, were in a sense sophisticated *vyavasthas*, geared to an audience of fellow pandits and their patrons. But this was only one register among several on which he was playing. Right at the beginning of the first *Bidhaba-bibaha* pamphlet, there is a memorable appeal to a conception of public, vernacular space that is fundamentally new. This was the space that he was simultaneously trying to create, through vernacular prose and reformed elementary education, in endeavours that, like widow remarriage, attained their climax precisely around 1855–6. Tired of the endless controversy on the matter that had been so long confined to pandits animated by mutual jealousy, Vidyasagar declares he has decided to present his views "in the language spoken by the people, to bring it to the notice of the general public [*sarbasadharan*]. Now let everyone read and discuss, in an impartial manner, whether widow marriage should

---

gives a brief history of the earlier campaigns against polygamy. Haldar, ed., *Vidyasagar Rachanabali*, vol. II, pp. 167–9.

[137] Sekhar Bandopadhyay, op. cit., p. 28.

[138] Vidyasagar reprinted this *vyavastha* in the second edition of his initial widow-remarriage tract (1857), at the same time pointing to its subsequent repudiation by most of the signatories as a crass instance of opportunism. Haldar, *Vidyasagar Rachanabali*, vol. II, pp. 15–19. Chandicharan Bandopadhyay, op. cit., pp. 224–5, lists a number of earlier attempts to get widow marriage accepted.

be introduced or not."[139] The shastric passages are therefore always translated, and the discussion, though inevitably complicated, is conveyed through a prose far simpler than what had been current in scholarly discussion in Bengali before Vidyasagar. And textual exegesis, ever so often, is interrupted by passages marked by deep compassion for suffering womankind, anger, and a profound sense of male guilt. The best known of these is of course the eloquent condemnation of *deshachar* at the close of the second *Bidhaba-bibaha* tract, highlighting (in that order) the sufferings of widows and the flood of immorality and abortion which is caused by male cruelty sanctioned by that custom. As in the *Balya-bibaha* pamphlet, an implicitly positive recognition of the naturalness of physical, sexual needs underpins Vidyasagar's polemic: "You think that with the death of the husband, the woman's body becomes like a stone . . ." The tract ends with the famous lines:

> Let not the unfortunate weaker sex [*abala*] be born in a country where the men have no pity, no dharma, no sense of right and wrong, no ability to discriminate between beneficial and harmful, where preservation of what has been customary is considered the only duty, the only dharma . . . By what sin do women come to be born in Bharatvarsha at all?[140]

There are other, less-known passages, too, that outstrip the limits of shastric interpretation. Space permits only one more reference. The first *Bahubibaha* pamphlet begins with the general proposition that women everywhere are subordinated to men, because "they are physically weaker, and because social rules are so bad" – "But in no country are the conditions of women so bad as in our unfortunate land, due to the excessive barbarism, selfishness, and thoughtlessness of men." And the long lists of Kulin men with many wives that Vidyasagar goes on to offer, giving precise names and locations, are interspersed with an angry sarcasm: "The younger [of two Kulin sisters] has a husband aged 25–26. He has not so far managed to marry more than 32 times."[141]

[139] Ibid., p. 21.
[140] Haldar, ed., op. cit., pp. 164–5.
[141] Ibid., pp. 171, 218–19.

The more purely textual sections of the widow-marriage and anti-polygamy tracts are unlikely to attract many readers today: a pity, for they have a brilliance of their own. Vidyasagar displayed here a mastery over text and interpretive logic that was able to subvert, or appropriate for his own purposes, a number of standard orthodox arguments. The example of "Kali-varjya" is particularly relevant for us, for once again we see Vidyasagar come close to the trope of Kaliyuga, and then move off in a completely different direction. Kali-varjya had been the method by which ancient texts had been modified or pruned, almost always in socially restrictive ways, and when with reference to controls over women, by medieval Smriti experts like Raghunandan.[142] Vidyasagar appropriated the same scholastic tool to prise open a textual space for widow marriage. The lynchpin of Vidyasagar's argument, as is well known, is a passage in the *Parasara-samhita*, permitting the remarriage of women in five specific cases, one of which is the death of the husband.[143] But there were many contrary texts which had to be got out of the way. Vidyasagar eliminated the *puranas* among these through the argument that Parasara as a *dharmashastra* had to be given precedence over them, and then made maximum use of the claim, made in the *Parasara-samhita* itself, that

---

[142] Raghunandan had listed, among practices allowed by some *Dharma-sastras* but no longer permissible in the Kaliyuga, sea voyages, twice-born *jatis* marrying women of lower castes, going on too-distant pilgrimages, Brahmans using Shudra cooks – as well as a practice which had often been interpreted as widow marriage. The relevant passage was quoted, and glossed differently, by Vidyasagar in his first widow-marriage tract: Haldar, ed., op. cit., p. 28.

[143] "A woman is permitted by the shastras to remarry if her husband has disappeared, has died, been found impotent, has abandoned the world, or has been outcasted." Haldar, ed., op. cit., p. 26. Biographers like Chandicharan Bandopadhyay (op. cit., p. 237) present Vidyasagar's discovery of this text in dramatic terms, as coming in a revelation after many nights of sleepless study of the shastras. This seems a bit unlikely, as the Derozian journal *Bengal Spectator* had already referred to the passage in July 1842 while advocating widow remarriage. Indramitra, *Karunasagar Vidyasagar* (Calcutta, 1969, 1992), pp. 242–3. A Sanskrit scholar like Vidyasagar would surely have known his *Parasara* anyway: the real problem was how the texts contradicting this passage could be shown to be irrelevant.

Vidyasagar and Brahmanical Society 297

this was the text specifically applicable to Kaliyuga: the other texts, where they contradict it, are Kali-varjya. Vidyasagar's use of Parasara, and not, say, Manu, which had been cited by pandits to allow the remarriage of Shyamacharan Das' daughter, indicates his desire to open the space for widow remarriage to the maximum degree possible within the shastric mode of argument. (Manu, it will be recalled, had been read by the pandits to permit only the remarriage of Shudra widows who were also *akshata-yoni*, i.e. *virgo intacta*.) Vidyasagar's second tract specifically controverted the argument that remarriage is only permitted for low-caste widows, and he also quietly dropped all reference to virginity as a prerequisite.

The shastric rejection of polygamy seems to have been a more difficult task. With all his obvious enthusiasm for monogamous conjugality, Vidyasagar could not prove a complete case for strict monogamy from the Hindu scriptures. All that he could establish, mainly on the basis of Manu, was that the texts had laid down a number of specific conditions under which a man could take more than one wife – there was no unlimited and arbitrary right to multiple wives, as had become the practice among Kulins in Bengal.[144] The argument in the first tract against polygamy then shifts rather quickly to non-shastric grounds: a highly derogatory sketch of the history of Kulinism in Bengal, followed by statistics giving the names, ages, number of marriages, and locations of prominent polygamous men in Hooghly district.[145]

[144] The permitted grounds in Manu are nearly all highly gender-unequal: the husband can marry again, not only if his wife dies, but also if she is barren, bears daughters only, drinks, is unfaithful, extravagant, always ill, and even if she talks back at him. Contrary to today's widespread communal stereotype which somehow associates Islam uniquely with many wives, the scriptural-cum-customary grounds for monogamy in Hindu traditions have been quite remarkably weak, and only postcolonial legislation has made a partial change. See the passages cited in Vidyasagar's two *Bahubibaha* tracts (1870, 1873), reprinted in Haldar, ed., op. cit., pp. 173–5, 413–15.

[145] One hundred and thirty-three are listed for Hooghly district, with the number of marriages ranging from 80 to 5. A list follows for the single village of Janai, near Calcutta, with 64 names of men having from 2 to 10 wives. Ibid., pp. 201–12.

Vidyasagar's shastric arguments justifying widow remarriage and restricting polygamy provoked a flood of attempted refutations from pandits, mostly it seems from the Nadia-Jessore and 24 Parganas belt of solid Brahmanical orthodox scholarship, but joined in later by some erstwhile allies, notably Taranath Tarkavacaspati. Vidyasagar plunged with zest into the scholastic debate, making his sequels far longer than the initial tracts, and carrying on the battle right into his last days. Leafing through his voluminous replies to critics (the second tract against polygamy runs to nearly 200 closely printed pages in the edition I am using), one does at times get the impression of the reformer trapped in a scholastic morass, lost in an endless polemic of interest to fellow pandits alone, moving away in fact from that vision of widening, lay, public space that had animated him in 1850 and 1855. There is a sense of helpless anger, too, finding vent perhaps in bouts of violent, even vulgar, abuse that Vidyasagar sometimes published under pen-names, replying in kind to no doubt equal or greater scurrility on the other side.[146]

A more crucial problem lay in the built-in limits of a strategy of reform "from within", by shastric exegesis. A number of areas dear to Vidyasagar's heart, as revealed by the 1850 pamphlet (notably, child- and arranged marriages) had to be left out as clearly validated by the scriptures, and the scholastic method also had a tendency to create problems for other, subsequent, reform agendas. Rammohan may have unwittingly added to Vidyasagar's difficulties by hunting up and publicising texts praising austere widowhood in order to controvert those that insisted on sati. Vidyasagar sought to eliminate one kind of polygamy which Manu had permitted (marrying a woman of lower caste) by emphasising that in Kaliyuga inter-caste marriage was strictly prohibited.[147] His polemic against Kulinism also used the argument

---

[146] See for instance the passage in *Ratnapariksha* (1886) where Vidyasagar, writing under the alias of "Worthy Nephew", expresses regret that his earlier polemic has led to the death of "Uncle Vidyaratna" (Brojobilas Vidyaratna, the Nadia Smriti scholar who had been opposing him from 1855), and now he doesn't know whether this should be classed as Brahman-slaughter or cow-slaughter. Haldar, ed., op. cit., p. 512.

[147] Ibid., p. 176.

that it often led to delayed marriages for girls in the absence of suitably high-status bridegrooms – and this, Vidyasagar emphasised, clearly contradicted the shastric command that marriage had to be consummated before the first menses.[148] Perhaps it was this passage in his own earlier writing that contributed to Vidyasagar's surprising ambiguity on the Age of Consent issue, when his opinion was officially asked for shortly before his death.[149] And finally, as Bankimchandra acutely pointed out in 1873 in a critique of Vidyasagar's demand for a law against polygamy, scriptural arguments were in a sense redundant, as Hindus guided themselves far more by custom, and texts at times prescribed rules which it would be quite impossible to implement strictly.[150]

We have been looking at Vidyasagar's reform initiatives so far in terms of texts and polemics. But this can be no more than a partial view, for with all its obvious limitations the issue of widow marriage did become for a time something like a movement, not confined to

---

[148] Ibid., p. 188.

[149] Vidyasagar found it impossible to support the bill in its existing form, as he thought fixing the minimum age of consent at twelve could go against the *garbhadan* rite immediately after menses. His alternative suggestion was to make consummation before first menses a penal offence, irrespective of age. As girls can menstruate very early, this would not have given protection against physical and emotional injury in many cases. Subolchandra Mitra, who enthusiastically gives long extracts from this note of 16 February 1891, rejects however a widespread opinion that it represented a kind of recantation of earlier attitudes: for two months before his death Vidyasagar warmly welcomed the marriage of the Brahmo activist Durgamohan Das (who had earlier tried to get his own widowed stepmother remarried) with a widow with several children: Mitra, op. cit., p. 652–5.

[150] Bankim, however, used this potentially radical argument to reject Vidyasagar's demand for an anti-polygamy law, which he thought to be unnecessary. A passage in his article was quite prophetic in the way it anticipated what later became, and remains, a recurrent argument: it was unfair to pass a law curtailing Hindu (male) rights unless a similar restriction was imposed on Muslims too. *Bahubibaha (Bangadarshan*, 1280/1873), reprinted in Jogeshchandra Bagal, ed., *Bankim Rachanabali*, vol. II (Calcutta, 1954, 1969), pp. 314–19.

pandits or even always only to highly literate people. Vidyasagar, as is well known, did not stop with getting widow marriage legalised. From November 1856 onwards he went to enormous trouble, expenditure, and sometimes real physical danger to organise widow marriages, and by 1867 had personally arranged about sixty of them.[151] Most of the big names, the rajas and zamindars who had joined him in petitioning the government for the law, quickly backed out, often defaulting on earlier commitments of financial help. He did continue to get enthusiastic and active support from a number of young men, most of them Brahmos, through the late 1850s and 1860s and beyond, and much of the information we do have about specific widow marriage cases in fact comes from Brahmo biographies and histories.[152] During and just after the campaign for legalisation of widow remarriage, interest and excitement was high enough to generate a large number of poems and songs, some ridiculing the move, others hailing it, and even "cultivators, street-porters, cab-men and other lower-class people indulged in" them.[153] The best known of the verses is of course the one wishing long life to Vidyasagar, which appeared on the borders of some saris woven at Santipur. (As weavers have been a low-status group in caste society, this in itself is an indication of a reach beyond the *bhadralok*.) But more significant perhaps than such momentary excitement, yet peculiarly difficult to recuperate, are the long-term personal experiences into which a movement like widow marriage necessarily translated itself. For widow marriage meant, above all, young men, and girls growing up into young women,

---

[151] Vidyasagar mentioned this figure in a letter published in *Hindoo Patriot*, 1 July 1867, in connection with a proposal that had been made to raise a public fund to help him repay the debts he had incurred while organising these marriages. He rejected the offer, but evidently felt it necessary to explain how so much had been spent.

[152] In his preface to the third edition (1863) of his first widow-marriage tract, Vidyasagar referred to the excitement and agitation generated in the Dacca region by his pamphlet, necessitating the reprint. Vidyasagar is not known to have many contacts in East Bengal, but the Brahmo movement acquired some of its principal bases in the areas of *bhadralok* concentration there, like Bikrampur, Barisal, and parts of Mymensingh and Sylhet.

[153] Subolchandra Mitra, op. cit., p. 279.

Vidyasagar and Brahmanical Society

entering into a domesticity that flouted traditions, in the face of an enormous amount of everyday petty slander, persecution, ostracism.

Here our sources tend to fail us, for nearly all accounts stop with the first few highly publicised marriages in Calcutta, followed by some discussion of Vidyasagar as lonely, tragic hero. The flood of anecdotes, so voluminous on philanthropy, also narrows down quite suddenly. Indramitra's *Karunasagar Vidyasagar*, which brings together the largest number of anecdotes, is a collection of 737 pages: only sixty-two of them deal with widow marriage.

We can get a few stray and momentary glimpses, however, of developments that should have called into question a number of very well-established assumptions but that have been almost entirely ignored. Vidyasagar has usually been seen as a reformer of urban, educated *bhadralok* society whose work had Calcutta as its focus. Yet the *Tattvabodhini Patrika* of Bhadra (August–September) 1858 contrasted the five widow marriages that had been achieved in Calcutta over the twenty months since the wedding of Srishchandra Vidyaratna in November 1856 with the seven in just two months in Hooghly villages (or very small towns) around Birsingha, beginning in June 1858. It mentioned Ramjibanpur, Khirpai, Chandrakona, Basuli; there were two more at Chandrakona next month, and the first widow marriage in Vidyasagar's home village in July 1862. By August 1862 *Somprakash* could report some twenty to twenty-two marriages in three years in this really small corner of Hooghly district, where Vidyasagar clearly had established some kind of a rural base.[154] Widow marriage, further, was not all an entirely high-caste matter: thus Sambhuchandra Vidyaratna describes the "20–25" marriages that took place during 1864–5 as involving "Brahmans, Kayasthas, Tantubay (weavers), Vaidyas, Telis, etc."[155]

---

[154] Indramitra, op. cit., p. 292. Sambhuchandra Vidyaratna mentions "nearly fifteen" widow remarriages organised in Jehanabad villages like Ramjibanpur, Chandrakona, Sola, Srinagar, Kalikapur, and Khirpai in Asar–Sravana 1265 (June–July 1858). Numerous such marriages, he states, took place in this area down to 1865. Sambhuchandra Vidyaratna, op. cit., p. 104.

[155] Ibid., p. 116.

Vidyasagar's letter in *Hindoo Patriot* of July 1867 gives some hints about how the movement had been organised in the villages – as well as the kind of problems it was facing. Explaining why widow marriage had proved so expensive, Vidyasagar stated that apart from the heavy sums he had spent on the first wedding to establish its respectability, "*dals* or parties" were being "maintained in several villages in the Mufassil", and anyone "acquainted with the constitution of Hindoo society" would know that this was an expensive proposition "even ordinarily". But this was not an ordinary situation: many cases had been brought against "the promoters of the movement in the Mufassil", and sometimes physical force was also being deployed. All this was demanding heavy litigation expenses.

Most remarkable of all, illuminating in concrete detail one instance of what Vidyasagar described in general terms in his letter, are the notes he had kept (in English) among his papers about a series of incidents in Kumarganj village, adjoining Birsingha. Long extracts from these are tucked away in a corner of Subolchandra's biography, but seem to have somehow gone unnoticed by later scholars.[156] The party at Kumarganj supporting widow marriage had been excluded from the ceremonies in the village Siva temple at the time of "Churrukpooja", at the end of the Bengali year. When they tried to enter the temple to offer puja separately, they "were beaten back with great violence", and local police officials at first refused to record their complaints. Worse was to come, for then the "Zamindar of the village Baboo Shib Narain Roy" of Jurul began "oppressing with impunity those of the Royors of his Talook Comergunj who belong to the widow marriage party." Shib Narayan sent *durwans* to forcibly round up the

---

[156] Subolchandra Mitra, op. cit., pp. 511–16. There is a passing reference to the Kumarganj developments also in Biharilal Sarkar, op. cit., p. 282, From Vidyasagar's autobiographical fragment, we learn that Kumarganj was the weekly marketplace (*haat*) for Birsingha, located in Chandrakona police station, Jehanabad (Arambagh) subdivision. There is no indication of date, but it must have been before 1869, when Vidyasagar left Birsingha permanently. Subolchandra places the extracts just after his account of Vidyasagar's relief work during the 1866 famine, and a date, *c.* 1867, seems indicated also by the reference in general terms to similar developments in the letter of 1 July 1867.

pro-reformers, who were dragged to his presence and "dismissed with 10 strokes of shoes and a fine of Rs 10 each . . . Several of them have left the village with their respective families." The terror had a wider impact: "The news having reached the inhabitants of pergonnas Burda and Chandrakona, those who are willing to marry their sons and daughters have fallen back, through fear of consequences." Further, the zamindar was clearly being backed by not only subordinate police officials but the deputy magistrate of Jehanabad: the local state apparatus, in other words. Numerous complaints to the latter, including several lodged by Vidyasagar himself, had had no result. The deputy magistrate passed orders against continuation of the acts of oppression, but Vidyasagar had learnt from a friendly police *amla* that "the Khan Bahadur" had told his subordinates to ignore these, render no help to the widow marriage party, but "endeavour to give them trouble if possible . . . It is notorious that Baboo Shib Narain Roy often calls on the Deputy Magistrate at an advanced hour of the night." The net result was that "the party at Coomergunge" which had "consisted of about 60 families" was reduced to four or five. Vidyasagar concluded his notes in a mood of complete despair. As "those who joined the cause at my solicitation and are suffering from their act" are not being relieved and their oppressors are going unpunished, "I must leave the world, for what is the good of my remaining in it when there is no chance of success of the cause. I have resolved to devote my existence to it and if it fails, life would have no charm to me and existence would be useless."

There is a little bit of data also in Vidyasagar's notes about the social composition of the two parties in the Kumarganj region. The deputy magistrate would of course be high caste, and the zamindar probably also so. Some names are given of Vidyasagar's "Royot" supporters: Damoo, Sriharee, Nilcomal, Gopal, and a "sreenibas Doss". The one surname, as well as its absence in the other cases, suggests a subordinate, probably lower-caste status. But the peasants are clearly divided, for Vidyasagar's supporters at one point get beaten up by the "Goallas [Sadgops] of the opposite Party". An anthropological study of Birsingha in the 1950s located the Sadgops as an upwardly mobile *jati*, dominant in the neighbouring villages and becoming so in Vidyasagar's home village, where the other major groups were Brahmans and Bagdis.[157] One is tempted to speculate about a link between the "Goalla" hostility to widow marriage and possible sanskritising aspirations at work already in the 1860s, but of course this is no more than guesswork.

The Kumarganj affair certainly raises some questions regarding the common stereotype about nineteenth-century social reform being an affair of the English-educated high *bhadralok* alone, generally backed by the foreign rulers and confined to issues which did not affect the rural masses. Despite Vidyasagar's contacts with leading British officials, an informal alliance between the state machinery at the local level and landlord power evidently frustrated all his initiatives in an area where he would have been most influential.[158] The implicit caste dimensions are equally interesting. In an important article some years ago, Lucy Carroll pointed out that for lower castes already practising widow marriage, Act XV of 1856 could have been unwittingly retrogressive, and indeed in some ways may have represented a paradoxical extension of Brahmanical norms. It deprived widows who married of all succession rights to the property of the deceased husband, lower-caste customs having been more liberal in that respect at times.[159] But, at least in Bengal where Brahmanical norms had penetrated fairly deep into lower-caste society, it is dangerous to associate the "popular" with any unqualified realm of freedom from upper-caste taboos and restrictions. The Kumarganj data seem rather to indicate that the ambiguities and divisions on reform issues

---

[157] The study, made incidentally by a descendant of Vidyasagar, found the village Siva temple controlled by a Brahman family, surnamed Ray (a relation of Shib Narayan Roy, perhaps), who had land granted by the Maharaja of Burdwan. Village religious festivals were still the foci of social conflict. Gouranga Chattopadhyay, *Ranjana: A Village in West Bengal* (Calcutta, 1964).

[158] There seems to have been a brief spell earlier where the local authority at Jehanabad had been helpful. Interestingly, the deputy magistrate who Sambhuchandra remembers as helping Vidyasagar then was the well-known Muslim intellectual Abdul Latif. Sambhuchandra Vidyaratna, op. cit., p. 104.

[159] Lucy Carroll, "Law, Custom and Statutory Social Reform: The Hindu Widow Remarriage Act of 1856", in J. Krishnamurty, ed., *Women in Colonial India* (Delhi: Oxford University Press, 1999).

could have their counterparts at other social levels, too, with some of the upwardly mobile seeking to "sanskritise" themselves by imposing greater controls on women, while at the same time the problems and misery caused by the widow marriage ban could also stimulate quite contrary tendencies. In 1922, a big Namasudra conference broke up partly through a bitter controversy as to whether widow marriage should be prohibited or encouraged, and during the mid 1920s Digindranarayan Bhattacharya, the rebel Brahman closely identified with lower-caste movements, revived and indeed extended Vidyasagar's programme by campaigning against the practice of widows being made to go without water on *ekadosi*.[160]

Vidyasagar had sought respectability for widow marriage by making their forms as conventional as possible, and in his letter of July 1867 claimed to have spent no less than Rs 10,000 on the marriage of Srishchandra, giving massive presents to pandits, *ghataks*, and Kulins. The reference to go-betweens confirms the obvious: these were presumably all arranged marriages, independent of the bride's consent. Yet, despite this strategic emphasis on conventionality, something entirely unconventional was happening, with implications that could at times go a bit beyond the norms set by the founder of the movement. In "normal" marriages, the child or very young girl was doing what every rule and custom of her society told her to do: in widow marriage she, along with the man she was marrying, was engaged in a violation of norms which no amount of apparent conformity could really disguise. And though the emphasis was always on getting child widows remarried, neither Vidyasagar's arguments nor the law itself made any mention of age or virginity being a condition. In practice, widows marrying again would have been likely to be of somewhat maturer age than first-time child brides. It is unlikely that a socially dangerous second marriage could have been imposed on them.

Some of the verses composed during the height of the agitation do convey a real sense of rebellion: mostly in ridicule and outrage,

---

[160] Sekhar Bandopadhyay, "Social Mobility in Bengal in the late-19th–early-20th century" (unpublished thesis, Calcutta University, 1985), p. 480; Digindranarayan Bhattacharya, *Bidhabar Nirjala Ekadosi* (Serajgunj, 1923, 1926).

but just occasionally in what seems to be celebration. Take some of the lines of the song said to have been inscribed on Santipur saris, of which only the first is commonly remembered. "O when will that day dawn, when the law will be proclaimed/ Orders will be passed in every district and region/ Widow marriages will come in a rush/ We will live happily, with husbands of our own choice/ When will the day come, when the sufferings of widows will end . . ."[161]

That, of course, was optimistic imagination, not reality: but an autobiography by a little-known Brahmo from Bikrampur, Gurucharan Mahalanobis (1833–1916), does reveal an instance of woman's agency. Gurucharan, unusual among Brahmos in never having formal English education, married a widow in 1862. Remarkably, as described in detail by Gurucharan, he had known her for some time before the marriage, and it was she who had taken the initiative. Indeed, there is a hint of a bit of romantic competition over the young man between her and another young girl who had also lost her husband. Vidyasagar, Gurucharan reports, was quite pleased when told of these unusual happpenings, and commented that an intelligent person should never agree to marry someone s/he had never seen. He did not come to the wedding – for Gurucharan, as a fervent young Brahmo who had discarded his sacred thread, refused to follow the Hindu forms – but remained close to the Mahalanobis family.[162]

The limits of Vidyasagar's ideas and reform activities still remain clear, particularly from today's feminist perspectives. The problems did not consist only in the kind of inconsistencies that we have seen emerging from his reform-through-texts strategy. The fundamental impulse, as in all nineteenth-century male *stri-swadhinata* (women's freedom – "freeing women" would perhaps convey the implicit meaning better) initiatives, was "protectionist" rather than egalitarian.[163] It sought through legal reform to improve the lot of the

---

[161] The full text of this song is given in Subolchandra Mitra, op. cit., pp. 279–80.

[162] Gurucharan Mahalanobis, "Atmakatha", manuscript, *c.* 1913, ed. Nirmalkumari Mahalanobis (Calcutta, 1974), pp. 46–53.

[163] See the useful theoretical distinctions drawn in Ratna Kapur and Brenda Crossman, op. cit., pp. 22–33.

abala (weak), a term much in use in reformist discourses. Paternalist concern certainly differed from conventional patriarchal discipline, but it could slide towards ideologies of control. Vidyasagar was not entirely free, perhaps, from a certain fear of the "over-independent" woman going beyond the bounds of (reformed and humanised) conjugality. All his tracts do have a moralising strand, though to be sure usually in a minor key, which portrayed theoretically austere widowhood as in practice a realm of sexual licence. (A licence, it should be added immediately, that basically men enjoyed at the expense of widows, who would be left to bear the costs in terms of illicit abortion, infanticide, and scandal: Vidyasagar's moralism did also have a point.) Such fears probably help to explain the most obvious limit, even contradiction, in Vidyasagar's programme. It made no attempt at all (unlike Digindranarayan later on) to improve the lot of the widow who could not, or maybe did not wish to, marry again. When his own daughter returned home as a widow, Vidyasagar is said to have imposed the same austerities on himself for some time. A moving tale, within limits: there is no report that Vidyasagar ever asked her to defy the traditional rules, the inhumanities of which had been a major impulse behind his entire reform drive. There are also a few indications that by the late 1860s and 1870s an increasingly frustrated and cynical Vidyasagar was falling behind some of the younger Brahmos in the extent to which he was prepared to endorse radical patterns of behaviour. He rejected Miss Carpenter's proposal for starting a normal school to train women teachers on the grounds that "respectable Hindus" would not allow "their grown-up female relatives to follow the profession of tuition", while "unprotected and helpless widows", whose services might be available, might not be "morally . . . fit agents for educational purposes . . ."[164]

A last, very personal, inconsistency: there are many instances of husbands educating their wives in the nineteenth century, but Dinamoyee Devi, wife of the great educator and champion of

---

[164] Vidyasagar to William Grey, 1 October 1867, reprinted in Subolchandra Mitra, op. cit., p. 466.

companionate conjugality, seems to have remained virtually illiterate, spending much of her time looking after Vidyasagar's parents in Birsingha.

The failure, indeed absence of effort, to modify the conditions of most married women, as well as of widows who did not remarry, may help us to understand the somewhat paradoxical appeal of a figure like Ramakrishna by the closing decades of the century. The saint's conversations were full of references to the dangers flowing from womankind: yet middle-aged and elderly wives and widows flocked to Dakshineswar. Like the men caught in the toils of *chakri*, they sought solace from the burdens of household routine in the message of *grihastha bhakti*, which promised a certain distancing through the cultivation of an inner devotional space, even while remaining immersed outwardly in the mundane everyday. Similarly, the withering of hopes in the transformative potential of education, as pressures on the middle class increased, may have had something to do with the resonance of Ramakrishna's denigration of formal learning, precisely among the educated.[165]

The biggest limit of all, so far as prospects of change in gender relations were concerned, was of course the absence, as yet, of autonomous, organised women's initiatives. Domestic domination and injustice – located "within the precincts of their own respective domiciles", to use again Maheshchandra Deb's clumsy but expressive phrase, has always been peculiarly difficult to organise against, which is one reason why self-conscious feminist movements and even perceptions have been fairly rare in history. A few of the preconditions for them did start to emerge in Vidyasagar's time, however, sometimes as distant consequences of his work.

The spread of women's education, combined with the questioning of norms that Vidyasagar had provoked, led on towards the beginnings of a female literary public sphere in the decade that immediately followed the peak of his educational and reform initiatives. Three instances will have to suffice. The *Bamabodhini Patrika* was founded in 1863, run by reformist Brahmo men but greatly stimulating writings

---

[165] See Sarkar, *Writing Social History*, chapter 8.

by women.[166] The same year saw the publication of Kailasbashini Devi's *Hindu Mahilaganer Heenabastha*. Kailasbashini had initially become literate at the behest of her husband, but her learning process still included an element of subversion, for it had to be kept a secret from her parents-in-law. Its results, as her husband confessed in his preface to the book, had surprised him, for the text by this neo-literate woman had needed no correction from her erstwhile teacher. In the sheer range of its survey of women's disabilities *Hindu Mahilaganer Heenabastha* rivals Vidyasagar's polemic against child marriage, for it includes within its sweep unequal treatment from childhood onwards, keeping girls uneducated and immersed in female rituals (*vratas*) which Kailasbashini considered meaningless, marrying them off in childhood into loveless conjugality, and exposing them to the miseries of Kulin polygamy. The accounts of married life and austere widowhood are especially poignant: child-brides torn from parental homes live as if in a prison, she says, caged like birds and animals. The agony of widows observing *ekadosi* provoked Kailasbashini to remark that only God can understand the wonders of the Hindu religion.[167] And then in 1868 there was Rashsundari Devi's *Amar Jivan*, the product of the lone, heroic efforts of an obscure, otherwise entirely conventional housewife, who had learnt her letters in fear and secrecy and gone on to publish the first "autobiography" in the Bengali language.[168]

Vidyasagar failed, insofar as the number of widows daring to remarry has remained almost negligible, and much social obloquy persists even today. But the legal reform he was able to push through, and even more the debates he provoked, did unsettle grossly unjust gender norms that had been part of a doxa of common sense, immune from rational debate and questioning. That, maybe, is where reformist

---

[166] Bharati Ray is editing a valuable collection of extracts from this journal: Ray, ed., *Sekaler Narishiksha: Bamabodhini Patrika, 1270–1329/1863–1922* (Calcutta, 1994).

[167] Kailasbashini Devi, *Hindu Mahilaganer Heenabastha* (Calcutta: Gupta Press, 1863).

[168] For Rashsundari, see Tanika Sarkar, "A Book of Her Own, A Life of Her Own: Autobiography of a Nineteenth-Century Woman", *History Workshop Journal*, 36, 1993.

efforts to change laws can help, even when they remain largely unimplemented, or much misapplied.

There is also a paradoxical way in which the extent of resistance to widow remarriage itself bears witness to the significance and radical implications of Vidyasagar's crusade. Whatever the degree of their continued prevalence in practice, child marriage and polygamy are no longer considered normative, but the widow who remarries still generally invites criticism or worse. Widow remarriage was, and remains, disturbing, because it had implications that went some distance beyond what is quite often assumed in feminist circles today to have been the outer limit of nineteenth-century male reformism: a notion of companionate marriage that in essence represented yet another form of control over feminine sexuality. Vidyasagar's campaign, and the law it was able to push through, implicitly challenged the basic Hindu notion of the pure woman as *ardhangini*, half her husband's body, even after the latter's death (and hence entitled to a share in his property as long as she did not remarry), who is permitted to have sex in the entire course of her life with one male partner, her husband, alone. (Here lay also the core of the double standard in Hindu conjugality, for there was no corresponding restraint on men.) The subversion implied in Vidyasagar's work was that he achieved the legalisation of the remarriage, not of child-widows or virgins alone, but of adult women who would have had full-fledged sexual relations with their husbands, and may have borne children. The "Great Unchastity Case" of 1873 drove the point home more sharply. It decided, going against general Hindu public opinion, that a widow who had not remarried but was proved to have committed "adultery" subsequently (i.e. been "unfaithful" to her deceased husband after his death) would retain her share of her husband's property. Vidyasagar, somewhat hesitantly, supported the majority judgment: "I do not want to condone immorality. But how can property, once inherited, be taken away again?"[169] Bourgeois property rights clearly triumphed in his mind in this case over customary norms of chastity.[170] It is also

---

[169] Biharilal Sarkar, op. cit., p. 332.
[170] My assessment of the significance of widow marriage has been greatly

noteworthy that Vidyasagar's tracts on marriage sedulously avoided the standard language of describing the husband as the supreme, near-divine preceptor of the wife. It emphasised repeatedly, rather, the dimension of mutuality, the meeting of adult minds and bodies. Vidyasagar obviously remained far from any questioning of the limits of ideal monogamous marriage, but he was still an uncompromising critic of double standards, and the weight he was prepared to give to theoretical equality of rights remains quite remarkable.[171]

The protectionist compassion of Vidyasagar was recuperable into socially innocuous philanthropy, and that quickly became, and remains, the dominant way of representing him. But his was a compassion associated above all with anger, and a deep sense of male guilt. It is this which distinguishes his widow-marriage campaign from apparently similar later moves, notably under Arya Samaj auspices, where there was a shift in emphasis to the need for breeding faster and better for religious community and/or country. Anger and guilt, too, have been often diffused or displaced on to external targets, in the heyday of anti-colonial nationalism, but also, in much more recent times, through writings where Western "post-Enlightenment modernity" becomes the primary polemical target.

We cannot afford to lose touch with Vidyasagar's anger and guilt, directed primarily towards gender relations in his own society. For we live in times when wives are regularly burnt for dowry, a lower-caste woman activist is raped for campaigning against child marriage, and the murderers of Roop Kanwar, burnt as sati at Deorala in 1987, are acquitted in court.

---

helped by Tanika Sarkar, "Talking about Scandals: Religion, Law and Love in Late Nineteenth Century Bengal", *Studies in History*, 13(i), 1997.

[171] The second widow-remarriage tract, for instance, did some skilful bending of the shastras to reach the conclusion that "carefully studied, the makers of the shastras may be seen to have wanted the same rules for men as for women." Haldar, op. cit., vol. 11, p. 156.

8

The Kalki-Avatar of Bikrampur
A Village Scandal in Early-Twentieth-Century Bengal

Browsing through the rich collection of Bengali tracts in the National Library of Calcutta, I came across an intriguing title: *Kalki-avatarer Mokaddama Bikrampure Bhishan Vyabhichari!* (Dacca: Chaitra 1311; March–April 1905). This translates as Trial of the Kalki-avatar – Terrible Immoralities in Bikrampur! The pamphlet, published by Madhusudan Chaudhuri on behalf of the weekly *Dacca Prakash*, described through seventy-five pages of extracts from court proceedings the remarkable events in Doyhata village, Munshigunj subdivision, Dacca district, on 23 Agrahayan 1311 (mid December 1904). Lalmohan Majumdar, an upper-caste householder of Doyhata, had invited into his house a poor Brahmin sadhu hailing from a village in the adjoining Madaripur subdivision of Faridpur district.[1] This Kalachand sadhu occasionally claimed to be the Kalki-avatar, the tenth incarnation of Vishnu, with whose coming Koli-yuga would end and the world set right side up again. Two untouchable disciples, the Chandal Prasanna and Ananda Bhuinmali,

---

While finalising this essay I have benefited greatly from the criticism and comments of Pradip Dutta, Tanika Sarkar, Dipesh Chakrabarty, and Ranajit Guha. I am grateful also to the colleagues in the Subaltern Studies editorial board present at the Delhi discussion in January 1988.

[1] "Majumdar" is usually a Brahmin or a Kayastha surname; that the Doyhata Majumdars were upper caste is confirmed by the desecration of the sacred thread of a relative of theirs, Upendrachandra Ghoshal (normally a Brahmin title).

followed Kalachand into the Majumdar house. Under circumstances for which several different explanations were given later, Prasanna killed Ananda on the afternoon of 23 Agrahayan, in the presence and with the probable complicity of Kalachand and Lalmohan. Somehow Ananda had been identified with Yama, the god of death; with his murder, therefore, the new era had begun. In a mood of apocalyptic frenzy, the Chandal now went around setting fire to neighbouring houses. He had been calling Lalmohan "Dronacharya", and himself, at times, "Hanuman"; what he was doing now, he declared, was burning "Lanka". Nudity was a second motif: the women of the Majumdar family were made to strip, touch a (presumably purifying) fire, and then pay obeisance to Kalachand. Rajlakshmi, Lalmohan's wife, had her pubic hair burnt, a *kalki* (pipe for smoking ganja) was thrust into her vagina, and Prasanna made her kick her husband three times on the forehead. Some of the men were also insulted and stripped, and one had his sacred thread burnt. All this went on for much of the evening and night. Prasanna was eventually overpowered by some neighbours a little before dawn the next day. At the trial before the Dacca sessions court in March 1905, the Indian jury acquitted Lalmohan and Kalachand, and found Prasanna guilty of culpable homicide, not murder. The British judge disagreed, there was an appeal to the Calcutta high court, and in June 1905 much stiffer sentences were passed against all the three accused.

The pamphlet (henceforth KM) contains the depositions of the three accused before the honorary magistrate of Srinagar and the Munshigunj deputy magistrate, the evidence of twenty-two witnesses, and the jury recommendations of the Dacca sessions trial of 9–16 March 1905. I was able to cross-check and get a few additional details from the Calcutta daily *Bengalee*, while the much scantier reporting about Doyhata in the *Amrita Bazar Patrika* includes what appears to be the full text of the Calcutta high court judgment of 28 June 1905.[2]

Calcutta's reporting of the affair was on the whole cursory and more than a little inhibited: certainly the matter never reached the

---

[2] *Bengalee*, 14–19 March 1905; *Amrita Bazar Patrika*, 15 March and 29 June 1905.

front-page headlines. I could find no reference at all in the *Report on Native Papers* (the weekly official summary of the Indian press). A local history of Bikrampur published in 1909 had only one brief shocked sentence about the case: "The scandalous story of the 'Kalkiavatar' of Doyhata has ruined the good reputation of a civilised place like Bikrampur."[3]

Somehow the incident had failed to attain the status of a scandal: more precisely, it quickly became the kind of scandal that one knows but does not talk about, as distinct from those incessantly recalled and retold, for purposes of reform or titillation.[4] This happened despite the build-up by the *Dacca Prakash*, and even though one could have expected the case to have had enough potential in terms of violence and salaciousness. And if it did not make the grade into contemporary *bhadralok* discourse, the chances of it entering conventional historical narratives were even slimmer. Doyhata raised no major point of legal significance; the local *bhadralok* historian Jogendranath Gupta was highly embarrassed by it; and the case obviously could find no place at all in the rich patriotic memory of a Bikrampur which in 1904–5 was entering the era of Swadeshi upsurge and revolutionary terrorism.[5] The Chandals or Namasudras of East Bengal in the late-nineteenth and early-twentieth centuries were engaged in a series of movements for education, respectability, and political status: the story of Prasanna could hardly contribute to the "sanskritising" upward mobility of a despised caste. Even radical historians of peasant or subaltern protest are likely to have had serious difficulties with a man whose plebeian fury found vent mainly against helpless women and a person of even lower social status than himself.

And yet historians today are getting interested precisely in such fragments of the past, "unimportant" events of no obvious consequence

---

[3] Jogendranath Gupta, *Bikrampurer Itihas* (Calcutta, 1316/1909), p. 373.

[4] Jogendranath clearly took it for granted that his single cryptic reference would make sense for his readers.

[5] In the course of my work in the 1960s on the Swadeshi movement in Bengal, I went through the *Bengalee*, *Amrita Bazar Patrika*, and a large number of contemporary pamphlets. I failed to notice the Doyhata case then: it did not engage the attention of a historian busy at the time with reconstructing the narrative of *bhadralok* nationalism.

which stick out and refuse to fit into any of the established patterns of historical reconstruction – akin, perhaps, to the Freudian slips of psychoanalysis and central to much social-anthropological work for quite some time. They afford oblique entry points into social history and can throw light upon dimensions obscured by dominant – all too often teleological – analytical frameworks.[6] Doyhata interested me, first, as a study in the problems of constructing historical narrative. Historians are becoming increasingly aware of the problematic nature of even the most conventionally "authentic sources", that is to say documents which are contemporary, which do not contradict each other, and whose bias can be easily discovered and discounted. "Sources" are always "texts", it has been increasingly realised, and no text is "innocent". It always embodies power relations and contains implicit principles or strategies of construction and deployment. Yet total relativism, a complete absorption in the enchantments of a kind of epistemological hall of mirrors, is hardly viable either for the discipline of history. The craft does seem to require the construction of narratives of the "as-if-true" kind, constructions which should remain open-ended and which are privileged only within the text the historian is engaged in composing at that moment.[7]

The information about Doyhata is, in conventional terms, both unusually detailed and fairly "reliable". It is true that it comes through the double filter of judicial proceedings as reported in the KM pamphlet and two Calcutta newspapers. I have failed to trace so far the original court records, and the issues of *Dacca Prakash* from which KM was collated also do not seem available. But there is a high degree of correspondence – even, given the difference of language, near-identity – between the pamphlet and the *Bengalee* account of

---

[6] See, for example, David W. Sabean, *Power in the Blood: Popular Culture and Village Discourse in Early Modern Germany* (Cambridge, 1984); Robert Darnton, *The Great Cat Massacre and Other Episodes in French Cultural History* (Penguin, 1984); and Ranajit Guha, "Chandra's Death", in Ranajit Guha, ed., *Subaltern Studies V* (Delhi, 1987).

[7] For valuable accounts of similar problems in contemporary anthropology, see George E. Marcus and Michael M. Fischer, *Anthropology as Cultural Critique: An Experimental Moment in the Human Sciences* (Chicago, 1986); and James Clifford and George E. Marcus, ed., *Writing Culture* (California, 1986).

the Dacca court proceedings. We may assume also that British justice here was trying to be reasonably "impartial": Doyhata had no political importance, and there was no need whatsoever for the prosecution to construct any "approver's testimony".[8] Prasanna in fact admitted straightaway his principal role in the series of actions construed by the prosecution as murder, arson, and "affront to feminine modesty", and even his otherwise surprising claims that Ananda had consented to his own murder was confirmed by several *bhadralok* witnesses. There was little dispute, then, about the basic "facts". The differences of opinion turned around the degree of complicity of Lalmohan and Kalachand, and as to whether the killing of Ananda was culpable homicide or murder.

Together with the very detailed account of the climactic events of 23 Agrahayan coming from some twenty witnesses, all this permitted the construction of a narrative of the "as if true" kind (see below section III). Yet my primary interest was never in the reconstruction of what may have really happened. The Rankean past "as it actually was" is both methodologically dubious and, in this study of an "unimportant" event, akin to sheer antiquarianism. My interest lay in what was remembered about it, what forgotten, and why. The witnesses at Dacca were recalling events of three months back, in the unfamiliar atmosphere of a criminal court; most of them were relatives or neighbours of Lalmohan. What they recalled now about the pattern and meaning of events which culminated on 23 Agrahayan must have been influenced by the totally unexpected denouement of that evening and night. The predominantly *bhadralok* witnesses, *bhadralok* jurymen and newspaper reporters, and British judges, would all have tacit assumptions colouring their memories and assessments. What we have, in other words, is a series of representations of Doyhata which do not, in the end, build up into a scandal, and which do not enter markedly into either *bhadralok* or British official discourse. What is excluded from discourse often throws considerable light

---

[8] For a detailed discussion of the ways in which colonial justice constructed approver's testimony in a case of overriding political importance, see Shahid Amin, "Approver's Testimony, Judicial Discourse: The Case of Chauri Chaura", in R. Guha, ed., *Subaltern Studies V*, op. cit.

on the assumptions underlying it, and this for me has been a principal source of interest in the entire affair. Why precisely the *bhadralok* were embarrassed by Doyhata is a question, we shall see, which has to be tackled at a variety of levels.

"Kalki-avatar" was the shorthand title given to the Doyhata affair by the *Dacca Prakash* pamphlet, Calcutta newspapers, and Jogendranath Gupta alike. Yet the Dacca evidence does not quite bear out this centrality. Several witnesses stated that they had been unaware of Kalachand's claim to be Kalki, and the Chandal who abruptly became the chief protagonist on 23 Agrahayan does not seem to have used the phrase. I found copious evidence about the importance of Koli-yuga and Kalki-avatar themes, however, not in the well-known high-*bhadralok* culture of the nineteenth century, but in what has been called the "low-life of literature":[9] all but forgotten tracts, stories, plays, and farces churned out by printing presses like those of Bat-tala in north Calcutta, as well as in some of the bazaar paintings of Kalighat. It became important for me to locate the social groups principally concerned in the late nineteenth century with producing and appropriating the kind of culture of which Koli-yuga seemed to be a major signifier. Tentatively, I found a distinction between "high" and "low" culture within the *bhadralok* more relevant here than a dichotomy of *bhadralok*/"popular" (or "present"), for it helped me to focus upon an intermediate world of poor rustic Brahmins as well as their city counterparts, the clerks –the world which produced not only Kalachand but also Ramakrishna.

The Koli-yuga theme itself goes back to the Mahabharata: what was interesting were the specific readings of it in colonial Bengal and, in particular, plays based upon it, at least one of which became part of the repertoire of a *jatra* company which toured the *mofussil* in the early years of the twentieth century. Nineteenth-century versions of Koli-yuga gave a crucial centrality to women: more precisely to two contrasting figures of women – the disorderly "modern" wife who dominates the husband and ill-treats the mother-in-law, and the

---

[9] I am borrowing this phrase from Robert Darnton, "The High Enlightenment and the Low-Life of Literature in Pre-Revolutionary France", *Past and Present*, no. 51, May 1971.

positive alternative of the pure mother or wife who helps to restore norms through a fascinating pattern of assertion-within-deference. The first emerges in some plays as a metaphor for sons neglecting the "mother"-land through enthralment to foreign ways; the second, by the 1920s, had become a standard figure in nationalist pulp literature.[10] The insubordinate Shudra, at least as prominent in earlier Koli-yuga texts as the women on top, is hardly ever mentioned in nineteenth-century versions; we do have, however, occasional plebeian figures contributing to the restoration of norms through a similar figure of deferential assertion. Quite unexpectedly, it appeared, I had stumbled upon one of the cultural roots of passive resistance or satyagraha – simultaneously mobilising and keeping under controls of deference peasants and women alike.

Doyhata now emerged as both related to as well as, in a more important sense, disjointed from this evolving pattern of feelings. Its significance lay precisely in its "irrelevance", its failure to enter dominant middle-class forms of discourse. What had happened that December night had been a conflict of meanings, of vastly different readings of a "common" Hindu religious tradition of Puranas and epics – for Prasanna's actions on 23 Agrahayan were all embedded in a kind of inverted appropriation of the motifs and values of brahminical culture. The *bhadralok* did not want to talk about Doyhata, for over it loomed the dark, terrifying yet fascinating, figure of the Chandal who, invited in by one of themselves, had for one night turned their world upside down.

II

Doyhata village adjoins the police station of Srinagar, which is sixteen miles west of the subdivisional headquarters of Munshigunj. Munshigunj, and the northern part of Madaripur subdivision of Faridpur from which it is divided by the Padma River, together make up the Bikrampur region, a classic heartland of the Bengali

---

[10] Tanika Sarkar, "Nationalist Iconography: Image of Women in 19th Century Bengali Literature", *Economic and Political Weekly*, xxii, 47, 21 November 1987.

Hindu *bhadralok*. The local historian Jogendranath Gupta in 1909 enumerated in loving detail its past and present achievements: this was the land of Ballal Sen, supposedly the founder of Bengali caste hierarchy and Kulinism, of Kedar Roy who had fought the Mughals, of Rajballabh in the eighteenth century. Bikrampur had been a centre of Sanskrit learning as reputed as Nabadwip, and it was the birthplace of a whole series of nineteenth- and early-twentieth-century *bhadralok* worthies.[11] Gupta claimed that virtually every Munshigunj village had its university graduates, and he was proud of the twenty-four High English schools in the subdivision. He made a special mention of the absence of big zamindaris in Munshigunj as a positive feature, conducive to broader development of the *madhyabitta* (middle class), and attributed it to certain administrative policies of the eighteenth-century nawabs.[12]

British representations of the Bikrampur *bhadralok* aimed at greater statistical precision, but were otherwise broadly similar. Officials were struck by the density of population of Munshigunj and Madaripur, extraordinary for an overwhelmingly rural tract.[13] They noted that Bikrampur was a land of small, highly fragmented zamindaris rather than big estates and/or multiple intermediate tenures, as in Mymensingh to the north and Bakhargunj to the south.[14] For the

[11] Ballal Sen is supposed to have had his capital in Rampal, six miles west of Munshigunj. The list of nineteenth-and early-twentieth-century luminaries given by Gupta include Rashbehari Mukhopadhyay, the campaigner against Kulin polygamy; the militant Brahmo Dwarkanath Ganguli; literary figures like the poet Gobindachandra Roy; Congress leaders like Lalmohan Ghosh and Chittaranjan Das; and the scientist Jagadishchandra Basu. Jogendranath Gupta, op. cit., *passim*.

[12] Ibid., p. 129.

[13] Munshigunj in 1901 had a density of 1654 per sq. mile, with 978 villages in an area of only 386 sq. miles. There was nothing classifiable as a town, for even the subdivisional headquarters had a population of only 964. Madaripur's statistics are similar: a density of 913, with a town of 17,463, and 1806 villages spread over 993 square miles. B.C. Allen, E.A. Gait, C.H. Allen, H.F. Howard, *Gazetteer of Bengal and North-East India* (n.d.; repr. Delhi, 1979), pp. 300, 341.

[14] Hunter noted these features of Dacca zamindari tenure in his *Statistical Account of Bengal*, vol. V (London, 1877; repr. Delhi, 1973), pp. 97, 118.

British, the achievements of Bikrampur *bhadralok* culture were less administratively relevant than the fact that Munshigunj subdivision alone supplied "nearly a third of the subordinate native officials in the Government offices of Bengal"[15] – a preponderance attributed to small estates, a heavy concentration of *bhadralok* castes, and a high level of English education.[16]

The Majumdars of Doyhata seem to have been gentlefolk similar to so many others in Bikrampur, quite unknown to the historical record but for that strange winter night of December 1904. Lalmohan referred in his testimony to a *praja* (tenant) of his, and a couple of witnesses described him as their *manib* (master, employer).[17] But the total helplessness of the Majumdars in face of the terror unleashed by just one man, Prasanna, indicates that they could only have been petty zamindars or *talukdars*: evidently they commanded no *lathials* (wielders of clubs) or *durwans* (guards).

Jogendranath Gupta's cryptic sentence about the Kalki-avatar of Doyhata is followed immediately by a comment deploring the absence of Bikrampur *bhadralok* menfolk from their homes for the greater part of the year due to the jobs they held outside the district. The *chotolok* (as well as, presumably, the women), he said, consequently live without *shashan* (order, discipline), and some of them become preachers of *andha dharma mat* (blind religious beliefs).[18] Certainly the Dacca court reports reveal the Majumdar household to have

---

Of the 7215 permanently settled zamindari estates in Dacca district in the early twentieth century, only 192 paid an annual revenue of more than 50 (roughly Rs 500), and there were seldom more than two middlemen between the zamindar and the raiyats. Faridpur had 5998 zamindari estates with only 5 paying revenue of more than Rs 10,000. Allen, *et al.*, op. cit., p. 342.

[15] Ibid., p. 311.

[16] Of the 988,000 (in round figures) classified as Hindus in Dacca district by the 1901 census, 66,000 were Brahmins, 86,000 Kayasths, and 11,000 Baidyas; 57,125 out of a population of 638,351 were literate in Munshigunj subdivision, as against a Dacca district literacy rate of 6.5 per cent. The district had 171 secondary and 1632 primary schools. Ibid., pp. 301, 309.

[17] KM, pp. 10, 67.

[18] Jogendranath Gupta, op. cit., p. 373.

been full of women. The family house had three *dalans* or wings, held by Lalmohan (father presumably deceased), Rajani, and Mathur (Lalmohan's father's younger brothers). Only two men of the immediate household appeared in the trial: Lalmohan himself, who practised medicine in the village with or without a proper degree, and the sixty-five-year-old Rajani.[19] Two other male relatives who lived in neighbouring houses figured among the witnesses: the seventeen-year-old Jitendramohan Majumdar (nicknamed Tona), a nephew of Lalmohan, and Lalmohan's cousin Upendrachandra Ghoshal, a zamindari employee. The women who gave evidence easily outnumbered the men: Lalmohan's wife Rajlakshmi; Rajani's wife Sashimukhi and daughter Jogmaya; Mathur's wife Sarala; and Barada, a sister of Rajani and Mathur. The other women directly involved were Lalmohan's sister-in-law Hemangini; Kalitara (an aunt of Lalmohan's by marriage); Kusumkumari (wife of Rajani's son Jasoda); Prabasini (widow of Rajani's deceased son Pramod); the mothers (unnamed) of Lalmohan and Tona; and Chapala, described as the wife of a *nafar* (bonded servant) of Rajani. All of them were stripped by Prasanna, or at least insulted in some way. Only the two daughters of Sarala, Sailo and Charubala, seem to have been spared. It was their illness, as we shall see, which in a way precipitated the crisis.

So far we have been talking about the *bhadralok* alone, but gentry cannot live or prosper without the labour of others. Bikrampur was also the land of a far larger number of subordinate groups. Actual cultivation would be the job of Muslim or lower-caste tenants or sharecroppers, and the gentry by the turn of the century were increasingly preferring produce-rent terms in the context of rising prices.[20]

The silence of Jogendranath Gupta is symptomatic here: no-one would guess from his book that Muslims constituted 51.1 per cent of the population of Munshigunj,[21] that Chandals (or Namasudras, as their upwardly mobile sections had started calling themselves) were

[19] "A small unqualified medical practitioner", was the Calcutta high court judgment's description of Lalmohan. *Amrita Bazar Patrika*, 29 June 1905.
[20] Partha Chatterjee, *Bengal 1920–1947: The Land Question* (Calcutta, 1984), pp. 50–2.
[21] Hunter, op. cit., p. 118, citing the 1872 census.

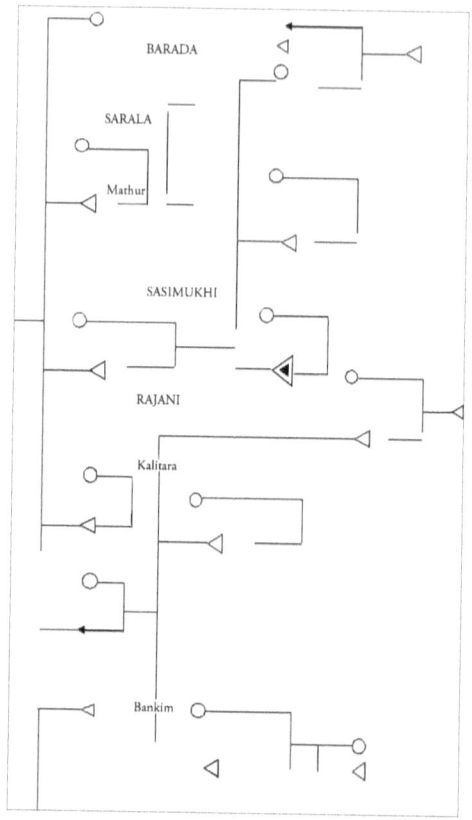

nearly a quarter of the Hindus of Dacca district,[22] and three-sevenths of the Hindus of Faridpur.[23] The *bhadralok* local history of Bikrampur was not about people like them.

[22] The demand for the new, more respectable name was gradually accepted by the British. Hunter (1877) used the term Chandal throughout. H.H. Risley, *Tribes and Castes of Bengal*, vol. I (Calcutta, 1891, repr. Calcutta, 1981) did the same, but added that the more successful Chandals preferred to call themselves Namasudras. Allen *et al.*, op. cit., speak only of the Namasudras, and the census of 1911 dropped the use of the term Chandal. Both Chandal and Namasudra were used in the Dacca case to describe Prasanna.

[23] The Chandals or Namasudras numbered 236,000 in Dacca District in 1901. In Faridpur the bulk of the Namasudra populace (245,000 in 1881)

British administrative and ethnographic accounts are more forthcoming about these lower depths. Hunter described Chandals in 1877 as "very low and despised . . . cultivators, grass-cutters, gardeners, boatmen and palanquin-bearers".[24] An upper crust of substantial peasants and traders, however, was emerging among them, particularly in the marshlands of south Faridpur and north-west Bakharganj (Gopalganj and Firozepur police stations), which Chandals had colonised and where they were overwhelmingly predominant. This became the centre of a Namasudra upthrust, beginning with the foundation of a new Vaishnava sect called Matua by the rich-peasant Biswas family of Orakandi village in Gopalganj. There were efforts at "sanskritisation" through the introduction of child-marriage and of the widow-remarriage taboo, as well as occasional refusals of service to the upper castes — as in Gopalganj and Muksudpur thanas in 1872–3. Schools were founded with missionary help, insistent claims made for the Namasudra title, and a struggle waged against *dhankarari* (fixed produce-rent) tenancies. Eventually, full-fledged caste organisations emerged, with a Namasudra Hitaishini Samiti, periodic conferences from 1908 onwards, and journals. The Biswas family of Orakandi remained the core of this developing movement.[25] As *bhadralok* patriotism gathered strength, the British exhibited a certain sympathy for such aspirations; concern within limits for the underdog in Indian society in any case fitted well with the self-image of the paternalist Raj. Risley's comment in 1891 reveals the early stage in the construction of a stereotype: the Chandal is "one of the most lovable of Bengalis . . . a merry, careless fellow, very patient and hard-working . . . a peaceful and exemplary subject of the English government."[26]

---

was concentrated in Madaripur subdivision and the marshy region to its south. Risley, op. cit., p. 189; Hunter, op. cit., p. 342.

[24] Hunter, op. cit., p. 50.

[25] Sekhar Bandopadhyay, *Caste and Politics in Eastern Bengal: The Namasudras and the Anti-Partition Agitation, 1905–1911* (Centre for S.E. Asian Studies, Calcutta University, 1981); Hunter, op. cit., p. 285; Risley, op. cit., p. 188.

[26] Risley, op. cit., pp. 188–9.

The Bhuinmali were a much smaller and even more despised group – 12,581 in Dacca and 8263 in Faridpur in 1881. Cultivators, musicians, palki-bearers and scavengers, they were "village servants employed in cutting brushwood, repairing footpaths, sweeping the outside of the zamindar's house, removing carcasses from the village... obliged to live on the outskirts of villages apart from the Hindus, and to perform any menial work that is required of them."

Bhuinmali women swept courtyards and were employed as midwives and domestic servants. Like the Chandals, Vaishnavism was strong among them, and, like the Chandals again, they had become by the 1880s "most anxious to represent themselves as Sudras, by aping the prejudices of the higher ranks." Possibly relevant for the Doyhata incident is the fact that Bhuinmali efforts at social ascent immediately brought them into conflict above all with the Chandals/Namasudras. Much "secret jealousy" and some "open feuds" were reported between them, and the Bhuinmali started refusing to eat with Chandals and became reluctant to work for them.[27]

Literacy rates among Chandals and Bhuinmalis were abysmally low, while, in yet another inversion of the *bhadralok* stereotype, both groups had a reputation of great physical strength.[28] Along with Muslims, they provided the bulk of *lathials* and *chaukidars* (watchmen). There are indications, however, of a rich oral culture: "singing is a favourite amusement, and a Chandal crew is rarely without some musical instrument." Music was one of the caste occupations of the Bhuinmali.[29] Even Jogendranath Gupta broke his silence about the lower orders to write a couple of pages about Bikrampur popular religious life: significantly, he placed it in his text just before the sentence about Doyhata. Gupta mentioned particularly the low-caste worship of Trinath, a syncretist cult combining adoration of Brahma, Vishnu and Siva. Ganja and religious songs, presumably of the kirtan type, were its principal ingredients, and the song which he records declares

---

[27] Ibid., pp. 105–7, 188.
[28] The percentage of literacy among Namasudras in 1901 was 3.3. See Sekhar Bandopadhyay, op. cit., p. 10.
[29] Risley, op. cit., pp. 189, 106.

that through the worship of Trinath "the people of Koli-yuga – all these figure notably in our Doyhata story.

The scanty information available about the Chandal and the Bhuinmali involved in the case permits few inferences about their possible linkages with the broader life of their communities. Ananda Bhuinmali's father, Krishna, did appear in court to state that his son had been a stay-at-home type till Kalachand and Prasanna turned up in their village (in Piyarpur thana, near Kamarkhali, in the extreme north-west of Faridpur) during the previous Baisakh and again in Agrahayan (April–May, November–December 1904). The two were staying on both occasions in low-caste houses, of a Das and a Patuni (boatman), and "used to sing, smoke ganja, and talk like sadhus." Ananda used to sit with them and occasionally stay over for a night or two, and one day in Agrahayan he slipped away from his father's house and village without explanation.[31] About Prasanna Chandal's background we know even less, for no relative or friend of his came to testify at Dacca. Presumably he had long since broken free of ties of kin and locality. We are told only, by Kalachand, that his surname was Dhetamandal, his father's name Bhagirath, and that he came from Jainasar (the Dacca district gazetteer mentions a post office of that name). The sadhu met him for the first time at the "last Langulbandh (Nangalbandh) bathing festival".[32]

Both Ananda and Prasanna evidently shared a leaning towards some kind of Vaishnavism, in common with many Chandals and Bhuinmalis. Ananda's father was named Krishna, the two had left home to follow someone who, as we shall see, insisted on devotion to Hari alone, and they called their guru Gossain, as Vaishnavas do.[33] The other impression we get is of a highly mobile, fluid world of wandering sadhus and their predominantly lower-caste devotees, knitted together by meetings at religious festivals (among which Nangalbandh, a few miles north of Munshigunj, is one of the most

[30] Jogendranath Gupta, op. cit., p. 372.
[31] Evidence of Krishna Bhuinmali, KM, p. 59.
[32] Testimony of Kalachand Sadhu at Srinagar, ibid., p. 5.
[33] Testimony of Prasanna at Srinagar and Munshigunj, ibid., pp. 7, 16.

popular), and developing through ganja and devotional songs a conviviality or communitas which could cut across barriers of caste and class. The devotional focus, however, would normally be provided by a high-caste sadhu.

Two very different worlds, then, with relations governed by firmly established norms of strict subordination and deference – the Bikrampur *bhadralok*, inordinately proud of their formal learning and culture; and the illiterate and despised low castes and untouchables. And yet they came together, briefly and explosively, in the house of the Majumdars of Doyhata. The link figure was Kalikumar Chakrabarti, or Kalachand sadhu, from an unnamed village in Madaripur subdivision. The wife, elder brother, and father-in-law of Kalikumar came to his trial. Pratapchandra Chakrabarti, the father-in-law, described himself as a *tahsildar* (minor revenue official), and the family evidently had the resources to engage some legal help. Kalikumar, the court was told, had taught in his village school for Rs 15. The pandit of that school made him a ganja addict, and he started beating up his wife and children and quarrelling with his father-in-law. Kalikumar had left home three years earlier. He had briefly returned the previous Aswin (September–October), and his elder brother, Laksmanchandra, had tried to keep him in chains – for "he was like a mad person . . . smoking a lot of *ganja* and taking rice from any and everybody" (i.e. breaking caste food taboos).[34] Lalmohan's uncle Rajani testified that the sadhu's message was "Kali is nothing, Hari is all",[35] and perhaps the way he changed his name is significant, for "Kalikumar" has Shakta associations, while Kalachand of cource is Krishna.

Figures like Kalachand were by no means rare in the Bengal countryside. In his account of Dacca, Hunter talks about "religious enthusiasts" who "leave their occupations and become itinerant preachers of Hari through *sankirtan*, who dispense faith-healing . . . as specific for all maladies."[36] Kalachand, too, claimed at Doyhata that his *charanamrita* and the ashes from his *kalki* had healing powers. More

---

[34] Ibid., p. 72.
[35] Ibid., p. 55.
[36] Hunter, op. cit., p. 56.

generally, and with or without specifically "religious" overtones, the poor (or at least not too well-off) village Brahmin dropout became a typical figure in much early-twentieth-century Bengali literature. The husband of Biraj-bau for instance, in Saratchandra Chattopadhyay's bestseller of that name (1914), responded to deepening financial crisis by immersion in the Mahabharata, ganja, and kirtan. In Saratchandra's semi-autobiographical novel *Srikanta* (1917) the Brahmin youth escapes from respectability to seek adventure in a shifting, relatively uninhibited, plebeian world, and the wandering Brahmin recurs, though in a more etherealised form, in Rabindranath's short-story "Atithi".

The householder, seeking solace from the tedium of a humdrum existence and genteel poverty in ganja, kirtan, and unfamiliar cults; the village youth who runs away to a dangerous and therefore attractive underworld; the wandering sadhu with lower-caste disciples who eventually acquires *bhadralok* patrons and wins respectability, maybe even fame – all these figures slide into each other and are marked fundamentally by the crossing and recrossing of social frontiers. Such fluidity, almost certainly, was nothing new, but colonial conditions could have enhanced it in several ways. The upper-caste literati which stuck to old forms of learning, whether out of choice or lack of opportunity, lost patronage and prestige as English education penetrated deeper into the rural *bhadralok*. Its landholding too could be pulverised over time, given an active land market. The new learning was not a guarantee of success, for it was soon producing its own quota of relative failures – depressed clerks or humble town or village schoolteachers. The myth of a Koli-yuga painted in lurid colours and occasional dreams of an apocalyptic Kalki-avatar were likely to take root precisely in such a milieu.

A bit of "modern" education and a smattering of brahminical culture – such as the ex-schoolteacher Kalikumar presumably had – could go some way, however, towards winning admirers from lower down the social scale, while a devotion to Hari, expressed mainly through *ganja* and song, fitted in well with established patterns of popular religion in Bikrampur, both Vaishnavism in its more plebeian manifestations and cults like that of Trinath. Kalachand's subsequent success in entering the Majumdar household indicates an ability to straddle two worlds. What seems important in such cases of crossing of margins, however, is the direction and ultimate destination of the journey, for on that apparently depends success or failure in conquering respectability. Way back in the seventeenth century, a Brahmin youth named Rupram Chakrabarti ran away from his *tol* to live among the untouchable Hadi community. He picked up from their oral traditions the stories about Lausen, and re-emerged after many years to win the patronage of a zamindar and write a famous Dharma-mangal Kavya. Sukumar Sen has suggested a parallel between Rupram and the early life of Saratchandra,[37] and in the mid nineteenth century the life of the celebrated *panchali* composer Dasarathi Roy reveals a similar pattern of descent followed by ascent.[38] It was perfectly respectable, even laudable, for a Brahmin religious leader to have low-caste disciples: that Chaitanya had extended his bounty even to Chandals was a much-quoted saying in the late nineteenth century. And Ramakrishna is only the best-known example of the sadhu with rustic poor Brahmin origins conquering parts of the *bhadralok* world. Another instance, not far from Doyhata, was Loknath Brahmachari of Barudi, a village in Dacca district.[39] What went wrong with the Doyhata Kalki-avatar, however, was that the direction of movement and influence got abruptly reversed when the Chandal Prasanna took over on 23 Agrahayan.

III

"In Aswin or Kartik", some two months before the denouement of 23 Agrahayan, Lalmohan recalled in his initial deposition, a low-

---

[37] Sukumar Sen, *Saratchandrika*, Preface to Sen, ed., *Saratsahityasangraha* (Calcutta, 1988).

[38] Haripada Chakrabarti, *Dasarathi o Tnahan Panchali* (Calcutta, 1960), chapter II.

[39] Loknath, a wandering sadhu of many years, eventually set up an ashrama in Braudi patronised by the local Nag zamindar family. To Satyacharan Mitra, author of one of the earliest biographies of Ramakrishna, "the Brahmachari of Barudi" was an equal of Ramakrishna himself. Satyacharan Mitra, *Sri Sri Ramakrishna Paramhansa* (Jivani o Upadesh; Calcutta, 1304/1897), pp. 2, 69; Saratkamini Basu, *Sri Sri Satguru-Kathamrita* (Dacca, 1335/1928), pp. 43–5.

caste *praja* of his named Nabin Mistri asked him "to come and see a sadhu who had turned up in his house accompanied by a Prasanna Namasudra". Lalmohan went and saw "the sadhu singing with an *ektara* . . . I looked at his face, it seemed like that of a boy, and Vatsalyabhava (paternal feeling) was evoked in me."[40] Kalachand also "talked like a proper sadhu", but apparently Lalmohan was not at first so impressed by his words. He invited the sadhu to come over to the Majumdar house, for "a Brahmin's son should not stay with a Chandal".[41] Lalmohan joined the singing and ganja sessions, began losing interest in his medical practice, and "spent much time in idleness . . . saying, if asked about anything, "The Sadhu will provide everything, there is nothing to worry about."[42] Until then he had been treating poor people without taking fees, and was fond of his wife and only son.[43]

The initial encounter, then, was conventional enough. The boyish, even childlike appearance and behaviour of many sadhus often constituted a major attraction for the middle-aged of both sexes, and this could be easily structured into the well-known Vatsalya form of Vaishnava devotion. The devotee searching for a guru often looks for a kind of elective affinity rather than a new message, and so for Lalmohan the appearance and personality of Kalachand were more important than this teaching. An early biography of Ramakrishna, for instance, included an entire section on the saint's "Balak-bhava".[44] The deliberate "feminization" associated with many forms of Vaishnava devotion often involved a turning away from external activity. Ramakrishna, in sharp contrast to Vivekananda, condemned social activism, even philanthropic work, and several of the characters in

---

[40] Deposition of Lalmohan at Srinagar, KM, p. 10.

[41] Ibid.

[42] Evidence of Lalmohan's wife Rajlakshmi at Dacca, ibid., p. 46.

[43] Evidence of Jitendramohan Majumdar (Tona), Lalmohan's nephew, ibid., p. 31.

[44] Satyacharan Mitra, pp. 150–2. Loknath Brahmachari made Bijoykrishna Goswami's wife Jogmaya feed him with her own hands, insisting that she scold him if he stopped eating. Saratkamini Basu, *Satprasanga* (Dacca, 1327/1920), p. 37.

Girishchandra Ghosh's plays clearly modelled on him wander around preaching passive acceptance of Hari.[45] "When there is someone to worry for you, why worry yourself? Think, when you were a child, you happily sucked your mother's breasts, your mother did all the worrying; today, if you stop worrying, Hari will worry for you . . . Let them take you where they will, you go reciting Hari's name."[46]

Lalmohan's uncle, the sixty-five-year-old Rajani Majumdar, testified that "I, too, used to go to the sadhu, and discussed matters of dharma with him": the relationship here seems to have been slightly more "intellectual" than in the case of Lalmohan. The sadhu did not like the Majumdar family practice of holding Kali-puja, and Rajani asked him to leave the day before Deepanwita Puja (i.e. Diwali).[47] Like many sadhus, Kalachand claimed miraculous healing powers, dispensing them through his *charanamrita* and, less conventionally, ashes from the pipe (*kalki*) that he used to smoke ganja.[48] the verbal coincidence here with Kalki-avatar seems to have had a strange fascination for both Kalachand and Prasanna.[49] During this first stay with the Majumdars, however, Kalachand made little or no reference to the Kalki-avatar, and nor did Prasanna leave much of an independent impression that time. But Rajani recalled that Prasanna "talked so fast that it was often difficult to follow him":[50] not really a trivial detail if we remember that ordinarily a Chandal would have

---

[45] See particularly Ramakrishna's account of his conversation with Sambhu-charan Mallik, which is repeated six times in the *Kathamrita* but is omitted from the later *Lilaprasanga*: Sumit Sarkar, "The *Kathamrita* as Text: Towards An Understanding of Ramakrishna Paramhansa", Occasional Papers, no. 22, New Delhi, Nehru Memorial Museum and Library, April 1985.

[46] Nasiram's words in the paly *Nasiram* (1888), III.ii, *Girish Rachanabali* (Calcutta, 1969), vol. iv, pp. 239–40.

[47] Ibid., p. 55; *Bengalee*, 17 March 1905.

[48] Evidence of Tona, KM, p. 31.

[49] For an example of similarity in sounds helping to constitute a whole alternative plebeian cosmogony, see Sudhir Chakrabarty's work on the Balarami sect of Nadia among the untouchables. "Hadi" resembles Had (bones), and this coincidence is central to the mythology of this sect. Sudhir Chakrabarty, *Balarami Sampraday Tadar Gan* (Calcutta, 1987).

[50] *Bengalee*, 17 March 1905.

remained deferentially silent in a gentry house if allowed to enter it at all. Certainly, he could never have dreamt of smoking ganja with upper-caste people. Incessant speech was an indication of the sense of liberation and self-confidence which the new cult was bringing to this untouchable devotee and speech in his case would later develop into abuse directed at superiors.[51]

Kalachand went off around Diwali to stay for some time with Purna Sarkar, another Doyhata devotee whose house lay three fields away.[52] Lalmohan often went to visit the sadhu there.[53] Prasanna seems to have left the village for a time, and Kalachand, too briefly went back home; the two also visited Ananda's village in early Agrahayan.[54]

With the return of Kalachand to the Majumdar house some seven or eight days before Thursday, 23 Agrahayan, the pace of events quickened and took a different turn. Several members of the family fell ill around this time: Lalmohan's wife Rajlakshmi as well as Charubala and Sailo, the two daughters of Mathur and Sarala, who may have had cholera.[55] Lalmohan refused to treat them and asked them to "trust in Kalachand". "I have surrendered my dispensary itself at the sadhu's feet," he told his relative and neighbour Upendrachandra Ghoshal.[56] Lalmohan also started telling some neighbours – Upendrachandra and a moneylender named Mahimchandra Sarkar – that the sadhu was Kalki-avatar, and "a *yugapralay* (cataclysmic end of the epoch) was coming, many will fall ill." He even mentioned a date for the apocalypse, 18 Paus, "when my sadhu will assume his real form".[57]

---

[51] For speech and abuse as in indicator of the plebeian inversion of social order, see Ranajit Guha, *Elementary Aspects of Peasant Insurgency in Colonial India* (Delhi, 1983), chapter II.

[52] Tona, KM, p. 24. Purna Sarkar did not give evidence at Dacca, and little more can be learnt about him.

[53] Evidence of Lalmohan's wife Rajlakshmi Devi at Dacca, ibid., p. 46.

[54] Evidence of Kalachand and Ananda's relatives, ibid., pp. 72, 59.

[55] *Bengalee*, 14 March 1905.

[56] Evidence of Upendrachandra Ghoshal, KM, p. 62.

[57] Evidence of Upendrachandra Ghoshal and Mahimchandra Sarkar, ibid., pp. 63, 66.

Incidentally, the women of the family seem to have remained on the whole more hard-headed about Kalachand than the resident menfolk. Rajlakshmi recalled at Srinagar that the sadhu had failed to cure her fever, and Sarala, when her daughter Charubala fell ill, tried to get some medicine from Upendra Ghoshal first, despite Lalmohan's insistence that the sadhu could cure everything.[58]

Ananda Bhuinmali turned up on Monday 19 Agrahayan, very dark and frightening in appearance.[59] With Prasanna's return next day, "the singing and the music stopped." The Chandal had started abusing those who did not show sufficient respect to Kalachand, particularly the women, while Tona recalled him flaunting a bow.[60]

The apocalypse became associated with Ananda: "The sadhu has come to our house, and brought Yama here . . . No-one would have to worry about anything once Yama has been killed. No-one on the earth will have to fear Yama . . ."[61] This identification as well as the entry of the Yama theme remains the most obscure aspect of the entire affair. All that we are told is that Ananda had a "fearsome" appearance (according to Kalachand); that Prasanna on the day of the murder had a fight with him at mealtime for refusing to remove his own plate after eating (there is a trace here, possibly, of the contemporary quarrels over precedence between Namasudras and Bhuinmalis);[62] that "everybody called Ananda Yama",[63] and that somehow both the ending of the chain of illnesses which had beset the Majumdar family and the impending *yugapralay* had got associated with the killing of Ananda-Yama. As for Ananda himself, it seems unlikely that he accepted, or maybe even knew of, this identification with the god of death. Prasanna, however, in his deposition at Munshigunj,

---

[58] Ibid., p. 21; *Bengalee*, 17 March 1905. Sarala started beliving, however – or so Rajlakshmi asserted – after Sailo improved a bit through the sadhu's treatment. KM, p. 46.

[59] Testimony of Kalachand at Srinagar, ibid., p. 5.

[60] Evidence of Rajani's wife Sashimukhi, and of Tona, ibid., pp. 50, 25.

[61] Mahimachandra Sarkar, reporting a conversation with Lalmohan, ibid., p. 66.

[62] Rajani's evidence, *Bengalee*, 17 March 1905.

[63] Tona's evidence, *Bengalee*, 14 March 1905.

claimed that Ananda had agreed to his own ritual murder: "Brother, why does Gossain keep himself hidden for so long? You kill me, and make manifest the *satyadharma*. Gossain is Jagatguru; he will bring me back to life if you kill me, and then the English and everyone else will know about his greatness (*mahima*)."[64] Tona confirmed that Ananda had made such a suggestion, and Lalmohan added that Prasanna had told the Bhuinmali disciple: "Surrender yourself to Kalachand, you will receive a divine body (*dibyadeha*)."[65]

On the afternoon of 23 Agrahayan, Prasanna killed Ananda in the presence of Kalachand, Lalmohan and Tona, with Jogmaya seeing it happen from behind a hedge while she was cutting fish. He attacked him first with the sadhu's trident and then with the knife they used to prepare ganja, and slit what Lalmohan with his medical knowledge recognised to be the "carotid artery". At Kalachand's orders Prasanna, Lalmohan, and Tona threw the dead body outside the house.[66] Prasanna then proclaimed his intention of making "the world red", to smash and burn everything around, describing this in court as "burning Lanka".[67] "I'll burn all the wife's sisters" (*shali* – used at times as a term of abuse), and he also declared, "All the women will have to come naked before the Gossain, or else none of them will be spared."[68]

Apart from a brief abortive bid to set fire to Rajani's house, the targets of Prasanna's arson efforts were *raiyat* homesteads: those of Mahim Mandal and Harachand De, both *prajas* of Lalmohan, and of Rajmohan Bhuinmali.[69] He had planned also, as Prasanna stated at Munshigunj, to set fire to the Muslim quarter ("Musalman *para*").[70]

---

[64] Prasanna's deposition at Munshigunj, KM, p. 16. In his first deposition, at Srinagar, Prasanna had merely stated that he had had a quarrel with Ananda over matters of worship and ritual ("*sadhana-bhajan*"), ibid., pp. 7–8.

[65] Tona, ibid., p. 31; Lalmohan's deposition at Srinagar, ibid., p. 10.

[66] Depositions of Prasanna, Lalmohan, and Jogmaya, KM, pp. 8, 11–12, 35.

[67] *Bengalee*, 14 March 1905; deposition of Barada Devi at Dacca and of Prasanna at Srinagar, KM, pp. 39–42.

[68] Prasanna's deposition at Munshigunj, ibid., p. 68.

[69] All three appeared as witnesses at Dacca, ibid., p. 68.

[70] Ibid., p. 19.

The women of the Majumdar household, about a dozen in all, were made to take off their clothes, touch a fire, and prostrate themselves before Kalachand. This done, they were allowed to dress and leave. When Tona's mother tried to resist, Prasanna urinated on her. Lalmohan's wife Rajlakshmi got special treatment: Prasanna forced her to stand naked on his knees "in the posture of Kali", burnt her pubic hair, thrust a *kalki* into her vagina, and made her kick her husband three times. Lalmohan was punished thus because he had refused to kill his son Nanda, despite Prasanna's promise that he would get "a golden son" in return.[71] The other *bhadralok* men around were not spared either. Umesh Kabiraj, a passerby who had caught a glimpse of the murder, was hit on the head by Prasanna and made to flee. Upendrachandra Ghoshal, the nextdoor neighbour and relative, was stripped, had his sacred thread torn, and was told to walk back naked to his house, an order he meekly obeyed.[72]

Prasanna claimed in his deposition at Srinagar that the "burning of Lanka", as well as the other actions, had been planned beforehand by "Thakur" (Kalachand), Lalmohan, and himself.[73] Many witnesses mentioned the active role of Lalmohan and the complicity of the sadhu, despite their efforts in court to wriggle out of responsibility. Lalmohan helped to bring in the women before Kalachand, and Upen Ghoshal recalled that he had made him do a *pranam*, after which Lalmohan put his feet upon his head.[74] Kalachand and Lalmohan assured the women: "You come naked to the world, you have to leave it naked – why be afraid? . . . How does this ruin *satitva* (purity, chastity)?"[75] It is evident, however, that the Chandal was calling all the tunes from the time of the murder onwards. Lalmohan, too, received some kicks and blows, though no disrespect seems ever to have been shown by Prasanna to the sadhu.

[71] The treatment of women that night is described in KM, pp. 6–9, 12–13, 15, 19, 21–2, 28, 36–7, 41, 45, 49–50, 61–2.
[72] Evidence of Umesh Kabiraj and Upendrachandra Ghoshal, ibid., pp. 60–1.
[73] Ibid., pp. 8–9.
[74] Ibid., p. 61.
[75] Deposition of Prasanna at Munshigunj, and evidence of Jogmaya and Sashimukhi, ibid., pp. 19, 37, 50.

The terror continued till early next morning, when Prasanna was at last overpowered by a group of villagers led by Mahim Sarkar after what is said to have been a two-hour fight. Prasanna was shouting then: "All the soldiers of Bharat together will not be able to do anything to me."[76] Lalmohan and Kalachand had already slipped away to the house of Purna Sarkar, from where the police arrested them.

In general, the *bhadralok* menfolk cut remarkably poor figures in the Doyhata evidence. Umesh Kabiraj did not complain to the police about Prasanna's assault and the fracas he had seen, for "he wanted to avoid getting involved in a case".[77] Upen Ghoshal submitted to the humiliation of walking back to his house naked, carrying his dhoti in his hands. Tona's complicity is clear: he helped to throw away Ananda's body, and his evidence reveals that he was present virtually throughout. Returning home later that evening, Rajani Majumdar was told by Umesh and then by his own daughter Jogmaya about what was happening. Rajani smoked, went out to relieve himself, had dinner, had some inconclusive discussion (*paramarsha*) with Upen Ghoshal as to what could be done, and only several hours later tried to get help from the "*raiyatpara*" (peasant quarter). Prasanna stopped him on the way, took off his clothes, and tied him to a tree. Rajani managed to cut the bonds with his teeth (lack of physical strength was clearly not the problem for this sixty-five-year-old), but then went off for some more *paramarsha*. Cross-examination revealed that the Srinagar police station was only a quarter of a mile from Rajani's house.[78]

The women who testified at Dacca, in sharp contrast, conveyed a certain independence and dignity. Several resisted, and Jogmaya emphasised that "we were unwillingly and by force taken by Lalmohan" to be stripped.[79] It was Jogmaya and her mother Sashimukhi who eventually went to Mahim Sarkar's house and persuaded him to come with a rescue party: the decisive action which ended the night of terror came from the initiative of women. Sashimukhi

[76] Evidence of Tona and Mahim Sarkar, ibid., pp. 30–1, 65.
[77] Ibid., p. 60.
[78] Evidence of Rajani Majumdar, ibid., pp. 55–8.
[79] *Bengalee*, 16 March 1905. Jogmaya was quite explicit about the role of Lalmohan in the version printed in the Calcutta newspaper: "Both Lalmohan and Prasanna took away our clothes."

and Jogmaya made it clear that they had not liked or respected the sadhu even before that afternoon.[80] Sometimes a strong note of half-suppressed anger at the behaviour of their menfolk came out from the testimonies of the women. Sashimukhi stated that "her husband did not turn up in time to save her from the whims of the ruffians."[81] Rajlakshmi made it amply clear that her husband Lalmohan had done nothing to save her, had in fact actively helped Prasanna and actually laughed when she had appealed for help. Yet he did protest, she recalled with evident bitterness, when Prasanna suggested that his son Nanda be sacrificed. Earlier, when Lalmohan had refused to treat her for fever and insisted that she seek help from the sadhu, Rajlakshmi had complained: "What kind of game is this – please give me some medicine, otherwise I will tell my *debar*" (husband's younger brother).[82] There are hints here of a fairly typical joint-family syndrome where the married son retains much greater concern for his mother and develops a strong interest in the male heir, but the wife remains somewhat of an outsider, a borrowed womb, important as child-bearer and household drudge but not for herself.

Tona, Jogmaya, Sashimukhi, and Barada recounted in detail the kicking of Lalmohan by his wife.[84] The husband did not mention it, and Rajlakshmi's otherwise very detailed account of her sufferings also maintained an interesting silence here. Kicking the seated Lalmohan on the forehead represented an exact inversion of the *pranam*, the normal ritual gesture of deference. Does Rajlakshmi's failure to mention this incident among the indignities she had suffered that night indicate that she may not have been entirely unwilling, just at that moment?

The two upper castes and the Chandal accused also presented a study in contrast at court. Lalmohan, by the end of the Dacca proceedings, had become a totally abject figure: "I am innocent, I did

[80] KM, pp. 33–8, 49–53; *Bengalee*, 16 and 17 March 1905.
[81] *Bengalee*, 16 March 1905.
[82] Evidence of Rajlakshmi Debi, at Srinagar and at Dacca, KM, pp. 21, 49.
[83] The wife could develop more affectionate relations, however, with her younger brother-in-law. Rajlakshmi's *debar* Brojendar, on that night, did try to rescue Nanda when Prasanna was threatening to kill him. Ibid., p. 49.
[84] KM, pp. 29, 37, 44, 53.

nothing, I had become like something inert then . . . Please forgive me."[85] Kalachand, in his first deposition at Srinagar, made a desperate attempt to pass the entire blame on to Prasanna, claiming, against all the evidence, that both Lalmohan and he himself had become "half-dead with shame and fear" and had been mere helpless observers of the disrobing of the women. Subsequently, at Munshigunj and in the Dacca court, the sadhu retreated into an enigmatic eccentricity, real or feigned. Once a schoolteacher, he now claimed to have forgotten how to write, and so refused to sign the *vakalatnama* needed for him to have a lawyer. He kept on repeating: "I am *nirguna*, there is no *guna* in me. I live by begging."[86] The pun might just possibly indicate an acquaintance with a famous passage in Bharatchandra's *Annadamangal* – where Parvati describes Siva through a similar double entendre – but otherwise contributed nothing to the proceedings.

Prasanna remained defiant till the end. "We have been amazed," the KM commented, "by his demon-like (*danabochita*) behaviour and words . . . in the open court that day this Chandal's son kicked a guard and threw him on to the ground." He made no attempt at all to shift the blame on to the others, and even declared in his last statement in Dacca: "I do not want to say anything more. I did everything alone."[87] The *Bengalee* noted with surprise that "Prasanna appears quite unconcerned with what is going around, commenting freely and gaily on the depositions of several witnesses."[88] His comment about Lalmohan's final plea for innocence is worth recording: "No, he did nothing, he just had three or four *kalkis* of ganja with us."[89] The sense of liberation brought to the Chandal through faith in Kalachand and impending *yugapralay* persisted even in court: he seems to have looked upon the trial as an opportunity for sarcastic comments about his social superiors. Such sarcasm and gaiety is reminiscent almost of the well-known genre of gallow speeches in eighteenth-century England and France, through which the condemned occasionally turned the spectacle of royal punitive authority into its opposite, giving it an

[85] Ibid., p. 74.
[86] Ibid., pp. 6–7, 14, 74.
[87] Ibid., pp. 3, 73.
[88] *Bengalee*, 17 March 1905.
[89] KM, p. 74.

"aspect of the carnival transformed into heroes".[90] What would have been missing in the urban *bhadralok*-dominated Dacca courtroom, however, was the ambivalent plebeian audience, scandalised, terrified, and yet fascinated by the criminal hero.

The Dacca jury consisted of three schoolteachers, a college lecturer, and a local zamindar.[91] A village doctor of a gentry family would be someone like themselves, though considerably less successful. Kalachand, for witnesses and jury alike, would be a marginal figure: a Brahmin ex-schoolteacher but distanced by ganja and low-caste associates, with sadhu claims discredited now by the violence and horror of 23 Agrahayan. Prasanna, for everyone in court, was bound to remain totally alien, a figure of crude, plebeian violence, unmitigated by any signs of repentance. Alone of the three accused, he also went without any legal defence.[92] Predictably, perhaps, despite ample evidence of complicity or worse, the *bhadralok* jury acquitted Lalmohan, by majority decision, of all charges. Kalachand was found guilty of abetting "homicide" and "affront to feminine modesty". But not of committing either; he was acquitted of the other charge of arson. Prasanna was unanimously condemned for "culpable homicide" (not murder), affront to feminine modesty, and arson (sections 304, 354 and 436 of the Criminal Procedure Code).[93] Sustaining the murder charge against Prasanna would probably have made the acquittal of Lalmohan more difficult.

Dissatisfaction with the relatively mild jury recommendations – "the judicial wisdom of which many have not been able to admire" – led the *Dacca Prakash* to collate its earlier reports into the KM

---

[90] Michel Foucault, *Discipline and Punish: The Birth of the Prison* (Paris, 1975; Peregrine, 1979), pp. 61, 57–69. See also Peter Linebaugh, "The Tyburn Riot Against the Surgeons", in Stephen Hay, *et al.*, *Albion's Fatal Tree* (Penguin, 1977).

[91] KM, pp. 1–2.

[92] Lalmohan had a lawyer to defend him. Kalachand's relatives brought several legal aides; despite his refusal to sign the *vakalatnama*, the British judge (Nicholls) permitted them to exercise "an informal watchdog brief as friends of the court". *Bengalee*, 14 March 1905.

[93] KM, p. 74; *Bengalee*, 19 March 1905.

pamphlet.⁹⁴ The motivation here was clearly a "reformist" exposure of religious corruption and superstition: "we shall be happy if the eyes of even one person are opened . . . The inhabitants of Bikrampur, so proud of their education, are very satisfied with themselves", but "They have colluded so long with the horrible things being done by such religious imposters (*dharmadhwajigana*) . . . We feel that the stream of immorality (*byabhichara*) which has been trickling so long through the heart of Bikrampur has now acquired the terrible form of the Kalki-avatar."⁹⁵

Dacca town, along with the gentry of adjoining Bikrampur, had been a major centre of Brahmoism, and in 1877 Hunter had cited the *Dacca Prakash* as representing the "views of the educated natives generally".⁹⁶ Social reform by 1905 had lost much of its centrality for the *bhadralok*, but something of the old zeal clearly remained.

Excitement had run high when the Doyhata case began before the Dacca sessions court: "The courtroom and the adjoining streets were crowded with spectators. The whole town seemed to be in a state of excitement. No schoolboy was permitted to enter the courtroom. The crowd sometimes was so great that the District Judge himself had to go out and clear the verandah . . .", and "such crowds have been seen rarely before in the court . . . The whole town seemed agog to see the strange trio (*apurba jivatroi*) and learn their fate."⁹⁷

Initially, then, Doyhata seemed well on the way towards becoming a major scandal. It was certainly sensational, and it could serve as a target for "reformist" exposure. Yet the Calcutta papers failed to take it up in a big way. The *Bengalee* of Surendranath Banerjea, the

---

⁹⁴ KM, p. 74.

⁹⁵ Ibid., p. 3.

⁹⁶ Brahmos numbered about a thousand in Dacca, according to Hunter, "comprising nearly all the English-speaking Hindus" of that district. There had been only one cultivating-class Brahmo, however, and he had gone mad. Hunter, op. cit., pp. 117, 158. The extreme narrowness of the *bhadralok* world is indicated by the circulation figures of *Dacca Prakash*: 300 by Hunter's account, 500 according to the official estimates in *Report on Native Papers (Bengal)*, January 1905.

⁹⁷ *Bengalee*, 17 March 1905; KM, p. 4.

mildly reformist mouthpiece of the Moderate Congress, gave fairly detailed coverage to the Dacca court hearings but no front-page or editorial space. Sisirkumar and Motilal Ghosh's *Amrita Bazar Patrika*, rival of Surendranath's paper since the 1870s and somewhat more militant and socially orthodox in its nationalism, allowed only one brief paragraph for the case and said nothing about women being stripped: "the case is nasty from beginning to end, and we withhold further details."[98] It subsequently published without comment the Calcutta appellate judgment on Doyhata as part of its regular court news section.

An interesting feature of the representation of Doyhata in the Calcutta press was an attempt to attribute responsibility primarily to the women: "It seems the women of the family had great faith in the sadhu Kalachand and implored him to save the girl" (Sailo). "The Sadhu was telling the women of the house that the end of the world was come and unless they implicitly followed him and his followers there would be no chance of his saving them from Destruction."[99] Such attribution of a special credulity to the Majumdar women, however, was clearly not borne out by the Dacca evidence as presented in KM or even in the *Bengalee*, and the point was not pressed further. Silence soon descended on the Doyhata affair.

The Calcutta *bhadralok* press was not always so reticent about scandals involving sex, murder, and corrupt religious figures. The Tarakeswar case of 1873, for instance, which like Doyhata had all these three ingredients, had remained a *cause célèbre* for years.[100]

Why, then, did Doyhata fail to make the grade? That social reform had lost its centrality is not too convincing as an answer: the exposure of abuses remained important also from points of view conventionally labelled "Hindu revivalist" or "patriotic". One explanation could be that for the Calcutta, as distinct from the Dacca or Bikrampur, public, the Doyhata Kalki-avatar was too distant and insignificant a figure to require "exposure", unlike, say, the Tarakeswar *mohanta*.

---

[98] *Amrita Bazar Patrika*, 15 March 1905.
[99] Ibid., 15 March 1905; *Bengalee*, 14 March 1905.
[100] Sripantha, *Mohunt-Elokesi Sangbad* (Calcutta, 1984), pp. 71–2, lists no less than thirty-four plays about this scandal.

The Kalki-Avatar of Bikrampur 341

But we can speculate about deeper reasons, and these lead on to the heart of our subject.

A scandal that gets talked about always involves transgressions – but transgressions which are not too uncomfortable, which remain within limits set by the dominant discourse. Doyhata seems to have gone beyond these limits in a number of ways, and, unlike many scandals, it proved impossible to derive any moral message from it. The Majumdar menfolk had cut very sorry figures indeed in the Doyhata case. They had allowed the Chandal to rage unchecked for a whole evening and night, even though the Srinagar police station was less than a mile away. Lalmohan, and possibly also Tona, had actually handed over the women of the household to be stripped. A cult of physical strength and courage had been developing for some years among Bengali *bhadralok* youth: publicity for Doyhata could certainly tarnish that self-image of male prowess.[101]

The attribution of a special superstition to the Majumdar women, attempted briefly by the two Calcutta dailies, may not necessarily have been a deliberate effort to pass responsibility. This, after all, was one of the standard stereotypes about women: they are often assumed to be exceptionally devout or credulous, depending on the point of view. Cults originally plebeian might gain social respectability through the conversion of upper-caste women as happens, for instance, in the medieval *Manasa-mangal*. Women, in other words, are supposed to have a liminal relationship *vis-à-vis* the dark, ambiguous, fearful, yet fascinating underworld of society and religion.

Once again, however, Doyhata refused to fit in, for here it was the men who were more credulous and the women much more hardheaded. "None of us wanted to strip . . . I did not respect the sadhu, I don't know whether anyone else did so."[102] Again, though the KM pamphlet in its preface related Doyhata to the preponderance of

---

[101] Physical culture centres (*akharas*) were being set up in many places, and Sarala Debi in 1902 had started a Birastami *vrata*. Sumit Sarkar, *Swadeshi Movement in Bengal, 1903–1908* (New Delhi, 1973), pp. 394, 397, 470; J. Rosselli, "The Self-Image of Effeteness: Physical Education and Nationalism in Nineteenth Century Bengal", *Past and Present*, no. 86, February 1980.

[102] Evidence of Barada and Jogmaya, KM, pp. 38, 41.

"*ghor koli*" (the depths of Koli-yuga), actually neither of the standard figures of women of nineteenth-century Koli-yuga literature were quite appropriate for the case.[103] Rajlakshmi, forced to kick her husband by Prasanna, and just possibly doing it half-willingly, was hardly the disorderly woman on top, while the self-sacrificing, assertive yet deferential mother or wife was also conspicuously absent. The Majumdar women, sceptical of the sadhu and expressing in open court their resentment at the behaviour of their menfolk, could not be caught in the net of any of these male constructions of gender. Even salaciousness lost its bite in such a situation.

The nineteenth- and early-twentieth-century *bhadralok* male self-image concerning relations with women and social subordinates comprised a whole range of attitudes: paternalist head of the family, social reformer spreading enlightenment and trying to uplift the status of women (and, less often, lower castes), "orthodox" or "revivalist" religious mentor, philanthropist benefactor of the *daridra-narayan*, patriot inspiring "his" people. What all these images had in common was an implicit retention of initiative. In Doyhata, however, a cult started by a poor Brahmin wanderer among lower castes, which seemed on the point of gaining a respectable *bhadralok* audience, had been suddenly hijacked by a Chandal. The normal distance between *bhadralok* and Chandal, reduced initially at the initiative of the sadhu in a quite acceptable manner (for Chaitanya, too, had untouchable disciples), had been not only eliminated but fundamentally reversed, with Prasanna imposing his own meanings, levelling and burning down distinctions of caste, class, and gender.[104] It was this fundamental reversal of initiatives, perhaps, that made Doyhata a subject too uncomfortable to be talked about.

The British judge disagreed with the verdict of the Dacca jury, and the consequent appeal to the Calcutta high court enables a glance at yet another set of representations of the events of 23 Agrahayan. Pargiter and Woodhoffe's judgment of 28 June 1905 attributed no

---

[103] "We would have found it difficult to imagine such things happening even in these times of complete domination of ghor Koli." Ibid., p. 1.

[104] For a fuller discussion of the possible meaning of Prasanna's action that night, see below, section V.

special superstition to women. Their summary of the evidence did not even mention Sailo's illness, and presented the women as helpless victims of "various forms of ill-treatment, the details of which being of an obscene character, it is unnecessary to repeat here." In sharp contrast to the *bhadralok* jury, there was a total lack of sympathy for the "small unqualified medical practitioner", Lalmohan and "the Brahmin sadhu". The latter was considered "greatly responsible for what occurred . . . owing to his position and the influence he possessed over his disciples . . . [he] could have, but did not, exercise any control over them . . ." Prasanna, however, got a certain amount of paternalist sympathy — "the whole blame is sought to be laid on Prasanna, a low-caste man, who is undefended."[105] Not too much sympathy, though, for this Chandal hardly fitted the British stereotype of "patient and hardworking . . . a peaceful and exemplary subject of the English Government."[106] And so Prasanna and Kalachand were given identical life sentences while Lalmohan, acquitted by the Dacca jury, now got ten years' rigorous imprisonment.

British judicial discourse was interested primarily in classification, drawing clear dividing lines, calculating precise degrees of guilt, and, in particular, establishing whether the accused were sane, legally responsible individuals or madmen — whether their appropriate destination should be the prison or the asylum. The decision was that exemption from liability under section 94 of the Penal Code was not possible: there could have been "some momentary mental derangement and religious delusions owing probably . . . to their being Ganja smokers. There is no evidence, however, that the Ganja had caused actual mental disease . . . We cannot therefore say that the accused did not by reason of unsoundness of mind know the nature of the acts which they did . . ."

The discussion about madness arose in the context of the insanity plea put forward by the lawyers acting for Kalachand. It is legitimate to suspect some legal tutoring behind the assertion by the sadhu's relatives that they had tried to chain him up as a madman for breaking caste food rules and beating his wife and children. The first is not

[105] *Amrita Bazar Patrika*, 29 June 1905.
[106] Risley's comment in 1891, see above, n. 26.

usually considered lunacy, and is often permissible for a *sannyasi*; the second, unfortunately, is common and "normal" enough. The suspicion is strengthened by the shift in Kalachand's behaviour – from the collected and "rational" effort to pass the blame on to Prasanna at Srinagar, to enigmatic irrelevancies at Munshigunj and Dacca. The strange claim by an ex-schoolteacher that he could not sign the *vakalatnama* did not harm Kalachand, for his lawyers remained in court; it could, however, have strengthened the insanity plea.

Madness as a permanent or long-term total condition, the mad entirely distinct from the sane or normal, subject to medical authority, preferably locked up in an asylum – the presuppositions of British Indian law, as well as the unsuccessful efforts by some Indian lawyers to make use of them, form part of modern "common sense". Yet, as Foucault has warned, madness too has a history, and the culture of Bengal contains ample evidence about quite different perceptions of the *pagal*: not someone to be confined, but a free wanderer, whose discourse could at times contain intimations of higher truths and values. We have indications of a world where, as in Europe prior to the "great confinement" of the seventeenth century, "the sensibility of madness was linked to the presence of imaginary transcendences."[107] Perhaps the range of meanings in Indian traditions is even more multi-layered than in pre-modern Europe. "Pagal" often conveys not a sense of alienness and fear, but affection as well as reverence: one can become *pagal* for love – human or more often divine (as in many of Meera's *bhajans*, or in Baul songs) – for knowledge, or, by the early twentieth century, out of self-sacrificing devotion to one's country. A wandering religious enthusiast like Kalachand could well be called *pagal* in this sense, with a connotation very different from the modern concept of madness. The nineteenth-century literature around the Koli-yuga and Kalki-avatar themes, we shall see, often includes such figures. The Doyhata evidence gives few indications that the Majumdar household had felt that they were confronting certifiable madmen in Kalachand, Prasanna, or Lalmohan. There are signs, however, that one or two of Lalmohan's relatives and friends – like Kalachand's family – tried to

---

[107] Michel Foucault, *Madness and Civilization: A History of Insanity in the Age of Reason* (Paris, 1961; London, 1967), p. 58 and *passim*.

The Kalki-Avatar of Bikrampur 345

utilise the ambiguities of the term *pagal* to help the accused.[108] *Pagal*, after all, in one of its many nuances, could mean – at least by 1905, perhaps much earlier – something similar to the concept of madness in the modern West.

The high court summary of evidence remained silent about the religious presuppositions of the Doyhata accused, apart from a single passing reference to Kalki-avatar claims. There was no attempt, in other words, Christian missionary-style, to classify the case as an instance of rank Hindu superstition, nor were there efforts to use the affair to discredit the *bhadralok*. Doyhata, in fact, did not enter British official discourse. Perhaps the judges wanted to avoid giving any impression of interference with religion. Political tempers were already rising in the context of plans for partitioning Bengal, and Tilak in Maharashtra had recently revealed the possibilities of the combination of aggressive Hinduism and patriotic fervour. It may have seemed wiser to attribute the "religious delusions" of the accused entirely to an external physical agent, ganja, rather than to "superstitious" beliefs.

Ganja can certainly produce delusions, but the precise forms of the latter would tend to be culturally constructed. We cannot, therefore, dismiss the religious dimensions of Doyhata as easily as did the British judge, nor should we – on the basis of court evidence coloured by hindsight coming from what happened on 23 Agrahayan – underestimate the possible initial faith in Kalachand's claims as miraculous healer of illness or Kalki-avatar. Traces of that faith, in fact, persist even in the evidence. Lalmohan recalled at Munshigunj: "My gurudeva had come to my house. I was then in a state of supreme happiness."[109] Several witnesses described Lalmohan's ecstasy on the night of 23 Agrahayan: "Lakshminarayan has come to our house, the women must all take off their cloths" . . . "None of you recognised him, but I have attained my Thakur, the *yugapralay* has begun."[110] The general mood of compliance, Tona's unexplained acquiescence,

---

[108] Rajlakshmi Debi and Mahim Sarkar occasionally used the term *pagal* in connection with Lalmohan. KM, pp. 22, 47, 66.

[109] KM, p. 14.

[110] Evidence of Prasanna, at Srinagar and of Barada Devi at Dacca, ibid., pp. 8, 40.

the remarkable timidity of Rajani, all these make a little more sense given a certain belief in, or at least ambivalence towards, Kalachand's miracle-working and Kalki-avatar claims. Prasanna, at least, never seems to have lost faith. He invariably referred to his guru or *gossain* with respect, which contrasted sharply with his usual sarcasm and abuse. Nor did he express any regret whatsoever for the killing of Ananda: no doubt it still represented for him the ritual slaying necessary for the coming of the new *yuga* and/or for the manifestation of the sadhu in his true form.

Yugapralay, Kalki-avatar, and the other epic or *pauranic* terms used by or implicit in the actions of the Doyhata accused therefore had deep roots and had considerable contemporary resonance in Bengal around the turn of the century.

The related themes of Koli-yuga and Kalki-avatar go back to the Mahabharata. In the third, Vana-Parva, volume of that epic (sections 187-90 of the Markandeya-Samasya), the sage Markandeya tells Yudishthira that the Satya of Krita, Treta, and Dwapar *yugas* will be followed by a Koli-yuga of a thousand years, when "the low will become the high, and the course of things will look contrary." The order of the world of nature will be upset, kings – many of them *mlecchas* – will turn terrible oppressors, avarice and lust will reign supreme, and Brahmins will become corrupt and have "their understanding clouded by the science of disputation." The text repeatedly associates Shudras with women as the two sources of disorder. Shudras "will expound the scriptures" and "cease to wait upon and serve the Brahmins", and they will have Brahmins to serve them. Girls will choose their own partners, wives will disobey and deceive their husbands and have intercourse with menials, slaves, and even animals. Thus, "all men . . . will become members of one common order, without distinction of any kind."

At the end of Koli-yuga, the world will be destroyed by a terrible fire coming from "seven blazing suns", followed by a universal flood. Then, in a famous and eerie tale, Markandeya will meet a boy playing under a tree in the midst of the endless ocean. He will find the whole universe again inside the mouth of this boy, who is Narayana or Vishnu – and so, with the Satya-yuga restored, with the upper castes purified and back at the top, and Shudras again "devoted to the service of the three (higher) orders", another identical cosmic cycle will begin.

In a brief coda, attached a bit loosely to this detailed account of Koli-yuga and world destruction, Markandeya offers an alternative version. He refers to the birth in a Sambhalgram Brahmin family of Kalki, who "will glorify Vishnu", exterminate all *mleccha* rulers, become "the king of kings", and, by giving the earth to the Brahmins at a great Aswamedha Yajna, properly inaugurate the new *yuga*.[111]

The account of Koli-yuga is elaborated in a number of later Sanskrit texts, as for instance the *Vishnudharma* and *Brhannaradiya upapuranas*, ascribed to the third and eighth centuries AD, respectively. The challenge from Shudras and women is often conflated now with Buddhist, Tantric, and Lokayata tendencies.[112] The theme cropped up in vernacular literature too: Tulsidas, for instance, talks of Shudras reading the Gita while pandits suffer, whores flourishing while the sati (chaste women) starve: "The *tamasha* of Koli-kal is wonderful, one has to weep and laugh at the same time."[113]

The *Kalki-purana*, a very late Sanskrit text, composed perhaps as recently as in the eighteenth century and possibly originating in Bengal, renders the myth much more concrete by giving it local habitations and names.[114] Koli-yuga is embodied now in the rule of

---

[111] As I have no Sanskrit, I am using an English prose translation of the *Mahabharata* by Pratap Chandra Roy (Calcutta, n.d.), vol. III, pp. 397–413. I have also consulted the most detailed and authoritative nineteenth-century Bengali translation, that by Kaliprasanna Sinha, Gopal Halder, *et al.*, ed., *Mahabharata* (Calcutta, 1974), vol. II, pp. 194–200.

[112] "The heretics, decrying the system of the four stages of life, will create delusions . . . by means of the power of argumentation . . ." *Vishnudharma*, chapter 105. 'shudras bearing the signs of mendicancy will instruct dharma to dwija". *Brhannaradiya*, chapter 38. There are many references to "Pasandas" worshipping the linga. R.C. Hazra, *Studies in the Upapuranas*, vol. I (Calcutta, 1958), pp. 140, 324–5, 332–5. See also R.S. Sharma, "The Kali Age: A Period of Social Crisis", in S.N. Mukherjee, ed., *India: History and Thought – Essays in Honour of A.L. Basham* (Calcutta, 1982).

[113] Quoted in Jayanta Goswami, *Samajchitre Unabinghsha Satabdhir Bangla Prahasan* (Calcutta, 1974), pp. 194–5.

[114] ". . . almost all its manuscripts, hitherto discovered, are written in Bengali script."R.C. Hazra, op. cit., p. 308.

King Koli of "Bishasanpur", whose lineage, personality, and reign signify a wide range of sexual transgressions, all bracketed together as more or less equally heinous: incest, masturbation, bestiality, couples mating by free choice and disregarding caste rules, wives behaving like whores and dominating their menfolk.[115] Kalki, the avatar of Vishnu, has his Sambhalgram setting carefully described now;[116] he is trained in the Vedas and archery, receives a white horse and sword from Siva, marries Padma (the incarnation of Lakshmi), and defeats in battle the Buddhists of Kikatpur and then Koli, whose city is destroyed by fire. The views described as Buddhist often recall those normally ascribed more to Carvaka: *pratyaksha* (sense perceptions) as the sole source of valid knowledge, a consequent *deha-vada* (rejection of any *atma* or soul apart from the body), denial of caste, gods, and life after death. Women soldiers are prominent in the Kikatpur army, and Koli is helped by *mlecchas* and "Chandals", while in the Satya-yuga as restored by Kalki Shudras will serve the *dwijas* and recite Hari-nama, and women will be "devoted to husbands and faithful to dharma".[117] The text is obviously Vaishnava, but in a manner very different from bhakti traditions, for it emphasises both rigorous caste hierarchies and, quite explicitly, the need for brahminical rituals, not bhakti or Hari-nama alone.

For almost two thousand years, then, the myth of Koli-yuga and Kalki-avatar has been a recurrent and powerful vision, reminiscent in some ways of its Christian counterparts from the Book of Revelations onwards, of the world turned upside down, and of a variety of

---

[115] Thus Koli's descent is traced through a succession of brother–sister unions, and he himself mates with his sister Durukti and sits holding his penis with his left hand. In Bishasanpur, "the mutual choice by man and woman is sufficient for marriage . . . wives behave like whores . . . whoever lives there is under the command of women." The two interesting omissions seem to be homosexuality and lesbianism. *Kalki-Purana*, translated into Bengali by Kaliprasanna Vidyaratna (Calcutta, 1899; 10th edn, 1982), pp. 8, 10–11, 173.

[116] Kalki's parents are Vishnuyasha and Sumati; he has three brothers: Kabi, Prajnya, and Sumantu. The Brahmin family is befriended by a king named Bishakhayupa.

[117] *Kalki-Purana*, pp. 113-17, 126, 173, 233 and *passim*.

millenarian dreams. There are, however, two cardinal differences. Time here is predominantly cyclical, not linear;[118] at the most fundamental level there is no innovation, order is endlessly disrupted and then restored, epoch after epoch, and the return is not on a higher plane. The ideal is hierarchical order – emphatically not the lost equality and freedom which inspired so many plebeian heresies and rebellions in medieval and early modern Europe. But both visions have provided forms and legitimacy to a variety of social anxieties and aspirations. What is relevant for us here is their specific forms in nineteenth-century Bengal.

As in early modern Europe, the development of print culture in colonial India broadened the potential audience and appeal of religious literature of a predominantly "traditionalist" type.[119] The publication of classical Sanskrit texts and their translations, started by Western Orientalists and indigenous reformers like Rammohun, was quickly taken up also by "orthodox" groups like the Bharatvarshiya Sanatan Dharmarakshini Sabha or the newspaper *Bangabasi*.[120] Editions of the

---

[118] Cyclical conceptions of time do not, however, necessarily rule out linearity: in this case, there is a linear progression from Satya through Treta and Dwapar to Koli-yuga. The two can coexist within the same cognitive system, but generally not on an equal footing. See L. Howe, "The Social Determination of Knowledge: Maurice Bloch and Balinese Time", *Man*, 16, II, 1981; and Nancy M. Farriss, "Remembering the Futute, Anticipating the Past: History, Time and Cosmology Among the Maya of Yucatan", *Comparative Studies in Society and History*, 29, III, July 1987.

[119] Forty-five per cent of the books printed in Europe before 1500 were religious works, and the latter comprised 105 out of 198 titles printed in Paris in 1515. Printing, it has been argued, "could not be said to have hastened the acceptance of new ideas and knowledge in any unqualified sense." Lucien Febvre and Henri-Jean Martin, *The Coming of the Book: The Impact of Printing, 1450–1800* (London, 1976), pp. 249, 264, 278.

[120] Thus the inaugural meeting of the Bharatvarshiya Sanatan Dharmarakshini Sabha in Calcutta in 1868, patronised by big zamindars like Maharaja Sir Digvijay Singh and Digambar Mitra, announced as one of its main objectives the translation of religious texts into Gauriya *sadhubhasha* (chaste Bengali). *Report of Inaugural Meeting* (Calcutta, 1868), p. 2. The "orthodox" Bangabasi set up a separate translation department for this purpose in 1886, under Panchanan Tarkaratna. Chintaharan Chakrabarti, "Bangla Sahitya sabhay

Sanskrit text of the *Kalki-purana* came out in 1873 and 1890. Bengali translations included those by Sureshchandra Samajpati in 1886, Kaliprasanna Vidyaratna in 1899 (which I am using), and Panchanan Tarkaratna in 1908.[121] Its continued popularity is indicated by the publication in 1962 of the tenth edition of Kaliprasanna Vidyaratna's version. Meanwhile the traditional oral media for propagation of religious and moral values like *jatras, panchalis,* and *kathakatas* remained as important as ever.[122]

The recurrent motifs of the Koli-yuga myth – *mleccha* rulers, corruption among the twice-born, insubordinate Shudras, disorderly "women on top", corrosion of faith by rationalist critiques – could obviously provide a convenient format for certain types of responses to developments in nineteenth-century Bengal. It is equally evident that the myth would attract some social groups more than others. The world of *bhadralok* high culture – the so-called Bengal Renaissance – on the whole concerned itself little with Koli-yuga, except as an occasional catch-phrase with little deep meaning, or as a peg for some fairly mild and not too serious satire.[123] Social reformers were unlikely to be attracted by a myth which flayed *dwija* corruption only to exalt caste hierarchy and the strict subordination of women. Nor were groups conventionally labelled "conservative"or "orthodox"necessarily attached to it. The lurid, black and white contrasts of the *Kalki-purana*, with its vision of an abrupt and total change, did not fit too well with the ameliorative and gradualist perspectives common on the whole to "reformers"or "conservatives" coming from established gentry or successful professional groups.[124]

Sanskrita Pandit-samaj", in *Sahitya-Sadhak-Charitmala*, vol. xI, no. 107 (Calcutta, 1971).

[121] *Catalogue of Bengali Publications*, National Library of India (no place, no date); R.C. Hazra, op. cit., p. 303.

[122] See Haripada Chakrabarti, *Dasarathi o Tnahar Panchali* (Calcutta, 1960), chapter I, for a useful account of such forms.

[123] Dwijendralal Roy, *Samaj-bibhrata o Kalki-avatar* (Calcutta, 1895), typifies this kind of non-serious handling of the myth.

[124] Thus the inaugural address of Chandrasekhar Mukhopadhyay to the Sanatan Dharmarakshini Sabha briefly referred to "Koli-yuga, which should be

The Koli-yuga theme leaps into prominence as soon as we try to explore the products of what is often generically described as "Bat-tola", the Calcutta equivalent of Grub Street.[125] Jayanta Goswami's voluminous study of plays and farces lists 505 of them between 1858 and 1899. Among these no less than 31 have Koli in their titles, while the texts summarised by him contain many more references.[126] The authors, most of them forgotten today, are generally upper caste, and quite often Brahmin. But clearly theirs is the world of the unsuccessful *bhadralok* – obscure hack-writers, clerks, humble schoolteachers, pandits losing patronage in the new era, very different from the elite families or upwardly mobile, highly educated "middle-class" gentlemen of the Brahmo Samaj, Indian Association, or Sanatan Dharmarakshini Sabha. Meanwhile, similar themes were finding expression in the bazaar paintings of Kalighat: "sold by thousands in stalls near the shrine of Kalighat in the neighbourhood of Calcutta as also in other places of pilgrimage and public fairs . . . at a price ranging from a pice to an anna."[127] From about the 1870s onwards, a strongly satirical note becomes evident in the Kalighat paintings – "the world", the *patuas* seem to have felt, "was passing through a dark age, a Koli yug." Mildred Archer has described this as a mood of "popular disgust with modern life."[128]

The term "popular" here probably requires some qualification. Bat-tola farces and Kalighat paintings no doubt satirised babu culture, but they do not offer any unmediated access to a distinct level of popular culture any more than, say, the *Bibliotheque bleu* or the chapbooks of seventeenth–eighteenth-century France or England. Their patrons and consumers could include many of the *bhadralok*, while the

---

obeyed." The apocalyptic note embodied in the Kalki myth is conspicuously absent here.

[125] For a brief description of Bat-tola literature, see Sukumar Sen, *Banglar Chhapa o Boi* (Calcutta, 1984).

[126] Jayanta Goswami, op. cit., pp. 1233–55.

[127] T.N. Mukherji, *Art Manufactures of India* (Calcutta, 1888), quoted in W.G. Archer, *Bazar Paintings of Calcutta* (London, 1953), pp. 12–13.

[128] Mildred Archer, *Indian Popular Paintings in the India Office Library* (London, 1977), p. 143.

strongly hierarchical values they embody would seem to suggest a culture imposed on rather than coming from the popular classes.[129] Insofar as a specific strata can be distinguished at all – always a problematic venture in matters of culture – it would be rather the world of genteel poverty, depressed upper-caste literati within a kind of pre-industrial lower middle class.[130] Precisely, in fact, the kind of milieu from which our Bikrampur Kalki-avatar came; and it is surely not stretching historical imagination too far to think of *jatras* embodying Koli-yuga themes and Kalighat paintings reaching a religious fair like that of Nangalbandh, where Kalachand met Prasanna.

The bulk of the farces surveyed by Jayanta Goswami are set firmly in the present, earthly – as distinct from *pauranic* or cosmic time. The evils of Koli-yuga, consequently, are far more prominent than the Kalki-avatar counterpoint, references to which are in fact rather rare. A principal target, as one would expect, was the anglicised, often Brahmo, young man.[131] The vices of corrupt *purohits* and Vaishnava *goswamis* are attacked with vehemence, at times in the same play, a reminder that sharp "reformist"/"orthodox" disjunctions are often irrelevant.[132] But the central figure, at least from the mid 1860s

---

[129] For important discussions concerning problems with the concept of "popular culture", see Carlo Ginzburg, *The Cheese and the Worms* (Harmondsworth, 1982), pp. xix–xx; and Roger Chartier, "Culture as Appropriation: Popular Cultural Uses in Early Modern France", in Steven Kaplan, ed., *Understanding Popular Culture* (The Hague, 1984).

[130] A Czech historian has warned against the imputation of an unqualified "popular" character to medieval European utopian or millenarian thinking. The "Land of Cockayne", he argues, is "most likely to be found among the wandering scholars and students who were familiar with village life but also had a certain literary education". F.F. Graus, "Social Utopias in the Middle Age", *Past and Present*, 38, December 1967.

[131] See, for example, Kanailal Sen, *Kolir Dashdasha* (Calcutta, 1875); Surendranath Haldar, *Kolir Sang* (Calcutta, 1880); and Mahendra Nath's *Kolir Avatar*, Jayanta Goswami, op. cit., pp. 404–8, 193–8, 893.

[132] Thus Kalikumar Mukhopadhyay's *Bapre Koli* (Calcutta, 1886) has as its twin targets the anglicised youth Ambicacharan, who tries to steal his elder brother's wife, and the guru Mahesh Vidyachandchu, who plans to seduce a servant girl. Most of the twenty-two farces on the Tarakeswar scandal of

onwards, is undoubtedly the disorderly woman: the prostitute who gets priority over the wife, or, more often, the modern wife herself, who ill-treats the mother-in-law, enslaves the husband, wastes money on luxuries for herself, and prefers reading to household duties.[133] The fears expressed through this recurrent figure seem too deep to be explained merely by "the *stri-swadhinata*" (women's emancipation) efforts – at their height in the 1860s and 1870s – of Vidyasagar, Keshab Sen, or the Young Brahmos. Reformist discourse in fact always combined emancipation with insistence upon puritanical restraint, freedom with discipline, and in any case the impact of reform efforts on everyday gender relations was extremely limited.[134] Perhaps we have here, as in Elizabethan and Jacobean England, "a displacing of change in general on to women in particular", with women bearing "the brunt of a general social uneasiness".[135]

The great unsaid of much of this literature, namely colonial subjection (it is significant that *mleccha* rule and oppression, very much of the Koli-yuga myth, is hardly ever directly mentioned in these farces), in fact makes an unexpected and indirect entry precisely through the woman-on-top. In Harishchandra Bandopadhyay's *Kaler Bau* (1880), for instance, the husband complains: "We have

---

1873 summarised in Goswami are bitterly critical of the *mohunt* Madhavgiri: ibid., pp. 1134–7, 254–300.

[133] In Bholanath Mukhopadhyay's *Bhyalare mor bap, arthat streebadhya prahasan* (Calcutta, 1876), to take only one example, the mother-in-law has to go around in tatters and is eventually thrown out, the wife (Bijoykali) spends all her husband's money on clothes for herself, the husband (Kalirkap) describes his wife as "my master, my guru, my object of worship and devotions" and even drinks her *charanamrita*. The farce ends with Bijoykali dressing up Kalirkap in sheep's clothes. Exact iconographic equivalents exist in Kalighat painting – a woman leads a sheep with a human head in a *pat* dated around 1865, and a woman boldly strides on top of a prostrate man. Mildred Archer, op. cit., p. 147; W. Archer, op. cit., plate 42, p. 70.

[134] For a brief discussion, see Sumit Sarkar, "Women's Question in Nineteenth Century Bengal", in *A Critique of Colonial India* (Calcutta, 1985).

[135] Lisa Jardine, *Still Harping on Daughters: Women and Drama in the Age of Shakespeare* (Sussex, 1983), pp. 49, 182.

no happiness, whether at home or outside. Slaves to government officials, we have to spend our time in homes as slaves to the wives." Subordination to wives gets conflated in an extremely interesting manner with political subjection to "the sons of the English queen": "Bangamata" has "become the slave [*dasi*] of the London queen". Thus the figure of the suffering mother neglected by sons who have been entrapped by the wiles of the modern wife become a metaphor for the enslaved "mother"-land.[136] Political themes quickly overshadow misogynist satire in *Meye Parliament ba Bhagnitantraraj* (1886, 1893), a farcical counter-utopia where women rule and men sit behind the purdah, deprived of equal rights since they are not yet fit for them: "Licking the feet of their superiors has become [their] only occupation . . . slavery is their only source of livelihood . . . the entire nation [*jati*] has become a nation of supplicants [*umedar*]."[137]

The disorderly wife promotes the neglect of kinship obligations, and thus enhances the corrosive impact of the "modern" craze for money. The theme of worship of money disrupting family ties is a recurrent one in the theatre of Girishchandra Ghosh, the one major literary figure of the nineteenth century who had roots in lower-middle-class urban life.[138] A related motif is the time-bound, and therefore unbearably rigorous, work characteristic of Koli-yuga from which solace is sought in drink – as by the ruined old-fashioned businessman Jogesh in *Prafulla* – or in a religion of simple bhakti through the recitation of Hari-nama alone, the only kind appropriate for busy times.[139] The discourse of Ramakrishna, Girishchandra's

---

[136] Jayanta Goswami, op. cit., p. 1036.

[137] *Sri Kono Ek Aitihasik, Meye Parliament ba Bhagnitantraraj* (Calcutta, 1886, 1893), pp. 180–2.

[138] See, for example, his *Srivatsa-Chinta* (1884) and *Prafulla* (1889), in Rathindranath Roy and Debipada Bhattacharji, ed., *Girish Rachanabali* (Calcutta, 1969), vols IV, III. Girish failed in his school-leaving examination and worked as a clerk till the 1880s. He wrote for a public stage, and his theatre took over many elements of the popular *jatra* form. Utpal Dutt's *Girish-manas* (Calcutta, 1983) contains an interesting discussion of such themes, but greatly exaggerates the "popular" and "progressive" aspects of Girishchandra.

[139] *Srivatsa-Chinta*, I. ii; *Prafulla*, I.i; *Nasiram* (1888), i.iii, ii.iii; *Kalapahar* (1896), II, I, III: *Girish Rachanabali*, vols III, IV.

guru – a poor rustic Brahmin who captivated a largely clerical *bhadralok* audience – becomes redolent of deeper layers of meaning in this context: for Ramakrishna, as is well known, repeatedly brought together the evils of *kamini*, *kanchan*, and the *dasatya* of *chakri* in offices.[140] *Natun Babu ba Kolir Abatar* (1904), written by a minor playwright obviously influenced by Girishchandra, identified "*Kolir karkhana*" – the factory of Kali – with craze for money, selfish sundering of kinship ties, and contempt of the *nouveau riche* babu for relatives who have remained clerks.[141]

From around the 1880s onwards, counterpoints start developing to the evils of Koli-yuga, and once again the women provide the central metaphor. The disorderly woman is partially displaced by the pure, suffering mother, wife, or even at times prostitute with heart of gold, ennobled by suffering and reasserting the moral order in ways that somehow combine boldness with deference. Prafulla, in Girish's play named after her, pious wife of the villainous Ramesh who has ruined his older brother Jogesh, provides a notable example of this genre. It is she who resists her husband, not Jogesh – who remains sunk in total passivity and drink – and yet she combines deference with resistance.[142] In Satischandra Chattopadhyay's *Annapurna* (1904), the wife insists on helping her ailing brother-in-law against the wishes of her husband Bhupen. A drunk Bhupen beats his wife, who responds

---

[140] For a preliminary discussion of these themes, which I no longer find entirely satisfactory, see Sumit Sarkar, "The *Kathamrita* as Text: Towards an Understanding of Ramakrishna Paramhansa", Occasional Paper xxii, New Delhi, Nehru Memorial Museum and Library, 1985.

[141] Bilas, the "*natun* babu", neglects his mother, refuses to help his brother, and is full of contempt for his old-fashioned father who had kept open house for poor relatives: "They are worthless clerks! Poor! And I am now a well-known *baralok* . . . The *baralok* of today doesn't care for brothers and such-like!'satischandra Chattopadhyay, *Natun Babu ba Kolir Abatar* (Calcutta, 1904), scenes xii and xiii.

[142] "Do you think I care for my own life so much that I'll let my husband do such a devilish thing . . .? Dharma has tolerated a lot, take care, it will not permit this: . . . I will not criticise you – I pray that God will accept my death as atonement (*prayashchitta*) for your sins . . . my dying prayer is – God forgive you." *Prafulla*, v.iv.

characteristically: "You have every right to beat me, but I am pleading at your feet . . . Do not get so excited . . . let me fan you a little."[143] The nature and limits of this kind of deferential assertion are clearly spelt out in a slightly earlier play by the same author: "We are women, our only intelligence is our husband's . . . but if at times the husband's thinking has gone astray (*vipareet buddhi*), the duty of the intelligent wife is to correct that, otherwise we disgrace our name as partners in dharma (*sahadharmini*)."[144] In both plays women relatives and neighbours are shocked by the boldness of the wives. What we have here is not a simple revival of the tradition of Sati-Savitri-Sita, but a new construction, different from yet related to the old.

The Koli-yuga literature we have been surveying is virtually silent about that other obsession of the earlier text, the insubordinate Shudra. This is perhaps because there were few self-consciously anti-caste movements among plebeian groups in nineteenth-century Bengal.[145] There are, instead, occasional plebeian trickster figures helping wronged wives to take revenge upon dissolute husbands,[146]

---

[143] *Annapurna*, III.vi.

[144] Satischandra Chattopadhyay, *Chandiram* (Calcutta, 1901), II.iv. The wife was protesting against her husband's plans to force their daughter Madhavi to marry the old king. In a happy ending, with change of heart all around, Madhavi marries the young man of her choice, and then promptly falls at his feet: "I am the servant (*dasi*) protected by you." The son also protests against his father, but within the same deferential mode. Ibid., VI.

[145] Brahmo criticism of caste spent itself in surrogate actions like removing the sacred thread from *acharyas* presiding over Brahmo prayer meetings, and in any case remained a strictly *bhadralok* affair; inter-caste marriages seldom went beyond Brahmin-Vaidya-Kayastha. Nineteenth-century Bengal never produced a Jyotiba Phule.

[146] Ramnarayan Tarkaratna, *Chakshudan* (Calcutta. 1869); Jogendranath Bandopadhyay, *Ami Tomari* (Calcutta, 1979); Mir Musaraff Husain, *Er Upay Ki?* (Calcutta, 1892). In Ramakrishna Chattopadhyay's *Chhere de Ma Knede Bnacchi* (Calcutta, 1881), two prostitutes sincerely devoted to their poor lovers turn the tables on a rich client: one rides on his back, the other spanks his behind. Jayanta Goswami, op. cit., pp. 201–4, 208–11, 216–19. Girishchandra's plays sometimes have plebeian women-trickster figures who energetically carry forward the action – the reformed prostitute Sona in *Nasiram*, the Shudra Chanchala in *Kalapahar*.

The Kalki-Avatar of Bikrampur   357

as well as old-world servants in choric roles ridiculing their anglicised masters and assisting, in properly subordinate ways, the restoration of the moral order.[147] Figures like Batul or Bhajahari in Girishchandra's *Srivatsa-Chinta* and *Prafulla* add an interesting dimension of plebeian comment. Peasants evicted and ruined by tax collectors and zamindars, they put in perspective the less acute misery of their masters. But concern for plebeian misery is never allowed to overstep its limits to become sympathy for rebellion. Batul in fact actively helps in the restoration of King Srivatsa after he has been overthrown by a popular uprising. Poverty ceases to remain abstract or marginal only when it becomes a matter of clerks, or – as in many early-twentieth-century Bengali novels about rural life – of the life of poor Brahmin families in villages.[148] For the rest, we have once again the figure of deferential assertion, for plebeians as for women. Deference is pushed to its limits, all but transgressed, turned into its opposite, but eventually restored in a purified form.

In several of Girishchandra's plays the restoration of the moral order takes place under the aegis of wandering Brahmins who appear mad (*pagal*) to the conventional world but convey profound truths in an earthy language. Nasiram in the play named after him (1889), or Chintamani in *Kalapahar* (1896), are clearly modelled on one kind of representation of Ramakrishna: they preach the complete surrender of rationalistic calculation, the rejection of any social activism, and repeatedly condemn *kamini*, *kanchan*, and, the *dasatya* of *chakri*.[149] The *pagal* of Girishchandra brings together elements of Indian religious traditions (the Baul, as well as bhajans, where love for the divine becomes indistinguishable from madness) with the Shakespearian fool.[150] Satischandra Chattopadhyay, too, has his "mad"

---

[147] Sailendranath Haldar, *Kolir Sang* (Calcutta, 1880); Jasadanandan Chattopadhyay, *Kolir Kap* (Calcutta, 1895). Jayanta Goswami, op. cit., pp. 195, 233–9.

[148] A good example of this genre would be the sufferings of Harihar and Sarbajaya in Bibhutibhushan Bandopadhyay's *Pather Panchali*.

[149] *Nasiram*, II.Iii; *Kalapahar*, I.v.

[150] In *Nasiram*, II.Iii, the Kapalik explains to Sona why the king likes Nasiram: "Kings like to keep such a *pagal* with them, to see what madness

religious wanderers – Chandiram, and in *Annapurna*, Ramakrishna himself as Gadadhar, a *pujari* in a rich man's temple, along with a *thakurda* (grandfather) who roams the streets singing devotional songs. The importance of this theme in contemporary culture might help to explain the ease with which Kalachand gained entry into the Majumdar household.

So far we have not encountered the Kalki myth at all. Its apocalyptic and martial mood did not fit in too well with the dominant motif of a restoration of moral order through a kind of passive resistance, and the plays we have surveyed are firmly set in earthly time. In 1888, however, a play was written about a rumour in Bengal that a golden tile had fallen from heaven on the Kasi Viswanath temple of Banaras, predicting that "soon Vishnu will be born as an avatar to punish the atheists (*nastik*)."[151] Ramakrishna was far from being a millenarian figure, yet the *Kathamrita* does contain one startling aside. Recalling insults suffered at the hands of a Dakshineswar temple official, he once remarked: "The Kalki-avatar will come at the end of Koli-yuga. A poor Brahmin's son, he will know nothing – suddenly a horse and sword will come . . ."[152] The striking thing here is the identification of Kalki with a poor Brahmin – totally absent in the Mahabharata or the *Kalki-purana* – which surely tells us something about the social location of the myth in late-nineteenth-century Bengal.

There are, however, a few plays which unlike the rest try to combine mythical with historical time. Two of these, dated 1859 and 1902, explicitly base themselves on the *Kalki-purana*, and the gap in time between them affords some insights into the way the theme was being modified in late-nineteenth-century Bengal. Narayan Chattoraj's *Koli*

---

is." He adds, however, "Oh, that madman, don"t you know how he cured the king of his illness once?"Elizabethan fools, in contrast, provide a commentary on the ways of the world – they seldom affect the course of the action in any fundamental way.

[151] R.N. Sarkar, *Kasidhame Visweswarer Mandire Swarga Hoite Sonar Tali Patane Kalki Avatar* (Calcutta, 1888), Jayanta Goswami, op. cit., p. 1218 (unfortunately no further details are given).

[152] "M", *Sri Sri Ramakrishna Kathamrita*, vol. IV (Calcutta, 1919, 1980), p. 101 (20 June 1889).

kautuk Natak (Serampur, 1859) describes the various evils of Koli-yuga, but does not mention Kalki or any *pagal* saviour at all; nor are women – whether disorderly or deferentially assertive – particularly prominent. The play ranges in time from the reign of Parikshit down to "Koli coming to Bengal, and setting up, through Clive sahib, the city of Koli-karta [where Koli is master] or Calcutta." The agents of Koli are many: Buddhists, Muslims destroying temples (only a passing reference, however), Tantriks, plebeian groups like the Bauls and the Kartabhaja, lecherous orthodox pandits, Kulin polygamists, anglicised young men, Rammohun, Vidyasagar. Special attention is given to materialist and hedonist arguments, which are expounded with such care that one is almost tempted to suspect some ambiguity in the author's own beliefs.[153]

An interesting study in contrast is offered by *Kolir Abashan, ba Kalki-abatarer Geetabhinoy* (Calcutta, 1902), written by a "poor Brahman" from Jessore working as head pandit in a Calcutta school (Mitra Institution), and particularly important for us because it was made into a *jatra* and performed often in the *mufussil*.[154] "Nastik" arguments remain important,[155] but an equally prominent feature of the reign of the incestuous Koli-Durukti couple is now the emancipated and therefore disorderly women.[156] The really striking innovation, however, is that Kalki is born in an abjectly poor village Brahmin

[153] Narayan Chattoraj, *Kolikautuk Natak Arthat nattyachhale Kolir arambhaabadhi bartaman kalparjyanta ghatanar sangkhipta bibaran* (Serampur, 1859), pp. 37–42. The arguments are put in the mouth of Buddha, but many of them are taken straight from descriptions of Carvaka's teachings in the *Vishnupurana* and Madhava's *Sarva-Darshan-Sangraha*: see Debiprasad Chattopadhyay, *Lokayata: A Study in Ancient Indian Materialism* (New Delhi, 1978), pp. 22, 41, 45. The ironic style is reminiscent also of Caryapada verses, and at the time of Kabir, while the more immediate context might well be the rationalistic iconoclasm of "Young Bengal".

[154] Aghorchandra Kabyatirtha, *Kolir Abashan, ba Kalki-abatar-Geetabhinoy* (Calcutta, 1902), Preface.

[155] Ibid., pp. 11, 111–20, 205–7. They include the well-known saying attributed to Carvaka: "As long as you live, live happily; borrow, if necessary, to have *ghi*."

[156] At the beginning of his reign, Kali assures Durukti that women will be completely free (*swadhin*): "In learning and wisdom/ men will be defeated by

household. His elder brother, Sumantu, almost dies of hunger, but is miraculously saved by "Gobin-pagla", a typical figure of holy madness preaching the power of Hari-nama.[157] And the deferentially assertive pure woman turns up again and again. Kalki's father Vishnuyasha, on the point of killing himself due to poverty, is given sustenance and faith by his wife Sumati, who asserts in the same breath that "the chief dharma of women is to serve their husband".[158] In heaven, Saraswati quarrels with Lakshmi, for in Koli-yuga virtuous learning (embodied no doubt in the poor Brahmin) has been overcome by the fickle power of money.[159] A Brahmin widow, dragged by soldiers into the court of the lustful Koli, heroically defends her chastity by killing herself. Though the play discreetly avoids any direct reference to *mleccha* rule as a feature of Koli-yuga, we are here trembling on the verge of a clear-cut patriotic statement.[160]

Biharilal Chattopadhyay's *Naba Rah aba Yuga-Mahatmya* (Calcutta, 1897) begins with the reign of Koli-raj and disorder in Siva's family, but quickly passes on to scenes of peasant poverty and plague. Significantly, a young male hero now appears to defend the honour of a village girl being pawed by an English doctor on the pretext of medical examination: "I will knock down your head", he thunders in English, "and examine your deranged brain wherein germinates the mania of Bubonic fever."[161] We are entering the era of Vivekananda, Swadeshi young men, and revolutionary terrorism.

V

By the turn of the century Koli-yuga and Kalki-avatar had thus come to signify a set of images, emotions and beliefs, an entire "structure of

---

women/ men will remain in fear/ at the feet of women, day and night/... the mother will be servant (*dasi*) to the daughter-in-law . . ." Ibid., pp. 6–7.

[157] Ibid., pp. 27–45.
[158] Ibid., p. 36.
[159] Ibid., pp. 12–19.
[160] Ibid., pp. 55–6.
[161] Jayanta Goswami, op. cit., pp. 1140–2.

feeling".[162] Its apparently traditionalist idiom was open to, and able to incorporate, moments of self-assertion by women and a concern for poverty: more specifically, the anguish of preindustrial "lower middle class" groups – poor Brahmin literati in villages and small towns, schoolteachers, clerks. More detailed analysis of the implications of this pattern of assertion-within-deference lies beyond the scope of the present essay. But the figure we have been tracing does seem to offer a striking preview of many dimensions of Gandhian satyagraha, and the low life of literature of Bengal in the 1920s would repeatedly return to it; merely spelling out explicitly its nationalist implications.[163] In its praxis, too, middle-class male nationalism would relate to subaltern groups in ways strikingly similar: peasants and women would be simultaneously mobilised and controlled through a strategy and language which modified, adjusted, but never fundamentally overturned the hierarchies and norms of deference of caste, class, and gender. We encounter here, perhaps, a crucial affective component of a pattern of "passive revolution".[164] Analysis of this structure of feeling might help the critique of nationalism to get beyond the crudities of conspiracy or betrayal models. Deferential assertion could be internalised, to a considerable extent, among subordinate groups. It had its linkages, after all, with pre-existing patterns of bhakti.

[162] Raymond Williams defines "structure of feeling" as "characteristic elements of impulse, restraint and tone; specifically affective elements of consciousness and relationships." He distinguishes this term from concepts like "worldview" or "ideology" because of the need to "go beyond formally held and systematic beliefs", and out of a concern for "meanings and values as they are actively lived and felt". Williams, *Marxism and Literature* (Oxford, 1977), p. 132.

[163] See in particular the analysis of the novel *Charka-Rani* in Tanika Sarkar, "Nationalist Iconography . . .", *Economic and Political Weekly*, xxii, 47, 21 November 1987.

[164] Antonio Gramsci, *Selections from Prison Notebooks* (New York-London, 1971), pp. 106–14. For attempts to apply the "passive revolution" concept to Indian nationalism, see Sumit Sarkar, *Popular Movements and Middle Class Leadership in Late Colonial India* (Calcutta, 1983), pp. 71–3, and Partha Chatterjee, *Nationalist Thought and the Colonial World: A Derivative Discourse?* (Delhi, 1987).

Meera's revolt against the norms of court life and patriarchy had found expression, it may be recalled, in a passionate willed submission: "*Mein chakor rakho, chakor rakho, chakor rakho ji.*"[165]

How, if at all, does Doyhata relate to all this? The linkages remain inevitably obscure. We know nothing about the reading abilities and habits of the Majumdar household or of Kalachand, about the plays they or the illiterate Prasanna may have seen, the cheap pictures they might have brought back from temples or fairs. More specifically, we do not know whether Kalachand saw the *jatra* about the Kalki-avatar, then touring the *mofussil*, which had been written by another poor Brahmin schoolteacher. All that the case record tells us is that bits and pieces, not only of the Kalki-avatar myth but of the Mahabharata and the Ramayana, coloured and structured the happenings at Doyhata. *Yuga-pralay*, Yama, Dronacharya, Hanuman, Lanka, all somehow entered the story. They entered it in different ways, in and through a conflict over meanings – that is the important point – and the sum total, after Prasanna's takeover, became something which middle-class discourse could not absorb.

A curious mismatch is apparent in the evidence about the four central figures of 23 Agrahayan: Lalmohan, Kalachand, Prasanna, and Ananda. We know, or can guess, a reasonable amount about the background of people like Lalmohan, or even Kalachand, but next to nothing about the everyday cultural life of Prasanna or Ananda. Yet Lalmohan and Kalachand remain more mysterious as individuals, for both in different ways tried to evade responsibility in court through reticence. Prasanna, in contrast, was evidently proud of most of the things he had done that night, and talked with apparent frankness. It is somewhat easier to tease possible meaning out of his actions, but very difficult to place them in a broader context.

Were the actions of the trio planned beforehand, as Prasanna claimed in court? The events stretched out over a fair length of time, from late afternoon or early evening to well past midnight. Lalmohan and Tona helped to throw away the corpse, no-one seems to have objected seriously to the fires, no family member or neighbour tried

---

[165] I owe this point to Tanika Sarkar.

The Kalki-Avatar of Bikrampur

to get help from the police station a mere quarter-mile away. Absent from the bulk of the evidence, also, is any marked tone of surprise or dismay. It was only around and after midnight, with the enforced stripping of the womenfolk and Prasanna's orders to Lalmohan to kill his son, that tensions apparently reached breaking point. Compliance till then out of cowardice alone is not entirely satisfactory as an explanation. Prasanna's amazing power that night could not have been purely innate: presumably it had some roots in the already established interrelations between Kalachand, Lalmohan, Prasanna himself, and the other members of the Majumdar household. We do at times get the impression, almost, of a kind of sacred theatre, with some sort of "script" – a script, however, into which Prasanna inserted improvisations, which shattered in the end the earlier unity of the protagonists.

What that script could have meant to its authors remains more than a little obscure, for we know nothing about the details of Kalachand's teaching. All that appears reasonably certain is that the cult initially involved a devotion to Hari explicitly placed above that the sadhu's *charanamrita* and ashes from his *kalki* were supposed to cure miraculously; and that, shortly before 23 Agrahayan, Kalachand started claiming to be Kalki-avatar and predicting some kind of *yuga-pralay*. Beyond that, the differences in reading begin, and these require some exploration, however tentative.

Prasanna on the night of 23 Agrahayan at first sight appears to signify a moment of uninhibited plebeian fury: smashing and burning houses; insulting, beating up, and stripping his social betters; burning a Brahmin's sacred thread and urinating on a *bhadramahila*; defying the police and army of British India. But we must not forget that Prasanna got the chance of entering the Majumdar house only because he had become the disciple of a Brahmin sadhu, and so was in a sense no longer quite the usual Chandal. He was rather what the KM pamphlet called a "Chandal sadhu".[166] His fury expressed itself

---

[166] During their first stay at the Majumdars, Rajani recalled Prasanna performing the appropriate subordinate function of preparing ganja for the sadhu and Lalmohan. KM, pp. 1, 55.

through picking up and rearranging, bricoleur-fashion,[167] fragments of dominant culture. It signifies, therefore, not a totally independent level or set of texts and beliefs, but autonomous ways of appropriation.[168]

Lalmohan, the best educated in the circle around Kalachand, was called "Dronacharya" by Prasanna – someone from whom sacred knowledge had to be acquired. The Chandal made a special point of asking "Dronacharya" to recite a mantra before starting the fire, which to him was a "*yajna*".[169] Prasanna had been seen brandishing a bow two days before the murder – he was Ekalavya, perhaps, but unlike the deferential Adivasi of the Mahabharata he did not hesitate to bully, insult, or even beat "Dronacharya".[170] He was simultaneously Hanuman, burning Doyhata as Lanka had been burnt or possibly also the capital of Koli, which too had been destroyed by fire. Once again, what was conspicuously absent was the note of deferential bhakti so characteristic of Hanuman in the Ramayana.

The event of 23 Agrahayan turned around the three nodal points of the killing of Ananda, fire, and nudity. Death rituals in Hinduism have a strong sacrificial element, through which the quotidian is elevated to the sacred and liminality is reintegrated. The murder of Ananda, too, was possibly a kind of sacrifice, though a very different one from the conventional "offering of the dead person . . . to the gods and ancestors" at the purified cremation ground, governed by caste rules and mantras.[171] The high castes Lalmohan and Tona displayed

[167] The analogy of the bricoleur is developed in Claude Levi-Strauss, *The Savage Mind* (London, 1981), pp. 16–36. For an application to the history of popular culture, see David W. Sabean, *Power in the Blood: Popular Culture and Village Discourse in Early Modern Germany* (Cambridge, 1984), pp. 90–1.

[168] "The search for a specific and exclusively popular, often a disappointing quest, must be replaced by the search for the differentiated ways in which common material was used." Roger Chartier, "Culture as Appropriation: Popular Cultural Uses in Early Modern France", in Steven Kaplan, ed., *Understanding Popular Culture* (The Hague, 1984), p. 235.

[169] Barada and Sashimukhi recalled Prasanna's request to Lalmohan, and Mahim Sarkar quoted Prasanna as saying, "Today I will perform yajna wth fire". KM, pp. 42, 52, 63.

[170] Evidence of Jogmaya at Dacca, ibid., p. 33.

[171] Veena Das, "The Uses of Liminality: Society and Cosmos in Hinduism", *Contributions to India Sociology*, NS, 10, ii, July–December 1976.

no qualms in helping the Chandal carry the body of the murdered Bhuinmali. Kalachand, however, seems to have ordered some kind of cleansing of the site of the murder immediately afterwards, which may or may not have had a ritual significance. No proper death ritual is permitted anyway in cases of unnatural death, and one might also speculate that the association of untouchables (Doms in particular, who are sometimes loosely called Chandals) with funerals and executions might have somewhat reduced the transgressive elements here for the upper-caste protagonists.[172]

The killing of Ananda provided a kind of meeting place for several different conceptions of *yuga-pralay*. For Kalachand and Lalmohan, *yuga-pralay* meant the coming of Kalki, and Ananda, identified by them curiously not with Koli but with Yama, had to be killed or sacrificed as the necessary prelude. How Yama got into the scenario remains extremely mysterious. The god of death does not figure in the Kalki myth at all, and the restoration of Satya-yuga never promised any deliverance from death or purely physical suffering of the kind Lalmohan had been talking about.

Prasanna, however, never referred to Kalachand as Kalki-avatar: to him, the sadhu was always "guru" or "*gossain*". Maybe the Kalki myth, with its insistence on rigid caste subordination, had little appeal to the Chandal, less certainly than Vaishnava bhakti which at least promised a certain mitigation of hierarchy, a level of devotion where Brahmin and untouchable could be momentarily one in a communion of ganja and song. Nor did Prasanna ever justify Ananda's murder as the killing of Yama. His version, confirmed by Tona, was that Ananda had offered himself as a victim (the note of sacrifice again, but in a different sense) to prove Kalachand's greatness to the world. The sadhu would bring about a miraculous physical resurrection: according to Lalmohan, Prasanna had promised Ananda a *dibyadeha* (divine body). Lalmohan himself was later offered "a son of gold" by Prasanna, in return for killing Nanda. When he refused, Prasanna declared that he had turned into a goat.[173]

---

[172] H.H. Risley, *Tribes and Castes of Bengal*, vol. I (Calcutta, 1891), pp. 184, 240.

[173] Evidence of Jogmaya, *Bengalee*, 16 March 1905.

It is just possible that we are encountering here traces of belief structures quite distinct from the Koli-yuga and Kalki tradition – a discordant physical note, embodied perhaps also in Lalmohan and Kalachand's assertions that the killing of Yama would end death in the world. The Nath cult, influential among plebeian groups in East Bengal for centuries, had sought to make the physical body immortal through various yogic practises; its myths include references to errant men being turned into goats or sheep.[174] Such practices, however, were eminently esoteric, conducted normally in secret and away from everyday household life. Their possible importation into a *bhadralok* household was deeply transgressive.

Kalachand, we know, had disparaged the worship of Kali, and yet the first thing Prasanna did after the murder was to smear his guru, Lalmohan, and himself with Ananda's blood, an obviously Shakta rite.[175] He also made Rajlakshmi stand naked on his lap in what a witness described was "the posture of Kali".[176] The juxtaposition of Shakta and Vaishnava elements in Prasanna is not really surprising: the two had been intermingling at least from the eighteenth century, as evident notably in the Shyamsangit of Ramprasad and the entire phenomenon of Ramakrishna.

The fires were started at Prasanna's initiative, but "Dronacharya" Lalmohan apparently blessed this *yajna*, and no-one seems to have been too worried by them: the Majumdar house was never seriously in danger. That Bhuinmali and Muslim houses were principally affected by Prasanna's arson efforts could have been accidental. *Raiyat* homesteads would burn more easily than a *bhadralok* house. Alternatively, one could argue that subaltern identity is quite often also defined in terms of groups lying still lower in the social hierarchy.[177] Chandals and Bhuinmalis, we know, were quarrelling over precedence

---

[174] Sashibhushan Dasgupta, *Obscure Religious Cults* (Calcutta, 1946, 1976), pt III, and Appendix C.

[175] Deposition of Prasanna at Munshigunj, KM, pp. 18.

[176] Jogmaya's evidence, ibid., p. 37.

[177] Tanika Sarkar, *Bengal 1928–34: The Politics of Protest* (Delhi, 1987), p. 148.

at that time, and Namasudra–Muslim relations in subsequent years were marked by occasional conflicts.[178]

The stripping of women (and of one or two men) had a purificatory significance for the sadhu and his *bhadralok* disciple. "*Astapash mukta boa*", liberation from the eight sins, was how Lalmohan described it, and he seems to have taken off his own clothes, too.[179] Liberation from worldly dross through nudity does have an important role at times in the sadhana of the ascetic or *sannyasi*: we are as yet not beyond the limits of high Hinduism. There was obviously a difference, however, between Lalmohan and Kalachand disrobing their caste equals, and Prasanna stripping off the clothes from his social superiors. It is difficult not to suspect layers of meaning here apart from an ascetic rejection of worldly superfluities. Clothes are a major significata of social rank and class, the obvious indicators even today in Bengal of the *bhadralok* and the *chotolok*. A man like Prasanna might well have been going around in a loincloth.

The central act in the peculiar kind of sacred theatre Prasanna conducted that night was the purification of women, and he had been abusing women in particular for not respecting the sadhu for some days before. They were stripped, made to touch a fire, had their pubic hair burnt, and Rajlakshmi had a *kalki* thrust into her vagina. No attempt was made to castrate or abuse male genitalia in any way. Prasanna, in other words, seems to have shared the pervasive male high-culture suspicion about women as the gateway to hell, and feminine sexuality as specially impure and dangerous. The Nath-yogi literature, too, is full of tales of feminine malignity.[180]

Purification involved inversion: nudity, as well as the penetration of the vagina by the *kalki* (not dissimilar in shape to the penis), far from

---

[178] Namasudra-Muslim riots affected eighteen villages along the Jessore-Khulna border in May 1911. Namasudras and Muslims had combined, however, against upper-caste Hindu landlords in Jessore and Khulna in 1908. Sumit Sarkar, "The Conditions and Nature of Subaltern Militancy: Bengal from Swadeshi to Non-Cooperation, *c.* 1905–22", in Ranajit Guha, ed., *Subaltern Studies III* (Delhi, 1984), p. 283.

[179] KM, p. 61.

[180] Sasibhushan Dasgupta, op. cit., pp. 244–9, 398.

having any sexual implications, had precisely the opposite significance that night in Prasanna's mind, and there is not the slightest hint of any attempt at rape. There are also indications that women purified came close to the sacred for him: once again, we have an echo of a high-culture theme. He addressed Rajlakshmi as "mother" while stripping her, used a term of respect for the women touching the fire, and claimed to have seen "two devatas" himself while this ritual was being performed.[181] Incidentally, the only time Prasanna showed any regret in court was about the way he had "infringed the modesty of women".[182]

Prasanna's inversions had a ritual character. Men and women were stripped; asked to salute the sadhu, and then allowed to put on their clothes and leave. Levelling down through nudity was purely temporary. Prasanna, after all, was not enacting an established ritual, but, perhaps, groping towards a new one. For one night, he did achieve the remarkable feat of a kind of double inversion. The Koli-yuga myth was an inverted world set right side up again, restoring proper caste and gender hierarchy and deference. Its nineteenth-century forms had not even considered Shudras the major source of disorder. Not only had the Chandal burst into and taken over a re-enactment of the myth by a Brahmin sadhu and a *bhadralok* disciple, he had appropriated bits of it, along with fragments from epics equally deferential in intent, to terrorise the Doyhata *bhadralok* and make a wife kick her husband on the forehead. It is fitting, then, that Prasanna be given the last word. Asked by the judge to sign the statement taking full responsibility for all that had happened, Prasanna replied: "*Jadi likkhai jantam, to be to panch-shat-shata taka mahinae joj-i-hoyitam.*" (If I had known how to write, why then, I would have become a judge and earned five to seven hundred rupees).[183]

---

[181] Deposition of Prasanna, KM, pp. 9, 19.
[182] Ibid., p. 24.
[183] Ibid., p. 74.

9

Nationalism
Ideology and Mobilisation

SOUTH ASIAN HISTORY-WRITING about the late colonial era has suffered from both too much and too little engagement with nationalism.[1] Too much because a single binary opposition between colonialism and nationalism has been dominant for a very long time, revealing a surprising tenacity amidst many changes in forms. Such binaries often homogenise both poles, ignoring differences within both categories and underestimating changes over time. Obvious instances would include the country/city dualism that has been common in many cultures for at least the past two centuries, gaining strength from the spread of industrialisation and the concomitant rise of romantic values, or, for that matter, West and non-West or "Oriental". There has also been a strong tendency to virtually enfold the entire terrain of the decades from roughly the 1870s till the 1940s within what then becomes a single narrative framework. Initiatives and developments get evaluated solely in terms of their relationships with this dichotomy, and the questions repeatedly foregrounded concern the "contributions" of particular initiatives towards strengthening or weakening political or cultural nationalism. Other kinds of implications or consequences, in terms of impact on more "internal" social-cultural relationships and values, tend to get ignored.

It might seem that I am oversimplifying, for the distinctness of much Muslim political mobilisation in the later colonial era is surely obvious, culminating in the emergence in 1947 of not one but two

[1] This essay was written in 2005.

independent nation-states. Perhaps, then, it might be argued, the standard framework has been of a triadic rather than a binary pattern, colonialism / Indian nationalism / Muslim nationalism. But in practice the third element has repeatedly been elided, in otherwise very different, indeed mutually opposed, historiographical traditions. In Indian history-writing, Muslim political mobilisation, even when on a countrywide scale and perspectives, has seldom been given what is assumed to be the honour of "legitimate" or "proper" nationalism. The terms preferred have been "Muslim breakaway", "Muslim separatism", or "communalism". Their counterparts in Pakistani scholarship follow the same assumption, though of course with reversed values. For them, the nationalism that culminated in the realisation of Pakistan is the only legitimate claimant to that honourable term. The Indian or anti-colonial nationalism that is written or spoken about and glorified across the border is for them no more than Hindu communalism in borrowed and illegitimate plumes. The homogenisation and the domination of a single narrative framework therefore persists, and along with it the problem which is really my central theme. What has been little explored, I feel, and precisely because of the domination of this single binary, are the ways in which nationalism(s) and a host of identity formations mutually inflected each other in late colonial times.

Too little of nationalism, at the same time: for the precise and varied meanings of that category in South Asia, its different types, have been seldom explored. It has remained far too much of an unitary concept. In the words of a recent commentator, South Asian historiography still lacks "a suitable register within which to locate incipient and formative nationalisms under the conditions of colonial and imperial domination", in significant contrast to nineteenth-century Europe where distinctions between "primordialist, ethnic, republican and civil nationalisms" have been well-established.[2] In both respects, I am tempted to suggest, "Orientalism" still flourishes amidst and through its many repudiations, for histories of the non-West often get portrayed in simplistic, unitary terms that would be

[2] Chetan Bhatt, *Hindu Nationalism: Origins, Ideologies and Modern Myths* (Oxford, 2001), p. 7.

unacceptable in the historiography of Western countries, and get typecast in entirety under the label of "nationalism".

The power of this silence is perhaps best indicated by the fate of the one major – if also highly controversial – attempt to disrupt it, made by Partha Chatterjee in two works dated 1989 and 1993, along with some associated late Subaltern Studies writings.[3] These did try to explore and critique South Asian nationalism theoretically, and have come to enjoy great renown internationally, as well as within the more prestigious academic circles within the country (though they have had little impact so far on the bulk of Indian syllabi and textbooks). I shall argue, however, that the significance of what could have heralded a major break has not been really grasped, for there was also a parallel process of recuperation, to which the scholars who brought about the potential rupture have also contributed. The binary model, I suggest, still continues, though in considerably modified forms, notably a shift from political and socio-economic, to cultural registers. And so does the tendency to enfold the bulk of South Asian history within that dichotomy, to a possibly enhanced extent.

But this is to begin intolerably in midstream, tempted by what today appears most prominent and theoretically exciting and controversial. I need to retrace my steps, through a conjoint historiographical and historical survey. This will be very brief about the initial decades, and begin to be more detailed, with some references to specific writings, from the climacteric of the 1970s and '80s, the era of the "Cambridge School" and early Subaltern Studies. My main focus, however, will be on the most recent years, when, I shall suggest, there are signs that the long-persistent binary framework is being complicated through a combination of empirical research and theoretical developments.

II

Even the briefest of looks at earlier frameworks shows the necessary connection of different phases of historiography with the nature of

---

[3] Partha Chatterjee, *Nationalist Thought and the Colonial World: A Derivative Discourse?* (Delhi, 1986), and idem, *The Nation and Its Fragments* (Princeton, 1993; Delhi, 1994).

source materials available at particular times, the changing assumptions of scholars and commentators, and political conjunctures. In histories of nationalisms, more obviously perhaps than elsewhere, the present keeps moulding the past, in ways both fruitful and problematic. Till the late 1960s the official archives most directly relevant for the study of Indian nationalist movements were inaccessible to historians, notably documents about the entire Gandhian era, due to a fifty-year rule. Private paper collections, whether of officials or Indians, were also mostly inaccessible. Academic history-writing about anti-colonial nationalism therefore had a rather later start, and patriotic sentiments of rather problematic kinds, we shall see, found expression in studies and the literature about movements against medieval Muslim rulers. Professional scholarship entered that so far neglected domain on a large scale only from the 1950s, at a time when there was considerable confidence in the possibilities of independent development along "Nehruvian" lines, and the dominant mood among Indian historians was nationalism of a rather conventional kind, though complicated by occasional Left-oriented writings. "Nationalism", per se, was assumed to be a good thing in a people fighting for independence from foreign domination. That it could also at times be problematic or repressive, in terms of its effects on class, caste, regional, religious, or gender relationships, literature and art, tended to get ignored, provided it could be shown to have been genuinely and sufficiently anti-colonial. Left writings did highlight some kinds of internal tensions, notably of course of class. But there remained, even in the more radical kinds of historiography, a persistent tendency to read into otherwise admired figures or movements elements of conscious, anti-colonial nationalism. So a pioneer social reformer of the early nineteenth century like Rammohan had to be termed embryonically nationalist in his ideals, the "father of modern India" with a precocious national vision, despite his well-known basic loyalism and considerable praise of British rule. Conversely, a certain Left-oriented line of criticism of Roy and similar nineteenth-century middle-class figures emphasised above all the inadequacies of their awareness of British exploitation, and not, say, the possible limits of their programmes of social reform. Similarly, the peasant rebels glorified particularly in another strand of Left history-writing had to have conscious nationalism read back into them, even if they were fighting purely local Indian oppressors and on occasion had looked up to British officials for sympathy and intercession. It was as if everyone had an obligation to be nationalist or anti-British right from the beginning of colonial rule, irrespective of evidence indicating much more complicated and contradictory patterns.

Such histories tended to be written "from above", in terms of leaders or parties mobilising followers. Left writing was not too different in this respect, leading to the later Subaltern Studies critique of having been "elitist" too, for the focus was on the "correctness" or otherwise of leading groups or programmes in mobilising from above – through trade union, peasant association, or party – what remained generalised categories of "masses", "peasants", the "working class". This resulted in enthusiastic surveys, usually all-India but occasionally region-based, of the achievements of great nationalist heroes effectively energising the masses, particularly from 1919 onwards. A standard, entirely linear, periodisation became firmly established, which still provides the framework for most textbook surveys, and remains useful for some purposes. It merits a brief outline.

The saga began with a series of anti-British "popular" movements, of which the 1857 Rebellion was thought to mark the climax. Whether these could be called "national", and therefore the real beginning of the "freedom movement", however, was the subject of a rather tedious and sterile controversy. This centred, above all, on the undoubtedly major landmark of the 1857 anti-British rebellion, started by the Indian soldiers in the East India Company army but spreading to dispossessed or disgruntled princes, nobles, and large numbers of peasants and other ordinary people across much of North and Central India. The stimulus to research on 1857 that came about on the occasion of its centenary, however, got bogged down in the controversy as to whether it could or could not be called "The First Indian War of Independence", to the exclusion of other possible questions.

In the narrative I am now summarising, the defeat of 1857 was followed after an interval of a couple of decades by the nationalism of the educated middle class. Initially quite loyalist, growing sections among them became critical of specific aspects of British rule, notably the "drain of wealth" and other policies contributing to repeated famines and immiserisation, deepening racism, and the refusal to make concessions to middle-class demands for ending discrimination in administrative appointments and providing a measure of political representation. This was the "Moderate" phase, from around the 1870s–80s till *c.* 1905, marked by the foundation of the Indian National Congress (1885), prayers and petitions primarily to win over public opinion in Britain, and a failure (or refusal) to attempt mass mobilisation around more radical demands, leave alone independence. British obduracy, combined with a series of provocations under Curzon, notably the partition of Bengal (1905), resulted then in an "Extremist" phase, most evident in Bengal, Maharashtra, and Punjab. Extremism experimented with new techniques like the boycott of British goods, the promotion of indigenous enterprises (swadeshi), and national education free of British control – anticipating some Gandhian methods – and occasionally raised a demand for self-government (swaraj). But the Extremist phase failed as a whole to achieve effective mass mobilisation, indispensable for the success of the new techniques, and, in the face of intensified repression (combined with some limited concessions by the British to win over the Moderates), gave way to "revolutionary" methods. These meant in practice the assassination of oppressive officials and occasional conspiracies to get arms from abroad, notably from Germany during the First World War. Extremism and revolutionary terrorism were marked also by a strong Hindu note. Unlike the broadly social-reformist and secular outlook of their Moderate predecessors, religion was thought by the Extremists to be the road to win over the masses.

From *c.* 1915–19 on, the simple and linear narrative went on to argue, Gandhi's charisma and skill in developing effective methods of peaceful mass struggle energised large numbers of peasants and important segments of Indian business groups, in three great waves of national upsurge, Non-Cooperation-Khilafat (*c.* 1919–22), Civil Disobedience (1930–4), and Quit India (1942). The Congress under the Mahatma thus became something very different from what it had been in the Moderate and Extremist phases. There was however an unfortunate dimension, which did not quite fit into this triumphalist narrative, and therefore tended to be played down in conventional nationalist accounts. This was what Indian historians usually described as a "Muslim breakaway" or "Muslim separatism", greatly encouraged by British divide-and-rule strategies, and in the combination of these two strands, it was assumed, lay the origins of the Partition of 1947. Their counterparts in Pakistan, equally predictably, described the same phenomena as signs of the growth of a legitimate and honourable "Muslim nationalism". That chauvinist Hindu-nationalist or communal elements also made a "contribution" towards the ultimate division of the country, working both outside and within the Congress, was generally ignored on the Indian side of the border. Communalism in Indian high school or college courses tended to get collapsed into Muslim separatism. Particularly from the mid 1920s onwards, communal riots between Hindus and Muslims became a regular feature of Indian life, and there was a significant decline in Muslim participation in the later stages of Gandhian nationalism. The consequence in 1947 was a freedom combined inextricably with a veritable communal holocaust and the partition of the country.

With access to new sources, such a simple narrative came to be questioned and complicated in the years from the late 1960s to the mid 1980s, in two very different and mutually hostile ways. Earlier studies, based mainly on autobiographies and biographies of all-India leaders, and the published statements of parties, had tended to possess a countrywide and therefore often over-generalised scope. The sudden expansion of access to central and provincial archives under the new thirty-year rule, coinciding with the opening up of more and more collections of private papers of British officials and prominent Indians, now stimulated research on regions and sometimes localities. A group of historians based in Cambridge – who came to be called the Cambridge School – were the first to make methodologically novel use of this expansion. What they brought was not just additional details based on this new material, but certain general alternatives to the standard, highly eulogistic and often starry-eyed, nationalist narrative. The first impact of the use of private correspondence or diaries, inevitably for the major part of "elite" figures, was to impart a note of cynicism about the idealism and purely patriotic motivations of many of the cult figures of the national movement who had so long been taken at face value, in terms of publicly proclaimed intentions alone. Even Gandhi began to seem to some of these scholars not much more than an effective political manipulator, mobilising his followers through intermediary "sub-contractors". Patriotic ideals appeared no more than a veil for the pursuit of selfish group or individual interests. These were initially conceptualized most notably in the pioneering work by Anil Seal's *The Emergence of Indian Nationalism* (Cambridge, 1968) as regional "elites" blending Western education and high-caste status. These elites had sought material benefits through a combination of collaboration and conflict with the British while engaged in simultaneous competition with other regional groups. Five years later, the collection titled *Locality, Province and Nation* edited by Jack Gallagher, Gordon Johnson, and Anil Seal (Cambridge, 1973) proclaimed the need for disaggregation of the category of "elite" into locality-based "patron–client" linkages ("factions"), equally animated by selfish interests. Their occasional, ephemeral combinations on a regional or even national basis were explained in terms of the pressures and/or opportunities offered at certain times by the colonial state. It is fair to add, though, that the Cambridge analysis of British officialdom was usually as cynical. But this "Namierite" shift – collapsing patriotic ideals into the narrowest of interests – aroused very hostile reactions among most Indian historians (myself included), some of whom even suspected a "neo-colonialist" motivation or conspiracy. They felt, with some justice, that the basic features of colonial exploitation and domination seemed to be obscured in a maze of detail about the selfish machinations of rulers and ruled alike. I now feel that our hostility was somewhat excessive, though there was an undoubtedly major problem in collapsing what after all did become for a time one of the biggest mass movements of the early twentieth century into the occasional coming together of otherwise quite disparate factional groupings of patrons and clients, explicable purely in terms of narrowly materialistic pressures and stimuli from changing official structures and policies. Significantly, periods of mass struggle tended to be largely ignored in the Cambridge School scholarship. But a cutting down to size of nationalist icons was perhaps ultimately helpful, and most Cambridge School scholars soon moved away from pure faction analysis and excessive cynicism. And the argument that the tightening of the structures of the colonial state had been a crucial factor in conditioning late-colonial Indian developments did prove subsequently quite fruitful, as we shall see, for it came to be extended to processes beyond nationalism, too, and taken beyond its constricted, conventionally "administrative" and "constitutional" beginnings.

The reactions to the Cambridge School took two divergent forms. One was a simple reassertion of the old nationalist verities, occasionally backed up by more empirical research than had been possible earlier but not very interesting from the point of new perspectives. The other was the Subaltern Studies project, now by far the best-known internationally of all South Asian historiographical trends, about the changing trajectory of which much has been written over the past decade, and is readily available. Briefly, and for the moment about early Subaltern Studies alone, before the major shift within the project in the late 1980s: its undoubted contribution was in exploring and complicating the relations and tensions between institutionalized political activities and popular, part-autonomous, initiatives. Effective (or ineffective) mobilisation had been studied so far in a top-down, "elitist" manner, and explained in terms of charismatic patriotic leadership and ideals, skilful manipulations, colonial pressures and stimuli, or (in early Marxist writing) by economic conjunctures and "correct" or "incorrect" applications of Marxist strategy. Such interpretations, whether nationalist or orthodox Marxist, were now critiqued for an elitism which went along sometimes with economic determinism; in both, the possibility of "subaltern" agency remained unexplored. The new approach sought moments of popular (in practice, most often, peasant) autonomy, and its emphasis on subjectivity led towards efforts at studying the forms of subaltern consciousness and culture, no longer assumed as the mere derivatives of "elite" patterns of thinking.

In the 1970s and early '80s, the world of late colonial South Asian history was simultaneously enlivened, and often obscured, by the polemical fire and smoke which gathered around both the Cambridge School (in both its phases) and Subaltern Studies that was launched some fifteen years after Seal's founding text. I do not think much purpose would be served now by rehearsing these old and somewhat dated controversies, and in any case a copious literature about them is easily available.[4] Despite the important points that had sometimes emerged from them, the polemics seem by hindsight to have taken up too much of the attention and time of many historians, and often resulted in excessively polarised and simplified positions. But major research-based works did emerge during these years, from both the Cambridge and the early Subaltern lines of thought, as well as sometimes from historians less easily classed with either, and these retain much more abiding value and interest. Three themes, I suggest, stand out here.

The new sources enabled explorations of the social bases of evolving nationalist movements at regional levels, going beyond earlier, often over-simplified, and formulaic class categories applied without much distinction to all parts of the country and across times. One instance would be John McLane's carefully nuanced study of the Moderate nationalists, which interestingly related their moderation and refusal to think seriously about mobilising non-elite strata to both relative affluence amidst mass poverty and the fear of mass upheavals. His broadly class-based analysis simultaneously avoided the excessively debunking stance of some of his contemporary Cambridge scholars. My doctoral research on early twentieth-century Swadeshi Bengal, while sharply critical of the Cambridge School, also tried to move away from conventional nationalist digits, linking the decline in the open agitation against the Partition from around 1907–8 not primarily to British repression, as had been customary, but

---

[4] The first volume of *Subaltern Studies* came out in 1982, but some of the research studies of individual members of its editorial collective had started appearing from the late 1970s. Many of the key contributions to the intense debate which followed have been conveniently brought together in David Ludden, ed., *Reading Subaltern Studies* (Delhi, 2001).

internal, class- and community-related, limits. A movement primarily of higher-caste educated Hindus, often with rentier interests in land, it failed to mobilise the mostly Muslim and lower-caste Hindu peasants, and never extended, for instance, the methods of "passive resistance" formulated at the peak of Extremist enthusiasm to include no-rent movements. Among the Cambridge scholars, the studies of South India by David Washbrook and C.J. Baker combined narrow faction analysis with interesting suggestions about differences in the structures of politics related to the contrast between "wet" and "dry" zones of agriculture.[5] And it is interesting that the essay by Chris Bayly on late-nineteenth-century structures of politics in the Allahabad region, which was included in *Locality, Province and Nation* (1973) – the second, revised theoretical statement of the Cambridge School – appears today a part-critique of that school in highlighting the links between professional middle-class groups and local bankers and traders, in questioning the assumption of invariable connections between moments of agitation and administrative pressures or opportunities, and in emphasising rather the *dharmic* or quasi-religious dimensions of an emergent nationalist politics which was closely bound up with the growth of Hindu conservative and revivalist sentiments. There was an implicit internal criticism here, already, of the undue stress on narrow material and factional calculations and sole determining role of government policies.[6]

[5] John R. McLane, *Indian Nationalism and the Early Congress* (Princeton, 1977); Sumit Sarkar, *Swadeshi Movement in Bengal 1903–08* (Delhi, 1973); D.A. Washbrook, *The Emergence of Provincial Politics: Madras Presidency, 1870–1920* (Cambridge, 1976); C.J. Baker, *The Politics of South India, 1920–1927* (Cambridge, 1976). Washbrook and Baker suggested that in the "wet" areas, characterised by abundance of rain or, more commonly, irrigation, a broad stratum of relatively prosperous peasants could emerge, constituting the basis of wider nationalist mobilisation. In the "dry" lands with insufficient water, in contrast, a more skewed agrarian structure emerged with small groups of dominant rural "bosses", and such mobilisation as happened took place along narrow patron–client lines

[6] C.A. Bayly, "Patrons and Politics in Northern India", *Modern Asian Studies*, 1973. Bayly elaborated this line of research through his *The Local Roots of Indian Politics: Allahabad, 1880–1920* (Oxford, 1975), and *Rulers,*

Despite the major differences in approach, much of the most impressive work of early Subaltern Studies carried forward this strand of exploration of social dimensions at regional and local levels, most notably perhaps in David Hardiman's micro-study of the major Gandhian base of Kheda (Gujarat), based on a combination of local archives and about 170 interviews with activists and survivors of those times, most of them village-level people.[7] Such levels of exploration of oral data have seldom been equalled in South Asian history-writing. The focus of research on nationalism had by now shifted decisively and permanently to regions or smaller areas, as indicated for instance by the still valuable compendium of studies brought out by D.A. Low in 1977, *Congress and the Raj: Facets of the Indian Struggle, 1917–47* (London).[8] Such collections also helped to bridge the gap between alternative polemical positions, for they have usually included contributions from both standpoints, as well as many from neither.

The trade mark of Subaltern Studies in its first phase was the focus on an autonomy/leadership dialectic. This was perhaps not entirely as novel as sometimes claimed by the votaries of this dynamic new group of historians, for some earlier orthodox Marxist work, including R.P. Dutt's pioneering *India Today* (1940), had suggested that Gandhian nationalism appropriated and utilised already emergent mass militancy, perhaps "betrayed" it at times (the locus classicus for that being Gandhi's abrupt and unilateral calling off of Non-Cooperation after the violence at Chauri Chaura in February 1922). Such "extreme Left" denunciations alternated with more pro-Congress attitudes in Indian Marxist circles for many decades, but, like historical accounts and interpretations of nationalism generally till the 1960s, they suffered from over-generality and fairly limited grounding in

---

Townsmen and Bazaars: North Indian Society in the Age of British Expansion, 1770–1870 (Cambridge, 1983).

[7] David Hardiman, *Peasant Nationalists of Gujarat: Kheda District 1917–1934* (Delhi, 1981).

[8] There have been a number of such collections since then, associated particularly with anniversaries, like the centenary of the foundation of the Congress in 1985, and fifty years of Indian independence in 1997.

sources. Like historical studies generally in those times, they tended to be all-India surveys based on secondary material. The problem was approached now with considerably enhanced subtlety, as for instance in the argument, first developed in the context of the United Provinces of the 1920s and '30s by Gyanendra Pandey but extended elsewhere, of an inverse relationship: strengthening of Congress organisation (Civil Disobedience as compared to Non-Cooperation, for instance), leading to a decline in peasant enthusiasm.[9]

The simultaneous rejection of "elitism" and "economism", central to the early Subaltern project, led on to efforts to explore autonomous popular (in effect, primarily peasant) forms of consciousness and culture. Ranajit Guha led the way with a stimulating, if perhaps a bit too structuralist, study of the "elementary forms" of peasant consciousness in colonial India, and there was important work on, for instance, the construction of images of Gandhi "from below", a local cult in Gujarat, and the mentalities that could be teased out of the death of a village woman in a botched-up abortion and a strange incident in a rural gentry household in Bengal.[10]

Such initial explorations of culture were still sought to be embedded in rigorous studies of material conditions, but soon there developed, both within and beyond Subaltern Studies, a strong "culturalist" turn in history-writing.[11] Here there was an obvious parallel with worldwide intellectual trends. The early interest in popular movements, stimulated by hopes of radical transformations from below, characteristic of the era of China, Cuba, Vietnam, May 1968,

---

[9] Gyanendra Pandey, *The Ascendancy of the Congress in Uttar Pradesh 1926–34* (Delhi, 1978).

[10] Ranajit Guha, *Elementary Aspects of Peasant Insurgency in Colonial India* (Delhi, 1983); David Hardiman, *The Coming of the Devi: Adivasi Assertion in Western India* (Delhi, 1987); Ranajit Guha, "Chandra's Death", in Guha, ed., *Subaltern Studies V* (Delhi, 1987); Sumit Sarkar, "The Kalki-Avatar of Bikrampur: A Village Scandal in Early Twentieth Century Bengal", in Ranajit Guha, ed., *Subaltern Studies VI* (Delhi, 1989).

[11] I have tried to explore the ramifications of the change within Subaltern Studies in my "The Decline of the Subaltern in *Subaltern Studies*", in Sarkar, *Writing Social History* (Delhi, 1997).

had ebbed by the late 1980s, and the pasts and minds of peasants and tribals no longer seemed so enthralling. Within Subaltern Studies, there was in effect a return to the colonial middle-class intelligentsia, whose culture was after all so much more accessible than the ways of thinking and emotions of a largely illiterate peasantry. Partha Chatterjee's effort to explore colonial middle-class nationalism as an ideology became central to this endeavour. This was certainly an advance, for there had been a strange absence at the heart of the plenitude of earlier writings. Early Subaltern Studies, despite its primary focus on anti-colonial struggles, had not really tried to explore nationalism as a category: in effect, it had been collapsed into popular movements. (A similar criticism would not be irrelevant if made about my *Modern India 1885–1947,* Delhi, 1983). To Cambridge, nationalism had seemed a ramshackle, occasional, and reactive coming together of local factions, while stereotypical nationalist writing had remained content to assume their subject to have been a natural given for a subject people.

Chatterjee's two books inaugurated what amounted to a vast expansion, for nationalism, so long thought of primarily in political or economic terms, now acquired, with surprisingly little debate (some polemics apart), a much wider, "cultural" set of meanings. The expansion has been a source of strength – and weakness. The wider roots and implications of nationalism, notably ideological and cultural, came under a scrutiny absent earlier, and important work began on its manifestations in diverse realms of late-colonial experience: gender images, caste relationships, literature, and art. But a weakness, too, in terms of a certain amorphousness, for it is sometimes a puzzle as to who, within the colonial educated intelligentsia, depending on choice, cannot be considered a "nationalist". Nowadays virtually any kind of middle-class literati thought or practice in the colonial era can be described as nationalist, even if the people involved had been quite loyalist in their politics – provided that germs of notions of a wider country, or of a modern nation-state, can be found somewhere in their writings. Conversely, the cultural domains now being opened up to sophisticated historical investigation tended to be interpreted primarily, at times solely, in terms of the quality of their nationalism, the extent to which they could escape from the burden of colonial modernity. And the vogue for "postcoloniality" in effect sometimes extends broadly similar assumptions and stereotypes down to current times. Once again, there are both gains and losses from this endless expansion. It would be widely accepted today that too much has often been made of the 1947 rupture – yet there is also something curious that more than fifty years after formal British control had ended, the history of independent India is still often being categorised as being, primarily, post-colonial.

Why such a big change in the meaning of nationalism attracted so little attention or debate (some criticisms of Chatterjee apart), quickly becoming a taken-for-granted academic common sense, might repay a little attention. As I have suggested, the transformation passed unnoticed because it also contained an important continuity: the persistence, in different forms, first political and/or economic, then cultural, of a basic colonial–anti-colonial (or genuinely "indigenous") binary. Indeed, the polarity was even accentuated, for, at least in its initial phase, cultural domination by "modern", "Western", "post-Enlightenment" ways of thinking and values was often construed in a seamless and total manner and in almost entirely negative ways. Chatterjee in 1989 famously characterised the discourses of the colonized as fundamentally "derivative", though by 1993 he had quietly abandoned that position and moved towards a disjunction between "home" and the "world", where religion, culture, and family values are thought to have retained or developed a certain autonomy. A troubling consequence, at times, was a temptation to characterise the world of the "home" in predominantly positive ways, occasionally veering towards socially conservative positions.

Such binaries homogenised in two ways. The degree of efficacy or autonomy *vis-à-vis* the modern West, political or cultural, becomes often the basic, or even the sole, standard of judgement for evaluating the quality of political or cultural initiatives flowing from the "colonial-educated" middle class. The bigger problem, however, is that the expansion of the range of the term nationalist seems sometimes in danger of swallowing up virtually the whole of late-colonial history, even more completely than earlier. A striking instance would be the evident embarrassment displayed by some feminist historians writing about social reform efforts or measures concerning specific forms of gender oppression, limited and rare as such changes in Hindu law remained under British rule. The laws banning sati, legalising widow marriage, and imposing a minimum age for consent (1829, 1856, 1891), made by colonial rulers with some persuasion from quite loyalist Indian literati, would be the most obvious instance. The emphasis tends to be on pointing out the limits of such measures, or the possibly suspect quality of British motivations – aspects that needed to be probed, but still I find the evident lack of enthusiasm or even sympathy for reform a bit worrying. The history of late-colonial India is placed within a simplified mould, and the possibility or even need to explore multiple, even conflictual, narratives, gets brushed aside as too complicated. Indian reform efforts related to gender or caste oppression might well have been opposed to nationalism, and nationalism at times have been deeply implicated in patterns of patriarchal, caste, or class domination. Surely it is time, even in an ex-colonial country (after more than a half century of independence), to move away from the assumption that nationalisms, even when unimpeachably anti-colonial politically and culturally, are necessarily always "progressive" phenomena in any unqualified manner. The bulk of serious work on histories of Britain, European countries, or the USA, in contrast, have given up for quite some time the late-nineteenth-century tendency to collapse history into the single narrative of nation-state formation and evolution, and the possibility of untidy, mutually conflicting narratives is commonly accepted. One example would be the histories of working-class movements and efforts at women's emancipation, in Britain and many Western countries. It is generally accepted that the advance of industrial labour organisation had often been accompanied by a marginalisation of women's issues, in significant contrast to some early socialist thinking and practices. Socialist-feminist scholarship which helped to open up these problems did not feel any necessity for ignoring or dismissing either.

I might be charged with being unfair at this point, for there is no doubt that late Subaltern Studies writings have polemicised against modern nationalism often enough, and in a sense the whole project began with a trenchant critique of not just colonialist but also "bourgeois-nationalist elitism". Yet Ranajit Guha's initial programmatic statement then went on to define *"the central problematic of the historiography of colonial India"* as the *"historic failure of the nation to come to its own."*[12] The revised framework changed things, but not entirely, for the critique then shifted from what in effect were the class-related limits of "elite" nationalism, to adoption of the "nation-state project" of the modern West: Marx, one might say, was displaced by Said and to some extent Foucault. Colonial and post-colonial nationalisms came under attack primarily for being deeply complicit in a Western or colonial discourse, with similarly homogenising consequences The modern "nation-state project" certainly has been and remains highly problematic in many ways, but the key point of criticism seems usually to be its origin in the modern West. Surely this gives far too much priority to the question of the origins of institutions or ideas, as distinct from possibilities of creative appropriations or multiple deployments, or even its specific consequences in particular times and places. And then the desire for an indigenous counterpoint often becomes irresistible, sought for usually in an "authentic", "subaltern", or domestic world distinct from elite or middle class, and somehow more or less untouched by the Western taint. Political nationalism expressed through struggles for an independent Indian state is condemned, but nationalism of a sort continues in cultural forms.

Meanwhile, global intellectual currents of different forms of poststructuralism and postcoloniality, originating mostly from Paris and then spreading quickly to US universities and then virtually throughout the world of literary, cultural, and historical studies, had started attracting growing numbers of avant-garde Indian intellectuals. A contributory factor was that more and more of the latter were going to the West for their advanced studies, and sometimes settling there. Subaltern Studies in its modified form acquired a central place in such

[12] Ranajit Guha, "On Some Aspects of the Historiography of Colonial India", in Ranajit Guha, ed., *Subaltern Studies I* (Delhi, 1982), p. 7 (emphasis in the original).

thinking, and in fact contributed quite decisively to the evolution of postcoloniality. This has been largely responsible for its enormous reputation in the West, something which no other tradition of Indian history-writing has ever enjoyed. Yet here a little-noticed paradox needs to be noted. With the exception of some of the recent writings of Dipesh Chakrabarty, the hallmark of the work of late Subaltern Studies has been a thoroughgoing inversion of the once-standard assumption, shared by liberals, Marxists, and even many Indian nationalists, of "Enlightened" modernity as, fundamentally, cultural progress, however tainted by its introduction in South Asia through colonial power. But such inversion necessarily retained a similar unilinearity of approach, with unqualified progress only displaced by equally unqualified retrogression, and "modern" ideas and values being tainted from birth, so to say, by their undeniably Western origins. Yet rejection alike of unilinearity and of excessive emphasis on origins have been vital to much post-structuralism and postmodernism, and even of some of the more sophisticated strands of postcolonial theory, which see in them some of the worst features of modern European "historicism". One can think, for instance, of Derrida's famous critique of Levi-Strauss for his unacceptable "ethic of nostalgia for origins, an ethic of archaic and natural innocence", or the subtleties of the best of Homi Bhabha's concepts of "hybridity" and "mimicry", so different from any one-way "derivation".[13] Here a seldom-noticed gap seems to have emerged between late Subaltern Studies, and even more between the writings of many of its enthusiastic acolytes, and the patterns of thought with which it is usually associated.

Recently, however, something like a new wave seems to be emerging, where through a combination of concrete research and theoretical analysis binaries of all kinds are being sought to be complicated in very interesting ways. It is to this most recent work on South Asian history and nationalism that I now turn.

[13] Jacques Derrida, "Structure, Sign and Play in the Discourse of the Human Sciences", in idem, *Writing and Difference* (Paris, 1967; trans. Chicago, 1978); Homi Bhabha, "Of Mimicry and Man: The Ambivalence of Colonial Discourse", in idem, *The Location of Culture* (London/New York, 1994), pp. 85–92.

III

The broader contexts for the new turn in historical thinking have been constituted by major shifts in both international and South Asian conjunctures through the late 1980s and '90s. The link between the apparent collapse of movements for radical transformation, and the ascendancy of "culture" over more materialistic histories, has been mentioned already. The other major development, again worldwide, was the displacement of class by diverse forms of identity-based movements, with that term itself coming into wide use only from around these years. Among these the most prominent in India has been of course Hindu nationalism or Hindutva, culminating in the destruction of the Babri Masjid in December 1992, the rise of the Hindu Right to power in the central government between 1998 and 2004, and the state-sponsored anti-Muslim pogrom in Gujarat in March 2002. But beginning from the late-1970s and now more visible was also the rise of Dalit and "lower-caste" formations, in which some have tried to find a kind of counterpoint to the upper-caste-led Hindu Right. Women's movements, previously dependent on organized parties, led invariably by men, took more self-conscious, theoretically aware feminist forms. A variety of local grassroots movements around questions of environment (the curtailment of common property rights in forests, hydro-electric projects displacing large numbers in the name of development, etc.) helped very directly to constitute yet another new field of intellectual and historical work. The sheer suddenness and evident importance of these largely new movements forced historians of modern India to at last partly overcome the odd inhibitions that had kept them so long on the other side of 1947. Communalism, caste, gender, and environment, themes previously marginal or virtually non-existent in history-writing about modern India, became the key subjects of current research. The focus has been on recent times, but there is also a delving back before independence. The net impact was that it has become increasingly difficult to present late-colonial history as a single, linear narrative centred around anti-colonial nationalism alone. The latter, in fact, has lately fallen somewhat out of favour with younger scholars, though still remaining overwhelmingly predominant in textbooks and official propaganda. Each phase of shifting contexts has thus helped to add new dimensions, but also sometimes threatens to occlude others: "presentism", too, has its problems.

At the theoretical level, Partha Chatterjee, already by the early 1990s, had moved away from his "derivative discourse" framework of 1989, which had inserted into South Asian scholarship a rather simplified version of Edward Said's critique of Orientalism, with an initial overwhelming stress on Western cultural domination. But the recent work of Dipesh Chakrabarty provides the most sophisticated instance of signs of change within the Subaltern Studies collective. The more empirical chapters of his *Provincializing Europe*, dealing with particular aspects of nineteenth-century middle-class life and sociability in Bengal, still occasionally get limited by the effort to sustain a "provincialising" project, which seems to demand a continued evaluation in terms of the degree of distance from Western forms of modernity. But basically, Chakrabarty's is an effort to work within, and at the same time move beyond, the post-colonial problematic as previously understood by Subaltern Studies scholars. It rejects categorically the possibility of "shunning European thought" and seeks throughout to hold in creative tension its "simultaneous indispensability and inadequacy" in exploring the "mental and emotive world of the colonial intelligentsia." The concepts it deploys, to use the helpful term coined by Derrida, are usually "under erasure". One can neither fully accept nor totally abandon them, but need to work in and through the categories, even while never giving up one's critique.[14]

The instances in historical research would be many, and extend across very diverse fields. Let me begin with two, drawn from areas less directly related to nationalism. In the new surge in labour history in South Asia after a long period of relative neglect, the rigid polarities around which earlier work had evolved – formal and informal sectors, factory workers and the urban poor, a settled city

---

[14] Dipesh Chakrabarty, *Provincializing Europe: Postcolonial Thought and Historical Difference* (Princeton, 2000), pp. 255–6, and *passim*. For a clear exposition of Derrida's concept of "erasure", see Gayatri Chakraborty Spivak's Introduction to Derrida, *Of Grammatology* (Baltimore, 1976, 1997).

proletariat and village labourers, histories of labour and of Dalits and subordinated castes – have all come under fruitful scrutiny. Jan Breman, who pioneered in South Asian Studies the questioning of the formal/informal dichotomy way back in 1976, formulated later the striking category "footloose labour" which cuts across all these distinctions.[15] Here, as in many other contexts, recent developments have been forcing rethinking by scholars, in particular the new patterns of "globalised" neo-liberal capitalism which replaces big factories with a multitude of household-located units tied together by new forms of putting-out, and generally breaks down many of the earlier distinctions. Peasant and tribal movements, sadly, no longer attract much research attention, in sharp contrast to the moods of the 1970s and '80s. But, once again, over-rigid distinctions are being questioned, notably that between "peasant" and "tribal", and here the burgeoning field of environmental history is making a contribution by going beyond the divisions it had constructed earlier between settled cultivators, pastoralists, and forest-dwellers. Studies of tribal and peasant protest are no longer content with romanticised notions of an unified, egalitarian community protesting as a whole against exploitation by intruders, whether British or Indian: internal tensions within such formations are also being probed.[16]

More surprisingly, however, at least to someone like me, who has been (and remains) a critic of much postcolonial studies under the sign of Said's *Orientalism*,[17] what began with vastly strengthening the

---

[15] Jan Breman, "A Dualistic Labour System? A Critique of the 'Informal Sector' Concept", *Economic and Political Weekly*, 27 November, 4 December, 11 December 1976; ibid., *Footloose Labour: Working in India's Informal Economy* (Cambridge, 1996). For a notable effort at overcoming the long separation between labour history and caste studies, see Peter Robb, ed., *Dalit Movements and the Meanings of Labour in India* (Delhi, 1993).

[16] "Forests, Fields, and Pastures", Special Issue, *Studies in History*, vol. 14.2, July–December 1998, particularly Neeladri Bhattacharya's Introduction, and the articles by Archana Prasad and K. Sivaramakrishnan; Sangeeta Dasgupta, "Reordering a World: The Tana Bhagat movement, 1914–1919", *Studies in History*, 15.I, January–June 1999; Jacques Pouchepadass, *Champaran and Gandhi: Planters, Peasants, and Gandhian Politics* (1986; rpnt. Delhi, 1999).

[17] Though it is probably unfair to blame Said himself for this – I have done

colonial–Western / indigenous–cultural divide has occasionally started in recent times to question that binary, as it moves from the narrowly cultural-discursive towards a more "material" and institutional focus. This is happening primarily through studies of inputs from indigenous literati into the very formation of colonial discourses and disciplines, to the point where these sometimes appear as virtually joint products, with British or Western practices no longer even necessarily coming earlier than the allegedly derivative Indian. The entire monolithic construct of a finished modern West imposing itself through conquest on colonised minds – the first assumption was of course absurd right from the beginning, considering that Britain in the 200-odd years of its Indian empire went through by far the most dramatic changes of its entire history – is coming to be questioned. To take one instance among many, the assumption still often to be encountered among English Literature scholars turning to postcolonial history, about the Macaulay Minute of 1835 determining the entire later course of South Asian education, is clearly oversimplified. British Indian educational policies went through various phases and contained numerous regional diversities. What is attracting much interest now is the importance of unequal, but still significant alliances between Western rulers and shifting sections of indigenous elites.[18]

I am aware that work along such lines, stressing indigenous inputs, the collaborative aspects of the colonial encounter, and what sometimes becomes a kind of continuity thesis suggesting that colonial rule may not have constituted any major break with pre-colonial

---

that myself sometimes – for in *Orientalism* and elsewhere he also pointed to the need to overcome rigid binary assumptions.

[18] Chris Bayly's *Empire and Information* (Cambridge, 1996) was the pioneering empirical work in this regard. For two very recent essays, dealing with themes as disparate as colonial cartography and the constitution of the discipline of historical epigraphy, see Kapil Raj, "Circulation and the Emergence of Modern Mapping: Great Britain and Early Colonial India, 1764–1820", in Claude Markovits *et al.*, *Society and Circulation: Mobile People and Itinerant Cultures in South Asia, 1750–1950* (Delhi, 2003), and Phillip Wagoner, "Precolonial Intellectuals and the Production of Colonial Knowledge", *Comparative Studies in Society and History* 45.4, October 2003.

times, can occasionally lay itself open to the danger of becoming an apologia for colonialism. This becomes particularly so when terms like "dialogue" are used, tending to underplay the ultimately more crucial dimensions of domination and conflict. Several of the authors I have just referred to are quite aware of this possibility, with Kapil Raj for instance emphasising the "asymmetrical aspects" of the coloniser-colonised relationship, despite the former's need for local negotiations with indigenous literati or other elites. There is also a need to take full cognisance of the precise time we are speaking of, with the late-colonial era certainly marked both by ruptures with pre-colonial conditions not always so evident earlier, and a much-sharpened racial divide. The temptation of South Asian scholars, both Indian and foreign, nowadays is rather to be too appreciative of anti-colonial nationalisms, and sometimes of pre-colonial cultures. In general terms, though, we cannot really give up binary and other distinctions altogether: once again, there seems a need to work through categories while simultaneously never ceasing to put them under questioning and qualification.

Research initiated under the aegis of post-colonial theory has shown a repeated pattern of spilling over its initial limits. One major thrust, beginning with some kinds of "colonial discourse analysis" – that were often narrowly culturalist, over-polemical, and extremely prone to binary formulations – has developed into important studies of colonial/modern statecraft and governmentality, bearing the marks of Foucault rather than Said. Everyday details of administration, previously dismissed as tedious or unimportant, have acquired new significance, and their links with processes of identity formation are being intensively probed. To take the two most striking instances: the census had earlier been regarded as no more than an important kind of source, and British Indian law of interest and relevance to specialists of that subject alone. Now, both have come under scrutiny for their key roles in the formation of a wide range of more rigid identities, the potentials for which were being constituted around the same time by the qualitative leap in communicational integration. From the 1770s onwards, the British erected from more inchoate Mughal foundations a sharp distinction in family law between Hindu and Muslim, helping to make both these categories more homogeneous, and forcing a clear choice between them in everyday matters of marriage, death, and inheritance. (No such distinction was made in public or criminal law, where there was an effort to assert the modern notion of sovereignty, ascribing to the state a monopoly over the legitimate use of force.) The introduction of the decennial census a hundred years later accelerated notably solidarities of religion, caste, language, and ethnicity, for enumeration demanded sharp distinctions and uniformity within the categories chosen, once again enforcing firm choices. During the run-up to the 1911 census, for instance, an official in charge of census operations expressed an inability to locate a particular community in the Gujarat region within either of the two main religious categories, and suggested use of the omnibus term "Hindu-Muslim". His superior pulled him up sharply, and asserted that people had to be either Hindus or Muslims.

It needs to be added that the processes of identity formation were not just being imposed by British fiat, and driven solely by a administrative convenience and divide-and-rule machinations, as was occasionally implied in the early days of research on such matters. There were important, and growing, Indian inputs in both law and census operations, even if we leave aside the question of possible antecedents for both, though at much more local levels, in pre-colonial times. More and more Indians, beginning with the relatively privileged but spreading downwards, made autonomous and creative use of the new forms of communication introduced in colonial times: improved roads, railways, postal services, a gradual and limited spread of literacy and education and, above all, mechanical print enabling cheap reproduction of all manner of reading and visual material, amounting in their totality to the formation of one or several forms of public spheres not really feasible earlier.

What happened in the late colonial era was a simultaneous crystallisation of many collectivities – "Indian", with a growing anti-colonial slant – religious, caste, language and ethnicity, class, gender. But this meant also inevitable processes of mutual inflections of one by the others, interpenetration, undercutting. Identities, one might suggest, were simultaneously becoming harder and more potentially fragile. This in turn stimulated efforts, usually at the instance of leading groups within the communities-in-formation with resources for such projects, to strengthen solidarity through enemy images of powerful, ever-threatening others. Notable efforts at building a countrywide Hindu unity, for instance, and perhaps widespread internalisation of the notion of Hinduism itself, really started from the late-nineteenth century at the initiative mainly of higher-caste groups. Such efforts at what could be termed sanskritisation from above had a clearly conservative and integrative role, aspects often missed out in conventional social-anthropological deployments of that category which, from its initiator M.N. Srinivas onwards, has generally carried only a positive content. There is a sharp contrast here with the more-or-less simultaneous efforts to crystallise identities and organisations of subordinated castes and Dalits, and figures like Phule and later Ambedkar in Maharashtra and Periyar in Tamilnadu were very suspicious of such moves, and sharply critical of brahmanical domination. The transition to chauvinistic forms of Hindu nationalism (or what its critics termed communalism), foregrounding Muslims as a perpetual and growing threat, was probably connected with upper-caste efforts in such conjunctures to buttress a slipping hegemony. Unificatory moves by some sections of Muslims, becoming increasingly anti-Hindu over time and termed Muslim nationalism by its advocates and Muslim communalism or separatism by others, was similarly an effort to build and consolidate unity within a religious category far from homogeneous and linguistically and culturally diverse: as indicated for instance by Jinnah's problems with numerous provincial Muslim politicians in the run-up to Pakistan.[19]

Nor were the conflicts purely political. Two prominent theologians of Indian Islam in the first half of the twentieth century, Husain Ahmad Madani and Maulana Mawdudi, developed sharply different approaches to the problems faced by Indian Islam in the era of nationalism. Madani, head for several decades of the Deoband training

---

[19] Maulana Madani, *Composite Nationalism and Islam*, trans. and intro. by Barbara Metcalf (Delhi, 2005); Sayyid Vali Reza Nasr, *Mawdudi and the Making of Islamic Revivalism* (New York/Oxford, 1996).

centre for theologians, strongly supported Congress nationalism and the ideal of a composite nationalism within a united India, which he thought would be more conducive to the spread and prosperity of his community over the entire subcontinent than any partition on religious lines. Mawdudi, founder of Jama'at-i-Islami in 1941, came to be recognised in the second half of the century as the principal apostle of a fundamentalist and revivalist Islam, and revered as such by similar groups throughout the Islamic world. But neither liked Jinnah's ideal of Islamic nationalism and a Pakistan that would be non-theological in its political forms.

Perhaps a pattern broadly similar to that noticeable in the narrative of caste can be discerned in the history of gender relationships and images. Social reform efforts here during the nineteenth century had emanated almost entirely from middle-class men, but an increasingly autonomous women's role manifested itself in course of time, with the gradual empowerment of some through access to literacy and greater possibilities of mutual communication and organisation through the emergent public sphere based on print culture. Both discursive and imaginative writing by women, very rare earlier except for some religious poetry, emerged in many parts of the country from the 1860s and '70s. Women's associations began to be set up from the early twentieth century, raising demands more radical than those voiced by earlier male reformers. Votes for women, for instance, started becoming an issue from the 1920s mainly at the initiative of some (admittedly elite) women. But, as with caste, counter-thrusts were not slow to manifest themselves, expressed through opposition to reform and assertions that the true role of the Hindu, Muslim, or Indian woman was to preserve traditional patriarchal values within the home.

Where, and how, within this welter of crystallising and yet fragile solidarities, are we to locate nationalism(s)? The use of the plural seems advisable, and the term itself clearly requires more precision. The most obvious meaning for the colonial era, and the one that dominated till the turn in historical thinking I have already written about, would be opposition or resistance to British rule, plus some kind of conception of a "nation-state" goal. But there have always been ambiguities in the literature, often producing somewhat sterile controversies. Nineteenth-century Indian middle-class thinkers, and even the Moderates of the early Congress, combined loyalism with a growing sense of India as a national unit. Even the Congress adopted complete independence as its creed only as late as 1929. Many nineteenth-century tribal and peasant protests or rebellions, on the other hand, subsequently eulogised as anti-British and national, were directed initially and sometimes throughout against local, mainly Indian, oppressors, and hardly had a sense of a "modern" kind of nationhood: a problem that would largely apply also to the more complicated instance of the major Rebellion of 1857. Hindu or Muslim nationalism/communalism in the twentieth century thought in terms of uniting their coreligionists across the space of India, believing that not colonial rule but the other religious community was the principal or sole enemy. Indisputably anti-colonial nationalisms, as well as at times quite notoriously the Indian, Pakistani, Bangladeshi, and Sinhala nation-states that eventually emerged from out of the end of the British Empire in South Asia, have often tended to brand and brutally suppress ethnic and/or regional solidarities as separatist or anti-national. Yet the latter have been animated by what they themselves often think of as perfectly valid nationalisms.

Perhaps we need a deployment of the category of nationalism flexible enough to include numerous different kinds, and one that is able to abstract itself from any necessarily and uniformly positive (or, as in some post-colonial thinking, negative) value. The putative imagined space within which such a project is seeking to locate itself would have to be reasonably extensive (as distinct from loyalty to a village, district, or town), and within that the aim is a loyalty superior to differences (e.g. class, caste, gender, etc.) other than whatever has been taken to be the essential marker for a particular nation. That again has varied widely, often with sharply different implications: common ancestry or ethnicity, language, religion, culture (which in such a context can be a more anodyne term for the former, as with Hindutva today), or an ideal of common citizenship uniting many diversities. And of course, as Benedict Anderson had pointed out, nationalisms (or for that matter any kind of collective solidarity or identity) are never timeless but always "imagined", and yet commonly projected back as somehow always already in existence.

Narratives of nationalism today, then, have to locate their subject within a complex and shifting field of solidarities, which assert their distinct and often conflicting presences, and yet repeatedly interpenetrate and interanimate each other. This makes a concentration only on the relations of the colonised with the British rulers increasingly inadequate. There has not been much theoretical recognition of this sea change, and certainly the old model of colonial repression/heroic nationalist resistance still dominates the bulk of textbooks and official discourses. In historical practice, though, studies of particular phases or types of anti-British movements have clearly declined, more specifically work on their popular manifestations which had attained its point of maximum sophistication with early Subaltern Studies. There is considerable scope for regret in this turning away from radical political protest, but also compensations. The bulk of recent important research has been not directly on nationalism, but on other solidarities or dimensions of the late-colonial era. Yet nationalism enters virtually into all such discussions, sometimes perhaps even in an excessive manner, as I have argued. What the remaining part of this essay has to focus on, therefore, are the reciprocal inflections of nationalism(s) with other emergent solidarities, on which intensive work goes on nowadays. Work which by implication is often illuminating the tensions within nationalism, and the variety of meanings of that term, in very interesting ways.

The prism through which such relationships are looked at today is primarily, and predictably for our times, "culture", and so one must start there. The connections of different forms of nationalism with major literary figures, like Bankimchandra, Tagore, or Premchand, have of course provided important themes for quite some time, and important work is still going on in this high-culture domain. But with growing research on print-related public spheres, attention is no longer concentrated on prominent thinkers or writers alone, and whole new and more plebeian worlds of production of minor vernacular writings have been opened up – forgotten plays and farces, tracts and household manuals, and other ephemera. Studies of this "low life of literature", to borrow Robert Darnton's phrase, have enabled entry into previously unexplored domains of urban lower-middle-class strata, subordinated castes, less privileged rural Muslims, and, perhaps above all, women, who found through print, and a limited but not negligible spread of literacy, channels of expression and communication previously denied them.[20]

Print culture over time meant also, to an ever-increasing extent, a proliferation through mechanical reproduction of not just written but also diverse visual and aural forms of communication (the gramophone, for instance, reached India in the early twentieth century) – of obvious importance in what remained a predominantly illiterate country. These have become major new foci of historical study in recent years, with important work on the evolution of painting and architecture across the late-colonial era, as well as research on the more "popular" (more precisely, perhaps, mass-cultural, since definitely market-driven and commercialised) forms like lithographs of religious icons, or calendar art. Ravi Varma of Kerala and Bombay, and the Bengal School of Art founded by Abanindranath Tagore, have been perhaps the favoured subjects within "high" art. Both could claim a relationship with nationalism, and yet the Bengal School sharply condemned its predecessor as denationalised, in an artistic conflict roughly corresponding to the Moderate/Extremist rift around the time of the Swadeshi movement. Then, in the early twentieth century came films: silent, with Dadasaheb Phalke's *Raja Harishchandra* (1913), amazingly soon after the Lumiere brothers, and talkies from the early 1930s. The gap in time between Western innovation and Indian appropriation was clearly lessening, and yet the early films were often marked by a predominance of mythological themes with a strongly Hindu-revivalist message: modernity and tradition intermingled in complicated and shifting ways, as they still do in what since the 1940s has been by far the most popular art form, the Bombay film industry.[21]

---

[20] For two instances of such work, see Sumit Sarkar, *Writing Social History*, chapters 6 and 8, and Judith Walsh, *Domesticity in Colonial India: What Women Learned When Men Gave them Advice* (Oxford, 2004).

[21] For a sample of the rich and growing historical literature on the visual arts, see Christopher Pinney, *"Photos of the Gods": The Printed Image and Political Struggle in India* (London, 2004); Tapati Guha Thakurta, *The Making*

Of the many emergent solidarities the mutual inflections of which with nationalisms demand exploration, two have been rather neglected, or at least under-theorised. What might loosely be termed class affirmations around conflicts connected more or less directly with production relationships have of course received considerable attention in orthodox Marxist writings, and then in the first phase of Subaltern Studies and the considerable work it helped to stimulate. Marxists for long tended to oscillate between a stress on inevitable conflicts of movements of or on behalf of tribals, peasants, and workers with "mainstream", "bourgeois" nationalism, manifested through "betrayals" by the latter, or the need for anti-imperialist unity and consequent rejection of "sectarian" excesses. Early Subaltern Studies leaned more towards the first approach, but introduced a history from below perspective through categories of subaltern, most often peasant, nationalism distinct from elite forms. One significant exception (Dipesh Chakrabarty) apart, subalternists did not take up labour, whether by itself or in relation to anti-colonial movements. Both peasant and labour studies then went into a long decline, from which the latter, though, seems to be recovering lately. The revival, while seldom focused primarily on articulations with nationalism, has already started producing interesting material and insights, and one can hope for more soon.[22]

The relative poverty of work on the articulations, or their absence, of regional / linguistic /ethnic solidarities with nationalism is cause

---

of a New Indian Art: Artists, Aesthetics and Nationalism in Bengal, c.1850–1920 (Cambridge, 1992); Partha Mitter, *Art and Nationalism in India, Occidental Orientations* (Cambridge, 1994); Ashish Rajadhyaksha and Paul Willemen, ed., *Encyclopaedia of Indian Cinema* (Delhi, 1994, 1999); and Madhav Prasad, *Ideology of the Hindi Film: A Historical Construction* (Delhi, 1998).

[22] See particularly Dipesh Chakrabarty, who began his career as a historian with a pioneering study of Bengal jute labour, *Rethinking Working-class History, Bengal 1890–1940* (Princeton/Delhi, 1989); Dilip Simeon, *The Politics of Labour under Late Colonialism: Workers, Unions and the State in Chota Nagpur, 1928–1939* (Delhi, 1995); Rajnarayan Chandavarkar, *Imperial Power and Popular Politics: Class, Resistance and the State in India, c.1850–1950* (Cambridge, 1998); and Chitra Joshi, *Lost Worlds: Indian Labour and Its Forgotten Histories* (Delhi, 2003).

for some surprise, since for a generation now the bulk of research has concentrated on specific regions (for only there can most historians readily access the vital vernacular material). What has been lacking on the whole is theoretical and methodological novelty. Similar, homogenised notions of nationalism seem to prevail in studies of both all-India and regional levels. We have had either a teleological perspective of regional identities ultimately merging with the national mainstream in tighter or looser forms of "integration" or at best "unity-in-diversity", or occasional assertions of near-independence in which the nationalist model is reproduced at the regional or even local level in an equal and opposite manner, with Indian nationalism replacing British domination as the Other. The articulations between identity formations at the many levels, local, regional, and national, in other words, have remained insufficiently explored. A related problem has been the way entire areas get totally neglected in textbook and pedagogical history: the north-east, most obviously. If modern South Asian history is equated virtually with the growth of anti-colonial nationalism or the freedom struggle, areas that did not visibly contribute all that much do not matter: nationalist teleology can hardly go further. But exceptions exist and are growing. The interanimations and tensions between anti-brahmanical impulses, language devotion, and Tamil and pan-Indian nationalisms, for instance, have been the subject of major historical studies. Another recent growth area has been the princely states that comprised a third of the country before 1947. Kashmir, for instance, has seen some very interesting work recently, highlighting a form of indigenous agency much less attractive than those once explored by Subaltern Studies. The Dogra Raj set up by the British flaunted an alleged Rajput ancestry, and appropriated some of the forms of centralised modern governance to work towards a definitively Hindu state in a Muslim-majority region. This was qualitatively different, Mridu Rai has argued, from the quite common juxtaposition of rulers and ruled differing in religion in many states of pre-colonial India, for then state power could not be concentrated quite so much at a single point.[23] South Asia lives with some of its consequences still, in

---

[23] Sumathi Ramaswamy, *Passions of the Tongue: Language Devotion in Tamil*

the form of violent conflicts between religious-cum-nationalist solidarities.

Movements critical of brahmanical hegemony among intermediate castes and Dalits that we have already touched upon were markedly different from earlier forms of protest, which had either sought sanskritising upward mobility, or evolved devotional, bhakti, religious forms without seeking this-worldly changes in the social or political order. Gandhian nationalism sought to build bridges with lower castes through humanitarian social work and bhakti, but the more radical and this-worldly "caste movements" of colonial and post-colonial times came to involve complicated, shifting, and fairly often conflictual relations with both pan-Indian and regional nationalisms.

Ideologies and organisations claiming to represent subordinated castes tended to suspect nationalism to be not only higher-caste led (which was largely indisputable), but engaged in promoting basically upper-caste interests. British rule for some among them could seem an asset, with its promise of legal equality, and so preferable to the tighter upper-caste domination which they feared might result from an independence movement led by the latter: fears which nationalism in its early-twentieth-century Extremist and aggressively Hindu phase did nothing to alleviate. Legal equality, it needs to be added, was extremely limited in practice (as indeed it often remains today even after fifty years of democracy), through the combination in British times of European racism and the continued importance of higher-caste elements in the lower sections of the bureaucracy and educational apparatus. But then it is promises held out but deferred that often have the greatest radical potential, in a pattern discernible in relation to Indian counter-elites *vis-à-vis* their European overlords, subordinated castes, and women. And linkages and reciprocal modulations did develop over time between caste movements and nationalisms, and here several different kinds of patterns might be discerned.

To start with the regions – the locus of most caste movements till at least the rise of Ambedkar in the 1920s. Lower-caste upthrusts became

---

India, 1891–1970 (California, 1997; Delhi, 1998); Mridu Rai, *Hindu Rulers, Muslim Subjects: Islam, Rights, and the History of Kashmir* (Delhi, 2004).

most effective where they could relate themselves to, and partly merge or take over, regional identity formations. The price was often a certain dilution of the initial, anti-Brahman and anti-caste message. Thus the Satyashodhak Samaj tradition founded by Phule began with powerful denunciations of Brahmins as outsiders who had established their supremacy over the warrior-peasant intermediate caste cluster of Marathas by force and fraud. By the 1930s, however, a still basically upper-caste Gandhian Congress had been able to establish its hegemony over this initially very anti-caste trend, but only through certain accommodations and limited openings towards lower-caste pressures. In Tamilnadu, the critique of brahmanical supremacy was perhaps sharpest, manifesting itself through a "Dravidian" ideology that, like Phule's, condemned Brahmins as conquerors coming from the North. After a moment of extreme radicalism under Periyar during the inter-war years, when the critique of upper-caste Hinduism had veered towards atheism, what developed was a regionally unifying cult of Tamil, a linguistic nationalism which reduced somewhat the sharpness of the attack on brahmanical domination.

Bengal and the bulk of the Hindi-speaking belt were marked by patterns significantly different from Maharashtra or Tamilnadu. Bengali regional identity remained identified with upper-caste Hindu *bhadralok* culture, and the occasionally powerful movements of intermediate and lower-caste groups (Mahishyas, Namasudras, Rajbansis) withered away after freedom and Partition. A key factor here may have been the large-scale migration of lower castes like the Namasudras from East to West Bengal after 1947, followed by their dispersal as refugees among whom the regional basis for unity was no longer present. The Hindi belt, lacking a clear regional focus and more easily identifiable with all-Indian nationalism, was marked by a late development of assertive, politically prominent caste movements – in sharp contrast to the heavily intermediate caste-based politics of more recent, post-independence decades, coalescing under the central plank of extension of affirmative action to the Other Backward Castes (OBCs). Kerala embodies yet another pattern, with its history of peculiarly extreme caste oppression, a powerful movement of lower-caste Ezhavas from the early twentieth century related to the spread of literacy through Christian missionary activity, and eventual partial take-over of that upthrust by the Communists.

In general, upper-caste groups were able to retain their predominance through the late-colonial era, but only through certain accommodations, limited openings towards lower-caste and, increasingly, Dalit pressures. The classic embodiment of such adjustments, in face of the Ambedkarite near-breakaway of significant sections of Dalits in the inter-war years, was the Gandhian condemnation of untouchability, emphasis on "Harijan welfare", and reluctant grant of a measure of affirmative action through reserved quotas in government jobs, educational opportunities, and electoral representation. Such concessions came in every case under lower-caste and particularly Dalit pressure and hard bargaining, as indicated by the Poona Pact of 1932 when Ambedkar gave up his initial support for separate electorates for his community in face of Gandhi's fast unto death by surrendering the British concession of a separate electorate for Dalits, but obtained in return a larger number of reserved seats in legislatures. Voters here would include many besides Dalits, though, and in a property-based franchise Dalits favoured by the much more prosperous upper castes would be likely to win.

But the changes brought about through Gandhian nationalism were not insignificant. Extremist nationalism had tried to postpone all social reforms concerning caste (and gender) relations till the achievement of political independence. Gandhi in contrast made abolition of untouchability the prerequisite of swaraj. But the dissatisfaction felt by many Dalits found expression through Ambedkar's fluctuating but always tense relationships with the Congress, and more recently through a major political formation (the Bahujan Samaj Party) as well as some significant historical works by Dalit scholars.[24] Several decades of reservation in government jobs and educational opportunities, won through Ambedkar's movement, have produced today an increasingly restive Dalit

---

[24] See, for instance, G. Aloysius, *Nationalism without a Nation in India* (Delhi, 1997), and D.R. Nagaraj, *The Flaming Feet: A Study of the Dalit Movement in India* (Bangalore, 1993).

intelligentsia and a political stratum capable of acting effectively on an all-Indian plane.

Studies of gender relationships and images, which were almost non-existent in Indian history-writing till around the early 1980s, received a major fillip from the rise of self-consciously feministic activism and scholarship, in India as well as on a world scale, and today represent a major growth area. The general trajectory here would be familiar already: an initial focus on more material and political dimensions, followed by a culturalist turn towards perceptions and images, studied primarily through women's writings and more recently visual forms. Undoubted advances in scope and sophistication, as elsewhere, were accompanied by certain losses, for the culture brought under scrutiny inevitably pertained to middle-class segments, and studies of labouring women and political movements have tended to lag behind.[25]

Previous, overwhelmingly male, accounts of nineteenth-century social reform and twentieth-century nationalism were generally laudatory about the achievements of reformist or patriotic men, with women occupying at best a marginal, also-ran position. Even the early 1970s critique of the so-called Renaissance model had failed to foreground the "women's question", focusing rather on the illusions of that era about British rule, and the initial volumes of Subaltern Studies included little about gender. Feminist writings made a difference from the beginning, highlighting, notably, the tensions within Gandhian nationalism between the twin dimensions of stimuli from nationalist upsurges (with large numbers of women coming out from domestic confines, facing police repression, going to prison, and even becoming comrades-in-arms of revolutionary men), and constraints, through the strongly patriarchal elements in much nationalist ideology which ultimately relegated women once

---

[25] Two collections of essays, published in the same year, but the first a bringing together of somewhat earlier articles in the *Indian Economic and Social History Review*, bring out this contrast: J. Krishnamurty, ed., *Women in Colonial India: Essays on Survival, Work and the State* (Delhi, 1989), and Kumkum Sangari and Sudesh Vaid, ed., *Recasting Women: Essays in Colonial History* (Delhi, 1989).

again to a (perhaps marginally modified) domestic sphere. Gandhi certainly inspired large numbers of women towards nationalist activism, but primarily through an idiom that emphasised Hindu piety, sacrifice, and the icons of Sita and Savitri. Such icons, drawn from high-Hindu epics, had a predominantly patriarchal ambience. Feminist scholarship, in a development which has been seldom noted, actually anticipated by several years the dialectic that lay at the heart of the early Subaltern Studies breakthrough. The note of criticism sharpened over time, as much writing about women came under the sway of post-colonial moods. Social reform now came to be described as no more than a "recasting" of patriarchy under colonial conditions, while Partha Chatterjee put forward what became a very influential generalisation about a "nationalist resolution of the women's question" by the early twentieth century. Questions about women, he suggested, came to be relegated to the private sphere of the home and were eased out of the public-political domain, where the struggle against foreign rule and cultural domination was given total priority.

Recently, though, there are signs of moves away from what had become at times an excessively critical and negative emphasis, amounting to a kind of cultural-nationalistic rejection of all forms that could be branded as derivative from the modern West. Intensive studies of nineteenth-century women's writings is one factor explaining the new shift, highlighting the sheer courage and novelty of women, in small but ever-growing numbers, learning to read and write and so violating age-old taboos, editing journals, beginning to go in for higher and professional education within a generation or so of middle-class Indian men, and braving social ostracism to contract marriages after widowhood (and occasionally even taking some initiative in such matters). And while the actual impact of the specific legal reforms concerning women during the nineteenth century (the banning of widow immolation in 1829, the legalisation of widow marriage in 1856, the Age of Consent Act of 1891) was extremely limited and at times shot through with contradictions, there seem to have been some unintended and ultimately far-reaching consequences. What was emerging, it has been recently suggested, was something like a "pre-history of rights" or individual entitlements – indicated paradoxically by the fact that even conservative opponents of reform from the sati debates of the 1820s onwards repeatedly deployed an argument of "consent": the bereaved woman voluntarily plunging into her husband's funeral pyre, widows preferring out of love not to marry again, child-brides attracted by the charm of early marriages.[26]

At the same time, the presence of contradictory tendencies cannot be ignored, and Chatterjee's nationalist resolution did contain an important point, though one perhaps presented in a somewhat overgeneralised and linear form. Nascent notions of individual rights were (and are) repeatedly sought to be countered through an emphasis on the necessary solidarities of "community": Hindu, Muslim, caste, or anti-colonial nationalist. Regional variations are also important: in some parts of the country, notably Kerala and some north-eastern tracts (as well as Ladakh in the far north), prevalent forms of matriliny, permitting a possibly more equal status of women, came to be eliminated through the prevalent modernising legal thrust towards monogamy and patrilineal succession.

The counterflows were at their strongest during the Extremist phase, and here a certain continuity can be observed with the subsequent rise of Hindutva nationalism, even an occasional continuity of persons (as when some of the erstwhile followers of the best-known Extremist leader, Tilak, helped to set up the core organisation of the Rashtriya Swayamsevak Sangh in 1925, with an ideology most clearly formulated by the ex-revolutionary nationalist Savarkar). But, once again, we have to emphasise contradictory strands. As Extremism declined, new intellectual-cultural openings became visible, manifested notably in the post-Swadeshi writings of Rabindranath Tagore in Bengal. Two novels by him, *Gora* and *Home and the World*, vividly portrayed the tensions of that era, while a sheaf of short stories around 1914–15 contained a sharper note of protest about conditions of women than ever before in his writings.[27] Politically, too, the need for

---

[26] An argument elaborated by Tanika Sarkar: see particularly her "A Pre-history of Rights? The Age of Consent Debates in Colonial Bengal", in *Hindu Wife, Hindu Nation: Community, Religion and Cultural Nationalism* (Delhi, 2001).

[27] See, for instance, the essays of Tanika Sarkar, Sumit Sarkar, and the

mass mobilisation in the Gandhian phase of anti-colonial nationalism (the insistence on strict non-violence making the widest possible active participation indispensable) demanded a degree of opening towards subordinated castes, classes, and women. Meanwhile reformist groups among women, however elitist and small in number, pressed ahead with demands for specific legal reforms on questions like raising the minimum age of marriage, changing elements of Hindu and Muslim family law, and, notably, extending votes to women. Their sustained work helped to lay the basis for the broadly progressive changes in Hindu family laws after Independence. The women's question, then, never became a pure matter of the home, and the nationalist resolution remained shot through with contradictions.

The relatively few recent works on the era of high nationalism and mass politics (roughly from the early 1920s to the '40s) indicate a sensitivity towards gender issues largely absent in such work earlier. In their totality, the impression which emerges is again the presence of contradictory strands. Space permits only two or three specific instances. Douglas Haynes' study of Surat has explored the ways in which Gandhian ideology meshed with fairly traditional notions of patriarchal *stridharma* (conduct proper to women). Another local study based on fieldwork, of the Darbhanga region of North Bihar in the 1930s by Wendy Singer, however, indicates how in that storm centre of both Gandhian mass nationalism and Left-leaning peasant associations, the Gandhian village centres could at times become much-needed shelters for women oppressed in their homes, and being pressurised to marry men they did not want to – so much so that nationalism came to be locally called by women the "anti-*parda* movement" (movement against the seclusion of women). The additional income earned by village women through the Gandhian stimulus to rural crafts, notably spinning, seems to have been partly responsible for such assertiveness: a pattern noticed also in the rural Gandhian centres in parts of Bengal studied by Hites Sanyal. But Singer's exploration of oral sources also reveals the existence

---

Introduction by Pradip Datta in P.K. Datta, ed., *Rabindranath Tagore's Home and the World: A Critical Companion* (Delhi, 2003).

of tendencies, in the end more effective, towards conservative recuperation. The socially radical moods have been largely forgotten today, and instead the moments of violent anti-British struggle (notably, the 1942 Quit India struggle) are highlighted, in part because the latter is invariably foregrounded in post-colonial, statist evocations of an undifferentiated nationalism bereft of much of the social radicalism it had occasionally possessed.[28] The Congress local activists recuperated in Darbhanga by Singer, for instance, are still honoured, but for their role as militant fighters against British rule in 1942. The anti-*parda* movement, however, has been almost entirely forgotten in this still highly patriarchal region.

A not dissimilar pattern, though one marked at times by greater initial rebellion, can be discerned in the mass struggles beyond the constraints and discipline of the Congress led by Left or other radical formations. Telengana, in the highly autocratic princely state of Hyderabad with marked feudal and patriarchal structures of landlordism, represents a striking instance. Here the peasant guerrilla struggle spearheaded by Communists over 1946–51 contributed greatly to the defeat of the Nizam's bid for an independent state and to the merger with India – after which the Indian state suppressed the insurrection through a combination of great repression and a marginal dose of land reform. The revolt had actually been sparked off by the mistreatment of a village washerwoman, Ailamma, in the summer of 1946 by the local landlord. Women participants in interviews conducted several decades later still recalled the days of the insurrection as "that magic time", imbued with a promise of many forms of equality and comradeship, not excluding gender relationships. But they also spoke with some bitterness of their specific grievances being often sidelined by the overwhelmingly male leaders and cadres, and of conventional division of labour within the household persisting even in life in the forests where guerrillas had been forced to take shelter in the last days of the insurrection.

---

[28] Douglas Haynes, *Rhetoric and Ritual in Colonial India: Public Culture in Surat City, 1852–1928* (California, 1991); Wendy Singer, *Creating Histories: Oral Narratives and the Politics of History-making* (Delhi, 1997).

Another, different kind of instance of the radicalism of women comes from the markedly different social milieu of Manipur, where women seem to have been noticeably independent and prominent in everyday social and economic life. Here there were the two "Nupilals" (Women's Wars) of 1904 and 1939. Despite subsequent efforts to assimilate them into the grand narrative of the anti-British freedom struggle, these movements led by women had as their prime targets the local court, which combined exactions with attempts to impose the more rigid norms of orthodox Hindu society on more relaxed local customs, as well as immigrant Marwari traders. The second Nupilal ultimately merged with a Communist-led movement which actually brought about universal suffrage as early as the summer of 1948, several years before the rest of India. The tradition of women's militancy in Manipur lives on: in 2003, they were in the forefront in highly innovative protests against oppression and rape by Indian paramilitary forces.[29]

Our sketch of the interactions of caste and gender with nationalism have had occasion to touch upon what recent developments have made extremely crucial for India, Pakistan, and Bangladesh today: the questions of religious identity, communalism, and secularism. Both these terms represent specific historically conditioned usages of Indian English. "Communalism" in South Asia, from the early twentieth century, lost the fairly positive connotation that words derived from "community" have often had in the West, and became entirely pejorative (no one admits to being communal, not even the most rabid communalist). It implies not just an emphasis on community solidarity or consciousness (itself largely a product in South Asia of numerous developments in late-colonial times, as we have seen) but further assumptions regarding conflicts between (usually religion-

---

[29] Vasantha Kannabiran and K. Lalitha, "That Magic Time: Women in the Telengana People's Struggle", in Sangari and Vaid, ed., op. cit.; John Roosa, "Passive Revolution Meets Peasant Revolution: Indian Nationalism and the Telengana Revolt", *Journal of Peasant Studies* 28.4, July 2004; Saraj N. Arambam Parrott and John Parrott, "The Second 'Women's War' and the Emergence of Democratic Government in Manipur", *Modern Asian Studies* 35.4, 2001.

defined) communities as inevitable, total, and more vital than any other conflict. For communalism, Hindu or Muslim, such conflicts became far more important than the struggle against foreign rule; for Hindus freedom came to mean liberation from a thousand years of alleged Muslim oppression and threat, and for Muslims the re-establishment of the glories of (equally alleged) medieval Muslim domination. Heavily mythologised versions of "history" provided sustenance for both creeds, at once mutually opposed and analogous to each other. Localised clashes between Hindus and Muslims (as well as occasional quarrels of both with Christians, mostly over missionary proselytisation) go fairly far back into the past, and became more frequent from around the 1890s (the riots over cow protection, probably the first time when conflict around the same issue led to violent conflicts over a large part of the country, from Bombay to Bihar). But communalism as a self-conscious ideology, both Hindu and Muslim, really became a significant force only in the early twentieth century, and more precisely from the mid 1920s. In the wake of the break-up of the impressive anti-imperialist unity briefly achieved through the Non-Cooperation–Khilafat upsurge, riots became and remained endemic in South Asian life, and organisations like the RSS, the Hindu Mahasabha, and the Muslim League emerged or became more aggressive. The specific Indian usage of "secular" also became prominent from around that time. It connotes being not anti-religious or even necessarily indifferent to religion (the deeply religious Gandhi in fact became in 1948 the greatest martyr for the cause of South Asian secularism), but anti-communal. The distinctions, it has to be added, have been clearer at the level of theoretical formulation than in actual historical practice. Teleological readings that assume a neat disjunction between secular and communal nationalisms going far back into the past are best avoided. We need to work, rather, with a logic that allows for both real distinctions, and frequent affinities and overlaps. Many major Hindu literary figures in the nineteenth century, for instance, grounded their emergent patriotism in an evocation of medieval Hindu resistance to Muslim kings (a mythologised history that was actually derived heavily from British Orientalist writings, which subsequently fed into developed communal stereotypes). They have remained icons for communal and anti-colonial nationalisms alike.[30] The central "secular" political formation, the Indian National Congress, again, has always contained communal Hindu elements, prominent particularly at local and provincial levels – despite the undoubtedly anti-communal, if significantly different, standpoints of the devoutly Hindu Gandhi and the agnostic Nehru.

Perhaps the most meaningful way of looking at the secular/communal divide within South Asian nationalisms might be to connect this logical disjunction to alternative ways of looking at and seeking to transcend the problem, common to both, of other, simultaneous and interpenetrating identity formations. Implicit in such alternatives, again, were distinct ways of imagining the very idea of an Indian nationhood and its history.

The Moderate phase of the Congress tried to tackle the question through what in today's terms might be called a narrow public sphere, from which divisive issues relating to religion, caste, social reform, regional, and class conflicts would be deliberately excluded. Objections raised by a significant section of Hindu or Muslim delegates, for instance, was made sufficient for exclusion from Congress sessions of any resolution on a matter affecting religious sentiments, while questions of social reform (relating primarily to gender or caste) were left to a separate National Social Conference. The nation, again, was often thought of as a goal to be achieved, still in the womb of the future: Surendranath Banerjea, for instance, gave the title *A Nation in Making* to his political autobiography. These could be termed incipient forms of secular nationalism, and elements going back to the Moderate phase remain discernible in post-colonial Indian constitutional provisions and political practices, where secularism is often understood, in a weak sense, as equal proximity to, rather than equal indifference towards, all religious loyalties. (In practice, the equal element has often proved difficult to preserve, given the fact

---

[30] Bankimchandra Chattopadhyay would be the most obvious example, his hymn "Bande Mataram" having inspired anti-colonial nationalism from the Swadeshi era onwards, but he has also frequently served as a rallying-cry for Hindus in anti-Muslim communal riots.

that the Congress has always had a preponderance of Hindu leaders and members.)

The Social Conference had at first met at the same venue and time as the annual Congress, and often included many of the Congress delegates. Tilak in the 1890s, the foremost leader of Extremism, insisted on its removal as part of his programme of aggressive and orthodox Hindu nationalism, while at the same time organising a Ganesh festival just at the time of Muharram, as well as an annual celebration of Shivaji, projected as the heroic champion of the Hindu cause against the villainous Aurangzeb. The aim was to mobilise a much wider circle than had been touched by the elitist policies of the Moderates against foreign rule, but the failure to really achieve such a breakthrough, as has been mentioned already, led to Extremism often passing over to methods of revolutionary terrorism. In practice, these remained equally elitist, with activists drawn entirely from the middle-class Hindu literati of regions like Bengal, Maharashtra, and Punjab, though not bereft of wider imaginative appeal through its undoubted heroism and self-sacrifice. By the 1920s, some among the Extremists and revolutionaries, notably Savarkar and a section of the erstwhile followers of Tilak, had come to constitute the core of what today is Hindutva nationalism, with one significant departure. Muslims had now displaced the British as the enemy that had to be overcome in the cause of achieving true Hindu freedom. An opposite but analogous trajectory from a prioritisation of Muslim religious community to aggressive Muslim communalism took place around the same time. The nation, Hindu or Muslim, came to mean for communalists an always already existent sacred entity, grounded in fetishised and chauvinistic constructions of religion and culture (the second in practice often an anodyne term for the first). Savarkar's *Hindutva: Who is a Hindu?* (1923) summed up this basic communal creed through defining the Hindu as possessed of an unique identity of fatherland and holy land. The Muslim or Christian might also claim or think themselves patriots, but their holy land, for this Hindutva ideologue, had to be Palestine or Mecca. True membership of the nation, therefore, was determined by religious and cultural origin alone. Non-Hindus could exist only on sufferance, on unequal terms, and Golwalkar, the second supreme head of the RSS, subsequently ridiculed as an "amazing doctrine" the idea, central to all forms of secular nationalism, that the nation was an entity in the process of formation, "composed of all those who, for one reason or another happen to live at the time in the country."[31] For Hindu and Muslim communalism alike, other communities were to be cowed into submission by threat and periodic use of force. Such ideals and strategies would also help to overcome all divisions of caste, gender, ethnicity, or class internal to the religious communities, without seriously modifying their often deeply unjust and hierarchised patterns. Their outcome, in practice, became the partition of the country, accompanied by a veritable holocaust of Muslim and Hindu minorities in what became independent India and Pakistan, continuing tensions and occasional wars between these successor states, periodic riots, and, in more recent times, events like the destruction of the Babri Masjid in 1992 and the state-sponsored pogrom in Gujarat in 2002.

The anti-communal alternatives to such exacerbation of identity conflicts have taken two different forms. From the 1920s onwards, Left-leaning formations – Communist, Socialist, the section within the Congress close to Nehru (particularly in his more radical, 1930s phase) – have sought to undercut religious and other loyalties thought to be divisive through emphasising the united interests and aspirations of toilers and radical socio-economic change through class struggle. Their evident decline or stagnation by the 1990s sometimes led to a too-hurried and over-generalised dismissal of such possibilities, that had been, and might still become, quite effective in some areas and times. Numerous powerful movements of peasants and workers,

---

[31] M.S. Golwalkar, *We or Our Nationhood Defined* (1939; 3rd edition, Nagpur, 1945), p. 64. Quite logically, Golwalkar went on to attribute the spread of such false ideas to "Western" democratic values, and openly praised (in this text which had been written shortly after the first major pogrom against Jews in Nazi Germany, the Kristalnacht of November 1938) the policies of Hitler. Such frankness became difficult after 1945 and the establishment in 1949 of India as a parliamentary democracy based on universal franchise, but they have never been repudiated by the RSS or its affiliated organisations.

Telengana over 1946–51 for instance, indicate the occasional existence of such potentials.

It is not difficult, and perhaps inadmissibly presentist, to adopt a similar total scepticism towards the Gandhian way, too. Gandhi's lifelong prioritisation of the question of non-violence, and conflict resolution through effective yet peaceful methods, can only be explained in terms of an agonised realisation of the great potential of escalation of violence in late-colonial India – between British rulers and Indian subjects, but also notably among Indians themselves – as well as in what he thought were the inevitable evils of contemporary industrial civilisation. Resolution of conflict through ahimsa and satyagraha sought a very difficult combination of rejection of violence and total confrontations, and real, if limited, change in relationships which Gandhi recognised to be deeply unjust – without the exacerbation of conflicts, barriers, permanently hardened identities. Gandhi's basic text, *Hind Swaraj* (1909), represents the opposite pole to Savarkar's programme and values, and it was not an accident that its author was murdered by a close associate of the latter who had once been in the RSS.[32]

Such methods did help to constitute what at its peak moments could become one of the biggest of mass movements of the twentieth century. Its limits and failures in practice remain equally clear. The old Left and early Subalternist critique, that Gandhian non-violence also rejected methods like labour strikes or peasant no-rent that had nothing intrinsically violent about them (any more than picketing of foreign goods, which he advocated), and that therefore Gandhism had a pronounced tilt towards propertied groups in its conception of the Congress as an unificatory umbrella, still has considerable resonance. The tilt, many have felt, was also towards the higher castes (rejection of untouchability being combined with refusal to repudiate caste in its entirety), and high-Hindu strata and values. By the 1930s, there was an important and worrying breakaway by considerable sections

[32] Some recent work also indicates that the immediate provocation for *Hind Swaraj* came from Gandhi's encounter during the preceding months with the Savarkar group in London. See Antony Parel's Introduction to Gandhi, *Hind Swaraj* (Cambridge, 1997).

among the Dalits, led by Ambedkar, while Gandhi's continued reliance on Hindu imagery and symbols, even while emphasising their syncretistic and non-violent elements, also aroused suspicion among many Muslims. His "double-edged use of Hindu imagery", seeking to utilise Hindu symbolism to push for reform from within, was also not understood or internalised by possibly the bulk of his followers, who took that language as uncritically celebratory.[33] Not too dissimilar patterns manifested themselves with respect to questions of family and gender relationships, leading to considerable later feminist criticism.

But perhaps there still is a need to distinguish between Gandhi as a specific historical figure, conditioned by his location in given class, social, religious, and patriarchal structures and values, and the long-term and continued relevance of some among his ideals and methods. Nothing else can explain how certain strands related to Gandhian values live on, both in India (not because but despite of his elevation into a statist icon), and mainly through the surge in recent times of a variety of grassroots activists and environmentalist movements abroad (the early African National Congress, the civil rights movement in the United States in the phase of the Students Non-Violent Coordination and Martin Luther King).

As for the continued significance of Indian nationalism as a whole, I would like to suggest in conclusion that this lay not so much in the achievement of independence – which, given the weakening of British military and political power after the Second World War, would have happened even in the absence of such a countrywide movement, as the experience of some colonies indicates – or even the heroism and self-sacrifice of its activists. Other peoples – settler colonies, Vietnam, Iraq today – have had to face much greater repression: unhappy the land, as Brecht memorably wrote, which has need for heroes. What was remarkable was the capacity for internal debate, change, and auto-critique, even at the height of anti-colonial movements. Such debates, combined with a persistent concern for mass poverty from

---

[33] A perceptive point made by a Dalit intellectual, D.R. Nagaraj, *The Flaming Feet: A Study of the Dalit Movement in India*, op. cit., chapter 1.

the early Moderate phase onwards and the need for mass mobilisation that was heightened by the adoption of Gandhian methods (as distinct from conspiratorial armed struggle where only some could be active), led to a progressive broadening of the meanings of freedom. One need only note that none of the four features central to the Constitution adopted by independent India in 1949 – democracy based on universal suffrage, secularism, elements of federalism, and social justice through affirmative action – had been present in the early programmes of mainstream nationalism. They came to be incorporated only through a dialectic of change through internal debates, pressures, conflicts. Hindutva nationalism, in sharp contrast, has changed little in its basic objectives since the 1920s, and is also marked by the absence of any deep concern with mass poverty. Here there is a fit, though, with present-day elite attraction for neo-liberal values the world over. Perhaps most remarkable of all, there was a persistent realisation among many of the key figures of the dangers of narrow forms of nationalism, and a quest in different ways for a combination with broader internationalist and humanist critiques. This was very evident in three of the most outstanding figures of the nationalist era. Gandhi's *Hind Swaraj* was utterly different from a conventional nationalist tract. Tagore around the same time launched a powerful critique of the dangers of nationalism, and Nehru – though perhaps the most statist among them – still sought to introduce and retain an international dimension. It is precisely such strands that are in danger of getting lost through the current domination of linear and homogenised views about nationalism, where its icons are projected as unchanging and uniform knights in shining armour. Few nationalisms, it needs to be emphasised, have been capable of such change through internal tensions, and of working simultaneously within, yet beyond, the confines of its chosen ideology.

10

The Conditions and Nature of Subaltern Militancy

Bengal from Swadeshi to Non-Cooperation, c. 1905–1922

"If we sit idle, and hesitate to rise till the whole population are goaded to desperation, then we shall continue idle till the end of time ... Without blood, O patriots! Will the country awake?" – *Yugantar*, 26 August 1907.[1]

"The events of the first quarter of 1922 confirmed the fear that the movement had got beyond the control of the leaders ... The spirit of violence and contempt of all authority, which now began to show its head, was not of the leaders, but of the masses." – Confidential official report on Non-Cooperation and Khilafat in Bengal, 1924.[2]

THE QUOTATIONS WITH WHICH I begin indicate an interesting contrast between the Swadeshi movement in Bengal (1905–8) and the Non-Cooperation–Khilafat upsurge in the same region (1919–22) from the point of view of the nature, extent, and consequences of "subaltern" participation in nationalist politics. During the anti-Partition agitation the masses appeared irritatingly inert to the more radical activists, for despite the formulation of a theory of "extended boycott" or "passive resistance" which

---

[1] Report on Native Papers (Bengal), hereafter RNP(B), week ending 28 August 1907, West Bengal State Archives (hereafter WBSA).
[2] Government of Bengal, Political (Confidential), hereafter GOB Poll (Conf.), F.N. 395, i–iii/1924: History of the Non-Cooperation and Khilafat Movements in Bengal, p. 13, WBSA.

demanded popular participation and often anticipated the methods of Gandhism,[3] the movement in practice seldom went beyond the confines of *bhadralok* groups. The politics of mass contact consequently soon became transformed into revolutionary terrorist activity by a handful of educated youth. Non-Cooperation–Khilafat in sharp contrast revealed a picture of masses outstripping leaders, particularly in the winter of 1921–2, and popular initiative eventually alarmed leaders into calling for a halt. C.R. Das may have been unhappy about the timing of Gandhi's Bardoli retreat,[4] but Calcutta and district newspapers had become nervous about the radical social implications of the upsurge months back.[5] The *Amrita Bazar Patrika*, a newspaper with a radical nationalist reputation, explicitly praised the clauses in the Bardoli resolution which gave assurances to zamindars as helping to remove the misunderstanding "that the movement of Mahatma Gandhi is aimed at the destruction of the rights of all property-owners."[6]

[3] This was developed above all in Aurobindo Ghosh's famous articles in *Bande Mataram*, 9–23 April 1907, later reprinted as *Doctrine of Passive Resistance* (Pondicherry, 1948). See also *Sandhya*, 21 November 1906: "if . . . the chaukidar, the constable, the deputy and the munsif and the clerk, not to speak of the sepoy, all resign their respective functions, feringhee rule may come to an end in a moment. No powder and shot will be needed, no sepoys will have to be trained . . ." RNP(B), 1 December 1906, WBSA.

[4] A compromise on favourable terms, possibly including a round-table conference to discuss more constitutional concessions, had been blocked in December 1921 by Gandhi against the wishes of Das and others. Reading to Montagu, telegrams of 15, 17, and 18 December 1921, Reading Collection, India Office Library (hereafter IOL), MSS Eur, E.238/4.

[5] ". . . once the masses raise their heads, we do not know what will happen to us Babus." *Nayak*, 3 September 1921. The *Hitavadi* of 25 November 1921 warned of the "grim shadow of Bolshevism" due to "the manner in which the swarajists are exciting the labourers." The *Nayak* of 1 December 1921 complained that "in Dinajpur it has become difficult to maintain zamindaries" and the *Tippera Guide* of Comilla of 24 January 1922 and the *Rarh Dipika* of Rampurhat of 8 February 1922 sounded similar notes of alarm. RNP(B), weeks ending 10 September, 3 December, 10 December 1921, and 4 and 18 February 1922, WBSA.

[6] *Amrita Bazar Patrika*, 25 February 1921.

I am using this contrast as the entry point into an analysis of the conditions and nature of subaltern militancy in the anti-imperialist movement. Certain preliminary points about concepts and methods require clarification here. The categories of "elite" and "subaltern" have aroused some misgivings as allegedly assuming a simplistic twofold division of society, and as a departure from the familiar digits of Marxist class analysis. Judging from the theoretical explication given by Ranajit Guha in the first volume of the *Subaltern Studies* series, this was very far from the intentions of the group responsible for the introduction of this Gramscian concept into modern Indian historiography.[7] There is surely a danger of prejudging the existence of distinctly articulated and self-conscious classes in a largely pre-industrial society, and we do need some omnibus terms for such situations. "Subaltern" is no more free of ambiguities and problems than its rough equivalents (for example "popular", "mass", "lower-class"); it does have the advantage however of emphasising the fundamental relationships of power, of domination and subordination. Nor does the subaltern concept exclude more rigorous class analysis where the subject or material permits it.

I am employing the term "subaltern" as a convenient shorthand for three social groups: tribal and low-caste agricultural labourers and sharecroppers; landholding peasants, generally of intermediate-caste status in Bengal (together with their Muslim counterparts); and labour in plantations, mines, and industries (along with urban casual labour). It will be obvious that we must expect considerable overlapping, indeed conflicts, between these groups as well as subdivisions. This is because the subaltern category includes exploiters as well as exploited – the *jotedars* for instance, or even fairly poor peasants employing agricultural labourers or getting their land cultivated by sharecroppers. The fundamental rationale for using an omnibus term also constitutes one of my principal arguments: that the subaltern groups so defined formed a relatively autonomous political domain

[7] See Ranajit Guha, *On Some Aspects of the Historiography of Colonial India*, in idem, ed., *Subaltern Studies I* (Delhi, 1982), pp. 5, 8, for passages emphasising "the diversity of . . . social composition" of subaltern groups as well as the ambiguities inherent in the concept as applied to the concrete realities of colonial India.

with specific features and collective mentalities which need to be explored, and that this was a world distinct from the domain of the elite politicians who in early-twentieth-century Bengal came overwhelmingly from high-caste educated professional groups connected with zamindari or intermediate tenure holding.

Charges of conceptual inexactitude apart, a serious problem in some "subaltern" writing has been the tendency to concentrate on moments of conflict to the relative exclusion of much longer timespans of subordination or collaboration – a trend it may be argued which really goes against Gramsci's own emphasis on the control exercised over such strata by more or less hegemonic dominant classes.[8] Subaltern groups normally enter the world of conventional historical sources at moments of explosion, consequently breeding a tendency either towards an assumption of total passivity or an opposite stereotype of heroic revolt. What one needs to keep in mind is a vast and complex continuum of intermediate attitudes of which total subordination and open revolt are only the extreme poles. James M. Freeman's fascinating "life history" of Muli, an untouchable Bauri living in what is now a suburb of Bhubaneswar, provides important data in this context. "Muli's ambivalent responses reflect respect for, affection for, resentment of, and rebellion against the same person." That the acquiescence of this Bauri pimp to his superiors did not mean that he accepted his lot[9] is indicated by his attitude towards upper-caste men to whom he supplied prostitutes.[10]

So far we have talked only about the formal aspect of subaltern attitudes; in practice subordination/rebellion and all that might lie in between would naturally always develop in relation to specific

---

[8] Guha's preface to *Subaltern Studies I* quotes Gramsci's well-known comment that "subaltern groups are always subject to the activity of ruling groups even when they rebel and rise up" (p. vii), but this aspect tends to get somewhat neglected in the text of the volume and even in Guha's own paper.

[9] James M. Freeman, *Untouchable: An Indian Life History* (London, 1979), pp. 54, 384.

[10] "To keep their prestige, they avoid us in public, but in private they screw our women, 'hu hu', panting like dogs": ibid., p. 22. And Muli does in the end become "the first untouchable of his village to publicly challenge and insult a Brahman" (p. 354) over a harvest dispute.

issues, grievances, and social relationships. Here the essential point requiring emphasis and explanation is the coexistence and complex interpenetration of extremely varied types of consciousness and activity: caste, communal, class, regional, or national. One might recall here the first item in Gramsci's six-point programme for studying subaltern classes: ". . . the objective formation of the subaltern social groups . . . and their origins in pre-existing social groups, whose mentality, ideology, and aims they conserve for a time."[11] The worker active in a strike might well have participated in a communal riot before and might do so again; the interpenetration of issues logically very different but in practice almost indistinguishable is even more evident in peasant movements; and similar complexities or contradictions are apparent often in the politics of the elite, too.[12] Some of the East India Railway workers who were to go on a massive strike in February–March 1922 following an alleged assault by a white driver on an Indian fireman had gone on strike in January of the previous year demanding an end to cow slaughter.[13] Swami Biswananda, extremely active as a pioneer labour organiser in the Non-Cooperation

---

[11] Antonio Gramsci, *Notes on Italian History*, in Q. Hoare and N. Smith, ed., *Selections from the Prison Notebooks* (New York, 1971), p. 52.

[12] Bipinchandra Pal's concept of "composite patriotism" leading up to a "federal" India with religious communities as its units clearly attempted a kind of combination between nationalism and religious-communal affiliations. See Sumit Sarkar, *Swadeshi Movement in Bengal, 1903–1908* (New Delhi, 1973), pp. 422–4. A biography of Chittaranjan Das, to take another example, repeatedly emphasises his loyalties towards Bikrampur as well as pride in being a Baidya. A Baidya Sammelan was held in 1914 by Das in his house at his own cost. Hemendranath Dasgupta, *Deshbandhu-Smriti* (Calcutta, 1926, 1959), pp. 24, 27. And the novelist Saratchandra Chattopadhyay has recorded how the face of the architect of the Bengal Pact paled "at the thought of what will happen ten years from now" as the percentage of Muslims went up further. *Swadesh o Sahitya* (Calcutta, 1933), pp. 50–1. I owe this reference to Partha Chatterjee.

[13] *Mussalman*, 10 February 1922, 7 January 1921. The January 1921 strike took place at Agra Junction with cooks, butlers, and sweepers of the town joining railway menial staff in a demand for an end to cow slaughter and closing down of the local slaughterhouse.

days and again in the late 1920s, preached cow protection in Purulia in August 1921,[14] and was prominent in the Calcutta communal riots of 1926.[15] Stephen Henningham's valuable study of anti-zamindar and anti-British peasant movements in north Bihar, which pays very little attention to caste or communal conflicts,[16] consequently appears so much less comprehensive than Satinath Bhaduri's novel *Dhorai Charitmanas* located in a part of the same region. Bhaduri has described in vivid detail the complex (and very far from unilinear) development of the consciousness of Dhorai in relation to the lowly casual labour Tatma community of Purnea into which he was born and the Koeri sharecroppers of Biskandha, the village to which he migrated. The rumour of the coming of "Gandhi-bawa", a holy man with wondrous powers, leads on to efforts at self-purification and "sanskritizing" caste upliftment among the Tatmas, conflicts with the neighbouring Dhangars (as well as with a Muslim hide concern) are occasionally sharpened, and yet in the end Civil Disobedience, anti-landlord struggle, and Quit India all impinge vitally on the life-history of Dhorai and his community.[17] Bhaduri's Dhorai was based on a real-life figure but there are still obvious dangers in reading off too directly the attitudes of the rural poor from a text composed by an upper-class patriotic novelist with a strong social conscience. The author in fact admitted later that he had somewhat exaggerated the "positive" features of his hero as well as the extent of change in peasant consciousness.[18] *Dhorai Charitmanas* is valuable therefore not

[14] Ibid., 26 August 1921.
[15] Kenneth McPherson, *The Muslim Microcosm: Calcutta 1918 to 1935* (Wiesbaden, 1974), chapter 5.
[16] There is only one reference to communal conflict (on p. 15) in Stephen Henningham, *Peasant Movements in Colonial India: North Bihar 1917–1942* (Canberra, 1982).
[17] Satinath Bhaduri, *Dhorai Charitmanas*, 2 vols (Calcutta, 1949–51), *Satinath Granthabali*, vol. II (Calcutta, 1973), pp. 25–34, 36, 62–4, and *passim*.
[18] "I completely suppressed certain major defects in Dhorai's character . . . The traditional values of the Dhorais have not changed – not as much as had been hoped for or as depicted in the book." *Satinath Granthabali*, appendix, pp. 495, 498. My translation.

for providing additional data about exploitation or dawning patriotic awareness, but precisely because it does focus to a considerable extent on "negative" or contradictory dimensions, elements which the novelist had no reason to invent or overemphasise.

A final methodological point emerges as a corollary from the above discussion. Subaltern participation in anti-imperialist struggle is a sub-set within the broader theme of subaltern awakening: the one does not automatically lead to the other without a variety of complex mediations in which the specific socio-economic structure of a region, historical traditions, efforts at mobilisation by elite nationalist groups and ideologies, and British strategies all play a part. The distance or otherwise of a specific subaltern group from the white overlords is rather crucial here. Thus the Patidar landholding peasants of a *raiyatwari* area like Kheda paying revenue directly to the colonial state could gravitate much more easily towards nationalism than their Baraiya subordinates who often proved more militant but were seldom consciously anti-imperialist.[19]

I intend to put two types of questions before a selection of the available data concerning subaltern attitudes and activities in early-twentieth-century Bengal. In the first place I feel that a comparative study of Swadeshi and Non-Cooperation can provide a useful test for the relevance or otherwise of some of the existing explanations of popular entry into nationalist politics. The "Cambridge" assumption that factions explain everything since local "patrons" have a kind of inherent and automatic capacity for mobilising their "clients", as well as the standard nationalist interpretation in terms of mobilisation from the top by patriotic leaders or ideologies, share in common a serious underestimation of the extent of popular initiative. A point brought out by much recent research on other regions and periods, this is abundantly confirmed by the data from early-twentieth-century Bengal. Nor can popular outbursts be explained by immediate economic factors like price fluctuations alone. What needs to be questioned is the central assumption underlying all these approaches:

---

[19] David Hardiman, *Peasant Nationalists of Gujarat: Kheda District, 1917–34* (Delhi, 1981), pp. 45–50, 65, 110–13.

that subaltern groups lack any relatively autonomous culture or mind of their own, and only respond mechanically to economic pressures or are mobilised through initiatives from the top.

But mere reiteration of the fact of subaltern autonomy together with an emphasis on the interpenetration of its diverse forms do not take us very much beyond the level of pure description. The second, much more speculative and provisional but to my mind more important, part of my analysis consists of an attempt to utilise data to explore some of the dimensions of collective mentality underlying apparently very different forms of popular militancy in the period under study. Certain recurrent patterns do seem to emerge, whether we study mass participation on a national issue or a communal riot or a caste movement or an apparently pure "economic" struggle. Something like a very tentative "structure" of popular mentality can be reconstructed in the Lévi-Straussian sense of an implicit, perhaps largely unconscious logical system lying beneath the surface of myths, beliefs, values, and activities.[20] One must hasten to add that reconstruction on the basis of militant outbursts alone cannot but be extremely provisional and incomplete and needs to be followed up by much deeper research, not attempted here, into popular cultural and religious traditions. Revolt as I have already argued is only an extreme and exceptional pole in the continuum of subaltern attitudes; it provides a convenient starting point only because it tends to be so much better documented.

In attempting the difficult but vitally necessary adventure of exploring popular consciousness, historians need to develop a fruitful dialogue with other social sciences, particularly perhaps with social anthropology in a country where mass illiteracy makes first-hand documentation of the world of the subaltern so very limited. "Structural"

---

[20] Claude Lévi-Strauss, "History and Anthropology", in his *Structural Anthropology*, vol. I (Harmondsworth, 1979). "Structure" has been used in a very different sense in the more narrowly empiricist British anthropological tradition, for example, as "an arrangement of persons in institutionally controlled or defined relationships . . . a system of social positions." A.R. Radcliffe-Brown, *Structure and Function in Primitive Society* (1952; rpntd London, 1976), p. 11.

analysis has often been accused, not unjustly perhaps at times, of underestimating the importance of change in the quest for synchronic patterns. But structure to my mind certainly does not exclude variations, both vertically in relation to the different strata coming under the omnibus subaltern category, and horizontally over time. Reconstruction of structures may indeed pose interesting problems for diachronic analysis. In the concluding section I raise certain questions regarding the extent to which mass movements from the 1920s of a more "modern" type (the Gandhian Congress in its later, more organised and disciplined form, or kisan and trade unions under Left and particularly Communist leadership) were able to bring about significant modifications in the collective mentality patterns I have tried to trace on the basis of early-twentieth-century data.

II

Down to 1919 the autonomy of the subaltern domain found expression through two distinct forms: general passivity *vis-à-vis* efforts at patriotic mobilisation from the top, and a variety of more or less militant actions distant from and sometimes directly opposed to the nationalism of the *bhadralok*.

Despite much talk about the need for mass awakening, the Swadeshi movement of 1905–8 seldom got beyond the confines of Hindu upper-caste *bhadralok* groups – students, journalists, teachers, doctors, and lawyers who very often had a link with rentier interests in land in the form of zamindari or intermediate tenure holding. The main centres of the upsurge reveal a strong correlation with the presence of large numbers of educated upper-caste Hindu gentry: Barisal (Backergunj), Madaripur, Bikrampur, Kishoreganj, the Brahmanbaria subdivision of Tippera, as well as of course Calcutta with its heavy *bhadralok* concentration.[21] The peasant seldom if ever appears in Swadeshi plays:[22] the volunteers in Mukunda Das *jatra*

---

[21] For details about the location of the Swadeshi movement, see Sarkar, *Swadeshi Movement*, pp. 26, 72, and chapter 7.

[22] A good example would be Amritalal Bose's play *Sabash Bengali*, in which Pashdanga village never becomes quite as real as the scenes of Calcutta life,

The Conditions and Nature of Subaltern Militancy   425

Palli Seva declare that they all have some land and hence do not have to worry about "mere rice and *dal*",[23] and police statistics about the social origins of Samiti members in Backergunj firmly establish the link with intermediate tenure holding.[24] A few Calcutta lawyers with nationalist affiliations did develop an interest in the labour movement, and Aswinikumar Dutta's Swadesh Bandhab Samiti could briefly acquire some kind of mass base in Barisal villages through sustained humanitarian constructive work. Yet the limits remain very evident, particularly in comparison with Non-Cooperarion–Khilafat days. The strikes led or unions formed were mainly of white-collar employees of printing presses and railways or of Bengali (and seldom Hindustani) workers in jute mills. The plantations and mines were entirely unaffected and, with the exception of something like a hartal on 16 October 1905, there were no instances of political strikes.[25] Even Barisal village *samitis* consisted "of the *bhadralok* of the village",[26] and an Anushilan militant turned Communist has recalled in his memoirs how peasants were occasionally mobilised for Swadeshi meetings, shy and silent participants in loincloth roped in by the well-dressed babus to prove Hindu–Muslim unity.[27] And evidence about the considerable use of caste, religious, and class pressures by the patriotic Hindu gentry to enforce the boycott in the countryside is really far too extensive to be dismissed as official or Muslim propaganda.[28]

---

no peasant appears on the stage, and the village movement is presented as a matter of schoolboys led by their patriotic headmaster: ibid., p. 300.

[23] Ibid., pp. 358–9.

[24] Thus in Sarupkhati police station of Backergunj, "nearly half the volunteers are said to be talukdars, that is to say, persons with a tenure holding interest in the land." Government of India Home Political Deposit (hereafter GOI Home Poll Dep.), October 1907, no. 19, National Archives of India (hereafter NAI), quoted in ibid., p. 72.

[25] For details, see Sarkar, *Swadeshi Movement*, chapter 8.

[26] Resume of Affairs in Backerganj for 1907, para 27, GOI Home Poll A, April 1908, no. 24, NAI.

[27] Satis Pakrashi, *Agni Diner Katha* (Calcutta, 1947), recollecting his boyhood days in a village in Dacca.

[28] Sarkar, *Swadeshi Movement*, chapters 6, 7, and *passim*.

Yet subaltern passivity can be overemphasised, and I now feel that I erred somewhat in that direction in my earlier work on Swadeshi Bengal. So far as labour is concerned, nationalist leadership generally entered the scene well after "spontaneous" initiative had led to a strike. Patriotic barristers like Aswinikumar Banerji or Apurbakumar Ghosh began their brief careers as labour leaders only when in the autumn of 1905 arrested clerks and tram workers sought legal help.[29]

In many cases Swadeshi involvement never came into the picture at all.[30] The fact that the bulk of the working class in Bengal was employed in foreign-owned concerns and that a Bengali industrial bourgeoisie hardly existed, permitted, however, considerably greater nationalist interest and sympathy in labour affairs than could be seen on questions of rent or rural indebtedness. Surendranath Banerjea's *Bengalee* on 13 May 1906 for instance did praise Rabindranath for giving rent remissions and loans to his tenants at Shelaidaha due to the prevailing scarcity, but it apparently saw no contradiction when, a fortnight later, it stoutly defended the zamindars of Muktagaccha for rejecting a petition complaining about a new 50 per cent *abwab* (cess). The Muktagaccha landlords had argued that "lately the ryots of this quarter have conceived an idea that their rents will be reduced and that their representation will be favourably considered by the government", and the *Bengalee* found in this evidence that Fuller, the strongly anti-Swadeshi lieutenant governor of East Bengal and Assam, had "demoralized the Mussalman ryots of Mymensingh".[31] That peasant protest could be construed as demoralisation is a revealing comment on the class inhibitions of *bhadralok* nationalism in Bengal.

The scattered and limited data available on lower-class unrest during the Swadeshi years indicate the existence of three strands, distinct in logic though much less so in practice. In the first place

---

[29] As when Banerji and Ghosh in September 1905 defended a clerk arrested for assaulting a strike-breaker at Burn Company. Next month they were reported as appearing for two tram conductors in a similar case: ibid., pp. 201–2.

[30] A four-month-long strike at Hooghly Jute Mill by 4000 workers, for instance, apparently aroused no nationalist interest at all: ibid., pp. 230–1.

[31] *Bengalee*, 13 May, 27 May, 30 May 1906, quoted in ibid. p. 334.

rumours about conflict between the government and patriotic gentry seems to have led peasants to feel that the time was suitable for some action on their grievances concerning rent or cesses. An official report noted in November 1906 that zamindars "in some cases . . . are afraid to appear before their tenants in definite opposition to government lest this should endanger their collection of rents."[32] An enquiry in February 1908 by the SDO of Jamalpur in Mymensingh district about the relations between the well-known Swadeshi zamindar Brojendrakishore Roychaudhuri and his tenants produced similar consequences: "As a result of these enquiries Brojendra Babu's tenants have got it into their heads that he has somehow become an object of official displeasure . . . Those of the tenants who had agreed to pay an enhanced rent are now refusing to do so."[33]

Over large parts of East Bengal the discontent of the largely Muslim peasantry found articulation in the form of communalism, with Hindu gentry, traders, and moneylenders as the principal targets. The *Charu Mihir* of Mymensingh started complaining from early 1906 onwards that "illiterate low class cultivators" were harbouring "wild ideas" that "they should pay rents at the low rates which obtained years ago", while Muslim sharecroppers were "refusing to work under Hindus, and cultivate lands of which the latter are proprietors."[34] Destruction of debt-bonds, attacks on landlord houses, and desecration of images constructed through an *Iswar-britti* cess figured prominently in the riots at Iswargunj in Mymensingh district in April–May 1906, in Brahmanbaria subdivision of Tippera in March 1907 and in the Jamalpur region of Mymensingh in April–May 1907. Some of the complexities of the situation were revealed a few months later at Sherpur in Jamalpur subdivision where a Muslim crowd attacked a

---

[32] Fortnightly Report, E. Bengal and Assam, no. 1331, 23 November 1906, GOI Home Public A, December 1906, no. 311, NAI.

[33] *Daily Hitavadi,* 11 February 1908, RNP(B) for week ending 15 February 1908, WBSA. The SDO of Jamalpur in 1908, interestingly enough, was A.K. Fazlul Huq. See Humaira Momen, *Muslim Politics in Bengal: A Study of Krishak Praja Party and the Elections of 1937* (Dacca, 1972), p. 37.

[34] *Charu Mihir,* 23 January, 27 February, 13 March 1906, RNP(B) for weeks ending 3 February, and 10 and 29 March 1906, WBSA.

contingent of additional police posted there in the context of earlier riots; no Chinese wall evidently separated "communal" disturbances from an anti-government outburst.[35] Manifestations of lower-class discontent took place mostly in the countryside, but there were certain urban parallels too. In the looting of Hindu shops in Comilla town in March 1907 Muslim "*gariwallas* who earn a large part of their living by driving Hindus of the better classes" were very prominent.[36] In Calcutta during 2–4 October 1907, following a clash between the police and a Swadeshi crowd at Beadon Square, the Bengali *bhadralok* found themselves being beaten up and their property looted by what a non-official enquiry committee described as "large numbers of low-class people, such as mehtars, dhangars, sweepers, etc."[37] The standard nationalist explanation for all such incidents in terms of official-cum-Muslim communalist instigation from above ignored pre-existing structures of exploitation and social envy without which divide-and-rule methods could have made little headway.

If Islam provided the key vehicle for Muslim peasants in the expression of their socio-economic grievances, one could expect caste movements to perform somewhat similar functions for rural Hindu society.[38] The first two decades of the twentieth century in fact witnessed a large number of "sanskritising" caste movements and associations in Bengal. The most significant among these were the

[35] For details, see Sarkar, *Swadeshi Movement*, chapter 8.

[36] Chittagong Divisional Commissioner Luson's Report, 11 G, 15 March 1907, Home Public A, May 1907, no. 163, NAI.

[37] "Report of the Unofficial Commission of Inquiry into the Riots in Calcutta on the 2, 3 and 4 October 1907". The commission, headed by the Moderate politician Narendranath Sen, examined 7 witnesses, including 72 shopkeepers, 29 clerks, 19 merchants, 10 zamindars – but only 4 "menials": GOI Home Poll A, January 1908, nos 75–80, NAI.

[38] In a recent article Partha Chatterjee has made the interesting point that East Bengal Muslim landholding peasants behaved in many ways like intermediate castes in other parts of the country, with the difference that religion permitted easier extensions of the movements both upwards and downwards to include Muslim gentry and the Muslim landless or poor peasants: Chatterjee, "Caste and Politics in West Bengal", in *Teaching Politics: Special Number on Land, Caste and Politics in Indian States* (Delhi, 1982).

The Conditions and Nature of Subaltern Militancy 429

movements among the Mahishyas of Midnapur, Howrah, Hooghly, and 24 Parganas, the Rajbansis of Jalpaiguri, Rangpur, and Dinajpur, and the Namasudras of Jessore, Khulna, and Faridpur – the three major castes below the level of the *bhadralok* in a province otherwise marked by unusually great fragmentation among intermediate and low castes.[39]

The Mahishyas of Midnapur and the Rajbansis of north Bengal included large numbers of gentry and *jotedars* as well as peasants. The Namasudras in contrast were overwhelmingly cultivators or sharecroppers subordinate to *bhadralok* zamindars or tenure holders.[40] The movements organised by the Bangiya Mahishya and Rajbansi Kshatriya Samitis consequently remained confined to claims to higher caste status and "sanskritising" changes in surnames or social customs; agrarian issues were hardly ever raised.[41]

Among the Namasudras of Jessore however a conference in 1908 which discussed educational and social improvement and set up a structure of village, union, and district committees financed by weekly rice collections was followed up the next year by moves "not to work as menial servants" in upper-caste houses in Narail subdivision and a refusal to cultivate the lands of the latter in Magura. The Jessore Namasudras got some support from "Muslim cultivators occupying a similar socio-economic position", and in 1909 Muslims in a village of Sadar subdivision "combined not to cultivate the lands of their Hindu landlords, unless the latter agreed to allow them to retain a

---

[39] See ibid.; also, *Census of India 1931 Volume V (Bengal and Sikkim), Part I*, statement XII-10, giving the district-wise number per mille of the five most numerous Hindu castes: Brahman, Kayastha, Namasudra, Mahishya, and Rajbansi.

[40] The proportion of Brahmans, Kayasthas, and Baidyas per mille of the Hindu population in 1931 was 184 in Faridpur, 141 in Jessore, 118 in Khulna – but only 71 in Midnapur, 51 in Rangpur, 28 in Dinajpur, and 27 in Jalpaiguri: *Census 1931*, chapter 12, statement XII-8.

[41] Hitesranjan Sanyal, "Congress Movements in the Villages of Eastern Midnapur, 1921–1931", *Asie du Sud: Traditions et Changements* (Paris, 1979). For information about Rajbansi caste movements I am indebted to Ranajn Dasgupta's unpublished "Nationalist and Left Movements in Bengal: Jalpaiguri 1905–1947".

two-thirds share of the produce instead of a half-share" – fascinating evidence of an anticipation of the *tebhaga* demand of the 1940s.[42] A Madaripur pleader in June 1909 reported similar refusals to cultivate *barga* lands and render menial services on the part of the Namasudras of Faridpur.[43] At Telak village near Khulna town in May 1908 a Namasudra–Muslim combination allegedly challenged Brahman control over the local festival of Kali in a conflict which quickly led to a confrontation with the police on the Sherpur pattern. Three years later, in a contrast which once again reveals the interpenetration of diverse issues, Namasudras and Muslims along the Jessore–Khulna border came into conflict with each other, with riots and looting affecting eighteen villages. Details of both incidents unfortunately do not seem available.[44]

A Government of India unpublished "Note on serious disturbances and political trouble in India from 1907 to 1917" provides interesting confirmation of the distance of mass upheavals from the world of organised national politics during this entire period. The section on "political disturbances" is confined virtually to a survey of revolutionary-terrorist activity, while the only incidents with something like a mass character included in the list for the Swadeshi years in Bengal are the Mymensingh riots of April–May 1907 and the Calcutta

---

[42] O. Malley, ed., *Jessore District Gazetteer* (Calcutta, 1912), pp. 50, 83. Tanika Sarkar in her unpublished thesis has already drawn attention to anticipations of *tebhaga* in 1909 and again in the 1920s: see "National Movement and Popular Protest in Bengal, 1928–34", unpublished thesis, Delhi University, 1981, pp. 111–21.

[43] Binod Lal Ghosh (Pleader, Madaripur), "What can be Done for the Namasudras", *Modern Review*, June 1909. Ghosh pleaded for better treatment by upper-caste Hindus of Namasudras on the social plane, as well as efforts to start schools and dispensaries, but remained characteristically silent about remedies for agrarian tensions.

[44] There are very brief references to both incidents in GOI Home Poll Deposit, February 1918, no. 31. The GOI files on the 1908 affair are not available, those on the Namasudra–Muslim riots of May 1911 (GOI Home Poll B, July 1911, 76–83, NAI) are not particularly illuminating. See also RNP(B), week ending 6 June, 13 June, and 20 June 1908 for some scattered information about the Telak village incident: WBSA.

clashes of October 1907. For the years from 1908 to 1917, apart from the two Namasudra disturbances already mentioned, the only other Bengal reference is to a communal riot at Titagarh and Serampore on the occasion of Bakr-Id in January 1909.[45]

Our sample for the years separating the decline of open Swadeshi politics from the beginning of the 1919–22 upsurge must include the Kamariarchar peasant conference in early 1914. The conference, organised by Khan Mohammed Sarkar of Jamalpur subdivision in Mymensingh with the help of some Calcutta-based Muslim leaders (Fazlul Haq, Abdul Kasem, Muhammed Akram Khan, Moniruzzaman Islamabadi), raised a number of specific demands of the upper stratum of the tenantry *vis-à-vis* the zamindars,[46] and marked the beginning of what came to be called the Praja movement in Bengal. We have to note also the development of Pan-Islamic sentiments in Calcutta which had acutely alarmed the government already by early 1913,[47] and the Calcutta riots of September 1918 in which lower-class Muslims clashed bitterly with the police and army and looted houses and shops of Marwari businessmen in Burra Bazaar.[48]

The two recurrent and salient features seem to be the potential strength of peasant solidarity in East Bengal and of millhands and casual labour in and around Calcutta, and the extreme volatility of popular sentiments and actions. The Praja movement throughout its history would combine in ever-varying proportions anti-zamindar class sentiments with appeals for Muslim solidarity, and the Kamariarchar conference presaged both aspects by its expression of purely agrarian demands through a meeting in which all the speakers were Muslims. In the riots of January 1909, following a clash over cow slaughter at Titagarh, "Muhammadan emissaries" were able "to get their co-religionists in all the mills on the right bank of the Hooghly to march together and cross the river to wreak vengeance on the

---

[45] GOI Home Poll Dept, February 1918, no. 31, NAI.

[46] Jatindranath De, "The History of the Krishak Praja Party in Bengal 1919–47", unpublished thesis, Delhi University, 1978.

[47] GOB Poll (Conf.) F.N. 66/1913: Mohammaden Feeling in Bengal, NMML, microfilm.

[48] Kenneth McPherson, op. cit., chapter 3.

Hindus", while "a large number of Muhammadan workers in the Calcutta mills as far south as Garden Reach struck work and commenced to march in various bands on Titagarh."[49] In 1913, however, in the context of the Balkan wars, pan-Islamist agitators like Ismail Husain Shiraji, Mujibur Rahman, Moniruzzaman (all three with Swadeshi backgrounds, incidentally) and Muhammed Akram Khan were co-operating actively with extremist veterans like Krishnakumar Mitra and Shyamsundar Chakrabarti, and some radical Hindus of Telinipara and Chandernagore were allegedly employing an agent named Hyder "to preach a regular Jehad against the British . . . among all the Mussalman millhands belonging to the mills on both sides of the river between Hooghly and Calcutta."[50] The September 1918 riots again saw "the coolie class . . . giving trouble . . . a large crowd of coolies made incessant attempts . . . to break through from Garden Reach and obtain entry into Calcutta."[51] Though ultimately directed against Marwaris, the riots had been preceded by bitter anti-British propaganda in the course of which Fazlur Rehman, one of the principal non-Bengali agitators involved in the affair, had even "eulogised the action of Kshudiram Bose and other revolutionaries". Governor Ronaldshay in his diary juxtaposed the provocation offered by the alleged insult to the Prophet in the Anglo-Indian journal *Indian Daily News* with memories of the Shahabad riots of 1917, the "misfortunes of Turkey, the internment of Indian Muhammaden leaders, and the high price of cotton cloth leading during the past winter to a considerable outbreak of *hat*-looting . . ." as causes of the riots.[52]

The reference in Ronaldshay's diary to cloth prices is a reminder that economic-determinist explanations of popular outbursts have

---

[49] Officiating Chief Secretary, Bengal to GOI Home, 4 January 6 January, 9/10 January 1909, GOI Home Police A, February 1909, nos 149–55, NAI.

[50] Extracts from Intelligence Branch Secret Reports for weeks ending 12 March, 30 April, 23 July 1913; Chief Secretary, Bengal, to Presidency and Burdwan Divisional Commissioners, 8 February 1913, GOB Poll (Conf.) F.N. 66/1913.

[51] Bengal Diary of Governor Ronaldshay, entries for 10 September 1918, Zetland Collection, IOL, MSS Eur. D. 609, NMML microfilm.

[52] Bengal Diary, undated, ibid.

been fairly common. They have been put forward by contemporary officials and later historians alike as supplements to or sometimes alternatives of the interpretation in terms of mobilisation from the top alone, and pride of place in such analysis has usually gone to price fluctuations. British officials often tried to relate *bhadralok* involvement in Swadeshi and terrorism to the impact of the post-1905 price rise cutting into relatively inelastic and sometimes inadequate incomes from fragmented zamindaris, tenure holdings, and services, while the link with the labour upsurge of 1905–8 appeared obvious. The indifference of the peasantry to Swadeshi agitation was conversely sought to be explained by the alleged benefits to agriculturists from high prices of foodgrains and jute, while landless labourers it was argued also did not suffer since they were paid mainly in kind.[53] A closer look compels numerous qualifications. I have argued elsewhere that sheer economic distress fails to explain *bhadralok* unrest in the Swadeshi age.[54] Allegedly beneficial high prices did not prevent considerable agrarian rioting during 1906–7, and an alternative economic explanation of this in terms of a less optimistic view of the impact of price rise on the peasantry does not go all the way either. The objectives of the Mymensingh rioters included such "non-economic" aims as the "rescue" of Muslim prostitutes, and as for labour strikes the Swadeshi data indicates that an assertion of human dignity against racist insult was a not unimportant element in their causation.[55] Narrowly economic interpretations are of no help at all in understanding the multiplicity of types of subaltern activity and their interpenetration.

With the Rowlatt upsurge of April 1919 we are at first sight in a very different world. The multitude of mass initiatives in the immediate post-war years, most of them combining briefly into an

[53] Sarkar, *Swadeshi Movement*, pp. 25–6, 510–12. The *Annual Report on the Administration of Bengal* (1906–7) noted that there had been "no serious agrarian disturbances during the year . . . strained relations . . . are the exception rather than the rule." The "real sufferers" from the abnormally high prices were the "so-called *bhadralok*": pp. v, 4.

[54] Sarkar, *Swadeshi Movement*, pp. 510–12.

[55] Ibid., chapter 5 .

anti-imperialist torrent, seems to bear ample witness to the success of the nationalists in breaking through to and effectively mobilising the masses. An economic explanation also appears attractive. Price rise equals labour unrest once again, and though a slight inconsistency might be noted in relating high prices this time to rural upheaval (the official argument in 1905–8 had been just the reverse), an escape route for the economic determinist is provided by the fact that industrial prices rose much faster than agricultural. Such interpretations abound in contemporary archival documents and have been echoed by recent historians like Judith Brown and Rajat Ray.[56] The two assumptions, political and economic, are fairly easily combined: elite politicians successfully manipulated an economic conjuncture favourable for agitation through "sub-contractors" or organisation-cum-propaganda to bring into existence a mass movement.[57]

Yet the correlation between price rise and popular militancy was by no means exact even in 1919–22. At the all-India level Judith Brown's figures show prices to have started *declining* by 1921–2, the climactic year for Non-Cooperation–Khilafat.[58] In Bengal the price rise was most acute during the lean pre-harvest months of 1919, but Ronaldshay was reporting at that time that "apart from a certain amount of *hat*-looting which has been due entirely to economic causes, the situation in Bengal continues satisfactory."[59] In very sharp contrast

---

[56] "Economic pressure supplies a background of unrest: the high cost of living has caused suffering and discontent and the sufferers . . . are inclined vaguely to attribute their misfortunes to Government or their employers, who in the case of the concerns employing large bodies of industrial labour, are mainly European firms." Chief Secretary, Bengal, to GOI Home, D.O. 2087P, Calcutta, 19 February 1921, GOB Poll (Conf.) F.N. 39 (1–2)/1921, WBSA.

[57] Judith Brown, *Gandhi's Rise to Power 1915–1922* (Cambridge, 1972); Rajat Ray, "Masses on Politics: The Non-Cooperation Movement in Bengal, 1920–22", *Indian Economic and Social History Review*, December 1974. Ray for instance begins with a brief discussion of economic pressures, but his account of the whole movement is heavily coloured by the assumption that leaders manipulate the masses.

[58] Taking 1873 as 100, the price level went up to 281 in 1920, but fell to 236 in 1921 and 232 in 1922: Judith Brown, op. cit., p. 125.

[59] Ronaldshay to Montagu, 24 September 1919, Zetland Collection.

The Conditions and Nature of Subaltern Militancy 435

a contemporary official report noted the winter of 1921–2 as being marked in Bengal by a slow recovery from the post-war economic crisis, with a bumper rice crop and raw jute prices recovering after six lean years[60] – and yet it was precisely during these months that the "mufassil . . . [was] . . . seething with unrest",[61] and that the upsurge in the countryside attained its point of climax. On the micro level too at least one official report related rural militancy to the relative *absence* of economic distress: "The inhabitants of Contai thana are capable of bearing the cost . . . [of punitive police] . . . There has been a very good rice crop and the people are generally well-to-do."[62]

As for mobilisation from the top, a very significant though seldom noticed feature of the Non-Cooperation–Khilafat days was in fact the distance between the expectations, political methods, and frames of reference of the patriotic intelligentsia leading the movement, and what really happened lower down the social scale and ultimately provided the upsurge with most of its real momentum. In Bengal the collective mentality of this intelligentsia was still very largely set in the mould constituted during Swadeshi years. There was considerable continuity at this level in personnel, methods, and social inhibitions.

Though the two top leaders of 1905–8, Surendranath Banerjea and Bepinchandra Pal, now played very different roles (Aurobindo Ghosh had retired from politics into mysticism), Chittaranjan Das and his barrister friends had provided considerable financial and legal support to earlier extremism. Shyamsundar Chakrabarti, Das' "Gandhian" rival in 1920, had been deponed in 1908 and Das built up the Congress organisation from 1921 onwards, relying heavily on released terrorist detenus. Among Khilafat leaders Azad later claimed some vague terrorist connections in youth, and Akram Khan, Mujibur Rahman, Moniruzzaman Islamabadi and Ismail Husain Shiraji had been noted for their Swadeshi sympathies.[63] It needs to be emphasised

[60] *Report on Adrministration of Bengal*, 1921–2, p. iv.
[61] Ronaldshay to Montagu, 26 January 1922, Zetland Collection.
[62] L. Birley, ADM, Midnapur, to Burdwan Divisional Commissioner, 27 January 1922, GOB Poll (Conf.) F.N. 87 (1–9)/1922, WBSA.
[63] Maulana Abul Kalam Azad, *India Wins Freedom* (New York, 1960), pp. 5–6; Muhammad Waliullah, *Yuga-Bichitra* (Dacca, 1967), pp. 272–7.

that very many of the Gandhian forms: boycott and swadeshi, national education, arbitration courts, populist calls for village reconstruction, and work in the countryside, an anti-industrial and anti-urban mood, peaceful violation of laws through a "satyagraha" – not perhaps all that different from the "passive resistance" creed of Pal and Aurobindo – were much less of a novelty in Bengal than in provinces like Gujarat, U.P., or Bihar, which had been untouched by extremism. Official attitudes were equally conditioned by memories of 1905–8 and subsequent terrorism. Though "revolutionary crime" virtually disappeared from the scene between 1919 and 1924, Ronaldshay in June 1919 had to express alarm for the "mental balance" of a top police official who was busy deciphering from the pages of the *Amrita Bazar Patrika* a terrorist code based on Conan Doyle,[64] and the Non-Cooperation–Khilafat volunteer movement for a long time excited alarm largely in terms of its alleged terrorist connections.[65] As for social inhibitions, Das' famous Bhowanipur address (1917) had combined passionate pleas for village work with total silence about rent issues or zamindari exploitation, and a scheme of village organisation announced in January 1921 by Das, Azad, and other Congress and Khilafat leaders was marked by a similar silence.[66]

On the eve of the Rowlatt satyagraha in Calcutta Ronaldshay found the scene at a Town Hall protest meeting "redolent of the anti-

---

[64] Bengal Diary, 29 June 1919, Zetland Collection.

[65] A fear greatly enhanced by the undoubted role of revolutionaries in building up the Congress and volunteer organisations in the districts following Das' agreement with them in late 1920. Thus Madaripur subdivision in Faridpur, an old Swadeshi and later terrorist base, excited much official alarm in the spring and summer of 1921 due to its regular drilling of volunteers headed by ex-revolutionaries. Intelligence Branch (Bengal) reports for weeks ending 7 April, 7 July 1921, GOI Home Poll 327/V/1922, NAI. And yet popular violence, as we shall see, generally developed in 1921–2 in areas very different from Madaripur or other strongholds of the *bhadralok*.

[66] Both the address of April 1917 and the January 1921 statement talked about co-operative banks and grain stores (*dharmagolas*), sanitation, drainage, and medical efforts, arbitration courts, relief work, and reduction in jute acreage. R. & B.K. Sen, *Deshbandhu Chittaranjan Das* (Calcutta, 1926), contains the text of the Bhowanipur address; *Mussalman*, 28 January 1921.

The Conditions and Nature of Subaltern Militancy 437

Partition agitation", but was assured privately by Das and Byomkesh Chakrabarti that "provocative language" would be avoided, shops would not be closed, and that passive resistance to specific laws "was not favoured" in Bengal.[67] The actual course of events in April 1919 proved startlingly different from Swadeshi patterns and leadership expectations alike. In the disturbances in Calcutta on 11–12 April following the news of Gandhi's arrest, educated Bengali Hindu youth, so prominent in 1905, were much less in evidence than Muslims and Marwaris whose "fraternisation" so soon after the September 1918 riots naturally appeared "mysterious" and "disconcerting" to Ronaldshay.[68] Except for this brief flare-up, Bengal was much less affected by the Rowlatt satyagraha than Delhi or the Punjab, and in general the Khilafat–Non-Cooperation movement took a rather long time to get off the ground in the province. Bengal extremists now led by C.R. Das resisted Gandhi's plunge into Non-Cooperation till the Nagpur Congress of December 1920. The Khilafatists were more enthusiastic and active, calling for hartals (not very successfully) on 19 March and 1 August 1920, helping to make boycott of elections very effective in Muslim-majority districts, and bringing a large number of Muslim students out of government schools by November–December 1920. Yet Khilafat leaders too had their inhibitions, indicated for instance by the announcement on the eve of the 19 March hartal "that the coolie class was not to cease work . . . for more than a hour at the time of midday prayer."[69]

Even during 1921–2, it was precisely the forms of agitation sanctioned by Gandhi and well integrated with the Swadeshi memories of the intelligentsia which proved surprisingly ineffective in Bengal. At times their impact seems to have been even less than in 1905–8. A numerically small but culturally very significant part of

[67] Bengal Diary, 21 March, 4 April 1919, Zetland Collection.

[68] The governor sought to explain it by alleged Marwari expectations of a Muslim *quid pro quo* (giving up cow-slaughter), veneration for Gandhi as "a supporter of orthodox Hindu aspirations", and Marwari resentment about the excess profits tax: Ronaldshay to Montagu, 19 May 1919, ibid.

[69] History of the Non-Cooperation Movement in Bengal, GOB Poll (Conf.) F.N. 395 1-3/1924, WBSA.

the intelligentsia headed by Rabindranath Tagore was openly hostile to Gandhian Non-Cooperation, and it is significant that the flood of patriotic songs which constituted such a notable feature of the Swadeshi era found no counterpart in 1919–22. Boycott did evoke a somewhat greater response from trading groups now, with sections of the Marwari community in a new patriotic mood, swayed by Gandhi and no doubt influenced also by the sharp fluctuations in the rupee–sterling exchange ratio which made the keeping of contracts with Lancashire often a hazardous business.[70] But boycott was reported to be "lukewarm" in Bengal in August 1921, and by November some of the Calcutta Marwaris who had promised Gandhi not to indent foreign cloth for six months (till February 1922) had started breaking their pledge.[71] In sharp contrast to 1905 there was no spurt this time in indigenous entrepreneurship, while charkha propaganda was officially described as not very successful "except in fashionable non-cooperation circles in Calcutta".[72] What caught the popular imagination and alarmed the authorities was not the concrete economic impact of boycott or Swadeshi but the mass courting of arrest in November–December 1921 through token sales of khadi by a cross-section ranging from the wife of C.R. Das to millhands and boatmen. As for the educational boycott, Das' spectacular gesture of January 1921 did for a time produce a real exodus from government colleges and schools,[73] but the emphasis was now on youth abstention from education for a year, not the starting of alternative national

---

[70] Sabyasachi Bhattacharya, "Cotton Mills and Spinning Wheels: Swadeshi and the Indian Capitalist Class 1920–22", in K.N. Panikkar, ed., *National and Left Movements in India* (New Delhi, 1980).

[71] Viceroy to Secretary of State, 25 August, 9 November 1921, Reading Collection, MSS Eur. E.238/4, IOL.

[72] *History of the Non-Cooperation Movement in Bengal*, p. 5.

[73] By March 1921, 11,157 out of 103,107 attending government or aided institutions had left, though about one-third rejoined later on: ibid., p. 4. The statistics of student enrolment given by Vice Chancellor Asutosh Mukherji to the Calcutta University Senate may be more complete: he reported a 23 per cent fall in recognised schools and 27 per cent decline in colleges in July 1921 as compared to July 1920: *Mussalman*, 30 September 1921.

schools.[74] Arbitration courts were more successful, totalling 866 in all for the period from February 1921 to April 1922; at their height in August 1921 "they considerably outnumbered the Government courts".[75] The other major plank in the official Non-Cooperation–Khilafat rural programme, a campaign among peasants against jute cultivation, had once again Swadeshi precedents in theory if not practice.[76] Started in February 1921 it did have some impact for a time, but had to go against the economic fact that raw jute prices though unusually low in 1921 were still higher than those of paddy. The later official survey makes the interesting point that the one significant result of the anti-jute agitation "was to make the cultivator think of other methods in which he might improve his position and to prepare the way for the no-taxes and no-rent movement . . ."[77]

Official files and private papers make abundantly clear that what really alarmed the authorities and made of Non-Cooperation–Khilafat a movement vastly different from that of 1905–8 was the large-scale adoption of such "other methods" through popular initiative and not anything deliberately worked out by Gandhi or the Calcutta leaders. The vast range of such initiatives extended from sporadic *haat* looting through a massive labour upsurge to jail-breaks, resignations by policemen, non-payment of *chaukidari* and Union Board taxes, hostility to settlement operations, no-rent, and virtually total disavowal of British authority by peasants fired by a conviction that Gandhi raj was coming or even already in existence.[78]

---

[74] Hitendranath Datta, veteran of the 1906 national education movement, issued a notice in January 1921 proposing a revival of arts and science departments in the Bengal National College, provided 150 students were available. An education board was set up under Jitendralal Banerji to conduct "national examinations", and we hear of a Kalikata Vidyapith with Subhas Bose as principal: *Mussalman*, 28 January, 11 February, 23 September 1921. National schools were set up in nearly every district in early 1921, but most of them quickly withered away: GOB Poll (Conf.), 395, 1.3.1924, p. 4, WBSA.

[75] Ibid., p. 6.

[76] Sarkar, *Swadeshi Movement*, p. 270.

[77] GOB Poll (Conf.) 395 1.3.1924, p. 4.

[78] *Haat*, the indigenous term for village or small-town markets, usually held on a specific day in the week.

Among all these forms, *haat* looting was the one most directly related to economic distress. The high price of cloth led to one such outbreak in the winter of 1917–18.[79] In August–September 1919 a very sharp rise in rice prices (due to large-scale exports from Bengal to feed other famine-stricken areas) was accompanied by eighty-two cases of *haat* looting.[80] The available extremely scanty data unfortunately provide no information about the climate of popular opinion which conditioned such *haat* looting; we have no information for instance as to whether the food rioters were animated by any definite conception of a "just price".[81] *Haat* and fish-pond looting by Santals in north-west Midnapur and Bankura in 1922 and 1923 however was clearly part of a broader upsurge and had more to do as we shall see with rumours of a crisis in authority than economic distress alone.[82]

Throughout 1920 and even part of 1921 the correspondence of the governor of Bengal indicates that labour unrest evoked maximum official concern, followed by the Khilafat agitation (itself connected with the presence "of a very large Muhammadan labour force employed in the jute mills"),[83] and specifically Gandhian Non-Cooperation came a poor third.[84] In a telegram to the secretary of state, Chelmsford attributed the unprecedented countrywide strike

[79] Bengal Diary, undated entry describing the Calcutta riots of September 1918, Zetland Collection.

[80] Ronaldshay to Montagu, 24 September 1919; Ronaldshay to King George V, 30 September 1919, ibid., *Annual Report on Administration of Bengal, 1918–1919*, p. 15.

[81] There are references to crowds enforcing lower prices (and not just looting) in north Bihar in 1921 and parts of Bengal in 1931–2. See Stephen Henningham, op. cit.; Tanika Sarkar, op. cit.

[82] GOB Poll (Conf.) 87, 1.9.1922, 181/1923, WBSA.

[83] The "proximity" of this labour force to Calcutta, Ronaldshay argued, was "the chief danger", for the Muslim worker "if aroused is capable of serious rioting as our experience in September 1918 showed": Ronaldshay to George V, 12 May 1920, Zetland Collection.

[84] "Gandhi's non-co-operation movement still falls flat in Bengal" (Ronaldshay to Montagu, 5 July 1920). "Apart from the activities of Kalam Azad and half a dozen of his tools in Calcutta, the situation in Bengal is entirely satisfactory": ibid., 19 July 1920. An earlier letter to Montagu (6 April) had identified some of these "tools" with "the group of Calcutta pan-Islamists

wave primarily to economic factors: soaring prices and the "general shortage of industrial labour" due to post-war industrial expansion, and the influenza epidemic. But he also mentioned as contributory elements the growing awareness "that capitalists, millowners in particular, are making very large profits", the impact of "world-wide political unrest . . . frequent reports of labour trouble in England and Europe", and "to some extent" encouragement "by political agitators in India".[85] The Bengal Committee on Industrial Unrest listed 137 strikes in the province in the nine months starting from July 1920, while the annual administrative reports chronicle 150 strikes involving 265,000 workers in 1921 and 91 strikes involving c. 160,000 next year.[86]

Comparison with Swadeshi labour unrest is again illuminating. Trade unions were far more numerous, though still often somewhat ephemeral, than in 1905–8; an Intelligence Branch list recorded forty "labour unions and associations" in Bengal in 1920, fifty-five in 1921, and seventy-five in 1922.[87] Barristers with nationalist connections were once again fairly prominent, men like I.B. Sen, S.N. Haldar, and N.C. Sen, all three close to Chittaranjan Das. But the government was much more worried by the activities of Khilafat agitators like Muhammed Osman trying "to spread disaffection on religious grounds among the mill coolies",[88] and recruiting volunteers from jute labourers via contacts with sardars.[89] The spate of swamis or "political

---

which gave us trouble in September 1918" – yet another indication of the interpenetration of logically very different forms of political activity.

[85] Telegram from Viceroy to Secretary of State, no. 8C, 25 October 1920, in reply to a query from the Secretary of State dated 16 October, GOI Home Poll B, November 1920, no. 281, NAI.

[86] *Report of Committee on Industrial Unrest* (Calcutta, 1921), p. 2; *A Report on Administration of Bengal, 1920–1* (p. xi) and *1921–2* (p. xi).

[87] *List of Labour Unions and Associations in Bengal 1920, 1921, 1922* (Bengal Government confidential publication). I am grateful to Rajat Ray for giving me access to these documents.

[88] History of the Non-Cooperation Movement in Bengal, p. 1, GOB Poll (Conf.) F.N. 395, 1.3.1924, WBSA.

[89] Officiating Chief Secretary Bengal, to GOI (Home), no. 16410 P of 17 November 1921, GOB Poll (Conf.) F.N. 333, 11.26.1921, WBSA.

sannyasis" also made officials nervous. As in 1905, strikes, unions, and nationalist barrister connections were at first most noticeable among white-collar employees of printing presses and mercantile firms, along with railway clerks and tramway men.[90] But the upsurge in the jute mills far outstripped Swadeshi precedents, plantations and the coal belt were affected for the first time, and among millhands, tea garden coolies, miners, and railway menial staff alike a more "religious" style of leadership was apparent. Apart from Muhammed Osman, Swami Iswar Das from Chapra was active among jute millhands. Swami Biswananda (Rasul Singh), Swami Dinanada (ex-professor of Sibpur Engineering College), and Swami Darshanananda figured prominently in strikes in the coal belt in the winter of 1920–1 as well as in the Assam–Bengal rail and steamer strikes of mid 1921 and the EIR strike of early 1922. Official reports attributed the exodus from tea plantations in the Chargola valley partly to the preaching of sadhus like Bisamber Das Guru of Central Provinces and Siyaram Das of Ayodhya.[91]

Initiative from below however remained far more important than organisation through outsiders in the strike wave of 1919–22. The Committee on Industrial Unrest statistics reveal the striking fact that labour unrest was at its height in the last quarter of 1920,[92] i.e. before the Non-Cooperation–Khilafat movement really got into its stride

---

[90] Thus an Employees Association of merchant office clerks was set up in August 1919, with Sachindranath Basu, son of the Swadeshi labour leader Premtosh Basu, as office bearer. The Journalists and Press Employees Association of January 1920 had C.R. Das as President and Bipin Pal, Jitendralal Banerji, I.B. Sen, S.N. Haldar, Hemantkumar Sarkar, and Maulvi Akram Khan among its office bearers. Tram workers went on strike repeatedly during 1920 and 1921, and N.C. Sen and S.N. Haldar figured among the office bearers of the Tramway Employees Union set up in October 1920. See *List of Labour Unions and Associations in Bengal*.

[91] Notes by Intelligence Branch, CID, Bengal, 9 July 1921, 7 November 1921, and by CID Assam, 21 October 1921, *Reports on Activities of Political Emissaries Disguised as Sadhus and Fakirs*, GOI Home Poll 118/1922, NAI.

[92] Of the 137 strikes listed by the Committee on Industrial Unrest, 11 per cent took place in the third quarter of 1920, 65 per cent in the last quarter of the same year, and 24 per cent in the first quarter of 1921. Quoted in Sanat

in Bengal. Political agitation and labour militancy followed parallel but largely separate paths, intermingling only on two occasions: the East Bengal railway and steamer strikes following the belabouring of tea garden coolies at Chandpur in May 1921, and the use of millhands as volunteers courting arrest in Calcutta in December 1921–January 1922. Yet statements that leaders like J.M. Sengupta "brought off" the East Bengal strikes grossly oversimplify a more complex reality.[93] These began really as a more or less spontaneous protest against Gurkha atrocities taking place "before the very eyes of the railway employees".[94] The strikes were no doubt encouraged by the Bengal Congress decision to provide "advice and financial help",[95] but they continued mainly on the basis of specific labour demands for strike pay and recognition of the Assam–Bengal Employees Union.[96]

It is interesting that Das' defence of the railway strike was more than a little embarrassed.[97] The use of millhands to court arrest did bring about a startling though short-lived change in the social composition

---

Bose, "Industrial Unrest and Growth of Labour Unions in Bengal 1920–24", *Economic and Political Weekly*, Special Number, November 1981.

[93] Rajat Ray, op. cit., p. 367.

[94] Statement of J.M. Sengupta at Chandpur, 14 July 1921, *Mussalman*, 22 July 1921. Following the Gurkha attack on the night of 20 May, sympathy strikes began among Chandpur and Laksham railway staff on 24 May; the decision for a general strike was taken by the Chittagong-centred Assam–Bengal Railway union next day. The steamer strike began on 27 May, following the arrest of the Secretary of the Sarangi Association, Abdul Majid. *Indian Annual Register*, 1922, p. 144.

[95] "Each station staff should go to the nearest Congress Office for advice and financial help." Statement by J.M. Sengupta, *Mussalman*, 17 June 1921.

[96] J.M. Sengupta's statement of 14 July pointed out that the railway employees were "holding out on three points" – strike pay, no break in service, recognition of their union (of which Sengupta was President). *Mussalman*, 22 July 1921.

[97] C.R. Das in a statement at Chandpur on 12 June declared that the strikes were "not labour or political strikes ... they are national", examples of "spontaneous non-cooperation" similar to the hartal by lawyers of Comilla, Chittagong and Noakhali courts following news of the Chandpur incident. "If it had been a labour strike, a mere question between the employer and

of the Calcutta agitation.[98] But even if we disregard repeated official charges that the labourers were no more than mercenaries hired through Khilafat funds,[99] one does get the impression that the politicians were really using the proletariat as cannon fodder at a time when student and *bhadralok* enthusiasm for going to jail was fast ebbing.[100] There was little or no nationalist interest in the major East India railway strike of February–March 1922, and certainly no effort at all to co-ordinate it with the Civil Disobedience programme.[101] And

---

the employed, I should have certainly discouraged it from the Congress point of view, I mean I would not have allowed it to interfere in any way with the ordinary work of the Congress." *Mussalman*, 17 June 1921.

[98] Of the 349 arrests in Calcutta during the week ending 5 January 1922, only 39 were students, "123 were mill hands from Telipara, Metiabruz, Kankinara, Champdeney, Barrackpore, Shamnagore, Khurda, Kamarhatty, Gondalpara and Bhadreswar. The remaining persons arrested were boat manjhis and low class Mohammedans from the suburbs." Calcutta Police Commissioner to GOB Chief Secretary, 5 January 1922, GOB Poll (Conf.) 14 (1-20)/1922, WBSA. It would be difficult to imagine a greater contrast with Swadeshi days.

[99] The volunteers courting arrest were mostly students till 17 December, Ronaldshay noted in his diary, "but since then nearly the whole has been millhand, paid for the purpose": Bengal Diary, 20 December 1921, Zetland Collection. The *Amrita Bazar Patrika* of 21 December 1921 tried to refute the charge of the *Englishman* that millhands were being paid by the Khilafat Committee: "Our information is that the millhands raised money by subscription among themselves . . ." Court reports of statements by arrested millhands and boatmen carried in the same issue were somewhat ambiguous. Some stated "they were volunteers, but they could not say what was the object of the organization of the hartal on 24th. An elderly mill coolie said that his conscience told him to organise hartal on the 24th and so he was preaching this among his countrymen."

[100] The difficulties in recruiting middle-class Bengali volunteers are recalled in Hemendranath Dasgupta, op. cit., pp. 218–19.

[101] There was a brief strike of the EIR menial staff from Mughalsarai to Asansol in early January 1922, following the alleged high-handedness of a foreman. A bigger strike began on 2 February 1922 after a case of assault by a white on Indian firemen at Tundla at a time when Civil Disobedience had not yet been countermanded by Gandhi: *Amrita Bazar Patrika*, 3, 5, 6 January

The Conditions and Nature of Subaltern Militancy   445

Gandhi himself as is well known denounced the East Bengal strikes,[102] while in December 1921 the arrest of Biswananda evoked from him the following hasty telegram to the Jharia coal belt: "Coolies must not strike. They may discard foreign clothes in earnest of their devotion. They must be absolutely peaceful."[103]

Though most strikes took place on specific economic demands, other dimensions were not entirely absent. Racist insults and assaults at Jhajha and Tundla provided the immediate occasions for the two E.I.R. strikes in early 1922. At Kumardhati in January 1921 the men left work after a similar incident, and when the management tried to lay off some of them they declared "that they would either go back to work in a body or not go back at all."[104] In November 1921 in a striking demonstration of working-class solidarity tramwaymen were "joined by millhands from neighbouring mills" in picketing Belgachia depot (north Calcutta) and in subsequent clashes with the police."[105] Five thousand Calcutta dock labourers went on strike on 14 December after an officer had removed a man's Gandhi cap; they demanded the immediate release of C.R. Das and the right to "shout Gandhi Maharaj ki Jai" while working on board.[106] And in a fascinating combination of patriotic millennial rumours and hardheaded collective bargaining jute mill workers in the last week of December 1921 demanded an end to the common practice "to keep

---

1922; *Mussalman*, 10, 24 February 1922. The *Servant* of 24 February 1922, the Calcutta journal closest to Gandhism, commented apropos of the EIR strike "that it is an unpardonable mistake to suppose that labour strikes are either necessary or can in any way avail to advance the cause of non-cooperation." RNEP(B) for week ending 4 March 1922, WBSA.

[102] "In India we want no political strikes": "Lessons of Assam", *Young India*, 15 June 1921.

[103] Telegram to G.K. Gadgil, *Amrita Bazar Patrika*, 28 December 1921.

[104] Swami Biswananda in his speech to Kumardhati and Kulti workers at Barakar on 17 January 1921 emphasised this dimension: ". . . although there was need for food in this world, there was also need for honour . . ." GOI Home Poll Dept, February 1921, no. 5, NAI.

[105] Viceroy to Secretary of State, 14 November 1921, Reading Collection.

[106] *Mussalman*, 16 December 1921.

three days wages in hand while paying a week's wages. The reason of such a demand is, we are told, that the workers are in the belief that they will get Swaraj on the 24th."[107]

The rumour of imminent swaraj in fact worked wonders repeatedly during 1921 and early 1922. Apart from the famous exodus of 6000–7000 coolies from Chargola tea estates in May 1921,[108] the most spectacular instance was probably the jailbreak by 669 prisoners from Rajshahi on 24 March 1921. This had been preceded by rumours that Gandhi was coming to Rajshahi on 25 March to end the British Raj. The prisoners before breaking out "bound *rakhis* or threads on their wrists as a sign of unity", thus reviving the symbolism of 1905 in a totally different context, and marched openly in a body through the streets of the town after overpowering their guards.[109] Smaller jailbreaks occurred or were attempted at Sirajganj, Netrokona, Dinajpur, Rangpur, Midnapur and Barisal.[110] Even more serious from the government point of view was large-scale disaffection among the police with thirty Calcutta Muslim constables and head constables resigning after a Maidan meeting of 200 policemen on 13 November 1921, pro-Non-Cooperation sentiments among upcountry constables in Howrah, and reports of police unrest flowing in from Noakhali, Rangpur, Mymensingh, Khulna, Bogra, and 24 Parganas.[111] A Hindi

---

[107] *Amrita Bazar Patrika*, 23 December 1921.

[108] The Chargola labourers demanded large pay increases "with shouts of Gandhi Maharaj ki Jai", and then left the plantations in a body. Viceroy to Secretary of State, 21 June 1921, Reading Collection. The *Sanjivani* complained on 7 July that the tea coolies were rejecting offers for agricultural employment in Bengal. ". . . unfortunately the idea has become rooted in their minds that Gandhi has become king of their province and that his Raj is free from sorrow and want. They are not therefore prepared to go anywhere but their native villages." RNP(B) for week ending 16 July 1921, WBSA.

[109] Official account of the Rajshahi jail-break, published in *Mussalman*, 20 May 1921.

[110] *Report on Administration of Bengal, 1920–21*, p. x.

[111] Reports on Political Situation (Bengal), GOI Home Poll 18/November 1921, 18/December 1921. Note by DIG, Intelligence Branch, 31 December 1921, GOB Poll (Conf) 39/137/1921. In February 1922, two Nepali women were reported as spreading disaffection among Gurkha armed policemen in

newspaper quoted a moving statement by one disaffected constable: "We shall all go home giving up our service and till land and spin *charkha* and pass our days happily. Mahatmaji has opened our eyes."[112]

Turning to more specifically rural movements, one might perhaps distinguish three strands. The very successful anti-Union Board agitation in Contai subdivision of Midnapur and the boycott of settlement operations in Bogra and Birbhum were organised and controlled movements under local nationalist leaders (Birendranath Sasmal in Midnapur, Jitendralal Banerji in Birbhum), taking up grievances which were specific, occasionally long-standing,[113] and above all without divisive potential so far as the rural community was concerned. Barring an isolated assault on a white settlement officer in Bogra,[114] such movements were both united and remarkably peaceful. Thus at Contai *tahsildars* were invited by villagers to attach their property "amidst shouts of Haribole and blowing of conchshells", "labourers and cartmen . . . refused everywhere to carry the attached moveables",[115] and union boards had to be withdrawn from Midnapur district as it was "impossible to realize union board rates by distraint, since no one will come forward to bid at the sales."[116] In

---

Calcutta. "I beg to point out that it is now impossible to deal with these women", complained the Deputy Commissioner of Police: GOB Poll (Conf.) 14/21–30/1922, WBSA.

[112] *Hindustan*, 16 November 1921, RNP(B) for week ending 26 November 1921, WBSA.

[113] Thus the introduction of union boards into Contai meant a possible sevenfold increase, from Rs 12 to a maximum of Rs 84 in a *chowkidari* tax which a Bengal chief secretary had admitted way back in 1908 as falling "too heavily on poor communities which really cannot afford whole time chowkidars". B.N. Sasmal's report on the Contai movement, *Mussalman*, 7 October 1921; GOB Poll (Conf.) 187(1–2)/1908. As for settlement operations, there was widespread fear that these would affect the standing crops, already rather poor in Birbhum in 1921.

[114] Report on Political Situation (Bengal), GOI Home Poll, 18 November 1921, WBSA.

[115] See B.N. Sasmal's report, op. cit.

[116] See Report on Political Situation, op. cit.

the four northern police stations of Birbhum centred around Rampurhat (J.L. Banerji's home town), settlement operations "almost completely stopped" in November 1921 due to a social boycott of officials. It was "impossible to procure coolies locally for the work" and moves by the authorities to get zamindar support failed: "the resident landlords are for the most part petty and would be unable even if they were willing to put a stop to the opposition of the people."[117] The dominant Swadeshi pattern of patriotic zamindars rallying their tenants had clearly been reversed to a considerable extent.

But it would be a serious mistake to assume an extension of the Contai pattern everywhere or to think that Gandhian restraints and social harmony could be maintained always in 1921–2. The Bengal Congress leadership in general remained as always very allergic to the raising of rent issues. The most "radical" leadership statement was probably that at the Barisal Provincial Conference in April 1921, and even this limited itself to requesting zamindars not to levy *abwabs* and to limit the filing of rent suits "even at a sacrifice."[118] Some newspapers in the Non-Cooperation period did give greater coverage to zamindari exploitation than at all common in Swadeshi days, but most of these journals tended to be somewhat aloof and at times positively hostile towards the political movement.[119] A special

[117] Report on F.W. Robertson, Settlement Officer, Bankura–Birbhum, to F.A. Sachse, Director of Land Records, Suri, 17 November 1920, GOB Poll (Conf.) 347(1–5)/1921, WBSA.

[118] The conference went a bit further on labour issues by extending "cordial support to the movement for organising labour unions . . . while deploring the necessity for strikes: *Mussalman,* 1 April 1921.

[119] Of the three newspapers giving noticeable coverage to agrarian disputes, the *Raiyat* clearly warned that "the raiyat movement will be stifled if it is mixed up with politics" (3 September 1921). The *Navyug* was edited in part by the future Communist leader Muzaffar Ahmed, but its owner was A.K. Fazlul Huq, who opposed Non-Cooperation. At least some of its articles could be frankly communal, as when it accused Khilafatists of trying to submerge "Musalmans as a race . . . into the community of idolators" (25 November 1921). The *Hitavadi,* which had earlier carried a lot of news about zamindari oppression, changed its line abruptly around November 1921 to warn about the "grim shadow of Bolshevism" and the danger that "swaraj would mean

The Conditions and Nature of Subaltern Militancy 449

case was presented however by the Midnapur Zamindari Company, a white-owned concern with extensive estates in central Bengal as well as in Midnapur. Newspapers carried frequent reports about the oppressive ways of this company, and more particularly of its branches at Bilimaria in Rajshahi and Shikarpur at Nadia,[120] areas where tensions had been sharpened by a bid to revive indigo cultivation taking advantage of the wartime elimination of German synthetic dye competition. Das privately encouraged Someswarprasad Chaudhuri, a young medical student who had joined the educational boycott, to try and organise peasant resistance to the company along the Rajshahi-Pabna-Nadia-Murshidabad border, though he made it clear that the Congress formally could give no support as the movement could very well adversely affect Indian zamindars who followed not dissimilar practices. Someswarprasad's autobiographical account gives vivid and fascinating details about the pattern of initial contacts (through Marwari traders and village *pramaniks* or headmen) and the forms of struggle (mass recording of grievances followed by a *dharmaghat* or collective refusal to do *begar* or work for the company) – as well as about the inevitable social problems when no-rent spread to the neighbouring estate of the zamindar of Rifaitpur in Nadia, in whose house a top Congress leader happened to be staying just at that time.[121]

While the central Bengal peasant agitation still retained a somewhat tenous lin[k with the Congress leadership through Someswarprasad's

---

Khilafat raj" (25 November 1921): RNP(B) for weeks ending 10 September and 3 December 1921, WBSA.

[120] *Raiyat*, 16 April and 3 September 1921; *Navyug*, 24 May 1921; *Hitavadi*, 24 June, 8 July, 15 July, 19 August, 26 August, 2 September, and 16 September 1921, RNP(B) for relevant weeks, WBSA.

[121] Someswaraprasad Chaudhuri, *Nilkar Bidroha* (Calcutta, 1972), pp. 6–8, 9–10, 16–19, 22–4, 29–43, 48–62. There are some clear parallels with the Champaran movement of 1917, where too the Indian trading element resented white planter rivalry and collective recording of grievances played an important role. See Jacques Pouchepadass, "Local Leaders and the Intelligentsia in the Champaran Satyagraha (1917): A Study in Peasant Mobilization", *Contributions to Indian Sociology*, 1974.

personal connections with and loyalty to C.R. Das, more elemental and uncontrolled movements had started developing in the winter of 1921–2. There is considerable evidence that what frightened the authorities most were not movements of the controlled Gandhian variety of which Birendranath Sasmal's Contai is the best-known prototype, but the "great wave of lawlessness which swept over the affected areas of east and west Bengal" in which the authority of district Congress committees was "rapidly lost" and there was a drift toward "civil disobedience", though no leader had ever sanctioned it.[122] Ronaldshay reported to Montagu in real alarm on 9 February 1922: "it is being widely stated in the villages that Gandhi Raj has come and that there is no longer any necessity to pay anything to anybody. They are consequently not only refusing to pay rent and taxes but also repudiating their debts!"[123]

British officials had repeatedly warned local Congress leaders with land who were heading the movement for non-payment of *chowkidari* taxes that "the next step the people will take will be the refusal to pay rent".[124] Despite a formal statement by the publicity board of the Provincial Congress warning the districts against no-rent,"[125] reports of such movements were flooding in by the winter of 1921–2 amidst a general collapse of authority in a number of regions. The four areas principally affected were Midnapur, parts of Rangpur, and Jalpaiguri, Chittagong, and Tippera – mostly outlying regions, it is interesting to note, relatively distant from the metropolis. We also hear of incidents in Mymensingh where a Kishoreganj Marwari trading firm with extensive landed property became the principal target, and Noakhali where zamindars were reported by the district magistrate to be in terror of their own tenants.[126] Peasants in Mymensingh

---

[122] *History of Non-Cooperation Movement in Bengal*, op. cit., p. 13.
[123] Zetland Collection.
[124] Notes by Midnapur Sadar SDO, Manicharan Bose, 13 January 1922, and by Midnapur ADM, L. Birley, 16 January 1922, GOB Poll (Conf.) F.N. 87(1–9)/1922, WBSA.
[125] Report on Political Situation, Bengal, 2nd half of January 1922, GOI Home Poll F.N., 18 January 1922, WBSA.
[126] Report of Mymensingh District Magistrate, 1 January 1922, GOB Poll

district were said to have declared "that they live in the land of God and are His creation and they are not to pay anything to anybody in the world."[127]

In Midnapur the district Congress urged paying up of *chowkidari* taxes once the union board had been withdrawn in December 1921, but there were still widespread refusals in regions like Contai, Panskura in Tamluk, Daspur in Ghatal, Debra in Sadar, and Gopiballavpur in Jhargram subdivisions. The SDO of Ghatal reported that "the masses" absolutely refuse to listen to local Congress committees, using the argument that payment to the Swaraj Fund exempted them from all other claims, while the Santals of Gopiballavpur claimed "that the chaukidari tax had been abolished by Gandhi Maharaj's order".[128] Meanwhile in semi-tribal north-west Midnapur (Jhargram subdivision) Santals and Mahatos (Kurmis) went about looting *haats*, destroying liquor shops amidst shouts of "Gandhi Maharaj ki Jai", searching for foreign cloth but taking "all kinds of cloth indiscriminately", and forbidding the export of paddy but (interesting evidence of some sort of underlying "moral economy") not "taking any away" . . . "everyone at Silda, including the non-co-operators, was very much afraid", and there was panic in Jhargram town on 29 January. The Santals had been inflamed also by a dispute with the Midnapur Zamindari Company over "wood for houses and agricultural purposes". No additional police was ultimately required for Contai but Jhargram had to be pacified by a route-march of the Eastern Frontier Rifles.[129] There was also a spate of dacoities, thirty-

───────────────

(Conf.) F.N. 14 (21–30)/1922; Report of Officiating District Magistrate, Noakhali, 28 December 1921, GOB Poll (Conf.) F.N. 39(118–28)/1921, WBSA.

[127] GOI Home Poll F.N., 18/January 1922, WBSA.

[128] L. Birley to Divisional Commissioner, Burdwan, 27 January 1922, pleading for additional punitive police for Contai and Daspur thanas, GOB Poll (Conf.) F.N. 87 (1–8) 1/22, WBSA. It is interesting that many of these areas were to figure very prominently in later militant movements – Daspur in 1930 (the Chechuahat incident – see Tanika Sarkar, op. cit., pp. 212–17), Contai and Tamluk in 1942, Debra and Gopiballavpur in the Naxalbari days.

[129] L. Birley to Burdwan Divisional Commissioner, 28 January 1922; A.W.

three in Midnapur district in January 1922 out of a total of 111 in the province that month.[130]

At Madarihat in Jalpaiguri district on 21 February, following a market quarrel between a Marwari shopkeeper and a Santal coolie, police attempts to arrest some Santals led to an attack by a crowd wearing Gandhi caps which "demanded the release of the prisoners, shouting all the time that they were immune from bullet wounds as they were wearing Gandhi Maharaj's caps."[131] Three Santals were killed by police firing. No-rent movements developed in neighbouring Rangpur, affecting the estates of Maharaja Manindra Nandy of Kasimbazar in Kurigram subdivision.[132] Marwari and Shaha merchants and moneylenders became principal targets along the Rangpur–Assam border, and in Batashan pargana the district magistrate persuaded the zamindar to give concessions to his tenants as there was "some danger that Raiyats' Samiti might be captured by the non-cooperators."[133]

In Chittagong there was widespread violation of forest laws in Banskhali, Satkania, and three police stations in Cox's Bazar subdivision. A ten-day permission to collect building material after the cyclone of May 1921 was extended indefinitely by popular action, eight out of twelve forest offices burnt in Cox's Bazar, and "until about May 1922 the Forest Department might have been said to have ceased to function . . . This widespread looting was not the work of volunteers, but of ordinary villagers out to help themselves . . ."[134]

Cook, District Magistrate, Midnapur, to Burdwan Divisional Commissioner, 1 February 1922, ibid.

[130] *History of Non-Cooperation Movement in Bengal*, op. cit., p. 15.

[131] *Mussalman*, 10 March 1922.

[132] Additional Superintendent of Police, Rangpur, to Deputy IG of Police, Intelligence Branch, Bengal, 12 February 1922, GOB Poll (Conf.) F.N. 14(21–30)/1912, WBSA.

[133] Reports of Rajshahi Divisional Commissioner, 13 August, 18 October 1921, GOB Poll (Conf.) F.N. 333 (30–46)/1921, WBSA.

[134] *History of Non-Cooperation Movement in Bengal*, op. cit., p. 15.

The Conditions and Nature of Subaltern Militancy 453

In Chaudagram police station of Tippera, a part of the district untouched by previous organised agitation (unlike Brahmanbaria or Chandpur), the rural police system had collapsed by November 1921: "No taxes were being paid, and no agricultural rents collected . . . the agitation was entirely Muhammaden, but not religious. The people were simply out to assert themselves . . ." Efforts to restore authority led to five clashes with the police in February–March 1922, culminating in a confrontation on 9 March in which three villagers were killed. An official report noted that "volunteers tried to restrain the mob but without effect", and that educated nationalist reaction to the firing was much less evident than after Chandpur in May 1921 "where the amount of force used was very much less."[135] Rural Tippera incidentally would again witness a powerful agrarian movement with a nationalist content during Civil Disobedience.[136]

It is noteworthy that unlike more organised movements, popular outbursts of this sort went on happening even after Non-Cooperation had been abruptly called off by the Congress Working Committee at its Bardoli session on 12 February 1922. In April 1923 for instance there was a wave of looting of fish ponds and violation of forest rights over an area of 200 square miles extending from Jamboni and Gopiballavpur (Jhargram subdivision, Midnapur) westwards to Ghatsila (in Singhbhum district of Bihar) and northwards through Silda and Binpur to Raipur police station in Bankura district. The situation was aggravated in Jamboni by a dispute between the local zamindar and his rival Pratap Dal of Dhalbhum, and in Silda by the activities of the local Congress leader Sailajananda Sen – very different types of politics producing interestingly similar results. However, the real roots lay not in any outsider instigation, but in the encroachment on traditional Santal rights to free use of forests by the Jamboni Raj and the Midnapur Zamindari Company once the construction of railways had made timber commercially profitable. Crowds of up to 5000 consisting of Santals as well as low-caste Bengali peasants looted fish ponds in daylight, asserting what they felt was a

---

[135] Ibid., p. 14. See also *Mussalman*, 31 March 1922.
[136] Tanika Sarkar, op. cit., pp. 301–6.

natural right. The Santal, an official reported, "will tell you how in his father's time all jungles were free, all *bandhs* (ponds) open to the public . . . Sometimes he is right." On one memorable occasion they made Additional District Magistrate Peddie flee for his life: "It is the first time I have had to run away and I did not like doing so – but there was nothing else possible."[137]

Agrarian conflicts of various types – tenant–zamindar disputes over rent and tenure, *bargadar* claims to a two-thirds share of the produce – in fact remained a major feature of Bengal life in the mid 1920s, particularly in the context of the rumours and debates which preceded the passage of the Tenancy Amendment Act of 1928.[138] But the link with nationalist politics, always a bit tenuous, had once again broken down – a rupture made blatant by the Swarajist pro-zamindar stance in the 1928 assembly discussions.[139] Peasant movements consequently tended to revert to their Swadeshi or post-Swadeshi pattern, finding articulation through forms of communalism or caste.

Thus the abrupt withdrawal of Non-Cooperation and the breakdown of Hindu–Muslim unity at the top with the abrogation of the Bengal Pact after C.R. Das' death did have serious repercussions on the world of the subaltern. Relative autonomy is very different from total disjunction and, as Peter Burke has recently argued, "peoples' history", however crucially important, has to be seen as part of a more all-embracing "total history".[140] An example of such interaction is provided by intelligentsia reactions to the spectacle of mass awakening in 1919–22. Characterised in the main by panic and retreat, the same

---

[137] Fascinating details about the whole affair are given in GOB Poll (Conf.) F.N. 181/1923, NMML microfilm.

[138] For details see Tanika Sarkar, op. cit., chapter 2, and Partha Chatterjee, "Agrarian Relations and Communalism in Bengal 1926–1935" in R. Guha, ed., *Subaltern Studies I* (Delhi, 1981).

[139] A detailed analysis of this significant episode has been made in Partha Chatterjee, *Agrarian Relations and Politics in Bengal: Some Considerations on the Making of the Tenancy Act Amendment 1928*, Centre for Studies in Social Sciences, Calcutta, Occasional Paper no. 30, 1980.

[140] Peter Burke, "Peoples' History or Total History", in Raphael Samuel, ed., *Peoples' History and Socialist Theory* (London, 1981).

years also saw the beginnings of constructive work in scattered village centres (Tamluk-Contai, Arambagh, Bankura, Comilia, etc.) along Gandhian lines leading up to the gradual formation of more stable peasant bases for the national movement.[141] It is not a coincidence furthermore that the first Communist groups emerged in Bombay, Calcutta, and Madras in the wake of Non-Cooperation and its Bardoli anticlimax.

An unpublished diary written by a young man who would develop later into a pioneer Marxist teacher and intellectual can be used to illustrate my point about the far-reaching impact of popular militancy on the intelligentsia. A Presidency College student named Susobhan Sarkar, immersed throughout much of 1921 in the poetry of Tagore and the internal quarrels of the Sadharan Brahmo Samaj, quite sharply critical of Gandhi along the lines worked out by Tagore in his *Call of Truth*, was yet sufficiently stirred by the spectacle of thousands courting arrest in the streets of Calcutta in November–December 1921 to start wearing *khadi* for a while as a token of protest, and to give up once and for all earlier plans formed under family pressure to take the I.C.S. examination. What was breaking down above all under the pressure of mass militancy was the legitimacy of foreign rule, its acceptance as sacrosanct even by groups otherwise very distant from nationalist politics and affluent enough to be personally untouched by economic distress.[142]

Conversely, it is again in terms of a weakening of the legitimacy or hegemony of the existing order that we can best understand the impact of certain phases of nationalist agitation on the world of the subaltern. In 1919–22 direct organisational or ideological mobilisation was still rather minimal; as one official report put it, the "particular

---

[141] Hitesranjan Sanyal, "Arambage Jatiyabadi Andolan" (*Anya Artha*, Calcutta, 1974–5), and "Dakshin-Paschim Banglay Jatiyatabadi Andolan" (*Chaturanga*, Calcutta, 1976–7).

[142] Sarkar's diary says nothing about price-rise, is generally very nonpolitical, and incidentally reveals no awareness as yet of the significance of the Bolshevik Revolution. All the more interesting, however, are the references to the September 1918 riots, the Rowlatt disturbances, Chandpur, the hartal of 17 November 1921, and subsequent mass courting of arrest.

form of lawlessness, which depended on organisation and a constant supply of speakers, was shortlived."[143] What was crucially important was the spread of rumours, potent in their very vagueness about the impending collapse of British rule and the coming of "swaraj" or "Gandhi Raj" within a year. The predominant rumour in the Swadeshi period in contrast had been that the babus were quarrelling with the government, and not that the sarkar itself was going down. An understanding of the impact of such things requires something in the way of an analysis of the "structure" of popular mentality underlying the multifarious forms of militancy we have been studying so far.

III

Taking our sample of popular movement as a whole, I think it is possible to construct a system of correlations and oppositions, structures of collective mentality conducive to rebellion or its opposite. The impact of economic pressures and middle-class political movements can best be understood in terms of their impinging on and activising such pre-existing structures.

Central to most of the popular outbreaks of our period is a concept of *breakdown*, real or more often rumoured, in the pattern of coercion/hegemony which "normally" keeps the subalterns in their place despite misery and exploitation. Oppression in "normal" times is cloaked by a certain legitimacy which makes rebellion seem not only too dangerous in view of the force at the command of the dominant classes and the state, but also morally wrong. A rumour of breakdown is needed to weaken this hegemonic control. Breakdown again can have two dimensions: a more or less sudden change in the conditions of life (predominantly, though not necessarily solely, economic) of the oppressed, and rumours of weakening of authority structures due to external threats to or divisions within the dominant strata. In colonial India war or rumours of war with Afghanistan, Russia, Germany or the Ottoman empire repeatedly sparked off such developments, and the early impact of middle-class nationalism was perhaps not qualitatively different.

---

[143] *History of Non-Cooperation Movement in Bengal*, op. cit., p. 13.

The first type of breakdown is obviously related to the economic pressures we have been talking about: price-rise and/or poor harvests bringing in their train *haat* looting, dacoity, and labour unrest, and contributing to communal riots with a significant economic dimension as in Mymensingh in 1906–7 or Calcutta in September 1918. It is a characteristic feature of such disturbances that relatively "new" oppressors, or at least people considered for various socio-religious or cultural reasons to be "outsiders", tend to become the principal targets. Thus Hindu landlords and Shaha and Marwari traders-moneylenders, felt to be outside the moral community of a predominantly Muslim peasantry, became objects of attack in parts of eastern and northern Bengal in 1906–7 and again in 1921–2 – though there must no doubt have been equally oppressive Hindu zamindars, *jotedars*, and usurers exploiting Hindu peasants in other parts of the province. Partha Chatterjee has recently argued that a Muslim element was by no means unimportant even among rentier groups in East Bengal.[144] *Bargadar* movements seem to have developed earlier in Jessore, Khulna, and Faridpur, where Namasudras confronted upper-caste *jotedars*, then in Midnapur where Mahishya caste ties helped to keep the countryside more united for a time. In north-west Midnapur in 1923 the Santals blamed newcomer "Bengalis" for their troubles and displayed a loyalty towards the dispossessed Pratap Dal in preference to the zamindar of Jamboni who had recently taken over the Dalbhum estate from the former.[145] As the protests were usually against what were felt to be new developments, evocations of earlier norms tended to be extremely common, at times developing into golden-age myths. Peasant rioters in Mymensingh in 1906 recalled an old pargana rate of rent,[146] while Santals in 1923 "believed that they were simply carrying on an

---

[144] Partha Chatterjee, "Agrarian Relations and Communalism in Bengal, 1926–1935".

[145] Bengal Chief Secretary to GOI (Home), 10 May 1923, enclosing extract from report of Deputy Commissioner, Singhbhum, to Chief Commissioner, Chota Nagpur, 28/29 April 1923, GOB Poll (Conf.) F.N. 181/1923, NMML.

[146] Before and during the Iswarganj riots of May 1906, there were "wild and extravagant expectations" that rent would be reduced to Rs 3–6 as per *ata* (a local unit of about five *bighas*). An identical demand had been raised in the

old tradition", bringing back a "golden age" when "all jungles were free".[147] A nice sense of discrimination was sometimes displayed in actions conditioned by such memories. Thus Gurusaday Dutt, the district magistrate of Bankura, reported in 1923 that Santals freely admitted looting of fish ponds to be illegal, but "they considered tank-raiding might act as an inducement to zamindars to concede their old customary rights over jungles".[148]

Yet for resistance to develop, a change for the worse in the conditions of exploitation is often less important than rumours of breakdown of the second type: the Santals of Jhargram and Bankura after all had been losing their forest rights for decades. Within the concept of breakdown of authority, I think it is useful to distinguish further between a less and a more "extreme" form. In the first the rumour is that of a conflict among the superiors: the zamindars or the babus have quarrelled with the government, the latter's officials consequently would be more sympathetic towards our grievances (or conversely the immediate superior would help us in our struggle). The more extreme variety is that *all* existing authority is collapsing, usually through the emergence of a new symbolic power centre like the Gandhi Raj of 1921–2.

Examples of the first type include the refusal of enhanced rent in the Swadeshi period by tenants of patriotic zamindars like Brojendrakishore Roychaudhuri of Mymensingh, the Muslim attacks on Hindu gentry in 1906–7 fired by rumours that officials were on their side, and the beating up of Swadeshi babus by plebeian elements in Calcutta in October 1907. In the Sherpur incident of September 1907 we meet the alternative version too: the Muslim crowd attacking the police shouted "that the nine-anna zamindar [a Hindu, and quite a "well-behaved" one] had ordered them to beat the police and loot

---

same area way back in 1882–3, and the Dacca commissioner felt that this was "a reminiscence of a former pargana rate": Sarkar, *Swadeshi Movement*, p. 458.

[147] Report of Deputy Commissioner, Singhbhum, GOB Poll (Conf.) F.N. 181/1923, NMML.

[148] Report from District Magistrate, Bankura, enclosed in report of Divisional Commissioner, Burdwan, to Chief Secretary, GOB, 11 May 1923, ibid.

their quarters." The local superintendent of police drew "a rather apt parallel between the shouting of the crowd and the cry of the Musalman rioters in the Dewanganj and other looting cases that the Government and the Nawab [of Dacca] had ordered them to loot the Hindus. It is quite probable that the mob had as little foundation for the one cry as for the other. . ."[149] In the Midnapur Santal rising of April 1923 the dispossessed Raja, Pratap Dal, was rumoured to have given permission to take wood and fish freely, and so there was a "genuine belief by 90% of the crowds that they were doing nothing illegal."[150] Some corroboration of the significance of this kind of conflict of authorities in triggering-off peasant movements comes from Satinath Bhaduri's *Dhorai Charitmanas*: Dhorai tells the sharecroppers of Biskandha that the time for action has come, since the "babusaheb" has lost the support of the officials as his son has joined the Congress.[151] There may well be insights worth exploring here for historians of the Kisan Sabha movement which acquired such strength in Bihar immediately after the Civil Disobedience years.

Glimpses of the myth of an alternative power centre displacing the existing structure can be seen on a few occasions even in the Swadeshi period, in the appeal of Muslim peasant rioters to the alleged authority of Salimulla, the nawab of Dacca. A Muslim communal leaflet, *Nawab Sahaber Subichar*, portrays the nawab as taking over, in fact conquering, large parts of Bengal from the British.[152] A fantastic and ludicrous vision, for Salimulla in reality was a notorious sycophant of the British, and yet the emphasis on conquest is surely an interesting pointer to certain subterranean structures of popular mentality. Such

---

[149] Telegram from Commissioner of Dacca Division, Jamalpur, 24 September 1907; letter of District Magistrate, Mymensingh to Commissioner, Dacca Division, 10 October 1907, Government of Eastern Bengal and Assam, Poll (Conf.) F.N. 513(1–22)/1907, WBSA.

[150] See GOB, Poll (Conf.) F.N 181/1923.

[151] "Why should we be afraid any longer? The *daroga*, *hakim*, and *chaukidar* are all against the *babusaheb* now." *Satinath Granthabali*, II, p. 173. My translation.

[152] The nawab, the pamphlet claimed, has conquered Assam, Sylhet, Chittagong – and, Allah permitting, he might conquer the whole world some day. For details, see Sarkar, *Swadeshi Movement*, pp. 456–7.

dimensions rose to the surface in an incomparably more massive and direct manner during Non-Cooperation–Khilafat with its dominant myth of the coming of Gandhi Raj.

A crucial feature of the concept of breakdown of authority in its more extreme form is its predominantly magico-religious character, natural and indeed inevitable in a peasant society which has not undergone the process of "disenchantment of the world" partially brought about in the West in the post-Reformation era. Religion in such societies, as Marx emphasised in a magnificent passage of which only the last sentence is commonly remembered, "is the general theory of that world, its encyclopaedic compendium, its logic in a popular form, its spiritualistic *Point d'honneur*, its enthusiasm, its moral sanction, its solemn complement, its universal source of consolation and justification." "The *protest* against real distress" consequently also takes on the alienated form of religion.[153] In a world largely untouched by secular creeds of progress, total breakdown involves a change of such magnitude that it can usually be conceived only in supernatural terms. I feel that the religious dimension is vital for an understanding of at least four crucial features of popular movements in the early Gandhian era: the nature and significance of rumour, the ethical norms and ritual obligations imposed by the emerging cult of Gandhi, the mood of renunciation and sacrifice evoked by the Mahatma, and the persistence of faith in him despite repeated instances of hopes deferred or frustrated.

Religion, particularly at its more popular levels, may promise the magical removal of specific ills; occasionally at moments of high excitement it can also hold out the apocalyptic vision of an immediate total transformation. Thus Max Weber distinguished between "the massive and archaic growth of magic" engulfing "the masses ... everywhere", and the occasional "prophetically announced religion of redemption".[154] Brian Wilson in his recent comparative

---

[153] Karl Marx, *Contribution to the Critique of Hegel's Philosophy of Law*, Introduction (1844), in Marx and Engels, *Collected Works*, vol. III (Moscow, 1973), p. 175.

[154] Max Weber, *Social Psychology of the World Religions*, in H.H. Gerth and C. Wright Mills, eds, *From Max Weber: Essays in Sociology* (London, 1967), pp. 274, 277.

study of primitive and Third World religious protest movements has attempted to conceptualise this distinction through the categories of "thaumaturgical" and "millennial".[155] To him these are variants of what he calls, not very happily perhaps, "deviant" religious forms as distinct from religious orthodoxies which try to absorb both removal of specific ills and hope of salvation into a basic sanctification of the status quo. Catholic orthodoxy for example has always sought to maintain a priestly monopoly over magic,[156] while relegating the hope of redemption to the life after death or a safely distant Second Coming. "Deviant" movements, however, naturally take over many forms and symbols from the orthodoxy prevalent in the concerned area, and sects in their "introversionist" phase, as Peter Worsley shows in detail for Melanesian cargo cults,[157] can once again emphasise a purely internal or distant salvation and so contribute to passivity.

Wilson's categories perhaps assume an over-sharp dichotomy between magic and religion, common in the days of Frazer or Max Weber but rather discredited now among social anthropologists.[158] The distinctions between healing of specific ills, hope of immediate apocalypse, and waiting for a distant salvation do seem to have some relevance, however, for understanding certain Indian popular movements. Birsa Munda for example began as a faith-healer; the movement he led briefly touched a flashpoint of rebellion against all authorities felt to be alien to the Mundas and then transformed itself into a quietist sect which still survives around Ranchi.[159] The thaumaturgical/millennial distinction appears helpful also for an analysis of early rumours about Gandhi in Bengal and possibly elsewhere.

[155] Brian Wilson, *Magic and the Millennium: A Sociological Study of Religious Movements of Protest among Tribal and Third World Peoples* (London, 1973), chapters 1, 2, and *passim*.
[156] Keith Thomas, *Religion and the Decline of Magic* (1971; rpntd London, 1980), chapter 2 and *passim*.
[157] Peter Worsley, *The Trumpet Shall Sound: A Study of Cargo Cults in Melanesia* (2nd edn, London, 1970), *passim*.
[158] For an effective critique, see Mary Douglas, *Purity and Danger* (London, 1966).
[159] K. Suresh Singh, *Dust-Storm and Hanging Mist* (Calcutta, 1966).

The Bengal material I have seen so far does not have the earthiness and local colour of Shahid Amin's recent collection of rumours from a Gorakhpur journal.[160] They come from sources more distant from the ground: the Calcutta-based *Mussalman* and *Amrita Bazar Patrika* translated extracts from other newspapers in the official *Report on the Native Press* and, above all, the diary and correspondence of Lord Ronaldshay, who in March 1921 was sufficiently impressed by "the making of miracles . . . going on here before one's eyes" to comment that "precisely such things as are recorded in the New Testament are being told of Gandhi here."[161] Yet certain tentative but interesting points do seem to emerge from this limited data.

The rumours seem to fall into three main categories. The first and by far the biggest group in my collection presents Gandhi as an avatar who breaks with impunity the normal laws of nature, is indestructible, and bestows miraculous gifts to believers which relieve individual ills – performing what Brian Wilson would call a thaumaturgical role. Gandhi "has been shot by the British but has appeared again and again . . . has been thrown into a prison but . . . the locks fall from the doors and he walks out."[162] From Champaran a rumour was reported in a Calcutta Hindi newspaper that sepoys fired a volley at Gandhi "but the bullets instead of piercing his body, deflected from it".[163] Among Calcutta mill-workers the story was current that British soldiers threw a bomb at Gandhi but "it melted like snow as soon as it touched his person".[164] The miracle-worker is able not only to preserve himself from every danger but (along occasionally with close associates like Muhammed Ali) also gives miraculous gifts to his devotees. Gandhi and Muhammed Ali "possess heavenly bread which when hung up by a pious maulvi in a Mosque is found to have doubled itself on the following Friday and also to have produced holy water which is a panacea for all disease."[165] But Gandhi also

---

[160] I am grateful to Shahid Amin for letting me read a draft version of his paper on the background to Chauri Chaura.
[161] Bengal Diary, entry for 17 March 1921, Zetland Collection.
[162] Bengal Diary, 17 March 1921.
[163] Hindustan, 9 July 1921, RNP(B) for week ending 16 July 1921, WBSA.
[164] Ronaldshay to George V, 1 June 1921, Zetland Collection.
[165] Bengal Diary, 11 July 1921.

The Conditions and Nature of Subaltern Militancy 463

"possesses the power of turning people to stone by breathing on them"[166] – indication that the new deity can also punish those who do not accept him. The theme of punishment is very noticeable in Amin's collection. I would expect further research to unearth much more data on this in Bengal too, for the reward/punishment syndrome is always very common in stories about the rise of new deities. One might recall the medieval Bengali myth of Mansa the serpent-goddess who establishes herself through inflicting a series of disasters on Chand-Saudagar, while her devotees prosper.

Rumours of this first type present Gandhi alone, or at most a colleague like Mohammed Ali who is also a national figure, as miracle-workers. At a second level, however, thaumaturgical power may pass on to the followers or minor local leaders too. Someswarprasad Chaudhuri has recorded how at the height of the movement against the Midnapur Zamindari Company peasants started acknowledging this young ex-medical student as their "*guru*, whose *mantra* is *dharma ghat* [strike]". The accidental death of Panja Pramanik, a powerful village headman who had opposed the movement, led to Someswar's orders being considered to be the commands of "Khoda or Iswar".[167] And by February 1922 as we have seen Santals of Madarihat in Jalpaiguri had come to believe that they were immune from bullets "as they were wearing Gandhi Maharaj's caps".[168] A recurrent feature in tribal and peasant uprisings both in India and in other parts of the world has been the belief that bullets turn into water.[169] One notices

---

[166] Ronaldshay to George V, 1 June 1921, ibid.
[167] Someswarprasad Chaudhuri, *Nilkar Bidroha*, pp. 74, 111.
[168] *Mussalman*, 10 March 1922.
[169] A few scattered examples out of many: the movement led by Korra Mallaya in the Vizagapatnam Agency in 1900 promised "that he would arm his followers with bamboos, which should be turned by magic into guns, and would change the weapons of the authorities into water." E. Thurston and K. Rangachari, *Castes and Tribes of South India*, vol. III (Madras, 1909), pp. 350–3. In the revolt headed by Enoch Mgijima in South Africa in 1920 the expectation was that "Jehovah would protect them and give them victory, turning the bullets of the soldiers to water." In the much bigger Maji Maji rebellion in German Tanganyika in 1905–6 the rebels used a "protective water" which they believed "changed bullets into water". Brian Wilson, op. cit., pp. 62, 244.

once again the characteristic pattern of inversion: red-hot bullets or bombs turn into innocuous water or snow, for the world itself is being turned upside down. And the Gandhi cap has become the equivalent of the amulets or the sign of the cross of more conventional religions, or of the protective water of the Maji-Maji rebels.[170]

In rumours of the third, so to say highest, type, it is this theme of sudden miraculous *total* transformation or reversal, as distinct from supernatural removal of specific personal ills, which predominates, and the transition from thaumaturgical to millennial is accomplished. In May 1919 Ronaldshay was informed about an Islamic prophecy that loss of Constantinople to the infidel would be followed by the coming of the Mahdi to restore Islam.[171] Throughout 1921 Gandhi's promise of Swaraj within a year led to dates being predicted repeatedly when a total transformation would come about: 25 March at Rajshahi, leading to the jailbreak,[172] 26 July among Darjeeling tea labourers,[173] 24 December among millhands in and around Calcutta.[174] And the content of this swaraj as we have seen went on broadening, embracing by early 1922 visions at times of a total repudiation of taxes, rents, and interest payments.

A cult usually imposes ethical and ritual obligations on its devotees, and the existence of a strong religious dimension in many of the popular movements we have been considering is indicated also by the fact that the actions undertaken often went beyond the removal of the specific concrete grievances which underlay them in a purely material sense. Thus agrarian tensions were certainly very important in the Mymensingh riots of 1906–7 but the objectives included the "rescue" of Muslim prostitutes, the withdrawal of menial services

---

[170] One might be permitted a brief speculative aside on the significance of the Gandhi cap as a possible counter-symbol to the sahib's hat: Western attire has become much more widespread in India after Independence, but the hat – better suited to a hot climate than suits or ties – seems to have disappeared completely.

[171] Bengal Diary, 17 May 1919, Zetland Collection.

[172] *Mussalman*, 20 May 1921.

[173] Ronaldshay to Montagu, 2 August 1921, Zetland Collection.

[174] *Amrita Bazar Patrika*, 23 December 1921.

The Conditions and Nature of Subaltern Militancy 465

to Hindus, and at places a general destruction of images. As a contemporary official report pointed out about the Iswarganj riots of 1906, "the object of the mob was not plunder, but what, according to the maulvis, religion demanded of them".[175] A strong note of internal moral purification was very prominent in Gandhian movements. The Tatmas of *Dhorai Charitmanas*, converted to the new cult by the miracle of "Gandhi-Bawa's" face appearing in a pumpkin, decide to give up meat, fish, and tobacco, wash every day, and stop working on Sundays in the houses of the babus – and only the last decision had any possible "economic" connotations.[176] Gandhi's anti-liquor campaign did hit British revenues, but there can be little doubt that much of its appeal lay in its purificatory "sanskritising" role. An early report of Non-Cooperation meetings in Rajshahi, for instance, describes how "Mehtars, Doms and Chamars... promised in a body to give up drinking", after which the local Congress leader Provash Lahiri publicly embraced a sweeper.[177] Similarly the symbolic value of things like khaddar and charkha far outstripped the rather limited material gains villagers could be expected to derive immediately from a revival of archaic crafts. The *Dhorai Charitmanas* interestingly enough refers to a song which identifies the charkha with the Sudarshan-chakra with which Krishna destroyed enemies in the Mahabharata war.[178]

Rumours and ritual obligations alike invariably centred around the image of Gandhi, and the most varied of popular actions were all undertaken in his name. The historical problem then is really twofold: the extraordinarily open nature of the "reception" of the Gandhian message, the way in which it became what in Roland Barthes' terminology might be called a text without an author,[179] and the fact that at the same time a mythical "authorship" is being constantly

---

[175] Deputy Magistrate Debendraprasad Roy to District Magistrate, Mymensingh, 25 May 1906, GOI Home Public A, July 1906, no. 124. See Sarkar, *Swadeshi Movement*, pp. 445–6, 458–9.
[176] *Satinath Granthabali*, vol. II, pp. 28–34.
[177] *Mussalman*, 18 March 1921.
[178] *Satinath Granthabali*, vol. II, p. 207.
[179] Roland Barthes, "The Death of the Author", in *Image-Music-Text* (Glasgow, 1982).

imputed to the Mahatma. To take an example from another province, an Allahabad police report in early 1921 asserts that Gandhi was being revered by villagers mainly because he was supposed to have stopped *bedakhli* (eviction) in neighbouring Pratapgarh.[180] The peasants' own achievements under their local leader Baba Ramchandra were thus being attributed by them to Gandhi: an example perhaps of the peasants' need for representation through a master, their dependence on a saviour from above which Marx talked about in his *Eighteenth Brumaire*.

As for the choice of Gandhi (and at a more local level of a large number of political sadhus like Ramchandra, Vidyananda in Darbhanga, Biswananda and Darshanananda among Bengal and Bihar workers, etc.), the religious dimension ("code" might be a better term) can once again provide part of an explanation. It is not sufficient here to talk about Gandhi's "use" of religion in the abstract, or merely to emphasise his effective combination of "modern", "traditional", and "saintly" political idioms.[181] Extremist leaders had also "used" religion and sought to give to patriotism the colours of a Hindu revival. Yet no equivalent popular cult developed around Bipinchandra Pal or even Tilak, and Aurobindo's post-1909 mysticism led his devotees away from active politics. Perhaps the comparative method can again provide a hint towards an answer. The Swadeshi (and terrorist) identification of patriotism with religion emphasised the centrality of *puja*: Durga or Kali as the Motherland, a symbolism going back to Bankimchandra.[182] Gandhi evoked rather the mood of renunciation, austerity, and sacrifice: the giving up of fashionable garments and the prospect of comfortable jobs through official education, going to jail, unflinchingly facing lathis and bullets without retaliation, the ritual

---

[180] GOI Home Political Deposit, February 1921, no. 13, NAI. The report has been reprinted in Gyanendra Pandey, "Peasant Revolt and Indian Nationalism: The Peasant Movement in Awadh, 1919–22", appendix, in R. Guha, ed., *Subaltern Studies I*.

[181] W.H. Morris Jones, *India's Political Idioms*, in C.H. Philips, ed., *Politics and Society in India* (London, 1963).

[182] Lawrence Babb, *Divine Hierarchy: Popular Hinduism in Central India* (Columbia, 1975), chapter 2 and *passim*.

of fasts so deeply ingrained in Hindu tradition. One might tentatively suggest that while the concept and imagery of puja is integrally bound up with social and divine hierarchy, the path of *sannyasa* is open to all and might even represent a moment of controlled rebellion.[183] Dumont's reference to the contrast between the figures of the emaciated sadhu and the pot-bellied Brahman in the north gate of Sanchi emphasises the greater and wider respect that *sannyasis* have on the whole evoked as compared to priests.[184] Muslims would not come near a puja, the presence of lower castes would pollute worship in temples or upper-caste households, but there have been innumerable holy men, local sadhus or pirs, devotion to whom has cut across barriers of caste and creed. Gandhi's link with the Muslim masses did remain tenuous, for the persistent use of Hindu imagery could not but be an irritant. But that problem still lay in the future in 1921, thanks to the close alliance of Non-Cooperation with a Khilafat movement which emphasised hostility towards the British as the prime religious duty of the moment.

As for the virtue of sacrifice in the context of Indian tradition, it is significant that the wealthy epicurean barrister Chittaranjan Das won enormous popularity and the title of Deshbandhu precisely by two such actions: giving up practice in January 1921 and going to jail along with women of his household towards the end of that year. The first evoked a storm of student withdrawal from colleges and schools; the second revived enormously the flagging enthusiasm for the courting of arrest.

It would be dangerous to press this point too far, for the path of renunciation in Gandhi's case obviously led not to an escape from the world but towards efforts at remodelling it. The religious dimension has to be placed alongside other aspects of the total Gandhian "message". In the context of 1921–2, however, I would still argue that

---

[183] "With his negation of the world and his asceticism, he [the *sannyasi*] represents that very reversal of values which we expected to find in festivals ... he is the safety-valve for the Brahmanic order." Louis Dumont, "World Renunciation in Indian Religions", in idem, *Religion/Politics and History in India* (Paris/The Hague, 1970), p. 51.

[184] Ibid., p. 44.

the secret lay not so much in Gandhi's specific political programmes or techniques, organisational abilities, or the undoubted peasant appeal of his anti-industrial populism (relatively little known before the spread of constructive-work centres in the countryside), but in the combination of his reputation for saintliness with two rather different elements. Gandhi was a holy man with an already acquired reputation for effectively doing something about specific "wrongs" (South African pass laws, Champaran indigo exploitation, Kheda revenue burdens), who was now promising a total change which enthralled by its very vagueness: "swaraj" within a year. If an analogy may be permitted from a very different milieu, the combination here of the particular (including mythical particulars like stopping *bedakhli* at Pratapgarh) with the general recalls Barthes' analysis of the subconscious codes underlying the efficacy of modern advertising.[185]

Part of the strength of a religious faith is derived from the kind of built-in explanation it tends to contain about failure. If the devotee does not obtain the specific benefits he has been praying for, the fault lies not in the deity but in himself. He has not observed the rites properly, or in the true spirit required of him. A millennial movement, once the flashpoint of maximum hope in immediate deliverance has come and gone, can still survive therefore, though in a transformed, "introversionist" manner, emphasising internal salvation through self-purification. Returning to the Gandhian context the religious dimension can perhaps help us to understand why despite so many "betrayals" Gandhi could retain so much more authority among the peasant masses than was ever enjoyed by his radical Left critics. Gandhi himself made ample and very effective use of this aspect of religious faith, fixing the responsibility for the retreats he so often ordered on the inadequacies of himself and of his followers with respect to issues like non-violence or untouchability. The explanation proved all the more effective because to a considerable extent Gandhi believed in it himself. This is indicated by his repeated expiatory fasts, and above all perhaps by that curious episode in Noakhali when the Mahatma risked a break with close followers and a public

---

[185] Jonathan Culler, *Barthes* (Glasgow, 1983), pp. 75–6.

scandal by undertaking some very controversial experiments in sexual abstinence in order to develop in himself the moral power to fight back communalism and Partition.[186] Persistence of faith in a new cult despite the fading away of millennial hopes – because devotees blame themselves for the failure – corresponds to the survival of orthodox religious faith even though rituals, pilgrimages, bathing in the Ganges, etc. seldom obtain for the faithful the hoped-for boons. Popular explosions of the type we have been discussing consequently tend to have a sporadic and intermittent character, sudden brief explosions alternating with longer periods of relative passivity without building up into continuous and really effective movements.

I would like to emphasise in conclusion that the structure of correlations and oppositions I have tried to set out is a very provisional one, not a definite statement but rather a starting point for further research directed towards greater concreteness and the study of variations and change. I emphasise this precisely because "structuralist" analysis does tend at times to overemphasise unchanging or "synchronic" elements, leading to the absurdities so effectively pilloried by E.P. Thompson in his *Poverty of Theory*.

Five types of variations, I feel, would be particularly relevant for developing and concretising the framework sketched out here. First, as already emphasised in the first section, subordination and revolt constitute only the extreme poles in a complex continuum of varying attitudes. "Breakdown" in my model is related to popular explosions, as distinct from various forms of protest which may not be uncommon even in normal or "stable" times. Isolation of specific elements underlying the extremes, however, may be of help precisely in analysing this continuum, in exploring for example the range of religious attitudes, symbols, myths, and norms lying between the opposite poles. What is needed above all is an ideal of totality: the study of popular movement in India has to break out of the confines

---

[186] "Ever since my coming to Noakhali, I have been asking myself the question, 'What is it that is choking the action of my Ahimsa? . . . May it not be because I have temporised in the manner of Brahmacharya?", Gandhi, Conversation with Thakkar Bapa, 25 February 1947, in Pyarelal, *Mahatma Gandhi: The Last Phase*, vol. 1 (Ahmedabad, 1956), p. 586

of the narrowly economic and narrowly political alike, and develop into social history in the broadest sense of that much-abused term.

In the second place, regional differences: my data here has been entirely from Bengal, but a study of popular movements in other provinces in the same period would no doubt bring out interesting and significant variations, particularly in the specific use of religious symbols and myths and their interactions in a complex pattern of continuity/inversion with the established structures of "orthodox" popular religion. Thus Crooke has some valuable pages on the role of hero cults in the popular religion and folklore of northern India,[187] and it may be interesting to consider the ways in which the cult of the Mahatma continued and/or deviated from the established patterns.

The third, and to my mind very important, variation would be the modifications in the structure of beliefs, emotions, and actions related to the differences among the varied social groups we have been lumping together under the omnibus categories of "subaltern" and "popular". I confess I find it difficult to go all the way with Partha Chatterjee when he talks about a specific "peasant-communal mode of politics",[188] both distinct and presumably more or less homogeneous. Attempts at dividing up the peasantry into distinct strata are admittedly hazardous and quite often very mechanical. Yet the differences remain vital, and particularly, as I have tried to argue elsewhere, the gap in Indian conditions between landholding peasants – usually of intermediate castes – and low caste, untouchable, or tribal agricultural labourers often debarred by religious and social tradition from holding land even in land-surplus situations.[189] One might hazard a tentative hypothesis for instance that rumours of a conflict of authorities and movements with specific, limited goals would tend to be more typical among landholding peasants. Examples

---

[187] W. Crooke and R.E. Enthoven, *Religion and Folklore of Northern India* (London, 1925), chapters 5–6.

[188] Partha Chatterjee, "Agrarian Relations and Communalism in Bengal, 1926–35".

[189] Sumit Sarkar, *Popular Movements and Middle-Class Leadership in Late Colonial India: Perspectives and Problem of a "History from Below"*, Deuskar Lecture, Centre for Studies in Social Sciences, Calcutta, 1983.

from an earlier period would include the Pabna and Deccan "riots" of the 1870s, in both of which rumours were current that the ultimate superiors, the queen or British authorities, were on the side of the peasants against zamindars and moneylenders, while the demands were quite specific and limited. Tribal movements in contrast were both more far-ranging, at times millennial in their aims, and often inspired by rumours that British rule itself was coming to an end. It may be important to explore whether such distinctions are also valid within Gandhian popular movements.

The relative role of material pressures and rumours of breakdown appears to be another possible social variable. *Haat*-looting, many forms of rural crime, and labour strikes seem to have a closer correlation with economic indicators like price variations than peasant movements against their social or political superiors.[190] Crowds gather anyway on market days, industrial labour is concentrated at the place of work, but the peasants in their scattered fields and villages may be more in need of the stimulus of a rumoured breakdown before they go in for large-scale action on issues like rent.

The limited data presently at my disposal also hint at some differences in the way apparently identical symbols and myths were used by peasants and industrial workers. Take for example the symbolism of the Gandhi cap. The Santals of Madarihat were moved by a belief in the invincibility it was supposed to give to its wearers into what was after all a totally suicidal confrontation with the police. Industrial workers in contrast seem to have used the symbol as well as rumours of imminent Gandhi Raj in a more hard-headed way, sometimes to further what amounted to trade-union unity in a fairly effective pursuit of specific objectives – as when Calcutta jute workers wanted an end to the practice of holding back wages on the ground that Swaraj was coming on 24 December 1921.

This brings us to the question of variations over time, which structuralist analysis at times tends to neglect or treat in a cyclical manner.

[190] David Arnold's study of Madras police records brings out marked correlations between food riots and dacoity and years of seasons of scarcity. "Dacoity and Rural Crime in Madras, 1860–1940", *Journal of Peasant Studies*, January 1979.

Certainly any assumption of a unilinear development of popular consciousness in a "progressive" direction has to be abandoned. In labour history oscillation between class struggle and communal strife remains all too evident, while the united peasant actions of the Non-Cooperation–Khilafat period gave way by the mid 1920s to agrarian-communal riots very reminiscent of 1906–7. Yet certain shifts can be seen, if we take a long enough timespan, and the greatness of Satinath Bhaduri's novel lies precisely in its comprehension of the complex development of popular consciousness in and through interruptions and retrogressions. The national movement had very far from a unilinear development, and yet the legitimacy of foreign rule was eroded over time. To take another example, the importance of swamis in leading peasant and labour movements seems to have been an essentially time-bound phenomenon. Again, the importance of rumours of breakdown as preconditions for popular militancy is probably not a universal phenomenon, but related to the stability attained by British rule in the post-Mutiny phase.

Finally, the spread of Gandhian constructive-work cadres over the countryside, followed a little later by the penetration of Left-wing ideas and organisations, raises the problem of the extent to which the structure of popular mentality we have been analysing was modified by the entry of more "modern" ideological–organisational patterns. The crucial differences once again would lie in the conception of breakdown. For a militant of a modern party, breakdown (or in less radical terms some kind of significant overall change) would be not the starting point or presupposition for action but rather the objective aimed at, and sustained political work would attain priority over intermittent unorganised explosions interspersed with periods of subordination. One would also expect the religious dimensions to decline over time, along with the related dependence on outsider leaders conceived as deified masters rather than democratic representatives. Whether or to what extent such changes have actually taken place in India is worth investigating.[191] We would certainly expect to find complex interactions between such theoretically

---

[191] Dipesh Chakrabarty has argued the case for continuity even within the Communist-led trade union movements: see his "Trade Unions in a

distinct structures, most obvious in developed Gandhism with its combination of peasant-populist religious idiom with strong urban bourgeois links and hard-headed organisational discipline mastering and channelising autonomous outbursts. In the historiography of Gandhian nationalism as well as occasionally in studies of Left movements the focus has recently been on a kind of spontaneity–consciousness debate, with leaders presented either as heroes or betrayers. A more systematic analysis of variations in structures of collective mentality might go some way towards enriching the subject and broadening its perspectives.

Hierarchical Culture: The Jute Workers of Calcutta, 1920–50", in R.Guha, ed., *Subaltern Studies III* (Delhi, 1984).

11

Primitive Rebellion and Modern Nationalism

Forest Satyagraha in the Non-Cooperation and Civil Disobedience Movements

"FOREST SATYAGRAHA" – THE REASSERTION by poor peasants and tribals of traditional customary rights over forests "reserved" by the colonial state – represents an almost forgotten but fascinating aspect of the Gandhian era. While conventional nationalist historiography has tended to concern itself mainly with the ideals and activities of great leaders, the much-advertised recent shift in the work of the "Cambridge School" from nation and province to "locality" retains a basically elitist stance with its incessant search for relatively privileged groups whose "ambitions" are assumed to have "created" political movements.[1] Forest movements, involving in the main the lowest strata of rural society, quite naturally seldom get more than passing reference in such accounts.[2]

---

[1] D.A. Washbrook clearly states this basic assumption: "The leaders of the movement, that is to say the people who created it, require a careful analysis, for in their ambitions must lie its causes." *The Emergence of Provincial Politics: Madras Presidency 1870–1920* (Cambridge, 1976), p. 279.

[2] A partial exception is C.J. Baker's account of the violation of forest laws in Rayachoti *taluk* of Cuddapah and Palnad *taluk* of Guntur in 1921–2: "Non-Cooperation in South India", in C.J. Baker and D.A. Washbrook, *South India: Political Institutions and Political Change 1880–1940* (Macmillan, 1975), pp. 99–103. Baker however does his best to relate this movement to the vested

I have tried here to make a preliminary study of forest conflicts connected with nationalism during the decade 1921–31 on the basis of fairly obvious and easily available sources.³ I feel that apart from its intrinsic interest, the subject has some relevance to the current debate among students of Indian nationalism about the significance and the degree of autonomy of peasant and lower-class movements in Gandhian upsurges.⁴ At a more general level, a further theme suggests itself. A millenarian note was not uncommon in the reassertion of lost forest rights, and studies of forest satyagraha might hopefully contribute a little some day to the worldwide discussion among anthropologists and historians concerning the relations between "primitive rebels" and modern social movements.⁵

Conflicts over forest claims have been extremely common in feudal or early-capitalist rural societies in many parts of the world. If royal and aristocratic monopolies over hunting rights had been a major peasant grievance in the Europe of the ancient regime, the development of bourgeois conceptions of property soon posed an even

---

interests of prosperous Reddi cattle breeders and leaves it out altogether in his later detailed study, *The Politics of South India, 1920–1937* (Cambridge, 1976). Even more striking is his total silence about the "Rampa" rebellion of 1922–4, far more militant and obviously lower class.

³ The Home Political records of the Government of India, M. Venkatarangaiya's invaluable selection of Madras Government Records (*Freedom Struggle in Andhra Pradesh*, vol. III, Hyderabad, 1965), the AICC files, district gazetteers, and some anthropological literature.

⁴ Gyanendra Pandey has emphasised the autonomous role of "peasant nationalism" in his study of Civil Disobedience in the United Provinces (in press). I am grateful to him for permitting me to read his manuscript. I have also benefited greatly from my discussions on this point with Ranajit Guha (Sussex University).

⁵ E.J. Hobsbawm, *Primitive Rebels* (Manchester, 1959, 1974) and *Bandits* (London, 1969). See also Norman Cohn's *The Pursuit of the Millennium* (New York, 1961) and P. Worsley's fascinating study of Melanesian Cargo Cults: *The Trumpet Shall Sound* (London: Paladin, 1970). Virtually the only Indian contribution so far to the literature on millenarianism is Stephen Fuchs' *Rebellious Prophets: A Study of Messianic Movements in Indian Religions* (Bombay: Asia, 1965).

greater threat to the precious customary rights of poorer village folk to the timber, grazing, and other facilities of forest lands. It is interesting to recall that an article condemning legislation against theft of wood in the Rhinelands constituted one of the earliest publications of the young Marx.[6] Forest conflicts in Hanoverian England have been illuminated by E.P. Thompson's recent study.[7] Eric Hobsbawm has described the tragic impact of post-unification Italian forest laws on marginal small proprietors and the peasant millenarianism it helped to produce in Tuscany,[8] and Eugene Weber's *Peasants into Frenchmen* contains abundant information about the gradual erosion of peasant communal rights over woodlands in nineteenth-century France.

Forest rights have been particularly important in our country, with its peculiar coexistence of food-gathering, shifting cultivation ("*podu*" or "*jhum*"), and settled agriculture.[9] In colonial India, pressures on forest lands took the form of usurious exploitation by traders and money-lenders from more developed areas rather than the growth of capitalist property relations, and led to occasional tribal explosions, among which the great Santal rebellion of 1855 against Bengali "*dikus*" and their white protectors is the best known. From the last quarter of the nineteenth century, a further patent source of tension emerged as the colonial state tightened its control over forest zones for revenue purposes, banning or restricting shifting cultivation in "reserved" forests and trying to monopolise forest wealth. The correspondence of the Bombay governor with Lord Lansdowne in February 1890 reveals a vivid picture of fires underground. "The

---

[6] "Debates on the Law on Thefts of Wood", *Rheinische Zeitung*, October–November 1842.

[7] E.P. Thompson, *Whigs and Hunters* (London, 1975).

[8] E.J. Hobsbawm, *Primitive Rebels*, op. cit., p. 67.

[9] D.D. Kosambi was probably the first to draw attention to this peculiar feature. "People could and did survive in the food-gathering stage when their immediate neighbours had become food-producers centuries earlier." He attributed this to the "ease and survival of food-gathering in monsoon forests." See idem, *The Culture and Civilization of Ancient India in Historical Outline* (London, 1965), p. 34.

Forest policy, the Abkari policy, the Salt duty, the screwing-up of land revenue by revision settlements, all make us odious."[10] "We know pretty well what the educated natives want, but what the feelings are of the uneducated, I admit I don't know. That in these parts the Forest Department is hated is a fact and I have always considered an abrupt cessation of privileges (which in many cases are *rights*) a most dangerous policy . . ." The governor described peasants as complaining: "You make us pay more land revenue – and at the same time you prevent us from getting the branches we want for our ash-manure, and the grass we want for our cows . . ."[11] The continuity of popular grievances is striking, though seldom noted in conventional historiography: salt, land revenue, excise, and forests were precisely the issues around which Gandhi was to forge a countrywide movement a whole generation later.

Data on such conflicts happens to be particularly abundant for the hill areas of present-day Andhra Pradesh. The Chenchus of the Nallamalai hills (Cuddapah and Nellore districts) were described in 1909 as "constantly in debt to the Komatis . . . [and] practically their slaves as regards the supply of timber and other forest produce." From 1898 onwards the Forest Department was trying to reduce traditional Chenchu forest rights, restricting the amount of timber permitted for domestic purposes, reducing the area set apart for grazing, etc. – an effort inhibited, however, by the fact that a policy of pure repression might mean "the total destruction by fire of the Nallamalai forests".[12] Administration was further tightened after the 1913 Forest Committee Report, and this coincided with an extension of links with the coastal areas, cattle owned by prosperous Raddis being sent to graze in the upland forests under "Lambadi" graziers. A sharp rise in the number of forest offences was reported in 1920–1,

---

[10] Bombay Governor Reay to Lansdowne, 15 February 1890. Quoted from the Lansdowne Papers in B.L. Grover, *A Documentary Study of British Policy Towards Indian Nationalism* (Delhi, 1967), pp. 140–1.

[11] Reay to Lansdowne, 20 February 1890, ibid., p. 142.

[12] E. Thurston and K. Rangachari, *Castes and Tribes of Southern India* (Madras, 1909), vol. II, pp. 29–35.

and efforts were made to expel Chenchus aiding Lambadis in the Cuddapah forests. It is hardly surprising, therefore, that Rayachoti *taluk* of Cuddapah became a storm-centre of forest satyagraha under Non-Cooperation auspices in 1921–2.[13]

Even more revealing perhaps were the developments in the hill regions lying to the north and north-east of the Godavari, constituting under the British the Godavari and Vizagapatam Agency Tracts inhabited mainly by the Koyas, the Konda Doras, and the Kondhs. Thurston in 1909 found the Koyas "terribly victimised by traders and money-lenders from the low country". Shifting or *podu* cultivation was common in this entire area, not really because the tribals were ignorant or lazy as hasty administrators sometimes believed, but because most of them had "no ploughs or agricultural cattle".[14] At the heart of this region lay Chodavaram, the "Rampa" country (so-called by the British after the family name of its traditional chief or *mansabdar*), the centre of almost endemic rebellion for more than a hundred years. After this *mansabdar* had made a raid into the plains in 1813, the British came to an arrangement with him, allowing him to go on collecting rent from his subordinate hill chiefs (called *muttadars*). Conflicts soon developed between the *mansabdar* and the tribal villages led by their *muttadars* for the former had started "deriving a considerable revenue from taxes on fuel and grazing and other unauthorized cesses" while enjoying the protection of the British.[15] There were revolts in 1840, 1845, 1858, 1861, and 1862, culminating in a major rising in March 1879 to which police exactions, indebtedness of tribals to low country traders, and new Abkari regulations farming out toddy revenue to outsiders and restricting domestic drawing of toddy also contributed greatly. This became a really major affair, embracing 5000 square miles by July 1879 and spreading to the Golkonda hills in Vizagapatam to the north-east and Rekapelle in Bhadrachalam district to the west (where restrictions on *podu* cultivation were being

---

[13] The above account is based on Baker, "Non-Cooperation in South India", op. cit., pp. 100–3.

[14] Thurston and Rangachari, op. cit., vol. IV, p. 47; idem, vol. III, p. 363.

[15] F.R. Hemingway, *Godavari District Gazetteer*, vol. I (Madras, 1907), p. 272.

Primitive Rebellion and Modern Nationalism 479

imposed).[16] It could be suppressed only in November 1880 with the use of six regiments of Madras infantry and two companies of sappers and miners, and the "harassing guerrilla warfare" was effective enough to compel the removal of the *mansabdar* and a direct settlement with the *muttadar*. Unrest continued, however, with the tightening of forest rules providing an additional major source of discontent, now directly anti-British: the reserved forests of Bhadrachalam were extended from 68 sq. miles in 1874 to 942 sq. miles by 1901, forest revenues going up in the same period from Rs 21,000 to Rs 2 lakhs.[17] Risings were reported again in 1900 and 1916. That of 1900 in Vizagapatam Agency seems particularly interesting. It was led by a Kanda Dora named Korra Mallaya who

> pretended that he was inspired – gathered round him a camp of 4–5000 people from various parts of the agency – gave out that he was a reincarnation of one of the five Pandava brothers; that his infant son was the boy Krishna: that he would drive out the English and rule the country himself; and that to effect this, he would arm his followers with bamboos, which should be turned by magic into guns, and could change the weapons of the authorities into water.[18]

All the classic elements of millenarian primitive rebellion are clearly evident in this brief but strangely moving account.

In this explosive atmosphere came the spark of Non-Cooperation, with its rumour (necessarily vague and distorted but all the more potent) of the coming of an apocalyptic "Gandhi Raj". When Gandhi came to Cuddapah in September 1921, he was greeted by "enormous crowds" of villagers who believed "that he would get their taxes reduced and the Forest Regulations abolished – many returned home

---

[16] Ibid., pp. 264–74.

[17] Ibid., pp. 92–101. The "Rampa" area was not "reserved" for some time "for political reasons" (ibid., p. 93), but restrictions on *podu* were being enforced there, too, by the second decade of the twentieth century: T.G. Rutherford's report, 22 August 1924, in Venkatarangaiya, op. cit., document no. 101).

[18] Thurston and Rangachari, op. cit., vol. III, p. 353. The Koyas and Kanda Doras, it may be added, have a legend that they are the offspring of Bhima and a forest woman. Ibid., vol. IV, p. 56.

greatly disappointed."[19] Forest satyagraha as it developed in Rayachoti and Palnad (a forest *taluk* of Guntur district where the tightening of forest laws had coincided with a bad harvest in 1921) was marked by two distinct strands. Congress leaders like Konda Venkatappayya at the Palnad *taluk* Political Conference (August 1921) "were not very much in favour of the movement for the defiance of forest regulations" and wanted to confine the agitation to a social boycott of forest officials. But already from July on villagers had started sending their cattle into reserved forests without paying grazing fees and the movement in Palnad culminated with some forest villages proclaiming swaraj and violently attacking police parties in early 1922 at Veludurthi, Jattipalem, and Minchalapadu (where three were killed in police firing).[20] At Rayachoti from August 1921 "during a period of 3 or 4 months there was quite an epidemic of forest crime attended with violence." Village *munsifs* put up notices "saying that all the people were free to go into the forests and remove what they wanted."[21] The Forest Administration Report of 1921–2 admitted a virtual loss of control for some time over Palnad *taluk* and the Nallamalai hills in Rayachoti in face of "large bands of men imbued with the idea that Gandhi Raj was either being or about to be established and that the forest was theirs to work their will upon."[22] What was involved was evidently far more than an interested agitation of prosperous coastal cattle breeders acting through Lambadis, as Baker would like to have it.

Nor was forest satyagraha merely an Andhra affair. On 10 July 1921 Reading reported to the secretary of state that 250,000 out to 400,000 acres of forest in the Kumaon Division of U.P. had been burnt down.[23] Cavalry had to be sent to Muzaffarpur in north

---

[19] Cuddapah District Magistrate to Madras Government Judicial Department, 10 January 1922, in Venkatarangaiya, op. cit., p. 281.

[20] Ibid., pp. 37–8.

[21] Cuddapah District Magistrate's note, op. cit., p. 283.

[22] *Madras Forest Administration Report 1921–22*, p. 30, quoted in Baker and Washbrook, op. cit., p. 103.

[23] Telegraphic Correspondence of Viceroy with Secretary of State, April–December 1921, MSS Eur E. 238/10, Reading Collection, India Office Library.

Primitive Rebellion and Modern Nationalism

Bihar in December 1921 to tackle an agitation over grazing rights.[24] From Bengal, too, came reports of Santals reasserting their lost forest rights in the Jhargram region of Midnapur, and widespread looting of woodlands in Banskhali and Cox's Bazar areas of Chittagong.[25]

Forest movements died down quickly after the anti-climax of the Bardoli withdrawal, with one major exception – the old Rampa country north of the Godavari, scene of a veritable guerrilla war between August 1922 and September 1924.[26] It was led by a remarkable man, Alluri Sitarama Raju, still revered as a hero and martyr in his home district but almost unknown outside Andhra.[27] From the vivid account left by the Special Commissioner of Agency Operations in August 1924, the roots of this rebellion seem fairly familiar: forest laws, made particularly irksome by a corrupt *tahsildar* of Guden, coming on top of exploitation by *sowcars*. Peasants with some land and cattle were hit by the restrictions on grazing,

> ... as Kuda Ramayya put it, "we are fined Rs 15 for cutting a stick and have to pay + as for a calf so high to graze." Others who had no lands or cattle said they had been able to eke out a living by *podu* before it was restricted. *Podu* does seem to have been the resource of such though

[24] Viceroy to Secretary of State, p/1196 (Weekly Telegram), 6 December 1921, ibid.

[25] Rajat Ray, "Social Conflict and Political Unrest in Bengal, 1875–1927", unpublished manuscript, pp. 209–11, 327–8. I am grateful to Dr Ray for permitting me to consult his manuscript.

[26] Gautam Bhadra (Centre for Studies in Social Sciences, Calcutta) first drew my attention to the Rampa revolt. Baker preserves a remarkable silence about this movement, though elsewhere he makes considerable use of Venkatarangaiya's volume, which contains forty pages of documents on the rebellion of 1922–4.

[27] The Andhra government has published a Telugu edition of the life of Sitarama Raju which I have not been able to use. A collection of Bengali poems by Soumyendranath Tagore (*Biplab-Baisakhi*, August 1930), then a Communist, included one about "Shri Ramraju Alluri" (Government of India, Home Poll F.N. 29/X/1930). I owe this reference to Tanika Sarkar. I am told by Andhra Communists that Raju is still a folk hero. See also the picture of Raju in the frontispiece of V. Raghavaiah's *Tribes of India*, vol. I, New Delhi, 1969.

the *sowcar* probably got most of the profit, and also to some extent of the men with lands because they have not enough cattle to properly manure and cultivate the valley land – *podu* for 3 years at least gives good crops."[28]

The recorded grievances of individual rebel prisoners make fascinating reading. Thus Yendu Padal (a rebel leader) had not been paid for his work and constables had seized milk (and) fowls from him; four "landowning" rebels from Malamakaram had murdered a forest guard and joined Raju as desperate men (a classic beginning for social bandits, as Hobsbawm reminds us);[29] "Edem Pantayya had some of his old cultivated land included in the forest reserve and had been fined for illicit grazing"; "Boodu Chinnayya was fined Rs 40/- once for doing *podu* in a prohibited area."[30]

Yet certain new elements are at least equally striking. Sitarama Raju was not a local village *muttadar* unlike previous leaders, but "a man without family or interest",[31] an outsider coming from a group which claimed Kshatriya status and often some proficiency in Telugu and Sanskrit scholarship.[32] He had been wandering among the tribals from 1915 as a *sannyasi* claiming astrological and medicinal powers, and coming under Non-Cooperation influence in 1921 had started preaching against drink and organising village panchayats.[33] The deputy *tahsildar* of Malkanagiri who was summoned by the rebel leader in June 1923 described Raju as dressed in a "red coloured khaddar—he spoke highly of Mr Gandhi but considers that violence is necessary."[34] The *tahsildar* of Chodavaram reported in October

---

[28] T.G. Rutherford (Special Commissioner, Agency Operations) to Madras Chief Secretary, 22 August 1924. Venkatarangaiya, op. cit., pp. 366–9.

[29] Hobsbawm, *Primitive Rebels*, op. cit., pp. 15–16, and idem, *Bandits*, op. cit., chapter II.

[30] Rutherford, op. cit.

[31] A.P. Muddiman's Note, 18 June 1924, Home Poll F.N. 104/1924.

[32] Thurston and Rangachari, op. cit., vol. VI, pp. 247–50.

[33] Venkatarangaiya, op. cit., Introduction, p. 79; also Rutherford, op. cit., p. 366.

[34] Report of Malkanagiri Deputy Tahsildar to Agency Commissioner, 13 June 1923, Venkatarangaiya, op. cit., p. 388.

1922 that Raju in a meeting with him expressed sorrow "that he was not able to shoot Europeans as they were always accompanied and surrounded by Indians whom he did not want to kill",[35] and in fact at the Damarapalli ambush of 24 September 1922 the rebels allowed the advance party of Indians to pass and then shot down two British officers.[36] But anti-imperialist ideology was still accompanied by primitive messianic elements. "Raju hints he is bullet-proof," reported the Malkanagiri Deputy Tahsildar,[37] while a rebel proclamation in April 1924 claimed that "God Sri Jagannadhaswami . . . would incarnate very shortly as Kalkiavatara and appear before us . . ."[38] The rebellion began with a series of successful attacks on police stations to obtain arms, and developed into a remarkable guerrilla war. The rebel force numbered no more than a hundred, but had "super-numeraries all over the disturbed area who joined it whenever it was in their locality"[39] – fish in water, in other words, who enjoyed the sympathy "of the majority of the local hill population over an area of about 2500 square miles",[40] who had cost the Madras government Rs 15 lakhs by March 1924,[41] and who were able to defy the Malabar Special Police and Assam Rifles for nearly two years. The Madras government repeatedly pleaded for special powers from New Delhi, "to deal with what is virtually a rebel population."[42] Eventually, Raju was captured in an accidental encounter on 6 May 1924, and was promptly

[35] Godavari Collector's Report, 23 October 1922, cited in ibid., p. 83.
[36] D.O. from F.W. Stewart, Agency Commissioner, Narasapatam, to Madras Chief Secretary, 26 September 1922, ibid., p. 373.
[37] Venkatarangaiya, op. cit., Document no. 110.
[38] Madras Government Press Communique, 12 April 1924, ibid., p. 390.
[39] Ibid., p. 90.
[40] Madras Chief Secretary to Government of India (Home), No. 616-A-2, 18 April 1924, Home Poll F.N. 104/1924.
[41] Note by C.W. Guyenee in the Home Department, 20 March 1924, ibid.
[42] Report of Major A.J. Hamilton on the Military Operations in the Agency Tracts of Madras, 21 March 1924, Home Poll B107/1924. In October 1922, Madras pleaded for a blanket indemnity in advance for policemen fighting the rebellion; it asked for a special ordinance to "ensure rapid and effective punishment" for rebel sympathisers in April 1924 and again in June 1924. New Delhi, however, turned down these requests, at least partly in view

reported shot in an "attempt to run away"[43] – a formula that sounds unpleasantly familiar. Even then, resistance continued for another three or four months. The next great wave of forest unrest coincided with the Civil Disobedience upsurge of 1930–1, though research on Forest Administration Reports and judicial records might reveal many more incidents and a greater continuity than is possible to establish so far.[44] An intriguing shift in the location of forest movements becomes evident in 1930–1. Apart from a single ambush of a police party by Kondhs in the Vizagapatam Agency in January 1931,[45] "a dangerous, though isolated and quickly suppressed outbreak of defiance of forest grazing regulations" in Kangra (Punjab),[46] and extensive hunting of elephants and rhino in North Kamrup (Assam) by Kachari tribals allegedly inspired by the Congress leader Chandraprobha Saikiani,[47] the centres of forest agitation were all in the hill regions of Maharashtra, Karnataka, and the Central Provinces. One is tempted to suggest an inverse relationship between the strength of Congress organisation – most evident in 1930 in provinces like U.P., Bihar, and Gujarat, as well as parts of Andhra – and the development of more elemental and uninhibited forms of popular action like forest upheavals.[48] Despite (or maybe because of) the sustained work of

---

of possible embarrassments *vis-à-vis* the Legislative Council. Home Poll F.N. 898/1922 F.N. 104/1924.

[43] Telegram from Madras Government to Government of India (Home), 13 May 1924, Home Poll F.N. 104/1924.

[44] The history of crime has been almost entirely neglected in our country, though social historians elsewhere have long become aware of its possibilities as a guide to primitive and inchoate forms of social protest. Cf. E. Hobsbawm and G. Rude, *Captain Swing* (London, 1969, 1973), pp. 54–7.

[45] Instances of Congress violence in connection with the conduct of the Civil Disobedience campaign, Statement I, Home Poll F.N. 14/19/1931.

[46] Fortnightly Report from Punjab, first half of September 1930, Home Poll F.N. 18/X/1930.

[47] Fortnightly Report from Assam, second half of December 1930, Home Poll F.N. XIII/181/1930.

[48] This point has been first suggested by Gyanendra Pandey on the basis of his U.P. research.

Congress volunteers in the Bardoli region of Gujarat among the Raniparaj on forest issues as well as prohibition,[49] forest satyagraha caught on much more in the politically more "backward" regions like the Central Provinces, where a badly frightened governor in July 1930 described Civil Disobedience as "sweeping up from Bombay into Berar and Mahratta country. The popular attitude towards it is semi-religious..."[50] "I shall have to hit hard and may have to shoot a bit," he informed Irwin a few days later, referring to forest "maenads".[51]

As in 1921, two forms of phases can be distinguished in Civil Disobedience forest satyagraha. The element of centralised initiative, direction, and organisation is considerably more evident in 1930. Already in February 1930, a circular of Motilal Nehru had suggested breach of Central Provinces forest laws (though only as "an exception"),[52] and the Working Committee in May sanctioned forest satyagraha as a legitimate form of Civil Disobedience. Training camps were set up for volunteers (as at Sangamner in Ahmednagar district of Bombay),[53] satyagraha centres were carefully selected (106 in Berar, for instance, between July and September 1930),[54] and efforts were made to restrict the movement to boycott of Forest Department auctions and peaceful mass violations of grazing and timber rules[55] –

---

[49] Extract from Bombay Police Abstract No. 5, 2 February 1929, Home Poll F.N. 5/17/1931.

[50] Secret report of Simla Governor's Conference, 23 July 1930, included in the private papers of F.H. Sykes (Governor of Bombay)—Correspondence with Viceroy, etc., 1 July–31 December 1930, Mss Eur F. 150 264, India Office Library.

[51] Montagu Butler to Irwin, 30 July 1930, *Halifax Collection*, Correspondence with Persons in India, July–December 1930, Mss Eur C. 152, India Office Library.

[52] Text of circular in Home Poll F.N. 14/18/1931.

[53] P.V. Mahajan (Secretary, Maharashtra Provincial Congress Committee) to Vallabhbhai Patel, 28 July 1930, Maharashtra Satyagraha File, 1930–1, AICC F.N. G-1 48/1930.

[54] Report of the Congress Activities of the Berar Province, 9 November 1930, Berar Satyagraha File, AICC F.N. G-84/1930.

[55] In Bagalan *taluk* of Nasik district, for instance, on 5 August 1930, "more than 70 thousand persons took part in it [the forest satyagraha]. Grass was cut

with the forest produce being brought to towns and publicly sold there as with illegally manufactured salt. The Karnataka Satyagraha Mandal even tried to specify the kind of trees that were to be cut down.[56] The movement developed into a really formidable one over vast areas, so much so that the Bombay governor later recommended the head of the Forest Department for the Honours List on the grounds that he had "had a particularly difficult time" during the Civil Disobedience days.[57]

As repression intensified and removed the leaders, however, the movement soon acquired much less inhibited forms, most notably among the Gonds of the Central Provinces and the Kalis of the Western Ghats. Space does not permit detailed analysis of the very numerous attempted rescues of arrested leaders and violent attacks on police and forest guards, but the official catalogues of "Congress violence" list ten such instances in the Central Provinces between July and October 1930,[58] and twenty in the Bombay Presidency between May and October of the same year.[59] The Gonds of Banjaridhal (Betul district, C.P.), for instance, bitterly resisted police attempts to arrest their leader Ganjam Korku on 22–23 August.[60] The Kolis of Kanashi and Chankapur (Nasik district, Bombay), "filled with stories that the British Raj had been replaced by Gandhi Raj", after a ceremonial banquet "started to shout Congress slogans – refused to disperse (and)

---

in prohibited jungle, brought into the town and taken in grand procession..." Weekly report from Poona, 14 August 1930, AICC F.N. G-148/1930.

[56] Minutes of Karnataka Satyagraha Mandal, Hubli, 10 August 1930, AICC F.N. 2/1930.

[57] Brabourne to Willingdon, 19 February 1934, Brabourne Collection, MSS Eur. F. 97/9 – IOL).

[58] Home Poll F.N. 14/14/1981, Statements I and II.

[59] Forest incidents represented two out of the forty-seven clashes listed for the Northern Division of Bombay Presidency (i.e. Sind and Gujarat), nine out of twenty-one for Central, and nine out of thirteen for South—a significant distribution. Home Poll 14/19/1931.

[60] Central Provinces Chief Secretary to Government of India (Home, 1434/11, 25 August 1930), Civil Disobedience in Central Provinces, Home Poll F.N. 253/1930.

Primitive Rebellion and Modern Nationalism 487

hurled down stones" in face of police firing.[61] In Baglan *taluk* of the same district on 13 October, after some arrests had been made for refusal of grazing fees, "about 100 women from Tembhe suddenly came up and formed a cordon round the arrested men to prevent their being taken away. The party subsequently decided to give up the arrested men . . ."[62] Such men and women deserve a better fate than the total oblivion that has been their lot so far.

A Congress leaflet on one such incident (Bilashi in Satara district) rigidly demarcating peaceful forest satyagraha from violent tribal outbursts,[63] serves as a point to a conclusion which must already appear quite obvious. Though Gandhian nationalism directly or indirectly made a great and perhaps indispensable contribution to the forging of a movement out of longfelt but inchoate grievances, it made little effort to integrate poor peasant and tribal militancy into its mainstream. Where more permanent links were established with tribal movements, it was usually with the relatively moderate sects striving for internal reform (often on "Sanskritising" lines) which tended to appear after the flashpoint of millenarian hope had passed away.[64] The later stages of the Tana Bhagat sect among the Oraons on the Sapha Hor revival under Bangam Manjhi among Gumia Santals in 1930, might serve as examples.[65] For the rest, as with the not entirely dissimilar cases of communal riots springing out of agrarian discontent, tribal movements in isolation developed along "separatist" channels – the Nagas, for instance, or the Jharkhand agitation in Chota Nagpur. That the situation has had much greater potentialities in a revolutionary direction has been revealed, however,

[61] The Chanakapur incident took place on 20 October. Fortnightly Report from Bombay, second half of October 1930, Home Poll F.N. 18/xi/1930.
[62] Home Poll 14/19/1931.
[63] *The Bilashi Case*, printed leaflet included in AICC F.N. G-148/1930. Congress newspapers in Andhra, it may be added, had showed little sympathy for Raju in 1922–4: Venkatarangaiya, op. cit., p. 92.
[64] Peter Worsley's *The Trumpet Shall Sound* gives numerous instances of similar "reformist" sects developing in the later stages of Cargo cults in Melanesia: Worsley, op. cit.
[65] Stephen Fuchs, *Rebellious Prophets*, op. cit., pp. 42, 57–8.

in the occasional, sporadic, perhaps sometimes adventurist, but truly heroic instances of movements under Left guidance: the Hajongs of the Garo Hills organised by Moni Singh in the late 1930s, the Rajbansis who flocked to the Tebhaga banner in 1946–7, the Warlis of Maharashtra under Godavari Parulekar, the Koyas of the Godavari forest under Communist leadership in the great Telangana struggle of 1946–51,[66] Naxalbari and Srikakulam in more recent times.

As I conclude, news comes of forcible occupation of forest lands and uprooting of trees in West Midnapur, allegedly led by the CPI (M) and the CPI.[67] The issues raised by forest satyagraha, like so many other hopes that our national movement aroused but could not fulfil, remain with us today thirty years after Independence.

---

[66] P. Sundarayya, *Telengana People's Struggle and its Lessons* (Calcutta, 1942), pp. 246–51.

[67] *Statesman* (Delhi), 22 October 1977.

12

The Logic of Gandhian Nationalism
Civil Disobedience and the Gandhi–Irwin Pact 1930–1931

> "This is the way the world ends,
> Not with a bang but a whimper."

THUS JAWAHARLAL NEHRU recalled in 1936 his immediate reactions to the Gandhi–Irwin Pact, in a mood characteristically intellectual, wry, and resigned.[1] Right from his South African days, Gandhi had had the habit of disconcerting his followers by abrupt unilateral retreats.[2] But March 1931 was perhaps the greatest anti-climax of them all, since it called off a movement which had been launched for the first time under the banner of Purna Swaraj, and which was proclaimed by its official chronicler later on to have been a "fight to the finish".[3] It is true that the Viceroy had been forced

---

This is the revised version of a paper presented to the Nehru Memorial Museum and Library, New Delhi, in April 1976. I am grateful to Professor Asok Sen and Professor Barun De of the Centre for Studies in Social Sciences, Calcutta, for criticism of the earlier draft.

[1] Jawaharlal Nehru, *An Autobiography* (London, 1936), p. 259.

[2] Thus in January 1908 Gandhi withdrew his first satyagraha against the Transvaal registration ordinance on the basis of a verbal promise from Smuts, and an angry Pathan follower tried to beat him up as a traitor: Tendulkar, *Mahatma*, I, 2nd edn (Delhi, 1960), pp. 90–2.

[3] P. Sitaramayya, *History of the Indian National Congress*, vol. 1 (Bombay, 1936), pp. 429–67.

to treat the national leader on a quite novel basis of courtesy and equality, and the average Congress worker released from jail seems to have gone back to his village or town in a mood vastly different from the near-total disenchantment and frustration of 1822.[4] Yet even the official preface to the *Collected Works* of the Mahatma admits that the Delhi agreement "yielded no tangible gains to the nationalist cause; the Viceroy drove a hard bargain and secured all the immediate advantage."[5] Participation in the Round Table Conference on Irwin's terms was quickly revealed to have been a big mistake; a premium was put on all kinds of communal and sectional intrigues, and Civil Disobedience had to be resumed soon enough on a much less favourable and essentially defensive terrain. It is easy to share Nehru's sense of a "great emptiness as of something precious gone, almost beyond recall".[6] Perhaps he was remembering his bold words of March 1930: "One special feature of the struggle initiated by Mahatma Gandhi and the Congress is that there is no room for any compromise."[7]

The aim of the present essay, however, is not any debunking or "exposure" of the Gandhian leadership, for which purpose the choice of an admittedly weak moment would be polemically expedient but historically quite one-sided and unsound. The whole history of our nationalism is marked by a pattern of ups and downs, advances followed by retreats, and I feel that a study of some of the crucial turning points, the onset or the end of a particular wave of struggle, might help us towards a deeper understanding of the inner logic of the entire movement. Determined in the immediate sense by the decisions of leaders and by the personal influences working upon

---

[4] One might cite, for example, the official concern over the increased militancy of lower-level Congress cadres in Rae Bareli, Bara Banki, and Allahabad districts of the United Provinces after March 1931: Government of India, Home Political File 33/24/1931, National Archives of India (henceforth Home Poll F.N.).

[5] Gandhi, *Collected Works* (henceforth *CW*), vol. XLV (New Delhi, 1971), Preface, vi.

[6] Nehru, *op. cit.*

[7] Nehru, Speech at Allahabad, 14 March 1930, idem, *Selected Works*, ed. S. Gopal (henceforth *SW*), vol. IV (Delhi, 1973), p. 281.

them, this logic in the ultimate analysis must have been conditioned by deeper socio-political forces, and it is the business of the historian to try to remain aware of both these levels of analysis.

The Gandhi–Irwin Pact has on the whole received less scholarly attention than the withdrawal of Non-Cooperation after Chauri Chaura in February 1922. Reticence is natural enough for orthodox Gandhians. The two possible arguments in defence of Bardoli – the obvious and flagrant breach of non-violence, and Nehru's later plea that the movement was really "going to pieces"[8] – not entirely convincing in the context of 1922, seem largely irrelevant here. It is true that two weeks before the Delhi Pact, Gandhi had sent a telegram to Bombay criticising the use of violence in picketing and that he harped on this theme several times in the next few days.[9] But all this was after talks with Irwin had begun, and the viceroy had requested him "to get Bombay to go slow in picketing etc."[10] Gandhi had not been worried overmuch by earlier, and more serious, local outbursts of violence (for example, at Sholapur in May 1930): indeed, he seems to have given assurances to Jawaharlal and to the Communist prisoners at Meerut "that Civil Disobedience ... need not be stopped because of a sporadic act of violence."[11] As for the movement going to pieces, Nehru does not use this argument at all in the context of 1931, while Gandhi himself had declared on 31 January 1931: "I have no doubt that we can carry on this fight for any length of time."[12] Above all, the British would certainly not have bothered to negotiate with a defeated Congress.[13]

---

[8] Nehru, *An Autobiography*, p. 85.

[9] Telegram to Perin Captain, 17 February 1931. Also speech at Delhi (20 February), interview to *News Chronicle* (21 February), letters to K.M. Munshi and Shivabhai Patel (24–25 February), "Picketing" (*Young India*, 26 February), *What Should One Not Do?* (*Navajivan*, 1 March), *CW*, pp. xlv, 192, 210–11, 213, 225–6, 229–30, 236.

[10] Interview with Viceroy, February 1931 (Irwin's version), ibid., p. 188.

[11] Nehru, *An Autobiography*, p. 210. S.A. Dange's testimony, cited in G. Adhikari, ed., *Documents of the History of the Communist Party of India*, vol. II (New Delhi, 1974), p. 55.

[12] Speech to Congress leaders at Allahabad, *CW*, vol. XLV, p. 134.

[13] Subjective benevolence or change of heart played little or no part in the making of the Delhi Pact, as its aftermath was to reveal soon enough. Gandhi

Left critics of Gandhi have also concentrated fire mainly on 1922, no doubt largely because of the ready ammunition provided by the unusually frank and explicitly pro-zamindar nature of the Bardoli resolution.[14] Abuse tends to replace analysis in R.P. Dutt's account of Gandhi's role in the Civil Disobedience movement: "This Jonah of revolution, the general of unbroken disasters . . . the mascot of the bourgeoisie", seeking "to find the means in the midst of a formidable revolutionary wave to maintain leadership of the mass movement . . ."[15] Such a tirade ignores the undoubted role of Gandhi and of Gandhian ideology and methods in the making of this "formidable revolutionary wave". The assumption that all this could have happened without Gandhi is unproved and probably unprovable. And if we do grant that assumption, the success of Gandhi in arbitrarily calling off the movement becomes utterly inexplicable. Surely a revolutionary wave of totally independent origin should have proceeded better and along more radical courses once the bourgeois mascot had abdicated his role as leader.

A more balanced and helpful theoretical framework is that worked out by Bipan Chandra in his analysis of the national movement in terms of a basically continuous "pressure – compromise – pressure" strategy pursued by the leadership, a strategy which conformed, he argues, to the interests of the Indian bourgeoisie. This avoids the simplistic equation of compromise with total sellout or compradorism, emphasises the long-term contradictions between even moderate

---

declared himself impressed by Irwin's "inexhaustible patience and unfailing courtesy" (ibid., pp. 176, 250). In his private correspondence with Secretary of State Wedgwood Benn, during the Dandi March, however, Irwin had said Gandhi "continues regrettably hale and hearty" (Irwin to Wedgwood Benn, 26–27 March 1930, Halifax Papers, Nehru Memorial Museum and Library, microfilm copy, Reel No. 3). As for the Labour Secretary of State, Malcolm Hailey once congratulated Irwin on having such a congenial partner, so pleasantly different from Lord Malley or Mr Montagu (Hailey to Irwin, 13 May 1930, Halifax Papers).

[14] Cf. the well-known analysis of R.P. Dutt, *India Today* (Bombay, 1947), pp. 289–91.

[15] Ibid., pp. 295, 301.

bourgeois elements and imperialism, while at the same time pinpointing the deliberate avoidance of all-out mass confrontations (the alternative logic of "pressure-victory") in which bourgeois leadership might have been difficult to maintain.[16] I feel, however, that there is an unnecessary emphasis here on the existence of a consciously worked-out strategy, the proof of which requires a much more detailed study of the interests and aspirations of recognisably bourgeois elements functioning amidst the specifics of a colonial situation. We have to analyse in greater depth also the precise moments of time when pressure was unleashed or replaced by compromise, and the fourteen months between the Lahore Congress (December 1929) and the Gandhi–Irwin Pact (March 1931) seem particularly suitable from this point of view.

In a recent work, R.J. Moore has argued that the early enthusiasm of the Indian business community (and particularly of Bombay) for Gandhi's 1930 programme was soon replaced by pressures for compromise, as "civil disobedience was bad for business".[17] Here is a valuable hint which, however, requires much broader elaboration, particularly because the specific data cited by Moore (a few letters taken from the Purshottamdas Thakurdas and M.R. Jayakar Papers) date from the June–August 1930 period, when Gandhi was still rejecting any compromise.

A brief resume of the basic thesis of this paper may be helpful at this stage. I have tried to focus, first, upon the social forces at work in the Civil Disobedience movement and their changing interrelationships, and, secondly, the shifts in Gandhi's attitudes during 1930–1 and the influences upon him. The central theme that emerges from these two levels of analysis is the vastly enhanced role of distinctively bourgeois groups, both in contributing heavily to the initial striking

---

[16] Bipan Chandra, "The Indian Capitalist Class and British Imperialism", in R.S. Sharma and V. Jha, ed., *Indian Society: Historical Probings – In Memory of D.D. Kosambi* (New Delhi, 1974), pp. 390–413; "Elements of Change and Continuity in Early Nationalist Activity", Indian History Congress, Muzaffarpur, 1972; "Jawaharlal Nehru and the Capitalist Class, 1936", Indian History Congress, Jadavpur, 1974.

[17] *The Crisis of Indian Unity, 1917–1940* (Oxford, 1974), pp. 168–80.

power of Civil Disobedience and ultimately in its calling off. The extension to considerable sections of the peasantry was a second crucial feature; quantitatively of the highest significance, it remained, however, politically subordinate, as the bourgeoisie proved skilful enough to cash in on popular discontent and yet retain ultimate control over it. Towards the end of 1930, a contradiction was emerging at the heart of Civil Disobedience: certain forms of struggle more definitely in the control of the bourgeoisie or its dependent allies (for example, urban boycott, or the no-tax movement of *patidars* in Gujarat) were definitely weakening, while there was a possibility that other, less manageable forms (like no-rent, or tribal outbursts) might gather strength. It was at this point that bourgeois pressures for a compromise became insistent, and, given the nature of the Gandhian leadership (no mere bourgeois tool in any simplistic or mechanical sense, but still manifesting a certain coincidence of aims with Indian business interests at specific points) and the absence of a coherent Left alternative, the bang ended in a whimper.

II

The best recent work on Civil Disobedience and on Gandhian nationalism in general has taken the form of grassroots studies at the district or even village level, and has proceeded on the basis of fieldwork, interviewing participants, and collecting local data in the regional languages.[18] In the absence of a sufficient number of such detailed studies, however, generalisations about Civil Disobedience at the level required by our present theme still have to be grounded mainly on data of a more conventional type: Home Political records, AICC files, and the papers of a few prominent figures, British or Indian. A cross-section of the Civil Disobedience movement at its height (in the summer of 1930) on the basis of a partial study of such admittedly limited sources leads to three tentative conclusions: participation, on

---

[18] Cf. particularly the work in progress at the Centre for Studies in Social Sciences, Calcutta, under Hitesranjan Sanyal, Partha Chatterjee, and Barun De, as well as Gyanendra Pandey's research on the United Provinces.

The Logic of Gandhian Nationalism 495

a probably quite unprecedented scale, by large sections of a recognisably bourgeois class; the spread of the movement deep into rural, and sometimes even tribal areas through a variety of forms occasionally rather unexpected; and the relative passivity, in sharp contrast to the preceding two or three years, of industrial labour.

The modern Indian nationalist movement had had a "bourgeois" colour in a certain sense right from the beginning, for its intelligentsia leaders already in the so-called "Moderate" phase had formulated the ideal of independent development of the country along broadly capitalist lines.[19] Actual participation by distinctively bourgeois groups, however, was quite a different matter and a much later phenomenon. In the Swadeshi upsurge of 1905–8 which saw the first extensive use of the boycott weapon, the Marwari piecegoods importers of Calcutta deserted the nationalists once their own trade dispute with Manchester had been settled. Picketing by student volunteers was far more common than collective pledges by merchants, and local traders like the Sahas of East Bengal even became the principal targets of social boycott for unpatriotic behaviour. Bombay millowners utilised the new mood merely for some profiteering, and political leaders of Bombay with business connections like Pherozeshah Mehta or Dinshaw Wacha spearheaded the drive against Extremists.[20] Even bourgeois financial contributions to the Congress became significant only after 1920, when Bombay city supplied more than one-third of the total collections to the Tilak Swaraj Fund.[21] The Non-Cooperation era did mark a major advance from the point of view of bourgeois – and, more specifically, merchant and petty trader – participation, as has been pointed out in a recent paper. But we must still remember the Anti-Non-Cooperation Society headed by Purshottamdas Thakurdas, or Lalji Naranji's presidential casting vote

---

[19] Bipan Chandra, *Rise and Growth of Economic Nationalism in India* (New Delhi, 1966), chapter V.

[20] Sumit Sarkar, *The Swadeshi Movement in Bengal 1903–1908* (New Delhi, 1973), pp. 142–3, 321–2; A.P. Kannangara, "Indian Millowners and Indian Nationalism", *Past and Present*, no. 40 (July 1968).

[21] Judith Brown, *Gandhi's Rise to Power: Indian Politics 1915–1922* (Cambridge, 1972), pp. 320–1.

against the Prince of Wales boycott resolution at the Bombay Indian Merchants' Chamber meeting of November 1920.[22]

The middle and late 1920s saw a definite sharpening of the contradictions between most sections of the Indian bourgeoisie and British imperialism. The Tatas, heavily dependent on government protection, constituted perhaps the one major exception.[23] There were virtually unanimous protests against the 1s 6d rupee–sterling exchange ratio fixed by the Hilton Young Commission of 1926. Thakurdas spearheaded the protests, with his minute of dissent, and the Indian bourgeois spokesmen argued with considerable justice that the over-valued rupee encouraged foreign imports at the cost of Indian textiles, hindered raw material exports with inelastic demand schedules (Thakurdas' major business interests, it might be recalled, were in raw cotton exports), and led to deflationary measures which reduced investment possibilities.[24] A second major grievance was the refusal till 1930 to implement the 1927 Textile Tariff Board recommendation of a higher import duty. The Cotton Industries Protection Bill moved on 28 February 1930 did raise tariffs on British textiles from 11 to 15 per cent, but placed a 20 per cent duty on non-British goods – a note of Imperial Preference which aroused a lot of opposition.[25] In eastern India, the Birla group was trying to make headway against entrenched British jute interests, and this conflict helps to explain its generally pro-nationalist stance from the early 1920s.[26] Another

---

[22] Sabyasachi Bhattacharya, "Cotton Mills and Spinning Wheels: Swadeshi in the Non-Cooperation Era", Paper presented to the Indo-Soviet Symposium of Historians, New Delhi, January 1976.

[23] Amiya Bagchi, *Private Investment in India 1900–1939* (Cambridge, 1972), p. 198.

[24] Ibid., pp. 64–5; F. Moraes, *Sir Purshottamdas Thakurdas* (Bombay, 1957), pp. 74–107.

[25] Bagchi, op. cit., pp. 240–1; *Annual Report of Bombay Millowners Association* (1930), pp. 32–6, 182–205; G.D. Birla's Legislative Assembly speech opposing the Cotton Textile Industry (Protection) Bill, 25 March 1930, in idem, *The Path to Prosperity—A Collection of Speeches and Writings* (Allahabad, 1950), pp. 174–93.

[26] Bagchi, op. cit., p. 199.

The Logic of Gandhian Nationalism   497

point of tension was Walchand Hirachand and Lalji Naranji's Scindia Steam Navigation engaged in an uphill fight with British shipping interests headed by Lord Inchcape.[27] A Mercantile Marine Conference failed to settle the dispute in January 1930,[28] while Irwin stated the government's "most uncompromising opposition" to a Bengal National Chamber of Commerce demand of September 1929 for extension to eastern India of legislation similar to Haji's March 1928 Bill for the reservation of coastal traffic to Indian vessels.[29]

The repeated raising of demands like these at meetings of local business bodies (the Bombay Millowners Association, the Bombay Indian Merchants Chamber, the Calcutta Indian Chamber of Commerce dominated by the Birla group, etc.) as well as of course the very formation of the Federation of Indian Chambers of Commerce and Industry in 1927 by G.D. Birla and Thakurdas indicate the extent to which the bourgeoisie was fast developing all-India connections. Analysis in terms of caste or purely local interest groups, currently so very fashionable, seems not particularly relevant any longer, at least in periods of major developments. It can be argued that by the 1920s and 1930s the Indian bourgeoisie had started operating as a class, with an overall perspective of its relations with imperialism. And a comparison of the concrete issues raised by bourgeois spokesmen: exchange ratio, protection, shipping, with Gandhi's Eleven Points of January 1930, does make illuminating reading.

Yet all this represents only one aspect of a very complex reality. If some sections of the bourgeoisie had developed an all-India outlook (most notably perhaps certain Marwari businessmen with countrywide connections, and Gujarati merchants and millowners with a strong emotional loyalty towards Gandhi), local, regional, and religious pulls remained extremely powerful.[30] Above all, there were a series of

---

[27] Moraes, op. cit., pp. 44–6.

[28] Irwin to Wedgwood Benn, 9 January 1930, Halifax Papers.

[29] Memorandum enclosed with Irwin's letter to Wedgwood Benn of 19 March 1930, ibid.

[30] The most obvious example would be the support given to the Pakistan movement by Muslim business groups: see Bagchi, op. cit., pp. 428–37. The links between late-nineteenth-century Hindu revivalism and the United

specific constraints inhibiting the Indian capitalist groups from any all-out struggle against imperialism and its "feudal" allies (princes and landlords) along classic "bourgeois-revolutionary" lines.

If conflicts with imperialism had sharpened, these remained interwoven with relations of dependence and collaboration. This was most obvious in the case of that substantial section of the Indian trading community which was engaged in the Manchester piecegoods and other import business. As late as July 1928, the Marwari Association of Calcutta, speaking on behalf of a community "very greatly interested in the piecegoods and yarn trade", wanted to organise a conference "with a view to taking definite steps for the rehabilitation of this important branch of trade". The more far-sighted Indian Chamber of Commerce which it approached for this purpose, however, cold-shouldered the proposal.[31] Nor was it merely a question of "comprador" merchants as distinct from a purer "national" industrial capital; such a neat division is quite untenable in the Indian situation, given the complex interlocking of finance, trade, and industry in the managing agency system.[32] Indigenous cotton mills depended heavily on imports of machinery from the UK, so much so that machinery and millworks import figures have been used as the best available index of industrial investment in the standard work on that subject.[33] Tendencies towards collaboration were particularly evident in the Bombay textile industry; British machinery import firms had played

---

Provinces' commercial groups have been emphasised in C.A. Bayly, *Local Roots of Indian Politics: Allahabad 1880–1920* (Oxford, 1975), and F. Robinson, *Separatism Among Indian Muslims: The Politics of the U.P. Muslims, 1860–1923* (Cambridge, 1974).

[31] Letter from the Calcutta Marwari Association to the Indian Chamber of Commerce, 19 July 1928, *Annual Report of the Indian Chamber of Commerce, 1928* (Calcutta, 1929), pp. 570–1.

[32] See, for example, Bagchi, op. cit., pp. 206–8, 214–15 ; Michael Kidron, *Foreign Investment in India* (Oxford, 1965), p. 7; D.R. Gadgil, *Indian Economic Organization*, in S. Kuznets, *et al.*, eds, *Economic Growth: Brazil, India, Japan* (Duke University, 1958), pp. 461–2; and Kenneth L. Gillion, *Ahmedabad: A Study in India's Urban History* (California, 1968), pp. 78, 85.

[33] Bagchi, op. cit., pp. 71–80.

an important role in its development, and many mill agents also had foreign piecegoods import interests.[34] The ambiguous role of Bombay millowners, headed by Homi Mody, in the 1930s, is therefore not particularly surprising.

A second set of constraints are related to the "feudal" connections of the Indian capitalist groups, which have effectively inhibited consistent bourgeois support for radical agrarian programmes right down to the present day. The *Indian Year Book* of 1939–40 describes G.D. Birla as "millowner merchant and zamindar".[35] The traditional Bania elite of Ahmedabad which pioneered the textile industry there also had connections with trading and moneylending in the countryside,[36] while twelve out of the twenty-four major Allahabad commercial families listed by Bayly owned zamindaris.[37] A lesser known but possibly important kind of connection is suggested by a note by the loyalist Muslim politician, A.H. Ghuznavi, which advised the government to persuade native princes to pressurise nationalist-minded businessmen with homes in the native states: "For example, Mr Birla is a subject of the Jaipur State. His father, Raja Baldeodas Birla, is against the civil disobedience movement, and the Jaipur State authorities could bring pressure to bear on G.D. Birla through his father to stop financing the movement."[38]

Till late 1929 or early 1930 bourgeois political initiatives against the government must have been inhibited to a considerable extent also by the wave of labour unrest culminating in the great Girni Kamgar-led Bombay textile strikes of 1928 and 1929. The *Annual Report*

---

[34] P.S. Lokanathan, *Industrial Organization in India* (London, 1935), pp. 21, 30. See also letter of F. Stones of E.D. Sasson and Company to Rainy, Bombay, 14 August 1930, complaining about Congress pressures on mill-owners for undertaking not to use foreign yarn or import foreign piecegoods, Home Poll F.N. 201/40/1930.

[35] Cited in Bagchi, op. cit., p. 209 fn.

[36] Gillion, op. cit., pp. 85–8.

[37] Bayly, op. cit., pp. 186–9.

[38] Confidential Note by A.H. Ghuznavi, MLA, giving his views on the Civil Disobedience movement, 15 September 1930, Home Poll F.N. 190/1930. I owe this reference to Tanika Sarkar.

of the Bombay Millowners' Association (1928) presented by Homi Mody in March 1929 did complain about the non-implementation of the Tariff Board proposals, but was concerned far more with the "unprecedented general strike" of 1928.[39] The Millowners' Association and the Indian Merchants' Chamber repeatedly pressed the Bombay governor for "drastic action" against the labour movement,[40] and Mody in his 1929 report "naturally" supported the Trades Disputes Bill. He wanted to tighten it up further through anti-picketing clauses, and argued that "peaceful picketing does not really exist" – a point with very interesting implications for nationalist politics.[41]

The March 1930 annual report of the Bombay Millowners' Association, however, jubilantly described the defeat of the 1929 strike, and then went on "to deal with the subject which has almost become a matter of life and death to the industry": the refusal of protection against British and Japanese competition After the Meerut arrests, the smash-up of Girni Kamgar, and the defeat (in early 1930) of the GIP railway strike led by the other major Communist-influenced union,[43] the decks evidently seemed clear for a round of pressure tactics on the government. G.D. Birla in his presidential address of 14 February 1930 to the Federation of Indian Chambers of Commerce and Industry described British Indian fiscal policies as "discriminating free trade" rather than discriminating protection, and bitterly attacked the stranglehold of British capital on the Indian economy.[44] He was followed by Thakurdas, who moved a resolution (which was carried unanimously) denouncing the 1s 6d exchange ratio.[45] Birla was even more outspoken in his concluding speech on 16 February, where he openly called on "capitalists, the employers

---

[39] *Report of Bombay Millowners' Association, 1928* (Bombay, 1929), pp. ii–iv.

[40] F.H. Sykes (Bombay Governor, 1928–33) to Irwin, 27 December, 1928, 26 January 1929, F.H. Sykes Collection, India Office Library Mss Eur F 150 (1).

[41] *Report of Bombay Millowners' Association*, op. cit., p. iii.

[42] Ibid., pp. ii–iv.

[43] Home Poll F.N. 95/1930.

[44] Birla, *Path to Prosperity*, op. cit., pp. 133–4, 141.

[45] N.N. Mitra, ed., *Indian Annual Register (1930)*, pp. 404–7.

and the industrialists" in their own interests "to strengthen the hands of those who are fighting for Swaraj."⁴⁶ His close adjutant D.P. Khaitan made the same point two weeks later at a special meeting of the Calcutta Indian Chamber of Commerce: "at long last there is dawning upon our minds the realisation of the stubborn fact that unless India attains Self-Government it is difficult for her to improve her economic position."⁴⁷

In the first months of Civil Disobedience, there is ample evidence regarding this new, relatively far more militant stance of the leading representatives of the Indian bourgeoisie. The FICCI published a *Monograph on Common Salt* which Jawaharlal recommended to Congressmen.⁴⁸ In May 1930, the Federation decided to stay away from the Round Table Conference till the viceroy made a definite promise regarding Dominion Status and Gandhi agreed to attend it also.⁴⁹ Business associations like the Indian Chamber of Commerce repeatedly protested in strong language against police repression.⁵⁰

Most active of all was Ghanshyamdas Birla donating large amounts to Gandhi according to Intelligence Bureau sources (from one to five lakhs was Sir David Petrie's estimate),⁵¹ and actively trying to persuade the Marwari foreign piecegoods importers of Calcutta to establish contacts instead with Bombay and Ahmedabad cotton mills.⁵² Birla of course is a very exceptional figure, with his remarkable

---

⁴⁶ Quoted in Bipan Chandra, "The Indian Capitalist Class and British Imperialism", op. cit., p. 398.

⁴⁷ D.P. Khaitan's speech at a special meeting of the Indian Chamber of Commerce, Calcutta, 5 March 1930, *Annual Report for 1930* (Calcutta, 1931), p. 189.

⁴⁸ Circular to PCCs, 22 February 1930, *SW*, vol. IV, 272–37.

⁴⁹ FICCI Memorandum to Viceroy, 14 May 1930, signed by Lala Sri Ram, P. Thakurdas, G.D. Birla, Chunilal Mehta, Lalji Naranji, D.P. Khaitan, Ambalal Sarabhai, N.R. Sarkar, and others, *Indian Annual Register (1930)*, op. cit., pp. 408–11.

⁵⁰ *Indian Chamber of Commerce (Calcutta), Annual Report for 1930,* op. cit., pp. 433–45.

⁵¹ Note by Sir David Petrie showing what funds are at the disposal of the Congress, 26 May 1930, Home Poll F.N. 5/40/1931.

⁵² "You know Marwaris are mainly responsible for the establishment of

political foresight and close personal contacts with Gandhi. The attitudes of two loyalists of 1921 – Lalji Naranji and Thakurdas – are perhaps even more significant.

At the February 1930 annual meeting of the Bombay Millowners Association, Lalji Naranji bitterly attacked the 1s 6d ratio and praised Birla's "admirable analysis of the growing burden of foreign liabilities". The Indian depression, he argued, was essentially a product of British financial policies, and had become acute long before the American collapse.[53] Two years later, Naranji in a remarkably frank letter to M.R. Jayakar sharply criticised the Liberals and explained his support for Gandhi: "I in my commercial way of thinking, believe more in Gandhiji's policy... Gandhiji's 11 points or demands are more of economic nature than of mere political nature. It is therefore that commercial community have put more explicit faith in Gandhiji or his organisations."

Naranji went on to mention British efforts to corner Indian markets, foreign control over banking, shipping, insurance, and railways, and unfair currency exchange and fiscal policies as reasons why "Government indifference has driven... we capitalists [sic] to work with Socialistic organisations like Congress." He also drew up a kind of minimum charter of bourgeois demands,[54] and stated

---

the Manchester market in Calcutta. If they once decide to wash their hands clean of foreign piecegoods business and devote themselves to the Swadeshi cloth business, they can perform miracles. There are people in this town who could purchase the whole production of your mills for 12 months ahead... I wish you and Bombay millowners could take advantage of the situation... I am writing this letter at the suggestion of some of the big importers who are ready to help the mills... I ask you to discuss this problem with your Ahmedabad and Bombay friends": G.D. Birla to Ambalal Sarabhai (with copies to Thakurdas and Kasturbhai Lalbhai), 30 April 1930, Purshottamdas Thakurdas Papers, F.N. 100/1930, Nehru Memorial Museum and Library.

[53] *Annual Report of Bombay Millowners' Association, 1929* (Bombay, 1930), pp. x–xi.

[54] Reduction of government expenditure, end of gold exports and unbacked paper currency, concessions regarding banking, insurance, and shipping, a ban on cloth imports, while "other demands (were) to be discussed with commercial bodies."

that if these were granted, "I am sure no commercial member will ever think of Congress and we further believe that if we get what we want... Congress will be the foremost in withdrawing their civil disobedience. They are not fond of that civil disobedience movement, particularly Mahatmaji is sure to withdraw if we are given what we want."[55]

Thakurdas' standpoint was more equivocal, and his papers show him as maintaining very close connections with officialdom throughout. Yet he too for some months had to go with the tide to a considerable extent. "It is impossible in Bombay to think of having a public meeting to point out the dangers of the movement", Thakurdas regretfully informed the Viceroy on 28 April 1930. A few weeks later he wrote: "I am truly grieved that public opinion should leave the Committee of the (Indian Merchants') Chamber no option but to send any resignation to your Excellency"[56] (from the Central Legislative Assembly), since "my electorate are not merely the Indian Merchants' Chamber but the vast Indian commercial community outside."[57] He also kept away from the first session of the Round Table Conference, though after much hesitation and a long exchange of letters with Birla.[58] And even he in the first flush of Civil Disobedience wanted from Irwin full Indian control over "finance, currency, fiscal policy and Railways" so as to end the "economic exploitation of the country as it is called"; defence and foreign and political relations he was prepared to leave with the British.[59]

It was not therefore a question of the attitudes of a few prominent

---

[55] Lalji Naranji to M.R. Jayakar, 27 January 1932, M.R. Jayakar Papers, F.N. 456, National Archives of India. The letter has been already quoted in part in Moore, op. cit., p. 168.

[56] Thakurdas to Irwin, 31 May 1930, Thakurdas Papers, F.N. 99/1930.

[57] Thakurdas to J.W. Bhore, 14 May 1930, ibid.

[58] Thakurdas to Birla, 16 September 1930; Birla to Thakurdas, 20 September 1930. Birla by this time was evidently trying to widen his options, and described himself as "A man... who would not himself accept the invitation but would not mind your accepting same... I do not represent the Congress nor have I got the Congress mentality. But I wish to be loyal to my party." Thakurdas Papers, F.N. 104/1930.

[59] Thakurdas to Irwin, 12 May 1930, ibid., F.N. 99/1930.

businessmen, however influential, but a kind of groundswell of opinion in a class. "Sykes (the Governor of Bombay) tells me that in Bombay the mercantile community has already given to Gandhi a measure of support which it refused to him until the later stages of the Non-Cooperation Movement of 1921–2", Irwin reported to Wedgwood Benn on 24 April 1930.[60] Bombay city became in fact a real nightmare for the British for several months in the summer of 1930, while its image inspired even the otherwise rather unenthusiastic Rabindranath Tagore.[61] Despite the Chittagong armoury raid, the notorious Calcutta police commissioner, Tegart, was far more anxious about Bombay than his own province in July 1930,[62] and in a governors' conference held in the same month the reports from Bombay and the neighbouring Central Provinces struck a note markedly different from the general tone of moderate optimism.[63] In Bombay, reported Home Member H.G. Haig, the methods of non-violence were doing far "more harm to Government".[64] "Gandhi caps fill the streets, volunteers in uniform are posted for picketing with the same regularity and orderliness as police constables",[65] while massive processions (one of them, on 23 May, organised by twenty-eight Indian commercial bodies),[66] were "brushing aside ... the ordinary

[60] Halifax Papers.

[61] Tagore to P.C. Mahalanobis, 26 January 1930, written from Totnes, on his way to Russia, *Desh* (Calcutta), 23 August 1975. I owe this reference to Tanika Sarkar.

[62] Tegart claimed that his policy of hitting "hard and keep on hitting" was paying off in Bengal, but he "was becoming extremely anxious with regard to the situation in Bombay": T.M. Ainscough, H.M. Senior Trade Commissioner, to J.A. Woodhead, Commerce Secretary, Government of India, 7 July 1930, reporting a conversation with Tegart in Calcutta, Home Poll F.N. 201/40/1930.

[63] Secret report of Governors' Conference, Simla, 21–25 July 1930, F.H. Sykes Collection, MSS Eur F 150/2(6).

[64] H.G. Haig to J.E.B. Hotson, D.O. No. S-687 Poll, Simla, 25 May 1930, Home Poll F.N. 257/V and K.W./1930.

[65] Note by H.G. Haig, 13 June 1930, ibid.

[66] *Bombay Chronicle*, 25 May 1930; *Indian Annual Register* (1930), Chronicle of Events, entry for 23 May.

The Logic of Gandhian Nationalism 505

functions of police control of traffic".[67] Above all, though the crowds and volunteers, as almost always in such nationalist upsurges since 1905, consisted mainly of

> clerks and shopkeepers and young men, the educated lower middle class ... the movement has undoubtedly been receiving a backing from the Indian commercial classes as a whole ... Bombay businessmen have for a long time been dissatisfied with the economic and financial policy pursued by the Government of India ... They feel that it is worthwhile making appreciable sacrifices now, if this is going to secure for them the economic and financial autonomy which they strongly desire.[68]

As these reports indicate, the 1921 pattern was being repeated: merchants and petty traders were more enthusiastic about Civil Disobedience than industrialists.[69] Congress relations with millowners were bedevilled by the old problems of excessive prices, the passing off of mill-cloth as khadi, the use of foreign yarn, and sometimes also the foreign piecegoods import business of some mill agents. Twenty-four Bombay mills had been blacklisted as non-Swadeshi by the local Boycott Committee by August 1930, and fifty-six throughout India.[70] Motilal Nehru before his arrest was trying to settle such disputes through discussions with Ambalal Sarabhai, Kasturbhai Lalbhai, and others, and a FICCI sub-committee drew up plans for a Swadeshi Sabha with mills accepting certain Swadeshi conditions as members.[71] But it remained a very uneasy alliance, presaging sometimes the conflicts of 1932–3, when the Bombay millowners signed the Lees–Mody Pact, while a "Nationalist" group of merchants fought to oust the collaborating Thakurdas from the Indian Merchants' Chamber.[72]

---

[67] Note by Haig, 13 June 1930, op. cit.
[68] Ibid.
[69] Sabyasachi Bhattacharya, op. cit.
[70] Home Poll F.N. 201/40/1930.
[71] Exchange of telegrams regarding proposed meeting of millowners with Motilal Nehru, June 1930; FICCI pamphlet, entitled *Rules of Swadeshi Sabha* (1930), Thakurdas Papers, F.N. 100/1930.
[72] Stanley A. Kochanek, *Business and Politics in India* (California, 1974), pp. 145–9.

Merchants normally dealing in piecegoods imports, in contrast, made considerable sacrifices, through corporate undertakings not to indent foreign goods for specific periods. Marwari importers of Calcutta, for instance, were persuaded by Madan Mohan Malaviya to take such a pledge on 30 April,[73] and such undertakings were particularly common in Bombay and North Indian trade centres like Amritsar and Delhi.[74] This was really a more effective form of boycott than the spectacular picketing by (often largely women) volunteers. There were problems concerning the sale of existing stocks, often through agreements with local Congress committees which were frequently denounced by the leaders,[75] and the fall of prices due to the depression might have provided an economic incentive to what otherwise seems to be altruistic patriotism.[76] A recent study of Madras Presidency relates widespread merchant support for the Congress in Andhra coastal towns to the distress caused by falling prices.[77] Yet even official reports and correspondence sometimes hint at dimensions left unexplored by the current Namierite fashion in

[73] D.P. Khaitan's speech at Quarterly General Meeting of Indian Chamber of Commerce, 2 May 1930, *Indian Chamber of Commerce, Annual Report for 1930* (Calcutta, 1931), p. 533.

[74] Cf., for example, the resolution of the Bombay Piecegoods Native Merchants Association, 21 May 1930, and the letter of the Northern Indian Chamber of Commerce, Lahore, to the Chief Secretary of the Punjab Government, 16 August 1930, reporting the "very grave situation facing shippers and importers as a result of the general repudiation of contracts by dealers in India in consequence of the boycott movement, and the resultant total stoppage of trade": Home Poll F.N. 201/40/1930.

[75] J. Nehru, Speech at Allahabad, 12 October 1930, *SW*, vol. IV, p. 395; Working Committee Resolution, Allahabad, 1 February 1931, *CW*, vol. XLV, p. 135.

[76] "The wholesale dealers realize that owing to the greatly reduced purchasing power of the masses, they could not now or in the near future dispose of the enormous stocks they normally hold, and so they are content to wait before ordering from abroad": *Fortnightly Report* (henceforth *FR*) from Punjab, second half of October 1930, Home Poll F.N. 18/xi/1930. Sykes made the same point in his letter to Irwin, 25 September 1930, F.H. Sykes Collection, MSS Eur F 150/2 (b).

[77] C.J. Baker, *The Politics of South India 1920–1937* (Cambridge, 1976), p. 216.

historiography. The Bombay governor explicitly rejected "the theory that we are dealing with a limited political clique supported by only a section of the public. In Bombay City and most of Gujarat we have practically a mass movement..."[78] And even Petrie bore testimony to the strength of the ideological element inspiring Bombay merchants:

> ...a highly impressive feature is that many of the ordinary, sober and sensible businessmen seem quite prepared to continue the movement, even though ruin is staring them in the face. This is, perhaps, more particularly true of the Gujarati element with whom Gandhi's influence is paramount. Anyhow, all this serves as a forceful illustration of the ascendancy established by the Congress over people who seem to stand to lose everything by supporting it...[79]

The net impact was a remarkable fall in British cloth imports. Their value declined from £26 millions in 1929 to £13.7 millions in 1980.[80] Homi Mody triumphantly declared in March 1931: "Imports have considerably dropped, and from 1379 million yards in the 9 months ending 31 December 1929 they have dropped to 713 million yards in 1930." No doubt the depression contributed to this fall, but, as Mody pointed out, the decline was far more marked in the case of Lancashire imports, while "the Swadeshi movement... undoubtedly helped the [Indian] industry during a period of grave difficulty", so much so that now "the future may be regarded as full of hope".[81] The series of panicky reports which flooded the office of the British Trade Commissioner from May to August 1930 provide even more eloquent testimony.[82]

Boycott via associations of merchants as much or even more than

[78] Sykes to Irwin, 20 June 1930, F.H. Sykes Collection, MSS Eur F 150/2 (a).
[79] Petrie to Emerson, Home Secretary, Government of India, 20 August 1930, Home Poll F.N. 504/1930.
[80] Moore, op. cit., pp. 211–13.
[81] *Annual Report of Bombay Millowners' Association, 1930* (Bombay, 1931), pp. ii–iii.
[82] "Let Sir George Schuster, Sir George Rainy and other Ministers and Heads of Departments know that we are feeling it very badly": H. Abbot of Imperial Tobacco, Calcutta, to Ainscough, 11 June 1930. "It cannot be denied that the campaign against British piecegoods, cigarettes and other

through picketing had thus become the predominant form of the urban movement. The older, more purely intelligentsia, forms of protest like lawyers giving up professions and students their schools or colleges had fallen somewhat into the background. Jawaharlal's Lahore presidential address gave them little prominence,[83] and a Bihar Congress report of July 1930 did not seem particularly worried by the fact that there had been "practically no response from lawyers and students". Foreign cloth dealers of Bankipore, Patna City and Dinapur, in contrast, "were and have been sympathetic towards the Congress movement".[84] Nationalism had at last achieved firm anchorage with a basic social class, for worse as well as for better as March 1931 was to reveal.

The same Bihar report stated that "the movement is practically entirely in the villages and in the hands of village people", and the second major achievement of Gandhian nationalism was of course this mobilisation of the peasantry. Detailed, district- or village-level studies are available so far only for parts of Bengal,[85] the United Provinces,[86] and – with considerably greater qualifications – Madras,[87] and the obvious existence of regional and local variations makes generalisations particularly hazardous here. We might still attempt a

---

commodities in lesser degrees has met with considerable success": Bengal Chamber of Commerce President R.S. Laird's letter No. 1850–1930, 3 July 1930. "These gentry have now succeeded in bringing our business in Bombay Presidency practically to a close": Dunlop Manager E.L. Jones to Rainy, 11 August 1930, Home Poll F.N. 201/40/1930.

[83] *SW*, vol. IV, p. 196.

[84] "A Short General Report of the Working of the Civil Disobedience Movement in the Province of Bihar, 21 July 1930", AICC Files, G/80/1930 (Nehru Memorial Museum and Library).

[85] Hitesranjan Sanyal, *Arambagh-e Jatiyatabadi Andolan* (The Nationalist Movement in Arambagh), *Anya Artha*, nos. 6–7 (Calcutta, 1974–5).

[86] Gyanendra Pandey, "The Ascendancy of the Congress in the United Provinces: 1926–1934" (forthcoming PhD dissertation, Oxford University). I am grateful to the author for allowing me to consult his manuscript.

[87] C.J. Baker, op. cit. As in other works of the "Cambridge School", the emphasis here is on administrative pressures and factional manoeuvres.

tentative distinction between two broad forms or waves of struggle in the countryside: one spreading out from top downward, mobilising peasants through accepted Gandhian forms and restraints: the other a relatively autonomous "peasant nationalism", welling out from the depths of rural society, using Gandhi's name but interpreting his message in vastly varied and socially much less inhibited ways.[88]

The first, "official" type of Gandhian civil disobedience had its natural starting points and strongest bases in areas which had already witnessed some amount of Gandhian rural "constructive work" – khadi and prohibition, village improvements, occasional campaigns around local grievances. Bardoli is the best-known example, with its successful no-revenue campaign of 1928 and its numerous "Swaraj Ashrams and Chawries".[89] But recent research is bringing out the importance of pockets like Contai, Tamluk, or Arambagh even in Bengal,[90] a province where most top Congress leaders were urban-based "bhadralok" generally busy with infighting after the death of C.R. Das, on the strength of which the whole Congress movement has been supposed to be "in decline".[91]

Salt provided the initial catalyst in 1930, in sharp contrast to the expectations of British officials, and possibly many intellectual Congressmen. "At present the prospect of a salt campaign does not keep me awake at night," Irwin blithely wrote to Wedgwood Benn on 20 February 1930.[92] A year later, the viceroy is said to have admitted to Gandhi: "You planned a fine strategy round the issue of salt."[93]

[88] Gyanendra Pandey's thesis on Civil Disobedience in UP has emphasised this dual aspect of rural nationalism.

[89] Bombay Police Abstract, No. 5, 2 February 1929, quoted in Home Poll F.N. 5/17/1931.

[90] Here from the early 1920s Gandhian Congressmen like Birendranath Sasmal or Prafullachandra Sen had combined constructive village work with anti-Union Board and occasionally even anti-zamindar campaigns: Hitesranjan Sanyal, op. cit.

[91] J. Gallagher, "The Congress in Decline", in J. Gallagher, G. Johnson, and A. Seal, *Locality, Province and Nation* (Cambridge, 1973).

[92] Halifax Papers.

[93] Gandhi's version of interview with Irwin, 18 February 1931, *CW*, vol. XLV, p. 200.

Salt linked up in a flash the ideal of Swaraj with a most concrete and universal rural grievance and one which (unlike rent, for instance) had no socially divisive possibilities. Like that other intellectually dubious Gandhian fetish, *khaddar*, it gave its peasant adherents the possibility of an extra income, paltry in itself but psychologically very important. And there was of course also the tremendous emotional impact of the Dandi March and the heroic non-violence of Dharasana. The government, too, made a big contribution by senseless brutality, with "unresisting men being methodically bashed into a bloody pulp", of which some of the AICC files provide a vivid account.[94] Even a man like Thakurdas bitterly complained about "the beating of women and little children of ten and twelve years of age by the police", and said that such things made participation in the Round Table Conference impossible.[95]

Salt, however, could obviously provide the stable basis for a sustained campaign only in those limited areas where its large-scale (as distinct from merely token) production was possible, as in the coastal areas of Bombay Presidency, Balasore in Orissa, or Midnapur in Bengal. Elsewhere other forms were soon needed, and in fact the British had expected and feared this from the beginning. Irwin informed Wedgwood Benn on 19 March 1930 of a significant remark of the U.P. governor, Malcolm Hailey: "He said that in the UP – and I should guess this is likely to be true of other Provinces – this [the salt campaign] was only as it were a curtain-raiser to the real business that would be a 'no-rent and no-revenue' campaign. On that he thought we should have to jump immediately and heavily. I agree."[96]

Gujarat – or more precisely Anand, Borsad, and Nadiad *talukas* of Kaira district and Bardoli in Surat district – soon became once again the centre of a formidable no-revenue campaign based upon the

---

[94] Webb Miller's classic description of Dharasana, quoted in R.C. Majumdar, *History of the Freedom Movement in India*, vol. III (Calcutta, 1963), p. 362; Bengal Satyagraha Reports, AICC Files G/86/1930. Here, as with the bulk of the Bengal material, I have borrowed heavily from the current research of Tanika Sarkar on Bengal Politics and Society, 1927–1937.

[95] Thakurdas to Graham Pole, 9 July 1930, Thakurdas Papers, F.N. 99/1930.

[96] Halifax Papers.

relatively prosperous Patidars, and by May had become the viceroy's most serious headache.[97] A later official report admitted that only Rs 20,000 out of Bardoli *taluka*'s revenue demand of Rs 397,000 could be collected up to the signing of the Gandhi–Irwin Pact.[98] In the zamindari areas, however, as in 1921–2, the close connection between no-revenue and no-rent inhibited the Congress leadership, even though landlord associations from the beginning had adopted a definitely antinational stand.[99] The Working Committee in May 1930 restricted non-payment of land tax to *ryotwari* areas,[100] and the constraints working lower down in the Congress hierarchy are indicated in a letter from the Bihar PCC which, after emphasising the predominantly peasant character of the movement, went on to recommend for the Working Committee the new provincial "dictator" Deep Narain Singh as a "big zamindar and an old nationalist".[101]

Less socially divisive forms of struggle were therefore sought for in most areas. Picketing of liquor shops and of excise licence auctions were particularly widespread, and had brought about a Rs 20 lakh fall in excise revenue in Bihar by September 1930.[102] A second major issue was the *chowkidari* tax, around which by August 1930 Congress activities were "gradually centering ... in the districts of Champaran, Muzaffarpur, Bhagalpur, Saran and Monghyr" in Bihar.[103] Midnapur with its anti-Union Board no-tax experience became another major centre of this campaign and, as at Bardoli, the government response combined physical coercion with possibly more effective large-scale

[97] Irwin to Wedgwood Benn, 14 May 1930, ibid.
[98] Bell to Emerson, Poona, 6 August 1931, Home Poll F.N. 33/24/1931.
[99] A conference of Bengal and Assam landholders in Calcutta in January 1930 hailed the Round Table Conference announcement, and on 6 February the UP Zamindars' Conference denounced the Independence Resolution, *Indian Annual Register* (1930), Chronicle of Events, entry for 3 January, ibid., p. 379.
[100] Chronicle of Events, for 12–15 May, ibid.
[101] Brajkishore Prasad to Vallabhbhai Patel, enclosing a report on the Civil Disobedience movement in Bihar, 21 July 1930, AICC Files, G/80/1930.
[102] FR, Bihar and Orissa, second half of October 1930, Home Poll F.N. 18/xi/1930.
[103] Weekly Progress Reports of Satyagraha Movement from Bihar PCC, 8 August 1930, AICC Files, G/80/1930.

confiscation of property. In two Champaran police stations, property worth Rs 2023 was confiscated for a total tax arrear of Rs 174,[104] while a Midnapur villager whose annual *chowkidari* tax burden was only Re 1 and 8 annas is said to have lost Rs 350 through his homestead and granaries being burnt by the police.[105] The quiet heroism of such obscure village folk, in the face of an amount of repression which seems quite fantastic if we remember that the British were dealing with a predominantly non-violent movement, deserves to be far better remembered in the annals of our freedom struggle.[106] Such things also make interpretations of nationalism merely in terms of the interplay of relatively privileged interest groups seem curiously partial and unreal.

In Gujarat, the main Congress base was among the relatively privileged Patidars, and the British seem to have had some success in utilising the lower ranks of rural society against this recalcitrant group.[107] Another example of Gandhian nationalism catching on among a locally dominant group would be the Jats in Bulandshahr and Meerut districts of western UP.[108] But the generalisation sometimes made that the Congress everywhere attracted only dominant-caste

---

[104] Ibid.

[105] Satya Manna of Gokulnagar village, P.S. Moyna, Midnapur, Birendranath Guha, Secretary, Bengal Council of Civil Disobedience, to AICC President, 6 November 1930, AICC Files, G/1930. I owe this reference to Tanika Sarkar.

[106] One further illustration, taken from a slightly later period: in February 1932 peasants in Kaira district were being stripped and made to stand on all fours for the crime of non-payment of revenue: Typewritten Weekly Civil Disobedience Review, 31 January–6 February 1932, preserved in the papers of M.R. Jayakar, F.N. 482.

[107] "In one district they (the British) are fomenting a class war between the laboureres, who belong to a criminal tribe, and the farmers who are refusing land tax'": H.N. Brailsford to Wedgwood Benn, 2 November 1930, enclosed in Benn to Irwin, 17 November 1930, Halifax Papers. Transfer of Patidar lands to Dharalas was the issue which almost blocked the Delhi Pact at the last moment: Gandhi to Irwin, 4 March 1931 *CW*, vol. XLV, p. 245.

[108] Note of UP Police I.G. Dodd, D.O. 580/CO-30 of 3 September 1930, Home Poll F.N. 249/1930.

rich peasant support still seems extremely hazardous. Hitesranjan Sanyal's field study of Arambagh (a very backward pocket in West Bengal, which yet became a storm centre) has revealed that out of 371 activists jailed for more than six months between 1930 and 1942, only 9 per cent can be classified as rich peasants holding more than 15 *bighas* (5 acres), while out of another sample of 561 participants, a mere 11 per cent were Brahmans or Kayasthas.[109]

Even more significant is the development of pressures and movements from below. The catastrophic fall in agricultural prices played a vital part here, and from September or October onwards the Fortnightly Reports repeatedly mention the deepening depression as a possibly crucial factor in politics.[110] Despite the hesitations of most Congress leaders, pressures were mounting, as we shall see, for a no-rent campaign particularly in the United Provinces by the autumn of 1930. Another form with explosive possibilities was the forest satyagraha, encouraging the rural poor to satisfy their need for timber, fuel, and grazing facilities and thus particularly attractive to the lower ranks of peasants and, even more, tribal society. Violation of forest laws had been an important part of Non-Cooperation in parts of Andhra in 1921–2,[111] and it caught on like wildfire again for some months after the Working Committee had sanctioned it along with the anti-*chowkidari* tax campaign in May 1930. The tribal response to it seems to have taken violent and often millenarian forms quite distinct in tone from orthodox Gandhism. Between July and September 1930 there was forest satyagraha at 106 centres in Berar alone,[112] and official sources report large-scale movements among

[109] Hitesranjan Sanyal, op. cit.

[110] Cf., for example, FR, UP, second half of September 1930, Home Poll F.N. 18/x/1930; FR, UP and Punjab, second half of October 1930, Home Poll F.N. 18/x/1930; FR, UP, first and second half of November, and FR, Bihar, Orissa and Punjab, second half of November 1930, Home Poll F.N. 18/xii/1930.

[111] C. Baker "Non-Cooperation in South India", in C. Baker and D. Washbrook, *South India: Political Institutions and Political Change, 1880–1940* (Macmillan, 1975), pp. 99–103.

[112] Report of Congress activities in Berar Province, 9 November 1930, AICC Files, G/84/1930.

the Gonds of the Central Provinces, the Kolis of the Ghat regions of Maharashtra, the Santals of Bihar, the tribals of North Kamrup in Assam, and the hill people of Kangra in Punjab.[113] There is rich material for the social historian here, but Indian historiography still awaits its E.P. Thompson.[114] The image of Gandhi and the Congress certainly took on strange colours as it filtered down into the depths of rural India, as when the Santals of Chota Nagpur took to illegal distillation on a large scale under the banner of Gandhi.[115] Some day a fascinating study might he made of the various, and sometimes conflicting, images of Gandhi as adapted by vastly different strata of Indian society.[116]

From business magnates through the urban lower middle class down to peasants and even tribals – the rich spectrum of Civil Disobedience seems to lack just one colour: the red of the industrial proletariat. Otherwise alarmist official reports from Bombay drew some comfort from this fact: "The most satisfactory feature of the situation in Bombay City is that at present the mill population appears to be quite unaffected . . . the operatives have not forgotten the effects of the strikes of last year."[117] The once-mighty Girni Kamgar had split into pro- and anti-Congress factions, and was now "without influence and almost entirely without funds".[118] "Organised labour as a whole

---

[113] Civil Disobedience in Central Provinces, Home Poll F.N. 253/1930; FR, Bombay, CP and Berar, first and second half of September, Punjab, first half of September 1930, Home Poll F.N. 18/x/1930; FR, Bombay, first and second half of October, CP and Berar, first half of October 1930, Home Poll F.N. 18/xi/1930; FR, Assam, second half of December 1930, Home Poll F.N. 18/xiii/1930.

[114] *Whigs and Hunters* (London, 1975), a brilliant study of conflicts over forest laws in eighteenth-century England.

[115] *Indian Annual Register* (1930), Chronicle of Events, 10 November 1930, FR, Bihar and Orissa, September-October 1930, Home Poll F.N. 18/x–18/xi/1930.

[116] A Bengali novel, Satinath Bhaduri's *Dhorai-Charitmanas*, gives a fascinating picture of the way in which a lowly north Bihar village group responded to Gandhi.

[117] H.G. Haig, 13 June 1930, op. cit.

[118] Petrie to Emerson, 20 August 1930, op. cit.

has not identified itself with the Civil Disobedience Movement", and "labour in Calcutta seems to have behaved very well", Irwin reported to Wedgwood Benn on 24 April 1930.[119] There was one massive but short-lived outburst at Sholapur in May following Gandhi's arrest,[120] and some Congress efforts to woo Bombay industrial labour in August and September,[121] but the overall contrast with the immediately preceding period of labour upsurge is glaring.

The passivity of industrial labour rendered infructuous Jawaharlal Nehru's Lahore Congress hopes of combining general strikes with no-tax campaigns at the climax of Civil Disobedience.[122] But it was not unwelcome, to put it mildly, to the bourgeois supporters of Congress and, we might guess, to the bulk of the nationalist leadership. And to Jawaharlal, too, in Naini jail, things seemed on the whole to be going wonderfully well. As he put it: "Events of the last four months in India have gladdened my heart and have made me prouder of Indian men, women and even children (!) than I had ever been . . . May I congratulate you on the new India you have created by your magic touch!"[123]

A terrible anticlimax, however, was waiting in the wings.

III

Released from jail for eight days in mid October 1930, the ever-sensitive Jawaharlal felt: "Civil disobedience activities, though still flourishing everywhere, were getting a bit stale . . . The cities and the middle classes were a bit tired of the hartals and processions. Obviously something was needed to liven things up, a fresh infusion

---

[119] Halifax Papers.

[120] Eighteen thousand mill-workers had gone on strike from 7 May, burnt police stations and court buildings, and sacked liquor shops; they remained sufficiently disciplined, however, to avoid drunkenness: Home Poll F.N. 512/1930.

[121] Petrie to Emerson, op. cit.; FR, Bombay, first half of September 1930, Home Poll F.N. 18/x/1930.

[122] *SW*, vol. IV, p. 197.

[123] Jawaharlal Nehru to Gandhi, 28 July 1930, ibid., p. 370.

of blood was necessary. Where could this come from except from the peasantry? – and the reserve stocks there were enormous."[124]

Numerous official reports from September 1930 onwards amply confirm Nehru's estimate. They regularly counterpose urban decline to rural dangers, and relate the former time and again to shifts in the attitudes of commercial groups which a few months back had given such formidable support to Civil Disobedience.

In early September, the inspector general of police of the United Provinces found "enthusiasm for the Congress in cities . . . subsiding considerably" everywhere except in Kanpur. Dealers had broken Congress-imposed seals on foreign cloth at Banaras, for example,[125] and similar reports flowed in during the succeeding months.[126] In Punjab, though the great Amritsar market remained generally closed till the end of the year, large amounts of foreign cloth were being secretly dispatched for sale to smaller towns like Fazilka.[127] In Bengal, urban picketing was causing increasingly less concern to officials from September onwards – as contrasted to terrorism and numerous instances of rural militancy – though there was some revival in December after the Congress patched up its factional quarrels.[128] "Some of the cloth dealers are likely to revolt against the Congress," the PCC reported from Berar in November 1930.[129] There were rumblings even inside the Civil Disobedience fort of Bombay. "Congress Solicitude for Bombay's Premier Industry/Sardar Allays Fears of Local Cotton Magnates," ran the headlines of the *Bombay Chronicle* on 26 July 1930. Thakurdas had protested against repeated hartals, and Patel had hastened to allay business fears.[130] Two months later, as the new trading season

---

[124] *An Autobiography*, p. 232.
[125] Note of 3 September 1930, Home Poll F.N. 249/1930.
[126] FR, UP, September–December 1930, Home Poll F.N. 18/x-/18/xiii/1930.
[127] FR, Punjab, second half of November and December 1930, Home Poll F.N. 18/xii-18/xiii/1930.
[128] FR, Bengal, September–December 1930, Home Poll F.N. l8/x-18/xiii/1930.
[129] AICC Files, G/84/1930.
[130] Thakurdas to Patel, 25 July 1930, Thakurdas Papers, F.N. 100/1930.

The Logic of Gandhian Nationalism 517

(mid-October) approached, an official report stated that "merchants with large stocks of last year's goods on their hands have begun to show signs of rebelling against the Congress mandate."[131] And if merchants were having second thoughts, the millowners, never very enthusiastic, were busy balancing the gains from Swadeshi demand against the losses caused by "frequent *hartals* which dislocated trade and industry, and created a feeling of considerable uncertainty."[132]

In the countryside, too, there were some signs that the more purely Gandhian forms of struggle based on relatively propertied peasant groups were losing their earlier potency in the face of ruthless British policies of distraint. In October 1930, the divisional commissioner on tour met groups of Kaira Patidars living in misery across the Baroda border, driven from their villages by police terror. Most were still "quite decided that they would not go back till their 'Sardar' (Vallabhbhai Patel) ordered them", but "there is no sign of insolence, much less of violence, in their attitudes. They seem disheartened."[133]

The very same Fortnightly Reports speak of the anti-grazing fee movement of the Kalis in the ghat areas of Nasik, Ahmednagar, and Poona districts in a startlingly different tone. "Filled with stories that the British Raj had been replaced by Gandhi Raj", the Kalis at Chankapur (Nasik district) on 20 October, "armed with spears, swords and other weapons . . . started to shout Congress slogans . . . refused to disperse [and] hurled down stones" in the face of police firing.[134]

There had been instances of local outbursts of popular militancy, going well beyond Gandhian orthodoxy, right from the beginning: most notably at Peshawar in late April–early May, where Garhwali Hindu soldiers refused to fire on Muslim crowds, and sent the chief commissioner into "a state of mental prostration".[135] But there are

[131] FR, Bombay, second half of September 1930, Home Poll F.N. 18/x/1930.
[132] Homi Mody, 19 March 1931, in *Report of Bombay Millowners' Association, 1930*, p. iii.
[133] FR, Bombay, second half of October and first half of November 1930, Home Poll F.N. 18/xi-18/xiii/1930.
[134] Ibid., second half of October 1930.
[135] Irwin to Wedgwood Benn, 1 May 1930, Halifax Papers.

some indications that such things were getting more common towards the end of 1930. British repression, plus the counting-house mentality of the bourgeoisie, was weakening the movement at certain levels, but at the same time new possibilities were opening up, as Civil Disobedience percolated down to ever-lower levels of Indian society, and as mass arrests repeatedly removed the established Gandhian leaders, giving more scope perhaps for less inhibited elements.

In Bengal, the Fortnightly Reports of December 1930 described terrorism as a growing danger, "in grim contrast to the waning activities of the Civil Disobedience movement."[136] Less well known, but perhaps more significant, was a change in the character of the movement in Midnapur, where the early picture of police beating up strictly non-violent satyagrahis and villagers is considerably modified by June. An official report speaks of a crowd of 6000 villagers encircling a police party at Chechuahat, with "conch shells and whistles blowing in all the surrounding villages and fields and men running towards us . . . with lathis": the police fired, it seems, in sheer panic, yet "they did not retreat . . . rather they began shouting and jeering."[137] The Midnapur district magistrate saw "little hope of any measure of peace until we have had a few more shootings."[138] "Large bodies of low-class people, including Santals" in Dinajpur district (north Bengal), "are indulging in lawless demonstrations and no chowkidari tax can be collected," says another report, of October 1930.[139]

Similar instances can be found in a number of other provinces. Tribal unrest became quite formidable in the Central Provinces, where

[136] Writers Building itself had been raided by three armed young men on 8 December, while several Armoury Raid leaders were still working underground in Chittagong villages, where it was almost impossible to get any information about them from the people: FR, Bengal, December 1930, Home Poll F.N. 18/xiii/1930.

[137] Chief Secretary, Government of Bengal, to Government of India, Home Poll No. PSD, 4030 of 18 June 1930, Home Poll F.N. 248/1930.

[138] Memorandum No. 537C of 13 June 1930 from Midnapur District Magistrate, J. Peddie, enclosed in Government of Bengal Poll No. 430 PSD 4302 of 25 June 1930, ibid. It is not entirely unpleasant to recall that Peddie was called by revolutionaries not long afterwards. I owe these Midnapur references to Tanika Sarkar.

[139] FR, Bengal, second half of October 1930, Home Poll F.N. 18/xi/1930.

The Logic of Gandhian Nationalism

the Gonds repeatedly attacked police parties.[140] We hear of some tribal leaders, too: Ganjan Korku of the Gonds, Bonga Manjhi, and Somra Manjhi of the Chota Nagpur Santals.[141] In December 1930, an anti-*chowkidari* tax demonstration at Bihore (Saran district in north Bihar) defied twenty-seven rounds of buckshot, and next month an Independence Day crowd at Begusarai (Monghyr district) swollen with large numbers of villagers, chased the sub-divisional officer into a ditch before being dispersed by 146 rounds of firing.[142]

The province that was causing the greatest anxiety to the government, however, was UP, where a section of the Congress had been pressing for a no-rent campaign almost from the beginning. A Rae Bareli activist is said to have written to Jawaharlal Nehru in the early days of Civil Disobedience "that breaches in the Salt Act would lead to nothing in themselves and must be regarded merely as a preparation for a no-rent campaign."[143] In a powerful speech to peasants in the same district in February 1930, Jawaharlal had described the zamindar community as "quite superfluous" and he had pressed the UPCC for an economic programme including removal of landed intermediaries and annulment of rural debt.[144] During his brief spell of liberty in October, he was able to persuade the provincial executive to sanction a no-tax campaign. It was to "apply to zamindars as well as tenants, to avoid the class issue if possible . . . The average zamindar would probably pay up the revenue demanded from him by the Government, but that would be his fault"; the no-rent movement could still go

---

[140] Chief Secretary, Central Provinces, to Government of India (Home), 1434/II of 25 August, 544/1 of 2 September, CS 218 of 29 September, D7665/30 of 12 October 1930; CP Government Press Communique of 30 August 1930, Home Poll F.N. 253/1930.

[141] Ibid., FR, Bihar and Orissa, second half of September 1930, Home Poll F.N. 18/x/1930.

[142] FR, Bihar and Orissa, second half of December 1930, Home Poll F.N. 18/xiii/1930, Communique of Bihar and Orissa Government, 6 February 1931, Home Poll F.N. 252/i/1931.

[143] Intercepted letter, mentioned in D.O. No. 90P, 21 April 1930, from UP Civil Secretariat to the Commissioner, Northern India Salt Revenue, Home Poll F.N. 249/1930.

[144] Speech at Tangan, 5 February 1930; resolution moved by Nehru, 26 February 1930, *SW*, vol. IV, pp. 250, 255–6.

ahead.[145] Nehru's activities in connection with a kisan conference at Allahabad led to his prompt rearrest.[146] Official reports repeatedly expressed alarm about the possibilities of a no-rent campaign in UP, with its memories, of peasant upheaval in the early 1920s,[147] and the current slump in agricultural prices.[148] Trends towards no-rent were being reported also from Midnapur, while in December 1930 attempts were being made in parts of Maharashtra "to influence the Khots not to pay their revenue by inducing their tenants to withhold their rent . . ."[149]

Such signs of militancy in the countryside could not have appeared particularly attractive to businessmen often not unconnected with land. Nor was potential radicalism entirely a rural phenomenon. Nehru has testified to the amazing popularity of Bhagat Singh in North Indian towns,[150] and here was a movement of petty bourgeois urban youth which combined militant nationalism with a groping towards socialist ideology, and which included in its ranks a future general secretary of the Communist Party of India.[151] While industrial labour was still generally quiet, officials expressed alarm over the possible consequences of unemployment in Bombay caused by the general depression aggravated by political disturbances.[152] There

[145] *An Autobiography*, p. 232.

[146] Ibid., pp. 232–6.

[147] S. Gopal, *Jawaharlal Nehru: A Biography, Volume I, 1889–1947* (Delhi: Oxford University Press, 1976), chapter IV, based mainly on the researches of Majid Siddiqi.

[148] FR, UP, second half of September, October, November, and December 1930, Home Poll F.N. 18/x-18/xiii/1930.

[149] FR, Bengal, first half of September 1930; FR, Bombay, first half of December 1930, Home Poll F.N. 18/x-18/xiii/1930.

[150] ". . . each town and village of the Punjab and to a lesser extent in the rest of northern India resounded with his name. Innumerable songs grew up about him, and the popularity that the man achieved was something amazing": *An Autobiography*, pp. 176–7.

[151] Ajoy Ghosh, op. cit.; for the Hindustan Socialist Republican Association, see Bipan Chandra, "The Ideological Development of the Revolutionary Terrorists in Northern India in the 1920s", in B.R. Nanda, ed., *Socialism in India* (Delhi, 1972).

[152] Petrie to Emerson, 20 August 1930, Home Poll F.N. 504/1930.

The Logic of Gandhian Nationalism 521

were indications also that lower-level Congress cadres thrust into prominence by the arrests of their leaders were at times developing attitudes significantly different from their chiefs'. Ambalal Sarabhai as early as June 1930 was complaining bitterly to Birla about the "rotten mentality of many of Gandhiji's followers" who object to the "payment of a few pies more to millowners". "I am sure Gandhiji would have done differently if he were out of jail."[153] Thakurdas retained in his papers a cyclostyled bulletin of the Bombay City Congress dated 4 November 1930. Movingly entitled "Freedom Be Thou My Soul, Sedition Be My Song", this included a violent attack on him for giving a farewell dinner to the police commissioner: "We have always known Sir Purshottamdas as a consistent supporter of the Government who also has the cleverness to create an impression among the public that he is on their side."[154] Similar cyclostyled sheets two years later were to attack Birla, too.[155]

It was in this situation that the leaders of the Indian bourgeoisie began sending out alarm signals to the Congress high command, and pressures mounted for a compromise.

IV

As early as June 1930 Thakurdas had expressed his nervousness "about a crop of insolvencies and consequent disaster",[156] and had conveyed his alarm to Motilal Nehru.[157] Homi Mody, predictably, went a step further, two months later, and prepared a draft calling for "a revision of the present policy, such as would enable trade and industry to recover" – otherwise there was a danger of "a disaster from which Bombay may not recover for a decade."[158] Thakurdas,

---

[153] Ambalal Sarabhai to G.D. Birla, 4 June 1930, Thakurdas Papers, F.N. 100/1930.
[154] Bombay Congress Bulletin No. 167, 4 November 1930, ibid., F.N. 101.
[155] Bombay Congress Bulletin No. II, 247, 17 October 1932, ibid.
[156] Thakurdas to Rangaswami Iyengar (Editor, *The Hindu*), 4 June 1930, ibid., F.N. 91.
[157] Thakurdas to Motilal Nehru, 4 June 1930, ibid.
[158] Typed draft, undated, but probably sometime in August, as Thakurdas commented on it in a letter to Mody on 22 August 1930, ibid., F.N. 100/1930.

however, at this point refused to go along with him, "as I fear that the Government have again started their repressive policy and whatever you or I may say is bound to unnecessarily irritate the people."[159] Birla, it is interesting to note, supported Gandhi's stand at Yeravda.[160] The pressures for compromise in August 1930 thus still did not include the decisive section of the bourgeoisie. That supreme tactician also made the accurate prediction that the government would not accept even minimum Congress demands till the Round Table Conference had been held.[161]

During the succeeding months, however, bourgeois pressures for a settlement steadily intensified. The crucial factors here were business difficulties, combined with a growing pessimism about Civil Disobedience – justified from a bourgeois point of view, since the ways in which the movement could still have gone ahead would not have been very comfortable for it. Thakurdas approached Motilal again (via Lalji Naranji) on 22 September, and warned him that "the capacity of the commercial community for endurance" was reaching its limits. "We are anxious to prevent the Congress from having a setback . . ."[162] Even more significant was a letter of Thakurdas to Deviprasad Khaitan of Calcutta dated 8 October, marked "absolutely confidential" but "of course" to be shown to "Ghanshyamdasji": "My impression gathered on the journey is that at Delhi, Amritsar and Cawnpore etc. the piecegoods importer and dealer is getting tired of picketing and of the loss involved on the dealer of imported cloth . . . But for Bombay the rest of India is well under control and will on the whole die out before long . . . I fear that the Congress will have a setback and with it the country will suffer heavily."[163]

---

[159] Ibid.
[160] "I do not think that I can altogether blame Gandhiji. At first sight people may think Gandhiji to be very unreasonable, but stripped of all verbiage, his demand amounts to nothing else but Dominion Status. The Government by giving assurances to him could have easily won him over": Birla to Thakurdas, 6 September 1930, ibid., F.N. 104/1930.
[161] Birla to Thakurdas, 20 September 1930, ibid.
[162] Thakurdas to Motilal Nehru, via Lalji Naranji, 22 September 1930, ibid.
[163] Thakurdas to Deviprasad Khaitan, 8 October 1930, ibid. F.N. 99/1930.

The Logic of Gandhian Nationalism   523

The tone is very significant: what is involved evidently is not a sellout but a compromise, not compradorism but the dual policy of a highly intelligent bourgeoisie. A few days after the Delhi Pact, a business delegation under Walchand Hirachand met Gandhi to ask for clarification regarding the boycott restriction clause in the agreement, and urged him to demand "protection for Indian industries at the next Conference".[164] The bourgeoisie was calling for a retreat, but it was also careful that this should not go too far.

By January or early February 1931, developments in London were providing the occasion for a further stepping up of pressures for a settlement. More important perhaps than the fairly minimal political concessions – a half-promise of responsible government at the centre, balanced by "reservations and safeguards" and a federal structure weighted in favour of princes[165] – was the understanding which the business delegates at the Round Table Conference headed by Mody seem to have reached with their British counterparts through private discussions.[166] A surcharge of 5 per cent was imposed on cotton piecegoods imports in February 1931, despite protests from depression-affected Lancashire and much cabinet opposition.[167] By 28 January an official estimate of the political situation was mentioning as a major factor in favour of a settlement (the prospects of which were stated to be "by no means hopeless") the "increasing unwillingness on the part of the commercial community to contribute towards the movement."[168] Ten days later, the Bombay governor's

---

[164] Gandhi's interview with the Indian Merchants' Chamber deputation, Bombay, 17 March 1931, *CW*, vol. XLV, p. 303.

[165] Ramsay MacDonald's statement at the Round Table Conference, 19 January 1931, ibid., Appendix I.

[166] Wedgwood Benn informed Irwin on 19 January 1931 that Reading had "got a form of words agreed between Mody and Sir Hubert Carr safeguarding the European trade interests. Mody told me that, on the whole, he was satisfied with this and thought he could persuade the Indian merchants to the same effect ... Hubert Carr rather warmly repudiated a suggestion that he had anything to do with Inchcape or his interests": Halifax Papers.

[167] Wedgwood Benn to Irwin, 11 February 1931, Halifax Papers; Moore, op. cit., pp. 211–13.

[168] Government of India, Home Department, Express Letter to all Local

telegram to the viceroy stated that "there are clear indications that a number of Gandhi's followers, particularly among mercantile community, are contemplating a breach with him unless he adopts reasonable attitude."[169]

The relevance of all this becomes clear if we consider now the evolution of Gandhi's views regarding a possible settlement. The *Collected Works* permit an almost day-to-day study of Gandhi's recorded opinions, and the impression they convey is that of a really startling change, sometime in the middle of February 1931.

In the round of discussions set off by the mediation bid of Sapru and Jayakar (July–August 1930), Gandhi had declared: "Jawaharlal's must be the final voice . . . I should have no hesitation in supporting any stronger position up to the letter of the Lahore resolution."[170] He did wobble a bit in his initial note to the Nehrus via Sapru (23 July), which admitted a possible discussion of transitional "safeguards" at the Round Table Conference,[171] but the 15 August joint letter from Yeravda was extremely firm in its unequivocal demands for the right of sessions, a "complete national government" with control over defence and finance, and an "independent tribunal" to settle British financial claims.[172]

Gandhi's initial stand after his release on 26 January was also quite uncompromising. Though he had agreed not to take a final decision before talks with Sapru and other Indian delegates returning from the Round Table Conference,[173] he still declared to the Working Committee on 31 January that there was no question of giving up "even one of the demands put forward in the negotiations carried on

---

Governments, No. D 797-31-Poll of 28 January 1931, Home Poll F.N. 5/45/1931.

[169] Sykes to Irwin, telegram, 7 February 1931, F.H. Sykes Collection, MSS Eur F. 150/3(a).

[170] Gandhi to Motilal Nehru, 23 July 1930, *CW*, vol. XLIV, p. 44.

[171] Ibid., p. 42. Jawaharlal found "Bapu's note disappointing . . . I wish we had definitely stopped all talk of peace": Prison Diary, 27–28 July 1930, *SW*, vol. IV, p. 373.

[172] *CW*, vol. XLIV, p. 83.

[173] 26 January 1931 *CW*, vol. XIV, p. 125.

from Yeravda."[174] In interviews with the *Times of India* and Reuters, Gandhi denounced the idea of any agreement behind the backs of the masses.[175] Right up to 11 February, in numerous private letters (and not just in public statements possibly made with a bargaining intention) he repeatedly expressed deep pessimism concerning the prospect of any agreement,[176] and pointed to the constantly growing tally of police atrocities even while the leaders were being released.[177]

Yet from 14 February (the letter to Irwin seeking an interview) began a retreat which at times became very nearly a rout. In talks with the viceroy, surprisingly little disagreement seems to have occurred over the scope of the next Round Table Conference with Congress participation. Irwin at the first meeting insisted on three "lynchpins . . . Federation; Indian responsibility; reservations and safeguards."[178] By 27 February Gandhi had accepted all this, and, if the viceroy is to be believed, had even admitted that the raising of the "academic" issue of session at the Conference would serve little purpose.[179] Clause 2 of the Delhi Pact of 5 March, which gave Nehru such "a tremendous shock", firmly pegged down the scope of future discussions to the scheme outlined at the first RTC session, and defined "reservations and safeguards" to cover "such matters as, for instance, defence; external affairs; the position of minorities; the financial credit of India, and the discharge of obligations."[180] The rider that such safeguards were to be "in the interests of India" meant precious little, and might even be termed hypocritical, as the secretary

---

[174] Ibid., p. 133.

[175] 28 January and 1 February 1931, ibid., pp. 128, 138.

[176] "Whatever settlement is reached, I have little hope that any will be reached . . .": Gandhi to Chhaganlal Joshi, 11 February 1931. A similar mood is expressed in his letters to Narandas Gandhi (2 and 10 February), V.S. Srinivasa Sastri (7 February), T. Rangachari (8 February), and Gangadharrao Deshpande (10 February), ibid., pp. 147, 160, 163, 169–70, 173.

[177] In particular the lathi-charge on women of Borsad in Gujarat (21 January) and the Begusarai firing in Bihar (26 January): Gandhi to Irwin, 1 February 1931, ibid., pp. 136–8.

[178] Interview with Viceroy, 17 February 1931 (Irwin's version), ibid., p. 185.

[179] Interview with Viceroy, 27 February 1931 (Irwin's version), ibid., p. 234.

[180] *An Autobiography*, p. 257.

of state pointed out in a telegram to Irwin.[181] The contrast to the Yeravda conditions could not have been more blatant.

Gandhi did put up a tougher fight over the immediate *quid pro quos* for a withdrawal of Civil Disobedience, and there were strenuous negotiations concerning picketing, salt, the demand for an enquiry into police excesses, and the return of confiscated lands in Gujarat. Yet here too in the end the nationalist gains were minimal. The concession regarding salt was a token one, while the viceroy was frankly exultant about Clause 7 concerning peaceful and non-political Swadeshi propaganda and picketing.[182] As for Clause 8 with its reference to Gandhi's demand for enquiry into police atrocities, Irwin explained to Wedgwood Benn that the "substantial point appears to be that demand is definitely dropped".[183] Gandhi fought longest over the issue of confiscated lands,[184] but even here eventually properties already sold to third parties were not restored. It is interesting, by the way, that the secretary of state at first objected to every one of these admittedly very minor concessions; so much for Labour Indophilism.[185]

What had happened after 11 February, and particularly perhaps on the two days between 11 and 14 February (since to argue that

---

[181] "It cannot be contended that proposed safeguards are solely in interests of India": Wedgwood Benn to Irwin, No. 801, 4 March 1931, Home Poll F.N. 5/45/1931.

[182] "Emerson had got Mr Gandhi hitched to the abandonment of the boycott as a political weapon and an assurance of complete freedom for cloth merchants to do what they liked. These seem pretty substantial gains . . . I have very little doubt that, if you can get rid of the political-weapon drive of it, and have it purely as an economic and social thing, it will be dead in three weeks": Irwin memorandum after interview of 1 March 1931, *CW*, vol. XLV, p. 241.

[183] Irwin's telegram to Wedgwood Benn, No. 662S, 5 March 1931, Home Poll F.N. 5/45/1931.

[184] Gandhi to Irwin, 5 March 1931, *CW*, vol. XLV, p. 245.

[185] Telegram No. 801, op. cit. For an opposite view arguing that the Labour Government of 1929–31 "tried hard, within the limits of its minority position, to undo some of the damage done to Indo-British relations", see P.S. Gupta, *Imperialism and the British Labour Movement 1914–1964* (London, 1975), p. 101.

Gandhi was simply converted by Irwin's alleged charm and courtesy would be to insult the stature and wisdom of an undoubtedly great political leader)? No record apparently survives of the Working Committee proceedings of 13 February. It had been preceded, as is well known, by a meeting of Gandhi with the Liberal leaders back from London, Sapru, Jayakar, and Srinivasa Sastri, and no doubt Gandhi was referring primarily to them when in his letter to Irwin of 14 February he mentioned "suggestions from friends whose advice I value that I should seek an interview with you . . . I can no longer resist this advice."[186] But these "professional mediators" had been pleading for a settlement almost from the beginning – why did their appeals, firmly rejected at Yeravda, command so much greater weight now?[187] No doubt they presented to Gandhi a rosy picture of the Round Table Conference, but the latter had been extremely sceptical just a few days back.[188] Jayakar, Sastri, and particularly Sapru were respected as individuals, but a British visitor in November 1930 had estimated the total political support of these Liberals as no more than "a few hundred".[189]

Indications are not wanting, however, of the presence of a much stronger force. There is, for instance, Gandhi's cryptic telegram to Purshottamdas Thakurdas, dated 9 February: "Your letter, Thanks, Earlier you come better."[190] On the very same day, Irwin was writing a really fascinating letter to Wedgwood Benn, which deserves quotation *in extenso*:

> Purshottamdas came to see me yesterday on return from his visit to Bombay. The original idea had been that Gandhi should have been in Bombay to meet Sapru and the men of commerce. The intention of the latter had been to put all the pressure on him that they could, and thus assist the efforts of Sapru and Co. . . . (Gandhi had to cancel the

[186] Gandhi to Irwin, 14 February 1931, *CW*, vol. XLV, pp. 175–6.
[187] S. Gopal's very apt phrase, op. cit., p. 144.
[188] "I do not believe that Macdonald's statement grants us anything": 31 January 1931, *CW*, vol. XLV, p. 134.
[189] H.N. Brailsford to Wedgwood Benn, Delhi, 2 November 1930, enclosed in Wedgwood Benn to Irwin, 17 November 1930, Halifax Papers.
[190] *CW*, vol. XLV, p. 165.

Bombay trip due to Motilal Nehru's fatal illness) . . . Purshottamdas told me however that he was pleased with the trend of opinion in commercial circles and thinks that they now definitely want to find ways of peace. This view is also supported by Sykes. Purshottamdas will probably go to see Gandhi at Allahabad in order to try to put commercial pressure on him . . .[191]

Thakurdas incidentally was in Delhi during at least part of the Gandhi–Irwin talks and contributed to the resolving of the final hitch over the Gujarat confiscations issue on 4 March.[192] And while Birla himself seems to have remained in the background during these crucial days, his adjutant D.P. Khaitan in his presidential speech to the Indian Chamber of Commerce declared: "it may not be amiss to suggest to Mahatma Gandhi and the Congress that the time has come when they should explore the possibilities of an honourable settlement. The Indian Mercantile Community would invite them to share its belief that the Premier's statement does not preclude the possibility of the suggested modifications . . . We all want peace."[193] The date is significant: 11 February.

In the face of all this evidence, it is surely not going beyond the bounds of historical inference to suggest that business pressures played a crucial role in bringing about a change in Gandhi's political stance in mid February 1931.

V

Two questions remain to be answered: why Gandhi bowed to this pressure, and how he could carry his ranks with him.

To argue, on the basis of a single decision, that Gandhi was no more than a bourgeois mascot or agent, would be quite unhistorical. For that one would have to prove, at the very least, the existence of a large number of similar coincidences of views. Gandhi obviously

---

[191] Irwin to Wedgwood Benn, 9 February 1931, Halifax Papers.
[192] Irwin's memorandum, *CW*, vol. XLV, p. 247.
[193] D.P. Khaitan's presidential address to the Indian Chamber of Commerce, Calcutta, 11 February 1931, *Indian Chamber of Commerce, Annual Report for 1930* (Calcutta, 1931), p. xliii.

The Logic of Gandhian Nationalism 529

was a much more complex figure with very diverse appeals, and his ideology was far less directly or obviously bourgeois than that of Moderates like Pherozeshah Mehta or Dinshaw Wacha or of Liberals like M.R. Jayakar. A man who could persuade capitalists to donate to a khadi programme, or who in the end was to sacrifice his life fighting against a Hindu communalism particularly strong among traders, was hardly a puppet. What we do have, however, is an occasional significant coincidence of subjective attitudes and inhibitions with bourgeois interests.

What Gandhi had felt about developments in the movement outside his prison walls is difficult to assess, since apart from the Yeravda negotiations, his jail correspondence is singularly silent on political matters. This seems to have been a point of principle with him,[194] and he kept himself busy with spinning, reading the Gita and Tulsidas, and writing innumerable letters to his disciples on subjects often extremely intimate but always far removed from Civil Disobedience.[195]

But Gandhi's general views on no-rent movements or labour strikes outside the Ahmedabad pattern – the two forms through which, as we have seen, Civil Disobedience could have gone ahead – are of course no secret. Way back in May 1921, Gandhi had repudiated no-rent moves,[196] and ten years later, on the day after the Delhi Pact, he gave an assurance to the UP Zamindars' Association: "We do not want that the tenants should stand against the zamindars . . . We assure the zamindars that their rights would be given due consideration in a swaraj constitution. I appeal to them to be generous to the Congress."[197] And again, in his 24 May 1931 "manifesto" to the UP

---

[194] "Being temperamentally so built, I cannot give a decisive opinion on matters happening outside the prison walls": Gandhi to Motilal Nehru, 23 July 1930, *CW*, vol. XLIV, p. 44.

[195] A not entirely unfair sample: "I cannot think of one simple remedy which will help Madhu and all others who suffer from constipation": Gandhi to Gangabehn Vaidya, 22 December 1930, *CW*, vol. XLV, p. 16.

[196] *Young India*, 18 May 1921, quoted in S. Gopal, op. cit., pp. 56–7.

[197] Interview with S. Hasan Ali Khan of UP Zamindars' Association, 6 March 1931, *CW*, vol. XLV, p. 262.

kisans he wrote: "We aim not at destruction of the zamindars and taluqdars, nor of their property. We only aim at its lawful use."[198]

During the Bombay strike of 1925, Gandhi is said to have told Ahmedabad workers that "faithful servants serve their masters even without pay".[199] He reiterated his opposition to "class war" in another speech at Ahmedabad on 11 March 1931, arguing further that the legitimate labour demand for "the necessaries of life . . . does not mean that you should have palaces like theirs."[200] One is tempted to suggest, as Subhas Bose did in his *Indian Struggle* later on, that Gandhi had refused to sanction any all-out movement in 1928–9 at least partly because of the labour militancy of those years.[201] Perhaps he also waited for the collapse of the GIP strike before launching the salt satyagraha. Thus, Gandhi in 1930 was prepared to lead only certain kinds of movements and not others. In the cross-pressures to which he must have been subjected immediately after his release, therefore, Jawaharlal's suggestions for overcoming "the staleness in the towns by stirring up the rural areas" never had any real chance of being accepted.[202] Such things were all too likely to go against the logic of non-violence and trusteeship as Gandhi conceived them. But how can we explain the fact that "the huge organisation (Congress) accepted in practice the new role, though many criticised it."[203] The Karachi Congress submitted to Gandhi as usual despite the additional provocation of the execution of Bhagat Singh. The answer seems to lie in the lack of any alternative leadership which could have tried to convert the scattered potentially radical manifestations into a coherent movement. In its absence, rural militancy remained either entirely spontaneous and uncoordinated, or under the leadership of village Gandhians with a basically limited outlook.

---

[198] Quoted in Jagdish Prasad, UP Chief Secretary, to Emerson, 16 July 1931, Home Poll F.N. 33/24/1931.

[199] *Masses of India*, November 1925; G. Adhikari, op. cit., p. 540.

[200] *CW*, vol. XLV, 280.

[201] Subhas Chandra Bose, *The Indian Struggle* (London, 1934; Calcutta, 1964), p. 148.

[202] S. Gopal, op. cit., p. 150.

[203] *An Autobiography*, p. 263.

The Logic of Gandhian Nationalism

During the late 1920s, the Left had been rapidly gaining ground among urban workers and youth, with Communist nuclei functioning through the peasants' and workers' parties. A unity-cum-struggle policy had been followed vis-à-vis the Congress, with the strategic objective remaining an anti-imperialist united front. As the Executive Committee of the Bengal Peasants' and Workers' Party had put it in its report for 1927–8, care should be taken not to oppose the Congress except on well-defined issues, "or we shall enable our opponents to claim that we are anti-Congress or even anti-national and that we stand merely for the sectional claims of labour".[204] The sharp "Left" turn brought about at the Sixth Comintern Congress (1928) in the wake of the Chinese debacle and in the context of Stalin's campaign against Bukharin's "Right Opposition" changed all that with disastrous consequences for Germany,[205] and the loss of a great opportunity in India. The Communists, already greatly weakened by the Meerut arrests, kept aloof from Civil Disobedience, spent most of their energies quarrelling among themselves,[206] and even concentrated their fire on Left-leaning nationalists like Nehru who was expelled from the League Against Imperialism in April 1930.[207] And even in the earlier period, a basic weakness had been the relative neglect of the countryside – the Bengal unit, for instance, could claim some activity only in the Tangail region.[208]

Among top Congress leaders with some Left leanings or reputations, Subhas Bose was already consistently critical of Gandhi (who even described him as his "opponent" in a conversation with

---

[204] Meerut Conspiracy Files, Sl. 459, p. 52. I owe this reference to Tanika Sarkar.

[205] For the best contemporary analysis of the responsibility of the Comintern for the victory of Hitler, see Trotsky's articles, recently reprinted as *The Struggle Against Fascism in Germany* (Pelican, 1975).

[206] See, for example, Ranen Sen, "Communist Movement in Bengal in the Early Thirties", *Marxist Miscellany*, no. 6 (New Delhi, January 1975).

[207] Nehru wrote to V. Chattopadhyay and Willi Munzenberg, more in sorrow than in anger, on 30 January 1930: "It is curious that you should have chosen a moment to attack us when the Congress is more advanced in its views, both political and social, than it has ever been before": *SW*, vol. IV, p. 237.

[208] Meerut Conspiracy Files, op. cit.

Irwin[209]) but unfortunately showed much less consistency in less personal matters. Though he later attacked Gandhi's attitudes towards labour, his own standpoint had not been all that different till 1929.[210] A request for financial support to jute workers on strike at Bauria, sixteen miles from Howrah, had to be relayed to him via Jawaharlal Nehru.[211] The Bengal Provincial Congress Committee, controlled by his faction in 1930, concentrated mainly on the urban boycott, and Midnapur rural leaders frequently complained of being neglected.[212] Bose's Lahore Congress speech had been a fiery one, calling for "non-payment of taxes campaign and general strikes wherever and whenever possible" and even for "establishing a parallel Government in India".[213] In practice Bose remained deeply involved in Calcutta Corporation politics throughout 1930, and, elected Mayor in September 1930, pleasantly surprised Wedgwood Benn by a "very civil" address.[214]

Jawaharlal Nehru was far more consistent at the intellectual level – unfortunately, all too often at that level alone. In jail again from October, he worked out a fairly radical "agrarian programme for the Congress", anticipated much of the Left-nationalist strategy of the mid 1930s by suggesting a Constituent Assembly as the central political slogan,[215] and then surrendered to Gandhi again. The breach with the Communist Left must have contributed to this vacillation. After a Congress–Communist clash in Bombay on 26 January 1930, Nehru had declared: "I honour and respect the red flag, because it represents the blood and suffering of the workers . . . There is, and should be, no rivalry between our national tri-colour flag and the workers' red flag."[216]

[209] Interview with Irwin, Gandhi's version (Mahadev Desai's manuscript diary), 18 February 1931, *CW*, vol. XLV, p. 200.
[210] I owe this point to Tanika Sarkar.
[211] Nehru to Subhas Bose, 24 January 1929, *SW*, vol. IV, p. 29.
[212] Civil Disobedience at Tamluk, AICC Files, G/86/1930.
[213] *Report of the Indian National Congress*, 44th Session, Lahore, 1929, p. 93.
[214] He was also praised by the Governor of Bengal. "Jackson told me that Bose had always been personally well-disposed towards him": Wedgwood Benn to Irwin, 26 September 1930, Halifax Papers.
[215] Notes made in Naini prison, December 1930, *SW*, vol. IV, pp. 437–51.
[216] Statement of 28 January 1930, ibid., p. 232.

The Logic of Gandhian Nationalism 533

But evidently this was not a hope which could be realized in 1930–1. Nehru, in addition, was extremely diffident about his organisational abilities: "I have not the politicians' flair for forming groups and parties," he had told Gandhi in July 1929.[217] Above all, he was acutely aware, that despite all his popularity, he lacked Gandhi's empathy with the peasantry and felt himself to be too much of an anglicised intellectual to understand the peasant outlook. It is hardly accidental that in the *Autobiography* a discussion of the Delhi Pact is immediately followed by a long appreciation of Gandhi as representing "the peasant masses of India".[218]

A similar sense of helplessness is evident in the speeches of the delegates who did oppose the Gandhi–Irwin Pact at the Karachi Congress (March 1931): Jamnadas Mehta, Swami Govindanand, and, most notable of all, Yusuf Meherali. The future Socialist leader bitterly attacked the Pact as a "great triumph of British diplomacy" and "a great national mistake", denounced unequivocally "the politics of compromise" and of "change of heart", and made a bitter reference "to the Birlas, Purshottamdas Thakurdass, Walchand Hirachands, Huseinbhai Laljis, who are now out and busy in making efforts to obtain the fruits of the suffering and sacrifices of others." Yet his concluding note is strangely passive: as the Round Table negotiations were bound to fail, Gandhi would again have to give the call to struggle, and then the radicals would get their chance. "We patiently await the call to fight. Inquilab Zindabad."[219]

Jawaharlal, as is well known, did not even go that far. Made acutely unhappy by the Delhi Pact, he yet agreed, after a bit of "wobbling" and some sleepless nights,[220] to move the resolution endorsing it at the Karachi Congress. Personal factors no doubt played some part here – the death of Motilal perhaps enhancing the psychological need for a substitute father-figure in Gandhi. Yet the implications of

---

[217] He mentioned in the connection the "hopeless failure" of the Independence for India League, Nehru to Gandhi, 13 July 1929, ibid., p. 156.

[218] *An Autobiography*, pp. 253–6.

[219] *Report of the Indian Notional Congress*, 45th Session, Karachi, 1931, pp. 67–80.

[220] *An Autobiography*, p. 261.

this surrender, destined to have so many counterparts in the years to come, far transcend the purely personal.

The significance of Civil Disobedience as compared to Non-Cooperation, it has been argued recently in a study of the United Provinces, lay both in the extension of mass participation in the countryside and the tighter organisational hold over it of the Congress high command.[221] We have seen that at crucial points this fitted in perfectly with the interests of a bourgeoisie, which needed to utilise mass discontent and yet wanted to keep it within bounds. The bourgeoisie had established a working understanding with the highly complex phenomenon of Gandhism, and would be able to use it till the need for that disappeared on the eve of the transfer of power. Helped on by the mistakes and weaknesses of the Left, it was asserting its leading role through a process of "transformismo" akin to that analysed by Gramsci for post-1848 Italy, bringing about "the gradual but continuous absorption . . . of the active elements produced by allied groups – and even of those which came from antagonistic groups and seemed irreconcilably hostile."[222] As in nineteenth-century Italy, again, this was only a relatively leading position, not a classic "hegemony" conducive to a total transformation of society.

Such a transformation – the working out of the full logic of a consistent anti-imperialist and anti-feudal revolution, something like an Indian counterpart of 1789, in other words – remained beyond the capacity of our colonial bourgeoisie, with its continued relative dependence on foreign capital, its links with pre-capitalist production relations in agriculture, and its fear of organised labour. A Gramscian analysis would also emphasise the lack of cultural hegemony, the absence of any permeation of modern bourgeois values throughout society. Far from that happening, as is well known, modernism in our country was and is largely confined to a colonial middle class with little roots in production, while the mental world of the bulk

---

[221] Gyanendra Pandey's forthcoming work on Civil Disobedience in the United Provinces.

[222] Antonio Gramsci, *Notes on Italian History: Selections from Prison Notebooks*, ed. Q. Hoare and N. Smith (New York, 1971), p. 59.

of Indian traders and industrialists – the "modest egoism" of the pre-1848 German burgher estate described by Marx – remained bound to pre-modern caste and religious loyalties. Men like Birla or Thakurdass were at best capable of writing,[223] not of the world-transforming revolutionary zeal of the French bourgeoisie of 1789.

At the same time, unlike China or Vietnam, there was no development in course of the national movement of an alternative, more radical leadership capable of mobilising the peasant masses and also, perhaps, of utilising the populist elements in Gandhism, as Mao used the heritage of Sun Yat-sen. The result was a curious stalemate: an independence which was also a deferment of so many of the more generous hopes aroused by the struggle for freedom.

---

[223] Karl Marx, Introduction to *Towards a Critique of Hegel's Philosophy of Right* (1844), in David Mc-Lellan, ed., *Karl Marx: Early Texts* (Oxford, 1971), p. 126.

13

Popular Movements and National Leadership 1945–1947

THE LAST TWO YEARS OF British rule have been both well served and ill served by historians. Thanks to the *Transfer of Power* series edited by Mansergh, certain types of official documents are more easily available for the 1940s now than for any other period of Indian history, and a mass of historical literature exists on the tortuous negotiations between British, Congress, and League politicians which culminated in a freedom which was also a tragic Partition.[1] In very sharp contrast, there is hardly any systematic historical research so far except for a few useful accounts by

This was first presented at a seminar on Aspects of the Economy, Society and Politics in Modern India 1900–1950, at the Nehru Memorial Museum and Library, New Delhi, December 1980.

[1] The published first-hand sources include N. Mansergh, ed., *Transfer of Power*, vols VI–VIII (London, various dates); Wavell, *The Viceroy's Journal*, ed. Penderel Moon (Oxford, 1973); Durga Das" edition of "Sardar Patel's Correspondence" (Ahmedabad, 1971); and the contemporary writings of Gandhi and Nehru. Among the well-known secondary works may be mentioned V.P. Menon, *Transfer of Power in India* (London, 1957), and *Story of the Integration of Indian States* (Bombay, 1956): A. Campbell Johnson, *Mission with Mountbatten* (London, 1951); Penderel Moon, *Divide and Quit* (London, 1961); H.V. Hodson, *The Great Divide* (London, 1969); Maulana Azad, *India Wins Freedom* (Bombay, 1959): Pyarelal, *The Mahatma: The Last Phase*, 2 vols (Ahmedabad, 1956, 1958); C. Khaliquzzaman, *Pathway to Pakistan* (Lahore, 1961); S. Ghosh, *Gandhi's Emissary* (London, 1967), as well as Collins and Lapierre's journalistic bestseller, *Freedom at Midnight* (Delhi, 1976).

Popular Movements and National Leadership 537

participants on the sporadic, localised, but often extremely militant and united mass actions which constitute the second major strand of these years: the I.N.A. release movement and the R.I.N. Mutiny of 1945–6, the massive post-war strike wave which was at its height in 1946, in 1946–7 the Tebhaga upsurge in Bengal Punnapra-Vayalar in Travancore and the Telangana peasant armed revolt in Hyderabad.[2] The tendency has been to consider the first theme in isolation from the second: indeed it is fatally easy, given the abundance of materials, to get engrossed in the world of the Simla Conference, Cabinet Mission, Interim Government, and Mountbatten Award, and tacitly assume it to have been more or less self-contained. Gopal's *Jawaharlal Nehru* (vol. I) contains many details about agrarian movements in the United Provinces in the 1920s and early 1930s, but very little about the popular upsurges of 1945–7 – a shift of interest which may appear not unjustifiable, for Nehru and other top Congress leaders had now little direct connection with grassroots movements.

It is my central argument, however, that in this as well as in other periods of modern Indian history the decisions and actions of leaders, British or Indian, cannot really be understood without the counterpoint provided by pressures from below. Certain obvious world developments apart, it was popular action, above all, which made the continuance of British rule impossible. Fear of popular "excesses" made Congress leaders cling to the path of negotiation and compromise, and eventually even accept Partition as a necessary price, while the limits of popular anti-imperialist movements made

---

[2] Sunil Sen, *Agrarian Struggle in Bengal 1946–47* (New Delhi, 1972); P. Sundarayya, *Telangana People's Struggle and Its Lessons* (Calcutta, 1972). *The R.I.N. Strike* by a group of victimised ratings (New Delhi, 1954), and K.C. George, *Immortal Punnapra-Vayalar* (New Delhi, 1975), represent valuable accounts by leaders or participants; none of the authors, however, had the opportunity of consulting official archival sources. See also Gautam Chattopadhyay, "The Almost Revolution", in B. De, *et al.*, *Essays in Honour of S.C. Sarkar* (New Delhi, 1976); Ravi Narayan Reddi, *Heroic Telengana-Reminiscences and Experiences* (New Delhi, 1973); and D.N. Dhanagare, "Social Origins of Peasant Insurrection in Telengana", *Contributions to Indian Sociology*, 1974.

the truncated settlement of August 1947 unavoidable. Detailed studies of popular movements demand much more research, yet it is my contention that even the easily available sources (like the Mansergh volumes, or Wavell's journal) really contain abundant evidence to substantiate my thesis, and can be used to throw some new light on vital decision-making processes.

To radical-minded contemporaries in the late 1940s, this argument – together with its concomitant, a somewhat unflattering picture in the national leadership – would have appeared acceptable and even rather obvious. Today, due to a variety of reasons, it is in contrast a bit unfashionable in many quarters. What had been the standard Left critique of "bourgeois betrayal" has become discredited, and in part rightly so, by its own crudities,[3] as well as by the disasters brought about by bouts of ultra-Left "sectarianism".[4] The reaction against the debunking of the Indian political leadership by the Cambridge School has also encouraged some of our top Left historians to take up a position at times rather difficult to distinguish from a conventionally nationalist standpoint. Yet even an initially healthy reaction can go too far, and perhaps a closer look at the events of 1945–7 can provide something like a corrective.

II

The framework for post-War developments was set by the aftermath of the 1942 revolt, together with the socio-economic impact of the last three years of the War.

The total confrontation of August 1942, paradoxically enough, ultimately strengthened forces preferring a compromise on both sides.

---

[3] Thus R.P. Dutt's assumption (*India Today*, Bombay, 1947, p. 474) that the Cabinet Mission decision was a direct result of the R.I.N. strike of 18 February 1946 is clearly false, for the Mansergh documents show that the former has been taken on 2 January. Charges of betrayal by leaders usually tend to ignore also deeper internal weaknesses of movements.

[4] As the Communists were to learn to their cost in 1949–51 the slogan of Yeh Azadi Jhut Hai, which seemed to follow logically from a "betrayal" thesis, cut remarkably little ice.

The British had required no less than fifty-seven army battalions to suppress what Linlithgow privately described as "by far the most serious rebellion since that of 1857, the gravity and extent of which we have so far concealed from the world for reasons of military security."[5] British policy during the early years of the War had often been deliberately provocative. From 1940 onwards, the bureaucracy had been planning a wholesale crackdown on the Congress on the pattern of 1942, compromise efforts had been repeatedly spurned, and Linlithgow, Wavell, and Churchill had successfully torpedoed the Cripps initiative at the last moment.[6] After Quit India, the British would never again risk such a confrontation, and that the decision in 1945–6 to try for a negotiated settlement was not just a gift of the new Labour government is indicated by the attitude of Wavell, the by no means ultra-liberal army commander who succeeded Linlithgow in October 1943. In a letter to Churchill dated 24 October 1944 Wavell pointed out that it would be impossible to hold India by force after the War, given the likely state of world opinion and British popular or even army attitudes (as well as the economic exhaustion of Britain, he might have added). "We have had to negotiate with similar rebels before, e.g. De Valera and Zaghlul", and it would be wise to start negotiations before the end of the war brought prisoners' release, demobilisation, and unemployment, creating "a fertile field for agitation, unless we have previously diverted their [Congress] energies into some more profitable channel, i.e., into dealing with the administrative problems of India and into trying to solve the constitutional problem."[7] Churchill's pig-headedness (Amery once commented in an aside during a cabinet meeting that the prime minister knew "as much of the Indian problem as George III did of the American colonies") delayed the process somewhat,[8] but this

---

[5] Linlithgow's telegram to Churchill, 31 August 1942; Government of India (Home) to Secretary of State, 12 September 1942, Mansergh, op. cit., vol. II, pp. 843, 952–3.

[6] R.J. Moore, *Churchill, Cripps and India 1939–45* (Oxford, 1979), and Mansergh, vol. I.

[7] Wavell, *The Viceroy's Journal*, pp. 97–8.

[8] Ibid., p. 12 (entry for 27 July 1943).

was precisely what the British were able to persuade the Congress leadership to do after 1945.

From the point of view of the Congress leaders, as D.D. Kosambi noted in a brilliant piece of contemporary history-writing in 1946, "the glamour of jail and concentration camp served to wipe out the so-so record of the Congress ministries in office, thereby restoring the full popularity of the organisation among the masses."[9] Rightist Congress leaders, who throughout the late 1930s had urged more and more co-operation with the British and pursued increasingly conservative policies as ministers and for whom 1942 had been something like an aberration (probably dictated in part by a belief that Japan and Germany were winning),[10] could now bask in the halo of patriotic self-sacrifice even while concentrating all their energies on a compromise settlement: 1942 became their electoral trump card as well as a very convenient stick for beating the Communists, though in private Patel would comment on 30 May 1946: "The Bombay atmosphere has been terribly spoiled by the underground and the Satara crowd."[11] Though the Socialists – who had done most of the actual fighting in 1942 – emerged with greatly enhanced prestige, the Left alternative as a whole had been weakened in two ways. The Left was now divided as never before, for the searing memory of charges and counter-charges of "treachery" and "fifth-columnist" activity erected a wall between the Socialists and followers of Bose on the one side, and the Communists on the other. Brutal repression must also have exhausted many peasant bases, built up through years of Gandhian constructive work or radical *kisan sabha* activity. It is significant that the principal centres of rural rebellion in 1942 – Bihar and eastern UP, Midnapur, Orissa, and the Maharashtra–Karnataka

---

[9] D.D. Kosambi, "The Bourgeoisie Comes of Age, in India", *Science and Society* (1946), reprinted in idem, *Exasperating Essays* (Poona, n.d.), p. 17.

[10] Nehru commented during the Working Committee session at Allahabad (27 April–1 May 1942) that "It is Gandhiji's feeling that Japan and Germany will win. This feeling unconsciously governs his decision." *Congress Responsibility for the Disturbances, February* 1943, Appendix I.

[11] Letter to Shankar Rao Deo in Manibehn Patel and G.N. Nandurkar, ed., "*Sardar's Letters – Mostly Unknown*", *Birth Centenary Volume IV* (Ahmedabad, 1977), p. 286.

countryside – played relatively little part in the anti-imperialist upsurge of 1945–7.

The economic impact of the last three years of the War on the whole aggravated this exhaustion of popular forces, even though it also led to acute discontent and occasional and sporadic near-revolutionary outbursts in 1945–7. Though India was spared actual military devastation (apart from the Kohima-Imphal border, and some air raids), mass suffering was none the less acute, for war meant rampant inflation (notes in circulation shot up from Rs 2300 million in 1939 to Rs 12,100 million in 1945), corruption and blackmarkets, and above all the terrible famine of 1943 in Bengal. As Amartya Sen has emphasised in a recent article, mortality figures remained higher than normal in Bengal for five or six years after 1943 for malnutrition left its population particularly susceptible to epidemics. It may not be irrelevant to note, also, that excess mortality (taking 1941–2 as "normal") in 1943 was the highest among all West Bengal districts in Midnapur (+ 137.6 per cent), the politically most militant region during Quit India.[12] The consequent breakdown of social mores must have greatly strengthened the "lumpen" elements in big cities who would provide ample combustible material for communal riots on a totally unprecedented scale from August 1940 onwards. Certainly, in contemporary Bengali literature, famine, riots, and Partition often merge into a continuum, all producing acute social dislocation and the breakdown of norms.

Yet War and famine also meant super-profits for some, and, as in 1914–18, a major step forward for the Indian bourgeoisie. War demand and enforced import-substitution led to advances in textiles, iron and steel, cement and paper, and some Indian entry into engineering and chemicals – though the British still obstructed the development of indigenous shipping, automobile, and aircraft production. Industrial growth, however, remained fairly slow, gross production rising only to 120 in 1945 if 1937 is taken as the base year (though steel rose to 142.9, chemicals to 134.1, and cement

---

[12] A.K. Sen, "Famine Mortality: A Study of the Bengal Famine of 1943", in E. Hosbawm, *et al.*, eds, *Peasants in History* (Oxford, 1980), pp. 198, 203, 207.

to 196.5).[13] The really fantastic increase was not in production, but in profits, particularly speculative gains through profiteering in food, sharemarket operations, war contracts, and the black market in general. The bourgeoisie was coming of age in India, Kosambi pointed out in 1946, but it was a specific kind of bourgeoisie, characterised by "ravening greed" and mania for speculation rather than initiative or efficiency in developing production.[14] Technological backwardness made it look for foreign collaboration, now that the changed economic and political situation promised to give it additional leverage in conducting negotiations. Birla and Tata led an Indian business delegation to the West in the summer of 1945 and concluded agreements with Nuffield and Imperial Chemicals. The same bourgeois leaders were quite willing to accept or even urge state investments in sectors like heavy industries, power, or irrigation where initial profits were bound to be low, even while haggling over specific types of state intervention and complaining about too many controls. Even the "Bombay Plan" drawn up by India's leading capitalists was prepared to accept a "temporary eclipse" in "freedom of enterprise" in the interests of development, and included a number of surprisingly warm references to the "Russian experiment".[15] A clear-cut split between a collaborationist or "compradore" and a "national" bourgeoisie is not too easy to establish even in China; it is certainly untenable for India.[16] To quote Kosambi's contemporary analysis again, the bourgeoisie "needs Nehru's leadership", just as in previous periods of mass struggle it had been intelligent enough "to exploit for its own purposes whatever is profitable in the Mahatma's

---

[13] P.A. Wadia and K.T. Merchant, *Our Economic Problem*, 6th edition (Bombay, 1959), pp. 359–60.

[14] Kosambi, op. cit., p. 14.

[15] P. Thakurdas, J.R.D. Tata, G.D. Birla, A. Dalal, Shri Ram, Kasturbhai Lalbhai, A.D. Shroff, John Mathai, *A Brief Memorandum Outlining a Plan of Economic Development for India* (Bombay, 1944), pp. 23, 25, 26, 38–9, 51–2.

[16] Marie-Caire Bergere, "The Role of the Bourgeoisie", in Mary C. Wright, ed., *China in Revolution: The First Phase 1900–1913* (New Haven, 1968), pp. 249–50.

teachings and to reduce all dangerous enunciations to negative philosophical points."[17]

As a class which had never had it so good amidst unprecedented mass misery, the bourgeoisie was naturally averse to any further round of popular struggle which could have unmanageably radical consequences and its formidable influence was cast firmly on the side of a negotiated compromise settlement after 1945. Fear of popular "excesses" has been of course a recurrent element in bourgeois behaviour in many other countries and times, and can be readily explained in terms of a rational calculation of class interest. Indian business groups, however, fell short of the "national bourgeois" ideal type also in their frequent preference of sectional over countrywide class interests. This became very important indeed during the last years of British rule, for, as the events of 1945–7 tragically proved, the price of a negotiated "transfer of power" was an encouragement of divisive forces culminating in Partition.

The rapid advance of the Muslim League, which took full advantage of the suppression of the Congress, in the closing years of the War certainly owed something to British encouragement. League ministries in Assam (August 1942) and the NWFP (May 1943) became possible only because most Congress MLAs were in jail. The pro-Congress Muslim premier of Sind was dismissed by the governor (October 1942) and European MLAs in Bengal propped up the Nazimuddin ministry from March 1943. But much more was involved in the League advance than assembly intrigues and official patronage. Pakistan was being presented to the Muslim peasants of Bengal and Punjab as the end of Hindu zamindar and Bania exploitation; Abul Hashem, for instance, the dynamic secretary of the Bengal Muslim League from November 1943, did his best to cultivate a radical image for his party. Pakistan at the same time promised "the hedging off of a part of India from competition by the established Hindu business groups or professional classes so that the small Muslim business class could thrive and the nascent Muslim intelligentsia could find

---

[17] Kosambi, op. cit., p. 18.

employment."[18] The economic muscle behind Muslim separatism thus no longer came only from old-fashioned *talukdars* and zamindars as in the days of the Aligarh Movement or of Nawab Salimullah of Dacca. The Ispahanis, a Calcutta-based Muslim business family with all-India connections, helped Jinnah in asserting his control over Bengal Muslim politics by ousting Fazlul Huq. Ispahani and Adamjee financed League papers (like the Calcutta *Star of India* and the Delhi *Dawn*), a Federation of Muslim Chambers of Commerce and Industry was started in April 1945 with Jinnah's blessings, and Muslim banks and an airways company were planned soon after the War.[19] Hindu business groups, on their part, had been often extremely orthodox, with strong revivalist, cow-protectionist, and Mahasabha links, and the two forms of communalism as usual fed each other. Hindu communalist opinion after 1946 came increasingly to accept Pakistan, provided Bengal and Punjab were also partitioned; this was felt to be a lesser evil, as compared to the inevitable "subordination" of Hindus to Muslim majorities in these two provinces in any democratic and regionally autonomous set-up. It is interesting, and little known, however, that G.D. Birla, the business magnate closest of all to the Congress, seems to have visualised something similar as early as July 1942: "You know my views about Pakistan. I am in favour of separation, and I do not think it is impracticable or against the interest of Hindus or of India."[20]

III

The complex interactions between British policies, Congress attitudes, and popular outbursts during 1945–7 can best be grasped through a firm chronological framework. Four phases can be distinguished here: (i) from the surrender of Germany and Japan (in May and

---

[18] Amiya Bagchi, *Private Investment in India, 1900–1939* (Cambridge, 1972), pp. 432–3.

[19] M.A.H. Ispahani, *Qaid-E-Azam Jinnah as I Knew Him* (Karachi, 1966), chapters VII–IX.

[20] G.D. Birla to Mahadev Desai, 14 July 1942, in G.D. Birla, *Bapu: A Unique Association Correspondence 1940–47* (Bombay, 1977), p. 316.

August 1945) to February 1946 (the R.I.N. revolt, coinciding with the announcement of the Cabinet Mission); (ii) February–August 1946 (from the Cabinet Mission to the Calcutta riots); (iii) August 1946 – February 1947 (when Wavell was replaced by Mountbatten and Attlee fixed a deadline for British withdrawal); and (iv) February–August 1947, the working out of the Mountbatten Plan.

Till the autumn and winter of 1945–6, British policy on the whole was marked by continuity rather than change. Though in June 1945 (with Germany defeated and British elections just a month ahead) Churchill at last permitted Wavell to release Congress leaders and start negotiations, the Simla Conference (25 June–14 July) was allowed to be wrecked on the rock of Jinnah's insistence that only the League had the right to choose the Muslim members of the proposed new Executive Council (which would be entirely Indian but for the viceroy and the commander-in-chief), but would still be within the 1935 structure of a central executive not responsible to the Assembly. This, it needs to be emphasised, was a fantastic demand in mid 1945, for the League then ruled (and that largely on Congress sufferance) only in Sind and Assam. The Punjab Unionist ministry under Khizr Hayat Khan had openly broken with Jinnah in mid 1944, the NWFP once again had a Congress government once its MLAs had been released, and even the Nazimuddin ministry in Bengal had fallen in March 1945. So far (till August 1946, in fact) there was little evidence that the League would be able to organise real mass sanctions behind its Pakistan demand. Yet by dissolving the conference, Wavell in effect gave Jinnah the veto he was asking for – in sharp contrast to British attitudes a year later, when the Congress would be invited, however reluctantly, to form an interim government on its own.[21]

The massive Labour victory of July 1945 initially did not bring about any major change, even though the new prime minister (along with Cripps) had been party to the informal Filkins agreement with Nehru in June 1938 by which Labour leaders had promised a complete transfer of power to a constituent assembly based on

---

[21] For details of the Simla Conference, see Mansergh, op. cit., vol. V, and Wavell, *Viceroy's Journal*, op. cit., pp. 111–58.

universal suffrage when they came into power.[22] Wavell's private fears that with "too big" a majority Labour might try to hand over "India to their Congress friends as soon as possible" were soon revealed as exaggerated. By December 1946 he would realise that most Labour leaders – like Foreign Secretary Bevin, for instance – were "in reality imperialists" who "like everyone else hate(s) the idea of our leaving India but like everyone else . . . (have) . . . no alternative to suggest."[23] The announcement of new central and provincial elections (last held in 1934 and 1937) made on 21 August 1945 was inevitable now that war had ended. It was welcomed by bureaucrats like the U.P. governor, Hallet, as the "first step" towards providing "constitutional activities for the agitators".[24] After consultations with the new Labour government, Wavell on 19 September merely reiterated the promise of "early realisation of full self-government" (the term "independence" was still being avoided). Post-election talks were promised with MLAs and Indian states for setting up a "constitution-making body" (a step back, this, from the Filkins acceptance of a constituent assembly based on universal franchise), and efforts would be made again to set up an Executive Council "which will have the support of the main Indian parties".[25] How little British policies had changed was indicated by the initial decision to put on trial no less than 600 of the 20,000 I.N.A. prisoners, while another 7000 would be dismissed from service and detained without trial.[26] Indian troops were sent out to help restore French and Dutch colonial rule in Vietnam and Indonesia, though about this Wavell did express some nervousness.[27]

---

[22] Subject only to an Indo-British treaty safeguarding British interests in India for a transitional period. See P.S. Gupta, *Imperialism and British Labour* (Macmillan, 1975), pp. 257–9.

[23] Wavell, *Viceroy's Journal*, op. cit., pp. 159, 169–71, 399 (entries for 26 July and 4 September 1945, and 24 December 1946).

[24] Hallet to Wavell, 14 August 1945, in Mansergh, op. cit., vol. VI, p. 68.

[25] Wavell, *Viceroy's Journal*, op. cit., pp. 170–1.

[26] GOI (War Department) to Secretary of State, 11 August 1945, in Mansergh, op. cit., vol. VI,1 pp. 49–51.

[27] Wavell to Secretary of State, 1 October, 17 October, ibid., pp. 305–10, 360.

Popular Movements and National Leadership 547

The decisive shift in British policies during the ensuing months obviously had an international dimension in the worldwide weakening of imperialist forces. Fascism had been routed, socially radical regimes with Communist leadership or participation were emerging throughout Eastern Europe and seemed on the point of doing so even in France and Italy, the Chinese Revolution was forging ahead, and a tremendous anti-imperialist wave was sweeping through SouthEast Asia, with Vietnam and Indonesia in the vanguard. A war-weary, economically ravaged Britain no longer had the resources to hold on to an entire subcontinent by force. That the British came to realise this, however, at this specific moment was above all due to mass pressure and not due to anything done by the top national leadership, Congress or League.

The autumn and winter months of 1945–6 have been perceptively described by Penderel Moon as "The Edge of a Volcano". The very foolish decision to put the I.N.A. men on trial, and that in the Red Fort with a Hindu, a Muslim, and a Sikh (P.K. Sehgal, Shah Nawaz, Gurbaksh Singh Dhillon) together in the first batch, unleashed a countrywide wave of protest. Nehru, Bhulabhai Desai, and Tej Bahadur Sapru appeared for the defence, the Muslim League also condemned the trials, and on 20 November an Intelligence Bureau note admitted that "there has seldom been a matter which has attracted so much Indian public interest and, it is safe to say, sympathy – this particular brand of sympathy cuts across communal barriers." A journalist (B. Shiva Rao) visiting the Red Fort prisoners on the same day reported that "There is not the slightest feeling among them of Hindu and Muslim . . . A majority of the men now awaiting trial in the Red Fort is Muslim. Some of these men are bitter that Mr Jinnah is keeping alive a controversy about Pakistan."[28] The British were extremely nervous about the I.N.A. spirit spreading to the Indian army, and in January the Punjab governor reported that a Lahore reception for released I.N.A. prisoners had been attended by Indian soldiers in uniform.[29] A second issue was provided by the use of the Indian

---

[28] Ibid., pp. 514, 564.
[29] Glancy (Governor of Punjab) to Wavell, 16 January 1946, ibid., p. 807.

army in Vietnam and Indonesia; the impact this had on popular (at least urban) sentiments as well as on sections of the army bore vivid testimony to the tremendous advance in anti-imperialist consciousness brought about by the War. Meanwhile the usual post-war problems of high prices and retrenchment were being sharply aggravated by a major food crisis, with Wavell in January 1946 estimating a deficit of three million tons. A drastic cut in rations in February reduced the calorie value to 1200 per head, while even wartime London in 1943 had got over 2800 calories.[30]

What the officials feared in the autumn of 1945 was another Congress revolt, a revival of 1942 made much more dangerous this time by the likely combination of attacks on communications with widespread agrarian revolt, labour trouble, army disaffection, and the presence of I.N.A. men with military expertise.[31] Violent speeches by Congress leaders (Nehru above all, but also at first Patel and regional leaders in Bihar, C.P., U.P., and elsewhere) initially aroused acute alarm, with their glorification of the heroes and martyrs of 1942, demands for stern punishment for official atrocities, and calls for the immediate release of I.N.A. prisoners. The British began to realise fairly quickly, however, that this sabre-rattling was essentially election propaganda combined with the need to accommodate the popular mood: 1942 after all was the electoral trump card of the Congress, and as for the I.N.A., Asaf Ali in a private conversation in October was reported to have explained that his party "would lose much ground in the country" unless it took up their cause, but if the Congress came to power it would certainly remove the I.N.A. men from the army and might even put some of them on trial."[32]

---

[30] Wavell to Secretary of State, 29 January, 18 February 1946, ibid., pp. 868–9, 1006.

[31] C.P. Governor Twynham to Wavell, 10 November 1945. On 24 November 1945, Commander-in-Chief Auchinleck in an appreciation of the internal situation expressed fears about a "well-organised revolution next Spring—if and when trouble comes it may be on a greater scale than in August 1942 . . ." ibid., pp. 468, 577–83.

[32] Jenkins to Turnbull, reporting a talk of a returned POW, Captain Badhwar (whose name was "*not* to be disclosed"), with Asaf Ali, 23 October 1945, ibid., p. 387.

Popular Movements and National Leadership 549

Another indication was the bitter campaign against the Communists, in which for the first time Nehru played a very active role, culminating in the expulsion of Communist A.I.C.C. members in December. That much more was involved here than legitimate anger about the C.P.I.'s wartime role is indicated by the fact that there was no such concerted campaign against the Hindu Mahasabha, some of whose leaders had actually been in ministries in August 1942,[33] while Rajagopalachari, whose attitude on the Quit India and Pakistan issues had been very similar to that of the Communists, remained a top Congress leader. In U.P. election meetings, reported an official source in November 1945, Congress speakers, "while condemning the invocation of religious issues by their Muslim rivals, concentrate upon the alleged atheist tenets of the Communists in their appeals to their audiences not to support them."[34]

The crucial shifts, alike in British policies and Congress attitudes, came in the wave of three major popular explosions – in Calcutta on 21–23 November 1945 and again on 11–13 February 1946, and in Bombay with the R.I.N. revolt of 18–23 February 1946. In Calcutta on 21 November 1945 a Forward Bloc student procession on Dharmtala Street demanding release of I.N.A. prisoners was joined by Communist Students Federation cadres (long considered their bitterest enemies) as well as by Islamia College students carrying the green flag of the League, and spontaneously the Congress, League, and Red flags were tied together as a symbol of all-India anti-imperialist unity. Police firing which killed a Hindu and a Muslim student was followed on 22 and 23 November by trouble all over the city: strikes by Communist-led tram workers and Sikh taxi drivers, in many factories the burning of police and army vehicles (150 were destroyed), crowds blocking trains, and veritable street fighting and

---

[33] Golwalkar's RSS had kept strictly aloof from the August Rebellion; Savarkar on 4 September 1942 had urged Mahasabha members of local bodies, legislatures and services to "stick to their posts and continue to perform their regular duties" (*Indian Annual Register, Chronicle of Events*, 1942) while Shyamaprasad Mukherji was actually a minister in Bengal while Midnapur was being ruthlessly suppressed.

[34] Fortnightly Report, UP, second half of November 1945; Government of India, Home Political (Internal), 11/11/45, hereafter Home Poll (I).

barricades: "the crowds when fired on largely stood their ground or at most only receded a little, to return again to the attack."[35] Order could be restored only after fourteen cases of firing, which killed thirty-three and injured about two hundred. Calcutta erupted again between 11 and 13 February 1946 in protest against the seven years' rigorous imprisonment sentence passed on Abdul Rashid of the I.N.A. This time the League student wing had given the initial strike call, and at least the appearance of total political unity was achieved by a mammoth Wellington Square rally on 12 February addressed by League leader Suhrawardy, Gandhian Congressman Satish Dasgupta, and the Communist Somnath Lahiri. But the real initiative in the strikes and street fighting, as in November, came from below, and to some extent from the Communists, described in an official account as "without doubt the most disruptive organisation concerned in the disturbances".[36] The situation was "worse than that in November 1945", with a Communist-led general strike paralysing industrial Calcutta, all jute mills in the city and suburbs closed for two days, train services disrupted up to Chinsura and Naihati, and bitter street clashes with the police and the army (two British and a Gurkha battalion had been deployed) which left eighty-four dead and three hundred injured.[37] As in November, the striking features were the total unity on the streets of Hindus and Muslims, students and workers, and violent anti-white feelings, with numerous attacks on sahibs, and attempts "to boycott everything European, to disaffect servants of Europeans and to prevent the sale of food to Europeans."[38]

The greatest explosion of all was the naval mutiny in Bombay and the accompanying mass upsurge from 18 to 23 February 1946, one

[35] Bengal Governor Casey to Wavell, 2 January 1946, summarising the enquiry report of the Calcutta Police Commissioner, in Mansergh, op. cit., vol. VI, pp. 724–7.

[36] Calcutta Police Commissioner's Report on Political Aspects of Calcutta Disturbances of February 1946, 3 April 1946, Home Poll (I), 22/5/46.

[37] Situation Report, 12 February 1946, ibid.; see also Gautam Chattopadhyay, "The Almost Revolution", in B. De, et al., eds, *Essays in Honour of S.C. Sarkar* (New Delhi, 1976).

[38] Situation Report, 13 February 1946, (3.30 p.m.), Home Poll (I), 22/5/46.

of the most truly heroic, if also largely forgotten, episodes in our freedom struggle. The R.I.N. ratings' strike began on 18 February in the signals training establishment "Talwar" as a protest against bad food and racist insults from white officers. It spread rapidly to Castle and Fort Barracks on shore and twenty-two ships in Bombay harbour, and, as in Calcutta in November, the tricolour, crescent, and hammer-and-sickle were raised jointly on the mastheads of the rebel fleet. The demands, as formulated by the elected Naval Central Strike Committee, combined service grievances with national political slogans: the release of I.N.A. and other political prisoners, the withdrawal of Indian troops from Indonesia, the acceptance of Indian officers alone as superiors. Desperately seeking advice and help from national leaders but getting little or nothing,[39] the ratings hesitated fatally on the borderline of peaceful strike and determined mutiny, and obeyed orders on the afternoon of 20 February to return to their respective ships and barracks, only to find themselves surrounded by army guards. Fighting broke out next morning at Castle Barracks when the ratings tried to break out of their encirclement, and there were remarkable scenes of fraternisation that afternoon as crowds thronged the Gateway of India with food for the sailors and shopkeepers invited them to take whatever they needed. The pattern of events in fact unconsciously echoed the course of the mutiny on the Black Sea Fleet during the first Russian Revolution of 1905: that, too, had begun over inedible food, and fraternising crowds had been shot down in a scene immortalised later on in the "Odessa steps" sequence of Eisenstein's film classic *Battleship Potemkin*. On 22 February the Bombay working class, already restive over a recent ration cut (three mills in Parel had gone on strike on this issue on 21 February), responded massively to a Communist call for a general strike, closing

---

[39] The ratings contacted Aruna Asaf Ali at her house in Dadar; she expressed sympathy and issued an appeal for "moral support" on 20 February. "She consulted Vallabhbhai Patel who snubbed her saying that it was no business of his or hers to interfere when the ratings did not abide by discipline. Mrs Aruna Asaf Ali left Bombay for Poona on the morning of February 20, 1946." Bombay Police Commissioner's Office (Special Branch) to Government of Bombay Home (Special), 20 February 1946, Home Poll (1), 21/5/46.

down all textile mills, railway workshops, and city transport. There was bitter street fighting throughout the 22nd and 23rd, with crowds "erecting road blocks and covering them from nearly buildings", particularly in the proletarian districts of Parel and Delisle Road. Armoured cars and four military columns were needed to restore order; official casualty figures were 228 civilians killed and 1046 injured (plus 3 police deaths and 91 wounded); 10 police outposts, 9 banks, 10 post offices, and 64 government grain shops had been attacked.[40] The strike spread to naval bases all over the country, there were serious clashes also in Karachi, and throughout February there was considerable unrest in the air force and army too. The Bombay ratings, however, surrendered on 23 February, not so much in face of British threats (though Admiral Godfrey had flown in bombers and warned that he was prepared to destroy the navy), but because Patel and Jinnah in a rare display of unanimity advised them to do so, giving an assurance that the national parties would prevent any victimisation – a promise soon quietly forgotten.

The R.I.N. ratings, in sharp contrast to the men of the Azad Hind Fauj, have never been given the status of national heroes, though their action involved much greater risk in some ways than joining the I.N.A. as alternative to an arduous life in Japanese P.O.W. camps. As in the Calcutta explosions, a striking feature was the total submergence of communal divisions – the Naval Central Strike Committee, incidentally, was headed by a Muslim, M.S. Khan. The last message of the committee deserves to be remembered far better than it is: "Our strike has been a historic event in the life of our nation. For the first time the blood of men in the services and in the streets flowed together in a common cause. We in the Services will never forget this. We know also that you, our brothers and sisters, will not forget. Long live our great people! Jai Hind !"[41]

Even apart from the massive political strikes in Calcutta and Bombay, the winter of 1945–6 marked the beginning of an unprecedented

---

[40] Bombay Governor Colville to Wavell, 27 February 1946, in Mansergh, op. cit., vol. VI, pp. 1081–4.

[41] *The R.I.N. Strike*, op. cit., p. 75.

wave of countrywide labour unrest as prices shot up and rations were cut. A glance through Wavell's journal and the Mansergh documents immediately reveals how worried British officials had become, particularly in the context of repeated strike threats by all-India organisations of railway workers, postal employees, and government clerical associations. The development of effective countrywide labour organisations in strategic sectors gave a new muscle-power to the Indian trade union movement; strikes in the 1920s and 1930s had been mainly confined to single industrial centres, primarily Bombay and Calcutta textiles.

For our purposes here, the main significance of the Calcutta and Bombay explosions and labour militancy lies in their impact on British and Congress attitudes. On 30 November 1945, a week after the Calcutta outburst, New Delhi informed London that while the original I.N.A. trials policy would have involved at least two or three hundred accused and possibly forty to fifty death sentences, it had to be recognised now that "abstract justice must to some extent give way to expediency." Future trials, it was announced on 1 December, would be "limited to cases of brutality and murder", instead of the sweeping charge of "waging war against the King" used in the first case,[42] and imprisonment sentences passed against the first batch were remitted in January. By February 1946, Indian soldiers were being withdrawn from Vietnam and Indonesia. On 28 November the British cabinet sub-committee on India decided on a parliamentary delegation; on 22 January the much more significant decision was taken to send a cabinet mission in March to negotiate with Indian leaders. Wavell meanwhile had started preparing a "breakdown plan". As presented to the Cabinet Mission on 30 May 1946, this visualised a withdrawal of the British army and officials to the Muslim provinces of north-west and north-east India, handing over the rest of the country to the Congress.[43] While evidently reflecting a desire in some high official circles to make of Pakistan an Indian Northern Ireland, the "plan" is

---

[42] Governor-General (War Department) to Secretary of State, 30 November 1945, in Mansergh, op. cit., vol. VI, p. 572.

[43] Wavell, *Viceroy's Journal*, op. cit., Appendix IV, pp. 485–6.

still interesting evidence of the British recognition that it would be impossible to suppress any future Congress-led rebellion.

On the Congress side, there were indications from November 1945 onwards that the forces which had restrained militancy in the past were at work again, while Wavell on 31 December would recognise the Calcutta disturbances of 21–23 November as the "turning-point", which "caused at least a temporary detente".[44] The point requires much further research, but it does seem that, as on some earlier occasions, business pressures played an important role here.[45] The governor of Sind on 3 November, Finance Minister Rowlands on 17 November, and Secretary of State Pethick-Lawrence on 30 November independently referred to G.D. Birla as getting "alarmed at the virulence of Congress speeches."[46] And Wavell informed Pethick-Lawrence on 5 December that "the strong capitalist element behind Congress . . . is becoming nervous about the security of its property . . . There have recently been indications that the Congress leaders want to reduce the political tension by making it clear that there must be no mass movement until after the elections."[47] Birla himself conveyed on the next day an interesting assurance and explanation to a London official: "There is no political leader including Jawaharlal who wants to see any crisis or violence . . . Popular

---

[44] Wavell to George VI, 31 December 1945, in Mansergh, op. cit., vol. VI, p. 713.

[45] For the role of business groups in the making of the Gandhi–Irwin Pact of 1931 and in the "taming" of Nehru in 1936, see Sumit Sarkar, "Legacy of Gandhian Nationalism: Civil Disobedience and the Gandhi–Irwin Pact 1930–31", *Indian Historical Review*, July 1976; and Bipan Chandra, "Jawaharlal Nehru and the Capitalist Class", reprinted in idem, *Nationalism and Colonialism in Modern India* (Delhi, 1979).

[46] Rowlands, as reported in Wavell, *Viceroy's Journal*, op. cit., p. 185. H. Dow (Governor of Sind) wrote to Wavell on 3 November that "Birla . . . is getting a little frightened of the Frankenstein's monster he has helped so much to create": Mansergh, op. cit., vol. VI, p. 438. The Secretary of State commented on 30 November: "I am glad to hear that Birla has told *Hindustan Times* to lower its tone. It rather looks as if the richer supporters of Congress may be beginning to wonder where the caravan is going." Ibid., p. 572.

[47] Ibid., pp. 602–3.

impatience and the prevalent atmosphere are responsible for these strong speeches. Even leaders are often led. But I think unrestrained language will be heard less and less in the future."[48]

In Calcutta on 21 November Sarat Bose, so long adored as the brother of Subhas, refused to come to address the students squatting on Dharmtala Street and later blamed the Communists for instigating violence.[49] Patel at a Bombay election rally on 24 November condemned the "frittering away" of energies in "trifling quarrels" with the police.[50] Gandhi began a fairly friendly dialogue with the Bengal governor, and the Calcutta A.I.C.C. Working Committee session of 7–11 December strongly reaffirmed its faith in non-violence[51] – in significant contrast to the September A.I.C.C. session where many members had glorified every aspect of the by-no-means non-violent 1942 struggle. During the February days in Calcutta, "the Indian National Congress, whatever individual members may have done, took no part . . . in the disturbance", while Suhrawardy's appearance at the Wellington Square meeting and the subsequent procession on 12 February were explained by the police commissioner in terms of his "intention of not committing the error of Sarat Bose who lost much popularity by not showing himself at Dhurrumtolla on the 21st November."[52] An official situation report on 13 February noted that there were "reassuring signs that the more well-to-do Indians are definitely annoyed by the riots and will bring pressure to bear to stop them. Congressmen are patrolling with loud-speakers telling the people to get off the streets . . ."[53]

---

[48] G.D. Birla to Henderson, 6 December 1945, ibid., p. 615.

[49] Fortnightly Report from Bengal, second half of November 1945, Home Poll (I), 18/11/45; Wavell to Secretary of State, 5 December 1945, in Mansergh, op. cit., vol. VI, p. 602.

[50] *Indian Annual Register*, July–December 1945.

[51] Ibid.

[52] The Commissioner added that Suhrawardy's foreknowledge (as a member of the League ministry) that the 12 February procession would not be stopped by the police "enabled him to pose with safety as a hero of liberty . . .": Calcutta Police Commissioner's Report, 3 April 1946, Home Poll (I), 22/5/46.

[53] Situation Report No. 7, 13 February 1946, ibid.

In Bombay during the R.I.N. upsurge, the governor reported to Wavell that "the Congress leaders had decried any share in the mutiny, and had advised people to preserve order. I received a message from Vallabhbhai Patel to this effect on Thursday" (21 February). Next day messages came from Chundrigar and S.K. Patil, heads of the provincial League and Congress units, "offering the help of volunteers to assist the police".[54] An official telephone message from Bombay on 22 February reported that "Congress were against today's hartal, and Vallabhbhai Patel was emphatic about this, but the Communists' call for sympathy with the R.I.N. ratings has won the day and the Congress Labour Union has been totally ineffective."[55] Patel explained his attitude clearly in a letter to Andhra Congress leader Viswanathan on 1 March 1946: ". . . discipline in the army cannot be tampered with . . . We will want Army even in free India."[56] Against Patel's advice, Nehru accepted Aruna Asaf Ali's invitation to come to Bombay, but quickly allowed himself to be "restrained from inflaming the situation, as on arriving here he had been impressed by the necessity for curbing the wild outburst of violence"[57] – though he did later hail the R.I.N. strike for breaking down the "iron wall" between army and people.[58] Gandhi, it has to be noted, was as unequivocally hostile as Patel. On 22 February he condemned the ratings for setting "a bad and unbecoming example for India", advised them to peacefully resign their jobs if they had any grievances, and made the very interesting statement that "a combination between Hindus and Muslims and others for the purpose of violent action is unholy . . ." Aruna Asaf Ali made the pertinent comment in reply that "It simply does not lie in the mouth of Congressmen who were themselves going to the legislatures to ask the ratings to give up their jobs." She also made a tragically accurate prophecy that it would be

---

[54] Colville to Wavell, 27 February 1946, in Mansergh, op. cit., vol. VI, pp. 1081–2.
[55] Home Poll (I), 21/5/46.
[56] *Sardar's Letters*, op. cit., vol. IV (Ahmedabad, 1977), p. 165.
[57] Colville to Wavell, in Mansergh, op. cit., vol. VI, p. 1084.
[58] Wavell to Secretary of State, 5 March 1946, quoting from *The Statesman*, 4 March, ibid., p. 1118.

far easier to "unite the Hindus and Muslims at the barricade than on the constitutional front."[59] It is tempting to set beside Gandhi's statement of 22 February Wavell's private comment of 30 May 1946: "We must at all costs avoid becoming embroiled with both Hindu and Muslim at once."[60]

The Congress rationale behind firmly rejecting mass confrontations was the need to concentrate energies on fighting the elections. The Congress did win a massive victory, polling 91.3 per cent of votes in the central assembly general constituencies, and winning majorities in every province except Bengal, Punjab, and Sind. The Hindu Mahasabha and other right-wing groups were routed, while Communists could capture only eight provincial assembly seats, all but one of them in constituencies reserved for labour (here they did put up a fairly tough fight, winning 112,736 votes against 321,607 of the Congress).[61] The most significant feature of the elections, however, was the prevalence of communal voting, in sharp contrast to the sporadic but quite remarkable anti-British unity forged so often in these very same months in the streets of Calcutta, Bombay, or even Karachi. The League swept all thirty Muslim seats in the Centre, and won 442 out of 509 provincial Muslim constituencies – a very major advance as compared to 1937, though it still narrowly missed a majority in Punjab, and was defeated in the NWFP.

Apart from the logic of separate electorates, it is possible that the extremely limited franchise (about 10 per cent of the population in the provinces, less than 1 per cent for the central assembly) may have had something to do with this stark contrast between united mass action and communal voting. The NWFP governor reported to Wavell in February 1946 that Muslim officials and the "bigger Khans" or landlords were all for the League, but the Congress was still getting the support of the "less well-to-do" Muslims due to its promises of economic reforms[62] – promises, however, which Congress ministries

---

[59] *Sardar's Letters*, op. cit., pp. 162–3.
[60] Wavell, *Viceroy's Journal*, op. cit., p. 485.
[61] Statistics in AICC FN G26/1946.
[62] Cunningham to Wavell, 27 February 1946, in Mansergh, op. cit., vol. VI, p. 1985.

did little to implement either after 1937 or in 1946–7. In this context, the tacit (and little-noticed) surrender by the Congress of its central slogan of the late-1930s – a constituent assembly elected on universal franchise – acquires crucial significance in understanding the course of events. Of all Indian political groups, only the Communists pressed this demand seriously in 1945–6, in their election manifesto *For the Final Bid For Power* (1945), for instance, or in P.C. Joshi's meeting with the Cabinet Mission on 17 April 1946.[63] Congress leaders, in contrast, quietly accepted the Cabinet Mission decision to have the constituent assembly elected by existing provincial legislatures based on limited voting rights. Much more was involved here than a mere question of abstract democratic principle. The League next year would win its claims to represent the majority of Muslims, being really tested, either in fully democratic elections or (as Congress claims had been) in sustained mass movements in the face of official repression (as distinct from occasional communal riots not unaccompanied often by official complicity). It may not be irrelevant to recall here that the Congress after 1947 would go on winning all-India elections for thirty years, while the League was routed in East Pakistan in the very first vote held on the basis of universal franchise (1954), and would fail to provide political stability even in West Pakistan.

In the long and tortuous negotiations which went on from 24 March to 29 June 1946, the Cabinet Mission at times seemed to lean marginally towards the Congress, arousing grave suspicions in the mind of the viceroy, who once even accused its members – and particularly Nehru's old friend Cripps – of "living in the pocket of Congress".[64] Yet this was due basically not to Labour pro-nationalist sympathies, but because, as Wavell himself pointed out in a note to the Mission on 29 March, the British had "an extremely difficult hand to play, owing to the necessity to avoid the mass movement or revolution which it is in the power of the Congress to start, and which we are certain that we can control."[65] It is difficult to avoid the conclusion

---

[63] Mansergh, op. cit., vol. VII, pp. 291–3.
[64] Wavell, *Viceroy's Journal*, op. cit., pp. 324–5.
[65] Ibid., p. 232.

Popular Movements and National Leadership 559

that the Congress leadership once again spiked its own guns in its eagerness for quick and easy power and desire at all costs to preserve social order. The spring and summer of 1946 marked the height of the greatest strike wave in the history of colonial India, and there is ample evidence that, apart from disaffection in the armed forces, it was urban labour unrest which alarmed British officials most. Strikes in 1946 totalled 1629, involving 1,941,948 workers and a loss of 12,717,762 man-days: in no previous year had stoppages exceeded 1000, or the workers involved numbering more than eight lakhs.[66] There were widespread police strikes in April (in Malabar-Andamans, Dacca, Bihar, and Delhi), threats of an all-India railway stoppage throughout the summer, a postal strike in July, and on 29 July, less than three weeks before the Great Calcutta Killing of 16 August, a total, absolutely peaceful, and remarkably united bandh in Calcutta under Communist leadership in sympathy with postal employees. The home member pointed out in a note dated 5 April that in the case of a break with the League, "even if they fight, they would be beaten", but "On the whole, I doubt whether a Congress rebellion could be suppressed". In such a situation, "by no means all units [of the army] could be relied on", "police over a large area would be likely to crack", and "a call to a general strike would be widely obeyed . . . labour is amenable mostly to Communist and Congress leadership."[67]

The Congress high command, however, had already opted for a different policy. Congress President Azad on 3 March publicly welcomed the ration cut (a major labour grievance) as "far-sighted", and declared that strikes were "out of place today", as the British were "now acting as caretakers".[68] Patel's correspondence reveals desperate efforts by local Congress labour leaders in May 1946 to prevent a strike ballot in the railways, "since if a ballot is taken it will be in

[66] J.B. Kripalani's analysis of post-war labour unrest, AICC FN G26/ 1946; V.B. Singh, "Trade Union Movement", in idem, *Economic History of India 1857–1956* (Bombay, 1965), p. 660.

[67] Note by J.A. Thorne, 5 April 1946, in Mansergh, op. cit., vol. VII, pp. 150–1.

[68] Wavell to Secretary of State, 5 March 1946, enclosing extract from the *Hindustan Times*, 3 March, in Mansergh, op. cit., vol. VI, p. 1116.

favour of the strike."[69] In August, the working committee meeting in Wardha condemned "hasty or ill-conceived stoppages" and the "growing lack of discipline and disregard of obligations on the part of the workers."[70]

There is some interesting evidence that fear of labour militancy, combined with a growing awareness of essential Congress moderation, played a crucial part in bringing about the next major shift in official policy: the decision to allow Nehru to form a purely Congress Interim Government on 2 September 1946. The brief agreement, always more apparent than real, between the Congress and the League in accepting the Cabinet Mission's long-term three-tier plan had broken down by the end of July, and Wavell had also failed in his efforts to set up a short-term coalition government in the centre. On 31 July, with the postal strike still on and two days after the Calcutta bandh, the viceroy wrote to Pethick-Lawrence: "I dislike intensely the idea of having an Interim Government dominated by one party but I feel that I must try to get the Congress in as soon as possible . . . If Congress will take responsibility they will realise that firm control of unruly elements is necessary and they may put down the Communists and try to curb their own Left wing. Also I should hope to keep them so busy with administration that they had much less time for politics."[71] The director of the Intelligence Bureau made the same point on 9 August: "the labour situation is becoming increasingly dangerous . . . Until a responsible Indian government is introduced at the Centre, there is little that can be done. The Communists are only part of a larger nettle which must be grasped. I am satisfied that a responsible government, if one can be achieved, will deal more decisively with Labour than is at present possible."[72] By an interesting coincidence, the DIB note enclosed a militant leaflet by the Delhi Electric Supply and Traction Employees Union, combined economic grievances with statements

---

[69] Shantilal Shah to Patel, 7 May 1946, in Durga Das (ed.), *Sardar Patel's Correspondence*, vol. III (Ahmedabad, 1971), pp. 64–5.

[70] J.B. Kripalani's note, AICC FN G26/1946.

[71] Mansergh, op. cit., vol. VII, pp. 154–5.

[72] Note by N.P.A. Smith, Director, Intelligence Bureau, Home Department, 9 August 1946, Home Poll (I), 7/12/46.

Popular Movements and National Leadership 561

like "We are soldiers of the RED FLAG . . . a part of the revolutionary army of the workers": on 20 September Wavell would be "cynically amused" to note that the new Congress minister Sarat Bose's "first reaction to a threatened strike of the Delhi electricity workers had been to make a plan for troops to be flown to Delhi to take over essential services and to summon certain British technicians."[73] By 5 August, Wavell had also received information that Patel was "convinced that the Congress must enter the government to prevent chaos spreading in the country, and was even prepared to threaten resignation from the Working Committee if his views were not accepted."[74]

From 16 August 1946 onwards, the whole Indian scene was rapidly transformed by communal riots on an unprecedented scale: starting with Calcutta on 16-19 August, touching Bombay from 1 September, spreading to Noakhali in East Bengal (10 October), Bihar (25 October), Garhmukteswar in U.P. (November), and engulfing the Punjab from March 1947 onwards. The British, who as late as June 1946 had been making plans to bring five army divisions to India in the context of a possible Congress movement,[75] made no such move while presiding over this awesome human tragedy. In Calcutta in August, in sharp contrast to November 1945 or February 1946, the army was called out only after twenty-four hours, though the governor was reminded of his First World War experiences in course of his early morning tour of the city on the 17th.[76] Two other examples, both taken from British sources, may suffice to indicate the extent of official passivity — if not deliberate connivance. Wavell commented on 9 November 1946 in the context of Bihari Muslim requests to use aerial bombardment to stop the riots: "Machine-gunning from the air is not a weapon one would willingly use, though the Muslims point out, rather embarrassingly, that we did not hesitate to use it in 1942."[77]

---

[73] Wavell, *Viceroy's Journal*, op. cit., p. 352.
[74] Ibid., p. 329.
[75] Mansergh, op. cit., vol. VIII, pp. 13–15.
[76] ". . . parts of the city on Saturday morning were as bad as anything I saw when I was with the Guards on the Somme." Governor Burrows to Wavell, 22 August 1946, ibid., p. 298.
[77] Wavell, *Viceroy's Journal*, op. cit., p. 374.

In March 1947, the two main bazaars of Amritsar were destroyed, while "not a shot was fired by the police" – and this, Penderel Moon pertinently recalls, was the city of the Jalianwallabagh massacre.[78]

The Interim Government of Nehru found itself presiding helplessly over this growing communal inferno. Collective functioning became all but impossible after Wavell had persuaded Jinnah to join the government on 26 October without the League giving up its Direct Action programme, its projection of the Cabinet Mission long-term plan, or its boycott of the Constituent Assembly. League obstructionism, in Congress eyes at least, included refusal to attend Nehru's "tea-party Cabinets" (informal sessions to co-ordinate policies before meeting the viceroy), and a rather demagogic budget moved in February 1947 by Liaquat Ali Khan imposing heavy taxes on (predominantly Hindu) big business – a "clever move", commented Wavell, since it "drives a wedge between Congress and their rich merchant supporters like Birla, while Congress cannot object to its provisions."[79]

Confronted by Calcutta, Noakhali, Bihar, and Punjab, the secular ideals of many within the Congress ranks and leadership tended to evaporate. If Nehru consistently denounced Hindu communalism in Bihar and elsewhere, and Azad blamed Wavell for not calling out troops promptly in Calcutta to suppress "the hooligans of Calcutta's underworld" unleashed by Suhrawardy,[80] Patel sympathised with hostile Hindu reactions to Nehru's condemnation of Bihar.[81] Communal riots, combined with the evident unworkability of the Congress–League coalition at the centre, compelled many by early 1947 to think in terms of accepting what had been unthinkable so far – Partition – and these came to include Nehru as well as Patel.

---

[78] Penderel Moon, *Divide and Quit* (London, 1961), pp. 76–81.

[79] Wavell, *Viceroy's Journal*, op. cit., 28 February 1947, p. 424.

[80] Interview with Wavell, 19 August 1946, in Mansergh, op. cit., vol. VIII, p. 261.

[81] "We would be committing a grave mistake if we expose the people of Bihar and their ministry to the violent and vulgar attacks of the League leaders": Patel to Rajendra Prasad, 11 November 1946, in Durga Das, op. cit., vol. III, p. 171.

The most insistent demands for this surgical solution had now started coming from Hindu and Sikh communalist groups in Bengal and the Punjab, alarmed by the prospect of compulsory grouping into Muslim-dominated sections (the League interpretation of the Cabinet Mission plan) which might very well later form themselves into Pakistan. But Nehru, too, was telling Wavell in private by 10 March 1947: "the Cabinet Mission plan was the best solution if it could be carried through . . . the only real alternative was the partition of the Punjab and Bengal."[82] A month later, Congress President Kripalani informed Mountbatten: "Rather than have a battle we shall let them have their Pakistan, provided you will allow the Punjab and Bengal to be partitioned in a fair manner."[83]

To one man, however, the idea of a high-level bargain by which the Congress would attain quick power in the major part of the country at the cost of a partition on religious lines still seemed unimaginably shocking and unacceptable. Gandhi had taken little part in the tortuous negotiations since 1945, while he had also condemned the united anti-imperialist outbursts in 1945–6 as tainted with violence. Increasingly isolated from the Congress leadership, as well as from business leaders like Birla who had now developed closer ties with Patel,[84] the old man of seventy-seven with undiminished courage now shaped his all in a bid to vindicate his life-long principles of change of heart and non-violence in the village of Noakhali, followed by Bihar and then the riot-torn slums of Calcutta and Delhi. Gandhi's unique personal qualities and true greatness were never more evident than in the last months of his life: courage to stand against the tide, total disdain for all conventional forms of political power which could have been his for the asking now that India was becoming free, and

---

[82] Wavell, *Viceroy's Journal*, op. cit., pp. 426–37.
[83] H.V. Hodson, *The Great Divide* (London, 1969), p. 236.
[84] Patel "had now taken the place of Bapu in my correspondence". G.D. Birla, *In the Shadow of the Mahatma* (Bombay, 1953), p. 328. Gandhi's letter to Birla on 6 December 1946 complained that Birla's letter to him of 2 December (unfortunately not included) revealed "a lack of genuine feeling of resentment of improper conduct" about the Bihar riots. G.D. Birla, *Bapu—Correspondence 1940–47* (Bombay, 1977), p. 421.

a passionate anti-communalism which made him declare to a League leader a month after Partition, while riots were ravaging Punjab: "I want to fight it out with my life. I would not allow the Muslims to crawl on the streets in India. They must walk with self-respect."[85] At times the presence of Gandhi really seemed to work miracles, as when peace returned to Calcutta after a whole year on the eve of 15 August, renewed riots were abruptly halted by his fast-unto-death in early September, or, even in Delhi, when on 27 January 1948 he was invited by Muslims to speak from the platform of the Quwaat-ul-Islam mosque, just three days before his death at the hands of a Hindu fanatic.

Intensely moving and heroic, the Gandhian way in 1946–7 could be no more than an isolated personal effort with a local and often rather short-lived impact. It is futile and dangerous to speculate on what might have been, but one might still argue that the only real alternative lay along the path of united militant mass struggles against imperialism and its Indian allies – the one thing which, as we have seen, the British really dreaded. Despite the obvious and major disruption caused by the riots, this possibility was by no means entirely blocked even in the winter of 1946–7.

Three months after the Calcutta riots, villages in many parts of Bengal (particularly Thakurgaon subdivision in Dinajpur and adjoining areas of Jalpaiguri, Rangpur, and Malda in North Bengal, as well as pockets in Mymensingh, Midnapur, and 24 Parganas) resounded to the slogans of *tebhaga chai* and *nijkhamara dhan tolo*, as sharecroppers responded to the call of the Communist-led Kisan Sabha to fight against the *jotedars* for the two-thirds share of the harvest promised by the Floud Commission (1940) but never implemented. Though Muslim-majority south-east Bengal was largely untouched by *tebhaga*, and its strongest base was among low-caste semi-tribal groups like the Rajbansis, many Muslims did participate in the strongholds of the movement, producing leaders like Haji Muhammad Danesh, Niamat Ali, and even some maulvis who quoted the Koran to condemn *jotedar* oppression.[86]

[85] C. Khaliquzzaman, *Pathway to Pakistan* (Lahore, 1961), p. 404.
[86] Sunil Sen, *Agrarian Struggle in Bengal 1946–47* (New Delhi, 1972).

A second major outburst was in the Shertalai-Alleppey-Ambalapuzha area of Travancore state where the close proximity of small-town industries with agricultural occupations made the formula of worker-peasant alliance more of a reality than in most areas, and where communist-led coir-factory, fishermen, toddy-tapper and agricultural labour unions had become powerful enough to control recruitment, establish arbitration courts, and even win the right to run their own ration shops. Economic grievances, sharpened by acute food scarcity, coincided in the autumn of 1946 with national opposition, spearheaded by the Communists, to Dewan C.P. Ramaswami Iyer's plans for an independent Travancore under an "American-model" constitution which would have perpetuated his own power. Intense repression led to violent clashes and attacks on police camps in Punnapra and Vayalar on 24–27 October 1946, which left about 800 killed and ultimately vastly enhanced the prestige of the Communists in Kerala. The massacre prevented the alliance with the totally discredited dewan towards which some right-wing Congress leaders had been moving and Ramaswami Iyer, in the next year, accepted integration with India fairly easily, no doubt because he had realised that the alternative might well be a violent revolution. In this sense it was Punnapra-Vayalar which really brought about the integration of Travancore with India, blocking the road towards Balkanisation.[87]

Where *tebhaga* and Punnapra-Vayalar had gone to the brink of armed struggle, but failed to cross it, Telangana in Hyderabad state between July 1946 and October 1951 saw the biggest peasant guerrilla war so far of modern Indian history, affecting at its height about 3000 villages spread over 16,000 sq. miles and with a population of 3 million. The beginning of the uprising is traditionally dated from 4 July 1946, when thugs employed by the *deshmukh* of Visunur (one of the biggest and most oppressive of Telangana's landlords, with 40,000 acres) murdered a village militant, Doddi Komarayya, who had been defending a poor washerwoman's mite of land. Unlike *tebhaga* and to a much greater extent than in Travancore, the Communist-led

[87] K.C. George, *Immortal Punnapra-Vayalar* (New Delhi, 1976); Robin Jeffrey, "A Sanctified Label – Congress in Travancore Politics, 1938–48", in D.A. Low, ed., *Congress and the Raj* (New Delhi, 1977).

agrarian revolt in Telangana against particularly gross forms of feudal oppression retained, till the entry of the Indian army in September 1948, the broader dimensions of a national liberation struggle to overthrow the nizam and his Razakar bands and unite Hyderabad with India. Another decisive advantage was the very slack enforcement of the Arms Act in Hyderabad, where, as Sundarayya recalls, "large numbers of country-guns . . . were available and . . . in common use", while till September 1948 arms could be collected more or less openly in the neighbouring Andhra districts of Madras, since everyone, including the Congress, wanted to block the nizam's bid to set up an independent and autocratic Muslim-dominated state. Incidentally, though the urban Muslim population, including many workers, remained generally outside the Telangana struggle, the Communist-led peasant revolt also succeeded in defusing what might have been quite an explosive communal situation in Hyderabad state, where the first political movements in the 1930s had been under Arya Samaj and Hindu Mahasabha inspiration.[88]

As Travancore and Hyderabad revealed, the situation in the princely states was full of radical possibilities, and 1946–7 in fact saw a major upsurge in states peoples' movements almost everywhere. The Congress high command, and particularly Sardar Patel, tackled the situation in what had become the standard practice of the party: using popular movements as a lever to extort concessions from princes, while simultaneously restraining radical elements (or even using force to suppress them once the prince had been brought to heel, as after "police action" in Hyderabad). Thus in Kashmir in June 1946, after Nehru had chivalrously rushed off to get arrested on hearing the news of the detention of Sheikh Abdullah by the very unpopular and despotic Hindu maharaja of a Muslim-majority state, Patel assured Wavell that Nehru had gone against his advice,[89] and soon began negotiations with Kashmir prime minister Kak to bring about a peaceful accession to India. "This alters the whole outlook for the states", the nawab of Bhopal declared on hearing of the appointments

---

[88] P. Sundarayya, *Telengana Peoples' Struggle and Its Lessons* (Calcutta, 1972), pp. 2, 7–9, 40.

[89] Patel's interview with Wavell, 27 June 1946, in Mansergh, op. cit., vol. VIII, pp. 1068–9.

of Patel and his civil servant friend V.P. Menon to head the new States Department. On 5 July 1947, Patel assured the princes: "The Congress are no enemies of the Princely Order, but on the other hand, wish them and the people under their aegis all prosperity, contentment and happiness."[90] Between July 1947 and September 1948, Patel and Menon brought off first the "accession" and then the "integration" of the states through a skilful combination of threats of mass pressure and baits – "surrender" only of powers of defence, external affairs, and communications in the first phase, which the princes in any case had never enjoyed under British paramountcy, and generous offers subsequently of privy purses and offices of Rajpramukhs. The rapid unification of India is certainly Sardar Patel's greatest and very real achievement, but we must not forget the considerable role played here, too, by the existence or at least the potential presence of mass pressures, as well as the way socially radical possibilities were blocked by this speedy "revolution" from the top.

Popular movements in urban areas were seriously disrupted by the riots, which began precisely in Calcutta and Bombay, the two main centres of the 1945–6 upsurge. Yet five months after the August riots the students of Calcutta were again on the streets on 21 January 1947 in "Hands off Vietnam" demonstrations against the use of Dum Dum airport by French planes, and all communal divisions seemed forgotten in the absolutely united and ultimately victorious 85-day tram strike under Communist leadership which began the same day, followed soon afterwards by port employees and Howrah engineering workers. January and February 1947, in fact, saw a new strike wave, with 100,000 out in Kanpur textiles, a threat of a coal stoppage, and strike in Coimbatore, Karachi, and elsewhere due "largely to Communist agitation".[91] "There are strikes everywhere – everybody wants higher wages and less work", Birla complained to Gandhi's secretary Pyarelal on 18 January.[92]

---

[90] V.P. Menon, *Story of the Integration of Indian* States (Bombay, 1956), p. 96.

[91] Wavell, quoting Labour Minister Jagjivan Ram, 14 January 1947, in idem, *Viceroy's Journal*, op. cit., p. 416.

[92] G.D. Birla, *Bapu—Correspondence 1940–47*, op. cit., p. 434.

The socially radical movements of which Telangana was the climax never coalesced into an organised and effective countrywide political alternative. The fear they undoubtedly inspired, however, helped to bring about the final compromise by which a "peaceful" transfer of power was purchased at the cost of Partition and a communal holocaust. V.P. Menon reported to Wavell in the wake of the early 1947 strike wave "that Congress leaders were losing popularity . . . there were serious internal troubles in Congress and great fear of the Left Wing: and that the danger of labour difficulties was acute."[93] A week later, Wavell's journal recorded a conversation with Patel "about the danger of the Communists. I got the impression he would like to declare the Party illegal",[94] a desire which the home minister would fulfil within a few months of Independence, in March 1948. The British government was also quick to come forward with a dramatic gesture when in February 1947 the League refusal to join the constituent assembly and co-operate in cabinet functioning led to a major political crisis, with the Congress demanding the resignation of the League ministers and threatening to withdraw its own nominees from the Interim Government if its demands were not met. This was the immediate context of Attlee's famous speech in the Commons on 20 February 1947, fixing June 1948 as the deadline for transfer of power and announcing the replacement of Wavell by Mountbatten. The hint of possible Partition or even Balkanisation into numerous states was very clear in this policy statement, but the bait of complete transfer of power by a definite and fairly early data proved too tempting to be refused, particularly as the only real alternative for the Congress was to plunge into another mass confrontation, difficult in the context of communal riots and very dangerous socially in view of what appeared to be a growing Left menace.

Something like a cult has developed around Mountbatten, depicting him as super-statesman-cum-Prince Charming who solved the subcontinent's problems in record time through a combination of military forthrightness, personality, and tact.[95] There is enormous

[93] Wavell, *Viceroy's Journal*, op. cit., entry for 9 January 1947, p. 408.
[94] Ibid., entry for 15 January 1947, p. 411.
[95] This is most blatant in L. Collins and D. Lapierre, *Freedom at Midnight* (Delhi, 1976).

Popular Movements and National Leadership 569

exaggeration here. The formula of freedom-with-Partition was coming to be widely accepted well before Mountbatten took charge, and the final draft of Wavell's "breakdown plan" in September 1946 had already envisaged complete British withdrawal by 31 March 1948.[96] The working out of the Mountbatten plan in fact revealed once again the potential strength of the Congress position, as well as the repeated failure of its leaders to use this fully due to their eagerness for quick and peaceful accession to power. Mountbatten's original "Plan Balkan" had envisaged transfer of power to separate provinces, which – along with princely states rendered independent by the lapse of paramountcy – would then have the choice of joining India, Pakistan, or remaining separate. A single outburst by Nehru in Simla on 10 May was sufficient for Mountbatten to give this up completely. Mountbatten himself, as well as his admirers, have been full of praise for the decision, on an "absolute hunch", of showing this plan privately to Nehru on the eve of seeking cabinet sanction for it. The historically much more significant point surely is that Nehru's opposition was sufficient to make Mountbatten abandon a plan on which British officials had been working for several weeks. The alternative then adopted owed its inception not to Mountbatten but to V.P. Menon, who had suggested in January 1947 a transfer to two central governments, India and Pakistan, on the basis of grant of Dominion Status with a right of secession. Vallabhbhai Patel, significantly enough, had privately agreed with this idea, even though formally it meant a retreat from the Lahore Resolution of 1929, since Dominion Status on the basis of existing political structures would obviate the need to wait for agreement in the constituent assembly, ensure a peaceful and very quick transfer of power, win for India influential friends in Britain by pandering to British sentiments about Crown and Commonwealth, and allow for continuity in the bureaucracy and army.[97] Unlike Plan Balkan, the revised scheme did guard against fragmentation of the country, but at the cost, it must be added, of blocking some interesting non-communal regional possibilities – moves towards a united, autonomous Bengal by

[96] Wavell, *Viceroy's Journal*, op. cit., p. 344.
[97] V.P. Menon, *Transfer of Power*, op. cit., pp. 363–4.

Suhrawardy and Abdul Hasham, which a few Congress leaders like Sarat Bose seemed prepared to consider, and the demand of Khan Abdul Ghaffar Khan for an independent Pathan state in the N.W.F.P. The Frontier Congress leaders felt that only such a slogan could counter the League bid to capture the province for Pakistan, now that anti-Muslim riots in Hindu-majority provinces had weakened the traditional Pathan identification with Indian nationalism. The Congress high command in 1947 let the Pathans down very badly indeed, signally failing to use its position of strength to block the decision to have a plebiscite on the India–Pakitsan issue alone, and that on the basis of the old limited electorate. The N.W.F.P. went to Pakistan, with the local Congress boycotting the plebiscite in protest, by the decision of just 9.52 per cent of its total population.[98] The Frontier Gandhi would later declare with justice that he and his movement had been "thrown to the wolves" by the Congress leadership.

IV

In conclusion, a few general comments may be attempted on two broad problems which emerge from the study of 1945–7 developments – the reasons behind the failure of the Left alternative, and the nature of the great but incomplete transition which was consummated on 15 August.

Within the Communist movement, a strong tendency had developed by late 1947 to attribute the Left failure to the allegedly "reformist" policies of the leadership, and particularly of P.C. Joshi; and at the Calcutta Party Congress in February 1948 Joshi was unceremoniously ousted as General Secretary and replaced by B.T. Ranadive with his much more militant line. Judging from official comments and reactions, Communist actions at least at local levels were hardly lacking in militancy in the 1945–7 period. A glance through the Home Political (Internal) files immediately reveals how completely the C.P.I. had displaced the Congress as Enemy No. 1 already by the end of 1945. It may also be argued that Communist militancy was often

---

[98] For details, see A.K. Gupta *North-West Frontier Province Legislature and Freedom Struggle 1932–47* (New Delhi, 1976).

Popular Movements and National Leadership 571

more effective during these years than in the "Ranadive period", which saw such complete fiascos as the call for a countrywide railway strike and rebellion on 9 March 1949, as well as the gradual decline even of the Telangana armed struggle. Party cadres and the leadership in fact showed unusual flexibility at times, as when the Students' Federation joined the Forward Bloc demonstration in Calcutta on 21 November 1945 and their action was endorsed next day by P.C. Joshi's telegram: "Get all war-time understanding out of your heads . . . New tactical line needed. Be with the people."[99] A considerable lag is noticeable, however, at the level of theoretical formulation and general slogans. Here the persistent calls for Congress–League–Communist unity made little sense and even sounded rather pathetic at a time when the Congress and the League obviously had no intention at all of coming together, and in fact seemed to agree only in a common detestation of the Communists. Another example would be the curious passage in the C.P.I. election manifesto which gave an assurance that the party "shall not touch the small zamindar or the rich peasant but shall open before them the prospect of becoming the best of the farmers and cattle-breeders, reputed members in their own village."[100] Less than a year after this programmatic statement, the party would be leading the Bengal sharecroppers in a struggle against the *jotedars*, who were not zamindars but big farmers.

As in other periods of "united front", the central problem was to combine broad multi-class objectives with retention of initiative and independence. The Chinese Communists under Mao, as everyone knows, did this brilliantly during the anti-Japanese war; an example less known would be the Bolsheviks, who up to the very eve of October 1917 had a very modest "bourgeois-democratic" minimum programme (an eight-hour day, a democratic republic, and return to peasants of Otrezki lands seized by the general), but certainly never expected bourgeois parties like the Kadets to carry out this programme

[99] Gautam Chattopadhyay, "The Almost Revolution", op. cit., p. 445.
[100] P.C. Joshi, *For the Final Bid for Power* (Bombay, 1945), p. 118. The document is thus very far from being an anticipation of Ranadive sectarianism as has been curiously misconstrued recently by Bhagwan Singh Josh in his *Communist Movement in the Punjab* (New Delhi, 1979).

for them. In colonial India, too, substantial advances were made in regions like Kerala and Telangana by Communists taking over the initiative and leadership in the national struggle, as when P. Krishna Pillai, E.M.S. Namboodiripad, and A.K. Gopalan during the 1930s simultaneously built up the Congress, the C.S.P. as legal cover, and the illegal Communist Party in Travancore and Malabar. But all too often united front came to mean a policy of waiting on bourgeois leaders and putting undeserved trust in their "progressive" intentions, an attitude which in turn repeatedly bred an equally disastrous relapse into ultra-Left sectarianism.

But failures in Communist leadership probably provide only a small part of the explanation for the Left defeat in the post-War years. The Communists, we must remember, were no more than a small, though in these years rapidly growing, force at the national plane, with only scattered pockets of real influence.[101] In addition, they still had to live down their 1942 regulation. The break within the Left over Quit India had pushed the Socialists much closer to the Congress high command, and a Fortnightly Report from U.P. noted with relief in November 1945 that "Congress Socialists as such have not come much to notice", since there was now "little difference in either the avowed objective or the outward means of attaining that objective between the Congress and the Congress Socialists."[102] The British, as we have seen, were alarmed above all by the militancy of urban labour; but with a few short-lived exceptions (Calcutta in November 1945 and February 1946, Bombay in February 1946, Punnapra-Vayalar in October 1946), all the strikes of the period were on economic demands alone. This may have been partly the responsibility of a trade union leadership sunk in "economism", but it remains more than a little dubious whether labour would have responded on a countrywide scale to a call for political action coming from the Communists alone. (A joint Congress–Communist call

---

[101] 15,000 members at the First Party Congress in May 1943, more than 100,000 at the Second in February 1948.

[102] "Fortnightly Report from UP first half of November 1945", Home Poll (1), 18/11/54.

would have been quite a different thing, as the British were well aware, but the Congress high command had no intention of going in the direction.) As for peasant movements, a crucial limitation here came from the marked, and growing, regional variations. All-India peasant unity against landlords was possible only in regions like Telangana, with its crude and blatant forms of feudalism. Regions like Punjab or Gujarat, where considerable rich peasant development coincided with the absence of zamindari, had in sharp contrast kept largely aloof even from the 1942 rebellion, while Communists naturally found entry difficult for a time into the quiet India strongholds of Bihar or east U.P. Poor peasants, sharecroppers, and agricultural labourers, often of low-caste or tribal origin, still provided combustible material. But, as the experience of the later stages of *tebhaga*, 1948–9, and Naxalbari has repeatedly indicated, movements of such sections alone, however militant and heroic, tend to end in a self-defeating isolation in which guerrilla war degenerates into sporadic individual terrorism. The Telangana "spark" thus failed to kindle a "prairie fire".

Controversies about Communist policies naturally lead on to the broader question of evaluating the real significance of August 1947. The problem lies in combining recognition of the very real and fundamental changes associated with the coming of freedom with an awareness of the equally real limits and contradictions. Perhaps some guidance can be sought from Antonio Gramsci's very interesting concept, developed in the context of his study of Risorgimento Italy, of "passive revolution": "passive" not in the sense of popular forces being inactive (as they were not in nineteenth-century Italy and even less so during the Indian freedom movement), but because the privileged groups in town and country were able to successfully detach attainment of political independence and unity from radical social change. Gramsci explained this in terms of the success of the leading bourgeois group, the Moderates headed by Cavour, in asserting its "transformismo", bringing about "the gradual but continuous absorption of the active elements produced by allied groups – and even of those which came from antagonistic groups and seemed irreconcilably hostile." If in Italy "the Action Party [of Mazzini and Garibaldi] was in fact indirectly led by Cavour", the Indian counterpart would be the subordination of Left elements within the Congress, best typified by Nehru and the C.S.P. in the 1930s, to the basically right-oriented high command. Such "hegemony" was however sharply distinct, according to Gramsci, from what he considered to have been the classic "Jacobin" model of successful and thoroughgoing bourgeois revolution based on mobilisation of the peasantry and total destruction of feudalism in the countryside. In Italy, despite unification and political independence, full-scale capitalist transformation proved very difficult to achieve, since the new ruling group was a bloc between northern industrialists and southern landlords established at the cost of peasant aspirations, and fundamental agrarian change remained a "rivoluzione mancata" (a "missing" or "absent" revolution). One major consequence was the perpetuation and sharpening of regional disparities, the north flourishing at the cost of the south – modern Italy's persistent "southern question". Historical parallels can never be exact, and a number of differences are evident in the Indian context (e.g. the absence of a Piedmont, or of direct foreign help in overthrowing alien rule, and the related much greater role of popular forces, which ensured the establishment of democratic forms far more quickly than in Italy); it would be labouring the obvious, however, to list the similarities. It is interesting that Gramsci in 1922 made a passing reference to the Gandhian as a "native theorisation of the 'passive revolution' with religious overtones."[103]

The millions who rejoiced throughout the subcontinent thrilled to Nehru's midnight speech on India's "tryst with destiny", and made of 15 August an unforgettable experience, had certainly not been entirely deluded, as subsequent developments abundantly proved. The Communist slogan in 1948–9 of "Yeh Azadi Jhut Hai" cut very little ice, for the new Indian government certainly did not act as an imperialist puppet; "a passive revolution" also implies fundamental, though slow and contradictory change. Yet it is possible to sympathise

---

[103] Antonio Gramsci, *Prison Notebooks*, ed. Q. Hoare and N. Smith (New York, 1971), pp. 59, 107, and *passim*. For a recent discussion by historians of the concept of passive revolution, see John A. Davis, ed., *Gramsci and Italy's Passive Revolution* (London, 1979).

with the many to whom independence seemed a sorry thing if compared to the generous dreams of the freedom fighters, and it is well known that Gandhi in great part shared this sense of disillusionment. The agony of many committed Leftists was well expressed in the last two poems Samar Sen has written: "The battleships [of the R.I.N.] lie silent in harbour, immobilised by treachery"; in Noakhali, Bihar, or Garhmukteswar, Hindus and Muslims find unity only after death; and "the passions of youth have become the lust of aging men."[104] A savage, but not entirely unjust, comment on the transformation of patriots into power-hungry politicians.

[104] *Samar Sener Kabita* (Calcutta, 1954), pp. 134–6.

14

The Return of Labour to South Asian History

SOME THIRTY YEARS AGO, Eric Stokes had hailed "the return of the peasant" to modern Indian history.[1] And, indeed, studies of peasant protest and of "autonomous" or "indigenous" forms of popular, predominantly rural, culture came to be prioritised in South Asian scholarship for a whole generation, above all through the impact of the Subaltern Studies project. Today, an important renewal of labour history has begun after years of neglect and marginalisation, though with much less fanfare and attention internationally or even within the country.[2] Significantly, this is not a revival in the sense of a mere return to old interests and approaches. It has been accompanied by intense debates, auto-critiques, the exploration of new themes, dimensions, methods. Raj Chandavarkar's two substantial volumes on the Bombay (Mumbai) textile industry, labour, and city life need to be located in the context of this renewal. The significance, as well as the limits, of his achievement can be best appreciated through

---

[1] Stokes 1978.

[2] There is now an active Association of Labour Historians, periodic conferences on labour history, and the building up of a central archival collection at the National Labour Institute near Delhi (accessible at <www.indialabourarchives.com>). There are signs also that the research interests of younger scholars, for long focused successively on anti-colonial popular movements, predominantly rural "subaltern" protest, and then questions of culture somewhat abstracted from material conditions, are beginning to move towards labour history.

a simultaneous look at certain other works of recent scholarship. Among the latter, I have chosen four: Ian Kerr on railway labour, Dilip Simeon on Jamshedpur steel workers and Chota Nagpur coal miners, Janaki Nair's comparative study of the Kolar gold mines and Bangalore textiles, and, most recently, Chitra Joshi's masterly work on Kanpur.[3]

Early research on capitalist industry and labour in late-colonial India followed patterns reminiscent of the preliminary phases of scholarship in other parts of the world. There was, first, a certain amount of research with a "managerial" kind of thrust, notably Morris David Morris' study of the Bombay cotton textiles labour force in terms of recruitment, adaptation of rural migrants to the conditions of modern industry, and the evolution of mechanisms of labour control and discipline.[4] Development along broadly unilinear, rightly and properly "modernising", capitalist lines was assumed to be the norm. Indian departures from it – slow or distorted growth of industry, an unstable, inefficient, and volatile working class, backward styles of management – needed to be explained. Here, the big debate turned around whether the impediments came primarily from colonial constraints, or from the persistence of indigenous structures and values. Scholarship of a second kind started from a very different kind of commitment, one given to the cause of labour, and often to socialist revolution. Activists, present or past, of labour movements and trade unions made significant contributions to this other kind of work. As in labour histories of this type elsewhere, in the pre-Thompsonian era, the focus tended to be on strikes, the rise and fall of trade unions, debates on Communist or other leadership strategies – on all of which there would be a considerable amount of easily available and obvious data. Explanations for the ebb and flow of labour movements and organisations tended to be in terms of a combination of economic conjunctures and "correct" or "incorrect" styles of leadership: variants of what would soon come to be rejected

---

[3] Chandavarkar 1994, Chandavarkar 1998, Kerr 1995, Simeon 1995, Nair 1998, Joshi 2003.
[4] Morris 1965.

as histories that were economistic and written "from above" alone, blind towards key questions of culture and autonomy.[5]

The radical-populist turn of the generation, inspired worldwide by Vietnam and May 1968, brought about a major change in moods, in which disillusionment with orthodox left-wing forms of party and trade-union organisation went along with soaring hopes in the potentials of "subaltern" self-activity. Publication dates indicate what proved to be a rather brief spell of interest in South Asian labour history during the late 1970s and early 1980s. This was also the time when South Asian labour historians began to become aware of the importance of the Thompsonian transformation of their subject. Instances of the scholarship of these years would include work produced in some Australian universities (the studies of Newman on Bombay labour, and Murphy on four textile centres in South India), the dedicated research over many years of Ranajit Dasgupta (a rare instance of a Communist activist who was able to combine basic adherence to orthodox Marxism with a remarkable openness to new ideas), and the beginning of the research activities of a group of young scholars gathered together by Sabyasachi Bhattacharya at Jawaharlal Nehru University, New Delhi – some of which have borne fruit only in quite recent times.[6]

But academic interest in labour studies proved rather evanescent, for the vogue for "histories from below" manifested itself, in India as well as in most other Third World countries, mainly through the valorisation of peasant movements and their histories. This was, of

---

[5] Two instances would be Karnik 1967 and Sen 1970.

[6] Newman 1981, Murphy 1977. Ranajit Dasgupta's numerous research papers on Bengal labour history, spread over several decades, are most conveniently gathered together (Dasgupta 1994). See, also, his important dialogue with Dipesh Chakrabarty (about whom more soon), in Chakrabarty and Dasgupta 1981. A sample of work located at the Jawaharlal Nehru University during these years (articles, rather than books) would include Bhattacharya 1981, Bhattacharya 1986; Joshi 1981, Joshi 1985; Mohapatra 1985. It may be noted that the origins of industrial labour attracted considerable research attention during these years: apart from Mohapatra, and several essays in Dasgupta, one needs to mention particularly Gupta 1974, and a seminal essay by Lalita Chakrabarti (Chakrabarti 1978).

course, the predominant note in the early volumes of the Subaltern Studies series, the project which ultimately came to acquire an international reputation that has been both unprecedented and unique for the world of modern Indian history. The peasant focus in radical scholarship was not unnatural, given the apparent triumphs of rural insurrections in China, Vietnam, and elsewhere. India, too, had in the late 1960s and 1970s its share of Maoist peasant rebellion in the Naxalbari movement, embers of which seemed to simmer on in some parts of the country – indeed, still do. India, during these years, saw also considerable labour militancy, notably the railway strike of 1975 and the heroic, year-long struggle of Bombay textile workers of 1982–3. But the defeat of 1983 marked the end of an epoch, for soon came the "structural adjustments" and globalising pressures which have led, in India as elsewhere, to the decline of many old industrial centres and what seems sometimes to be a virtual elimination of the old kind of working class.

The logic underlying the trajectory of Indian labour studies during these years is perhaps best appreciated through a brief look at the work of the one member of the Subaltern Studies editorial collective whose research area, initially, was the modern industrial working class. Dipesh Chakrabarty published his book on Calcutta jute mill workers in 1989, but the core of his thesis had already been conveyed through a series of research essays in the early 1980s.[7] Chakrabarty's work, though controversial, was widely acknowledged as highly original and almost seductive in its brilliance. Yet, in hindsight, it seems clear that, far from inaugurating any new surge in labour history, it may have acted as a positive dampener for further research. Chakrabarty himself, after 1989, moved away decisively from labour studies, refusing even to enter into debate with his later critics (among whom, as we shall see, Raj Chandavarkar has been the most persistent and aggressive).

Thompsonian in his rejection of reductive economism and focus upon cultural dimensions, Chakrabarty's work still veered away from many of the stresses and values of *The Making of the English Working*

---

[7] Chakrabarty 1981a, Chakrabarty 1981b, Chakrabarty 1983.

Class. The basic emphasis was on the reproduction of pre-bourgeois, "semi-feudal", deeply hierarchised assumptions within colonial factories as well in workers' organisations. Thus, capitalists managed their workers not through the procedures of a Foucauldian disciplinary regime, but via "sardars" or "jobbers" rooted in caste, religious, and rural structures of domination. The emergence of class consciousness, in the full Marxist sense, Chakrabarty argued, rested on the premise of a "hegemonic bourgeois culture" – and this colonialism could never create, governed as it was by what Chakrabarty's Subaltern Studies colleague Partha Chatterjee would soon term the basic "rule of colonial difference".[8] Trade-union organisers were, no doubt, often sincere and dedicated, but they, even the Communists among them, still necessarily came from educated, "respectable" (in Bengali, *bhadralok*) strata, and they, too, could not escape the insidious pulls of a semi-feudal culture. The assumption of a trajectory similar to that in the advanced bourgeois West, governed by the supposedly uniform and inexorable laws of capitalist economic development, only made them blind to the ways in which their own relations with "their" workers remained hierarchical, undemocratic, akin to that between the "babu" and the "coolie". Worker attitudes towards their employers and overseers oscillated sharply between the poles of deference and defiance. Militant moments were not rare, but what remained absent were stable, long-lasting trade-union structures.

The enduring significance of Chakrabarty's work is undeniable. No serious South Asian labour history after him has been able to ignore the questions he raised, in particular the intersections of community ties of religion and caste with class. Nor could a simple, unilinear progression towards higher levels of proletarian class consciousness be assumed any longer to be somehow natural. But three kinds of problems appear relevant at this point. Chakrabarty implicitly postulated a Western/non-Western dichotomy, where Indian factory and trade-union realities were counterposed against what was really a model at a very high level of abstraction read off directly from Volume I of Marx's *Capital*. One is left in some doubt as to whether

---

[8] Chakrabarty 1989, p. 4; Chatterjee 1993, p. 10.

a not-dissimilar gap might not emerge if the empirical details of nineteenth-century England are compared directly with Marx's initial abstract model. (To take one instance: there may have been more domestic servants, no doubt entangled within "semi-feudal" connections, in many mid-Victorian cities, than factory workers.) Did not such an approach do some violence to what Marx had explicitly proclaimed to be a method of moving from the abstract towards the concrete, only through a whole series of mediations? Then there was also the interesting fact of a leading member of the Subaltern Studies collective developing such a critical, not to say near-cynical, view of labour protest and organisation precisely when his other colleagues were writing histories of peasant movements of a much more eulogistic kind. Doubts regarding the limits of "semi-feudal" modes of leadership, for instance, were not allowed entrance into Ranajit Guha's *Elementary Aspects* – in some ways, the flagship of the entire project. "Peasant" insurgent consciousness was probed here in a structuralist manner, through a series of rebellions, most of which had been headed by local chiefs, landlords, sometimes even kings, with little attention to possible internal tensions between leaders and followers.[9] Most directly relevant for my present argument, however, are the ways in which Chakrabarty's prioritisation of what might be called the "backward linkages" of labour culture – its rootedness in caste, religious, rural, pre-modern traditions – may have discouraged subsequent studies of workers in their grappling with the new conditions of city and factory environments. If culture was the decisive dimension, and that culture needed to be explored in terms of its roots in the countryside, surely a shift in focus from the city worker to the peasant made ample sense.

But, fairly soon, attention began moving away even from peasants, as dominant strands within Subaltern Studies moved towards more pronounced "culturalist" positions. The problematic shifted towards questions of cultural domination by the modern, "post-Enlightenment" West, acting primarily on and through the colonial middle class. As I have suggested elsewhere, a decline of the "subaltern" was

---

[9] Guha 1983.

taking place within Subaltern Studies: or, more precisely, the elite/subaltern polarity had come to be abstracted from its initial, quasi-class moorings and made implicitly equivalent to a Western cultural conquest/indigenous cultural autonomy binary.[10] Meanwhile, the old kind of industrial working class and its organisations, in India as well as nearly everywhere, seemed to have entered into terminal decline, and the collapse of "actually-existing" socialist regimes in 1989–91 appeared to cap the process. The years during and just after "the Fall" marked the nadir of labour history, a time when even getting publishers to agree to bring out works on such an unfashionable theme became a matter of some difficulty.

II

How, then, did a renewal become possible? Certainly, current conditions in India do not indicate any prospect of a major upturn in the fortunes of organised labour. Quite the reverse, in fact, for the right-wing regime in Delhi between 1998 and May 2004 was more committed to neo-liberal strategies than any of its predecessors, and labour and trade-union rights came to be threatened on a massive scale. (There were protests, demonstrations, occasional one-day strikes, but nothing particularly effective.) But, maybe the very depth of the crisis, some of the forms it has taken, and the crassness of the present worldwide triumphalism of the votaries of the "free" market, have had some paradoxical consequences for sensitive academics. The withering away of expectations of any kind of ultimately inevitable "forward march" of labour has occasionally stimulated a more nuanced historical understanding, where empathy is finely balanced with critical detachment.[11] In more specific terms, what has become impossible to retain today, as so many old centres of reasonably effective labour organisation enter into apparently terminal decline, is an earlier frequent radical disdain for organised trade unionism as catering to a privileged minority with wages and conditions so obvi-

---

[10] Sarkar 1997.

[11] The premier instance, so far, of such fine-grained research is Chitra Joshi's *Lost Worlds* (Joshi 2003).

ously superior to the mass of urban casual labour and rural toilers. The very distinction, for long assumed as a given, between the organised/formal and unorganised/informal sectors of non-agricultural employment seems to be vanishing.[12] And a questioning of this and related polarities, we shall see, has been quite central to the work of Chandavarkar and other recent historians of labour.

Raj Chandavarkar first attracted scholarly attention through two articles in *Modern Asian Studies*, in 1981 and 1985. The arguments and supportive data presented in these remain crucial to his subsequent books and have been incorporated in unchanged form as chapters four and two in *Imperial Power and Popular Politics*. The 1985 essay questioned the model of a linear, "normal" track of development from handicrafts, through forms of putting-out and manufacture, to large-scale, machine- and factory-based industry. Despite their manifold other differences, theorists of "modernisation" and Marxists had for long shared such an assumption. Deviations and retardations from this norm, derived from what was then thought to have been the paradigmatic British model of industrialisation, were assumed to be lags, signs of persistent backwardness. In the Bombay textile industry, however, the point of origin and for long the heart of Indian capitalist development, what remained characteristic virtually

[12] The formal sector has been conventionally defined as that governed by state laws fixing minimum wages, hours of work, etc. From the initial factory acts of the late-colonial era onwards, such regulations had been made applicable only to units that used power and employed a minimum number of workers. During the post-Independence Nehruvian era, with trade unions gaining strength and the passing of a series of reasonably progressive labour laws, capitalists developed strategies whereby production shifted to smaller units. Textiles provide the clearest example. Particularly after the defeat of the strike of 1982–3, power-looms came to be shifted massively from big weaving factories in old industrial centres like Mumbai and Ahmedabad to a new kind of widely scattered "domestic" or "cottage" production, largely outside the scope of labour regulations, where unionisation was much more difficult. Today, the globalised free trade régime threatens also this renovated kind of "domestic" industry, while the state is in the process of removing the vestiges of the "formal"/"informal" distinction by drastically curtailing the old regime of limited, but real, labour protection and welfare.

throughout was the combination of large factories with a considerable degree of putting-out forms, small workshops, and petty or artisanal units of production. Even in the 1920s and 1930s, seventy years or more after the foundation of the industry, one-third or more of the workforce was hired on a daily or casual basis, and "independent" industrial investment in factories went along with often the same businessmen engaged in putting-out as well as in "comprador" trading in British piecegoods imports. A major portion of even second- or third-generation industrial workers retained strong links with their village homes. Instead of the perennial search for explanations in terms of assumed backwardness, Chandavarkar suggested, one should rather explore the considerable degree to which such flexible forms may not have been reasonably successful adaptations by both capitalists and workers to specific circumstances. Thus frequent short-term fluctuations in the price of raw cotton as well as in the demand for yarn and cloth made "flexible" investment by capitalists an eminently sensible strategy. The highly oppressive conditions of factory work and uncertainties of urban employment made workers who still had some land prefer circular movements between village and city to one-way migration to industry. They tended to invest whatever they could save on land, kept their families in the villages (living conditions in the city slums were generally atrocious), tried to go back there during harvests and festivals, and looked forward to returning permanently upon retirement.

In more general terms, Chandavarkar sought to shift the focus of attention away from the usual concentration on constraints limiting Indian capitalist development, whether colonial or indigenous-cultural, and giving it an allegedly peculiar, "colonial" character. He emphasised, rather, instances of success through effective adaptations: as with South Indian handlooms in the early twentieth century. It may be important to note, at this point, that assumptions of linear development were coming under attack even in British economic history from around the mid 1980s, and this may have emboldened Chandavarkar to embark on his revisionist enterprise. One is tempted to suggest a link between this interpretive shift and the transition on a world scale from around the 1970s, away from Fordism towards scattered, flexible forms of investment and production. The lineaments of contemporary capitalism are probably making historians more aware of the non-linear and more variegated features even of the era of the classic "industrial revolution", for the big factory no longer appears such an inevitable end product of historical development.[13]

Chandavarkar's 1981 essay raised important questions about another standard thrust in labour studies, homologous in many ways with the formal/informal disjunction. Attention had been concentrated on conditions and conflicts within factories, in virtual abstraction from the neighbourhoods or *mohallas* where industrial workers lived, embedded within an amorphous and highly varied mass of poor as well as lower-middle-class people. The neighbourhood, further, was usually identified as the locus for elements of heterogeneity, cultural and religious sectionalism, rural continuities – all hindering the growth of ideal-typically "pure" proletarian consciousness the seedbed for which would be necessarily the factory. Chandavarkar was able to go beyond both these stereotypes, through a vivid study of "Girangaon", the area within Bombay city where most textile workers lived (often within walking distance of their places of work), with its slums, vibrant street life, and patterns of entertainment. The neighbourhood was the site of multiple dependencies, binding workers to the markets for housing, credit, and labour recruitment in interrelated ways. The jobber or labour contractor through whom mill owners usually recruited and disciplined workers often doubled as house agent, moneylender, petty trader, or shopkeeper in the neighbourhood. Chandavarkar thus emphasised the interrelations between

[13] See, for instance, Cannadine 1984, and Sabel and Zeitlin 1985. There can be a more and less "optimistic" reading of these dimensions, however, whether of past times or the present, and it may not be entirely irrelevant to note that Chandavarkar, who cites the above two articles in his 1994 volume, makes no mention of the important and pioneering study of Berg 1985, with its quasi-Thompsonian emphasis on the exploitative dimensions and the everyday life of working men and women in such continuations or revivals of "domestic" forms of capitalist production. (E.P. Thompson himself is a surprising omission from the otherwise very comprehensive bibliographies of Chandavarkar's two volumes, which contain a large number of references to studies of industrial and labour history of countries outside South Asia.)

the forms of hierarchical domination on the shop floor and in the *mohalla*. But the 1981 essay simultaneously probed the possibilities of part-reversals of such connections. The neighbourhood was far from being always a source of weakness, from the point of view of labour militancy and class consciousness. It was also the social arena within which workers exercised a degree of counter-pressure and autonomy, much more so than in the factory with its quasi-despotic forms of control and repression and ever-present threats of dismissal for insubordination. Even the jobber was not quite the omnipotent figure sometimes imagined by historians. The hierarchies of domination were multiple, occasionally conflicting, and the jobber was not immune from everyday neighbourhood pressures and sanctions. Jobbers recruited and controlled workers through caste, religious, kinship, or village connections, but these, too, were ambivalent, becoming, on occasion, channels for counter-pressures. Neighbourhood connections and pressures were particularly vital during strikes, with strike-breakers being subjected, for instance, to various forms of social ostracism.

Chandavarkar urged the need to go beyond the common assumption that the persistence of working-class connections with the countryside and with pre-modern patterns of social life and culture was necessarily a hindrance to labour consciousness or militancy. Quite often, it was the worker with land and village connections who could fall back upon them for sustenance during long strikes or lock-outs: the more "proletarianised" were obliged to surrender and serve as blacklegs. The 1981 essay was also prepared to explore certain more novel possibilities, and provided some details about the ways in which the Communist-led Girni Kamgar Union, which helped to organise and sustain two massive strikes in Bombay textiles during 1928 and 1929 and, at its peak, had 65,000 members, effectively intervened in the neighbourhoods to subvert jobber and other forms of "normal" control. For a brief moment, it was also able to set up elected mill committees of workers. Unfortunately, however, as we shall see, Chandavarkar later moved away somewhat from this early interest in the details of labour autonomy and protest, as he became engrossed in building up a polemical counter-model to Dipesh Chakrabarty.

Let us turn now to Chandavarkar's two major works. *Origins of Industrial Capitalism in India* presents empirically and analytically rich accounts of the growth of Bombay city, its working population in their relationships with their rural origins, and the conditions of life in "Girangaon". The focus, inevitably, remains on textiles: the evolution of the industry from the 1850s; workplace structures; business initiatives in the inter-war decades to "rationalise" and "standardise" labour in order to maintain and enhance profits; and the powerful resistance mounted by workers to such efforts. Colonial state policies, of course, enter centrally into all these narratives, and there is also a closing chapter about the shifting and ambiguous relations between millworkers and the politics of national, class, religious, and caste identities. The collection of essays, old and new, that Chandavarkar brought out in 1998 as *Imperial Power and Popular Politics* in part covers similar ground. But there are important extensions: a critique of the widely held stereotype about Indian workers as perpetually immature proletarians peculiarly prone to sporadic violence, and excellent studies of police and public order in Bombay and the plague panic of the late 1890s. The volume begins with a valuable introduction summing up the author's approach and methods, but ends with two rather pedestrian and over-general essays on Gandhian nationalism and "South Asia and World Capitalism".

Running through the volumes is the sustained questioning of a series of interrelated and homologous polarities, which, Chandavarkar suggests, have bedevilled the entire field of South Asian industrial and labour history through assumed total oppositions: rural and urban; informal and formal sectors; neighbourhood and shop floor; "semi-feudal" domination of workers through jobber intermediaries versus "proper" capitalist managerial methods. Similarly, the alleged tendency of Indian workers to swing between deification and defiance, acceptance of paternalist ties and sporadic bouts of militancy or violence, was counterposed against "mature" proletarian consciousness, stable trade unions, self-activity and, perhaps, socialist politics. The important, and to a considerable extent, convincing point made by Chandavarkar is that acceptance of this set of polar oppositions has been common to modernising theorists, orthodox Marxists, and the culturalist turn embodied in Chakrabarty and late Subaltern Studies alike. His polemic, therefore, is directed simultaneously against all three, but most vehemently against Chakrabarty, who, he implies, has retained the old discursive structure while inverting its values. Thus, advocates of modernisation, and orthodox Marxism, had assumed and largely welcomed a unilinear, if maybe often belated, transition from tradition towards modernity, from feudalism through capitalism towards socialism, on a world scale. The subalternist stress on "colonial difference" questions the possibility as well as the value of such progression, and at times veers towards a preference for the premodern, the indigenous, the authentic: but the assumed disjunctions remain very similar.

The polarities are evidently grounded in a Western/non-Western, colonial/colonised binary opposition which, depending on the associated value judgements, can have both orientalist and anticolonial-nationalist implications. Chandavarkar does not elaborate this theme much, but the introductory essay to his 1994 volume does make an important point about South Asian labour history having been hindered for long by the domination of the entire field by a single, imperialist/nationalist binary.[14] Questioning of this central paradigm of Indian-nationalist as well as much Marxist historiography tends to evoke suspicions – not always entirely groundless, it has to be added – of apologetic, neo-colonial motivations. Any such charge, however, would be quite unfair to Chandavarkar. His analysis of the hindrances to indigenous capitalist growth, in fact, follows lines similar to the standard, vigorously anti-imperialist, left-nationalist-Marxist account of Amiya Bagchi.[15] Indeed, at one point, he adds to that critique in an important way. Drawing on the research of Marika Vicziany, Chandavarkar explains the well-known shift of big Indian export merchants of Bombay towards investment in the cotton textile industry from the 1850s by the gradual easing out of indigenous traders from external commerce (notably the China opium trade) by growing British domination.[16] He also emphasises the many ways in which the peculiarities of capital investment in Bombay textiles – continual shifts between factories and putting-out forms,

[14] Chandavarkar 1994, p. 4.
[15] Bagchi 1972.
[16] "... the development of the cotton textile industry was a response to the subordination of the Indian capital and not a function of its linear progression from trade to industry": Chandavarkar 1994, p. 65.

large-scale use of casual labour, and so forth – were related to the structural constraints imposed by colonial domination. These included a home market limited by mass poverty, Lancashire competition backed by British refusal to give any tariff protection till well into the 1920s, and a dependence on textile machinery imports virtually till Independence (the first indigenous ring-frame was manufactured only in 1946). The structures of high finance, commerce, and shipping, dominated by British banks and firms and regulated by a state tilted in favour of British businessmen, was inadequate and largely beyond the control of the Indian bourgeoisie.[17]

Chandavarkar deploys two kinds of arguments in his effort to undermine the binary structures which he feels have been the bane of South Asian historiography. Insofar as "colonial difference" has come to be construed in principally cultural terms, he uses a kind of rational-choice theory to argue that culturalist interpretations are redundant, since the same phenomena can be more easily explained by the commonsensical responses of capitalists or workers to specific, material, economic, and/or political determinants and conjunctures.[18] More impressive, perhaps, is the skilful deconstruction of some of the binary categories, revealing their roots in official presuppositions, stereotypes, and policies. The formal/informal sector disjunction that has been mentioned already is the most obvious example. Chandavarkar demonstrates in a fairly convincing manner that "historians ... in quest of the 'mind' of the working classes, have often unwittingly taken over and replicated [the categories of colonial] discourse and sometimes even elevated it into grand explanatory frameworks and transcendent sociological truths."[19]

---

[17] Ibid., pp. 241–4.

[18] "[T]he history of capitalism and of the working class in India could most fruitfully be investigated, not as an exception – neither as a case of 'pre-capitalist' development nor as the product of a peculiar and unique 'Indian culture' – but firmly in relation to what are deemed to be the 'rules' or expectations of sociological discourse" (Chandavarkar 1998, p. 1). This is about the closest the author comes to defining his own methodological postulates, and it can hardly be taken to be particularly explicit: an important area of weakness to which I will return.

[19] Chandavarkar 1998, p. 14.

The great critics of colonial discourse have, in effect, uncritically surrendered to many of the terms it had constituted. The critique of culturalism, predictably, is focused upon Chakrabarty, and I do feel that here Chandavarkar on the whole has been able to put forward a more convincing thesis. He takes up the paradox with which Chakrabarty had started – that of labour militancy going along with persistent weakness of organisation – and suggests that sporadic outbursts were not the result of any peculiarly pre-modern "deify/defy" combination, but no more than a rational response to material conditions. Cultural explanations have tended to implicitly underestimate the sheer extent and efficacy of capitalist-cum-colonial state repression, making stable yet militant trade unionism almost impossible. Again, worker dependence on outsider "babu" leaders need not have been related to the persistence of "semi-feudal" culture. Actual workers in leadership positions often faced immediate dismissal, or worse, while the low level of literacy also made dependence on outsiders with education and some knowledge of law quite indispensable.

The deconstruction of official categories is at its most effective in three chapters of *Imperial Power and Popular Politics* that range beyond labour history, strictly defined, and take up as polemical target another historian associated with Subaltern Studies, David Arnold.[20] Historians, he suggests, have merely taken over the assumption commonly held by policemen, civil servants, and employers that Indian workers were prone to sporadic bouts of violence, as a function of their pre-industrial character. A closer look reveals considerable variations in the usage of the term "violence" (extended at times to cover even wildcat strikes), and the conjunctural nature of the moments when this discourse became particularly prominent. One such moment, predictably, was Bombay in 1928–9, in the wake of the massive yet generally peaceful strike led by Communists, and the upshot of the panic whipped up by British officials as well as by Indian mill owners and substantial sections of "respectable" citizens was a draconian anti-labour law and the Meerut Conspiracy Case

---

[20] Specifically, two articles by David Arnold (Arnold 1980, Arnold 1987).

against left trade unionists. "Violence", thus, was not a given but constructed and shifting category, and its provenance could extend across colonial/indigenous divides. Chandavarkar goes on to make the interesting suggestion that "[C]olonialism in India might . . . be defined, in one of its characteristic aspects, as the process by which labour was cheapened and more fully subordinated to capital, both indigenous and imperial."[21] The subverting of over-sharp polarities is carried further in the succeeding two chapters of *Imperial Power and Popular Politics*, dealing with the Bombay police and with the plague panic of the late 1890s. The first attempts a kind of social history of the police, a subject that David Arnold had pioneered way back in 1986.[22] As one would expect, Chandavarkar refuses to focus solely on the police as a principal, if socially subaltern, agent of foreign rule, and highlights its everyday linkages also with indigenous structures of local power. He takes issue with the widespread assumption that colonial conditions made the police necessarily more authoritarian (except at moments of extreme danger, as in 1919 and 1942, when, in any case, the British relied much more on the army), and recalls, in respect of labour, the methods used in Britain to smash Clydeside workers in 1919 and the General Strike in 1926. Alien command in a non-settler colony with a massive indigenous population could also be a source of weakness and necessary caution. As indicated by the anti-labour legislation of the Congress ministry in Bombay during 1937–9, "increasing Indian control over the institutions and agencies of the state" could go along with "increasing state repression", with local elites deploying the resources of the state built by colonialism "to discipline and control labour, whether in the towns or the countryside". A tendency which, it must be admitted, has been fully continued under successive post-Independence regimes.[23]

Chandavarkar is perhaps at his deconstructionist best in the essay on the plague panic of the late 1890s in Bombay Presidency, where draconian segregation efforts led to massive unrest and culminated

---

[21] Chandavarkar 1998, pp. 143, 155 and 179.
[22] Arnold 1986.
[23] Chandavarkar 1998, pp. 224–5, and p. 231.

in the murder of two British officials, Rand and Ayerst, at Poona in 1897 in the first act of middle-class terrorist nationalism. Resistance to plague control, and, sometimes, Western colonial medicine in general has been widely portrayed in terms of a cultural conflict between aggressive modernism and indigenous popular traditions, "a reminder of the great cultural gulf which divided the colonisers and the colonised".[24] Here, as throughout his work, Chandavarkar prefers to focus upon specific, shifting conjunctures, seeking "hard", "rational" explanations in place of assumptions of cultural uniqueness. Both the scale of official restrictions, and resistance to them, were largely confined to a specific area and time, the province of Bombay between 1896 and 1902 – yet the mortality rate was considerably higher (twelvefold, in fact) during the period from 1903 to 1907, when its main target area had shifted to the Punjab countryside. But plague in the 1890s was a sudden intruder, affecting the premier port of British India, and raising fears of an international embargo which would hit European and elite Indian business profits as well as the British balance of payments. A decade later, plague had become much more of a poor people's disease, control measures were no longer so panicky and excessive, and resistance had become sporadic and attracted less attention. Chandavarkar goes on to argue that the extreme nature of the early segregation measures and their unimaginative implementation made resistance quite understandable, without benefit of any presumed deep cultural difference. Thus, it was surely perfectly "rational" for people to refuse to go to plague hospitals, considering that, in Bombay city, the mortality rate there had touched 80 per cent. Nor was there, really, any uniform or clear-cut elite/popular disjunction in Indian attitudes, as is often assumed: "Resistance was not the only response to the plague measures and collaboration was by no means confined to the elites." The disjunction has been sought to be substantiated by reports about rumours concerning the plague allegedly in "popular" quarters, for here Arnold found a "significant divergence . . . between the middle classes and the subordinate population."[25] Chandavarkar makes, here,

---

[24] Ibid., p. 236.
[25] Ibid., p. 251, quoting from Arnold 1987.

a point of wider significance, drawing attention to the fact that data about oral rumours generally enter historical discourse only through official reports, memoirs, and middle-class newspapers. In a largely illiterate country, rumours most often can be no more than "an elite discourse about popular attitudes", the constructions and implicit presuppositions of which need to be carefully explored. In general, he finds little evidence of any uniform popular hostility to Western medicine: attitudes were determined, rather, by "its efficacy, its accessibility and its cost".[26]

It should be evident that there is much in Chandavarkar that I find acceptable and valuable. His handling of official material, in particular, is often exemplary, reminiscent at peak moments of Richard Cobb's classic critique of over-facile use of the police archives of revolutionary Paris in exploring the history of the "crowd", without taking account of the processes of construction of official and other stereotypes.[27] But there are also major problems, to which I now turn. We may start with the less substantial. Chandavarkar has a rather irritating habit of claiming or implying excessive originality. This is surely quite unnecessary for a well-established scholar whose substantial contributions to South Asian industrial and labour history are not likely to be denied by anyone. The questioning of the formal/informal sector dichotomy, for instance, had begun with a much-cited article of Jan Breman way back in 1976. This had emphasised the persistent similarities and interflows between labour in "formal" and "informal" sectors, and sought to explain the survival or reproduction of allegedly "primordial" caste and religious loyalties within the Indian factory proletariat by the "advantages offered by such ties under highly unfavourable economic conditions."[28] Two years later, Lalita Chakrabarti's pioneering study of labour migration had similarly undercut many standard polarities, showing how the "labour catchment areas" for indentured "coolies" recruited for plantations in Assam or

---

[26] Chandavarkar 1998, pp. 251–3, 258.
[27] Cobb 1970.
[28] See Breman's summing up of almost thirty years of "micro-research within a macroframework", integrating anthropological with historical approaches, in Breman 1996.

overseas also came to supply a major part of "free" labour for factories. The emergence of the industrial labour force in late-colonial India, she suggested, "is a part of the story of so-called coolie migration".[29] Chandavarkar's emphasis on the "powerful connections . . . between factory proletarians, casual workers, rural migrants, agrarian labour, artisans, 'tribals', and dalits"[30] really falls within an already fairly established historiographical tradition. To take a second instance: an essay published in 1977 by E.D. Murphy had already suggested an inverse correlation between proletarianisation – in the sense of total uprooting from village connections – and labour militancy, for such detachment reduced staying capacity during strikes.[31] It would be unfair to suggest that these and other "anticipations" have been entirely ignored by Chandavarkar, for the articles I have mentioned are all included in his bibliographies. But the lay or unwary reader is still likely to assume an unwarranted degree of originality, for the text does tend to convey an impression of a lone pioneer struggling against the weight of previously unchallenged modernising or Marxist orthodoxies.

To turn to more substantial problems. The recurrent, yet never fully explicated premise of rational choice which underlies so much of Chandavarkar's argument is undoubtedly effective as polemic, but it also has a self-limiting dimension. The method seems to be to begin with "hard", material, pressures and constraints of specific economic or (more often) political conjunctures, and then suggest that questions of culture are more or less redundant, since the phenomena being scrutinised can be explained without them. But when, by what sorts of criteria, does an explanation become satisfactory or complete? Surely that depends crucially on the overall framework being used by the historian, and here complete agreement is unlikely. A scholar with "culturalist" leanings might well suggest that to posit individuals or groups across cultures and times acting always according to "the 'rules' or expectations of sociological discourse" is to universalise arbitrarily a specific, modern Western, culture, and that the whole procedure

[29] Chakrabarti 1978.
[30] Chandavarkar 1998, p. 7.
[31] Murphy 1977.

has an "Eurocentric" flavour.[32] Yet the opposite assumption, of a fundamental, indigenist cultural particularity, also has major pitfalls, as Chandavarkar sometimes shows very well. The case, on either side, can hardly be "proved" in any formal, positivistic sense.

If we still want to avoid the morass of complete relativism, perhaps a criterion of generative capacity, productiveness in terms of professional or scholarly consequences, might be helpful. Frameworks are not equal here, for some tend to stimulate more questions, extend our curiosity and understanding of previously unexplored dimensions of life of greater numbers of people. And, here, a paradoxical "unity of opposites" seems to emerge between Chandavarkar and Dipesh Chakrabarty, a limit they have in common and to which Chitra Joshi has recently drawn our attention.[33] Both, though in different, indeed opposite, ways, tend to underestimate, even ignore, the possibility of workers' agency. The culturalist determinism of the one is inverted into the economic or political determinism of the other, and what tends to get relatively missed out, in Chakrabarty and Chandavarkar alike, are the moments of labour self-activity, militancy, autonomy. These, of course, had been the central, almost the only foci for earlier radical historiography, and so, once again, there is an inversion common to both historians.

For Chakrabarty, Bengal jute workers were enmeshed in premodern, hierarchised relationships and values, which prevented stable organisations and self-activity. Labour protest consequently could never be more than spasmodic and ephemeral, while the persistence of traditional community ties of caste and religion kept workers inexorably fragmented, quite incapable of moving towards class consciousness in the "proper" Marxist sense. Bombay textile workers, for Chandavarkar, were equally entrapped, not through semi-feudal culture but by more material determinants of the labour market, managerial authority and disciplinary mechanisms, and police and state interventions. Disunion and fragmentation, once again, are assumed to have been the basic characteristic of labour history, with unities across such divisions being no more than conjunctural

[32] Chandavarkar 1998, p. 1.
[33] Joshi 2003, p. 8.

and momentary. The consequence that follows for both historians is a common tendency to leave relatively unexplored the moments of effective and united labour militancy. And, yet, these were far from uncommon during the inter-war decades: two general strikes in Bengal jute, in 1929 and 1937, and no less than eight of these in Bombay textiles, all lasting for at least a month and some of them much more prolonged (1919, 1920, 1923, 1925, 1928, 1929, 1934, 1940) – impressive by any standards, national or international. Perhaps even more remarkable is the history of the Communist-led Girni Kamgar Lal Bavta (Red Flag) Union, bitterly repressed almost throughout its history, by the British and then in 1937–9 under a Congress provincial ministry, not effective most of the time in the sense of bringing material gains for its workers, yet retaining their loyalty across a whole generation. With the partial exception of his early, 1981, essay, little of the atmosphere and emotions that must have accompanied such moments enter Chandavarkar's otherwise richly detailed narrative. Labour subjectivities are not his concern – but, then, Chakrabarty's culturalism has an essentialised, tradition-oriented tint which, in effect, produces a not dissimilar silencing.

The limits, for both historians, are set by an interaction of framework with the kind of source materials they have preferred to work with, or ignore. Chandavarkar makes no use of oral material, apart from a few interviews with well-known middle-class labour leaders. Chakrabarty's bibliography is even more sparse in this respect. More remarkable is the almost total neglect of contemporary vernacular material, indeed, by and large, of sources other than those of mill owner or official origin. Even the well-known depositions and other data (including pamphlets and other strike material) preserved in the Meerut Conspiracy Case files figure but rarely in Chandavarkar's volumes.[34] We shall see shortly how Chitra Joshi has been able to

---

[34] To cite a specific instance: more than twenty years ago, Sabyasachi Bhattacharya's paper on capital–labour relations in Bombay in 1928–9 (Bhattacharya 1981) had made some use of the proceeding of a Joint Strike Committee of workers in 1928, which he had found in the private papers of the labour leader N.M. Joshi. That had been a preliminary article, part of a study which Bhattacharya unfortunately has never completed. Chandavarkar

unearth a significant amount of contemporary material of direct labour origin about a rather brief moment of labour upsurge in Kanpur in 1937–8. I find it difficult to believe that the Girni Kamgar-led movements, undoubtedly more powerful and prolonged, did not leave in their wake many more traces and memories than have entered Chandavarkar's history.

For all their undoubted achievements, Chakrabarty and Chandavarkar's volumes leave us with a sense of incompleteness, a certain bloodless quality. It is as if both historians are primarily interested in establishing a thesis, and controverting the views of others, less in exploring the times and spaces and lived experiences of their subjects as human beings. Fortunately, for the future of South Asian labour history, Chakrabarty and Chandavarkar have been surpassed in these respects by a number of publications over the last decade, and it is to some of these that I would like to briefly turn in the concluding section of this review essay.

III

The first of the four recent works I want to look at, Ian Kerr's *Building the Railways of the Raj, 1850–1900*, is appropriately titled, for it has an unusual focus, not on the management and working of an industry assumed as already established, but on construction and maintenance as ongoing process. This, of course, is particularly relevant for the early history of railways across a subcontinent. Between 1850 and 1900, an average of 1405 miles were added every year to railways in India, and construction work employed from between 180,601 to 221,253 labourers. The bulk of this vast mass of men, women, and children were engaged in purely menial kinds of unskilled work, where the labour processes, as yet largely unmechanised, had remained virtually unchanged across centuries. Yet, on their toil rested an elaborate and immense hierarchy, highly capitalised and sophisticated in its upper reaches, and having at its command the latest in nineteenth-century

---

does include the N.M. Joshi Papers in his bibliography, but does not seem to have used such material.

engineering technology. Railway construction, maintenance, and operation, Kerr reminds us, has necessarily involved the bringing together of labour processes of the most diverse kinds, ranging from the most simple to the most complex, from the almost-primitive to the ultra-modern. Railways demanded the bringing together of the most diverse kinds of organisation and labour – skilled and purely manual, permanent and casual, formal and informal. Railway workers were hierarchised into relatively well paid and skilled engineers and drivers (for long, largely European or Eurasian), through a clerical intermediary strata, down to a mass of unskilled manual labourers.

Two interesting consequences follow from this unusual focus adopted by Kerr. The concentration on the everyday details of labour processes required for construction and maintenance highlights the usually forgotten "hewers of wood and drawers of water" – to borrow the striking Biblical phrase deployed recently by Peter Linebaugh and Marcus Rediker (in their study from below of the emerging Atlantic economy) to categorise those who "built the infrastructure of merchant capitalism".[35] Labour history thus gets extended beyond its usual concentration on artisanal, manufacturing, and mechanised-industrial forms of work. In the second place, Kerr's study is not just empirically rich: working within an explicitly Marxist framework, it goes on to suggest a rather interesting theoretical point. Marx, it might be recalled, had distinguished between two dimensions of the labour process within emergent capitalism. Capitalists could establish control over already-existing labour processes from the outside without major technological transformation, extracting absolute surplus-value from workers. This was a "formal subsumption" of labour to capital, conceptually distinct from "real subsumption", associated with technological change and a shift towards relative surplus-value.[36] The general assumption has been that these were chronologically

---

[35] Linebaugh and Rediker 2000, p. 49, and chapter 2.

[36] The distinction between formal and real subsumption had been introduced into Indian economic-historical discussion by Jairus Banaji, an important participant in what came to be known as the "mode of production debate" concerning the nature of the pre-colonial South Asian society and its transformation under colonialism (Banaji 1977).

successive phases. Kerr uses his Indian railway data to argue that the "two dimensions of the labour process could and did exist at the same work-site . . . with no necessary, unidirectional movement from the former to the latter."[37] He thus effectively undercuts the common assumption, made notably by Chandavarkar, that unilinear teleologies are necessarily built into all varieties of Marxist historical practice.

Kerr has an interesting chapter on instances of early worker resistance, which follows up an earlier article he had published a decade back.[38] But the bulk of the book is deliberately a study "from above", about which he is, rightly, unapologetic, feeling this to have been indispensable for its central theme of railway construction and operation as a "complex assembly of labour processes". Kerr suggests that socialist sympathies do not preclude, but rather demand, an understanding of the power and strategies of capital and management. The nature of his subject, and particularly its location in time more than a hundred years in the past, also preclude entry into labour perceptions through interviews or vernacular writings: the vast majority of the subalterns of labour who are his principal focus of interest would have been illiterate. In these respects, Kerr's work differs significantly from the other three recent works I have selected for my sample.

Dilip Simeon's *The Politics of Labour under Late Colonialism: Workers, Unions, and the State in Chota Nagpur, 1928–39* is a study of two sites of labour, geographically close to each other and with very close economic links, yet markedly different in many ways. Jamshedpur (Tatanagar) in South Bihar (today part of the recently formed Indian state of Jharkhand) is India's first steel city, built in the early twentieth century by indigenous capital though with considerable support from the colonial state. Its coal came from mines in the nearby Jharia-Dhanbad region, with Jharia alone accounting for more than half of India's coal production in the 1920s. The Tatas cultivated a self-image of being "modern" entrepreneurs, employing a necessarily large proportion of skilled, often high-caste workers along with smaller numbers of lower castes and tribals (Adivasis) as well as a

---

[37] Kerr 1995, pp. 7–9.
[38] Ibid., chapter 6.

reserve army of casual labourers. Unusually for Indian capitalism, they also built quarters for their employees, thus constructing a new, entirely company-controlled city with a reasonable standard of amenities. Jharia represented a different world: mines ruthlessly worked to exhaustion and then abandoned, a predominantly unskilled workforce dispersed across the countryside, recruited predominantly from low castes and tribals and including (unlike steel workers) large numbers of women and children. Labour conditions in the mines were – and largely remain – atrocious, with frequent accidents (one underground fire in this region has now been ablaze for some seventy years!). Simeon's thus is an interesting attempt to bring together within a single focus two quite different kinds of industry and labour: the sources available, though, have permitted more details about Jamshedpur than Jharia.

A distinctive, indeed rather unusual, feature of Simeon's book is its firmly chronology-based organisation of material pertaining to the limited time span of a single decade (1928–39). Thematic arrangement is usually preferred as indicating greater "sophistication", the author admits, but chronology permits a firmer grasp of the discipline of historical context. It has enabled a highlighting of the fluidity of positions and attitudes of capitalists, state officials, politicians of varied kinds, jobbers, union leaders, shop floor activists, a highly differentiated labour force, emphasising complex, conjunctural, shifting interactions, rather than fixed polarities. "Treating such matters as if one were observing a spectrum, makes it easier to observe distinctions without being tied to precise lines of demarcation, which can be left to emerge and dissolve within the account." This mode of presentation does have a problem, though. Numerous implications of general or theoretical interest remain embedded in the text (except for a concluding section, after three hundred pages of dense narrative), and might get lost for many readers amidst the detail.

Among these is a non-polemicised, but quite effective, raising of doubts about Dipesh Chakrabarty's model of "semi-feudal" labour leaders running unions as their landed estates (*zamindaris*), with the workers' representatives being also their masters. The detailed chronologically arranged narrative suggests, rather, that if leaders could instrumentalise workers' struggles, there were many occasions when "workers could no less instrumentalise their leaders and/or reject them".[39] But Simeon simultaneously rejects any "subalternist" romanticisation of worker autonomy as always contributing to more effective class struggle. Establishment of a single union would obviously have made collective bargaining more effective for the steel workers and coal miners. But this was almost never achieved, in significant part, it seems, because workers did not want to become overdependent on a unified body of outsider "controllers".[40] A related, interesting point, which Simeon leaves implicit rather than worked out, is the way Indian labour has often been attracted to maverick figures not bound by discipline or ideology, whether nationalist or left-wing. Of the two outstanding leaders of Jamshedpur workers during the period studied by Simeon, Maneck Homi had no stable political connections, while Abdul Bari, though initially sent to the area by the Congress, was drifting away from his parent organisation during his period of maximum popularity.[41] Mavericks remained a prominent and recurrent feature of the Indian labour landscape, right down to Datta Samanta, who led the last great struggle of Bombay textile workers in the early 1980s. The explanation perhaps lies not in "charisma" alone: individual leaders without stable external linkages could have seemed more amenable to local pressures, less likely to take decisions on "broader" grounds of national politics or ideology that often must have remained somewhat mysterious to many workers. But such leaders at times could also be quite irresponsible, letting down their followers in unforeseen ways.

Concentration on a brief time span enables Simeon to make a fairly exhaustive study of a mass of sources: official reports, archival material, Tata managerial files, private papers of businessmen and labour leaders, some interviews. Direct worker testimony is not very

---

[39] Simeon 1995, p. 5.
[40] Ibid., p. 344.
[41] Homi was a Parsi, and Bari a Muslim: the workers they led were largely Hindu. As Simeon suggests, this seems to indicate that Indian workers could be less bound by "primordial" attachments of caste or religion than historians have often assumed.

abundant, but the author has carefully included in appendices the texts of material of this kind which he was able to unearth – some leaflets, memorials coming from workers, and police records of a few speeches by labour leaders.

Politics of Labour begins with a moving acknowledgement of the "radical utopianism of the 1960s", and indeed its author has remained an activist all his life, in varying forms and in different spheres of life. Changing times and a determination to combine commitment with academic rigour have ensured that this does not result in a relapse into any teleological or celebratory mode. But some incidents linger particularly in memory, amidst the often tedious detail: most of all, perhaps, the martyrdom of the Communist Hazara Singh, standing in front of a lorry bringing in blacklegs to break a strike in July 1939. He was deliberately run over – it seems at the order of the owner's son, who, incidentally, later became independent India's defence minister. Forty years later, a retired worker told the author that "it came to be said that every drop of Hazara's blood produced Communists".[42] Simeon's narrative does not deny that such militant moments in labour history tend to be rare, evanescent, and quantitatively less prominent than periods of quiescence and fragmentation. But they can also sometimes acquire greater salience, in the memory of workers as well as in historical reconstructions. But that, of course, will depend on values, and circumstances of recall or writing. And, here, the choice made by Simeon, and indeed in different ways by all the historians I am looking at in this concluding section, differs significantly from those of Chandavarkar and Chakrabarty.

Like Simeon, Janaki Nair has attempted a study of two adjoining but contrasting locations in her *Miners and Millhands: Work, Culture and Politics in Princely Mysore*. To an even greater extent than the coal mines of Bihar, the Kolar gold mines represented colonial extractive methods at their most oppressive. Opened up by British capital in the 1870s, they were at their peak in the early twentieth century, but began declining from the 1920s, leaving Kolar a deindustrialised ghost town by the late twentieth century. The mines in their heyday had

---

[42] Simeon 1995, pp. 299–304.

been the deepest in the world, with workers made to labour 8000 feet underground without air-conditioning till 1936. In addition, the possibility of theft of the valuable product led to "extraordinary levels of surveillance", and so, the author suggests, Foucault might be more relevant than Thompson in understanding the nature of the structure of domination at Kolar. Foucault with a "colonial difference", however, targeting collectivities rather than constituting individuals, operating through contractor intermediaries, and aimed at producing not "disciplined *subjects*" but a "repressed and docile *workforce*".[43] Repression blocked formal trade unions till the 1940s, but failed to stamp out other, occasionally more violent, forms of protest. There were numerous sporadic attacks on the watch and ward staff, and an interesting sub-culture of anonymous notices. One of these, denouncing the taking of thumb impressions of workers, was put up on a rock in 1930, and led to a 21-day strike the organisers of which were never traced.

Bangalore, the capital of the kingdom of Mysore (one of the largest of the many "native states" of British-dominated India), had a different industrial and labour pattern. It became a major industrial centre after Independence, but had grown slowly in the colonial era, with a small and struggling textile industry which really took off only during the Second World War through manufacturing silk for parachutes. Mysore princes and their ministers were rather unusual in the interest several among them took in trying to foster indigenous industrial development through bureaucratic initiative. (Some scholars have even suggested that Mysore, along with a few other princely states like Baroda, provided an early version of what in post-1947 India became the Nehruvian pattern of state-promoted economic development.) The Mysore rulers, predictably, sought to combine such industrialisation "from above" with a markedly anti-democratic stance. Trade unions were legalised only in 1942, while in directly British-ruled India they had been so from 1926. But repression was never as intensive and thorough as at Kolar. Unlike in the mines, Bangalore factories did provide some opportunities for skill development

[43] Nair 1995, p. 42.

and a measure of upward mobility: strikes, too, could be more frequent.

Tanneries apart, the Bangalore industries employed somewhat upper- or "respectable"-caste workers, but an important feature of the Kolar gold mines was their heavy reliance on low-caste and untouchable (Adi-Dravida, in South-Indian parlance) migrant labour. Kolar in the early twentieth century was one of the major centres of lower-caste assertion, which took the forms of a neo-Buddhist religious revival and then a socially radical "self-respect" movement. The nature of her material thus obliged Nair to confront more directly than the historians discussed so far the difficult question of the relationships between identity formations of class and caste. Nair's theoretical discussion, however, remains somewhat unsatisfactory, for it ends up with a rather banal dualistic assertion: the importance of "cultural identities" has to be recognised, but "capitalist work-experience . . . [is] equally important".

More interesting is the argument that, despite the atrocious work conditions, Kolar low-caste miners do not fit into the general mould of "reluctant proletarians" nostalgic about their lost village moorings. Such an assumption, veering towards an occasional valorisation of pre-capitalist identities, has been common among South Asian labour historians.[44] Dalit life in South Indian villages, Nair suggests, produced instead "searing memories", and may have even contributed to a certain exaggeration of "the relative freedoms of the capitalist workplace".[45] Her main evidence here comes from some early-twentieth-century miners' songs printed in a Tamil journal, contrasting the "little gruel" and "tatters" of life in the "wild countryside" with the "mutton and rice" in the Kolar gold fields. But, unfortunately, Nair tells us nothing about the exact provenance of

---

[44] Dipesh Chakrabarty provides the most obvious instance, but Nair notes occasional traces of such valorisation also in Simeon, in a contrast between the rich "symbolic co-ordinates" of tribal or rural homes and the "subordination . . . drudgery and humiliation" of factory or mine work, making the "class existence" of labour itself a matter of resentment. Nair, p. 296; Simeon, pp. 2, 326.

[45] Nair 1995, p. 296.

these songs, whether anything is known about how they came to be collected and published at a surprisingly early date, and consequently how representative they may have been of miner values. One is left unsure whether her interesting hypothesis may not have been relevant only for a small section of relatively better-off miners, who would have been the ones most likely to be attracted by the improvement discourse of the self-respect movement. In more general terms, however, it should be added that like Simeon and, as we shall see shortly, Joshi, Nair has been able to gather some interesting first-hand data about worker experiences and perceptions through interviews. Around thirty of these are listed, mostly though with middle-class Communist leaders or activists. But there are also two brief life histories of workers, reconstructed through interviews. A woman tobacco worker still recalled her active participation in a strike, way back in 1936, as a brief moment of pride in a lifetime of drudgery and oppression. For a Communist activist of Kolar, likewise, the long strike in 1946 represented a very special moment. But there was a certain nostalgia also about a past that was not rural, but located in the mines of a bygone boom era, when employment was abundant, however exploitative. A mood quite characteristic, we shall see, also of deindustrialised Kanpur today, as explored by Chitra Joshi.

What had been an occasional or passing glimpse for Simeon or Nair has become a central and profound feature of *Lost Worlds: Indian Labour and Its Forgotten Histories*. The title is unusually appropriate, for the book is a meditation (and I am using this word, more common in literary or philosophical writings, quite deliberately) on shifting times and spaces, and the ways in which they mould and interact with experiences, memories, histories of labour. The lost worlds are not one but many. There is the world of the radical intellectual and historian, someone like Joshi herself, evoked in moving terms at the beginning of the book. She had been inspired by vestiges of the moods of May 1968 while studying in a university famed then (and to some extent even today) for its radicalism, and began research on Kanpur labour in the wake of a major strike at the Swadeshi Cotton Mills there in 1977. The research was completed, however, and the book published, a quarter-century later. A very different time, when the old kind of working class, concentrated in big factories and cities, appears to be fast disintegrating more or less everywhere, trade unions have become shadows of their former selves, and the ideals of socialism seem to have received a mortal blow. Kanpur, once described as a kind of Manchester of the East, is today a medley of "sprawling mill compounds – noiseless and deserted – majestic buildings worn down and crumbling, [where] tall and smokeless chimneys stand as silent reminders of the past . . . young and old, the unemployed waiting for jobs or for mills to reopen, sit around vacantly: others push carts, ply rickshaws, or work in cottage industries in alleys and bylanes."[46] Such scenes are common in many parts of the world today, in the burnt-out areas of inner cities or old industrial areas. Labour history itself has been a casualty of this decline, being deserted, as we have seen, by most radical scholars, first for research on peasants and then studies of "culture" or "colonial discourse". The efforts of historians such as Joshi to recover something of Indian labour's "forgotten histories" therefore becomes additionally significant. Failure, in this respect, would surely provide one more instance of that "enormous condescension of posterity" of which Thompson had written memorably in a very different context, forty years ago.

But Joshi's is not a simple, binary contrast between present and past, both imagined in homogenised ways and therefore open in equal measure to facile assumptions of linear progress, or nostalgic evocations of an undifferentiated "world we have lost". The strength of the book consists, in significant part, in its deconstruction of such imputed, essentialised unities. The disintegration of the old industrial working class is no doubt a "loss" of a qualitatively more tragic kind. Yet, in a profoundly original emphasis, Joshi suggests that the lives of workers, maybe everywhere but notably in South Asia, with its "footloose labour" and perpetually circular migration from villages to cities and back, have been, in a sense, always a history of worlds getting lost. Through complex and changing combinations of external compulsions and choice, men, women, and quite often children have been moving from the countryside to cities, from one factory to an-

[46] Joshi 2003, p. 3.

other, from regular to casual employment or joblessness. And this sense of movement – a part of capitalism itself, it may be added, as the *Communist Manifesto* had suggested way back in 1848 – is conveyed by Joshi, not primarily by formulaic presentations, but through vivid stories of the lives of individual workers that she has been able to recover through enormously impressive research. There is Shriram, for instance, who wrote an autobiography in the 1970s – moving from village to Kanpur, then through a mingling of need and sense of adventure to factories in Delhi and several other cities, returning in the 1930s to Kanpur and becoming a Communist trade unionist there. Shriram showed no inclination to go back to his original village home, but, for Ramcharan, who moved to Kanpur in more recent times, the village still represents a (somewhat uncertain) hope of comfort and security in old age. And, unlike much conventional labour history in India or elsewhere, the faces that we see are not just those of male workers: women, within factories or engaged as commonly nowadays in various forms of sweated "domestic" industries, figure prominently in Joshi's narrative. Throughout, experiences, memories, identities emerge as both diverse and shifting, in and through complex interpenetrations of structural determinants with elements of choice, an agency that is limited but not entirely or always illusory. And the rhythms of movement and change that pervade the entire book enable an exceptionally profound grasp of the fluidity of all identities, a firm historicisation that has been able to avoid all kinds of essentialism, whether of class, caste, religion, or gender.

It will be evident that, in broad terms, Joshi's affinities remain with the Thompsonian tradition of labour and social history. As we have already seen, it is from this perspective that she has mounted a most effective, simultaneous critique of the apparently opposed poles of Chakrabarty and Chandavarkar, pointing to a common occlusion of agency through assumptions of a reified traditional culture in the one, and by the emphasis on determinations through external labour market pressures and business strategies in the other. Both have inverted in similar ways the conventional Marxist assumption of linear change leading on teleologically towards working-class unity, to produce, however, an opposite kind of essentialism, one in which fragmentation and internal conflict is inevitable, and change, agency, moments of effective, class-conscious militancy, well-nigh impossible.[47] It should be added that Joshi has been able to fully incorporate within her vision the undoubted strengths of Chandavarkar, in particular his state-of-the-art awareness of recent trends in industrial and labour history and the questioning of the traditional polarities of rural and urban, informal and formal, factory and neighbourhood. What she adds, however, is a deeper perception of fluidities, the ability, I am tempted to suggest, to make rigid categories dance to a dialectical tune:

> How does one straitjacket people like Ramcharan? It would be simplistic to categorise them as either workers or peasants. In a sense they were labourers-in-between, living partially in both worlds and fully in neither. Just as the lines between city and village blurred, so did boundaries between the employed and unemployed, between substitutes and regulars, between factory jobs and other work.[48]

Lost Worlds is, evidently, a work imbued with a profound and sophisticated grasp of questions of theory. Yet its primary purpose is not the testing-out of one or other hypothesis, while, in sharp contrast again to both Chakrabarty and, even more, Chandavarkar, polemics figure very little within the text. What lingers in the mind, above all, is the sheer richness of the multiple narratives of labour and urban life, and, here, three features need to be highlighted. There is, first, a rare ability – missing, I think, even in Thompson – to convey through appropriate visual images the sense of changing locations and spaces. The illustrations are not mere accompaniment, as they so often remain in books by historians. Three series of sketches and photographs convey a vivid sense of the evolution of Kanpur, from a small riverside trading centre in a setting still predominantly rural, through the imposing, busy factories of the 1930s, down to today's images of disrepair and desolation.[49] Then there is the capacity to combine effective presentation of an abundant mass of "hard" data – statistics concerning industrial growth or decline, labour composition and

---

[47] Ibid., pp. 7–8.
[48] Joshi 2003, p. 99.
[49] Ibid., pp. 25–6, 40–1 and 322–5.

conditions, the reworking of urban spaces through municipal and sanitation policies – with a remarkably acute eye for vivid human detail. I have already touched on some of the life histories of workers, but Joshi's imaginative reach does not exclude the employers, or even their wives: the British wives in mid-nineteenth-century Kanpur, for instance, who waited with such eagerness for their "boxes" carrying European goods and delicacies from "Home". And, finally, what above everything else has made these many achievements possible: an extraordinarily rich abundance of material, collected over decades of necessarily intermittent but determined research, which includes a wealth of vernacular and oral data of direct worker origin that, I think, is quite unprecedented in South Asian labour history. Joshi has been able to unearth a large number of vernacular tracts and pamphlets, including some composed by workers themselves, which include an autobiography by Shriram, and several volumes of poems by a Communist worker, who calls himself Sudarshan Chakr (a take-off from a symbol associated with Krishna). And the list of "oral accounts" runs to more than fifty, among which only about half a dozen are interviews with middle-class trade-union leaders.

I have mentioned Joshi's affinities with Thompson. But a book dated 2003 instead of 1963 can only be Thompsonian with differences, of which two are particularly significant. The effective deployment of terms like "in-between" or "hybridity" – associated, of course, with Homi Bhabha – indicates an unusual ability to integrate within a basic Marxian perspective elements or insights of value drawn from today's poststructuralist, postcolonial intellectual currents. Marxist attitudes here have tended to oscillate wildly between rejection or surrender, both equally uncritical: Joshi is able to steer clear of both. And, while a high point of the book remains a vivid, not to say enthusiastic account of "Lal Kanpur" (Red Kanpur) – the brief moment in 1938 when workers on strike seemed to dominate the city – this obviously cannot be the concluding or dominant mood. Thompson could end on a semi-triumphalist note, with the achievement of a "working-class presence" in England by 1832. The final, intensely moving, and sad chapter of *Lost Worlds*, dealing with Kanpur today, is instead titled "Despair". It describes a time when workers unemployed for years have even begun to look back with a certain nostalgia towards the oppressive work discipline of the past, remembering everything "with a sense of male pride and achievement", regretting the passing of a world when capitalists, so to say, had been able to exploit them with "proper" efficiency. The memory of Lal Kanpur, in contrast, has almost vanished for the current generation. More generally, Joshi suggests that "the culture of worklessness in the present" can give "insights into the meanings of work", the ways in which it had once meant "a forging of relationships, bonds between wage earners, a sense of power of their collectivity in the city, a sense of pride and dignity."[50] Therein lies what is, perhaps, the deepest loss of all.

The book has to end with the admission that, faced with what really is "the death of a world, a whole way of life, of a cultural form which was once seen as the backbone of urban, industrial India", a labour historian can perhaps only make "what E.M. Forster might have termed 'one of the slighter gestures of dissent' – an attempt, against the grain, not to forget that world."[51] And, yet, in keeping with her ever-present emphasis on fluidity and rejection of essentialised closures, Joshi does hint towards a subdued counterpoint. There is the wonderfully evocative cover photo, of what had been once the bustling union office at Gwaltoli, the "fortress of the workers", now virtually deserted, with rickshaws plied today by unemployed workers drawn up in front of it. But a boy with a hauntingly quizzical, inquisitive expression looks forward towards us from one of the rickshaws. And there is also a dedication by the author, to her daughter, "and a world of new possibilities". The old kind of working class may be dead or dying, but surely not the struggle, in new forms, for a more just and better world.

Lost Worlds, I will be bold enough to suggest, is labour history at its best. And, with its ability to transcend both positivist naïveté, and that "lazy scepticism that refuses to see any distinction between history and fiction",[52] it is also a triumphant vindication of the abiding power of historical research and writing.

[50] Ibid., p. 11.
[51] Ibid., p. 329.
[52] The quote comes from what some might think an unexpected source: Chatterjee 2002, p. xi.

References

Arnold, David 1980, "Industrial Violence in Colonial India", *Comparative Studies in Society and History*, 22, 2: 234–55.

—— 1986, *Police Power and Colonial Rule: Madras, 1859–1947*, Delhi: Oxford University Press.

—— 1987, "Touching the Body: Perspectives on the Indian Plague, 1896–1900", in *Subaltern Studies V*, ed. Ranajit Guha, Delhi: Oxford University Press.

Bagchi, Amiya Kumar 1972, *Private Investment in India 1900–1939*, Cambridge: Cambridge University Press.

Banaji, Jairus 1977, "Capitalist Domination and the Small Peasantry: Deccan Districts in the Late 19th Century", *Economic and Political Weekly*, Special Number, August, 1375–1404.

Berg, Maxine 1985, *The Age of Manufactures, 1700–1820*, London: Fontana.

Bhattacharya, Sabyasachi 1981, "Capital and Labour in Bombay City, 1928–29", *Review of Political Economy*, 16: 36–44.

—— 1986, "The Colonial State, Capital and Labour: Bombay, 1919–31", in *Situating Indian History*, ed. Sabyasachi Bhattacharya and Romila Thapar, Delhi: Oxford University Press.

Breman, Jan 1996, *Footloose Labour: Working in India's Informal Economy*, Cambridge: Cambridge University Press.

Cannadine, David 1984, "The Present and the Past in the English Industrial Revolution, 1880–1980", *Past and Present*, 103: 131–71.

Chakrabarti, Lalita 1978, "Emergence of an Industrial Labour Force in a Dual Economy: British India, 1880–1920", *Indian Economic and Social History Review*, 15, 3: 249–328.

Chakrabarty, Dipesh 1981a, "Communal Riots and Labour: Bengal's Jute Mill Hands in the 1890s", *Past and Present*, 91: 140–69.

—— 1981b, "Conditions for Knowledge of Working-Class Conditions: Employers, Government and the Jute Workers of Calcutta", in *Subaltern Studies II*, ed. Ranajit Guha, Delhi: Oxford University Press.

—— 1983, "On Deifying and Defying Authority: Managers and Workers in the Jute Mills of Bengal, c. 1890–1940", *Past and Present*, 100: 124–46.

—— and Ranajit Dasgupta 1981, "Some Aspects of Labour History of Bengal in the Nineteenth Century: Two Views", *Occasional Paper No. 40*, Calcutta: Centre for Studies in Social Sciences.

Chandavarkar, Raj 1981, "Workers' Politics and the Mill Districts in Bombay between the Wars", *Modern Asian Studies*, 15, 3: 603–47.

—— 1985, "Industrialization in India before 1947: Conventional Approaches and Alternative Perspectives", *Modern Asian Studies*, 19, 3: 623–68.

———— 1994, *The Origins of Industrial Capitalism in India: Business Strategies and the Working Classes in Bombay, 1900–1940*, Cambridge: Cambridge University Press.

———— 1998, *Imperial Power and Popular Politics: Class, Resistance and the State in India, c. 1850–1950*, Cambridge: Cambridge University Press.

Chatterjee, Partha 1993, *The Nation and Its Fragments*, Princeton: Princeton University Press.

———— 2002, *A Princely Impostor? The Kumar of Bhawal and the Secret History of Indian Nationalism*, Delhi: Permanent Black.

Cobb, Richard 1970, *The Police and the People: French Popular Protest, 1789–1820*, Oxford: Clarendon Press.

Dasgupta, Ranajit 1994, *Labour and Working Class in Eastern India: Studies in Colonial History*, Calcutta: K.P. Bagchi.

Guha, Ranajit 1983, *Elementary Aspects of Peasant Insurgency in Colonial India*, Delhi: Oxford University Press.

Gupta, Parthasarathi 1974, "Notes on the Origin and Structuring of the Industrial Labour Force in India, 1880–1920", in *Indian Society: Historical Probings*, ed. R.S. Sharma, New Delhi: People's Publishing House.

Jagga, Lajpat 1981, "Colonial Railwaymen and British Rule: A Probe into Railway Labour Agitation in India, 1919–22", *Studies in History*, III, 1–2: 103–46.

Joshi, Chitra 1981, "Kanpur Textile Labour: Some Structural Features of Formative Years", *Economic and Political Weekly* 16, 44–6: 1823–38.

———— 1985, "Bonds of Community, Ties of Religion: Kanpur Textile Workers in the Early Twentieth Century", *Indian Economic and Social History Review*, 22, 3: 251–80.

———— 2003, *Lost Worlds: Indian Labour and its Forgotten Histories*, Delhi: Permanent Black.

Karnik, V.B. 1967, *Strikes in India*, Bombay: P.C. Manaktala and Sons.

Kerr, Ian 1995, *Building the Railways of the Raj*, Delhi: Oxford University Press.

Kumar, Radha 1983, "Family and Factory: Women in the Bombay Cotton Textile Industry, 1919–1939", *Indian Economic and Social History Review*, 20, I: 81–110.

Linebaugh, Peter and Marcus Rediker 2000, *The Many-Headed Hydra: The Hidden History of the Revolutionary Atlantic*, London: Verso.

Mohapatra, Prabhu 1985 "Coolies and Colliers: A Study of the Agrarian Context of Labour Migration From Chota Nagpur, 1880–1920", *Studies in History*, 1, 2: 247–304.

Morris, Morris David 1965, *The Emergence of an Industrial Labour Force in India: A Study of the Bombay Cotton Mills, 1854–1947*, Bombay: Oxford University Press and University of California Press.

Murphy, E.D. 1977, "Class and Community in India: The Madras Labour Union", *Indian Economic and Social History Review*, 14, 3: 291–322.

Nair, Janaki 1998, *Miners and Millhands: Work, Culture and Politics in Princely Mysore*, New Delhi: Sage.

Newman, R.K. 1981, *Workers and Unions in Bombay: A Study of Organization in the Cotton Mills*, Canberra: Austalian National University Monographs on South Asia No. 6.

Sabel, Charles and Jonathan Zeitlin 1985, "Historical Alternatives to Mass Production: Politics, Markets and Technology in Nineteenth Century Industrialization", *Past and Present*, 108: 133–76.

Sarkar, Sumit 1997, "The Decline of the Subaltern in Subaltern Studies", idem, in *Writing Social History*, Delhi: Oxford University Press.

Sen, Sukomal 1970, *Working Class of India: History of Emergence and Struggle, 1830–1970*, Calcutta: K.P. Bagchi.

Simeon, Dilip 1995, *The Politics of Labour under Late Colonialism: Workers, Unions and the State in Chota Nagpur, 1928–1939*, Delhi: Manohar.

Stokes, Eric 1978, "The Return of the Peasant", in idem, *The Peasant and the Raj*, Cambridge: Cambridge University Press.

15

Thinking about P.C. Joshi

LET ME BEGIN WITH SOME personal recollections as P.C. Joshi figures prominently in my childhood memories. He had become a close friend of my father, Susobhan Sarkar (a Marxist Professor of History at Presidency College, Calcutta), from the early 1940s, some years after he became General Secretary of the Communist Party of India (CPI). My uncle, P.C. Mahalanobis, was also his friend and he provided Kalpana Joshi with a job at the Indian Statistical Institute. During the War, our Elgin Road home became a meeting place for British and American communist soldiers posted in India, who helped to deepen the international contacts of Indian communists. Several from the International Brigade – formed to fight against the Fascist forces in Spain – were among the visitors, though I was then too young to remember their names. Joshi, too, was a participant in the endless political discussions of those times.

Then came 1948, and Joshi's abrupt and very brusque removal from leadership as the party line changed from efforts to build links with Congress nationalism to a decision to topple the Congress government in the immediate future. After his overthrow from the leadership, Joshi came to stay with us for a few days. He loved walking and I remember the long walks that he used to take with my father, talking incessantly for hours on political matters. I accompanied them, listening eagerly to what sounded like an enthusiastic and lively discussion, and trying to make some sense of what they said. Such were the beginnings of my political and Marxist education.

One morning, I woke up to strange sounds. Joshi was rushing around, packing his bag and muttering to himself: "I have to go, I have to go." Later I came to know that the party had just been declared illegal, and Joshi had to go underground immediately. Advance news about the impending ban, interestingly, reached the party from a very high-ranking police officer with well-concealed leftist sympathies. The party had, surprisingly, prepared little for this most likely eventuality, considering how loudly it had announced its decision to dislodge the Congress government. Many comrades had to spend nights in hiding at the Sealdah station. Only later, Nikhil Chakravartty gradually built up a remarkable tech apparatus to give them shelter and to carry on underground party functioning.

The Joshi family moved to Delhi. I had little to do with him for a number of years till I began to make frequent trips there to research in the National Archives, from the mid 1960s. Joshi's Delhi apartment was not very far from the archives. I would visit him virtually every evening after I had finished the day's work. Once again, there were long walks with him across the India Gate grounds, and once again he talked incessantly. His mood had now darkened. I particularly remember him saying once: "You know, Sumit, it is strange that I was far more influential in the country in my thirties than I am now in my sixties." I also remember how despondent he was as he told me on one of those walks, around 1967, that the Soviet Party had just okayed the Communist Party of India's decision to enter into coalition governments in some states with all anti-Congress forces including the Jan Sangh. It was a difficult decision for the Left. The long political domination of the Congress finally seemed to be ending, the post-Nehru Congress had lost much of its earlier stature, and yet the anti-Congress forces appeared something of a ragtag-bobtail, extending from convinced leftists and socialists to the extreme right. It was a situation that did not fit with his general faith in the historic necessity of broad unity among secular nationalist forces. Moreover, he was keenly aware of the danger from communalism. This was somewhat unusual at that time since the party then had not really begun to analyse communalism in a serious and informed manner.

My wife and I moved to Delhi in 1974, and very soon my parents and sister came to visit us. They were excited, above all, at the prospect of meeting the Joshis after a very long time. We spent a day with them at their home. Joshi seemed a broken man now, with very little to say about the political situation.

The last time I walked with Joshi was at his funeral procession. A class friend who walked with me said that our last links with the party had now snapped.

II

It is not inappropriate to bring in personal memories in the context of a discussion of P.C. Joshi. He was one of those rare communists whose warm personal touch and ability to communicate with all kinds of people, from all stages and ways of life – ranging from intellectuals, artists, scientists, to plebeian workers – were remarkable. While most communist leaders would enter the party headquarters at Ajay Bhawan in Delhi without more than a passing glance at the gatekeepers and guards, Joshi invariably stopped and chatted with them about their home and village life. The fact that this was something rather remarkable for communist leaders is significant in itself.

The political life of P.C. Joshi has its puzzles. Youth, for a start: born in 1907, he was arrested under the Meerut Conspiracy Cases at the age of twenty-two, and became General Secretary of the Communist Party when still in his twenties, in 1936. He was born in Almora and educated in Allahabad, both places far away from centres of labour militancy or communist activity. His first contact with the working class came only in the 1930s when he became a trade unionist at Kanpur for a brief while, after his release from prison. But distance from already established communist centres perhaps proved to be more of an advantage. It helped him to be independent of local political networks and develop an all-India perspective all the more effectively and quite early.

Joshi was a good writer and speaker, and an excellent journalist, but not perhaps a significant Marxist theoretician. Here he differed from Dange, for instance, who is revealed in the Meerut files as well read not only in Marx, but also in Utopian Socialism, even at that early date. He differed, too, from E.M.S. Namboodiripad, whose studies of Kerala history and society are intensive and acute. In contrast, a glance through the available writings of Joshi indicates that the vast bulk of them related to day-to-day organisational practicalities about the running of urgent political movements. There seems virtually no discussion of more general theoretical aspects of Marxism, nor fine-grained analysis of general or specific Indian political realities.

Joshi's main contribution clearly lay in mobilisation and the organisation of mass movements of varied kinds: cultural as well as political. Both required a truly exceptional ability to connect with and inspire a wide variety of people, from different regions and across social classes. In this ability to communicate lay his real strength.

Joshi's life was marked by two basic loyalties: to Marxian Socialism, which communists equated at the time with the Soviet Union; and to anti-colonial Indian nationalism. The two loyalties came into conflict when Hitler invaded the Soviet Union in 1941. Joshi initially found it very difficult to accept what come to be called the "People's War" line: full support for the war and therefore a certain playing down of immediate struggles against the British for the time being. After some hesitation, however, he was able to implement this new line effectively and innovatively. Under his leadership, Indian communists combined "People's War" with a whole range of local and regional movements against immediate oppressors, most of whom were Indians. Historians have shown that in practice they continued to accuse the British for wartime famine and repression, and government correspondence in the early 1940s reveals a string of British suspicion of communists even during that phase.

Remarkably, the 1940s – even with this "anti-nationalist" tactic – proved to be a period of rapid growth for the communist movement in India, despite the charges of collusion that nationalists brought against it. This was the time of the Tebhaga movement in Bengal, when sharecroppers protested powerfully against landlords and rich peasants, and of the Telangana armed struggles waged by peasants against landlords in Hyderabad who were backed by a despotic nizam. Through these massive struggles under conditions of brutal repression, Communist Party membership shot up from a few hundred in the late 1930s to almost a 100,000 on the eve of Independence. The C.P.I. emerged as the second largest party in India in the first general elections held under universal franchise. The expansion had happened largely in the Joshi era.

Joshi's achievements were most striking in the cultural field, demonstrating his unique ability to weave together intellectuals, writers, artists, and theatre and film personalities with militant mass struggles and popular movements. Even a necessarily brief list of such cultural figures would include Balraj Sahni, Prem Chand, Manik Bandopadhyaya, and Sambhu Mitra. They left an abiding impact on avant-garde cultural movements as well as on progressive strands in popular Bombay cinema. The consolidation of communist intellectual–cultural initiatives was most strikingly evident in the Progressive Writers Association (P.W.A.) and the Indian People's Theatre Association (I.P.T.A.). The latter travelled across the country, raising funds for the millions affected by the terrible Bengal famine of 1943. Its central slogan became *"Bhookha Hai Bengal"* (Bengal is Starving). What seemed be a fund-raising effort with cultural events grew into an amazing journey by middle-class left cultural activists to famine-ravaged villages, to reach out to and understand, at first hand, what imperialism, class oppression, and a new form of capitalism under war conditions meant as actual experience. The bridges that were built enriched communists as well as cultural activists and intellectuals, and brought different regional wings together in warm solidarity, for Joshi saw to it that this was a truly subcontinental anti-famine effort. Cultural troupes included women in significant positions. War-time communism began to reach out to women as a deliberate expansion of cadre bases and mass fronts. For the first time, communists encouraged the formation of specifically women activists' brigades, like the Mahila Atmaraksha Samiti in Bengal, which worked with destitute victims of famine and communal violence. Both the Tebhaga and Telangana struggles, too, saw remarkable participation by women activists, from peasant as well as middle-class backgrounds. The incorporation of women into party activities, however, had an interesting twist. As communist men and women came together in marriage at this time and began to produce babies, Joshi felt the need to provide shelters for the new generation at this time of grave risk of repression that parents faced. I recall hearing in political discussions at home that he now advised women to return to the larger family networks from which many of them had broken away. This was, obviously, not an easy matter for women who had chosen a life of social as well as political defiance.

III

The Joshi era in Indian Communist Party history ended abruptly and painfully in 1948, when he was removed from the leadership of the party at its Second Congress. Perhaps rendered overconfident by the advances in the preceding years, the party swung to a sectarian line declaring that the transfer of power was a sham – '*Yeh azaadi jhut hai*' (This independence is false). This was primarily a Soviet decision. The Soviet Union, threatened now by possible nuclear devastation, wanted an expansion of an exclusive communist influence as quickly as possible through insurrectionary methods. Later, the party line was reversed again when communists were told to follow a parliamentary path. But Joshi was never again restored to leadership.

The fall of Joshi underlines a larger paradox that is ingrained in party histories. The Soviet Union was both the greatest asset for international communism, fighting often desperate battles and armed only with the conviction that its continued presence meant that communism was destined to succeed. This teleology of success that the Soviet Union embodied gave its decisions paramount status for parties all over the world. Questions of leadership and strategies for all the different parties at different conjunctures were settled in Moscow. Sometimes this worked very well indeed. When the Indian Communist Party was virtually disintegrating under the weight of bitter inner-party struggles in the late 1940s and early 1950s, some of the leaders were called to Moscow and conflicts were resolved through Stalin's direct intervention. But such procedures of Stalinist authority left no room for either broad theoretical initiatives or for broad strategic innovations within individual parties. It is interesting to recall that the major breakthroughs in international communism took place in three countries where the Soviet influence was defied or bypassed: China, Yugoslavia, and Italy. Italian communists, inspired by Gramsci, were able to develop a distinctively different trajectory of Marxism. As an aside, I may add that the very peculiar absence of considerations of caste in Indian communist writings is, in large measure, due to such externality of formulations about communist social theories.

Indian communists were not defiant. Joshi would always obey Soviet commands, even when they militated against his own convictions and understanding – as in 1942. More remarkably, he accepted his own overthrow and yet remained in the party.

What, then, did Indian communist leadership precisely consist of, under such a structure of constraints and limits? Joshi had steered the party through difficult times, turning crisis into successful mobilisation. His stewardship saw some of the greatest mass upsurges that the C.P.I. had ever mobilized. He extended the party into many different, even contrary, directions and spaces. Yet, overarching strategies and theoretical guidance could never be his. We return, then, to an earlier point: the mismatch between organisational genius and an absence of theoretical creativity. Perhaps Joshi's entire understanding of Indian society and politics remained embedded in planning details of mobilisation and organization, into the creativity of shaping mass movements on the ground.

16

Edward Thompson

EDWARD THOMPSON (1924–1993) a truly rare combination of outstanding historian, creative socialist, Marxian thinker, and activist has come to be widely acknowledged as the principal progenitor of international trends towards writing "histories from below". The son of another Edward Thompson – the ex-Methodist missionary who sympathised with Indian liberal-nationalist causes and became a friend of Tagore and Nehru – E.P. Thompson, as a fervent anti-Fascist, fought in a tank brigade during the war. He was then for a decade an active member of the British Communist Party, helping to set up the extraordinarily fertile Marxist Historians' Group of the party. Fellow members included Christopher Hill, E.J. Hobsbawm, Rodney Hilton, as well as his lifelong partner Dorothy, who herself became a major historian of nineteenth-century Britain. Along with many of its most dedicated cadres, Thompson resigned from the party when it refused to condemn the Soviet intervention in Hungary in 1956, but his commitment to radical causes only deepened and took on more imaginative forms after this break. Thompson as activist will be remembered most for his outstanding role in peace and anti-nuclear movements; the Campaign for Nuclear Disarmament of the late 1950s and '60s in Britain, and the European Nuclear Disarmament campaigns during the second Cold War of the 1980s which for a few years became a powerful mass movement. Thompson's was a vision of alternative, democratic, and humane forms of socialism, fundamentally distinct alike from then-existing bureaucratic-socialist regimes and capitalist and consumerist societies and values. Thompson was very far removed from the stereotype of the basically ivory-tower, even if at times academically Marxist, professional scholar, and it is significant that he was never offered any university chair or formal honours in his own country. But he still came to be very widely acknowledged as possibly the most outstanding and influential historian of his generation, remarkable above all for combining passionate political commitment with the highest standards of professional rigour and originality, each feeding into the other, and both communicated through superb prose, argument, and richness of data.

Even before 1956, Thompson began elaborating notions of socialist history and ideals beyond the limits of Stalinist orthodoxy through a biographical study of William Morris (1955; rev. edn 1977), the late-nineteenth-century English romantic poet, artist, designer, and activist who tried to work for a different kind of socialism. An over-long biography, this attracted few readers when it appeared, but it already contained some of the key features of the "Thompsonian" stress on the ethical-cultural dimensions of the socialist project and history-writing alike. His real breakthrough into the historical world came with *The Making of the English Working Class* (1963), a true classic if ever there has been one, which inspired generations of labour and social historians across the world, not excluding India. What made *The Making* such a landmark, as well as endlessly controversial, was its novel handling of problems of class and class consciousness, bringing together materialist analysis with cultural history. Thompson rejected the then-dominant Marxist tendency to make class into a fixed "thing", easily translatable into a set of people having a determinate connection with a particular kind of production relations. Such a set, it was then assumed, "should" have a particular kind of "class consciousness" more or less determined by material conditions: if, as happens much more often than not, workers did not behave and act according to the script laid down by theory, various forms of substitutist vanguardism tended to take over. Economic determinism, Thompson was quick to add, was no monopoly of Marxists, and was as common in anti-Marxist "modernisation" theories. Against both types of reductionism, he tried to develop the alternative focus on a dialectic of structure and agency in which, in history and politics alike, Thompson tended to emphasise the importance of the second: human beings living in conditions and amidst presuppositions inherited from the past, and so not of their choice, but still striving to make their own history. Class, for Thompson, was what could be seen to happen sometimes, and in ever-shifting forms, in actual human relationships. It could not be grasped, at least in historical reconstruction, as a finished or isolable entity. This approach transformed the whole field of British and, indeed, world labour history, which had so long consisted either of narrowly economistic analysis and debates about the conditions and standards of living of workers, or, among the more radically committed, of studies of trade union and socialist organisations. The new focus upon the varied everyday experiences and cultures of toilers soon became standard historiographical common sense, but has also remained open to simplifications in which Thompson's own uncanny capacity to hold together material and cultural histories has proved difficult to maintain. Thus Thompson came to be both revered and attacked for inaugurating a "culturalist" turn – yet his *Making*, and indeed all his writings, remained steeped in economic history, and, far from neglecting politics, are rich in detailed analysis of radical or socialistic groups. Even its occasional gaps and flaws have at times proved fruitful. Thus, several distinguished feminist historians have said that the combination in *The Making* of a neglect of gender dimensions with the elaboration of tools and concepts clearly very relevant for exploring all those "hidden from history", above all women, set them off on their own distinct but not unrelated paths. Thompson's work, again, has often been criticised for being overconfined to England, as even in the title of his magnum opus: but it must be noted that some of his old students, notably Peter Linebaugh, have subsequently pioneered explorations of a wider "Atlantic" world from below through an extension of his methods.

The distinctive quality of Thompson's Marxism lay in a refusal to allow the economy to remain at the level of abstractions governed by inexorable, purely objective laws, as "bases" firmly separable from "superstructures" – terms which he firmly rejected. Thompson's commitment to "agency" also made him very angry about the late 1970s and early '80s turn in Western radical circles towards structuralist

Marxism, embodied for him in Althusser. *Poverty of Theory* (1978) was felt by many to be unnecessarily violent in its anti-Althusserian polemic, but it also contained a valuable exposition of Thompson's own conceptions of historical method.

Thompson had begun in the 1970s to extend back in time his distinctive approach, exploring eighteenth-century English history through a number of illuminating essays (among which "Moral Economy of the English Crowd in the Eighteenth Century" is the most famous), as well as a second major book, *Whigs and Hunters* (1975). The research was then interrupted by a decade of total involvement in the anti-nuclear struggle, from which he returned with his health broken by years of incessant activism. This was a moving sacrifice by a great historian to causes felt to be more urgent than academic work, in a world which in the Reagan era seemed to be on the brink of nuclear extermination.

His eighteenth-century studies, *Whigs and Hunters*, together with the revised version of the other essays – put together shortly before his untimely death – in *Customs in Common* (1991), once more transformed historical understanding of what so long had been considered a relatively placid era preceding the Industrial Revolution. It highlighted complex forms of plebeian crime, protest, and culture, situating them in the context of transformations in English law, state structures, and ruling ideologies. The posthumous *Witness Against the Beast* (1993), a study of the late-eighteenth-century Romantic poet, revolutionary, and mystic of artisan origin William Blake, in a sense brought together all his major concerns in ways that simultaneously illuminated the lost connections between the radical upsurge in mid-seventeenth-century England that Christopher Hill had explored, with the world of his own *Making*.

Thompson inherited from his father a lifelong interest in matters Indian, visiting the country twice, in 1976–7 and again as peace campaigner in the mid 1980s. The first visit, when he addressed a session of the Indian History Congress, provided a notable stimulus to new kinds of social-historical teaching and research in India. It is not always remembered that there was a Thompsonian impulse behind the initial Subaltern Studies project, though later its dominant trajectory moved in a different direction. It is fitting in some ways that the last of his books that Thompson was able to see in print was on an Indian theme, *Alien Homage* (1993), a collection of his father's correspondence with Rabindranath. It came with an unusually quiet, even modest Introduction, for Thompson was aware that he was writing about a country and culture about which he knew little. Even this relatively minor work did make, however, an important point about the dangers of reductionist oversimplification, in this case the way missionary and imperial origin is often assumed to determine all values and attitudes: "The limits must be noted . . . but what may merit our attention more may be what lies outside these limits or confounds our expectations."

MAJOR PUBLICATIONS

William Morris, Romantic to Revolutionary (1955; London: Merlin, 1977)
The Making of the English Working Class (London: Gollancz, 1963).
Whigs and Hunters (London: Allen Lane, 1975)
Poverty of Theory and Other Essays (London: Merlin, 1978)
Customs in Common (London: Merlin, 1991)
Alien Homage (Delhi: Oxford University Press, 1993)
Witness Against the Beast (Cambridge, etc., 1993)

Several collections of Thompson's political writings have also been published, combining brilliant polemic with historical insight: see, for instance, *Writing by Candlelight* (Merlin, 1980).

FURTHER READING

Perry Anderson, *Arguments within English Marxism* (London: Verso, 1980)
H.J. Kaye and K. McClelland, ed., *E.P. Thompson: Critical Perspectives* (Cambridge: Polity, 1990)
Kaye, Harvay J., *The British Marxist Historians: An Introductory Analysis* (Cambridge: Polity, 1984)
Bryan Palmer, *The Making of E.P. Thompson: Marxism Humanism and History* (Toronto, 1981)
J. Rule and R. Malcolmson, eds, *Protest and Survival, the Historical Experience: Essays for E.P. Thompson* (London: Merlin, 1993).
Sumit Sarkar, "The Relevance of E.P. Thompson", in Sarkar, *Writing Social History* (Delhi: Oxford University Press, 1997).

17

In Memory of Eric Hobsbawm

A LONG LIFE, AMAZINGLY RICH and productive till the very end, is now over. It is, indeed, the passing of an era: of a tradition of committed Marxist history-writing which peaked especially in post-War Britain. Hobsbawm belonged to the Historians' Group of the Communist Party of Great Britain which founded *Past and Present* and which, at one point, included Christopher Hill, E.P. Thompson, Rodney Hilton, and many other towering figures. It was a generation directly engaged with tumultuous world historical events in ways that had seldom been the lot of historians in other times and places.

Hobsbawm himself was born in 1917. He and his contemporaries saw the rise and fall of socialist revolutions the world over. Many fought in one of the bloodiest wars in history. They lived for very large stretches of their lives under the shadow of an imminent nuclear holocaust. They also saw some remarkable triumphs: the defeat of Fascism, of formal imperialism in Asia and Africa, the American defeat in Vietnam.

A historian's tribute, however, cannot rest with the iconic evocation of tradition or of great achievements alone. It needs to encompass paradoxes which set Hobsbawm apart from many of his other comrades.

I can recall three stories about Hobsbawm that might help situate him as a communist historian. The first two are ironical; the third, in contrast, speaks of the depth of his own kind of communist political conviction. They indicate, perhaps, an inner tension that could, ultimately, find no resolution.

Shortly after the Soviet invasion of Czechoslovakia in 1968, a group of us – leftists in Calcutta who ran a study circle called the Marx Club – invited Hobsbawm, then visiting the city, to speak about the Soviet "intervention". He condemned it unequivocally and openly. He then went on to remark that the Soviet Party should be seen as something similar to the Indian Civil Service: joining it was a lucrative job option. The meaning of party membership in a situation where the party ruled the state was vastly different, he said, from being a communist in a capitalist country.

His criticism of communisms in power was not restricted to the Soviet model. He extended it to the Chinese experience that had attracted so many across the world at the time. He once said that Mao's Little Red Book – brandished by all political rebels and radicals around the globe in those days – made him nostalgic even for Stalin's infamous Short Course on the History of the Soviet Party: a classic example of doctored, self-serving historical narrative. So extreme were the absurdities of the former that the lies of the latter seemed modest by comparison.

Taken together, these two stories establish Hobsbawm's growing scepticism about communist hopes of revolutionary change, and his acute awareness of the myths spun by Stalinism and adjacent ideologies to disguise the horrors of "actually existing socialist regimes". One may, perhaps, wonder if this sense of hopelessness – most acute and painful in someone who would not abjure the party – might not have influenced certain decisions that may seem cynical: his acceptance of the Order of the Companion of Honour is a case in point. More consequentially, his support for Neil Kinnock and the Labour Right in the 1980s, at the peak of Thatcherism, has been, justifiably, a subject of fierce criticism from the British Left.

The third story, by contrast, points in the opposite direction. It illuminates what appears to be the most puzzling of Hobsbawm's decisions: his retention, till his death, of his party membership. Unlike his associates in the Historians' Group of the Communist Party of Great Britain, his acceptance of the truths of Khrushchev's revelations did not lead him to publicly relinquish his party affiliation. Nor would he do so after the Soviet invasion of Hungary, when several

British Marxist historians – E.P. Thompson, most notably – left the party and founded their relationship with Marxist theory and praxis on very different terms. Hobsbawm neither revised his stance towards the party, nor did he formally reconstitute his older Marxist understanding about the mainspring of historical processes even after such catastrophic shocks.

The third story, perhaps, helps us to understand why it was so. It comes from his autobiography, *Interesting Times*, and it speaks of the precise moment at which his decision to become a communist became written in stone. It was in the middle of the last march of the German Communist Party through a dark Berlin just before Hitler came to power. A decision taken at such a momentous turning point in history, in the face of such odds, seems to have led Hobsbawm to see his communism as a political identity which simply could not be given up, however purely formal its presence in his public life increasingly became.

His historical practice is difficult to define very precisely. He continued to adhere to a largely orthodox economic determinism, organising historical processes around the structures of modes of production. In contrast, Thompson and Raymond Williams would develop powerful critiques of the base–superstructure model. At the same time, in his own research and writings, Hobsbawm was drawn, again and again, to historical figures and events which orthodox Marxism tended to ignore, marginalise, or dismissively castigate as residual elements, misfits in a neat and confident narrative of progress which moves from an anti-feudal to an anti-capitalist transformation in forces and relations of production, under organised working-class leadership. Some of his most profound and sensitive writings relate to outlaw figures: *Bandits*, *Primitive Rebels*, or his work on Luddite machine breakers. These people were not representatives of the vanguard revolutionary class and they belonged to defeated forces that, as Thompson famously said, had been seen at best with enormous condescension by posterity, including by progressive historians. Studying doomed rebellions was hardly a classically communist choice. His preference, or his irresistible attraction for such moments, then, indicates his position as lying outside of an orthodoxy that he never repudiated.

However, this tension was not uncharacteristic of British Marxist historians even in earlier times. Thompson wrote a study of William Morris' utopian socialism while he was still in the party; Morton had uncovered the history of the Ranters sometime previously, thus reorienting the history of the English civil war in ways which Christopher Hill would elaborate and enrich. Raphael Samuel once pointed out that, in a political life defined by constant exhortations to "scientific method" and an acceptance of the iron laws of progress, history furnished "the playground of the Communist unconscious". So if Hobsbawm wrote about subjects that were unorthodox from a communist political perspective, this choice was, in Britain at least, hardly unusual for a Marxist. It was an orthodox Marxist's undying passion for unorthodox themes.

In a slightly different vein, Hobsbawm also underlined occasions in Marx's own analytical practice when Marx departs from a fully economistic understanding of history. This is clearest in Marx's *Eighteenth Brumaire*, where the analysis of Bonapartism had to move away from a simple reduction of the state to class power. I also sometimes speculate that the rather abrupt entry of Bonapartism in Hobsbawm's late essay, "Marx, Engels and Politics", was possibly implicitly conditioned by his awareness of the nature of actually existing socialist regimes which, in their operation, could not be fully understood within strictly class digits.

There was a radical difference with other Marxist historians, nonetheless. The fact that Hobsbawm never broke with the party, and, further, that his particular brand of Marxism, unlike Thompson's or Hill's, was far more deliberately shaped by economic explanations of the big forces of historical change, imbued his work with certain specific qualities and strengths. Unlike Thompson's or Hill's, some of his greatest work spanned very big slices of time and space: the ages of revolution, capital and empire, moving from Europe to the globe: even though, strangely, the global history excluded any sustained engagement with India and China. He was a master of the grand narrative in the best sense of the term.

There were other productive differences. Hill, Hilton, and Thompson confined their detailed research to British, or even English, historical experiences. Hobsbawm, born of mixed European descent and staying on in Germany till the rise of Nazism, was the most European of British Marxist historians. His work, therefore, had a sweep and range, across both time and space, which his contemporaries could not claim. His life story, told by himself, is imbued with this cosmopolitanism.

What he shared with them, nonetheless, was his interest in detail and the smaller events which cohered to produce the larger picture. The details were important in themselves and not just as a prelude to large conclusions, such as those, for instance, in the work of Perry Anderson, the other British Marxist with a comparable sweep.

Hobsbawm's unswerving faith in Marxism depended on a very interesting paradox. This is indicated in a passage in one of his last essays, "Marx Today". He gave two reasons for what he saw as the abiding and ever-growing general interest in Marxism from the late twentieth century. He attributes it partly to the collapse of the erstwhile socialist countries: this emancipated Marx from the iron cage of official Marxism-Leninism. Second, the globalised capitalism of today is "uncannily" like the world predicted in the Communist Manifesto.

The worldwide triumph of capitalism becomes, ironically, in Hobsbawm, an argument for the perennial strength of Marxist analysis. It is a memorable point for us all.

Index

abhijat bhadralok, 67
Acharya, Poromesh, 277
achintabhedabheda, 190
Adam, William, 13, 43, 277
Addhya, Udaychandra, 41, 43
adhikaribheda, 116, 122, 126, 129, 200–2, 225, 226, 238, 258, 278
Adi Samaj Brahmos, 78
Advaita Vedantist philosophy, 201
Age of Consent, 261, 299
Age of Reason, 36
Agni-sanket (1984), 236
A.I.C.C. Working Committee, 555
Alaler gharer dulal, 42–3
Ali, Niamat, 564
Alien Homage (1993), 625
Aligarh Movement, 544
Amar Jivan, 309
Amherst, Lord, 3
Amrita Bazar Patrika, 67, 69, 74, 77, 313, 340, 417, 436, 462
Anandamath, 172, 212
Ananda Yama, 332
Ancient Rights of Females (1822), 13
Anderson, Benedict, 395

Anglo-Indian bureaucracy, 56
Anglophilism, 80
Annadamangal, 337
Annapurna, 223, 355, 358
Annual Report of the Bombay Millowners' Association (1928), 499–500
anti-British rebellion, 1857, 373
anti-*chowkidari* tax campaign, 513
anti-colonial nationalism, 311, 370, 372, 406
anti-imperialist ideology, 483
anti-jute agitation, 439
anti-*parda* movement, 406, 407
An Apology for the Pabna Rioters (1873), 84
arbitration courts, 439
Archer, Mildred, 351
aristocracy, 69
Arnold, David, 590–2
Arnot, Sandford, 9
Aryan civilisational myth, 116
Aryan cultural assimilation, 148
Asaf Ali, Aruna, 548, 556
ashtavakramsamhita, 191
Assam–Bengal Employees Union, 443

"*Astapash mukta boa*," liberation, 367
Aswamedha Yajna, 347
Atmajivani, 75
"Atmasakti" concept, 56
Atmiya Sabha, 8
Aurobindo Ghosh model, 78
Autobiographical Letter, 14
Autobiography (1952), 21
avowed atheism, 37
Azad Hind Fauj, 552

Bagchi, Amiya, 588
Baker, C.J., 379
Balak-bhava, 329
Ballantyne, J.R., 270, 271n79, 272
Balya-bibaha pamphlet, 295
Balyabibaher Dosh, 289, 292
Bamabodhini Patrika, 308
Bandopadhyay, Chandicharan, 254, 261
Bandopadhyay, Harishchandra, 180, 353
Bandopadhyay, Sekhar, 110, 131, 241–3, 293
Bandyopadhyaya, Bhabanicharan, 66
Banerjea, Surendranath, 68, 176, 339, 410, 426, 435
Banerji, Krishnamohan, 27, 28, 31, 40, 75
Banerji, Sasipada, 84, 93
Bangabasi, 258, 262, 349
"Bangadesher Krishak," 66, 83
Bangalee, 59
Bankim–Akshay Sarkar, 77
Banylal's revolt, 32
baralok, 165, 166
baramanush model, 164–5, 172, 183, 184, 188
Bardoli resolution, 417
Barisal Hitaishi, 130
Barisal Provincial Conference, 448
Bartaman Bharat, 229, 230, 232, 233
Basu, Loknath, 202
Basu, Rajnarain, 38
Basu, Ramram, 7
Battleship Potemkin, 551
"Battola," 351
Bayly, Chris, 379
Belur Math, 219
Bengalee, 69, 70, 73, 97, 121, 123, 313, 315, 337, 339, 340, 426
Bengal Herald, 15, 17
Bengal Hurkaru, 16, 50
Bengali entrepreneurship, 249
Bengal Namasudra Association, 131
Bengal peasant agitation, 449
"Bengal Proper," 112
Bengal Provincial Congress Committee, 532
Bengal Punnapra-Vayalar, 537

Bengal Renaissance, 2, 13, 14, 20, 21, 24, 26, 178, 350
Bengal Spectator, 39, 40, 46, 47, 90, 96
Bengal Tenancy Bill, 74
Benjamin, Walter, 143
Benn, Wedgwood, 504, 509, 515, 526, 532
Bentinck Papers, 34
Berkeley, Bishop, 270
bhadralok, 61, 124, 134, 135, 140, 152–8, 160, 162, 165, 166, 170–2, 175, 178, 179, 186, 187, 189, 190, 194, 198, 199, 203, 205, 207, 212, 213, 215, 217, 219, 224, 228, 234, 239, 251, 261, 280, 286, 287, 304, 314, 316–23, 326, 327, 334, 335, 338–43, 345, 350, 351, 366–8, 401, 417, 424–6, 428, 429, 433, 444
Bhaduri, Satinath, 421, 459, 472
bhagchasis, 136, 138
Bhakti, 151–236
Bharat Sramajivi, 73, 84, 93
Bharatvarsha, 161
Bharatvarshiya Sanatan Dharmarakshini Sabha, 349
Bhattacharya, Digindranarayan, 122, 305
Bhattacharya, Sabyasachi, 76, 578
"*Bhookha Hai Bengal,*" 618
Bhuinmali, Ananda, 324, 332
Bibliotheque bleu, 351
Bidhaba-bibaha tract, 295

Bihar Congress report, 508
Bilvamangal, 222
binary opposition, 369
Biographical Sketch of David Hare, 29
Birla, G.D., 499, 500, 544, 554
Biswananda, Swami, 420
Blake, William, 624
Blithely, Irwin, 509
Bodhoday, 281, 282
Bogra, 446, 447
Bolsheviks, 571
Bombay Chronicle, 516
Book of Revelations, 348
Bose, Amritalal, 58
Bose, Anandamohan, 68
Bose, Rajnarain, 4n8, 71
Bose, Subhas, 530, 531
bourgeois betrayal, 538
bourgeois liberalism, 102
"bourgeois" nationalism, 398
bourgeois-nationalist elitism, 385
bourgeois property rights, 310
bourgeois-revolutionary, 498
Brahmani, Bhairabi, 212, 221
Brahmanical society, 237–311
Brahmanism and the Sudra, or the Indian Labour Problem, 119
Brahmans, 6, 13, 111n11, 126, 301
Brahma-Pauttalik Sambad, 5
Brahmoism, 11, 76, 88, 95
Brahmo Public Opinion, 68
Brahmo Samaj, 10
breakdown plan, 553

Brief History of Bengal Commerce (1872), 65
British economic exploitation, 98
British Indian Association, 46
British Orientalism, 14
British repression, 518
Broomfield, J.H., 61n30
Brown, Judith, 434
Bryce, James, 19
Buckingham, James Silk, 16
Building the Railways of the Raj, 597
Burdwan fever, 163
Burdwan Provincial Conference, 59
Burke, Peter, 454
Burn, Martin, 220

Calcutta Courier, 44
Calcutta Journal, 16
Calcutta Monthly Journal, 49
Calcutta Review, 47, 65n45
Cambridge School, 377, 378, 378, 474
Capital, 580
capitalism, 87, 389, 585, 588, 630
Carroll, Lucy, 304
caste, 114
hierarchy, 116
movements, 125
catholic hierarchy, 11
catholicity, 198, 201, 226
Chaitanya-Lila (1884), 217

chakdars, 135, 136, 138
Chakrabarti, Biharilal, 167, 173
Chakrabarti, Lalita, 593
Chakrabarti, Shyamsundar, 435
Chakrabarti, Tarachand, 28
Chakrabarty, Dipesh, 386, 388, 579, 595, 600
Chakravartty, Nikhil, 615
Chakri, 151–236
Chanakya-slokas, 278, 284
Chandals, 125, 126, 126n36, 133, 321, 323, 325, 328, 336, 348, 366
Chandavarkar, Raj, 576, 583–6, 587–93, 594, 595, 596, 599
Chandra, Bholanath, 65, 67, 73
Chandra, Bipan, 54, 492
Charitabali, 281
Charter Act, 1833, 42
Chasi Kaibarta, 132
Chatterjee, Partha, 115, 155, 371, 388, 404, 470, 580
Chatterji, Haramohan, 30
Chattopadhyay, Bankimchandra, 212, 410n30
Chattopadhyay, Biharilal, 360
Chattopadhyay, Gadadhar, 163
Chattopadhyay, Gautam, 26, 42
Chattopadhyay, Sanjib, 236
Chattopadhyay, Satischandra, 223, 355, 357
Chattoraj, Narayan, 358
Chaudhuri, Asutosh, 59
Chaudhuri, Benoy Bhushan, 84
Chaudhuri, Madhusudan, 312

Chaudhuri, Nirad C., 2, 21
chaukidari tax, 18, 63, 451
child marriage, 231, 288, 290, 291, 309, 310
Chinese Revolution, 547
chowkidari tax, 450, 451, 511, 512, 518
Chuckervarty Faction, 28, 35
city life, 168
civil disobedience movements, 374, 450, 453, 474–535
civil nationalisms, 370
class consciousness, 622
Cobb, Richard, 593
coitus reservatus, 195
Collet, S.D., 9
colonial bourgeoisie, 534
colonial difference, 589
colonial discourse analysis, 391
"colonial-educated" middle class, 383
colonialism, 22, 102, 144, 174, 242, 369, 370, 391
colonial middle-class nationalism, 382
colonial modernity, 109
colonial rule, 96, 182
Comedy of Errors, 255
communalism, 370, 375, 387, 393, 395, 408, 409, 412, 615
communications, 109
Communist-led Girni Kamgar Union, 586
Communist-led Kisan Sabha, 564

Communist Manifesto, 607
Congress and the Raj: Facets of the Indian Struggle, 380
"Congress violence," 486
Congreve, Richard, 81
conjugality, 215, 252
consciousness, 423
Constructive Swadeshi, 56
contradictory consciousness, 144
coolie migration, 594
cosmopolitanism, 630
Cotton Industries Protection Bill, 496
cultural encounter, 243
culturalist determinism, 595
cultural nationalism, 120
culture's representational technology, 259
Customs in Common (1991), 624

Dabistan-i Mazahib, 8
Dacca Prakash, 312, 314, 315, 317, 338, 339
Dacca proceedings, 336, 338
Dainik-o-Samachar-Chandrika, 262
dakshinachara, 195
daladali, 67
Dalits, 107n3, 112n11, 117n18, 143, 389, 400, 402
Dandi March, 510
Danesh, Haji Muhammad, 564
daridra athaccha bhadra, 251

daridra-narayan, 161, 224, 235
Darnton, Robert, 396
Das, Chittaranjan, 435
Das, C.R., 417, 437, 438, 445, 450, 454
Das, Mukunda, 58
Das, Swami Iswar, 442
Das, Upendranath, 72
Dasgupta, Ranajit, 578
Dasgupta, Satish, 550
Datta, Michael Madhusudan, 173
Datta, Ramachandra, 219, 221
death rituals, 364
Deb, Maheshchandra, 14, 38, 40, 288, 308
Deb, Raja Rajendranarayan, 75
Deb, Sibchandra, 28
Debganer Marta Agaman (1889), 180
Debi, Sarada, 212, 218, 221, 227
Decennial Report, 73
defamiliarisation, 144
deferential assertion, 361
deindustrialisation, 63, 98
Deism, 37
Delhi Pact, 491, 533
demarcation, 600
Derozian iconoclasm, 280
Derozian ideology, 35
Derozian reformism, 47
Derozians, 51, 92, 101
Derozio, 27, 28, 33
Derrida, Jacques, 386, 388
Devi, Kailasbashini, 309

Devi, Rashsundari, 309
Dharma Ghut, 48
Dhorai Charitmanas, 421, 459, 465
dichotomy, 369
Digby, 4
disaggregation, 107
discrimination, 21
Doyhata, 315–18, 320, 326, 339–42, 344–6, 362
Doyle, Conan, 436
"drain of wealth," 374
Dramatic Performances Act in 1876, 72
dualism, 113
Duff, Alexander, 11, 27, 28, 36, 37
Dutt, Akshaykumar, 14, 47, 94
Dutt, Gurusaday, 458
Dutt, Kailashchandra, 64
Dutt, Nimchand, 32
Dutt, Rameshchunder, 84
Dutt, R.C., 84
Dutt, R.P., 54, 87, 380
Dutta, Akshoykumar, 276
Dutta, Aswinikumar, 425
Dutta, Kalikinkar, 11n33
dwija corruption, 350
early nationalist activity, Bengal, 53–85
East, Hyde, 13
Economic and Political Weekly, 151
economic determinism, 377, 622
economic pressure, 434n56

economism, 104, 107, 149n72, 381, 572
"The Edge of a Volcano," 547
Eighteenth Brumaire, 466, 629
E.I.R. strikes, 445
Ekei ki bole sabhyata? (1860), 32
Elementary Aspects, 580
elitism, 377, 381
Ellenborough, 4n6
The Emergence of Indian Nationalism, 376
Englishman, 45
Eurasian, 28
European racism, 400
European radicalism, 27
European-style Reformation, 12
Exemplary and Instructive Biography, 281
extremist nationalism, 402
Ezhavas, 401

false consciousness, 94, 96
fascism, 547
Father of Modern India, 1, 63, 372
Federation of Indian Chambers of Commerce and Industry in 1927, 497
feeling, structure of, 361n162
feminisation, 172, 175, 329
FICCI, 501, 505
Filkins agreement, 545
"The First Indian War of Independence," 373

First World War, 374, 561
Floud Commission, 564
footloose labour, 389
Forest Administration Reports, 484
Forest Committee Report, 477
forest conflicts, 475
forest movements, 474, 481
forest satyagraha, 474–88
Forster, E.M., 610
For the Final Bid For Power (1945), 558
fraternisation, 437, 551
Friend of India, 34, 45

Gallagher, Jack, 376
Gandhi, Mahatma, 417, 490, 528
Gandhian leadership, 494
Gandhian nationalism, 137, 141, 400, 403, 473, 487, 587
  logic of, 489–535
Gandhian Non-Cooperation Movement, 136
Gandhi–Irwin Pact (1930–1931), 489–535
Gandhi Raj, 456, 460, 471, 479, 480, 486, 517
garbhadan ritual, 215n189
Gaudiya Vaishnavabad, 190
Gaudiya Vaishnava scholasticism, 208
Geddes, James, 64, 81
gender issues, 115

gender paradox, 185
gender-related reformism, 145n67
gender relationships, 403
Ghosh, Benoy, 26, 240, 244n19
Ghosh, Girish Chandra, 176, 185, 217, 330, 354
Ghosh, Girish Chunder, 67, 69, 74, 97
Ghosh, Harachandra, 34, 50
Ghosh, Jogendrachandra, 120
Ghosh, Maheshchandra, 27
Ghosh, Ramgopal, 35
Ghosh, Sisirkumar, 72, 77
Ghoshal, Upendrachandra, 334
Ghuznavi, A.H., 499
"Gift to Deists," 4
"Gobin-pagla," 360
Gonds of Banjaridhal, 486
Gopalan, A.K., 572
Gora, 18, 405
Goswami, Bejoykrishna, 174
Goswami, Jayanta, 351
Gramsci, Antonio, 573, 574, 620
Gramscian language, 85, 101
Gramsci's language, 146
"Great Unchastity Case," 310
grihastha bhakti, 254, 308
grihastha sannyas, 207, 208, 213, 236
Guha, Ranajit, 284, 381, 385, 418, 581
Gunder Frank model, 87
Gupta, Iswar, 184
Gupta, Jogendranath, 314, 320, 321, 324, 325

Gupta, Mahendranath, 153, 167, 172, 237, 238, 258
Gupta, Rabindra, 20
Guruchand Carit, 128, 129, 131
gurumohasayas, 277

Haig, H.G., 504
Hailey, Malcolm, 510
Hale, Mary, 230
harassing guerrilla warfare, 479
Hardiman, David, 380
Hard Times, 50
Hare, David, 27, 29
Haribhakti, 189n111
Harijan uplift, 60
Harijan welfare, 402
Harileelamrita, 128, 131
Harischandra (1875), 72
Hasham, Abdul, 570
Hashem, Abul, 543
Hatcher, Brian, 241–3, 264, 283
Haynes, Douglas, 406
hegemonic bourgeois culture, 580
Henningham, Stephen, 421
Hill, Christopher, 621, 624, 626, 629
Hilton, Rodney, 621, 626
Hilton Young Commission, 496
Hindoo Community, 12
Hindoo Patriot, 67, 302
Hind Swaraj (1909), 413, 415
Hindu-dharma-marma, 202
Hindu Mahilaganer Heenabastha, 309

Hindu–Muslim riots, 199
Hindu–Muslim unity, 425
Hindu revivalism, 20
Hindu self-government, 120
Hindutva nationalism, 405, 411, 415
Hindutva: Who is a Hindu? (1923), 411
Hirachand, Walchand, 523, 533
History of Bengal (1948), 20
Hitopadesha, 284
Hobsbawm, Eric, 476, 621
memory of, 626–30
"Holy Mother," 218
Home and the World, 405
Humble Suggestions (1823), 11
Hunter, 323, 339

identities, 392
identity formations, 105–50
imaginary transcendences, 344
imperialist racism, 226
Imperial Power and Popular Politics, 587, 590, 591
India: A Review of England's Relations Therewith (1868), 64
India Gazette, 17, 50
Indian Daily News, 432
Indian National Congress (1885), 374
Indian nationalism, 370
Indian national movement, 53
Indian People's Theatre Association (I.P.T.A.), 618
Indian Struggle, 530
Indian trade union movement, 553
Indian Year Book of 1939–40, 499
India Today (1940), 380
industrial revolution, 585
intellectuals, radicalism of, 86–104
Interesting Times, 628
Iswarchandra Vidyasagar and His Elusive Milestones, 240
Iswarganj riots, 465

jalacharanya, 134
Jama'at-i-Islami, 394
Jatibheda, 122
jatis, 112n11, 114, 117
jatra Palli-Seva, 58
Jawaharlal Nehru, 537
Jayakar, M.R., 502, 529
Jivancharit, 281
Jnananvesana, 35, 38, 39, 41, 43, 44
Jnanasindhu Tarango, 37
John Bull, 19, 82
Johnson, Gordon, 376
Jones, William, 116
Joshi, Chitra, 577, 595, 596, 605, 606, 608–10
Joshi, Kalpana, 614
Joshi, P.C., 570, 571, 614–20
achievements, 618

Indian Communist Party history, 619
  loyalties, life, 617
  Marxism, 617
  Meerut Conspiracy Cases, 616
  "People's War," 617
  political life of, 616
  Utopian Socialism, 616
jotedars, 139, 142
oppression, 564

Kabiraj, Umesh, 335
Kabiranta, Nandakumar, 202
Kaibarta, 248
Kalapahar (1896), 222, 357
Kaler Bau (1880), 180, 353
Kalighat paintings, 180, 351, 352
Kalikata Kamalalay, 66, 250
Kaliprasanna Vidyaratna, 350
Kalir Abasan (1902), 187
Kaliyuga, 151–236
Kalki-avatar, Bikrampur, 312–68
Kalki-purana, 350, 358
"Kamtapur" movement, 145n67
Karachi Congress, 530, 533
karma doctrine, 10n32
Karnataka Satyagraha Mandal, 486
Karunasagar Vidyasagar, 301
Kathamrita, 153–6, 158, 160, 162, 166, 170, 175, 176, 187–9, 191, 194, 195, 197, 198, 205, 207, 213, 215, 221, 234, 235, 237, 238, 358

Kayasthas, 126, 301
Kenopanishad (1823), 9
Kerani-carit (1885), 180
Kerr, Ian, 577, 597–9
Khaitan, D.P., 501, 528
Khan, Khizr Hayat, 545
Khan, M.S., 552
Khan, Muhammed Akram, 432
Khilafat agitation, 440
Khilafat agitators, 441
Khilafat leaders, 435
Khilafat movement, 467
Khilafat–Non-Cooperation movement, 437
Khulna, 446
Kinnock, Neil, 627
Knight, Robert, 64
Koli kautuk Natak, 358–9
Kolir Abashan, ba Kalki-abatarer Geetabhinoy, 359
Koli-yuga literature, 356
Koli-yuga myth, 350, 353, 368
Kopf, David, 19
Kosambi, D.D., 540
Kshatriyas, 13, 111n11, 140
Kshatriya Samiti, 141
Kulinism, 298
labour indophilism, 526
labour militancy, 443
Labour return, South Asian history, 576–610
Lahiri, Ramtanu, 28
Laljis, Huseinbhai, 533
language, 159, 357, 361, 414, 494

late-colonial Bengal, identity formations, 105–50
Life of Vivekananda, 230
Lilaprasanga, 157, 205
Linebaugh, Peter, 598
Little Red Book, 627
Locality, Province and Nation (1973), 376, 379
London British India Society of 1839, 98
Lost Worlds: Indian Labour and Its Forgotten Histories, 605
Low, D.A., 380
lower-caste monotheism, 95
low-life of literature, 317
Ludtke, Alf, 207n169
Lyotard, J.F., 144

Macaulay-style literary education, 4
Madani, Husain Ahmad, 393
Madhusudan, Michael, 32, 176
madhyabitta crisis, 250
Madhyabitta sreni, 68
Mahalanobis, Gurucharan, 306
Mahalanobis, P.C., 614
Mahila Atmaraksha Samiti, 618
Mahishyas, 60, 108, 125, 127, 132–5, 137, 140, 429
Mahishya Sevika, 134
Maji-Maji rebels, 464
Majumdar, J.K., 20
Majumdar, R.C., 19

Majumdars of Doyhata, 320, 326
The Making of the English Working Class (1963), 622
Mallaya, Korra, 479
Mallik, Sambhu, 161, 163
Manusamhita, 126n36
Marwari Association of Calcutta, 498
Marx Club, 627
Marxism-Leninism, 630
Marxist approach, 20
"Marx Today," 630
Mashik Patrika, 43
Matuas, 127–9, 131, 132, 323
Mavericks, 601
Mawdudi, Maulana, 393, 394
Mayabad, 6
McLane, John, 378
mendicancy, 53, 56, 83
Menon, V.P., 567–9
Mercantile Marine Conference, 497
Meye Parliament ba Bhagnitantraraj, 354
middle-class leadership, 111
Midnapur District Gazetteer, 133
Midnapur Zamindari Company, 451, 453, 463
Miners and Millhands: Work, Culture and Politics in Princely Mysore, 602
Mirat-ul-Ukhbar, 13
missionary propaganda, 227
Mitra, Dinabandhu, 32, 52, 72

Mitra, Kishorichand, 25
Mitra, Nabagopal, 78, 80
Mitra, Pearychand, 29, 35, 42
Mitra, Satyacharan, 329n44
Mitra, Subolchandra, 258, 261
Modern Asian Studies, 583
modern Indian nationalist movement, 495
modernisation, 22
modernism, 57
modernity, 386
modern nationalism, 474–88
Modern Review, 123
Mody, Homi, 499, 521, 523
mofussil bhadralok, 68
moneylenders, 471
monism, 6
monogamous marriage, 311
Monograph on Common Salt, 501
monotheism, 6, 19
Moody-Adams, Michele, 150n73
Moon, Penderel, 547
Moore, R.J., 493
moral pedagogy, 241
Morley–Minto reforms, 55
Morris, Morris David, 577
Morris, William, 622
Moslem oppression, 64
Mountbatten Plan, 545, 569
Mugdhabodha, 268
Mughal bureaucracy, 182
Muhammadan emissaries, 431
Mukherjee, S.N., 66
Mukherji, Dakshinaranjan, 37–8

Mukherji, U.N., 121, 122, 147
Mukherji's Magazine, 64, 65
Mukhopadhyay, Joykrishna, 275
Mullick, Krishnamohan, 65
Mullick, Rasikkrishna, 27, 34, 37, 64
Murphy, E.D., 594
Muslim breakaway, 375
Muslim Chambers of Commerce and Industry, 544
Muslim League, 543, 547
Muslim nationalism, 370, 375, 393, 395
Muslim separatism, 370, 375
Muslim tyranny, 42, 79, 80, 96
Mymensingh riots, 62, 430, 464

Naba Rah aba Yuga-Mahatmya, 360
Nair, Janaki, 577, 602
Nakazato, Nariaki, 124
"Namasudra Awakening, 1907," 129
Namasudra conference, 60
Namasudra–Muslim relations, 367, 430
Namasudra-Muslim riots, 367n178
Namasudras, 108, 112, 118, 123, 125, 129–34, 140, 287, 314, 324, 429–31, 457
Namboodiripad, E.M.S., 572, 616

Namierite cynicism, 61
"Namierite" shift, 376
Naranji, Lalji, 502
Narayan, Shib, 302
Narodniks, 61
Narodnism, 101
Nasiram, 222
Nath-yogi literature, 367
nationalism, 369–415, 508
national leadership (1945–1947), 536–75
National Paper, 71, 78–80
national self-regeneration, 56
A Nation in Making, 410
Natun Babu ba Kolir Abatar (1904), 355
Nawab Sahaber Subichar, 459
Naxalbari movement, 579
Naxalite iconoclasm, 21
Neevel, Walter, 196n131
Nehru, Jawaharlal, 519, 524, 530, 532, 554
neo-liberal capitalism, 389
Nihar, 136, 138
Nil-Darpan (1860), 72, 83
nineteenth-century Bengal case study, 86–104
nitishastra, 284
Noakhali, 446
non-conformity, 8
Non-Cooperation-Khilafat upsurge, 374, 409, 416, 417, 422, 425, 434, 435, 439, 442, 460, 472

Non-Cooperation movements, 474–88
Notes on the Bengal Renaissance (1946), 21
Notes on the Sanskrit College, 270

obiter dicta, 153
odium theologicum, 95
On the Bengal Renaissance, 21n70
open-market fluidity, 204
oppression, 456
optimism, 82
orality, 192
organised labour, 514
organised philanthropy, 224
organised trade unionism, 582
orientalism, 370
Orientalism, 389
Orientalist scholarship, 116
Oriental Magazine, 25
Origins of Industrial Capitalism in India, 586
orthodox Hinduism, 10
Osman, Muhammed, 442
Other Backward Castes (OBCs), 401
Otherness, 155
Ottoman Empire, 13, 456

Pabna rent strike of 1873, 103
Paine, Tom, 36
Pal, Bipinchandra, 20, 81, 99, 435

Pandey, Gyanendra, 381
Paramahansa, Ramakrishna, 3, 152
Parasara-samhita, 258, 296
Parganas, 429, 446
parochial scholasticism, 274
partition of Bengal, 374
Partition Plan, 55
passive resistance, 416
Patel, Sardar Vallabhbhai, 556, 566, 567
paternalist concern, 307
Pather Panchali, 134n47
pathshalas, 277–9, 285
patriarchal prejudices, 183
"patron–client" linkages, 376
peasant consciousness, 381
peasant movements, 420, 454
peasant nationalism, 509
peasant-populist religious idiom, 473
Peasants into Frenchmen, 476
The Persecuted, 31
Peter Linebaugh, 623
Phalke, Dadasaheb, 397
philanthropy, 238, 256, 287, 301
Philo-Cleanthes dialogue, 29
Pillai, P. Krishna, 572
"plebeian" practicality, 169
political agitation, 443
political conformism, 142
political consciousness, 183
Political Extremism, 56, 72
political nationalism, 385

Politics of Labour, 602
The Politics of Labour under Late Colonialism: Workers, Unions, and the State in Chota Nagpur, 599
polygamy, 297, 309, 310
polytheism, 115
Poor Folk, 165
popular movements, 536–75
postcoloniality, 383
post-Enlightenment modernity, 311
potential radicalism, 520
poverty, 177, 244, 249, 357, 398
Praja movement, 431
pratakshyabad, 169
Press Regulation, 1823, 13
primitive rebellion, 474–88
print culture, 397
professional mediators, 527
professional scholarship, 372
Progressive Writers Association (P.W.A.), 618
prolific translator, 94
proselytisation, 229
"Prospect of Bengal," 17
Protestant Reformation, 11, 95
provocative language, 437
public speeches, 227
punctuality, 268
Puritan Revolution, 92
Purna Swaraj, 489

quid pro quos, 526
Quit India struggle (1942), 374, 407

racial discrimination, 82, 183
radicalism, 4, 89, 230, 401
radical nationalism, 83
radical utopianism, 602
Rai, Mridu, 399
raiyats, 74, 83, 96, 97, 333
Raj, Dogra, 399
Raja Harishchandra (1913), 397
Rajbansi Kshatriya Sabha, 145n67
Rajbansis, 108, 125, 127, 132, 139, 140, 429
Ramakrishna, Thakur, 151–236
Ramakrishna Mission, 216, 223, 225, 234, 235
Ramakrishna-Vivekananda Tradition, 151
Ramayat sadhu Jatadhari, 193
Ramtanu Lahiri o tatkalin Bangasamaj, 26
Ranadive, B.T., 570
Ranadive Period, 87n3
Rangpur, 446
Rangpur Dharma Sabha, 141
Rangpur District Gazetteer, 141
Rashid, Abdul, 550
rational discrimination, 10
rationalism, 7, 8
Ray, Rajat, 434
Ray, Satyajit, 134n47
Raychaudhuri, Brojendrakishore, 120

recuperation, 371
redemptive wife, 187
Rediker, Marcus, 598
reductionism, 108
Reform Bill, 30
Reformer, 44
reformist discourse, 353
Rehman, Fazlur, 432
Reid, A., 29
religious awareness, 168
religious materialism, 169
renaissance awakening, 240
renaissance concept, 1, 8, 18, 19, 75, 78, 86–9, 96, 98, 171
renaissance model, 403
Report on Native Papers, 314
Report on the Native Press, 462
repression, 53, 55, 603
reticence, 491
revivalism, 57
revolutionary crime, 436
revolutionary movement, 56
revolutionary terrorism, 111
R.I.N. strike, 556
ritual transgression, 195
Round Table Conference, 523, 524, 527
Rowlatt satyagraha explosion, 55
Rowlatt upsurge, 433
Roy, Dasarathi, 328
Roy, Rammohun, 1–24, 98, 115
Roychaudhuri, Brojendrakishore, 427
Roy–Lenin controversy, 87

rural hierarchy, 171
rustic barbarism, 274

Sabash Bangali, 58
Sadhabar ekadasi (1866), 32
Sadharan Brahmos, 80
Sadharan Brahmo Samaj, 28, 77, 455
Sadharani, 82
Sahajiya cults, 195
Sahibdhani, 195
Said, Edward, 106, 174, 385, 388, 389, 391
Samachar Chandrika, 16, 19, 33, 36, 41, 99
Samachar Darpan, 39, 243
Sambad Bhaskar, 247
Sambad Kaumudi, 12
Sambad Prabhakar, 36
Sambad Purnachandroday, 33
"samiti" movement, 57, 58
Sanatan Dharmarakshini Sabha, 293
sandeha-nirasana, 202
sandhya-bhasha, 204, 206
Sanjibani Sabha, 71
Sanskrit Press Depository, 256, 263
Santal rebellion of 1855, 476
Sanyal, Hitesranjan, 406, 513
Sarabhai, Ambalal, 521
Sarat-Sarojini (1874), 72
Sarbatattva-deepika Sabha, 12

Sarkar, Akshaychandra, 82
Sarkar, Akshaykumar, 78
Sarkar, Biharilal, 261
Sarkar, Jadunath, 20
Sarkar, Khan Mohammed, 431
Sarkar, Susobhan, 21n70, 614
Sarvadarshanasangraha, 269
Sasmal, Birendranath, 137
Sastri, Sibnath, 26, 38
sati, 19
satyadharma, 333
Satyashodhak Samaj tradition, 401
scepticism, 10
Seal, Anil, 376
Seal, Brajendranath, 7
Second World War, 414, 603
sectarianism, 538
secularism, 8
self-government, 77
"self-respect" movement, 604
"self-strengthening" movement, 23
semi-feudal labour, 600
Sen, Amartya, 541
Sen, Amit, 26n3
Sen, Asok, 88, 95, 240, 285
Sen, Keshabchandra, 77, 173, 194
Sen, Ramkamal, 29, 48
Sen, Sailajananda, 453
Sen, Samar, 575
Sen, Sukumar, 328
Sengupta, Kalyankumar, 69, 84

Shahabad riots, 432
Shakta doctrine, 209
Shakta–Vaishnava relations, 209
sharecropper movement, 130
Shivaji Utsava, 71
Shudras, 185, 229, 346, 347, 350, 368
Sikdar, Radhanath, 39, 42
Simeon, Dilip, 599
Simla Conference, 537, 545
Singer, Wendy, 406
Singh, Bhagat, 530
Singh, Deep Narain, 511
Singh, Hazara, 602
Sircar, Mahendralal, 211
"Sita-Savitri-Damyanti" model, 230
Sixth Comintern Congress (1928), 531
Sketch of the Condition of Hindoo Women, 40
smarta panchopasana, 201
smriti-shastras, 290
social activism, 171
Social Conference, 411
social-cultural relationships, 369
social degradation, 226
socialist-feminist scholarship, 384
social ostracism, 404
social radicalism, 39, 147
social reform, 92, 121, 242, 289, 372, 403, 404, 410
energies, 9
social revolution, 104

Society for Acquisition of General Knowledge (SAGK), 26, 40, 43
Society for the Acquisition of General Knowledge, 37
socio-religious reform movements, 99
solemnity, 220
Somprakash, 70, 83, 97, 301
South Asian historiography, 105
South Asian nationalisms, 371, 410
South Asian scholarship, 388
Speeches and Documents on British Rule, 20
Srikanta (1917), 326
Srinivas, M.N., 393
Sri Ramakrishna Samasamayik Drishtite, 155n7
Statesman, 239
stereotypes, 25, 229, 383
Stewart, Dugald, 30
Stokes, Eric, 576
stri-swadhinata, 115, 116, 160, 252, 306, 353
"subalternist" approach, 113n13
subalternity, 185
subaltern militancy, conditions and nature, 416–73
Subaltern Studies, 418
Sudras, 111n11
Sultan Mahmud II, 13
Surendra-Binodini (1875), 72
Sureshchandra Samajpati, 350

Sutherland, James, 10, 16
sutra-bhashya, 206
Swadesh Bandhab Samiti, 425
Swadeshi, meaning, 110n9
Swadeshi agitation, 433
Swadeshi intelligentsia, 61
Swadeshi labour unrest, 441
Swadeshi movement, 56, 80, 100, 104, 223, 416, 422, 424
Swadeshi nationalist militancy, 234
Swadeshi period, 55, 57, 81
Swami Saradananda, 154n5
"Swaraj Ashrams and Chawries," 509
Swaraj Fund, 451
synthesis, 3

Tagore, Debendranath, 75
Tagore, Dwarkanath, 102
Tagore, Dwijendranath, 66, 80
Tagore, J.M., 70
Tagore, Jyotirindranath, 72
Tagore, Rabindranath, 18, 123, 167, 263, 274, 405, 438, 504
Tantric-cum-Sahajiya "esoteric" cults, 206
tantrism, 195–7, 200, 209
Tantubay, 301
Tarkalankar, Madanmohan, 276
Tarkaratna, Panchanan, 258
Tarkavacaspati, Taranath, 276, 298

Tattvabhushan, Sitanath, 73, 84
Tattvabodhini Patrika, 47, 96–7
Taylor, Charles, 148
Tebhaga movement, 145n67, 617
Tebhaga upsurge, 537
Telis, 301
Tenancy Act of 1885, 62, 70, 83, 97
Tenancy Amendment Act of 1928, 454
tenancy amendment bill, 59
terrorism, 53
Textile Tariff Board recommendation, 496
Thakurdas, Purshottamdas, 502, 503, 516, 521, 522, 527, 533
Thompson, E.P., 469, 476, 514, 621–6, 628, 629
Thompson, George, 45, 46, 48, 98
Tilak Swaraj Fund, 495
trade union, 623
traditionalism, 57
"traditionalist–modernist" model, 76
transmission, 192
tribal movements, 471
The Triplicane Literary Society Address (1897), 233
Tuhfat, 8–10, 13
Tuhfat-ul-Muwahhidin (c. 1803–4), 4, 94

unity-in-diversity, 399
Upadhyaya, Biswanath, 164
UP Zamindars' Association, 529
utilitarianism, 102

Vacaspati, Sambhuchandra, 288
Vaidyas, 126, 301
Vaishnava, 159
Vaishnavbad, Gaudiya, 210
Vaishnavism, 195, 324, 327
Vaishyas, 111n11
Vajra-suchi translation, 9
Varma, Ravi, 397
Varnaparichay, 281, 282, 284
Vedanta Chandrika, 7
Vedantic monism, 202, 225
Vedantic philosophy, 6
Vedantism, 37
Vernacular Press Act, 54, 68
Vernacular schools, 47
Vidyabhushan, Dwarkanath, 70, 97
Vidyabhushan, Radhamohan, 255, 265
Vidyalankar, Mrityunjay, 7
Vidyaratna, Sambhuchandra, 301
Vidyasagar, Ishwarchandra, 93, 95, 153, 165, 171, 176, 237–311
Vivekananda, 218–20, 224–7, 229–33, 254
voters, 402

Ward, William, 248
war-time communism, 618
Washbrook, David, 379
Wavell, 539, 546, 548, 553, 554, 557, 560–2, 568
Weber, Eugene, 476
Weber, Max, 460
Westerner-Slavophile dichotomy, 89
"What Can be Done for the Namasudras," 123
What is to be Done?, 149n72
Whig perfidy, 102n58
Whigs and Hunters, 624
Widow Marriage Bill, 292
widow marriages, 252, 300, 301, 304–6
widow remarriage, 78n109, 92, 127, 291, 294, 310
widows' homes, 228
Williams, Raymond, 361n162, 628
Wilson, Brian, 460, 462
Wilson, H.H., 3
Witness Against the Beast (1993), 624
women, 159, 185, 217, 218, 309, 310, 334, 347, 361, 394, 403, 407
Worsley, Peter, 461

Yama theme, 332
Yavanas, 41

Young, Arthur, 130
Young, Gordon, 286
"Young Bengal," 194
complexities of, 25–52
unity of, 27
yugapralay, 331, 332, 337, 345, 346, 362, 365

Zamindar Darpan, 83
zamindar–peasant conflict, 124
zamindars, 15, 74, 139, 239, 244, 275, 300, 303, 357, 426, 427, 429, 448–50, 457, 458, 471, 519

www.ingramcontent.com/pod-product-compliance
Lightning Source LLC
Chambersburg PA
CBHW021111300426
44113CB00006B/114